Children's Writers' & Artists' YEARBOOK 2009

Children's Writers' & Artists'
YEARBOOK
2009

FIFTH EDITION

A directory for children's writers and artists
containing children's media contacts and
practical advice and information

A&C Black • London

© 2009 A&C Black Publishers Ltd
36 Soho Square, London W1D 3QY

Reprinted 2009

This book is produced using paper that is made
from wood grown in managed, sustainable forests.
It is natural, renewable and recyclable. The logging
and manufacturing processes conform to the
environmental regulations of the country of origin.

A CIP catalogue record for this book is available
from the British Library.

ISBN 10: 140810377X
ISBN 13: 9781408103777

Typeset by QPM from David Lewis XML
Associates Ltd

Printed in the UK by CPI William Clowes
Beccles NR34 7TL

'Whenever people ask me about how to get their work for children published, or how to find their way around the world of writing and publishing for children, the first words to come out of my mouth are always: *Children's Writers' & Artists' Yearbook*'
Michael Rosen

'I wish you all the luck in the world. Don't be a ninny like me, practically giving up at the first rejection. Consult the excellent *Children's Writers' & Artists' Yearbook* and get going!'
Jacqueline Wilson

'On the road to becoming a published author, every writer has to take a first step. Make the *Children's Writers' & Artists' Yearbook* yours'
Meg Cabot

'Between the covers of this book is everything you need to know to get published'
Julia Donaldson

'Every possible scrap of information needed by the upcoming or established writer is included'
Eoin Colfer

'Stuffed with advice and contacts for would-be children's authors and illustrators'
TESS

'When I first started out as a writer I wasted so much time knocking on the wrong doors! A book like this, containing all the information you need, would have been invaluable to me'
Diane Redmond

'Writing for children is a serious business and this is a serious book about it'
Jeremy Strong

Contents

Foreword – Michael Rosen   ix

Books
Getting started – Alison Stanley   1
Notes from Jacqueline Wilson   74
A word from J.K. Rowling   77
How it all began – Eoin Colfer   78
Notes from a successful children's author and
   illustrator – Lauren Child   80
Spotting talent – Barry Cunningham   83
Writing and the children's book market
   – Chris Kloet   86
The next big thing – Becky Stradwick   90
Year in view of children's publishing
   – Caroline Horn   94
Books for babies – Wendy Cooling   98
Writing books to read aloud – Anne Fine   102
Writing for boys – Russell Ash   105
Writing for girls – Louise Rennison   111
Writing for different genres – Malorie Blackman   114
Fiction for 6–9 year-olds – Alison Stanley   119
Writing humour for young children
   – Jeremy Strong   121
Writing horror for children
   – Anthony Horowitz   124
Writing historical novels for children
   – Michelle Paver   127
Writing for teenagers – Meg Rosoff   131
Teenage fiction – Gillie Russell   135
Writing for the school market – Jim Green   138
It could happen to you – Matthew Skelton   142
What does an editor do? – Yvonne Hooker   145
Marketing, publicising and selling children's
   books – Rosamund de la Hey   149
Notes from a successful self-publisher
   – John Howard   154
Children's books and the US market
   – Richard Scrivener   158
Categorising children's books – Caroline Horn   162

Listings
Children's book publishers UK and Ireland   5
Children's book publishers overseas   27
Children's audio publishers   60

Children's book packagers   63
Children's book clubs   68
Children's bookshops   70

Poetry
Riding on the poetry roundabout – John Foster   167
An interview with my shadow – Brian Patten   171

Listings
Poetry organisations – Paul McGrane   173

Literary agents
How to get an agent – Philippa Milnes-Smith   181
Do you *have* to have an agent to succeed?
   – Philip Ardagh   185
The role of a children's literary agent
   – Rosemary Canter   189

Listings
Children's literary agents UK and Ireland   192
Children's literary agents overseas   199

Illustrating for children
Creating graphic novels – Raymond Briggs   207
Eight great tips to get your picture book
   published – Tony Ross   209
Writing and illustrating picture books
   – Debi Gliori   213
The amazing picture book story – Oliver Jeffers   217
Illustrating for children's books
   – Maggie Mundy   221
Children's character licensing – Joel Rickett   224

Listings
Illustrators' agents   228

Publishing practice
Publishing agreements – Caroline Walsh   231
FAQs about ISBNs   236
Public Lending Right   238

Copyright
Copyright questions – Michael Legat   245
The Copyright Licensing Agency Ltd   248
Authors' Licensing and Collecting Society   250
Design and Artists Copyright Society   252

Magazines and newspapers

Writing for teenage magazines
– Michelle Garnett   255

Listings

Magazines and newspapers for children   259
Magazines about children's literature and
education   270

Television, film and radio

Commissioning for children's television
– Anna Home   275
Writing comedy for children's television
– Adam Bromley   277
Children's literature on radio and audio
– Neville Teller   281
Writing to a brief – Diane Redmond   287

Listings

BBC children's television   291
Independent children's television   292
Children's television and film producers   295
Children's radio   298

Theatre

Writing for children's theatre – David Wood   299
Adapting books for the stage – Stephen Briggs   304

Listings

Theatre for children   308

Resources for children's writers

Setting up a website – Suna Cristall   315
Learning to write for children – Alison Sage   320
Indexing children's books – Valerie Elliston   324

Listings

Children's writing courses and conferences   328
Online resources about children's books   330
Books about children's books   333

Societies, prizes and festivals

The Society of Authors   335
Booktrust   338
Seven Stories, the Centre for Children's Books   339
The Children's Book Circle – Katie Jennings   341
Federation of Children's Book Groups
– Sinead Kromer   342
National Year of Reading
– Honor Wilson-Fletcher   380

Listings

Societies, associations and organisations   344
Children's book and illustration prizes and
awards   364
Calendar of awards   373
Children's literature festivals and trade fairs   375

Finance for writers and artists

FAQs for writers – Peter Vaines   381
Income tax – Peter Vaines   383
Social security contributions
– Peter Arrowsmith   394
Social security benefits – K.D. Bartlett   402

Index   407

Foreword

Michael Rosen is the Children's Laureate for 2007–9. He is a poet, story-writer, broadcaster and performer who has been taking his one-man shows of stories and poems into schools, theatres and libraries for over 30 years.

I was brought up in a house that was full of books and people who loved literature. My friends used to come home from school with me and stand in the front room of our flat staring up at the shelves of books, their faces full of wonder. My parents were teachers – which doesn't necessarily mean that a home will be full of books, but their background seemed to have given them the idea that books represented a way of knowing about the world. This meant that I grew up with the idea that people who could string words together were special. This wasn't just confined to books. I was taken to see Shakespeare (Judi Dench as Juliet at the Old Vic was great), played recordings of poets (Robert Graves, Dylan Thomas) and we would gather together to enjoy Frank Muir and Dennis Norden on *Call My Bluff*, the *Goon Show* and Peter Ustinov.

Obviously, it doesn't necessarily follow that if you're exposed to all this, you'll turn into a writer (my brother became a palaeontologist), but it certainly seems to help. What also helped was that my parents were both involved in a constant hunt for poems and stories to interest the children they were teaching. This went so far as them taking part in putting together anthologies and broadcasts. Geoffrey Summerfield, who edited the ground-breaking *Voices* poetry collections, layed out strings of poems on our front room floor for my parents (and me) to pass comments on what we thought worked or didn't work. James Britton, who put together the Oxford University Press collections of poetry for schools, was a close friend and sought their advice and my mother used to present poetry programmes on BBC Schools.

From all this, I think I gathered that poetry was something that you could listen to, play with and rummage around in. There were also some kinds of poems that you could think were possible examples of the sort of thing you could write. I first made that thought concrete when I was about 16. The trigger point was reading James Joyce's *A Portrait of the Artist as a Young Man*. You'll remember that the book uses a literary device of changing the narrator's mode of address as the subject of the narration gets older. In effect, this marries the Proustian moment to 'stream of consciousness' in fiction. With that in my ear, I set about trying to write passages which imitated this method. I conjured up my first memories of being wheeled in a pushchair at Clacton-on-sea, of the gap between the ship and the quayside on the way to Brittany and turned them into Joycean prose. I also read D.H. Lawrence's poems and wormed around inside them, enjoying the way in which he describes the sensation of an event and interposes his critical voice. He wrote 'Bat' and 'Snake' so I wrote 'Moth'! There were also girlfriends who had to be written to, for and about, but I'm not sure whose voice was in my head for these.

I'm a little ashamed to say that my first outlet for all this was my mother's poetry programme on BBC Schools – shameless nepotism, eh? She would sit with a pile of poetry books on the table next to her typewriter, trying to construct a programme which flowed from one poem to another. Sometimes, there really didn't appear to be a link between the poems, no matter how hard she tried to push it. She would sit staring up at the ceiling. On more than one occasion, I asked what the problem was and the result of this was that I would dash off to another room, write a poem that I thought might be the link and turn up a couple of hours later, to ask her if this one would do the trick.

Because it did, my mother's producer, Joan Griffiths, asked my mother if young Michael had written any more poems, and so it came about that Joan asked me to present one of her programmes. In effect, I nicked my mother's job. More shame. Around this time, I was also trying to write plays. While I was first at medical school (yes, I did think I was going to be a doctor), and then at Oxford University, I spent an unbelievable amount of time directing, writing and acting in plays. One play I wrote won the NUS student drama award and this play went to be produced at the Royal Court and published by Faber. Off the back of this, I tried to get the poems I had written published, and in the end it was Pam Royds at André Deutsch who thought this was a goer. She married me up with Quentin Blake and so my first book of poems came to be published in 1974.

All this meant that by the time I was 28, I was in a position to write, perform poems, stories and radio programmes... which is more or less what I've been doing ever since.

Michael Rosen

Books
Getting started

You just have! By buying or borrowing the *Children's Writers' & Artists' Yearbook* you have taken the first step towards a potential new career in the field of children's publishing. Alison Stanley gives the benefit of her experience for success in this expanding market.

Whether you want to write for magazines, television, write or illustrate books, adapt for radio, get published in the UK or overseas, find an agent, illustrate greetings' cards, attend a festival, course or conference, or surf the children's literature websites, you will find the information on how to do it in this *Yearbook*.

But to help you on your way, here are ten top tips:

1. Read, read, read

• Read as many children's books as you can – picture books, young fiction, novels, teen reads, non-fiction, the classics, the prize-winners – and find out just what is being published… and what children like to read.

• Look at children's magazines and newspaper supplements as they will give you ideas about current trends.

• Read reviews in national newspapers, read children's literary magazines such as *Books for Keeps* and *Carousel* (see *Magazines about children's literature and education* on page 270).

2. Get out and about

• Visit your local bookshop and browse in the children's section.

• Go to your library and talk to the children's librarian. Children's books are read by children but usually bought by adults – so find out what parents, teachers, librarians and other professionals are recommending for young people.

• Visit Seven Stories, the Centre for Children's Books (see page 339).

• If you have children, don't just go by what they are reading, ask their friends too – children have wide reading tastes, just like adults. Ask permission to sit in on their school 'storytime' (or a literacy hour or a guided reading session if educational publishing is what you are interested in).

• Go to a festival! There are many literature festivals held throughout the year and most have children's literary events (see page 375). All children's literature festivals will have a sprinkling of new and well-known authors and illustrators in attendance, and most authors and illustrators will be accompanied by a representative from their publishing company. So you can see and hear the author/illustrator and even do a bit of networking with the publisher! You will also be guaranteed some fun. Festivals are also a useful way of seeing children's reactions to their favourite authors and books in an informal situation.

3. Watch, listen and … learn

• Familiarise yourself with the children's media: watch children's television and listen to children's radio programmes (see the *Television, film and radio* section beginning on page 275), and check out the websites listed throughout the *Yearbook*. Look at children's character merchandising and greetings cards.

• Enrol on a creative writing course where you can meet others who also want to write for children (see *Learning to write for children*, page 320). Or apply to do a postgraduate course in writing for young people, where you will be guided by published authors and other publishing professionals (see *Children's writing courses and conferences*, page 328).

4. Network
• Being an author or illustrator can be a lonely business – don't work in a vacuum. Talk to others of your discipline at festivals, conferences and book groups. Join the Federation of Children's Book Groups (see page 352) where you can network to your heart's content. Find out if there are any writer/illustrator groups in your area. If you are already published, join the Scattered Authors Society (see page 359).

5. Never underestimate the job in hand
• Writing and illustrating for children is not an easy option. Many people think they can dash off a children's story and a few sketchy illustrations and that they will be good enough to publish. But if you have researched the marketplace you will realise that it is a hugely competitive area and you have to be talented, have something original to say, have an unique style… and know how to persevere in order to get your work published and out to a wider audience.

6. Use your experiences
• Having your own children, or working in a child-related profession is helpful but shouldn't be relied on to bring you a new career as a children's writer or illustrator. (Never use this line when submitting a manuscript: 'I wrote this story for my children and they enjoyed it so please will you publish it?' Any story you write for your own children, grand-children, nieces, nephews, etc is likely to be enjoyed by them because children love attention.) Publishers will only want to take on something that has appeal for a wide range of children – both nationally and internationally – never forget that publishing is a business. However, do use your experiences in terms of ideas, especially the more unusual ones, like seeing your first alien fall from the sky!

7. Research catalogues and websites
• Look at publishers' catalogues and websites, not just to find out what they are publishing, but because many of them give guidance for new writers and illustrators. When submitting a manuscript or portfolio to a publisher, it is a good idea to let them know that you know (and admire!) what they already publish. You can then make your case about where your submission will fit in their list. Let them know that you mean business and have researched the marketplace.

8. Submit your material with care
• First decide whether to approach an agent or to go it alone and submit your material direct to a publisher (see *How to get an agent* on page 181, *Do you have to have an agent to succeed?* on page 185 and *Publishing agreements* on page 231 for the pros and cons of each approach.) Check that the agent or publisher you are thinking of approaching accepts (a) unsolicited material, and (b) is interested in the type of work you are doing. For example, don't send your potential prize-winning novel to an educational publisher, and don't send your ideas for a Guided Reading Series at Key Stage 1 to a 'trade' publisher without an educational list. And don't send your illustrations for a children's picture book to an agent

who only deals with teenage fiction – there will be zero interest from them and you will be very disappointed.

• Submit your work to the right publisher/agent and the right person within the company. Ring first to find out who the best person for your work might be, whether it be in a publishing company, an agency, a television production company or a children's magazine. Also ask whether they want a synopsis and sample chapters or the complete manuscript or, for artwork, a selection of illustrations or your whole portfolio.

• Presentation is important. For example, no editor will read a handwritten manuscript. It should be typed/word processed, using double spacing with each page clearly numbered. (Should an editor be interested in your work, it will be photocopied for all involved in the acquisition process to read. Photocopiers have a habit of chewing up pages and there's nothing worse than pages being missing at a crucial part of a novel.) If your manuscript is accepted for publication, the editor will want the text electronically.

• For illustrations, select work on a paper that can be easily photocopied – a white/cream background with no unusual textures for your first pitch (such as sandpaper or glass – yes it really has happened!) And remember, publishers' photocopiers are notoriously bad at reproducing colour accurately, so if you are relying on the vibrancy of your colour to wow an art director, bear in mind that by the time they have been photocopied a few times for interested parties to see, the colours will not be the same. If your artwork is computer generated, send hard copies with your disk – it saves time when being shown around.

9. Identify your USP

• Ask yourself what the unique selling point (USP) of the material you are submitting for publication is. You may have an original authorial 'voice', you may have a particularly innovative illustration style or technique, or you may have come up with an amazingly brilliant idea for a series. If, after checking out the marketplace, you think you have something truly original to offer, then believe in yourself and be convincing when you offer it for publication.

10. Don't give up!

• Editors receive hundreds of manuscripts, and art directors receive hundreds of illustration samples every day. For a publisher, there are many factors that have to be taken into consideration when evaluating these submissions, the most important of which is 'Can we publish it successfully?' – i.e. 'Will it sell?' Publishing is a big business and it is ever more competitive. Even after an editor or art director has seen and liked your work, there are many other people involved before something is acquired for publication: the marketing manager, the publicist, the rights director, the book club manager, the sales director and, of course, the financial director. You will find this mantra repeated again and again in many of the articles in this book: *Have patience, keep at it.* If you believe in your 'product' eventually someone else will too. And meanwhile, keep perfecting your craft. After all, you are doing it because you enjoy it, aren't you?

Alison Stanley has been a senior commissioning editor of children's fiction at Puffin Books and at HarperCollins Children's Books. She is now selling her USP as a freelance.

See also...

● *Notes from Jacqueline Wilson*, page 74
● *Notes from a successful children's author and illustrator*, page 80

4 Books

- *Spotting talent,* page 83
- *Writing for boys,* page 105
- *Writing for girls,* page 111
- *Writing for different genres,* page 114
- *Fiction for 6–9 year-olds,* page 119
- *Writing humour for young children,* page 121
- *Writing horror for children,* page 124
- *Writing historical novels for children,* page 127
- *Writing for teenagers,* page 131
- *Teenage fiction,* page 135
- *What does an editor do?* page 145
- *Writing for the school market,* page 138
- *Writing and illustrating picture books,* page 213
- *The amazing picture book story,* page 217

Children's book publishers UK and Ireland

*Member of the Publishers Association or Publishing Scotland
†Member of the Irish Book Publishers' Association

Abbey Home Media
435–7 Edgware Road, London W2 1TH
tel 020-7563 3910 fax 020-7563 3911
email info@abbeyhomemedia.com
website abbeyhomemedia.com
Chairman Ian Miles, Directors Anne Miles, James Harding, Emma Evans, Caroline Hansell

Activity books, board books, novelty books, picture books, non-fiction, reference books, audiotapes and CDs. Advocates learning through interactive play. Age groups: preschool, 5–10.

Philip Allan – see Hodder Education Group

Alligator Books Ltd
(Pinwheel Division)
Gadd House, Arcadia Avenue, London N3 2JU
tel 020-8371 6622 fax 020-8371 6633
email sales@pinwheel.co.uk
website www.pinwheel.co.uk
Directors Neil Rodol (commercial), Andrew Rabin (sales & publishing)

Children's non-fiction, picture books and novelty titles. Unsolicited MSS will not be returned. Wholly owned subsidiary of International Greetings Plc.

Andromeda Children's Books (imprint)
Creative Director Linda Cole
Illustrated non-fiction for children aged 3–12 years.

Pinwheel Children's Books (imprint)
Creative Director Linda Cole
Cloth and novelty books for children aged 0–5 years.

Andersen Press Ltd
20 Vauxhall Bridge Road, London SW1V 2SA
tel 020-7840 8703 (editorial) 020-7840 8701 (general)
fax 020-7233 6263
email andersenpress@randomhouse.co.uk
website www.andersenpress.co.uk
Managing Director/Publisher Klaus Flugge, Directors Philip Durrance, Joëlle Flugge, Rona Selby (editorial)

Picture books, and junior and teenage fiction. Recent successes include the Elmer series by David McKee and Doing It by Melvin Burgess. Other authors include Anne Fine, Michael Foreman, Tony Ross and Jeanne Willis. Illustrators include Ralph Steadman and Max Velthuijs, winner of the the 2004 Hans Christian Andersen Award for Illustration for his Frog series.

Submission details For novels, send 3 sample chapters, a synopsis and return postage. Juvenile fiction should be 3000–5000 words long, and older fiction about 15,000–30,000 words. The text for picture books should be under 1000 words long. No poetry or short stories. Do not send MSS via email.

Andrew Brodie Publications – see A&C Black Publishers Ltd

Andromeda Children's Books – see Alligator Books Ltd

Anglia Young Books – see Mill Publishing

Anness Publishing
88–89 Blackfriars Road, London SE1 8HA
tel 020-7401 2077 fax 020-7633 9499
email info@anness.com
website www.annesspublishing.com,
www.lorenzbooks.com, www.southwaterbooks.com
Managing Director Paul Anness, Publisher Joanna Lorenz

Practical illustrated books on lifestyle, cookery, crafts, gardening, Mind, Body & Spirit, health and children's non-fiction. Imprints: Lorenz Books, Southwater, Practical Pictures. Founded 1989.

Anova Children's Books – see Pavilion Children's Books

Anvil Books/The Children's Press†
45 Palmerston Road, Dublin 6, Republic of Ireland
tel (01) 4973628
Directors Rena Dardis (managing), Margaret Dardis (editorial)

Children's Press: adventure fiction for ages 9–14. Anvil: Irish history and biography. Only considers MSS by Irish-based authors and of Irish interest. Send synopsis with IRCs (no UK stamps); unsolicited MSS not returned. Founded 1964.

Arcturus Publishing Ltd
26–27 Bickels Yard, 151–3 Bermondsey Street, London SE1 3HA
tel 020-7407 9400 fax 020-7407 9444
email roberta.bailey@arcturuspublishing.com
Managing Director, Arcturus Children's Publishing Roberta Bailey

Children's non-fiction and school library books, including activity books, reference, education, geography, history and science.

Atlantic Europe Publishing Co. Ltd

Greys Court Farm, Greys Court, Henley-on-Thames, Oxon RG9 4PG
tel (01491) 628188 *fax* (01491) 628189
email enquiries@atlanticeurope.com
website www.atlanticeurope.com,
www.curriculumvisions.com
Director Dr B.J. Knapp

Educational: children's colour illustrated information books, co-editions and primary school class books covering science, geography, technology, mathematics, history, religious education. Recent successes include the *Curriculum Visions* series and *Science at School* series. Founded 1990.

Submission details Submit via email to contactus@atlanticeurope.com with no attachments. No MSS accepted by post. Established teacher authors only.

Atom – see Little, Brown Book Group

Autumn Publishing

Appledram Barns, Birdham Road, Chichester, West Sussex PO20 7EQ
tel (01243) 531660 *fax* (01243) 774433
email autumn@autumpublishing.co.uk
website www.autumpublishing.net

Activity books, novelty books and picture books to enable children to learn whilst they play. Also lift-the-flap board books, sticker books, wall charts, colouring books and colourful flash cards designed to help young children have fun while learning the alphabet and counting. Publishes approx. 200 titles each year and has 600 in print. Recent successes include *Travel Time for Kids* and *Wallchart* ranges. Founded 1976.

Submission details No responsibility is accepted for the return of unsolicited MSS.

Award Publications Ltd

The Old Riding School, The Welbeck Estate, Worksop, Notts. S80 3LR
tel (01909) 478170 *fax* (01909) 484632
email info@awardpublications.co.uk

Children's books: full colour picture story books; early learning, information and activity books. No unsolicited material. Founded 1954.

b small publishing limited

The Book Shed, 36 Leyborne Park, Kew, Richmond, Surrey TW9 3HA
tel 020-8948 2884 *fax* 020-8948 6458
email info@bsmall.co.uk
website www.bsmall.co.uk
Publisher Catherine Bruzzone

Activity books and foreign language learning books for 2–12 year-olds. No unsolicited MSS. Founded 1990.

Bantam Press (children's) – see The Random House Group Ltd

Barefoot Books Ltd

124 Walcot Street, Bath BA1 5BG
tel (01225) 322400 *fax* (01225) 322499
email info@barefootbooks.co.uk
website www.barefootbooks.co.uk
Editor-in-Chief Tessa Strickland, *Group Editorial Manager* Jo Collins

Children's picture books and audiobooks: myth, legend, fairytale, cross-cultural stories. Picture book MSS only with return p&p. Founded 1993.

Barrington Stoke*

18 Walker Street, Edinburgh EH3 7LP
tel 0131-225 4113 *fax* 0131-225 4140
email info@barringtonstoke.co.uk
website www.barringtonstoke.co.uk
Managing Director Sonia Raphael, *Editorial Manager* Kate Paice

Fiction for reluctant, dyslexic or under-confident readers: fiction for 8–12 year-olds with a reading age of 8+, fiction for teenagers with a reading age of 8+, fiction for 8–12 year-olds with a reading age of below 8, fiction for teenagers with a reading age of below 8, non-fiction for 10–14 year olds with a reading age of 8+, fiction for adults with a reading age of 8+, graphic novels. Resources for readers and their teachers. Publishes approx. 50 titles a year and has over 300 books in print. Founded 1998.

Submission details No unsolicited MSS. All work is commissioned from well-known authors and adapted for reluctant readers.

BBC Audiobooks Ltd

St James House, The Square, Lower Bristol Road, Bath BA2 3BH
tel (01225) 878000 *fax* (01225) 310771
website www.bbcaudiobooks.com
Directors Paul Dempsey (managing), Jan Paterson (publishing)

Large print books and complete and unabridged audiobooks. Does not publish original books. Children's imprint: Galaxy Children's Large Print. Recent successes include *Midnight* by Jacqueline Wilson, *Artemis Fowl: The Eternity Code* by Eoin Colfer and *Shadowmancer* by G.P. Taylor – all published in audio and large print. Formed in 2002 from the amalgamation of Chivers Press, Cover To Cover and BBC Radio Collection.

BBC Children's Books – see Penguin Group (UK)

Belair – see Folens Publishers

A&C Black Publishers Ltd*

38 Soho Square, London W1D 3HB
tel 020-7758 0200 *fax* 020-7758 0222

email enquiries@acblack.com
website www.acblack.com
Chairman Nigel Newton, *Managing Director* Jill Coleman, *Deputy Managing Director* Jonathan Glasspool, *Directors* Oscar Heini (production), Janet Murphy (Adlard Coles Nautical), Jayne Parsons (children's and music), David Wightman (sales), Chris Facey (finance)

Children's and educational books (including music); ceramics, art and craft, drama, ornithology, reference (*Who's Who, Whitaker's Almanack*), sport, theatre, books for writers. Imprints: Adlard Coles Nautical, Andrew Brodie, Featherstone Education, Christopher Helm, The Herbert Press, Methuen Drama, Pica Press, T&AD Poyser, Thomas Reed, Reeds Nautical Almanac. Subsidiary of Bloomsbury Publishing plc. Founded 1807.

A&C Black/Andrew Brodie/Featherstone Education (imprints)

Commissioning Editors Susila Baybars (fiction), Isabel Thomas and Helen Diamond (educational resources), Saskia Gwinn (non-fiction)

Fiction for 5–8 and 9–14 year-olds, non-fiction, reference, plays, poetry. A&C Black publishes approx. 180 titles each year. Andrew Brodie publishes educational books for primary and secondary schools; approx. 30 titles each year. Featherstone Education is a range of books for practitioners at Early Years and Foundation Stage; approx. 35 titles each year.

   Recent fiction successes include, for 5–8 year-olds: *Mouldylocks and the Three Clares* by Sally Grindley in the *Chameleons* series; fiction for 7–9 year-olds: Terry Deary's *Historical Tale*; fiction for 8–11 year-olds: *I am a Tree* by Kaye Umansky in the *Black Cat* series. Recent non-fiction successes include *You Can Save the Planet* by Rich Hough, and *My First Book of Garden Birds* by Sarah Whittley and Mike Unwin. Recent education successes include *100% New Developing Literacy* and *100% New Developing Mathematics, Assembly Today* by Andrew Brodie and the *Little Books* series from Featherstone.

   Submission details For fiction enquire about current guidelines before submitting work as the content of each seasonal list varies. Allow 8–10 weeks for a response. No submissions by email. Look at recently published titles and in catalogues to gauge a feel of current publishing interests. Much of the fiction list has been commissioned to appeal to the educational market and to be part of large series, but increasingly fiction books are being presented to appeal to the trade as standalone titles. For education and non-fiction books the focus is on materials related to the National Curriculum.

Blackwater Press – see Folens Publishers

Bloomsbury Publishing Plc*

36 Soho Square, London W1D 3QY
tel 020-7494 2111 *fax* 020-7434 0151

website www.bloomsbury.com
Chief Executive Nigel Newton, *Non-executive Chairman* Jeremy Wilson, *Executive Director* Richard Charkin, *Directors* Liz Calder (publishing), Alexandra Pringle (publishing), Michael Fishwick (publishing), Kathleen Farrar (international), David Ward (sales), Kathleen Farrar, Helen Garnons-Williams (editorial), Katie Bond (publicity), Ruth Logan (rights), Penny Edwards (production), Sarah Odedina (children's), Colin Adams (finance), Jill Coleman (A&C Black), Kathy Rooney (Berlin Verlag), Elisabeth Ruge (Berlin Verlag), Stephanie Duncan (Dot.com), Charles Black (non-executive), Mike Mayer (non-executive), *Company Secretary* Ian Portal

Fiction, biography, illustrated, travel, children's, trade paperbacks and mass market paperbacks. Founded 1986.

Bloomsbury Children's Books (imprint)

website www.bloomsbury.com/childrens
Chief Executive Nigel Newton, *Publishing Director* Sarah Odedina, *Deputy Editorial Director* Emma Matthewson, *Commissioning Editor* Ele Fountain, *Design Director* Val Brathwaite, *Publicity Manager* Ian Lamb, *Rights Director* Ruth Logan, *Children's Key Accounts Manager* Emily Monkton-Milne, *Sales Director* David Ward, *Marketing Managers* Colette Whitehouse, Joanne Owen, *Finance Director* Colin Adams

Baby books, picture books, fiction for children of all ages. Publishes approx. 100 titles a year and has over 500 books in print. Recent publications include the *Harry Potter* series, *Whispering to Witches* by Anna Dale and *Marvin Wanted More* by Joseph Theobalds (picture book). Company founded 1986; children's list launched 1994.

   Submission details Send a synopsis of the book together with 3 chapters. No unsolicited MSS.

Bodley Head Children's Books – see The Random House Group Ltd

Boxer Books Ltd

101 Turnmill Street, London EC1M 5QP
tel 020-7017 8980 *fax* 020-7608 2314
email info@boxerbooks.com
website www.boxerbooks.com

Innovative books for babies, toddlers and children: board books, novelty books, picture books and young fiction. Age groups: 0–12.

Brilliant Publications*

Unit 10, Sparrow Hall Farm, Edlesborough, Dunstable LU6 2ES
tel (01525) 222292 *fax* (01525) 222720
email info@brilliantpublications.co.uk
website www.brilliantpublications.co.uk
Managing Director Priscilla Hannaford

Practical resource books for teachers and others concerned with the education of 0–13 year-olds. All areas of the curriculum published, but specialise in modern foreign languages, art and design, developing thinking skills and PSHE. Some series of books for reluctant readers, aimed at 7–11 year-olds. No children's picture books, non-fiction books or one-off fiction books. See 'Manuscripts guidelines' on website before sending proposal. Founded 1993.

British Museum Company Ltd*
38 Russell Square, London WC1B 3QQ
tel 020-7323 1234 fax 020-7436 7315
website www.britishmuseum.co.uk
Director of Publishing Rosemary Bradley, Senior Commissioning Editor Carolyn Jones

The world's leading museum publisher, with a growing children's list encompassing authoritative illustrated reference and information titles as well as a range of activity and colouring books. Founded 1973.

Andrew Brodie – see A&C Black Publishers Ltd

Buster Books
9 Lion Yard, Tremadoc Road, London SW4 7NQ
tel 020-7720 8643 fax 020-7627 8953
email busterbooks@mombooks.com
website www.mombooks.com/busterbooks
Managing Director Lesley O'Mara, Publishing Director Philippa Wingate

Non-fiction and gift books for young children. Publishes approx. 40 titles a year. Recent successes include The Boys' Book, The Girls' Book, The Girls' Annual and The Boys' Annual.
Submission details Submit novelty and non-fiction (no fiction) with sae. Allow 1–2 months for response.

Cambridge University Press*
The Edinburgh Building, Shaftesbury Road, Cambridge CB2 8RU
tel (01223) 312393 fax (01223) 315052
email information@cambridge.org
website www.cambridge.org
Chief Executive of the Press Stephen R.R. Bourne, Managing Director, Europe, Middle East & Africa Andrew Gilfillan, Managing Director, Academic Publishing Andrew Brown, Managing Director, Cambridge Learning (ELT) Hanri Pieterse, Chief Executive, Cambridge-Hitachi, John Tuttle

For children: curriculum-based education books and software for schools and colleges (primary, secondary and international). Part of the National Grid for Learning. English language teaching for adult and younger learners.
For adults: anthropology and archaeology, art history, astronomy, biological sciences, classical studies, computer science, dictionaries, earth sciences, economics, e-learning products, engineering, English language teaching, history, language and literature, law, mathematics, medical sciences, music, philosophy, physical sciences, politics, psychology,

reference, technology, social sciences, theology, religion. Journals (humanities, social sciences, STM). The Bible and Prayer Book. Founded 1534.

Campbell Books – see Macmillan Publishers Ltd

Jonathan Cape Children's Books – see The Random House Group Ltd

Carlton Publishing Group
20 Mortimer Street, London W1T 3JW
tel 020-7612 0400 fax 020-7612 0401
email enquiries@carltonbooks.co.uk
website www.carltonbooks.co.uk
Managing Director Jonathan Goodman, Children's Editorial Director Jane Wilsher

No unsolicited MSS; synopses and ideas welcome, but no fiction or poetry. Imprints: Carlton Books, André Deutsch, Prion Books. Founded 1992.

Carlton Books (division)
Mass market illustrated interactive children's books.

Caterpillar Books – see Magi Publications

Catnip Publishing Ltd
14 Greville Street, London EC1N 8SB
tel 020-7138 3650 fax 020-7138 3658
website www.catnippublishing.co.uk
Directors Robert Snuggs (managing), Andrea Reece (publishing), Martin West (editorial)

Children's books. New and previously published titles for children up to the age of 11, with the emphasis on 5–7 year-olds, from foreign publishers or UK houses that have let them go out of print. New books in 2008 from Annette and Nick Butterworth, Joan Lingard, Dominic Barker and Sarah Matthias. Publishes 40 books a year. Created from the merger of Happy Cat Books and Southwood Books. Founded 2005.

CGP
Coordination Group Publications, Kirkby-in-Furness, Cumbria LA17 7WZ
tel (0870) 750 1282 fax (0870) 750 1292
email info@cgpbooks.co.uk, carolinebatten@cgpbooks.co.uk
website cgpbooks.co.uk

Educational books centred around the National Curriculum, including revision guides and study books for GCSE, KS3, KS2, KS1 and A level. Subjects include maths, English, science, history, geography, ICT, psychology, business studies, religious studies, child development, design and techology, PE, music, French, German, Spanish, sociology.
Submission details On the lookout for top teachers at all levels, in all subjects. Potential authors and proofreaders should email Caroline Batten with their name, subject area, level and experience, plus contact address, ready for when a project comes up in their subject area.

Paul Chapman Publishing – see SAGE Publications Ltd

Cherrytree Books – see Zero to Ten Ltd

The Chicken House
2 Palmer Street, Frome, Somerset BA11 1DS
tel (01373) 454488 *fax* (01373) 454499
email chickenhouse@doublecluck.com
website www.doublecluck.com
Managing Director & Publisher Barry Cunningham,
Deputy Managing Director Rachel Hickman

Picture books, fiction for ages 5–8 and 9–11 and teenage fiction. Publishes approx. 25 titles a year. Recent successes include *Tunnels* by Roderick Gordon and Brian Williams, *The Road of the Dead* by Kevin Brooks and *Waves* by Sharon Dogar. Part of Scholastic Inc.
Submission details Will consider unsolicited MSS. Send synopsis and 3 sample chapters. See website for submission guidelines. Allow 16 weeks for response.

Child's Play (International) Ltd
Ashworth Road, Bridgemead, Swindon,
Wilts. SN5 7YD
tel (01793) 616286 *fax* (01793) 512795
email office@childs-play.com
website www.childs-play.com
Chairman Adriana Twinn, *Publisher* Neil Burden

Children's educational books: board, picture, activity and play books; fiction and non-fiction. Founded 1972.

Christian Education*
(incorporating RE Today Services and International Bible Reading Association)
1020 Bristol Road, Selly Oak, Birmingham B29 6LB
tel 0121-472 4242 *fax* 0121-472 7575
email enquiries@christianeducation.org.uk
website www.christianeducation.org.uk

Publications and services for teachers of RE including *REtoday* magazine, curriculum booklets, training material for children and youth workers in the Church. Worship resources for use in primary schools. Activity Club material and Bible reading resources.

Chrysalis Children's Books – see Pavilion Children's Books

Claire Publications
Unit 8, Tey Brook Craft Centre, Great Tey,
Colchester, Essex CO6 1JE
tel (01206) 211020 *fax* (01206) 212755
email mail@clairepublications.com
website www.clairepublications.com

Publisher and manufacturer of educational books and equipment, specialising in mathematics and literacy for children aged 5–15.

Collins Education – see HarperCollins Publishers

Colourpoint Books
Colourpoint House, Jubilee Business Park,
21 Jubilee Road, Newtownards, Co. Down,
Northern Ireland BT23 4YH
tel (028) 9182 0505 *fax* (028) 9182 1900
email info@colourpoint.co.uk
website www.colourpoint.co.uk
Commissioning Editor Sheila Johnston

Educational textbooks for KS3 (11–14 year-olds), KS3 Special Needs (10–14 year-olds), GCSE (14–16 year-olds) and A-Level/undergraduates (age 17+). Subjects include English, geography, history and politics, home economics, ICT, maths and religious education. Founded 1993.
Submission details Because Northern Ireland is a small market, Colourpoint concentrates on pupil books which are bought in class set quantities. Potential authors should send some sample pages of their material to show that they can connect with their target age group, say how long they have been successfully teaching a particular subject and whether they have been involved in writing before. Include return postage.

The Continuum International Publishing Group Ltd
The Tower Building, 11 York Road,
London SE1 7NX
tel 020-7922 0880 *fax* 020-7922 0881
email info@continuumbooks.com
website www.continuumbooks.com
Ceo Oliver Gadsby, *Directors* Robin Baird-Smith (publishing), Bob Marsh (finance), Ken Rhodes (sales & marketing), Benn Linfield (publishing services)

Serious non-fiction, academic and professional, including scholarly monographs and educational texts and reference works in history, politics and social thought; literature, criticism, performing arts; religion and spirituality; education. Imprints: Burns & Oates, Continuum, T&T Clark International, Thoemmes Press, Mowbray.
Education books include *Getting the Buggers to Write* and *Getting the Buggers to be Creative* by Sue Cowley.

Corgi Children's Books – see The Random House Group Ltd

cp publishing
The Children's Project Ltd, PO Box 2, Richmond,
Surrey TW10 7FL
tel 020-8546 8750 *fax* 020-8974 5849
email info@childrensproject.co.uk
website www.socialbaby.com
Directors/Co-founders Helen Dorman, Clive Dorman

High-quality visual books that help parents and carers better understand and communicate with their children from birth. The Children's Project is dedicated exclusively to supporting the family and improved outcomes for children. It draws upon the experience and expertise of parents, health professionals and academics to provide up-to-date information in a form that is easily accessible to everyone – parents, carers and practitioners. Founded in 1995; first books published 2000.

Crown House Publishing Ltd

Crown Buildings, Bancyfelin, Carmarthen SA33 5ND
tel (01267) 211345 *fax* (01267) 211882
email books@crownhouse.co.uk
website www.crownhouse.co.uk
Chairman Martin Roberts, *Directors* David Bowman (managing director), Glenys Roberts, David Bowman, Karen Bowman, Caroline Lenton

Publishes a range of teacher resources detailing the latest and best techniques for enhancing learning and teaching ability. List includes accelerated learning, thinking skills, multiple intelligence, emotional intelligence, mindmapping and music. Also publishes titles in the areas of psychotherapy, business training and development, Mind, Body & Spirit. Founded 1998.

Dean – see Egmont Books

Dorling Kindersley – see Penguin Group (UK)

Doubleday Children's Books – see The Random House Group Ltd

Dref Wen

28 Church Road, Whitchurch, Cardiff CF14 2EA
tel 029-2061 7860 *fax* 029-2061 0507
Directors Roger Boore, Anne Boore, Gwilym Boore, Alun Boore, Rhys Boore, *Editor* Catrin Hughes

Welsh language publisher. Original, adaptations and translations of foreign and English language full-colour picture story books for children. Also activity books, novelty books, Welsh language fiction for 7–14 year-olds, teenage fiction, reference, religion, audiobooks and poetry. Educational material for primary and secondary schoolchildren in Wales and England, including dictionaries, revision guides and Welsh as a Second Language. Publishes approx. 50 titles a year and has 450 in print. Founded 1970.
Submission details No unsolicited MSS. Phone first.

The Educational Company of Ireland†

Ballymount Road, Walkinstown, Dublin 12, Republic of Ireland
tel (01) 4500611 *fax* (01) 4500993
email info@edco.ie
website www.edco.ie
Executive Directors Martina Harford (Chief Executive), Robert McLoughlin (Executive), *Financial Controller* Eugene MacCurtain

Educational (primary and post-primary) books in the Irish language. Publishes approx. 60–70 titles each

year and has 600–700 in print. Ancillary materials include CD-Roms, CDs and audiotapes. Recent successes include *Sunny Street/Streets Ahead* Primary English Langue Programme, *Fonn 1, 2, 3* (Irish language publications for post-primary) and *Geo* (geography publication for post-primary). Trading unit of Smurfit Kappa Group – Ireland. Founded 1910.
Submission details Send an A4 page outlining the selling points and proposal, a draft table of contents and a sample chapter. Allow 3 months for response.

Educational Explorers (Publishers)

Unit 5, Feidr Castell Business Park, Fishguard SA65 9BB
tel/fax (08456) 123912
email explorers@cuisenaire.co.uk
website www.cuisenaire.co.uk
Directors M.J. Hollyfield, D.M. Gattegno

Educational. Mathematics: *Numbers in colour with Cuisenaire Rods*; languages: *The Silent Way*; literacy, reading: *Words in Colour*; educational films. No unsolicited material. Founded 1962.

Egmont Books*

3rd Floor, Beaumont House, Avonmore Road, London W14 8TS
tel 020-7605 6600 *fax* 020-7605 6601
email initial.surname@euk.egmont.com
website www.egmont.co.uk
Directors Robert McMenemy (managing), Cally Poplak (press)

Children's books: picture books, fiction (ages 4–16), and Two Heads. Authors include Michael Morpurgo, Jenny Nimmo, William Nicholson, Helen Oxenbury, Enid Blyton, Andy Stanton, Julia Golding, Jan Fearnly and Lydia Monks. We accept unsolicited MSS but will not acknowledge or respond to individual sumissions unless successful. Founded 1878.

Egmont Publishing (imprint)

239 Kensington High Street, London W8 6SA
tel 020-7761 3500 *fax* 020-7761 3510
email d.riley@euk.egmont.com
tel 020-7605 6600 *fax* 020-7605 6601
website www.egmont.co.uk
Managing Director Robert McMenemy, *Director of Publishing* David Riley

Annuals, activity books, novelty books, film/TV tie-ins, licensed character list. Characters include Thomas the Tank Engine, Barbie, Mr Men, Miffy, Postman Pat, Action Man.

Evans Publishing Group*

2A Portman Mansions, Chiltern Street, London W1U 6NR
tel 020-7487 0920 *fax* 020-7487 0921
email sales@evansbooks.co.uk
website www.evansbooks.co.uk
Directors Stephen Pawley (managing), Brian D. Jones

(international publishing), A.O. Ojora (Nigeria), *UK Publisher* Su Swallow

Educational books, particularly preschool, school library and teachers' books for the UK, primary and secondary for Africa, the Caribbean. Submissions welcome but do not respond if unsuccessful. Part of the Evans Publishing Group. Founded 1908.

Faber and Faber Ltd*

3 Queen Square, London WC1N 3AU
tel 020-7465 0045 *fax* 020-7465 0034
website www.faber.co.uk
Chief Executive Stephen Page, *Publicity Director* Rachel Alexander, *Marketing Director* Jo Ellis, *Production Director* Nigel Marsh, *Rights Director* Jason Cooper, *Head of Children's Fiction* Julia Wells

High-quality general fiction and non-fiction, drama, film, music, poetry. For children: fiction for 5–8 and 9–12 year-olds, teenage fiction, poetry and some non-fiction. Authors include Paul McCartney, Ricky Gervais, G.P. Taylor, Ted Hughes, Philip Ardagh, Margaret Mahy, Pauline Fisk, Steve Voake, Harry Hill, Kenneth Oppel, Justin Richards, Betty G. Birney.
Submission details Only accepts submissions through an agent; no unsolicited MSS.

CJ Fallon

Ground Floor, Block B, Liffey Valley Office Campus, Dublin 22, Republic of Ireland
tel (01) 6166400 *fax* (01) 6166499
email editorial@cjfallon.ie
website www.cjfallon.ie
Executive Directors Brian Gilsenan (managing), John Bodley (financial)

Educational textbooks. Founded 1927.

David Fickling Books – see The Random House Group Ltd

First and Best in Education

Earlstrees Court, Earlstrees Road, Corby, Northants. NN17 4HH
tel (01536) 399005 *fax* (01536) 399012
email sales@firstandbest.co.uk
website www.shop.firstandbest.co.uk
Contact Anne Cockburn (editor)

Education-related books (no fiction). Currently actively recruiting new writers for schools; ideas welcome. Send sae with submissions. Founded 1992.

Flame Tree Publishing

Crabtree Hall, Crabtree Lane, London SW6 6TY
tel 020-7386 4700 *fax* 020-7386 4701
email info@flametreepublishing.com
website www.flametreepublishing.com
Managing Director Frances Bodiam, *Publisher/ Creative Director* Nick Wells

Children's novelty books. Also for adults: music, reference, art, cookery. Part of The Foundry Creative Media Company Ltd. Founded 1992.

Floris Books*

15 Harrison Gardens, Edinburgh EH11 1SH
tel 0131-337 2372 *fax* 0131-347 9919
email floris@florisbooks.co.uk
website www.florisbooks.co.uk
Children's Editor Gale Winskill

Children's activity books, picture books. Publishes approx. 40 titles each year and has 300 in print. Also for adults: religion, science, Celtic studies and craft books. Founded 1978.
Submission details No unsolicited picture books.

Kelpies (imprint)

Contemporary Scottish fiction for 8–12 year-olds. Recent successes include *The Chaos Clock* by Gill Arbuthnott, *Dragonfire* by Anne Forbes and *Chill* by Alex Nye, winner of the 8–11 years old category. Annual Kelpies Prize, see website and page 368.
Submission details Will consider unsolicited MSS. Send synopsis and sample chapter. Must be Scottish in theme.

Folens Publishers*

Waterslade House, Thame Road, Haddenham, Bucks. HP17 8NT
tel (0870) 609 1235 *fax* (0870) 609 1236
email folens@folens.com
website www.folens.com
Managing Director Adrian Cockell, *Director of Publishing* Peter Burton, *Primary Publisher* Zoe Nichols, *Secondary Publisher* Abigail Woodman

Primary and secondary educational books. Imprints: Folens, Belair. Founded 1987.
Submission details Will consider unsolicited MSS. Send synopsis, rationale and sample section by post or email. Material will be acknowledged on receipt; reply with decision to publish within 1–3 months.

Folens Publishers

Hibernian Industrial Estate, off Greenhills Road, Tallaght, Dublin 24, Republic of Ireland
tel (01) 4137200 *fax* (01) 4137282
email info@folens.ie
website www.folens.ie
Chairman Dirk Folens, *Managing Director* John O'Connor, *Primary Managing & Commissioning Editor* Deirdre Whelan, *Secondary Managing Editor* Margaret Burns

Educational (primary, secondary, comprehensive, technical, in English and Irish). Founded 1956.

Blackwater Press (imprint)

Fiction for 9–12 year-olds, teenage fiction, picture books and *Brainstorm* series of activity books. Recent successes include *Irish Lengend* series, *Kirsten* by Elspeth Cameron (teenage fiction) and *Bin Bling* by Aoileann Garavaglia (activity book). Founded 1993.
Submission details Will consider unsolicited MSS. Send synopsis and first chapter. Allow 6 weeks for response.

David Fulton – see Taylor and Francis Group

Galaxy Children's Large Print – see BBC Audiobooks Ltd

Galore Park Publishing Ltd*
19–21 Sayers Lane, Tenterden, Kent TN30 6BW
tel (01580) 764242 fax (01580) 764142
website www.galorepark.co.uk

Educational textbooks and revision guides for students studying at independent schools. *So You Really Want To Learn* range of textbooks for children aged 11+ and *Junior* range for 8–10 year-olds. Courses include Latin, French, English, Spanish, maths and science. Founded 1999.

Gardner Education Ltd
The Old Manse, Rothiemurchus by Aviemore, Inverness-shire PH22 1QP
tel (0845) 230 0775 fax (0845) 230 0899
email education@gardnereducation.com
website www.gardnereducation.com

Specialists in literacy books and resources.

Geddes & Grosset*
David Dale House, New Lanark ML11 9DJ
tel (01555) 665000 fax (01555) 665694
email info@gandg.sol.co.uk
Publishers Ron Grosset, Mike Miller

Popular reference, children's non-fiction and activity books. Founded 1988.

Ginn – see page 19

GL Assessment
The Chiswick Centre, 414 Chiswick High Road, London W4 5TF
tel (0845) 602 1937 fax 020-8996 3660
email information@gl-assessment.co.uk
website www.gl-assessment.co.uk
Group Education Director Andrew Thraves

Independent provider of tests, assessments and assessment services for education. Its aim is to help educational professionals to understand and maximise the potential of their pupils and students. Publishes assessments for the 0–19 age group, though the majority of its assessments are aimed at 5–14 year-olds. Testing and assessment services include literacy, numeracy, thinking skills, ability, learning support and online testing. Founded 1981.

Gomer Press
Llandysul, Ceredigion SA44 4JL
tel (01559) 363090 fax (01559) 363758
email gwasg@gomer.co.uk
website www.gomer.co.uk, www.pontbooks.co.uk
Managing Director Jonathan Lewis, *Publishing Director* Mairwen Prys Jones, *Editors* Sioned Lleinau, Helen Evans, Rhiannon Davies

Picture books, novels, stories, poetry and teaching resources in the Welsh language relevant to Welsh culture. No unsolicited MSS; preliminary enquiry essential. Founded 1892.

Pont Books (imprint)
email editor@pontbooks.co.uk
website www.pontbooks.co.uk
Editor Viv Sayer

Picture books, novels, stories, poetry and teaching resources with a strong Welsh connection or background written in English. No unsolicited MSS; preliminary enquiry essential.

W.F. Graham
2 Pondwood Close, Moulton Park, Northampton NN3 6RT
tel (01604) 645537 fax (01604) 648414
email books@wfgraham.co.uk
website www.wfgraham.co.uk

Activity books including colouring, dot-to-dot, magic painting, puzzle, word search and sticker books. Also picture books and story books.

Granada Learning*
The Chiswick Centre, 414 Chiswick High Road, London W4 5TF
tel 020-8996-3333 fax 020-8742-8390
website www.granada-learning.com

Educational multimedia company publishing innovative, curriculum-based resources for the UK and abroad. It has a catalogue of over 800 software and hardware products for preschool children, primary and secondary, through to A level and adult education. Products are developed by teachers and educationalists. The Granada Learning Group includes BlackCat (educational software for primary schools), Granada Learning Software, Granada Learning Professional Development, GL Assessment (see page 12), SEMERC and The Skills Factory.

Hachette Children's Books*
338 Euston Road, London NW1 3BH
tel 020-7873 6000 fax 020-7873 6024
website www.hodderchildrens.co.uk, www.hachettelivreuk.co.uk
Managing Director Marlene Johnson, *Chief Operating Officer* Catherine Newman

Hodder Children's Books (imprint)
Publishing Director Anne McNeil
Fiction, picture books, novelty, general non-fiction and audiobooks.

Orchard Books (imprint)
Executive Director Penny Morris
Fiction, picture and novelty books.

Franklin Watts (imprint)
Publishing Director Rachel Cooke
Non-fiction and information books.

Wayland (imprint)
Publishing Director Joyce Bentley
Non-fiction and information books.

Hachette Livre UK Ltd*
338 Euston Road, London NW1 3BH
tel 020-7873 6000 *fax* 020-7873 6024
website www.hachettelivre.co.uk
Chief Executive Tim Hely Hutchinson, *Directors*
Martin Neild (managing, Headline and Ceo H&S and
John Murray), Jamie Hodder-Williams (managing,
H&S General), Philip Walters (Ceo, Hodder
Education), Marlene Johnson (managing, Hachette
Children's), Peter Roche (deputy Ceo/Ceo Orion),
Malcolm Edwards (managing, Orion), Alison Goff
(Ceo Octopus), Ursula Mackenzie (Ceo Little, Brown
Book Group), Pierre de Cacqueray (finance), Richard
Kitson (commercial), Martin Evans (IT & logistics),
Susan Taylor (group hr), Malcolm Edwards
(managing, Hachette Livre Australia), David Young
(Ceo Hachette Book Group USA)

Part of Hachette Livre SA since 2004. Hachette Livre
UK group companies: Hachette Children's Books
(page 12), Headline Book Publishing, Hodder
Education Group, Hodder & Stoughton, Hodder
Faith, John Murray, Little, Brown Book Group
(page 15), Orion Group (page 18), Octopus Group,
Hachette Livre Ireland, Hachette Livre Australia
(page 27), Hachette Livre New Zealand.

Haldane Mason Ltd
PO Box 34196, London NW10 3YB
tel 020-8459 2131 *fax* 020-8728 1216
email info@haldanemason.com
website www.haldanemason.com
Directors Sydney Francis, Ron Samuel

Illustrated non-fiction books and box sets, mainly for
children. No unsolicited material. Imprints: Haldane
Mason (adult), Red Kite Books (children's). Founded
1995.
Submission details Interested in non-fiction only;
phone or email first to check interest.

HarperCollins Publishers*
77–85 Fulham Palace Road, London W6 8JB
tel 020-8741 7070 *fax* 020-8307 4440
also at Westerhill Road, Bishopbriggs, Glasgow
G64 2QT
tel 0141-772 3200 *fax* 0141-306 3119
website www.harpercollins.co.uk
Ceo/Publisher Victoria Barnsley, *Managing Director*
Amanda Ridout

For adults: fiction (commercial and literary) and
non-fiction. Subjects include history, celebrity
memoirs, biographies, popular science, Mind, Body
& Spirit, dictionaries, maps and reference. Imprints
include Collins Crime, Collins Dictionaries/
COBUILD, Collins/Times Maps and Atlases, Collins
Willow, Estates, Fourth Estate, HarperCollins,

HarperCollins Entertainment, Thorsons/Element. All
fiction and trade non-fiction must be submitted
through an agent, or unsolicited MSS may be
submitted to www.authonomy.com. Owned by News
Corporation. Founded 1819.

HarperCollins Audio (imprint)
Publishing Director David Roth-Ey
See page 61.

HarperCollins Children's Books
website www.harpercollinschildrensbooks.co.uk
Managing Director Mario Santos, *Publisher* Ann-
Janine Murtagh, *Publishing Directors* Gillie Russell
(fiction), Sue Buswell (picture books), Claire Harding
(brands & properties)
Annuals, activity books, novelty books, picture books,
painting and colouring books, pop-up books and
book and tape sets. Fiction for 5–8 and 9–12 year-
olds, teenage fiction and series fiction; poetry; film/
TV tie-ins. Publishes approx. 265 titles each year.
Recent successes include (picture books) *The Tiger
Who Came to Tea* by Judith Kerr, *Percy the Park
Keeper* by Nick Butterworth, and *Duck in a Truck* by
Jez Alborough; and fiction by Louise Rennison, Nicky
Singer, Darren Shan and Michael Morpurgo. Books
published under licence include *Mary-Kate and
Ashley, Noddy, The Hulk, Spiderman, The Simpsons,
The Magic Roundabout, Dr Seuss* and *Paddington
Bear.*
Submission details No unsolicited MSS: only
accepts submissions via agents.

Collins Education (division)
Managing Director Nigel Ward, *Secondary Publisher*
Andrew Freeman
Books, CD-Roms and online material for UK
primary and secondary schools and colleges.

Heinemann – see Pearson Education

Hippo – see Scholastic Ltd

Hodder Children's Books – see Hachette
Children's Books

Hodder Education Group*
338 Euston Road, London NW1 3BH
tel 020-7873 6000 *fax* 020-7873 6024
website www.hoddereducation.co.uk,
www.hachettelivreukco.uk
Directors Philip Walters (chief executive and acting
managing, trade & tertiary), Alyssum Ross (business
operations), Ian Cafferky (commercial), Alexia Chan
(editorial FE/HE; maternity cover Paul Cherry),
Joanna Koster (editorial, health sciences), Katie
Roden (consumer education), Tim Mahar (sales &
marketing, consumer education), Samantha Eardley
(tertiary sales & marketing), Patrick White
(managing, Chambers Harrap), Elisabeth Tribe
(managing, schools), Robert Sulley (business &

international), Janice Tolan (sales & marketing, schools), Steve Connolly (editorial, digital publishing), Jim Belben (editorial, humanities & modern languages), Martin Davies (editorial, English, Maths, Science), John Mitchell (Hodder Gibson), Ron Richardson (conferences, Philip Allan Updates), Philip and David Cross (magazines & books, Philip Allan Updates)

Medical (Hodder Arnold), consumer education and self-improvement (Hodder Education and Teach Yourself), school (Hodder Education, Hodder Gibson and Philip Allan), dictionaries and related titles. Part of Hachette Livre UK Ltd (see page 13).

Hodder Gibson*
2A Christie Street, Paisley PA1 1NB
tel 0141-848 1609 *fax* 0141-889 6315
email hoddergibson@hodder.co.uk
website www.hoddergibson.co.uk,
www.hoddereducation.co.uk,
www.madaboutbooks.com
Managing Director John Mitchell

Educational books specifically for Scotland. No unsolicited MSS. Part of Hachette Livre UK Ltd (see page 13).

Hodder Headline Ltd – see Hachette Livre UK Ltd

Hopscotch Educational Publishing Ltd
St Jude's Church, Dulwich Road, London SE24 0PB
tel 020-7501 6736 *fax* 020-7978 8316
email rebecca.h@markallengroup.com
website www.hopscotchbooks.com
Publishing Manager Angela Morano-Shaw, *Publishing Assistant* Rebecca Haworth

National Curriculum teaching resources for primary schools. Founded 1997.

Step Forward Publishing Ltd
Early years teacher resources.

John Hunt/O-Books Publishing Ltd
The Bothy, Deershot Lodge, Park Lane, Ropley, Hants SO24 0BE
email john.hunt@o-books.net
website www.o-books.net
Director John Hunt

Children's and adult religious full-colour books for the international market. Founded 1989.

Hutchinson Children's Books – see The Random House Group Ltd

Jolly Learning Ltd
Tailours House, High Road, Chigwell, Essex IG7 6DL
tel 020-8501 0405 *fax* 020-8500 1696
email info@jollylearning.co.uk
website www.jollylearning.co.uk
Director Christopher Jolly

Educational: primary and English as a Foreign Language. The company is committed to enabling high standards in the teaching of reading and writing. *Jolly Phonics* provides a foundation for reading and writing. Publishes approx. 25 titles each year and has 200 in print. Recent successes include *Jolly Dictionary*, *Jolly Readers* and *Jolly Phonics Starter Kit*. Imprint: Jolly Phonics. Founded 1987.

Submission details Unsolicited MSS are only considered for add-ons to existing products.

Miles Kelly Publishing
The Bardfield Centre, Great Bardfield, Essex CM7 4SL
tel (01371) 811309 *fax* (01371) 811393
email info@mileskelly.net
website www.mileskelly.net
Directors Gerard Kelly, Jim Miles, Richard Curry

High-quality illustrated non-fiction and fiction titles for children and family: activity books, board books, story books, poetry, reference, posters and wallcharts. Age groups: preschool, 5–10, 10–15, 15+. See also entry in *Book packagers*. Founded 1996.

Kelpies – see Floris Books

Kingfisher – see Macmillan Publishers Ltd

The King's England Press
Cambertown House, Commercial Road, Goldthorpe, Rotherham, South Yorkshire S63 9BL
tel/fax (01484) 663790
email sales@kingsengland.com
website www.kingsengland.com, www.pottypoets.com

Poetry collections for both adults and children. Successes include *The Spot on My Bum: Horrible Poems for Horrible Children* by Gez Walsh, *Always Eat Your Bogies and Other Rotten Rhymes* by Andrew Collett, *Wang Foo the Kung Fu Shrew and Other Freaky Poems Too* by Chris White and *Vikings Don't Wear Pants* by Roger Stevens and Celia Warren.

Also publishes reprints of Arthur Mee's *King's England* series of 1930s guidebooks and books on folklore, and local and ecclesiastical history.

Submission details See website for guidelines. Currently not accepting new unsolicited proposals. Founded 1989.

Kingscourt/McGraw-Hill*
McGraw-Hill House, Shoppenhangers Road, Maidenhead, Berks. SL6 2QL
tel (01628) 502500 *fax* (01628) 635895
website www.mcgraw-hill.co.uk/kingscourt
General Manager Rob Ince

Educational publisher of resources for KS1–3, including *Big Books for Shared Reading, Guided Reading, Story Chest, Literacy Links Plus* and *Maths Links Plus*. Resources support National Literacy and Numeracy Strategies, the Scottish Guidelines 5–14,

Northern Ireland curriculum and Curriculum 2000 in Wales. Part of the McGraw-Hill Companies. Founded in 1988.

Jessica Kingsley Publishers*
116 Pentonville Road, London N1 9JB
tel 020-7833 2307 fax 020-7837 2917
email post@jkp.com
website www.jkp.com
Managing Director Jessica Kingsley

Psychology, psychiatry, arts therapies, social work, special needs (especially autism and Asperger Syndrome), education, law, practical theology and a small children's list focusing on books for children with special needs. Founded 1987.

Kube Publishing Ltd
(formerly the Islamic Foundation)
Markfield Conference Centre, Ratby Lane, Markfield, Leics. LE67 9SY
tel (01530) 249230 fax (01530) 249656
email info@kubepublishing.com
website www.kubepublishing.com
Managing Director Haris Ahmad

Books on Islam for adults and children.

Ladybird – see Penguin Group (UK)

Leckie & Leckie*
3rd Floor, 4 Queen Street, Edinburgh EH2 1JE
tel (0131) 220 6831 fax (0131) 225 9987
email enquiries@leckieandleckie.co.uk
website www.leckieandleckie.co.uk

Educational resources. Dedicated to the ongoing development of materials specifically for education in Scotland, from Standard Grade Foundation to Advanced Higher Level. Over 200 titles are currently available in the study guide range. Part of Huveaux plc.

Letts Educational
4 Grosvenor Place, London SW1X 7DL
tel 020-7096 2900 fax 020-7096 2945
email mail@lettsed.co.uk
website www.letts-educational.com
Directors Andrew Ware (managing), Chris Glennie (publishing, education group), Helen Jacobs (publishing)

Study and revision guides for children of all ages, from preschool to A Level. Owned by Huveaux plc.

Frances Lincoln Ltd
4 Torriano Mews, Torriano Avenue,
London NW5 2RZ
tel 020-7284 4009 fax 020-7485 0490
email reception@frances-lincoln.com
website www.frances-lincoln.com
Directors John Nicoll (managing), Janetta Otter-Barry (editorial, children's books), Jon Rippon (finance),

Martin Oestreicher (sales), Andrew Dunn (rights), Tim Rix, David Kewley, Sarah Roberts (non-executive)

Illustrated, international co-editions: gardening, architecture, environment, interiors, art, walking and climbing, gift, children's books. Founded 1977.

Frances Lincoln Children's Books (imprint)
Novelty books, picture books, fiction for 5–12 year-olds, religion, poetry.
    Submission details Submit material either through an agent or direct to Antonia Parkin.

Lion Hudson plc*
Wilkinson House, Jordan Hill Road,
Oxford OX2 8DR
tel (01865) 302750 fax (01865) 302757
email enquiries@lionhudson.com
website www.lionhudson.com
Managing Director Paul Clifford

Books for children and adults. Children's books include fiction, picture stories, illustrated non-fiction and information books on the Christian faith. Also specialises in children's Bibles and prayer collections. Founded 1971 as Lion Publishing; merged with Angus Hudson Ltd in 2003.

Little, Brown Book Group*
100 Victoria Embankment, London EC4Y 0DY
tel 020-7911 8000 fax 020-7911 8100
email uk@littlebrown.co.uk
website www.littlebrown.co.uk
Ceo & Publisher Ursula Mackenzie, Coo David Kent, Directors Richard Beswick (editorial), Antonia Hodgson (editorial), David Shelley (editorial), Peter Cotton (design), Melanee Winder (export sales), Robert Manser (group sales), Roger Cazalet (marketing), Karen Blewett (commercial), Rosalie MacFarlane (publicity), Diane Spivey (rights)

Hardback and paperback fiction and general non-fiction. No unsolicited MSS. Part of Hachette Livre UK Ltd (see page 13). Founded 1988.

Atom (division)
website www.atombooks.co.uk
Publishing Director Tim Holman, Editorial Director Darren Nash
Teen fiction with a fantastical edge.

Little Tiger Press – see Magi Publications

Livewire – see The Women's Press

Longman – see Pearson Education

Macmillan Publishers Ltd*
The Macmillan Building, 4 Crinan Street,
London N1 9XW
tel 020-7833 4000 fax 020-7843 4640
website www.macmillan.com
Chief Executive Annette Thomas, Directors Julian

Drinkall, S.C. Inchcoombe, D.J.G. Knight, Dr A. Thomas, D. Macmillan, N. Byam Shaw, G. Elliot, J. Gutbrod (Germany), S. von Holtzbrinck (Germany), R. Gibb (Australia)

Pan Macmillan (division)
20 New Wharf Road, London N1 9RR
tel 020-7014 6000 fax 020-7014 6001
website www.panmacmillan.com
Managing Director Anthony Forbes-Watson, Publishers Richard Milner (Macmillan non-fiction, Sidgwick & Jackson, Boxtree), Maria Rejt (Macmillan fiction, Picador & Macmillan New Writing), Deputy Publisher Picador Ursula Doyle, Publishing Manager Alison Muirden (Macmillan Audio)

For adults: novels, literary, crime, thrillers, romance, science fiction, fantasy and horror. Autobiography, biography, business, gift books, health and beauty, history, humour, travel, philosophy, politics, world affairs, theatre, film, gardening, cookery, popular reference. Publishes under Macmillan, Tor, Pan, Picador, Sidgwick & Jackson, Boxtree, Macmillan Audio, Macmillan New Writing. No unsolicited MSS except through Macmillan New Writing. Founded 1843.

Campbell Books (imprint)
Editorial Director Sarah Fabiny
Early learning, pop-up, novelty, board books for the preschool market.

Kingfisher (imprint)
tel 020-7014 6000 fax 020-7014 6001
Director Emma Hopkin, Non-fiction Publishing Director Melissa Fairley
Novelty books, picture books, fiction for 5–8 and 9–12 year-olds, series fiction, reference and poetry. Publishes approx. 50 new non-fiction titles and 25 new fiction titles each year and has about 500 in print. Recent successes include Cleopatra by Adele Geras and Simon Basher's Periodic Table. The Kingfisher Book of Nursery Rhymes by Vivian French and Small Bad Wolf by Sean Taylor (from the I Am Reading series). Imprint of Macmillan Children's Books.
Submission details No unsolicited MSS.

Young Picador (imprint)
Editorial Director Sarah Dudman
Literary fiction in paperback and hardback for the young adult market.

Macmillan Education Ltd (division)
Macmillan Oxford, 4 Between Towns Road, Oxford OX4 3PP
tel (01865) 405700 fax (01865) 405701
email info@macmillan.com
website www.macmillaneducation.com
Chief Executive Julian Drinkall, Publishing Directors Alison Hubert (Africa, Caribbean, Middle East, Asia), Kate Melliss (Spain), Sharon Jervis (Latin America),

Sue Bale (Dictionaries), Angela Lilley (International ELT)
ELT titles and school and college textbooks and materials in all subjects for the international education market in both book and electronic formats.

Magi Publications
1 The Coda Centre, 189 Munster Road, London SW6 6AW
tel 020-7385 6333 fax 020-7385 7333
website www.littletigerpress.com
Publishers Monty Bhatia, Jude Evans, Editors Stephanie Stansbie, Jo Collins

Little Tiger Press (imprint)
email info@littletiger.co.uk
Children's picture books, novelty books, board books, pop-up books and activity books for preschool age to 7 years. Will consider new material from authors and illustrators via email only; see website for guidelines. Founded 1987.

Caterpillar Books (imprint)
email jasher@caterpillarbooks.co.uk
website www.caterpillarbooks.com
Publisher Jamie Asher, Editor Sarah Frost
Books for preschool children, including pop-ups, board books, cloth books and activity books. Will consider new material from authors.

Stripes (imprint)
email info@stripespublishing.co.uk
website www.stripespublishing.co.uk
Publisher Jane Harris, Editor Katie Jennings
Fiction for children aged 6–12 years. Mainly series publishing. Will consider new material from authors and illustrators; see website for guidelines. Founded 2005.

Mantra Lingua
Global House, 303 Ballards Lane, London N12 8NP
tel 020-8445 5123 fax 020-8446 7745
email sales@mantralingua.com
website www.mantralingua.com, www.talkingpen.co.uk
Managing Director M. Chatterji
Children's multicultural picture books; multilingual friezes/posters; dual language books and CD-Roms; sound-enabled teaching resources for literacy and language learning. Founded 1984.

Marshall Cavendish*
5th Floor, 32/38 Saffron Hill, London EC1N 8FN
tel 020-7421 8120 fax 020-7421 8121
email editorial@marshallcavendish.co.uk
website www.marshallcavendish.co.uk
Managing Editor Susan McGing
English language teaching. Founded 1969.

Kevin Mayhew Ltd
Buxhall, Stowmarket, Suffolk IP14 3BW
tel (01449) 737978 fax (01449) 737834

email info@kevinmayhew.com
website www.kevinmayhew.com
Directors Kevin Mayhew (chairman), Kevin Whomes
(managing)

Christianity: prayer and spirituality, pastoral care,
preaching, liturgy worship, children's, youth work,
drama, instant art. Music: hymns, organ and choral,
contemporary worship, piano and instrumental.
Contact Manuscript Submissions Dept before
sending MSS/synopses. Founded 1976.

Meadowside Children's Books

185 Fleet Street, London EC4A 2HS
tel 020-7400 1061 fax 020-7400 1037
email info@meadowsidebooks.com
website www.meadowsidebooks.com
Publisher Simon Rosenheim

Picture books and children's fiction. Founded 2003.

Gullane Children's Books (imprint)
Publisher Sophie Winter-Cole
Picture books for children aged 0–8 years.

The Mercier Press[†]

Unit 3, Oak House, Riverview Business Park,
Blackrock, Cork, Republic of Ireland
tel (021) 4899858 fax (021) 4899887
email pr@mercierpress.ie
website www.mercierpress.ie
Directors J.F. Spillane (chairman), C. Feehan
(managing), M.P. Feehan

Books for adults and children. Subjects include Irish
literature, folklore, history, politics, humour, current
affairs, health, mind and spirit and general non-
fiction. Founded 1944.

Mill Publishing

PO Box 120, 4 Balloo Avenue,
County Down BT19 7BX
tel (0800) 731 2837 fax (0800) 0272833
email info@motivationinlearning.com
website www.superstickers.com

Produces material to meet the needs of the National
Curriculum. The Skillbuilder system, in its separate
Literacy and Numeracy versions, provides schools
with a means of achieving the objectives required by
the National Literacy Strategy and National
Numeracy Strategy. The Write into History series
develops key writing skills using the approach set out
in Grammar for Writing. The Crosslinks series covers
reading, writing and thinking across the curriculum.
Part of the Motivation in Learning Group.

Anglia Young Books (imprint)
website www.angliayoungbooks.co.uk
Educational publisher. Historical fiction for use in the
KS2 classroom. Also publishes cross-curricular
material; the Write into History series delivers
grammar in the context of historical stories and

Crosslinks focuses on reading, writing and thinking
across the curriculum.Welcomes suggestions from
teachers for new resources. Authors and illustrators
should send a brief synopsis of their intended title or
portfolio.

National Association for the Teaching of English (NATE)

50 Broadfield Road, Sheffield S8 0XJ
tel 0114-255 5419 fax 0114-255 5296
email info@nate.org.uk
website www.nate.org.uk
Chair Simon Wrigley, Vice-chair Elaine Millard,
Company Secretary Lyn Fairfax, Development &
Communications Officer Ian McNeilly, Publications
Manager Anne Fairhall, Publications Coordinator Julie
Selwood

Educational (primary, secondary and tertiary):
teaching English, drama and media. Publishes
approx. 4 titles each year and has 70 in print. Recent
publications include Cracking Good Picture Books
(KS1 focus), Drama Packs (KS3/4 focus) and The Full
English (KS2–5). Imprint: NATE. Founded 1963.
   Submission details Submissions should be made via
a 'Publication Proposal' form for consideration by
the Publications Manager and 3 members of the
Editorial Board. Allow 3–6 weeks for response. Will
consider unsolicited MSS.

Neate Publishing

33 Downside Road, Winchester, Hants SO22 5LT
tel (01962) 841479 fax (01962) 841743
email sales@neatepublishing.co.uk
website www.neatepublishing.co.uk
Directors Bobbie Neate (managing), Ann Langran,
Maggie Threadingham

Non-fiction books, educational packs, CDs and
posters for primary schoolchildren. Founded 1999.

Nelson Thornes Ltd*

Delta Place, 27 Bath Road, Cheltenham,
Glos. GL53 7TH
tel (01242) 267100 fax (01242) 221914
email name@nelsonthornes.com
website www.nelsonthornes.com
Managing Director Lindeon Harris

Print and electronic publishers for the educational
market: primary, secondary, further education,
professional. Part of the Wolters Kluwer Group of
Companies.

Jane Nissen Books

Swan House, Chiswick Mall, London W4 2PS
tel 020-8994 8203 fax 020-8742 8198
email jane@nissen.demon.co.uk

Reprinted fiction for 5–8 and 9–12 year-olds, teenage
fiction and poetry. Publishes approx. 4 titles each year
and has 30 in print. Recent successes include My
Friend Mr Leakey by J.B.S. Haldane, Kings and

Queens by Eleanor and Herbert Farjeon and *Tennis Shoes* by Noel Streatfeild. Seeking to publish more children's 'forgotten' classics. Founded 2000.
Submission details Personal recommendations welcome.

Oberon Books
521 Caledonian Road, London N7 9RH
tel 020-7607 3637 *fax* 020-7607 3629
email info@oberonbooks.com
website www.oberonbooks.com
Managing Director Charles Glanville *Publisher* James Hogan *Editor* Dan Steward

New and classic play texts, programme texts and general theatre and performing arts books. Founded 1986.

The O'Brien Press Ltd†
12 Terenure Road East, Rathgar, Dublin 6, Republic of Ireland
tel (01) 492 3333 *fax* (01) 492 2777
email books@obrien.ie
website www.obrien.ie
Directors Michael O'Brien, Ide ní Laoghaire, Ivan O'Brien

For children: fiction for all ages; illustrated fiction series – *Panda Cubs* (age 3+), *Pandas* (age 5+), *Flyers* (age 6+) and *Red Flag* (8+); novels (10+) – contemporary, historical, fantasy; also non-fiction. Also for adults: biography, politics, history, true crime, sport, humour, reference. No adult fiction, poetry or academic. Founded 1974.
Submission details Unsolicited MSS (sample chapters only), synopses and ideas for books welcome – submissions will not be returned.

Orchard Books – see Hachette Children's Books

The Orion Publishing Group Ltd*
Orion House, 5 Upper St Martin's Lane, London WC2H 9EA
tel 020-7240 3444 *fax* 020-7240 4822
website www.orionbooks.co.uk
Directors Arnaud Nourry (chairman), Peter Roche (chief executive), Malcolm Edwards (deputy chief executive)

For adults: fiction and non-fiction and audio. Imprints include Everyman, Gollancz, Orion, Phoenix and Weidenfeld & Nicolson. Part of Hachette Livre UK Ltd (see page 13). Founded 1992.

Orion Children's Books (division)
Publisher Fiona Kennedy, *Editorial Manager* Jane Hughes

Picture books, fiction for 5–8 and 9–12 year-olds, teenage fiction, series fiction and audio. Publishes approx. 50 titles each year and has about 350 in print. Recent successes include books by Francesca Simon, Michelle Paver and Sally Gardner. Imprints: Orion Children's Books.

Submission details Will consider unsolicited MSS. Allow 2 months for response. Submissions via agents take priority.

Oxford University Press*
Great Clarendon Street, Oxford OX2 6DP
tel (01865) 556767 *fax* (01865) 556646
email enquiry@oup.com
website www.oup.com
Ceo Henry Reece, *Group Finance Director* David Gillard, *Academic Division Managing Director* Tim Barton, *UK Children's & Educational Division Managing Director* Kate Harris, *ELT Division Managing Director* Peter Marshall, *Publishing Director Journals* Martin Richardson, *UK Human Resources Director* Caroline James-Nock, *Sales Director* Alastair Lewis

Archaeology, architecture, art, belles-lettres, bibles, bibliography, children's books (fiction, non-fiction, picture), commerce, current affairs, dictionaries, drama, economics, educational (infants, primary, secondary, technical, university), encyclopedias, English language teaching, electronic publishing, essays, foreign language learning, general history, hymn and service books, journals, law, medical, music, oriental, philosophy, political economy, prayer books, reference, science, sociology, theology and religion; educational software; *Grove Dictionaries of Music & Art*. Trade paperbacks published under the imprint of Oxford Paperbacks. Founded 1478.

Children's and Educational Division
Managing Director, Children's & Education Kate Harris, *Business Director Trade & Children's* Richard Hodson, *Children's Publisher, Fiction & Picture Books* Liz Cross, *Dictionaries Publisher* Vineeta Gupta, *Non-Fiction Publisher* Gill Denton, *Schoolbooks: Business Director, Primary & Electronic* Rod Theodorou, *Business Director, Secondary & International* Phil Garratt, *Head of Publishing, Secondary English, Humanities, Languages & Cartography* Simon Tanner-Tremaine, *Publisher, Modern Foreign Languages & Classics* Dick Capel-Davies, *Publisher, Science Maths & Technology* Elspeth Boardley, *Head of Primary Literacy Publishing* Jane Harley.
Picture books, fiction, poetry and dictionaries. Authors include Tim Bowler, Gillian Cross, Julie Hearne and Geraldine McCaughrean.

Parragon Books Ltd
4 Queen Street, Bath BA1 1HE
tel (01225) 478888 *fax* (01225) 478897
email info@parragon.com
website www.parragon.com
Managing Directors Paul Taylor, Lutz Billstein, *Children's Publisher* Venetia Davie, *Children's Editorial* Jane Walker, *Children's Licensed* Ayshea Scharf

Activity books, novelty books, picture books, fiction for 5–8 year-olds, reference and home learning, book and CD sets. Licensed character list. No unsolicited material.

Pavilion Children's Books

10 Southcombe Street, London W14 0RA
tel 020-7605 1400 fax 020-7605 1401
website www.anovabooks.com
Publisher Ben Cameron

Children's books: from baby and picture books to illustrated classics and interactive books. Part of the Anova Books Group. Submissions via an agent only.

Recent successes include *The Story of the Little Mole* by Werner Holzwarth, *War Boy* by Michael Foreman, *What's in Your Tummy, Mummy?* by Sam Lloyd, *Michael Foreman's Classic Fairy Tales*, and Quentin Blake's *Ten Frogs*.

Payne-Gallway – see Pearson Education

PCET Publishing

27 Kirchen Road, London W13 0UD
tel 020-8567 9206 fax 020-8566 5120
email info@pcet.co.uk
website www.pcet.co.uk

Pictorial Charts Educational Trust (PCET) publishes visual resources for primary and secondary education: wallcharts, photopacks, activity books and other classroom accessories to support the National Curriculum. Also has a charitable arm which provides funding and teaching resources for the developing world.

Pearson Education*

Edinburgh Gate, Harlow, Essex CM20 2JE
tel (01279) 623623 fax (01279) 414130
email schools@longman.co.uk
email www.pearsoned.co.uk
President, Pearson Education EMA Rod Bristow

Materials for school pupils, students and practitioners globally.

Harcourt (imprint)
Educational resources for teachers and learners at Primary, Secondary and Vocational level. Provides a range of published resources, teachers' support, and pupil and student material in all core subjects for all ages. Imprints: Ginn, Heinemann, Payne-Gallway, Raintree, Rigby.

Longman (imprint)
Edinburgh Gate, Harlow, Essex CM20 2JE
tel (0800) 579579 fax (01279) 414130
email schools@longman.co.uk
website www.longman.co.uk

Educational: primary and secondary. Primary: literacy and numeracy. Secondary: English, maths, science, history, geography, modern languages, design and technology, business and economics, psychology and sociology.

Penguin Longman (imprint)
English language teaching.

York Notes (imprint)
Literature guides for students.

Penguin Group (UK)*

80 Strand, London WC2R 0RL
tel 020-7010 3000 fax 020-7010 6060
website www.penguin.co.uk
Group Ceo (Global) John Makinson, Penguin UK Ceo Peter Field, DK Ceo Gary June, Managing Directors Helen Fraser (Penguin), John Duhigg (travel), Stephanie Barton (brands and licences)

Books for adults and children (see below). Adult subjects include biography, fiction, current affairs, general leisure, health, history, humour, literature, politics, spirituality and relationships, sports, travel and TV/film tie-ins. Adult imprints include Allen Lane, Dorling Kindersley, Fig Tree, Hamish Hamilton, Michael Joseph, Penguin, Penguin Classics, Rough Guides, Viking. Owned by Pearson plc.

Puffin (division)
Managing Director Francesca Dow, Publishing Director Sarah Hughes (fiction), Editorial Directors Louise Bolongaro (picture books), Kate Hayler (characters)

Children's paperback and hardback books: picture books, board books, novelty books, fiction, poetry, non-fiction, popular culture; and audio. Series: *Puffin Classics* and *Puffin Modern Classics*.

Submission details No unsolicited MSS or synopses.

Brands and Licensing (division)
website www.funwithspot.com,
www.flowerfairies.com, www.peterrabbit.com,
www.ladybird.co.uk
Managing Director Stephanie Barton

Specialises in preschool illustrated developmental books for ages 0–6, non-fiction 0–8; licensed brands; children's classic publishing and merchandising properties. No unsolicited MSS. Includes Warne; Ladybird and BBC Children's Books.

Dorling Kindersley (division)
website www.dk.com
Ceo Gary June, Coo Andrew Philips, Global Publisher Miriam Farbey

Illustrated non-fiction for adults and children: gardening, health, medical, travel, food and drink, history, natural history, photography, reference, pregnancy and childcare, antiques.

Age groups: preschool, 5–8, 8+, family.

Penguin Longman – see Pearson Education

Phaidon Press Ltd

Regent's Wharf, All Saints Street, London N1 9PA
tel 020-7843 1000 fax 020-7843 1010
email enquiries@phaidon.com
website www.phaidon.com

2

Publisher Richard Schlagman, *Chairman* Andrew Price, *Directors* Amanda Renshaw (deputy publisher), James Booth-Clibborn

Visual arts, lifestyle and culture.

Piccadilly Press
5 Castle Road, London NW1 8PR
tel 020-7267 4492 *fax* 020-7267 4493
email books@piccadillypress.co.uk
website www.piccadillypress.co.uk
Managing Director & Publisher Brenda Gardner

Picture books, humorous tween/teenage fiction, series fiction, parental advice trade paperbacks. Publishes approx. 25–30 titles each year and has over 200 in print. Recent successes include *Mates Dates* series by Cathy Hopkins and *It's Not Fair!* by Anita Harper and Mary McQuillan. Founded 1983.
Submission details Will consider unsolicited MSS. Send synopsis and 3 sample chapters. Allow 6 weeks for response. Looking to publish humorous teenage books which deal with contemporary issues.

Picthall & Gunzi Ltd
21A Widmore Road, Bromley, Kent BR1 1RW
tel 020-8460 4032 *fax* 020-8460 4021
email chez@picthallandgunzi.demon.co.uk, chris@picthallandgunzi.demon.co.uk
website www.picthallandgunzi.com
Director Chez Picthall (managing director), *Publisher & Editorial Director* Christiane Gunzi

High-quality, photographically illustrated non-fiction for children: activity books, board books, novelty books, early learning. Age groups: preschool and Key Stage 1. See also page 66.

Pinwheel Children's Books – see Alligator Books Ltd

Pipers' Ash Ltd
Pipers' Ash, Church Road, Christian Malford, Chippenham, Wilts. SN15 4BW
tel (01249) 720563 *fax* (0870) 0568916
email pipersash@supamasu.co.uk
website www.supamasu.co.uk
Editorial Director Alfred Tyson

Poetry, contemporary short stories, science fiction stories; historical novels, biographies, plays, philosophy, translations, children's, general non-fiction. New authors with talent and potential encouraged. Founded 1976.

Point – see Scholastic Ltd

Pont Books – see Gomer Press

Poolbeg Press Ltd
123 Grange Hill, Baldoyle, Dublin 13, Republic of Ireland
tel (01) 8321477 *fax* (01) 8321430

email poolbeg@poolbeg.com
website www.poolbeg.com
Directors Kieran Devlin (managing), Paula Campbell (publisher), Brian Langan (non-fiction editor)

Children's and teenage fiction. Also adult popular fiction, non-fiction, current affairs. Imprint: Poolbeg. Founded 1976.

Priddy Books
4 Crinan Street, London N1 9XW
tel 020-7418 5515 *fax* 020-7418 85507
website www.priddybooks.com
Publisher Roger Priddy, *Publishing Manager* Claire Amos, *Art Director* Robert Tainsh, *Rights Manager* Isabel Rollings

Specialises in baby/toddler and preschool books: activity books, board books, novelty books, picture books.

Prim-Ed Publishing
PO Box 2840, Coventry CV6 5ZY
tel (0870) 876 0151 *fax* (0870) 876 0152
email sales@prim-ed.com
website www.prim-ed.com
Managing Director Seamus McGuinness

Educational publisher specialising in copymasters (photocopiable teaching resources) for primary school and special needs lower secondary pupils. Books written by practising classroom teachers.

Puffin – see Penguin Group (UK)

QED Publishing
226 City Road, London EC1V 2TT
tel 020-7812 8600 *fax* 020-7253 4370
email qedpublishing@quarto.com
website www.qed-publishing.co.uk
Publisher Steve Evans, *Creative Director* Zeta Davies

Education. High-quality curriculum-based books designed to stimulate early learning in the classroom, as well as in the home. Series include *QED Start Talking*, *QED Start Reading*, *QED Start Writing*. QED is from the Latin *quod erat demonstrandum* (that which was to be demonstrated). Imprint of the Quarto Group. Founded 2003.

Quarto Children's Books Ltd
226 City Road, London EC1V 2TT
tel 020-7812 8626 *fax* 020-7253 4370
email quartokids@quarto.com
website www.quarto.com
Publisher Sue Grabham, *Art Director* Jonathan Gilbert

Co-edition publisher of innovative Books-Plus for children. Highly illustrated paper-engineered, novelty and component-based titles for all ages, but primarily preschool (3+), 5–8 and 8+ years. Mainly non-fiction, early concepts and curriculum-based topics for the trade in all international markets. Opportunities for freelance paper engineers, artists, authors, editors and designers.

Ragged Bears Publishing Ltd

Unit 14A, Bennett's Field Trading Estate,
Southgate Road, Wincanton, Somerset BA9 9DT
tel (01963) 824184 *fax* (01963) 31147
email info@raggedbears.co.uk
website www.raggedbears.co.uk
Managing Director Henrietta Stickland, *Submissions Editor* Barbara Lamb

Activity books, picture books, novelty books and fiction for 5–8 year-olds. Publishes 5–10 titles each year and has 150 in print. Recent successes include *Big Dig* and *The Christmas Bear* by Paul Stickland, *Lovely Ruby & The Mermaid* by Nancy Trott, and *We're Going on an Aeroplane* by Steve Augarde. *Dinosaur Roar!* has sold over 10 million copies since its publication almost 10 years ago. *Little Robots* by Mike Brownlow is now an animated TV series on CBeebies. Founded 1994.
  Submission details Will consider unsolicited MSS. Allow 3–4 months for response. Takes very few unsolicited ideas as the list is small. Include sae for return of MSS; do not send original artwork. No email submissions.

Raintree – see Pearson Education

The Random House Group Ltd*

20 Vauxhall Bridge Road, London SW1V 2SA
tel 020-7840 8400
website www.randomhouse.co.uk
Chairman/Ceo Gail Rebuck, *Deputy Ceo* Ian Hudson, *Directors* Larry Finlay (RHCB and Managing Director, Transworld), Mark Gardiner (finance), Brian Davies (Ebury Publishing and Managing Director, overseas operations), Peter Bowron (CHA and Group Managing), Richard Cable (CCV and Managing Director Random House Enterprises), Garry Prior (sales), Mark Williams (Managing Director Distribution)

Subsidiary of Bertelsmann AG.
  Group consists of 5 publishing companies comprising 40 imprints.

Random House Audio Books (imprint)
tel 020-7840 8419 *fax* 020-7233 6127
Commissioning Editor Zoe Howes
See page 61.

Random House Children's Books (division)
61–63 Uxbridge Road, London W5 5SA
tel 020-8579 2652 *fax* 020-8579 5479
website www.kidsatrandomhouse.co.uk
Annie Eaton (Publisher, fiction), Fiona MacMillan (Publisher, colour and custom books), Charlie Sheppard (Editorial Director, fiction), Kelly Hurst (Editorial Director, fiction), Helen Mackenzie Smith (Editorial Director, picture books), Natascha Biebow (Senior Commissioning Editor, picture and novelty/preschool books), Alice Corrie (Commissioning Editor, colour and custom books), Margaret Hope (Art Director)

Picture books, novelty and gift books, preschool and pop-ups, fiction, non-fiction and audio CDs.
  Imprints: Bantam Press, Bodley Head Children's Books, Jonathan Cape Children's Books, Corgi Children's Books, Doubleday Children's Books, David Fickling Books, Hutchinson Children's Books, Red Fox Children's Books. No unsolicited MSS or original artwork or text.

Tamarind Ltd
61–63 Uxbridge Road, London W5 5SA
tel 020-8231 6800 *fax* 020-8231 6737
email info@tamarindbooks.co.uk
website www.tamarindbooks.co.uk
Managing Director Verna Wilkins
Multicultural children's books. Fiction: picture books (ages 4–8), board books for babies (ages 0–3), board books for toddlers (ages 2–5). Non-fiction: biography (ages 8–12). Books feature on National Curriculum. Founded 1987.
  Submission details Will consider unsolicited MSS with sae. Allow one month for response. Looking for books which give black children a high positive profile.

David Fickling Books (imprint)
31 Beaumont Street, Oxford OX1 2NP
tel (01865) 339000 *fax* (01865) 339009
email dfickling@randomhouse.co.uk
website www.davidficklingbooks.co.uk
Publisher David Fickling, *Editor* Bella Pearson
Picture books, fiction for 5–8 and 9–12 year-olds, teenage fiction and poetry. Will consider unsolicited MSS (first 3 chapters only); include covering letter and sae and allow 3 months for response. If possible, find an agent first. Founded 2000.

Ransom Publishing Ltd

51 Southgate Street, Winchester SO23 9EH
tel (01962) 862307 *fax* (05601) 148881
email ransom@ransom.co.uk
website www.ransom.co.uk
Directors Jenny Ertle (managing), Steve Rickard (publishing)

Books for reluctant and struggling readers covering high interest age/low reading age titles, quick reads, reading schemes, gifted and talented. Range of accompanying workbooks, teacher's guides and software. Series include Boffin Boy, Dark Man, Trailblazers, Siti's Sisters and Cutting Edge.
  Considers unsolicited manuscripts. Email in first instance. Founded 1995.

Reader's Digest Children's Publishing Ltd

The Ice House, 124–126 Walcot Street,
Bath BA1 5BG
tel (01225) 473200 *fax* (01225) 460942
email jo_o'hagan@readersdigest.co.uk
website www.rd.com, www.readersdigest.co.uk
Commercial Director Paul Stuart, *Contact* Jo O'Hagan

Innovative, high-quality books designed to encourage children to use their creativity and imagination. Board, novelty, cinema and TV tie-ins. Licensed characters and brands. Also a wide range of children's religious titles. Fully owned subsidiary of Reader's Digest Association Inc. Founded 1981.

Red Bird Publishing

Kiln Farm, East End Green, Brightlingsea, Colchester, Essex CO7 0SX
tel (01206) 303525 *fax* (01206) 304545
email info@red-bird.co.uk
website www.red-bird.co.uk
Publisher Marin Rhodes-Schofield

Innovative children's activity packs and books produced with a mix of techniques and materials such as Glow in the Dark, Mirrors, Stereoscopic 3D, Moiré and other optical illusions. Authors are specialists in their fields. Activity books, novelty books, picture books, painting and colouring books, teaching books, posters: hobbies, nature and the environment, science. Age groups: preschool, 5–10, 10–15. No unsolicited MSS.

Red Fox Children's Books – see The Random House Group Ltd

Red Kite Books – see Haldane Mason Ltd

Religious and Moral Education Press (RMEP)*

13–17 Long Lane, London EC1A 9PN
tel 020-7776 7540 *fax* 020-7776 7556
email admin@scm-canterburypress.co.uk
website www.rmep.co.uk
Chief Executive Andrew Moore, *Commissioning Editor* Valerie Bingham

Educational books and teachers' resources (primary and secondary): religious education, citizenship, PSHE, assembly resources (collective worship). Publishes approx. 10–20 titles each year and has about 150 in print. Division of SCM-Canterbury Press Ltd. Founded 1980.
Submission details Will consider unsolicited MSS. Send an outline or synopsis to the Commissioning Editor, indicating how the proposed publication would meet school curriculum requirements. Allow 4–6 weeks for a response. Most RMEP authors are, or have been, school teachers or college lecturers – mostly specialists in religious education. Welcomes work from children's book illustrators.

Rigby – see Pearson Education

Rising Stars

Rising Stars UK Ltd, 22 Grafton Street, London W1S 4EX
tel 020-7495 6793 *fax* 020-7495 6796
email publishing@risingstars-uk.com
website www.risingstars-uk.com

Educational publisher of books and software for primary school age children. Titles are linked to the National Curriculum Key Stages, QCA Schemes of Work, National Numeracy Framework or National Literacy Strategy. Approach by email with ideas for publishing.

SAGE Publications Ltd*

1 Oliver's Yard, 55 City Road, London EC1Y 1SP
tel 020-7324 8500 *fax* 020-7324 8600
email info@sagepub.co.uk
website www.sagepub.co.uk
Directors Stephen Barr (managing), Katharine Jackson, Ziyad Marar, Richard Fidczuk, Phil Denvir, Clive Parry, Carol Irwin, Blaise Simqu (USA), Sara Miller McCune (USA), Paul R. Chapman

Primary/elementary education, children's development. Social sciences, behavioural sciences, humanities, STM. Founded 1971.

Paul Chapman Publishing (imprint)

website www.paulchapmanpublishing.co.uk
Publisher Marianne Lagrange

Education: academic and professional books for students, practitioners and school leaders.

Salariya Book Company Ltd

Book House, 25 Marlborough Place, Brighton BN1 1UB
tel (01273) 603306 *fax* (01273) 693857
email salariya@salariya.com
website www.salariya.com
Director David Salariya

Children's non-fiction. Imprints: Book House, Scribblers. Founded 1989.

Schofield & Sims Ltd

Dogley Mill, Fenay Bridge, Huddersfield HD8 0NQ
tel (01484) 607080 *fax* (01484) 606815
email post@schofieldandsims.co.uk
website www.schofieldandsims.co.uk
Chairman C.N. Platts

Educational: nursery, infants, primary; posters. Founded 1901.

Scholastic Ltd*

Euston House, 24 Eversholt Street, London NW1 1DB
tel 020-7756 7761 *fax* 020-7756 7795
website www.scholastic.co.uk
Chairman M.R. Robinson, *Group Managing Director* Kate Wilson

Children's fiction and non-fiction and education for primary schools. Owned by Scholastic Inc. Founded 1964.

Scholastic Children's Books (division)

Euston House, 24 Eversholt Street, London NW1 1DB
tel 020-7756 7756 *fax* 020-7756 7795
email publicity@scholastic.co.uk
Managing Director Elaine McQuade, *Editorial*

Director, Non-fiction Lisa Edwards, *Editorial Director, Fiction* Elv Moody, *Editorial Director, Preschool* Katherine Halligan, *Rights Director* Antonia Pelari, *Sales & Marketing Director* Hilary Murray Hill

Activity books, novelty books, picture books, fiction for 5–12 year-olds, teenage fiction, series fiction and film/TV tie-ins. Recent successes include *Horrible Histories* by Terry Deary and Martin Brown, *His Dark Materials* trilogy by Philip Pullman and *Mortal Engines* by Philip Reeve. Imprints include Hippo, Point, Scholastic Fiction, Scholastic Non-fiction, Scholastic Press.

Submission details Will consider unsolicited submissions: send synopsis and sample chapter only.

The Chicken House
See page 9.

Scholastic Educational Publishing (division)
Villiers House, Clarendon Avenue, Leamington Spa CV32 5PR
tel (01926) 887799 *fax* (01926) 883881
Managing Director Denise Cripps

Professional books and classroom materials for primary teachers and magazines (*Nursery Education Plus, Child Education Plus, Junior Education Plus, Literacy Time Plus*).

Scholastic Book Clubs (division)
See page 69.

Scholastic Book Fairs (division)
See page 69.

SCP Publishers Ltd
(trading as Scottish Cultural Press)
Unit 6, Newbattle Abbey Business Park,
Newbattle Road, Dalkeith EH22 3LJ
tel 0131-660 6366 *fax* (0870) 285 4846
email info@scottishbooks.com
website www.scottishbooks.com
Directors Brian Pugh, Avril Gray

'Scottish books for children.' Picture books, history, reference and cookery. Publishes approx. 3 titles each year and has 32 in print. Recent successes include *Teach the Bairns to Cook/Bake* and *Classic Children's Games*. Also, for adults: Scottish non-fiction and Scots language. Founded 1992.

Submission details No unsolicited MSS. Send letter, phone or email before sending material. See website for submission guidelines.

Scripture Union
207–209 Queensway, Bletchley, Milton Keynes, Bucks. MK2 2EB
tel (01908) 856000 *fax* (01908) 856111
email postmaster@scriptureunion.org.uk
website www.scriptureunion.org.uk
Director of Publishing Terry Clutterham

Christian books and Bible reading materials for people of all ages; educational and worship resources for churches; adult fiction and non-fiction; children's fiction and non-fiction (age groups: under 5, 5–8, 8–10 and youth). Publishes approx. 40 titles each year for children/young people and has 200–250 in print. Recent successes include *No Angel* by Kathy Lee, *Out of the Shadows* by Steve Dixon and *The Day the Sky Opened* by Andrew R. Guyatt. Scripture Union works as a charity in over 120 countries and publishes in approx. 20. Founded 1867.

Submission details Will consider unsolicited MSS. Send sample and outline to Christina Simms in Publishing Dept. Authors should note that Scripture Union is a ministry as well as a publishing house. All books have an overt Biblical content.

SEMERC – see Granada Learning

SEN Press Ltd
7 Cliffe Street, Hebden Bridge,
West Yorkshire HX7 8BY
tel (01422) 844822 *mobile* 07733-193083
email info@senpress.co.uk
website www.senpress.co.uk
Publisher Peter Clarke

Specialises in books that are accessible to young people (14–19 years) with special educational needs. Founded 2003.

Short Books Ltd
3A Exmouth House, Pine Street, London EC1R 0JH
tel 020-7833 9429 *fax* 020-7833 9500
email emily@shortbooks.co.uk
website www.shortbooks.co.uk
Editorial Directors Rebecca Nicolson, Aurea Carpenter

Children's books: biographies of famous people from the past. Also non-fiction for adults, mainly biography and journalism. No unsolicited MSS. Founded 2000.

Simon & Schuster UK Ltd*
Africa House, 64–78 Kingsway, London WC2B 6AH
tel 020-7316 1900 *fax* 020-7316 0331/2
website www.simonsays.co.uk
Directors Ian Chapman (managing), Suzanne Baboneau (publishing), Charlotte Robertson (sales), Alex Maramenides (children's rights), Ingrid Selberg (children's publishing)

For adults: fiction (commercial and literary) and serious non-fiction. Subjects include biography, current affairs, history and science. Imprints include Free Press, Pocket Books, Scribner and Simon & Schuster Audio. No unsolicited MSS. Founded 1986.

Simon & Schuster Children's Publishing
Children's Publishing Director Ingrid Selberg, *Children's Rights Director* Alex Maramenides, *Fiction Editorial Director* Venetia Gosling, *Senior Commissioning Editor, Picture Books & Novelties* Emma Blackburn, *Art Director* Nia Roberts

Activity books, novelty books, picture books, fiction for 5–8 and 9–12 year-olds, teenage fiction, series fiction, film/TV tie-ins. Publishes approx. 180–200 titles each year. Recent successes include *Aliens Love Underpants* by Claire Freedman, *Vampirates* by Justin Somper and the *Spiderwick* series by Holly Black and Tony Di Terlizzi.

Submission details No unsolicited MSS. Will only consider MSS via agents.

Smart Learning
PO Box 321, Cambridge CB1 2XU
tel (01223) 477550 *fax* (01223) 477551
email admin@smart-learning.co.uk
website www.smart-learning.co.uk

High-quality teaching and learning resources for both teachers and children – from the Foundation stage through to Key Stage 3. Publishes software and books to enhance the teaching and learning of ICT, Phonics, Literacy, PSHE and Citizenship and English.

Stacey International
128 Kensington Church Street, London W8 4BH
tel 020-7221 7166 *fax* 020-7792 9288
email info@stacey-international.co.uk
website www.stacey-international.co.uk
Chairman Tom Stacey, *Managing Director* Max Scott

Illustrated non-fiction, encyclopedic books on regions and countries, Islamic and Arab subjects, world affairs, art, travel, belles-lettres, children's books (picture books, fiction for 5–8 and 9–12 year-olds and reference). Publishers of the *Musgrove* series.

Storysack Ltd
Resource House, Kay Street, Bury BL9 6BU
tel 0161-763 6232 *fax* 0161-763 5366
email hello@resourcehouse.co.uk
website www.storysack.com

Storysacks for children aged 3+. Storysacks are cloth bags of resources to encourage children and parents to enjoy reading together. Each sack is based around a picture story book with a supporting fact book on a similar theme, a parent guide, characters and a game. Founded 1999.

Stripes – see Magi Publications

Tango Books Ltd
PO Box 32595, London W4 5YD
tel 020-8996 9970 *fax* 020-8996 9977
email sales@tangobooks.co.uk
website www.tangobooks.co.uk
Directors Sheri Safran, David Fielder

Children's fiction and non-fiction novelty books, including pop-up, touch-and-feel and cloth books. No poetry. Submissions with sae or by email.

Tarquin Publications
99 Hatfield Road, St Albans AL1 4ET
tel (01727) 833866 *fax* (0845) 4566385
email editorial@tarquinbooks.com
website www.tarquinbooks.com
Director Andrew Griffin

Mathematical models, puzzles, codes and logic and paper engineering books for intelligent children. Publishes 7–8 titles each year and has 103 in print. Recent successes include *1000 Playthinks*, *Mathematical Merry-go-round* and *A Handbook of Paper Automata Mechanisms*. Founded 1970.

Submission details Do not send unsolicited MSS. Send a one-page proposal of idea.

Taylor and Francis Group*
2 and 4 Park Square, Milton Park, Abingdon, Oxon OX14 4RN
tel 020-7017 6000 *fax* 020-7017 6699
email info@tandf.co.uk
website www.tandf.co.uk, www.informa.com
Managing Director, Taylor & Francis Books Jeremy North

Academic and reference books, including education. Imprints include BIOS Scientific Publishers, CRC Press, Europa, Garland Science, Institute of Physics, Psychology Press, Routledge, Routledge-Cavendish, Spon and Taylor & Francis.

David Fulton (imprint)
website www.routledge.com/education
Education, Special Education Needs.

The Templar Company plc
The Granary, North Street, Dorking, Surrey RH4 1DN
tel (01306) 876361 *fax* (01306) 889097
email rebecca.beves@templarco.co.uk
website www.templarco.co.uk
Managing Director Amanda Wood, *Sales & Marketing Director* Ruth Huddleston, *Publishing Manager* Rebecca Elliott

Publisher and packager of high-quality illustrated children's books, including novelty books, picture books, pop-up books, board books, non-fiction and gift titles. Lightning Source Children's Publisher of the Year 2008; The Van Tulleken Independent Publisher of the Year 2008.

D.C. Thomson & Co. Ltd – Publications
2 Albert Square, Dundee DD1 9QJ
London office 185 Fleet Street, London EC4A 2HS

Publishers of newspapers and periodicals. Children's books (annuals), based on weekly magazine characters; fiction. For fiction guidelines, send a large sae to Central Fiction Dept.

Ticktock Media
2 Orchard Business Centre, North Farm Road, Tunbridge Wells, Kent TN2 3XF
tel (01892) 509400 *fax* (01892) 509401
email info@ticktock.co.uk
website www.ticktock.co.uk

Children's non-fiction.

Titan Books
144 Southwark Street, London SE1 0UP
tel 020-7620 0200 *fax* 020-7620 0032

email editorial@titanemail.com
website www.titanbooks.com
Publisher & Managing Director Nick Landau, *Editorial Director* Katy Wild

Graphic novels, including *Simpsons* and *Batman*, featuring comic-strip material; film and TV tie-ins and cinema reference books. No fiction or children's proposals, no email submissions and no unsolicited material without preliminary letter. Email or send large sae for current author guidelines. Division of Titan Publishing Group Ltd. Founded 1981.

Top That! Publishing plc
Marine House, Tide Mill Way, Woodbridge, Suffolk IP12 1AP
tel (01394) 386651 *fax* (01394) 386011
email info@topthatpublishing.com
website www.topthatpublishing.com
Directors Barrie Henderson (managing), Simon Couchman (creative), Stuart Buck (production), Douglas Eadie (financial), Daniel Graham (editorial), Dave Greggor (sales)

Tide Mill Press (imprint)
Children's novelty and picture books. Recent successes include *Millie the Millipede* (pop-up) and *Counting on the Farm*. Founded 2007.

Top That! Kids (imprint)
Activity books, novelty books, reference books and CD-Roms. Publishes 150 titles each year and has 300 titles in print. Recent successes include *Mini Maestro* activity series, *Fun Kits* and *Early Days* series (preschool). Founded 1998.
Submission details Phone the Editorial Dept before sending MS to ascertain interest.

Treehouse Children's Books
The Studio, Church Street, Nunney, Frome, Somerset BA11 4LW
tel (01373) 836233 *fax* (01373) 836299
email treehouse-books@btconnect.com
Editorial Director Richard Powell

Preschool children's books and novelty books. Imprint of Emma Treehouse Ltd (see page 67). Founded 1989.

Trentham Books Ltd
Westview House, 734 London Road, Oakhill, Stoke-on-Trent, Staffs. ST4 5NP
tel (01782) 745567 *fax* (01782) 745553
email tb@trentham.books.co.uk
Editorial office 28 Hillside Gardens, London N6 5ST
tel 020-8348 2174
website www.trentham-books.co.uk
Directors Dr Gillian Klein (editorial), Barbara Wiggins (executive)

Education (including specialist fields – multi-ethnic issues, equal opportunities, bullying, design and technology, early years), social policy, sociology of education, European education, women's studies.

Does not publish books for use by parents or children, or fiction, biography, reminiscences and poetry. Founded 1978.

Trotman Publishing
Westminster House, Kew Road, Richmond, Surrey TW9 2ND
tel 020-8334 1600 *fax* 020-8334 1601
email info@trotman.co.uk
website www.trotman.co.uk
Commercial Director Tom Lee

Independent advice and guidance on careers and higher education. Founded 1970.

Usborne Publishing Ltd
Usborne House, 83–85 Saffron Hill, London EC1N 8RT
tel 020-7430 2800 *fax* 020-8636 3758
email mail@usborne.co.uk
website www.usborne.com
Publishing Director Jenny Tyler, *Editorial Director, Fiction* Megan Larkin, *General Manager* Robert Jones

Activity books, novelty books, picture books, fiction for 5–8 and 9–12 year-olds, series fiction, reference, poetry and audio. Reference subjects include practical, craft, natural history, science, languages, history, art, activities, geography. Publishes 120 titles each year and has about 1200 in print. Recent successes include *That's Not My Penguin* (touchy-feely board book) and *Fairy Things to Make and Do* (activity book). Imprint: Usborne. Founded 1973.
Submission details Looking for high-quality imaginative children's fiction. Send correspondence to Jenny Tyler (non-fiction) and Megan Larkin (fiction).

Walker Books Ltd
87 Vauxhall Walk, London SE11 5HJ
tel 020-7793 0909 *fax* 020-7587 1123
website www.walkerbooks.co.uk
Directors David Lloyd (chairman), David Heatherwick (group managing), Helen McAleer (managing), Kevin Jones (finance), Jane Winterbotham (publishing), Jane Harris (sales), *Publishers* Deirdre McDermott, Caroline Royds, Loraine Taylor, Denise Johnstone-Burt, Gill Evans

Activity books, novelty books, picture books, fiction for 5–8 and 9–12 year-olds, teenage fiction, series fiction, film/TV tie-ins, plays, poetry and audio. Publishes approx. 300 titles each year and has 1500 in print. Recent successes include the *Alex Rider* series by Anthony Horowitz, *Tamar* by Mal Peet, *The Runaway Dinner* by Allan Ahlberg and Bruce Ingman, and *Butterfly, Butterfly* by Petr Horáček. Imprint: Walker Books. Founded 1980.
Submission details Write to the Editor. Allow 3 months for response.

Ward Lock Educational Co. Ltd
BIC Ling Kee House, 1 Christopher Road, East Grinstead, West Sussex RH19 3BT

tel (01342) 318980 *fax* (01342) 410980
email wle@lingkee.com
website www.wardlockeducational.com
Directors Au Bak Ling (chairman, Hong Kong), Au King Kwok (Hong Kong), Au Wai Kwok (Hong Kong), Albert Kw Au (Hong Kong), *Company Secretary* Eileen Parsons

Primary and secondary pupil materials, Kent Mathematics Project: *KMP BASIC* and *KMP Main* series covering Reception to GCSE, *Reading Workshops*, *Take Part* series and *Take Part* starters, teachers' books, music books, *Target* series for the National Curriculum: *Target Science* and *Target Geography*, religious education. Founded 1952.

Warne – see Penguin Group (UK)

Franklin Watts – see Hachette Children's Books

The Watts Publishing Group Ltd – see Hachette Children's Books

Wayland – see Hachette Children's Books

WingedChariot Press
7 Court Royal, Eridge Road, Tunbridge Wells, Kent TN4 8HT
tel (07791) 273374
email info@wingedchariot.com
website www.wingedchariot.com
Directors Neal Hoskins, Ann Arscott

Children's books in translation. Founded 2005.

Wizard Books Ltd
The Old Dairy, Brook Road, Thriplow, Cambridge SG8 7RG
tel (01763) 208008 *fax* (01763) 208080
email wizard@iconbooks.co.uk
website www.iconbooks.co.uk/wizard
Directors Peter Pugh (managing), Simon Flynn (publishing)

Gamebooks for 5–8 and 9–12 year-olds, reference and narrative non-fiction. Recent successes include *Fighting Fantasy Gamebooks* by Steve Jackson and Ian Livingstone, *Big Numbers* by Mary and John Gribbin and *Darkness Visible: Inside the World of Philip Pullman* by Nicholas Tucker. Imprint of Icon Books Ltd.

Submission details Will consider unsolicited MSS (non-fiction only).

The Women's Press
Top Floor, 27 Goodge Street, London W1P 2LD
tel 020-7636 3992 *fax* 020-7637 1866
email david@the-womens-press.com
website www.the-womens-press.com
Acting Managing Director David Elliott

Books by women in the areas of literary and crime fiction, biography and autobiography, health, culture, politics, handbooks, literary criticism, psychology and self-help, the arts. Founded 1978.

Livewire (imprint)
Books for teenagers and young women.

Wordsworth Editions Ltd
8B East Street, Ware, Herts. SG12 9HJ
tel (01920) 465167 *fax* (01920) 462267
email enquiries@wordsworth-editions.com
website www.wordsworth-editions.com
Managing Director Helen Trayler

Reprints of classic books: literary, children's; poetry; reference; Special Editions; mystery and supernatural. Founded 1987.

Y Lolfa Cyf.
Talybont, Ceredigion SY24 5AP
tel (01970) 832304 *fax* (01970) 832782
email ylolfa@ylolfa.com
website www.ylolfa.com
Director Garmon Gruffudd, *Editor* Lefi Gruffudd

Welsh-language popular fiction and non-fiction, music, children's books (recent successes include *Iawn Boi!* by Caryl Lewis and *Stori Dafydd ap Gwilym* by Gwyn Thomas and Margaret Jones); Welsh-language tutors; Welsh politics in English and a range of Welsh-interest books for the tourist market. Founded 1967.

York Notes – see Pearson Education

Young Picador – see Macmillan Publishers Ltd

Zero to Ten Ltd
2A Portman Mansions, Chiltern Street, London W1U 6NR
tel 020-7487 0920 *fax* 020-7487 0921
email sales@evansbrothers.co.uk
Publishing Director Su Swallow

Non-fiction for children aged 0–10: board books, toddler books, first story books, etc. Part of the Evans Publishing Group. Submissions welcome but don't respond to unsuccessful submissions. Founded 1997.

Cherrytree Books (imprint)
UK Publisher Su Swallow
Children's non-fiction illustrated books mainly for schools and libraries.

ZooBooKoo International Ltd
4 Gurdon Road, Grundisburgh, Woodbridge, Suffolk IP13 6XA
tel (01473) 735346 *fax* (01473) 735346
email karen@zoobookoo.com
website www.zoobookoo.com
Sales Director Karen Wattleworth

Designer/manufacturer of ZooBooKoo Original Cube Books, multi-level educational folding cube books. Recent successes include *World Football, Human Body, Kings and Queens, French Phrases* and *United Kingdom.*

Children's book publishers overseas

Listings are given for children's book publishers in Australia (below), Canada (page 29), France (page 32), Germany (page 33), Italy (page 34), the Netherlands (page 34), New Zealand (page 35), South Africa (page 36), Spain (page 37) and the USA (page 38).

AUSTRALIA

*Member of the Australian Publishers Association

ACER Press
19 Prospect Hill Road, Private Bag 55, Camberwell, Victoria 3124
tel (03) 9277 5555 fax (03) 9277 5500
email info@acer.edu.au
website www.acer.edu.au
Publishing Manager Andrew Wattson

Publisher of the Australian Council for Educational Research. Produces a range of books and kits.

Allen & Unwin Pty Ltd*
83 Alexander Street, Crows Nest, NSW 2065
postal address PO Box 8500, St Leonards, NSW 1590
tel (02) 8425 0100 fax (02) 9906 2218
email info@allenandunwin.com
website www.allenandunwin.com
Directors Patrick Gallagher (publishing), Paul Donovan (managing), David Martin (finance), Publishers, Children & Teenagers Erica Wagner

Picture books, fiction for 5–8 and 9–12 year-olds, teenage fiction, series fiction, narrative non-fiction and poetry. Also adult/general trade books, including fiction, academic, especially social science and history. Publishes approx. 40 titles each year and has about 310 in print. Recent successes include *Horrible Harriet* by Leigh Hobbs (picture book), *Think Smart, Hazel Green* by Odo Hirsch (junior fiction) and *How to Make a Bird* by Martine Murray. Imprint: Allen & Unwin. Founded 1990.
    Submission details Will consider unsolicited MSS (but not picture book texts). Prefers to receive full MSS by post, with a brief synopsis and biography. Allow 3 months for response. Seeking junior fiction, quirky non-fiction by wise, funny, inventive authors with a distinctive voice.

Michelle Anderson Publishing Pty Ltd*
PO Box 6032, Chapel Street North, South Yarra 3141
tel (03) 9826 9028 fax (03) 9826 8552
email mapubl@bigpond.net.au
website www.michelleandersonpublishing.com
Director Michelle Anderson

General health and mind/body. Recent successes include *Broken Beaks* (explaining homelessness to children), *What About Me?* (story for siblings of sick children) and *Who Am I?* (yoga for children).

Imprint: Michelle Anderson Publishing. Founded 2004.
    Submission details Will consider unsolicited synopses but not MSS. Allow 3 weeks for response.

Cengage Learning Australia*
Level 7, 80 Dorcas Street, South Melbourne, Victoria 3205
tel (03) 9685 4111 fax (03) 9685 4199
website www.cengage.com.au

Educational books.

Cygnet – see University of Western Australia Press

Hachette Children's Books
17/207 Kent Street, Sydney, NSW 2000
tel 612-8248-0800 fax 612-8248-0810
website www.hachettechildrens.com.au

Picture books, fiction for 5–8 and 9–12 year-olds, teenage fiction and series fiction. Publishes approx. 65 titles each year and has 750 in print. Recent releases include *The Arrival* by Shaun Tan.
    Submission details Will not accept unsolicited MSS. Submit MSS via an agent. List is full until 2009.

Hachette Livre Australia Pty Ltd*
Level 17, 207 Kent Street, Sydney, NSW 2000
tel (02) 8248 0800 fax (02) 2848 0810
email auspub@hachette.com.au
website www.hachette.com.au
Directors Malcolm Edwards (managing), Chris Raine, David Cocking, Louise Sherwin-Stark, Matt Richell, Sandy Weir, Fiona Hazard, Jodie Mann, Matt Hoy

General, children's. No unsolicited MSS.

HarperCollins Publishers (Australia) Pty Ltd Group*
postal address PO Box 321, 25 Ryde Road, Pymble, NSW 2073
tel (02) 9952 5000 fax (02) 9952 5555
website www.harpercollins.com.au
Managing Director Robert Gorman, Publishing Director Shona Martyn

Literary fiction and non-fiction, popular fiction, children's, reference, biography, autobiography, current affairs, sport, lifestyle, health/self-help, humour, true crime, travel, Australiana, history, business, gift, religion.

Little Hare Books*

8/21 Mary Street, Surry Hills, NSW 2010
tel (02) 9280 2220 fax (02) 9280 2223
email enquiries@littleharebooks.com
website www.littleharebooks.com

Publishes high-quality children's books in Australia, New Zealand and the UK: early childhood, picture books, fiction and puzzle/activity books. Recent successes include *Pirates* by Anna Nilsen.

Submission details Will accept unsolicited fiction and picture book MSS, and sample artwork. Send MSS in hard copy only (no disks or email); sample artwork on CD is acceptable. Include sae or IRCs for return of material. For junior fiction submissions, include only the first 3 chapters and a detailed outline of how the events unfold and how the plot is resolved. Allow 4–6 months to assess submissions. Send submission to the Commissioning Editor.

McGraw-Hill Education*

Level 2, The Everglade Building, 82 Waterloo Road, North Ryde NSW 2113
postal address Private Bag 2233, Business Centre, North Ryde, NSW 1670
tel (02) 9900 1800 fax (02) 9878 8280
website www.macgraw-hill.com.au
Publishing Director Nicole Meehan, *Managing Director* Murray St Leger

Educational publisher: higher education, primary and secondary education (grades K–12) and professional (including medical, general and reference). Division of the McGraw-Hill Companies. Founded 1964.

Submission details Always looking for new potential authors. Has a rapidly expanding publishing programme. See website for author's guide.

Macmillan Education Australia Pty Ltd*

Melbourne office Level 4, 627 Chapel Street, South Yarra, Victoria 3141
tel (03) 9825 1025 fax (03) 9825 1010
email mea@macmillan.com.au
Sydney office Level 2, St Martin's Tower, 31 Market Street, Sydney, NSW 2000
tel (02) 9285 9200 fax (02) 9285 9290
website www.macmillan.com.au
Managing Director Ross Gibb, *Managing Publisher* Angela Berry

Educational books.

New Frontier Publishing*

Forest Central Building 7, 4–49 Frenchs Forest Road, Frenchs Forest, NSW 2086
tel (02) 9453 1525 fax (02) 9975 2531
email info@newfronteir.com.au
website www.newfrontier.com.au
Director Peter Whitfield

Aims to uplift, educate and inspire through its range of children's books. Activity books, picture books, fiction, dictionaries, textbooks. Caters for 5–10 year-olds.

Submission details Unsolicited MSS accepted. Understanding of existing list crucial. Downloadable submissions pack available via website.

Pan Macmillan Australia Pty Ltd*

Level 25, 1 Market Street, Sydney, NSW 2000
tel (02) 9285 9100 fax (02) 9285 9190
email pan@macmillan.com.au
website www.macmillan.com.au
Directors James Fraser (publishing), Peter Phillips (sales), Andrew Farrell (publicity & marketing)

Commercial and literary fiction; children's fiction, non-fiction and character products; non-fiction; sport.

Pearson Education Australia*

Schools Division, 20 Thackray Road, Port Melbourne, Victoria 3207
tel (3) 9245 7111 fax (3) 9245 7333
email schools@pearsoned.com.au
website www.pearsoned.com.au/schools
Primary Publisher Corinne Atoune, *Secondary Publisher* Emma Roberts

Early fiction, non-fiction, geography, history, mathematics, textbooks, CD-Roms, interactive websites.

Penguin Group (Australia)*

250 Camberwell Road, Camberwell, Victoria 3124
tel (03) 9811 2400 fax (03) 9811 2620
postal address PO Box 701, Hawthorn, Victoria 3122
website www.penguin.com.au
Managing Director Gabrielle Coyne, *Publishing Director* Robert Sessions, *Publishing Director – Books for Children & Young Adults* Laura Harris, *Associate – Books for Children & Young Adults* Jane Godwin, *Executive Editor* Lisa Riley

Picture books, fiction for 5–8 and 9–12 year-olds, teenage fiction, series fiction and film/TV tie-ins. Also for adults: fiction and general non-fiction. Publishes approx. 85 titles each year and has about 500 in print. Recent successes include *Cuthbert's Babies* by Pamela Allen (picture book), *Rascal* books by Paul Jennings (younger readers) and *Saving Francesca* by Melina Marchetta (young adult). Children's imprints: Puffin (paperback). Founded 1935.

Submission details Will consider unsolicited MSS but submit only one MS at a time. Send proposals to The Editor, Books for Children and Young Adults at the postal address (above). Enclose an sae for the return of material. Does not accept proposals by email or fax.

Prim-Ed Publishing Pty Ltd

4 Bendsten Place, Balcatta, WA 6021
tel 618-9240-9888 fax 618-9240-1513
email mail@ricgrop.com.au
website www.prim-ed.com

Educational publisher specialising in blackline master or copymasters and student workbooks for schools and homeschoolers.

Puffin – see Penguin Group (Australia)

University of Queensland Press*
PO Box 6042, St Lucia, Queensland 4067
tel (07) 3365 7244 fax (07) 3365 7579
email uqp@uqp.uq.edu.au
website www.uqp.com.au
General Manager Greg Bain
Australian children's and young adult fiction. Via agents only. Founded 1948.

The Quentaris Chronicles – see Hachette
Children's Books

Random House Australia Pty Ltd*
20 Alfred Street, Milsons Point, NSW 2061
tel (02) 9954 9966 fax (02) 9954 4562
email random@randomhouse.com.au
website www.randomhouse.com.au
Managing Director Margaret Seale, Head of Publishing, Random House Jane Palfreyman, Head of Publishing, Bantam Doubleday Fiona Henderson, Children's Publisher Lindsay Knight, Illustrated Publisher Jude McGee, Sales & Marketing Director Carol Davidson, Publicity Director Karen Reid

General fiction and non-fiction; children's, illustrated. Imprints: Arrow, Avon, Ballantine, Bantam, Black Swan, Broadway, Century, Chatto & Windus, Corgi, Crown, Dell, Doubleday, Ebury, Fodor, Heinemann, Hutchinson, Jonathan Cape, Knopf, Mammoth UK, Minerva, Pantheon, Pavilion, Pimlico, Random House, Red Fox, Rider, Vermilion, Vintage, Virgin.Subsidiary of Bertelsmann AG.
Submission details For Random House and Transworld Publishing, unsolicited non-fiction accepted, unbound in hard copy addressed to Submissions Editor. Fiction submissions are only accepted from previously published authors, or authors represented by an agent or accompanied by a report from an accredited assessment service.

Scholastic Australia Pty Ltd*
76–80 Railway Crescent, Lisarow, Gosford, NSW 2250
tel (02) 4328 3555 fax (02) 4323 3827
website www.scholastic.com.au
Managing Director Ken Jolly, Publisher Andrew Berkhut
Children's fiction and non-fiction. Founded 1968.

Start-Ups – see Hachette Children's Books

University of Western Australia Press*
UWA, M419, 35 Stirling Highway, Crawley 6009, Western Australia
tel (618) 6488 3670 fax (618) 6488 1027
email admin@uwapress.uwa.edu.au
website www.uwapress.uwa.edu.au
Director Terri-ann White
Fiction, general non-fiction, natural history, contemporary issues. Founded 1935.

CANADA
*Member of the Canadian Publishers' Council
†Member of the Association of Canadian Publishers

Annick Press Ltd†
15 Patricia Avenue, Toronto, Ontario M2M 1H9
tel 416-221-4802 fax 416-221-8400
email annickpress@annickpress.com
website www.annickpress.com
Co-editors Rick Wilks, Colleen MacMillan, Creative Director Sheryl Shapiro

Preschool to young adult fiction and non-fiction. Publishes 8 picture books, 3 young readers, 3 middle readers and 8 young adult titles each year. Recent successes include – Fiction: *Baboon: A Novel* by David Jones (ages 10–14); *The Night Wanderer: A Native Gothic Novel* by Drew Hayden Taylor (ages 12 and up); *Shoe Shakes* by Loris Lesynski, illustrated by Michael Martchenko (picture book, ages 3–5); Non-fiction: *The Siege: Under Attack in Renaissance Europe* by Stephen Shapiro, illustrated by John Mantha (ages 10 and up); *The Inuit Thought of It: Amazing Arctic Innovations* by Alootook Ipellie with David MacDonald (ages 9–11); *The Big Book of Pop Culture: A How-To Guide for Young Artists* by Hal Niedzviecki, illustrated by Marc Ngui (ages 12 and up). Founded 1975.
Submission details Approx. 25% of books are by first-time authors. No unsolicited MSS. For illustrations, query with samples and sase to Creative Director. Responds in 6 months.

Boardwalk Books – see Dundurn Press

Doubleday Canada
1 Toronto Street, Suite 300, Toronto, Ontario M5C 2V6
tel 416-364-4449 fax 416-957-1587
website www.randomhouse.ca
Chairman John Neale, Publisher Maya Mavjee
General trade non-fiction; fiction; young adults. Division of Random House of Canada Ltd. Founded 1942.

Dundurn Press†
3 Church Street, Suite 500, Toronto, Ontario M5E 1MZ
tel 416-214-5544 fax 416-214-5556
email info@dundurn.com
website www.dundurn.com
President J. Kirk Howard
Popular non-fiction, fiction, scholarship, history, biography, young adult, art. Part of the Dundurn Group. Founded 1973.

Boardwalk Books (imprint); Sandcastle Books (imprint)
Young adult fiction.

Fitzhenry & Whiteside Ltd
195 Allstate Parkway, Markham, Ontario L3R 4T8
tel 800-387-9776 fax 800-260-9777

email godwit@fitzhenry.ca
website www.fitzhenry.ca
Publisher Sharon Fitzhenry, *Children's Publisher* Gail Winskill

Fiction and non-fiction (social studies, visual arts, biography, environment). Publishes 10 picture books, 5 early readers/chapter books, 6 middle novels and 7 young adult books each year. Founded 1966.
Submission details Approx. 10% of books are by first-time authors. Emphasis is on Canadian authors and illustrators, subject or perspective. Will review MS/illustration packages from artists. Submit outline and copy of sample illustration. For illustrations only, send samples and promotional scheet. Responds in 3 months. Samples returned with sase.

Harcourt Canada Ltd
55 Horner Avenue, Toronto, Ontario M8Z 4X6
tel 416-255-4491 *fax* 4416-255-0177
website www.nelson.com, www.psychorp.com

Educational materials from K–Grade 12, testing and assessment. Imprints: Harcourt Religion (formerly Brown-ROA), Harcourt Brace & Company, Holt, Rinehart and Winston, MeadowBrook Press, The Psychological Corporation, Therapy Skill Builders/Communications Skill Builders. Distributed by Thomson Nelson. Founded 1922.

HarperCollins Publishers Ltd*
2 Bloor Street East, 20th Floor, Toronto, Ontario M4W 1A8
tel 416-975-9334 *fax* 416-975-9884
email hccanada@harpercollins.com
website www.harpercollins.ca
President David Kent

Publishers of literary fiction and non-fiction, history, politics, biography, spiritual and children's books. Founded 1989.

Key Porter Books Ltd
6 Adelaide Street East, 10th Floor, Toronto, Ontario M5C 1H6
tel 416-862-7777 *fax* 416-862-2304
email info@keyporter.com
website www.keyporter.com
Publisher Jordan Fenn

Fiction and non-fiction for all ages. Recent successes include *Rosie in New York: Gotcha!* by Carol Matas (fiction, young adult), *The Dinosaur Atlas* by Don Lessem (non-fiction, ages 8–10) and *Rude Ramsay and the Roaring Radishes* by Margaret Atwood (non-fiction, ages 4–7). For adults: fiction and non-fiction (nature, history, Canadian politics, conservation, humour, biography, autobiography, health). Founded 1981.
Submission details Approx. 30% of books are by first-time authors. No unsolicited MSS: only interested in submissions via literary agents. Responds to queries/proposals in 6 months. Length:

picture books – 1500 words; young readers, fiction – 5000 words; middle readers, non-fiction – 15,000 words.

Kids Can Press Ltd†
29 Birch Avenue, Toronto, Ontario M4V 1E2
tel 416-925-5437 *fax* 416-960-5437
email info@kidscan.com
website www.kidscanpress.com/canada/
Publisher Karen Boersma

Juvenile/young adult fiction and non-fiction. Publishes 6–10 pciture books, 10–15 young readers, 20–30 middle readers and 2–3 young adult titles each year. Recent successes include *Alphabeasts* by Wallace Edwards, Melanie Watt's award-winning *Scaredy Squirrel, If the World Were a Village* by David J. Smith and *Ryan and Jimmy and the well in Africa which brought them together* by Herb Shoveller. Publishers of *Franklin the Turtle* and *Elliot Moose* characters. Founded 1973.
Submission details Approx. 10–15% of books are by first-time authors. Submit outline/synopsis and 2–3 sample chapters. For picture books, submit complete MS. Responds in 6 months. Only accepts MSS from Canadian authors. Fiction length: picture books – 1000–2000 words; young readers – 750–1500 words; middle readers – 10,000–15,000 words; young adult – over 15,000 words. Non-fiction length: picture books – 500–1250 words; young readers – 750–2000 words; middle readers – 5000–15,000 words.

McGraw-Hill Ryerson Ltd*
300 Water Street, Whitby, Ontario L1N 9B6
tel 905-430-5000 *fax* 905-430-5020
website www.mcgrawhill.ca
President & Ceo David Swail

Educational and trade books.

Madison Press Books
1000 Yonge Street, Suite 200, Toronto, Ontario M4W 2K2
tel 416-923-5027 *fax* 416-923-9708
website www.madisonpressbooks.com
Publisher Oliver Salzmann

Illustrated non-fiction for 8–12 year-olds.

Napoleon & Company†
178 Willowdale Avenue, Suite 201, Toronto, Ontario M2N 4Y8
tel 416-730-9052 *fax* 416-730-8096
email napoleon@napoleonandcompany.com
website www.napoleonandcompany.com
Publisher Sylvia McConnell, *Editor* Allister Thompson

Children's books and adult fiction. Founded 1990.

Orca Book Publishers†
Box 5626, Station B, Victoria, BC, V8R 6S4
tel 800-210-5277 *fax* 877-408-1551
email orca@orcabook.com
website www.orcabook.com

Books for children and young adults. No poetry. *Orca Echoes* (7–8 year-olds), *Young Readers* (8–11 year-olds), juvenile novels (9–13 year-olds), *Orca Currents* (intermediate novels aimed at reluctant readers with simple language and short, high-interest chapters), young adult fiction, *Orca Soundings* (high-interest teen novels aimed at reluctant readers). Recent successes include *Hero an Orca Young Reader* by Martha Attema and *The Puppet Wrangler* by Vicki Grant.

Submission details Currently seeking picture book MSS of up to 1500 words. Submit complete MS FAO Children's Book Editor. No queries.

Orca Echoes, Orca Young Readers (also called chapter books) and juvenile fiction: Contemporary stories or fantasy with a universal theme, a compelling, unified plot and a strong, sympathetic child protagonist who grows through the course of the story and solves the central problem him/herself. Well-researched stories dealing with, or taking their inspiration from, historical subjects, but not thinly disguised history lessons. Length: *Orca Echoes* 5500–6000 words; *Young Readers* 14,000–18,000 words; juvenile fiction 25,000–35,000 words. Send query with sample chapter FAO Children's Book Editor.

Stories for *Orca Currents* should have appropriate story lines for middle school (family issues, humour, sports, adventure, mystery/suspense, fantasy, etc) with strong plots, credible characters/situations. Awkward moralising should be avoided. Protagonists are between 12–14 years old and should be appealing and believable. Length: 14,000–16,000 words; 12–16 short chapters. Send a chapter-by-chapter outline and one sample chapter FAO Melanie Jeffs, Editor.

Teen or young adult fiction: Issue-oriented contemporary stories exploring a universal theme, with a compelling, unified plot and strong, sympathetic protagonist(s). Well-researched stories dealing with, or taking their inspiration from, historical subjects, but not thinly disguised history lessons. Length: up to 50,000 words. Send queries to Teen Fiction Editor.

Orca Soundings: Stories should reflect the universal struggles that young people face. They need not be limited to 'gritty' urban tales but can include adventures, mystery/suspense, fantasy, etc. Interested in humorous stories that will appeal to teens of both sexes. 'Disease-of-the-week' potboilers or awkward moralising should be avoided. Protagonists are between 14–17 years old and should be appealing and believable. Length: 14,000–16,000 words, 12–16 short chapters. Send a chapter-by-chapter outline and one sample chapter FAO Andrew Wooldridge, Editor.

Will consider MMS from Canadian writers only. No submissions by fax or email. See website for submission guidelines. Founded 1984.

Pearson Education Canada*
(formerly Prentice Hall Canada and Addison-Wesley Canada)

26 Prince Andrew Place, Toronto, Ontario M3C 2T8
tel 416-447-5101 *fax* 416-443-0948
email pearson.learning@pearsoned.com
website www.pearsoned.ca
President Allan Reynolds

Academic, technical, educational, children's and adult, trade.

Penguin Group (Canada)*
90 Eglinton Avenue East, Suite 700, Toronto, Ontario M4P 2Y3
tel 416-925-2249 *fax* 416-925-0068
email info@penguin.ca
website www.penguin.ca
President and Publisher David Davidar

Literary fiction, memoir, non-fiction (history, business, current events). No unsolicited MSS; submissions via an agent only. Imprints: Penguin Canada, Viking Canada, Puffin Canada. Founded 1974.

Pippin Publishing Corporation
PO Box 242, Don Mills, Ontario M3C 2S2
tel 416-510-2918 *fax* 416-510-3359
email cynthia@pippinpub.com
website www.pippinpub.com
President/Editorial Director Jonathan Lovat Dickson

ESL/EFL, teacher reference, adult basic education, school texts (all subjects), general trade (non-fiction).

Raincoast Books[†]
9050 Shaughnessy Street, Vancouver, BC V6P 6E5
tel 604-323-7100 *fax* 604-323-2600
email info@raincoast.com
website www.raincoast.com
Publisher Jesse Finkelstein

Non-fiction for adults. Fiction and non-fiction for children. Recent successes include *Waiting for Wings* by Lois Ehlert (picture book), *Genius Squad* by Catherine Jinks (juvenile fiction) and *Strange New Species* by Elin Kelsey. Imprints: Polestar, Press Gang.

Submission details Will not accept unsolicited MSS. Send a query letter via regular mail for the attention of the Editorial Department. For young adult fiction, submit query letter with a list of publication credits plus one-page outline of the plot. No queries via email. Allow up to 9 months for reply. Only accepts material from Canadian residents.

Random House of Canada Ltd*
1 Toronto Street, Suite 300, Toronto, Ontario M5C 2V6
tel 416-364 4449 *fax* 416-364-6863
website www.randomhouse.ca
Chairman John Neale

Adult and children's. Imprints: Canada, Doubleday Canada (page 29), Knopf Canada, Random House Canada, Seal Books, Vintage Canada. Subsidiary of Bertelsmann AG. Founded 1944.

Red Deer Press
Room 1512, 1800 4 Street SW, Calgary, AB T2S 2S5
tel 403-509-0800 *fax* 403-228 6503

email rdp@ucalgary.ca
website www.reddeerpress.com
Publisher Richard Dionne, *Children's Editor* Peter Carver

Literary fiction, non-fiction, drama, poetry, children's illustrated books, young adult fiction, teen fiction. Publishes books that are written or illustrated by Canadians and that are about or of interest to Canadians. Imprints: Discovery Books, Prairie Garden Books, History Along the Highway Books, Roundup Books, Writing West, Northern Lights Books for Children (illustrated books), Northern Lights Young Novels (juvenile and young adult fiction). Also series in Canadian drama, adult fiction, and children's first chapter books. Publishes 14–18 new books per year.

Submission details Children's picture books MSS from established authors with a demonstrable record of publishing success are preferred. Not currently accepting new MSS. Founded 1975.

Sandcastle Books – see Dundurn Press

Scholastic Canada Ltd*

Scholastic Canada Ltd, 175 Hillmount Road, Markham, Ontario L6C 1Z7
tel 905-887 7323
email custserv@scholastic.ca
website www.scholastic.ca
Publishing Director Diane Kerner, *Art Director* Ms Yüksel Hassan

Serves children, parents and teachers through a variety of businesses including Scholastic Book Clubs and Book Fairs, Scholastic Education, Classroom Magazines, Trade, and Les Éditions Scholastic. Publishes recreational reading for children and young people from kindergarten to Grade 8 and educational materials in both official languages. Its publishing focus is on books by Canadians. Wholly owned subsidiary of Scholastic Inc.

Submission details No unsolicited MSS. Call 905-887 7323 for information on current submissions policy. Artists may submit several photocopied samples of their work and a brief résumé plus sase to the art director. Never send originals or anything that cannot be replaced.

Thomson Nelson*

1120 Birchmount Road, Scarborough, Ontario M1K 5G4
tel 416-752-9448 *fax* 416-752-8101
email inquire@nelson.com
website www.nelson.com
President Greg Pilon, *Vice President, Market Development* Chris Besse, *Senior Vice President, Media Services* Susan Cline, *Vice President, Higher Education* James Reeve

Educational publishing: school (K–12), college and university, career education, measurement and guidance, professional and reference, ESL titles. Division of Thomson Canada Ltd. Founded 1914.

Tundra Books Inc.†

75 Sherbourne Street, 5th Floor, Toronto, Ontario M5A 2P9
tel 416-598-4786 *fax* 416-598-0247
email tundra@mccelland.com
website www.tundrabooks.com
Publisher Kathy Lowinger

High-quality children's picture books.

Whitecap Books Ltd†

351 Lynn Avenue, North Vancouver, BC V7J 2C4
tel 604-980-9852 *fax* 604-980-8197
website www.whitecap.ca
President Michael E. Burch, *Vice-President* Nicholas S.M. Rundall, *Publisher* Robert McCullough

General: cooking, wine and spirit, gardening, travel, health and well-being, history, biography, nature and the environment. Also publish juvenile fiction, young adult fiction, non-fiction, picture books for young children (nature, wildlife and animals). Recent titles include *Saddle Island* series No 3: *Race to the Rescue* by Sharon Siamon, *Take it to the Extreme* No 10: *Mountain Board Maniacs* by Pam Withers, and *Dogabet* written and illustrated by Dianna Bonder.

Submission details For children's illustrated fiction, send complete MS. For all other submissions, send a synopsis, a table of contents listing the chapters or stories and their length, information about the proposed illustrations or photographs (number planned, b&w or colour), 1–3 sample chapters and information about the author, including professional background and previous publishing credits. Include a sase with sufficient return postage, and if submitting from outside of Canada, include an international postal voucher.

Women's Press

180 Bloor Street West, Suite 801, Toronto, Ontario M5S 2V6
tel 416-929-2774 *fax* 416-929-1926
email info@cspi.org
website www.womenspress.ca
Editorial Director Megan Mueller

The ideas and experiences of women: fiction, creative non-fiction, children's books, plays, biography, autobiography, memoirs, poetry. Owned by Canadian Scholars' Press. Founded 1987.

FRANCE

L'Ecole des Loisirs

11 Rue de Sevres, 75006, Paris
tel (1) 42229410 *fax* (1) 45480499
email edl@ecoledesloisirs.com
website www.ecoledesmax.com
Managing Director Jean Fabre

Specialises in children's literature from picture books to young adult fiction.

Flammarion

87 quai Panhard et Levassor, 75647 Paris Cedex 13
tel (1) 40 51 31 00 *fax* (1) 43 29 43 43
website www.flammarion.com
Managing Director Danielle Nees

Leading French publisher. Children's imprints include: Albums du Père Castor, Castor Poche, Tribal, Etonnants Classiques, GF – Flammarion. Founded 1875.

Père Castor (imprint)
Children's Publisher Hélène Wadowski

Children's picture books, junior fiction, activity books, board books, how-to books, comics, gift books, fairy tales, dictionaries and records and tapes. Covers ages 0–16.

Gallimard Jeunesse

5 rue Sebastien Bottin, 75007 Paris
tel (1) 49 54 42 00 *fax* (1) 45 44 39 46
email premdec@gallimard-jeunesse.fr
website www.gallimard-jeunesse.fr
Children's Publisher Teresa Cremisi

Publisher of high-quality children's fiction and non-fiction including board books, novelty books, picture books, pop-up books. Founded 1911.

Hachette Livre/Gautier-Languereau

43 quai de Grenelle, 75905 Paris Cedex 15
tel (43) 92 30 00 *fax* (43) 92 33 38
website www.hachettejeuness.com
Director Arnaud Nourry, *Editorial Director* Brigitte le Blanc, *Artistic Manager* Maryvonne Denizet

Picture books and poetry. Publishes approx. 55 titles each year. Recent successes include *Cyrano* by Tai Marc Le Thanh and Rébecca Dautremer and *Princesses* by Philippe Lechermeier and Rébecca Dautremer. Founded 1992.
Submission details Will consider unsolicited MSS. Allow 2 months for response.

Kaléidoscope

11 Rue de Sèvres, F–75006 Paris
tel (1) 45 44 07 08 *fax* (1) 45 44 53 71
email infos@editions-kaleidoscope.com
website www.editions-kaleidoscope.com
Children's Publisher Isabel Finkenstaedt

Specialises in up-market picture books for 0–6 year-olds. Founded 1988.

Editions Sarbacane

35 Rue d'Hauteville, 75010 Paris
tel (1) 42462400 *fax* (1) 42462815
email e.beulque@sarbacane.net
website www.editions-sarbacane.com
Publisher Emmanuelle Beulque

High-quality activity books, board books, picture books and general fiction for children from preschool age to 15 years.

Le Sorbier

2 Rue Christine, 75006 Paris
tel (1) 40515200 *fax* (1) 40515205
website www.editionsdelamartiniere.fr
Publisher Françoise Mateu

High-quality picture books for children up to 10 years old and illustrated reference books for ages 9–12. Imprint of Editions de la Martiniere.

GERMANY

Carl Hanser Verlag

Vilshofener Strasse 10, 81679 München
tel (89) 998 30 191 *fax* (89) 944 03 6710
email info@hanser.de
website www.hanser.de
Children's Publisher Dr Friedbert Stohner

High-quality hardcover books for all ages from preschool to young adults. Board books, picture books, fiction and non-fiction. Age groups: 5–10, 10–15, 15+. Founded 1928.

Carlsen Verlag

Völckerssstrasse 14–20, D 22765 Hamburg
tel (40) 398040 *fax* (40) 39804390
email info@carlsen.de
website www.carlsen.de
Publisher Klaus Humann

Children's picture books, board books and novelty books. Illustrated fiction and non-fiction. Teenage fiction and non-fiction. Publishes both German and international authors. Publisher of the *Harry Potter* series. Age groups: preschool, 5–10, 10–15, 15+. Founded 1953.
Submission details Unsolicited MSS welcome but must include an sae for its return. Do not follow up by phone or post. For illustrations, submit no more than 3 colour photocopies and unlimited b&w copies.

Deutscher Taschenbuch Verlag (DTV)

Friedrichstrasse 1/A, D–80801 Munich
tel (89) 381 67281 *fax* (89) 346428
email verlag@dtv.de
website www.dtvjunior.de
Children's Publishing Director Anne Schieckel

Fiction and non-fiction for children and teenagers. Authors include Astrid Lindgren, Uwe Timm and Joan Aiken. Founded 1971.

Ravensburger Buchverlage

Robert-Bosch-Straße 1, 88214 Ravensburg
tel (49) 751860 *fax* (49) 751 861289
email buchverlag@ravensburger.de
website www.ravensburger.de

Managing Directors Renate Herre, Johannes Hauenstein, *Commissioning Editors* Ulrike Metzger, Sandra Schwarz, Sabine Zürn

Activity books, novelty books, picture books, fiction for 5–8 and 9–12 year-olds, teenage fiction, series fiction and educational games and puzzles. Publishes approx. 450 titles each year and has 1500 in print. Founded 1883.

Submission details Will consider unsolicited MSS for fiction only. Allow 2 months for response.

ITALY

Edizoni Arka srl
Via Raffaello Sanzio, 7–20149, Milano
tel (39) 02 4818230 *fax* (39) 02 4816752
email arka@arkaedizioni.it
website www.arkaedizioni.it
Publisher Ginevra Viscardi

Picture books and some general fiction for preschool children and up to 10 years.

De Agostini Editore
Via Giovanni da Verrazano, 15-28100, Novara
tel (39) 0321 4241 *fax* (39) 0321 47128/6
website www.deagostini.it
Publisher Matteo Faglia

Illustrated books, books for schools.

Edizioni El/Einaudi Ragazzi/Emme Edizioni
Via J. Ressel 5, 34018 San Dorligo della Valle TS
tel (040) 3880311 *fax* (040) 3880330
email edizioniel@edizioniel.it
website www.edizioniel.com
Children's Publisher Orietta Fatucci

Activity books, board books, picture books, pop-up books, non-fiction, novels, poetry, fairy tales, fiction. Age groups: preschool, 5–10, 10–15, 15+. Publishes over 270 new titles per year.

Giunti Editore SpA
Via Bolognese, 165–50139, Florence
tel (39) 055 50621 *fax* (39) 055 5062298
email info@giunti.it
website www.giunti.it
Publishers Sergio Giunti, Camilla Giunti

Activity books, board books, novelty books, picture books, colouring books, pop-up books and some educational textbooks.

Arnoldo Mondadori Editore S.p.A (Mondadori)
Via Durazzo 4, 20134 Milan
tel (02) 2121-3214 *fax* (02) 2121-3220

email info.ragazzi@mondadori.it
website www.ragazzi.mondadori.it
Editor-in-Chief Fiammetta Giorgi

Activity books, board books, novelty books, picture books, painting and colouring books, pop-up books, how-to books, hobbies, leisure, pets, sport, comics, poetry, fairy tales, education, fiction and non-fiction. Age groups: preschool, 5–10, 10–15, 15+. Founded 1907.

Adriano Salani Editore S.p.A.
Via Gherardini 10, 20145 Milano
tel (02) 34597624 *fax* (02) 34597206
email info@salani.it
website www.salani.it
Publisher Grazia Maria Mazzitelli

Picture books, how-to books, comics, gift books, fiction, novels, poetry, fairy tales. Age groups: preschool, 5–10, 10–15, 15.

THE NETHERLANDS

Lemniscaat BV
PO Box 4066, 3006 AB, Rotterdam
tel 31 10 2062929 *fax* 31 10 4141560
email info@lemniscaat.nl
located at Vijverlaan, 48-3062 HL, Rotterdam
website www.lemniscaat.nl
Publisher Boele van Hensbroek

Picture books, general fiction, fairy tales.

Rubinstein Publishing
Prinseneiland, 43-1013 LL, Amsterdam
tel 31 20 4200772 *fax* 31 20 4200882
email info@rubinstein.nl
website www.rubinstein.nl
Publisher Dik Broekman

Independent publisher specialising in audiobooks for children. Also produces novelty books.

Sjaloom & Wildeboer, Uitgevers
Postbus 1895, NL–1000BW, Amsterdam
tel (20) 6206263 *fax* (20) 4288540
email post@sjaloom.nl
website www.sjaloom.nl
Children's Publisher Willem Wildeboer

Board books, novelty books, picture books, pop-up books, non-fiction, fiction for ages preschool, 5–10 and 10–15.

Submission details Welcomes new submissions (no disks) and illustrations. Include sae for return of material.

Van Goor
Onderdoor, 7-3995 DW, Houten
tel 31 30 7998300 *fax* 31 30 7998398
website www.van-goor.nl
Publisher Marieke Woortman

High-quality picture books and activity books and literary fiction for age groups 6+ to young adults.

Zirkoon Uitgevers

Postbus 598608, 1040 LC, Amsterdam
tel (20) 6233426 *fax* (20) 6234031
email post@zirkoon.nl
website www.zirkoon.nl
Children's Publisher Iris Zuydewijn van de Roy

High-quality picture books, activity books, board books, novelty books, pop-up books, poetry, fiction and some non-fiction.

NEW ZEALAND

*Member of the New Zealand Book Publishers' Association

David Bateman Ltd*

30 Tarndale Grove, Albany Business Park, Bush Road, Auckland
tel (09) 415-7664 *fax* (09) 415-8892
email bateman@bateman.co.nz
postal address PO Box 100242, North Shore Mail Centre, Auckland 1330
website www.bateman.co.nz
Chairman/Publisher David L. Bateman, *Directors* Janet Bateman, Paul Bateman (joint managing), Paul Parkinson (joint managing)

Natural history, gardening, encyclopedias, sport, art, cookery, historical, juvenile, travel, motoring, maritime history, business, art, lifestyle. Founded 1979.

Blue Balloon – see Scholastic New Zealand Ltd

Dunmore Press Ltd*

PO Box 25080, Wellington 6146
tel (04) 472-2705 *fax* (04) 471-0604
email books@dunmore.co.nz
website www.dunmore.co.nz
Directors Murray Gatenby, Sharmian Firth

Education, history, sociology, business studies, general non-fiction. Founded 1970.

HarperCollins Publishers (New Zealand) Ltd*

31 View Road, Glenfield, Auckland
tel (09) 443-9400 *fax* (09) 443-9403
email editors@harpercollins.co.nz
postal address PO Box 1, Auckland
website www.harpercollins.co.nz
Managing Director Tony Fisk, *Commissioning Editor* Lorain Day

General literature, non-fiction, reference, children's.

McGraw-Hill Book Company New Zealand Ltd*

Locked Bag 2232, Business Centre, North Ryde, NSW 1670
postal address Private Bag 11904, Ellerslie, Auckland 1005
tel (61) 2 9900 1800 *fax* (61) 2 9900 1985
website www.mcgraw-hill.com

Educational publisher: higher education, primary and secondary education (grades K–12) and professional (including medical, general and reference). Division of the McGraw-Hill Companies. Founded 1974.
Submission details Always looking for new potential authors. Has a rapidly expanding publishing programme. See website for author's guide.

Mallinson Rendel Publishers Ltd*

Level 5, 15 Courtenay Place, PO Box 9409, Wellington
tel (04) 802-5012 *fax* (04) 802-5013
email publisher@mallinsonrendel.co.nz
website www.mallinsonrendel.co.nz
Publisher & Managing Director Ann Mallinson, *Editor* Katie Haworth

Picture books, fiction for 5–8 and 9–12 year-olds and teenage fiction. Publishes approx. 7 titles each year and has over 100 in print. Recent successes include *The Other Ark* by Lynley Dodd, *Right Where It Hurts* by David Hill and *The Real Thing* by Brian Falkner. Imprint: Mallinson Rendel. Founded 1980.
Submission details Will accept unsolicited MSS but is only interested in submissions from New Zealand authors.

MM House Publishing

752 Gladstone Road, Gisborne 3815, PO Box 539
tel (06) 8687769 *fax* (06) 8687767
email info@millymolly.com
website www.millymolly.com
Managing Director John Pittar

Picture books, gift books, fiction, education, interactive CD-Roms for preschool children and 4–8 year-olds. Promotes acceptance of diversity and sound values worldwide.

New Zealand Council for Educational Research*

Box 3237, Education House, 178–182 Willis Street, Wellington 6140
tel (04) 384-7939 *fax* (04) 385-8738
email info@nzcer.org.nz
website www.nzcer.org.nz
Director Robyn Baker, *Publisher* Bev Webber

Education, including educational policy and institutions, early childhood education, educational achievement tests, Maori education, curriculum and assessment, etc. Founded 1934.

Pearson Education New Zealand Ltd*

Private Bag 102902, Rosedale, North Shore 0745, Auckland
tel (09) 442-7400 *fax* (09) 442-7401
email firstname.lastname@pearsoned.co.nz
General Manager Adrian Keane

New Zealand educational books.

Penguin Group (NZ)*
Private Bag 102902, Rosedale, North Shore 0745,
Auckland
tel (09) 442-7400 *fax* (09) 442-7401
website www.penguin.co.nz
Managing Director Margaret Thompson, *Publishing Director* Geoff Walker

Adult and children's fiction and non-fiction. Imprints: Penguin, Viking, Puffin Books. Founded 1973.

Random House New Zealand Ltd*
Private Bag 102950, North Shore Mail Centre,
Auckland 0627
tel (09) 444-7197 *fax* (09) 444-7524
website www.randomhouse.co.nz
Managing Director M. Moynahan

Fiction, general non-fiction, gardening, cooking, art, business, health, children's. Subsidiary of Bertelsmann AG. Founded 1977.

RSVP Publishing Company*
PO Box 47166, Ponsonby, Auckland
tel/fax (09) 372-8480
email rsvppub@iconz.co.nz
website www.rsvp-publishing.co.nz
Managing Director/Publisher Stephen Picard

Fiction, metaphysical, children's. Founded 1990.

Scholastic New Zealand Ltd*
21 Lady Ruby Drive, East Tamaki, Auckland
tel (09) 274-8112 *fax* (09) 274-8114
email publishing@scholastic.co.nz
postal address Private Bag 94407, Greenmount,
Auckland 2141
website www.scholastic.co.nz
Publishing Manager Christine Dale

Picture books, fiction for 5–8 and 9–12 year-olds, teenage fiction and series fiction. Publishes approx. 50 titles each year and has over 200 in print. Imprints: Scholastic NZ, Blue Balloon. Founded 1962.
   Submission details Does not accept unsolicited MSS from writers not already published by Scholastic New Zealand. See website download for further details. For picture books send copies of illustrations (though not essential), *not* original artwork.

Weldon Owen Education*
6–10 The Strand, Takapuna, 0622
tel (09) 358-0190 *fax* (09) 358-0793
email info@weldonowen.co.nz
website www.weldonowen.co.nz

Supplementary educational titles for school systems internationally. Produces literacy-teaching programmes for kindergarten through to Grade 6. Also resources for home schooling. Series include *Shockwave* (8–10 year-olds), *Brainbank* (4–9 year-olds) and *Worldscapes* (8–10 year-olds). Founded 2001.

SOUTH AFRICA

Member of the Publishers' Association of South Africa

Cambridge University Press*
(African Branch)
Lower Ground Floor, Nautica Building,
The Water Club, Beach Road, Granger Bay,
Cape Town 8005
tel (021) 412-7800 *fax* (021) 419-8418
email capetown@cambridge.org
website www.cambridge.org
Director Colleen McCallum

African Branch of CUP, responsible for sub-Saharan Africa and English-speaking Caribbean. Publishes distance learning materials and textbooks for various African countries, as well as primary reading materials in 28 local African languages.

Chart Studio Publishing (Pty) Ltd
40 Long Street, Maitland 7405, Cape Town
tel (21) 510 7681 *fax* (21) 511 8797
email chartstudio@chartstudio.com
website www.chartstudio.com

Educational, fun-to-learn products including posters, flip-charts, fun-time fold-out books, flash cards, wooden puzzles, board books. Age groups: preschool, 5–10, 10–15, 15+.

Clever Books Pty Ltd*
PO Box 13816, Hatfield, Pretoria 0028
tel (012) 342-3263 *fax* (012) 430-2376
email cillierss@cleverbooks.co.za
Managing Director J. Steenhuisen

Educational titles for the RSA market. Owned by Macmillan South Africa. Founded 1981.

Human & Rousseau
PO Box 879, Cape Town 8000
tel (021) 406 3033 *fax* (021) 406 3812
email nb@nb.co.za
website www.nb.co.za

General Afrikaans and English titles. Quality Afrikaans literature, popular literature, general children's and youth literature, cookery, self-help. Founded 1959.

Best Books (imprint)
Education.

Jacklin Enterprises (Pty) Ltd
PO Box 521, Parklands 2121
tel (011) 265-4200 *fax* (011) 314-2984
email mjacklin@jacklin.co.za
Managing Director M.A.C. Jacklin

Children's fiction and non-fiction; Afrikaans large print books. Subjects include aviation, natural history, romance, general science, technology and transportation. Imprints: Mike Jacklin, Kennis Onbeperk, Daan Retief.

Maskew Miller Longman (Pty) Ltd*

PO Box 396, Howard Drive, Pinelands 7405, Cape Town 8000
tel (021) 532-6000 *fax* (021) 531-8103
email firstname@mml.co.za
website www.mml.co.za
Publishing Director Dorette Louw

Educational and general publishers.

NB Publishers (Pty) Ltd*

PO Box 879, Cape Town 8000
tel (021) 406-3033 *fax* (021) 406-3812
email nb@nb.co.za
website www.nb.co.za
Managing Director Eloise Wessels

General: Afrikaans fiction, politics, children's and youth literature in all the country's languages, non-fiction. Imprints include Tafelberg, Human & Rousseau, Pharos and Kwela. Founded 1950.

New Africa Books (Pty) Ltd*

99 Garfield Road, Claremont, Cape Town 7700
tel (21) 674-4136 *fax* (21) 674-3358
email info@newafricabooks.co.za
postal address PO Box 46962, Glosderry 7702
website www.newafricabooks.co.za
Publisher Jeanne Homnid

General books, textbooks, literary works, contemporary issues, children and young adult. Formed as a result of the merger of David Philip Publishers (founded 1971), Spearhead Press (founded 2000) and New Africa Educational Publishing.

Oxford University Press Southern Africa*

Vasco Boulevard, N1 City, Goodwood, Cape Town 7460
tel (021) 596-2300 *fax* (021) 596-1234
email oxford.za@oup.com
postal address PO Box 12119, N1 City, Cape Town 7463
website www.oxford.co.za
Managing Director E. Kotze, *Publishing Director* M.R. Griffin

Reference books for children and school books: Preschool and Foundation Phase, Intermediate Phase, Senior Phase, dictionaries, thesauruses, atlases and teaching English as a main and as a second language.

Shuter and Shooter Publishers (Pty) Ltd*

21c Cascades Crescent, Cascades, Pietermaritzburg 3201, KwaZulu-Natal
tel (033) 347-6100 *fax* (033) 347-6130
email sabeb@shuter.co.za
postal address PO Box 13016, Cascades 3202, KwaZulu-Natal

website www.shuters.com
Managing Director Mrs P. B. Chetty

Core curriculum-based textbooks for use at foundation, intermediate, senior and further education phases. Supplementary readers in various languages; dictionaries; reading development kits, charts. Literature titles in English, isiXhosa, Sesotho, Sepedi, Setswana, Tshivenda, Xitsonga, Ndebele and Siswati. Founded 1925.

SPAIN

Grupo Anaya

C/ Juan Ignacio Luca de Tena, 15 – 28027 Madrid
tel 34 91 3938700 *fax* 34 91 7424259
website www.anaya.es
Managing Director Carlos Lamadrid

Non-fiction: education textbooks for preschool through to 15+.

Editorial Cruilla

Balmes 245, 4t, 08006 Barcelona
tel (93) 292 21 72 *fax* (93) 238 01 16
email editorial@cruilla.com
website www.cruilla.com
Publishing Director Josep Herrero

Activity books, novelty books, fiction for 5–8 and 9–12 year-olds, teenage fiction and poetry. Publishes approx. 120–130 titles each year. Recent successes include El Vaixell de Vapor (series), Vull Llegir! and Molly Moon Stops the World/Molly Moon's Incredible Book of Hypnotism. Founded 1984. Subsidiary of Ediciones SM.

Destino Infantil & Juvenil

Edificio Planeta, Diagonal 662–664, 08034 Barcelona
tel (93) 496 7001 *fax* (93) 496 7002
email destinojoven@edestino.es
website www.edestino.es
Children's Director Bueno Marta

Fiction for ages 6–16 years old. Picture books, pop-up books, fiction and some unusual illustrated books. Age groups: preschool, 5–10, 10–15, 15+.

Libros del Zorro Rojo

Sant Joan de Malta, 39, 202A, 08018 Barcelona
tel/fax 34 93 3076850
email editorial@librosdelzorrorojo.com
website www.librosdelzorrorojo.com

Small independent publisher specialising in children's and young adult books. Main focus is picture books for young children and classics with high-quality illustrations for young readers.

Editorial Libsa

San Rafael 4, Poligono Industrail, 28102 Alcobendas/Madrid
tel 34 91 6572580 *fax* 34 91 6572583

email libsa@libsa.es
website www.libsa.es
President Amado Sanchez, *Children's Books Editor*
Maria Dolores Maeso

Publisher and packager of highly illustrated mass market books: activity books, board books, picture books, colouring books, how-to books, fairy tales.

Random House Mondadori
Travessera de Gracia 47–49, 08021 Barcelona, Spain
tel (34) 93 3660300 *fax* (34) 93 3660449
website www.randomhousemondadori.es

Preschool activity, novelty and picture books through to young adult fiction. Also a packager and printer.

Beasco (division)
Character publishing, including Disney and Fisher-Price.

Lumen (division)
Classics and illustrated books.

Montena (division)
Contemporary literary fiction including fantasy.

Vicens Vives SA
Avenida Sarriá 130–132, 08017 Barcelona
tel (93) 252 3700 *fax* (93) 252 3711
email e@vicensvives.es
website www.vicensvives.es
Managing Director Roser Espona de Rahola

Activity and novelty books, fiction, art, encyclopedias, dictionaries, education, geography, history, music, science, textbooks, posters. Age groups: preschool, 5–10, 10–15, 15+.

USA

*Member of the Association of American Publishers Inc.

Abingdon Press
201 Eighth Avenue, PO Box 801, Nashville, TN 37202–0801
tel 615-749-6290 *fax* 615-749-6372
website www.abingdonpress.com
President Neil Alexander, *Vice President* Tammy Gaines

General interest, professional, academic and reference – primarily directed to the religious market; children's non-fiction. Imprint of United Methodist Publishing House.

Harry N. Abrams Inc.
115 West 18th Street, New York, NY 10011
tel 212-206-7715 *fax* 212-519-1210
website www.hnabooks.com
Ceo/President Michael Jacobs

Art and architecture, photography, natural sciences, performing arts, children's books. No fiction. Founded 1949.

Harry N. Abrams Books for Young Readers
tel 212-519-1200
website www.abramsyoungreaders.com
Director, Children's Books Howard W. Reeves

Fiction and non-fiction: picture books, young readers, middle readers, young adult.
   Submission details For picture books submit covering letter and complete MS, for longer works and non-fiction send query and sample chapter with sase.

Absey and Co. Inc.*
23011 Northcrest Drive, Spring, TX 77389
tel 888-412-2739 *fax* 281-251-4676
email info@absey.biz
website www.absey.biz
Publisher Edward Wilson

Mainstream fiction and non-fiction, poetry, educational books, especially those dealing in language arts. Recent successes for young adult readers include *Where I'm From* by George Ella Lyon, *Poetry After Lunch* by Joyce Armstrong Carroll and *Just People and Paper, Pen, Poem* by Kathi Appelt; and picture books *Regular Lu* by Robin Nelson and *Stealing a Million Kisses* by Jennifer Skaggs.
   Submission details For fiction query with sase. For non-fiction query with outline and 1–2 sample chapters.

Action Publishing, LLC
PO Box 391, Glendale, CA 91209
tel 323-478-1667 *fax* 323-478-1767
email info@actionpublishing.com
website www.actionpublishing.com

Picture books and fiction for young, middle and young adult readers.
   Submission details See website for guidelines. Founded 1996.

Aladdin Paperbacks – see Simon & Schuster Children's Publishing Division

All About Kids Publising
9333 Benbow Drive, Gilroy, CA 95020
tel 408-846-1833 *fax* 408-846-1835
email mail@aakp.com
website www.aakp.com
Publisher Mike G. Guevara, *Editor* Linda L. Guevara

Fiction and non-fiction picture books and chapter books. Recent successes include *A, My Name is Andrew* by Mary McManus-Burke (picture book) and *The Titanic Game* by Mike Warner (chapter book). Founded 1999.
   Submission details See website for guidelines.

Alyson Publications, Inc.
PO Box 4371, Los Angeles, CA 90078
tel 323-860-6065 *fax* 323-467-0152
email mail@alyson.com
website www.alyson.com

Editor Angela Brown

Picture books and young adult titles that deal with gay or lesbian issues. Recent successes include *Daddy's Wedding* by Michael Willhoite.

Submission details Picture books are only considered if text and illustrations are submitted together. For young adult books submit synopsis and sample chapters with sase. See website for submission guidelines.

American Girl Publishing, Inc.
8400 Fairway Place, Middleton, WI 53562
email im_es@americangirl.com
website www.americangirl.com

Age-appropriate books and playthings to 'foster girls' individuality, intellectual curiosity and imagination'.

American Girl (imprint)
Advice and activity books for 8–12 year-old girls.

Submission details Publishes material to encourage girls' dreams and to reinforce their self-confidence and curiosity as they prepare to navigate adolescence in the years ahead. Invites proposals for well-focused concepts for activity books, craft books, or advice books. Also non-fiction specifically targeted to girls – if the approach would appeal to boys as well as to girls, submission is not appropriate. Proposals should include a detailed description of the concept, sample chapters or spreads, and lists or samples of previous publications, plus sase. Complete MSS are also acceptable. Founded 1985.

Amistad Press – see HarperCollins Publishers

The Julie Andrews Collection – see HarperCollins Publishers

Atheneum Books for Young Readers – see Simon & Schuster Children's Publishing Division

Avisson Press, Inc.
3007 Taliaferro Road, Greensboro, NC 27408
tel 336-288-6989 *fax* 336-288-6989
email avisson4@aol.com
Publisher Martin Hester

Biography for young adults. Recent successes include *I Can Do Anything* by William Schoell and *The Girl He Left Behind* by Suzanne Middendorf.

Submission details Submit synopsis and 2 sample chapters. Founded 1995.

Avon Books – see HarperCollins Publishers

Bantam Books – see Random House Inc.

Barefoot Books
2067 Massachusetts Avenue, Cambridge, MA 02140
tel 617-576-0660 *fax* 617-576-0049

email publicity@barefootbooks.com
website www.barefootbooks.com

Barefoot Books 'celebrates art and story with books that open the hearts and minds of children from all walks of life'. Recent successes include *The Boy Who Grew Flowers* by Jen Wojtowicz, illustrated by Steve Adams (age 4–9, picture book).

Submission details Length: 500–1000 words (picture books), 2000–3000 young readers. Accepts unsolicited MSS. Send full MS and SAE. Allow up to six months for a response. Founded 1993 in UK; 1998 in USA.

Barron's Educational Series Inc.
250 Wireless Boulevard, Hauppauge, NY 11788
tel 800-645-3476 *fax* 631-434-3723
email barrons@barronseduc.com
website www.barronseduc.com
Chairman/Ceo Manuel H. Barron, *President/Publisher* Ellen Sibley

Series books for children aged 7–11, 12–16. Publishes 20 picture books, 20 young reader titles, 20 middle reader titles and 10 young adult titles each year. Recent successes include *Everyday Witch* by Sandra Forrester and *Word Wizardry* by Margaret and William Kenda. Also for adults: cookbooks, Mind, Body & Spirit, crafts, business, pets, gardening, family and health, art. Founded 1941.

Submission details Approx. 25% of books are by first-time authors. For fiction, query by email. For non-fiction, submit outline/synopsis and sample chapters with sase for response. Responds to MSS in 8 months. Send to Acquisitions Manager. See website for full details.

Reviews MS/illustration packages from artists: send query letter with 3 chapters of MS with one piece of final art, remainder roughs. For illustrations only send tearsheets or slides plus résumé. Responds in 2 months. Send to Bill Kuchler, Art Director.

Bebop Books
95 Madison Avenue, New York, NY 10016
tel 212-779-4400 *fax* 212-683-1894
email general@bebopbooks.com
website www.bebopbooks.com

Multicultural fiction and non-fiction for young readers. Imprint of Lee & Low Books, Inc.

Submission details Child-centered stories that support literacy learning and provide multicultural content for beginning readers. Currently not accepting new submissions. Founded 2000.

Bick Publishing House
307 Neck Road, Madison, CT 06443
tel 203-245-0073 *fax* 203-245-5990
email bickpubhse@aol.com
website www.bickpubhouse.com

Adults: health and recovery, living with disabilities, wildlife rehabilitation. Non-fiction for young adults:

philosophy, psychology, self help, social issues, science. Recent successes include *What Are You Doing with Your Life? Books on Living for Teenagers* by J. Krishnamurti; *The Teen Brain Book: Who and What Are You?* and *Talk: Teen Art of Communication* by Dale Carlson. Founded 1993.

Bloomsbury USA

Suite 315, 175 Fifth Avenue, New York, NY 10010
tel 212-674-5151 *fax* 212-982-2837
email bloomsbury.kids@bloomsburyusa.com
Publisher, Children's Books Melanie Cecka, *Publisher, Walker Books* Emily Easton, *Editorial Director* Michele Nagler, *Associate Publisher* Diana Blough, *Publicity Director* Debra Shapiro

Publishers of literary fiction, general non-fiction and children's (picture books, early chapter books, middle grade fiction, teen fiction). A wholly owned subsidiary of Bloomsbury Plc. Adult division does not accept unsolicited MSS. Children's division will consider unsolicited MSS, no material will be returned, and only accepted MSS will receive a reply. Founded 1998.

Bloomsbury Children's (USA)

Novelty books, picture books, fiction for 5–8 and 9–12 year-olds, teenage fiction, series fiction and poetry. Publishes 40 titles each year and has 80 in print. Recent successes include *Pirates!* by Celia Rees, *Bill in a China Shop* by Katie McAllaster Weaver and Tim Raglin and *The Alphabet Room* by Sara Pinto. Founded 2002.

Submission details Approx. 25% of books are by first-time authors. Will consider unsolicited MSS with sase. Allow 6 months for response. Will review MS/illustration packages from artists; send query letter or submit MS with dummy.

Blue Sky Press – see Scholastic Inc.

Boyds Mills Press

815 Church Street, Honesdale, PA 18431
website www.boydsmillspress.com

Activity books, picture books, fiction, non-fiction, and poetry for ages 18 and under. Recent successes include *Drive* by Nathan Clement, *One Whole and Perfect Day* by Judith Clarke and *I'm Being Stalked by a Moonshadow* by Doug MacLeod. Publishes approx. 80 titles each year. Founded 1991.

Submission details Will consider both unsolicited MSS and queries. Send to above address and label package 'Manuscript Submission'. Looking for middle-grade fiction with fresh ideas and subject matter, and young adult novels of real literary merit. Non-fiction should be fun and entertaining as well as informative, and non-fiction MSS should be accompanied by a detailed bibliography. Interested in imaginative picture books and welcomes submissions from both writers and illustrators. Submit samples as b&w and/or colour copies or transparencies;

submissions will not be returned. Include sase with all submissions. Send art samples to above address and label package 'Art Sample Submission'.

Calkins Creek Books (imprint)
US history and historical fiction.

Front Street (imprint)
See page 44.

Wordsong (imprint)
Poetry.

Calkins Creek Books – see Boyds Mills Press

Candlewick Press

99 Dover Street, Somerville, MA 02144
tel 617-661-3330 *fax* 617-661-0565
email bigbear@candlewick.com
website www.candlewick.com
President/Publisher Karen Lotz, *Editorial Director/ Associate Publisher* Liz Bicknell

Books for 6 months–18 year-olds: board books, picture books, novels, non-fiction, novelty books. Publishes 160 picture books, 15 middle readers and 15 young adult titles each year. Recent successes include *The Earth, My Butt, and Other Big Round Things* by Carolyn Mackler (young adult fiction), *The Tales of Despereaux* by Kate DiCamillo (middle-grade fiction) and *Surprising Sharks* by Nicola Davies, illustrated by James Croft (non-fiction picture book). Subsidiary of Walker Books Ltd, UK.

Submission details Approx. 5% of books are by first-time authors. Submit MSS via a literary agent. No unsolicited MSS accepted. For illustrations, send résumé and portfolio for the attention of Art Resource Coordinator. Responds in 6 weeks. Samples returned with sase. Founded 1991.

Carolrhoda Books – see Lerner Publishing Group

Cartwheel Books – see Scholastic Inc.

Charlesbridge Publishing

85 Main Street, Watertown, MA 02472
tel 617-926-0329 *fax* 617-926-5720
email tradeeditorial@charlesbridge.com
website www.charlesbridge.com
President & Publisher Brent Farmer, *Vice President & Associate Publisher* Mary Ann Sabia

Board books, novelty books, fiction and non-fiction picture books and transitional books for preschool–12 year-olds. Lively, plot-driven story books plus nursery rhymes, fairy tales and humorous stories for the very young. Non-fiction list specialises in nature, concept and multicultural books. Publishes 60% non-fiction, 40% fiction picture books and transitional books. Recent successes include *The Searcher and Old Tree* by David McPhail, *Wiggle and*

Waggle by Caroline Arnold, *Hello Bumblebee Bob* by Darrin Lunde, and *Life on Earth – and Beyond: An Astrobiologist's Quest* by Pamela S. Turner. Founded 1980.

Submission details Send full MSS; no queries. Responds to MSS of interest. Length: 1000–10,000 words. For illustrations, send query with samples, tearsheets and résumé.

Chicago Review Press

814 North Franklin Street, Chicago, IL 60610
tel 312-337-0747 *fax* 312-337-5110
email frontdesk@chicagoreviewpress.com
website www.chicagoreviewpress.com
Publisher Cynthia Sherry

General publisher. Non-fiction activity books for children. Recent successes include *Exploring the Solar System: A History with 22 Activities* by Mary Kay Carson.

Submission details Interested in hands-on educational books. See website for submission guidelines. Founded 1973.

Chronicle Books

680 Second Street, San Francisco, CA 94107
tel 415-537-4200 *fax* 415-537-4460
email frontdesk@chroniclebooks.com
website www.chroniclebooks.com,
www.chroniclekids.com
Chairman & Ceo Nion McEvoy, *Publisher* Christine Carswell

Traditional and innovative children's books. Looking for projects that have a unique bent – in subject matter, writing style or illustrative technique – that will add a distinctive flair. Interested in fiction and non-fiction for children of all ages as well as board books, decks, activity kits, and other unusual or 'novelty' formats. Publishes 60–100 books each year. Also for adults: cooking, how-to books, nature, art, biographies, fiction, gift. Founded 1967.

Submission details For picture books submit MS. For older readers, submit outline/synopsis and 3 sample chapters. No submitted materials will be returned. Response approx. 3 months.

Clarion Books – see Houghton Mifflin Company

Clear Light Books

823 Don Diego, Santa Fe, NM 87505
tel 505-989-9590 *fax* 505-989-9519
website www.clearlightbooks.com
Publisher Harmon Houghton

For adults: art and photography, cookbooks, ecology/environment, health, gift books, history, Native America, Tibet, Western Americana. Non-fiction for children and young adults: multicultural, American Indian, Hispanic.

Submission details Looking for authentic American Indian art and folklore. Send complete MS with sase.

CMX – see DC Comics

Collins – see HarperCollins Publishers

The Continuum International Publishing Group Inc.

80 Maiden Lane, Suite 704, New York, NY 10038
tel 212-953-5858 *fax* 212-953-5944
email info@continuum-books.com
website www.continuum-books.com

General non-fiction, education, popular culture, philosophy, politics, linguistics, history, literary criticism, religious studies. Founded 1999.

David C. Cook

4050 Lee Vance View, Colorado Springs, CO 80918
tel 719-536-0100
website www.davidccook.com

Christian education resources for preschool to teenagers.

Joanna Cotler Books – see HarperCollins Publishers

Cricket Books

Carus Publishing Company,
Cricket Magazine Group, Suite 300,
70 East Lake Street, Chicago, IL 60601
email bookpublicity@caruspub.com
website www.cricketmag.net

Picture books, chapter books, poetry, non-fiction and novels for children and young adults. Recent successes include *Breakout* by Paul Fleischman and *Robert and the Weird & Wacky Facts* by Barbara Seuling, illustrated by Paul Brewer. Also publishes *Cricket*, the award-winning magazine of outstanding stories and art for 9–14 year-olds, and other magazines for young readers. Founded 1973. Division of Carus Publishing.

Submission details Not accepting MSS submissions at this time.

Crown Books – see Random House Inc.

Darby Creek Publishing

7858 Industrial Parkway, Plain City, OH 43064
tel 614-873-7955 *fax* 614-873-7135
email editorial@darbycreekpublishing.com
website www.darbycreekpublishing.com

Fiction and non-fiction for children and young adults. Recent successes include *Albino Animals* by Kelly Milner Halls (age 10+).

Submission details Interested in non-fiction works for ages 8–14 with themes that relate to sports, science, history or biography, and fiction from early chapter books through to young adult. For short projects submit entire MS. For longer works submit 2–3 sample chapters with a synopsis and brief chapter summary outline. Also include a CV and sase.

Interested in seeing illustration samples of all styles, in both colour and b&w. Do not send originals. Send to Submissions Editor. Founded 2002.

Dawn Publications
12402 Bitney Springs Road, Nevada City, CA 95959
website www.dawnpub.com
Editor & Co-Publisher Glenn Hovemann, Art Director & Co-Publisher Muffy Weaver

Picture books and biographies 'to assist parents and educators to open the minds and hearts of children to the transforming influence of Nature'. Recent successes include Near One Cattail: Turtles, Logs and Leaping Frogs by Anthony D. Fredericks (picture book), and Mammals Who Morph: The Universe Tells Our Evolution Story by Jennifer Morgan (picture book).
Submission details See website for guidelines.

DC Comics
1700 Broadway, New York, NY 10019
tel 212-636-5400 fax 212-636-5975
email askeditors@dccomics.com
website www.dccomics.com
Activity books, board books, novelty books, picture books, painting and colouring books, pop-up books, fiction, fairy tales, art, hobbies, how-to books, leisure, entertainment, film/TV tie-ins, calendars, comics, gift books, periodicals, picture cards, posters, CD-Roms, CD-I, internet for preschool age to 15+.
DC Comics has published and licensed comic books for over 60 years in all genres for all ages, including super heroes, fantasy, horror, mystery and high-quality graphic stories for mature readers. Imprints: WildStorm, Vertigo. A Warner Bros. Company.

CMX (imprint)
Translated manga from Japan in its original format.

MINX (imprint)
Original graphic novels for teenage girls.

Delacorte Press Books for Young Readers – see Random House Inc.

Dial Books for Young Readers – see Penguin Group (USA), Inc.

Disney Books for Young Readers – see Random House Inc.

Dog-Eared Publications
PO Box 620863, Middletown, WI 53562–0863
tel/fax 608-831-1410
email field@dog-eared.com
website www.dog-eared.com
Children's nature books.
Submission details No unsolicited MSS.

Tom Doherty Associates, LLC
175 5th Avenue, 14th Floor, New York, NY 10010
tel 212-388-0100 fax 212-388-0191

website www.us.macmillan.com/TorForge.aspx
Fiction and non-fiction for middle readers and young adults. Publishes 5–10 middle readers and 5–10 young adult books each year. Recent successes include Hidden Talents, Flip by David Lubar (fantasy, ages 10+), Briar Rose by Jane Yolen (fiction, age 12+), Strange Unsolved Mysteries by Phyllis Rabin Amert (non-fiction). For adults: fiction – general, historical, western, suspense, mystery, horror, science fiction, fantasy, humour, juvenile, classics (English language); non-fiction. Imprints: Tor Books, Forge Books, Orb Books, Starscope, Tor Teen. Founded 1980.
Submission details For both fiction and non-fiction, submit outline/synopsis and complete MS. Responds to queries in one month; MSS in 6 months for unsolicited work. Fiction length: middle readers – 30,000 words; young adult – 60,000–100,000 words. Non-fiction length: middle readers – 25,000–35,000 words; young adult – 70,000 words. For illustrations, query with samples to Irene Gallo, Art Director. Responds only if interested.

Doubleday Books for Young Readers – see Random House Inc.

Dover Publications Inc.
31 East 2nd Street, Mineola, NY 11501
tel 516-294-7000 fax 516-742-5049
website www.doverpublications.com
Activity books, novelty books, picture books, fiction for 5–8 and 9–12 year-olds, teenage fiction, series fiction, reference, plays, religion, poetry, audio and CD-Roms. Also adult non-fiction. Publishes approx. 150 children's titles and has over 2500 in print. Recent successes include Easy Noah's Ark Sticker Picture, How to Draw a Funny Monster and Pretty Ballerina Sticker Paper Doll. Founded 1941.
Submission details Will consider unsolicited MSS but write for guidelines.

Dragon Books – see Pacific View Press

Dragonfly Books – see Random House Inc.

Dutton Children's Books – see Penguin Group (USA), Inc.

EDCON Publishing Group
30 Montauk Boulevard, Oakdale, NY 11769–1399
tel 631-567-7227 fax 631-567-8745
email info@edconpublishing.com
website www.edconpublishing.com
Supplemental instructional materials for use by education professionals to improve reading and maths skills. Includes early reading, Classics series, Easy Shakespeare, fiction and non-fiction, reading diagnosis and vocabulary books. Recent successes include adaptations of A Midsummer Night's Dream and The Merchant of Venice. Founded 1970.

Edupress

W5527 State Road 106, PO Box 800, Fort Atkinson,
WI 53538
tel 800-835-7978 *fax* 800-558-9332
email edupress@highsmith.com
website www.highsmith.com
Educational materials. Founded 1979.
Submission details See website for guidelines.

Eerdmans Publishing Company

2140 Oak Industrial Drive NE, Grand Rapids,
MI 49505
tel 616-459-4591 *fax* 616-459-6540
website www.eerdmans.com
President William B. Eerdmans, Jr

Independent publisher of a wide range of religious
books, from academic works in theology, biblical
studies, religious history, and reference to popular
titles in spirituality, social and cultural criticism and
literature. Founded 1911.

Eerdmans Books for Young Readers (imprint)

website www.eerdmans.com/youngreaders
Acquisitions Editor Shannon White, *Art Director* Gayle
Brown
Picture books, biographies, middle reader and young
adult fiction and non-ficiton. Publishes 12–18 books
a year. Seeks MSS that are honest, wise and hopeful
but also publishes stories that delight with their
storyline, characters or good humour. Stories that
celebrate diversity, stories of historical significance,
and stories that relate to current issues are of special
interest.
Submission details Only considers exclusive
submissions; include sase for reply. Send to Shannon
White; responds in 3 months. For illustrations, send
photocopies or printed media and include a list of
books you have illustrated. Send to Gayle Brown.
Samples returned with sase.

Encyclopaedia Britannica Inc.

331 North La Salle Street, Chicago, IL 60610
tel 312-347-7000 *fax* 312-294-2162
email international@eb.com
website www.britannica.com
Encyclopedias, reference books, almanacs, videos and
CD-Roms for adults and children aged 5–15+.

Enslow Publishers, Inc.

Box 398, 40 Industrial Road, Dept F61,
Berkeley Heights, NJ 07922–0398
tel 908-771-9400 *fax* 908-771-0925
email customerservice@enslow.com
website www.enslow.com
President Mark Enslow, *Vice President/Publisher* Brian
Enslow

Non-fiction library books for children and young
adults. Founded 1976.

Eos – see HarperCollins Publishers

Evan-Moor Educational Publishers

18 Lower Ragsdale Drive, Monterey, CA 93940
tel 831 649 5901 *fax* 831 649 6256

email editorial@evan-moor.com
website www.evan-moor.com
President Linda Hange, *Publisher* Joy Evans

Educational materials for parents and teachers of
children (ages 3–12): activity books, textbooks, how-
to books, CD-Roms. Subjects include maths,
geography, history, science, reading, writing, social
studies, art and craft. Publishes approx. 50 titles each
year and has over 450 in print. Recent successes
include *Daily Paragraph Editing* (5-book series,
grades 2–5) and *Nonfiction Reading Practice* (6-book
series, grades 1–6). Founded 1979.
Submission details Less than 10% of books are by
first-time authors. Query or submit outline, table of
contents and sample pages. Responds to queries in 2
months; MSS in 4 months. See website for
submission guidelines. For illustrations, send résumé,
samples and tearsheets to the Art Director. Primarily
uses b&w material.

Farrar, Straus and Giroux, LLC

18 West 18th Street, New York, NY 10011
tel 212-741-6900 *fax* 212-633-9385
website www.fsgbooks.com, www.fsgkidsbooks.com
President/Publisher Jonathan Galassi

General publishers: literary fiction, non-fiction,
poetry, children's. Imprints: Books for Young
Readers, Faber and Faber Inc., Hill and Wang, North
Point Press, Sarah Crichton Books. Founded 1946.

Farrar, Straus and Giroux Books for Young Readers

Editorial Director and Co-publisher Margaret
Ferguson, *Frances Foster Books* Frances Foster,
Melanie Kroupa Books Melanie Kroupa, *Executive
Editors* Wesley Adams, Beverly Reingold, *Senior
Editor* Janine O'Malley, *Art Director* Robbin Gourley
Books for toddlers through to young adults: picture
books, fiction for 5–8 and 9–12-year-olds, teenage
fiction and poetry (occasionally). Publishes 70
hardcover originals plus 10 paperback reprints each
year and has approx. 500 titles in print. Recent
successes include *The Wall* by Peter Sís, *The Way
Down Deep* by Ruth White and *Someday This Pain
Will be Useful to You* by Peter Cameron. Imprints:
Frances Foster Books, Melanie Kroupa Books,
Sunburst (paperback).
Submission details Approx. 10% of books are by
first-time authors. Send query letter first but will
consider unsolicited MSS. Include a covering letter
containing any pertinent information about yourself,
your writing, your MSS, etc and a sase for return of
MSS. Address submissions to Children's Editorial
Department. Allow 3 months for response. Looking
to publish books of high literary merit. For
illustrations, send only 2–3 samples; do *not* send
original artwork.

David Fickling Books – see Random House
Inc.

Firebird – see page 52

Flux – see Llewellyn Worldwide

Walter Foster Publishing Inc.
23062 La Cadena Drive, Laguna Hills, Irvine,
CA 92653
tel 949-380-7510 *fax* 949-380-7575
email info@walterfoster.com
website www.walterfoster.com
Chief Executive Ross Sarracino

Instructional art books for children and adults. Also art and activity kits for children. A subsidiary of Quayside Publishing Group.

Free Spirit Publishing
217 Fifth Avenue North, Suite 200, Minneapolis,
MN 55401
tel 612-338-2068 *fax* 612-337-5050
email help4kids@freespirit.com
website www.freespirit.com
President Judy Galbraith

Award-winning publisher of non-fiction materials for children and teens, parents, educators, and counsellors. Specialises in SELF-HELP FOR KIDS® and SELF-HELP FOR TEENS® materials which empower young people and promote positive self-esteem through improved social and emotional health. Topics include self-esteem and self-awareness, stress management, school success, creativity, friends and family, peacemaking, social action, and special needs (i.e. gifted and talented, children with learning differences). Publishes approx. 18–22 new products each year, adding to a backlist of over 100 books, audio tapes, and posters. Free Spirit authors are expert educators and mental health professionals who have been honoured nationally for their contributions on behalf of children. Founded 1983.

Front Street
(An imprint of Boyds Mills Press)
862 Haywood Road, Asheville, NC 28806
tel 828-236-5940 *fax* 828-236-5935
email contactus@frontstreetbooks.com
website www.frontstreetbooks.com
Director of Institutional Marketing & Subsidiary Rights Nancy Hogan, *Publisher* Stephen Roxburgh, *Art Director* Helen Robinson, *Editor* Joy Neaves

Books for children and young adults: picture books, fiction (5–8, 9–12, teenage). Publishes 10–15 books each year. Recent successes include *Runaround* by Helen Hemphill, *What Happened* by Peter Johnson, *Baby* by Joseph Monninger, *Sneaking Suspicions* by Carolyn Coman, and *Isabel and the Miracle Baby* by Emily Smith Pearce. Founded 1994.
Submission details For fiction, submit 2–3 sample chapters and a plot summary. For picture books, do not send MSS but send a query letter describing your project as fully as possible. Include sase. Allow 3–4 months for response.

Fulcrum Resources*
4690 Table Mountain Drive, Suite 100, Golden,
CO 80403

tel 303-277-1623 *fax* 303-279-7111
email fulcrum@fulcrumbooks.com
website www.fulcrum-books.com

Books and support materials for teachers, librarians, parents and elementary through middle school children in the subjects of science and nature, literature and storytelling, history, multicultural studies, and Native American and Hispanic cultures. Imprint of Fulcrum Publishing.

Gale Cengage Learning*
27500 Drake Road, Farmington Hills, MI 48331–3535
tel 248-699-4253
website www.gale.cengage.com

Education publishing for libraries, schools and businesses. Serves the K–12 market with the following imprints: Blackbirch Press, Greenhaven Press, KidHaven Press, Lucent Books, Sleeping Bear Press, UXL.

Greenhaven Press (imprint)
High-quality non-fiction resources for the education community. Publishes 220 young adult academic reference titles each year. Recent successes include the *Opposing Viewpoints* series. Founded 1970.
Submission details Approx. 35% of books are by first-time authors. No unsolicited MSS. All writing is done on a work-to-hire basis. Send query, résumé and list of published works.

KidHave Press (imprint)
Non-fiction references for younger researchers.

Lucent Books (imprint)
Non-fiction resources for upper-elementary to high school students. Recent successes include *Women in the American Revolution* and *Civil Liberties and the War on Terrorism*.
Submission details No unsolicited MSS. Query with résumé.

Sleeping Bear Press (imprint)
email sleepingbearpress@cengage.com
website www.sleepingbearpress.com
High-quality picture books.

Laura Geringer Books – see HarperCollins Publishers

Golden Books for Young Readers – see Random House Inc.

Graphia – see Houghton Mifflin Company

Greenhaven Press – see Gale Cengage Learning

Greenwillow Books – see HarperCollins Publishers

Grosset & Dunlap – see Penguin Group (USA), Inc.

Gryphon House, Inc.
PO Box 207, Beltsville, MD 20704
tel 301-595-9500 *fax* 301-595-0051

website www.gryphonhouse.com
Early childhood (age 0–8) books for teachers and parents.
Submission details 'We look for books that are developmentally appropriate for the intended age group, are well researched and based on current trends in the field, and include creative, participatory learning experiences with a common conceptual theme to tie them together.' Send query and/or a proposal.

Hachai Publishing
527 Empire Boulevard, Brooklyn, NY 11225
tel 718-633-0100 *fax* 718-633-0103
email info@hachai.com
website www.hachai.com
Jewish books for children aged 0–8+.
Submission details Welcomes unsolicited MSS. Specialises in books for 2–4 year-olds and 3–6 year-olds. Looking for stories that convey the traditional Jewish experience in modern times or long ago, traditional Jewish observance, and positive character traits.

Handprint Books
413 Sixth Avenue, Brooklyn, New York 11215
tel 718-768-3696 *fax* 718-369-0844
email submissions@handprintbooks.com
website www.handprintbooks.com
Publisher Christopher Franceschelli, *Executive Editor* Ann Tobias
A range of children's books: picture and story books through to young adult fiction. Imprints: Handprint Books, Ragged Bears, Blue Apple.
Submission details Welcomes submissions of MSS of quality for works ranging from board books to young adult novels. For novels, first query interest on the subject and submit a 7500-word max. sample. Accepts MSS on an e-submission basis only, sent as attachments in a word processing format readily readable on a PC. Artwork should be sent as jpg files and total size should not exceed 200K and website addresses containing artists' illustrations may be submitted. Submission of the following is discouraged: series fiction, licensed character (or characters whose primary avatar is meant to be as licenses), 'I-Can-Read'- type books, titles intended primarily for mass merchandise outlets.

Harcourt School Publishers*
6277 Sea Harbor Drive, Orlando, FL 32887
tel 407-345-2000
website www.harcourtschool.com
Textbooks and related instructional materials for school and home use by students (grades PreK–6): reading, language arts, ESL, maths, science, social studies, art, health, professional development and electronic and online material. Division of Harcourt Inc. Founded 1919.

Harcourt Trade Publishers*
15 East 26th Street, New York, NY 10010
tel 212-592-1034 *fax* 212-592-1030
website www.harcourtbooks.com
President/Publisher Dan Farley, *Editorial Director* Liz Van Doren
Fiction and non-fiction (history, biography, etc) for readers of all ages. Imprints: Harcourt (hardcover books), Harvest Books (paperbacks), Harcourt Children's Books. A Harcourt Education company.

Harcourt Children's Books
Publisher Lori Benton, *Editorial Director, Harcourt Children's Books* Allyn Johnston
Quality picture books, contemporary and historical fiction for teen readers, board and novelty books, gift items, and non-fiction for children of all ages. Also reading and teacher guides for teachers of children aged 8–14+. The original publisher of such classics as *The Little Prince, Mary Poppins, The Borrowers, Half Magic, Ginger Pye,* and *The Moffats.* Recent successes include *Where Did That Baby Come From?* by Debi Gliori and *Juliet Dove, Queen of Love* by Bruce Coville (fiction, age 8–12). Imprints: Gulliver Books, Silver Whistle, Red Wagon Books, Harcourt Young Classics, Green Light Readers, Voyager Books/Libros Viajeros, Harcourt Paperbacks, Odyssey Classics, Magic Carpet Books.
Submission details Does not accept unsolicited query letters or emails, MSS and illustrations. Only accepts material via literary agents.

HarperCollins Publishers*
10 East 53rd Street, New York, NY 10022
tel 212-207-7000 *fax* 212-207-7145
website www.harpercollins.com
President/Ceo Brian Murray
Adult fiction (commercial and literary) and non-fiction. Subjects include biography, business, cookbooks, educational, history, juvenile, poetry, religious, science, technical and travel. Imprints include Amistad, Avon, Avon A, Avon Inspire, Avon Red, Caedmon, Collins, Collins Design, Ecco, Eos, HarperAudio, Harper Mass Market, Harper Paperbacks, Harper Perennial, Harper Perennial Modern Classics, HarperCollins, HarperEntertainment, HarperLuxe, HarperOne, William Morrow, Morrow Cookbooks, Rayo. No unsolicited material; all submissions must come through a literary agent. Founded 1817.

HarperCollins Children's Books Division
1350 Avenue of the Americas, New York, NY 10019
tel 212-261-6500
website www.harperchildrens.com
President/Publisher Susan Katz
Children's classic literature. Recent successes include *Goodnight Moon, Where the Wild Things Are, The Giving Tree,* and *Charlotte's Web.* Imprints: Amistad Press, the Julie Andrews Collection, Avon Books,

Collins, Joanna Cotler Books, EOS, Laura Geringer Books, Greenwillow Books, HarperChildren's Audio, HarperCollins e-books, HarperEntertainment, HarperFestival, HarperTeen, HarperTrophy, Rayo, Katherine Tegen Books, TOKYOPOP.

Submission details Does not accept unsolicited or unagented MSS.

Amistad Press (imprint)

Books by and about people of African descent on subjects and themes that have significant influence on the intellectual, cultural, and historical perspectives of a world audience.

The Julie Andrews Collection (imprint)

website www.julieandrewscollection.com
Books for young readers that nurture the imagination and celebrate a sense of wonder. Includes new works by established and emerging authors, out-of-print books, and books by Ms Andrews herself.

Avon Books (imprint)

Series and popular fiction for young readers: romance, mystery, adventure, fantasy. Series include *Making Out*, *Animal Emergency*, *Get Real*, and *Enchanted Hearts*, and authors include Bruce Coville, Beatrice Sparks and Dave Duncan.

Collins (imprint)

Non-fiction for toddlers to teens, including books published in conjunction with the Smithsonian Institution, the Emily Post Institute, and TIME for Kids, as well as Seymour Simon's award-winning titles and the classic *Let's-Read-and-Find-Out Science* series.

Joanna Cotler Books (imprint)

Literary and commercial picture books and fiction for all ages. Authors and illustrators include Clive Barker, Francesca Lia Block, Sharon Creech, Jamie Lee Curtis, Laura Cornell, Patricia MacLachlan, Barbara Robinson, Art Spiegelman, Jerry Spinelli and William Steig.

Eos (imprint)

Science fiction and fantasy.

Laura Geringer Books (imprint)

Publisher Laura Geringer
Fiction. Publishes 6 picture books, 2 young readers, 4 middle readers and one young adult title each year. Recent successes include *If You Take a Mouse to School* by Laura Numeroff, illustrated by Felicia Band (ages 3–7) and *The Dulcimer Boy* by Tor Seidler, illustrated by Brian Selznick (ages 8+). Authors and artists include William Joyce, Laura Numeroff, Felicia Bond, Bruce Brooks, Richard Egielski and Sarah Weeks.

Submission details Submissions via a literary agent only. Length: picture books – 500 words; young readers – 1000 words; middle readers – 25,000 words; young adult – 40,000 words.

Greenwillow Books (imprint)

Books for children of all ages. Publishes 40 picture books, 5 middle readers and 5 young adult books each year. Recent successes indlue *Olive's Ocean* by Kevin Henkes.

Submission details No unsolicited MSS or queries. Unsolicited mail will not be opened or returned.

HarperChildren's Audio (imprint)

Offers bestselling children's books and young adult favourites in CD and audio cassette formats.

HarperCollins e-Books (imprint)

Middle-grade and young adult fiction. Many titles contain ebook features not found in print editions.

HarperEntertainment (imprint)

Film and TV tie-ins, from preschool through to teens. Recent titles include *The Chronicles of Narnia*, *Ice Age 2*, *X-Men*, *Charlotte's Web*, *Spider-Man* and *Shrek*.

HarperFestival (imprint)

Books, novelties and merchandise for children aged 0–6. Classic board books include *Goodnight Moon* and *Runaway Bunny*.

HarperTeen (imprint)

Books that reflect teen readers' own lives: their everyday realities and aspirations, struggles and triumphs. From topical contemporary novels to lighthearted series books, to literary tales. Authors include Meg Cabot, Walter Dean Myers, Louise Rennison, Chris Crutcher and Joyce Carol Oates.

HarperTrophy (imprint)

Children's books. Authors and illustrators include picture books by Maurice Sendak, *I Can Read* books by Arnold Lobel, novels by Laura Ingalls Wilder, E.B. White, Katherine Paterson and Beverly Cleary.

Rayo (imprint)

Culturally inspired Spanish, English and bilingual books, as well as translations of award-winning and highly popular English titles. The list celebrates the rich Latino heritage.

Katherine Tegen Books (imprint)

Story books that entertain, inform, and capture the excitement, the joys, and the longings of life.

TOKYOPOP (imprint)

Manga titles based on existing HarperCollins works, as well as original manga titles conceived by HarperCollins authors.

Health Press NA Inc.

PO Box 37470, Albuquerque, NM 87176
tel 505-888-1394 *fax* 505-888-1521
email goodbooks@healthpress.com
website www.healthpress.com

Books for children and adults on a wide variety of medical conditions to meet the need for easy access to responsible, accurate patient education materials.

Submission details Not currently accepting new MSS submissions.

History Compass LLC

25 Leslie Road, Auburndale, MA 02466
tel 617-332-2202 *fax* 617-332-2210
email info@historycompass.com
website www.ushistorydocs.com

The history of the USA presented through the study of primary source documents. Recent successes include *Get a Clue!* (grades 2–8) and *Adventures in History* series (grades 4–8). Other series include *Perspectives on History* (grades 5–12+) and *Researching American History* (8–15 year-olds and ESL students). Also historical fiction for younger readers. Founded 1990.

Holiday House

425 Madison Avenue, New York, NY 10017
tel 212-421-6134
website www.holidayhouse.com
Vice President/Editor-in-Chief Mary Cash

General. Publishes 35 picture books, 3 young reader, 15 middle reader and 8 young adult titles each year. Recent successes include *Jazz*, illustrated by Christopher Myers.

Submission details Approx. 20% of books are by first-time authors. Send query letter with sase before submitting MSS. Responds in 3 months. Will review MS/illustration packages from artists: send MS with dummy and colour photocopies.

Henry Holt and Company LLC*

175 Fifth Avenue, New York, NY 10010
tel 646-307-5095 *fax* 646-307-5285
website www.henryholt.com
President/Publisher Dan Farley

Books for young readers. Publishes 20–40 picture books, 4–6 chapter books, 10–15 middle-grade titles and 8–10 young adult titles each year. Recent successes include *Baby Bear, Baby Bear, What Do You See* by Bill Martin Jr and Eric Carle. For adults: history, biography, nature, science, self-help, novels, mysteries, computer books. Founded 1866.

Submission details Approx. 15% of books are by first-time authors. For fiction and non-fiction, submit complete MS with sase to Laura Godwin, Editor-in-Chief/Associate Publisher of Books for Young Readers. Responds in 4 months. Will not consider simultaneous or multiple submissions. For illustrations, send tearsheets and/or slides to Patrick Collins, Creative Director. Responds in one month.

Houghton Mifflin Company*

222 Berkeley Street, Boston, MA 02116
tel 617-351-5000
website www.houghtonmifflinbooks.com

Fiction and non-fiction – cookbooks, history, political science, biography, nature (Peterson Guides), and gardening guides; reference, both adult and juvenile. No unsolicited MSS. Imprints: Mariner (original and reprint paperbacks); Houghton Mifflin Children's Books; American Heritage® Dictionaries. Founded 1832.

Houghton Mifflin Children's Books (imprint)

222 Berkeley Street, Boston, MA 02116-3764
tel 617-351-5000 *fax* 617-351-1111
email childrens_books@hmco.com
website www.houghtonmifflinbooks.com
Associate Editor Erica Zappy, *Managing Editor* Ann-Marie Pucillo, *Creative Director* Sheila Smallwood

Fiction and non-fiction for all ages. Recent successes include *Actual Size* written and illustrated by Steve Jenkins and *Just Grace* by Charise Mericle Harper. Imprints include Clarion Books and Graphia.

Submission details For fiction, submit complete MS. For non-fiction, submit outline/synopsis and sample chapters. Responds within 4 months only if interested. For illustrations, query with samples (colour photocopies and tearsheets). Responds in 4 months.

Clarion Books (imprint)

215 Park Avenue South, New York, NY 10003
tel 212-420-5800 *fax* 212-420-5850
website www.houghtonmifflinbooks.com/trade
Vice-President & Associate Publisher, Clarion Books Dinah Stevenson, *Director, Children's Rights* Rebecca Mancini, *Editor* Jennifer Green, *Art Director* Joann Hill

Board books, picture books, biographies, non-fiction, fiction, poetry and fairy tales for ages 5–15. Recent successes include *Flotsam* by David Wiesner. Founded 1965.

Submission details For fiction and picture books, send complete MSS. For non-fiction, send query with up to 3 sample chapters.

Graphia (imprint)

222 Berkeley Street, Boston, MA 02116-3764
tel 617-351-5000 *fax* 617-351-1111
website www.graphiabooks.com

Fiction and non-fiction for young adults, including poetry and graphic novels. Recent successes include *I Can't Tell You* by Hillary Frank and *Kid B* by Linden Dalecki.

Hunter House Publishers

PO Box 2914, Alameda, CA 94501–0914
tel 510-865-5282 *fax* 510-865-4295
email acquisitions@hunterhouse.com
website www.hunterhouse.com

Non-fiction books on physical, mental, and emotional health, including sexuality and relationships for adults and teens and life skills and activity books for teachers. Recent successes include *The Worried Child* and *101 Drama Games for Children*. Founded 1978.

Hyperion Books for Children

114 Fifth Avenue, New York, NY 10010–5690
tel 212-633-4400 *fax* 212-633-4833
website www.hyperionbooksforchildren.com

Board and novelty books, picture books, young readers, middle grade, young adult, non-fiction (all subjects at all levels). Recent successes include *Don't Let the Pigeon Drive the Bus*, written and ilustrated by Mo Willems, *Dumpy The Dump Truck* series by Julie Andrews Edwards and Emma Walton Hamilton (ages 3–7) and *Artemis Fowl* by Eoin Colfer (young adult novel, *New York Times* bestseller). Imprints include Michael di Capua Books, Jump at the Sun, Volo. Founded 1991.

Submission details Approx. 10% of books are by first-time authors. Only interested in submissions via literary agents. For illustrations, send résumé, business card, promotional literature or tearsheets to be kept on file to Anne Diebel, Art Director.

Ideals Publications LLC

535 Metroplex Drive, Suite 250, Nashville, TN 37211
website www.idealsbooks.com

Picture books and board books for young children. Imprints: Candy Cane Press, GP Kids, Guideposts Books, Ideals Children's Books, Ideals Press, Ideals Interactive, Riverton Press, Williamson Books. Division of Guideposts.

Submission details Send sase for submission guidelines.

Illumination Arts Publishing

PO Box 1865, Bellevue, WA 98009
tel 425-644-7185
email liteinfo@illumin.com
website www.illumin.com
Editorial Director Ruth Thompson

Picture books. 'Books to inspire the mind, touch the heart and uplift the spirit.' Successes include *All I See is Part of Me*. Founded 1987.

Submission details Length: 300–1500 words.

Impact Publishers Inc.*

PO Box 6016, Atascadero, CA 93423–6016
tel 805-466-5917 *fax* 805-466-5919
email info@impactpublishers.com
website www.impactpublishers.com

Psychology and self-improvement books and audio tapes for adults, children, families, organisations, and communities. Recent successes include *The Divorce Helpbook for Kids*, *The Divorce Helpbook for Teens* and *Jigsaw Puzzle Family* by Cynthia MacGregor and *Teen Esteem: A Self-Direction Manual for Young Adults* by Pat Palmer and Melissa Alberti Froehner. Founded 1970.

Submission details Only publishes books which serve human development. Written by highly respected psychologists and other human service professionals. See website for guidelines.

Incentive Publications Inc.

2400 Crestmoor Road, Suite 211, Nashville, TN 37215
tel 615-385-2934
website www.incentivepublications.com
President Blake Parker

Supplemental resources for educators and students. Founded 1969.

Submission details Send a letter of introduction, table of contents, a sample chapter, and sase for return of.

innovativeKids

18 Ann Street, Norwalk, CT 06854
tel 203-838-6400 *fax* 203-855-5582
email info@innovativekids.com
website www.innovativekids.com

Beginning reader books, activity books, infant/toddler books, preschool books and games, and science learning tools in a wide range of themes and subjects. Recent successes include *A Kid's Guide to Giving*, *Phonics Comics* series, *Groovy Tube* series and *iBaby* series. Founded 1999.

Just Us Books, Inc.

356 Glenwood Avenue East Orange, NJ 07017
tel 973-672-7701
email cheryl_hudson@justusbooks.com
website www.justusbooks.com
Publisher Cheryl Willis Hudson

'Publishers of Black-interest books for young people,' including preschool materials, picture books, biographies, chapter books, young adult fiction. Focuses on Black history, Black culture and Black experiences.

Submission details Currently accepting queries for young adult titles, targeted to 13–16 year-old readers. Work should contain realistic, contemporary characters, compelling plot lines that introduce conflict and resolution, and cultural authenticity. Also considers MSS for picture books and middle reader chapter books. Send a query letter, 1–2 page synopsis, a brief author biog that includes any previously published work, plus a sase. Founded 1988.

Kaeden Books

PO Box 16190, Rocky River, OH 44116
tel 440-617-1400 *fax* 440-617-1403
email info@kaeden.com
website www.kaeden.com

Educational publisher specialising in early literacy books and beginning chapter books.

Submission details Seeking beginning chapter books and unique non-fiction MSS (25–2000 words). Vocabulary and sentence structure must be appropriate for young readers. No sentence fragments. See website for complete guidelines.

Accepts samples of all styles of illustration but is primarily looking for samples that match the often humorous style appropriate for juvenile literature. Send samples, no larger than 8.5 x 11ins to keep on file. Founded 1986.

Kar-Ben Publishing – see Lerner Publishing Group

KidHave Press – see Gale Cengage Learning

Kingfisher – see Houghton Mifflin Company

Klutz – see Scholastic Inc.

Alfred A. Knopf Books for Young Readers – see Random House Inc.

Wendy Lamb Books – see Random House Inc.

Laurel-Leaf Books – see Random House Inc.

Lee & Low Books, Inc.
95 Madison Avenue, Suite 606, New York, NY 10016
tel 212-779-4400 *fax* 212-683-1894
email general@leeandlow.com
website www.leeandlow.com
Editor-in-Chief Louise May

Children's book publisher specialising multicultural literature that is relevant to young readers. The company's goal is 'to meet the need for stories that children of colour can identify with and that all children can enjoy and which promote a greater understanding of one another'.

Focuses on fiction and non-fiction for children aged 5–12 which feature children/people of colour. Of special interest are realistic fiction, historical fiction, and non-fiction with a distinct voice or unique approach. Does not consider folktales or animal stories.

Submission details MSS should be no longer 1500 words for fiction and 3000 words for non-fiction. Send MSS with a covering letter that includes a brief biography of the author, including publishing history, and stating if the MS is a simultaneous or an exclusive submission. No submissions via email. Writer will be contacted within six months if interested. Makes a special effort to work with artists of colour. Founded 1991.

Lerner Publishing Group
241 First Avenue North, Minneapolis, MN 55401–1607
tel 612-332-3344 *fax* 612-332-7615
email info@lernerbooks.com
website www.lernerbooks.com
Publisher Adam Lerner, *Non-fiction Submissions Editor* Jennifer Zimian, *Fiction Submissions Editor* Zelda Wagner

Independent publisher of high-quality children's books for K–12 schools and libraries: picture books,

fiction for 5–8 and 9–12 year-olds, teenage fiction, series fiction and non-fiction. Subjects include biography, social studies, science, sports and curriculum. Publishes approx. 200 titles each year and has about 1500 in print. Founded 1959.
Submission details no unsolicited submissions for any imprint.

Carolrhoda Books (imprint)
website www.carolrhodabooks.com
Picture books aimed at 5–8 year-olds; longer fiction for age 7+, including chapter books and middle-grade and young adult novels; biographies. Interested in unique, honest stories that stay away from moralising and religious themes; also science fiction/fantasy for young readers. Popular characters include Little Wolf and Harriet. Authors and illustrators include Nancy Carlson and Jan Wahl. Recent successes include *Almost to Freedom* by Vaunda Micheaux Nelson, illustrated by Colin Bootman. Founded 1969.
Submission details no unsolicited submissions for any imprint.

Kar-Ben Publishing (imprint)
website www.karben.com
Books on Jewish themes for children and families. Subjects include the High Holidays, Passover, Sukkot and Simchat Torah, Hanukkah, Purim, Selichot, Tu B'Shevat, crafts, cooking, folk tales, and contemporary stories, Jewish calendars, music, and activity books. Founded 1974.
Submission details no unsolicited submissions for any imprint.

LernerClassroom (imprint)
website www.lernerclassroom.com
Non-fiction books and teaching guides for grades K-8 in social studies, science, reading/literacy and mathematics. Books are paired with teaching guides that are correlated to national and state standards.

Millbrook Press (imprint)
Maths, science, American history, social studies and biography for a younger age bracket.

Twenty-First Century Books (imprint)
Maths, science, American history, social studies and biography for Secondary school age bracket.

Arthur A. Levine Books – see Scholastic Inc.

Little, Brown & Company
237 Park Avenue, New York, NY 10020
tel 212-364-2200 *fax* 212-364-0924
email publicity@littlebrown.com
website www.hachettebookgroupusa.com
Publisher Michael Pietsch

General literature, fiction, non-fiction, biography, history, trade paperbacks, children's.

Little, Brown Books for Young Readers
website www.lb-kids.com, www.lb-teens.com
Publisher Megan Tingley, *Creative Director* Gail Doobinin

Picture books, board books, chapter books, novelty books and general non-fiction and novels for middle and young adult readers.

Recent successes include *The Gulps* by Rosemary Wells, illustrated by Marc Brown, *The Gift of Nothing* by Patrick McDonnell; *Chowder* by Peter Brown, *How to Train Your Dragon* by Cressida Cowell, *Atherton* by Patrick Carman, *Nothing But the Truth (and a Few White Lies)* by Justina Chen Headley, *Story of a Girl* by Sara Zarr, *Eclipse* by Stephenie Meyer, *America Dreaming* by Laban Carrick Hill, and *Exploratopia* by The Exploratorium.

Submission details Only interested in solicited agented material. Does not accept unsolicited MSS or unagented material. For illustrations, query Art Director with b&w and colour samples; provide résumé, promotional sheet or tearsheets to be kept on file. Does not respond to art samples. Do not send originals; copies only.

Llewellyn Worldwide
2143 Wooddale Drive, Woodbury, MN 55125
tel (651) 291-1970 *fax* (651) 291-1908
email billk@llewellyn.com
website www.llewellyn.com
Publisher Bill Krause

New Age: alternative health and healing, astrology, earth-based religions, shamanism, Gnostic Christianity and Kabbalah; mystery novels and young adult novels. Founded 1901.

Flux (imprint)
email submissions@fluxnow.com
website www.fluxnow.com
Young adult: fiction for ages 12+ in all genres. Seeks to publish authors who see young adult as a point of view rather than a reading level. Looks for edgy, challenging books that try to capture a slice of teenage experience. Particularly interested in books that tell the stories of young adults in unexpected or surprising situations around the globe. Recent successes include *Blue is for Nightmares* and sequels by Laurie Faria Stolarz and *How It's Done* by Christine Kole MacLean.

Submission details Seeking high-quality novels of all genres for ages 12+. No middle-grade or picture books. See website for submission guidlines.

Lucent Books – see Gale Cengage Learning

Margaret K. McElderry Books – see Simon & Schuster Children's Publishing Division

McGraw-Hill Education*
2 Penn Plaza, 11th Floor, New York, NY 10121
tel 212-904-2000
website www.mhprofessional.com,
www.mgeducation.com
Publisher Chuck Wall

Shaum's Outlines, test preparation and study guides. Division of the McGraw-Hill Companies.

Marshall Cavendish Benchmark
Marshall Cavendish Corporation,
99 White Plains Road, Tarrytown, NY 10591
tel 914-332-8888 *fax* 914-332-1082
email customerservice@marshallcavendish.com
website www.marshallcavendish.us

Non-fiction books for young, middle and young adult readers. Subjects include activities, American studies, the arts, biographies, health, human behaviour, mathematics, science, social studies, world cultures. Imprint of Marshall Cavendish Corporation.

Submission details Non-fiction subjects should be curriculum related and are published in series form. Length: 4000–20,000 words. Either send complete MS or synopsis with one or more sample chapters.

Marshall Cavendish Children's Books
Marshall Cavendish Corporation,
99 White Plains Road, Tarrytown, NY 10591
tel 914-332-8888 *fax* 914-332-1082
email customerservice@marshallcavendish.com
website www.marshallcavendish.us/kids

Picture books, non-fiction and fiction for young readers. Imprint of Marshall Cavendish Corporation.

Milet Publishing, LLC
333 North Michigan Avenue, Suite 530, Chicago, IL 60601
email info@milet.com
website www.milet.com

Picture books in English; bilingual picture books; adventurous and international young fiction; language learning books.

Submission details Will consider unsolicited submissions by post only. No email submissions. See website for guidelines and profile of list.

Milkweed Editions
1011 Washington Avenue South, Suite 300, Minneapolis, MN 55415
tel 612-332-3192 *fax* 612-215-2550
email editor@milkweed.org
website www.milkweed.org
Publisher Daniel Slager

Children's novels (ages 8–13). Recent successes include *Perfect* (contemporary) and *Trudy* (contemporary). For adults: literary fiction, non-fiction books about the natural world, poetry. Founded 1979.

Submission details Full length novels of 90–200pp. No picture books or poetry collections for young readers. Submit complete MS. Responds in 6 months. Will consider simultaneous submissions.

Millbrook Press – see Lerner Publishing Group

MINX – see DC Comics

Mitchell Lane Publishers, Inc.
PO Box 196, Hockessin, DE 19707
tel 302-234-9426

email customerservice@mitchelllane.com
website www.mitchelllane.com
President Barbara Mitchell

Non-fiction for young readers, middle readers and young adults. Recent successes include *Art Profiles for Kids* series (middle-grade readers) and *Crisis in the Environment*.

Mondo Publishing*
980 Avenue of the Americas, New York, NY 10018
tel 212-268-3560 *fax* 212-268-3561
email info@mondopub.com
website www.mondopub.com

Classroom materials and professional development for K–5 educators.

Morgan Reynolds Publishing
620 South Elm Street, Suite 223, Greensboro, NC 27406
tel 336-275-1311 *fax* 336-275-1152
email editorial@morganreynolds.com
website www.morganreynolds.com

Biographies for juveniles and young adults. Recent successes include *Elizabeth I of England in the European Queens* series and *Ulysses S. Grant: Defender of the Union in the Civil War Generals* series. Founded 1993.
   Submission details MSS of 25,000–30,000 words, with 8–10 chapters of 2500–3000 words each. See website for submission guidelines.

Thomas Nelson Publisher
PO Box 141000, Nashville, TN 37214
tel 800-251-4000
email publicity@thomasnelson.com
website www.thomasnelson.com
President and CEO Michael Hyatt

Bibles, religious, non-fiction and fiction general trade books for adults and children. Founded 1798.

NorthWord Books for Young Readers
11571 K–Tel Drive, Minnetonka, MN 55343
tel 952-933-7537 *fax* 952-933-3630
email mbohr@nbnbooks.com
website www.nbnbooks.com

Picture books and non-fiction nature and wildlife books in interactive and fun-to-read formats. Imprint of Cooper Square Publishing. Founded 1989.

The Oliver Press, Inc.
Charlotte Square, 5707 West 36th Street, Minneapolis, MN 55416–2510
tel 952-926-8981 *fax* 952-926-8965
email queries@oliverpress.com
website www.oliverpress.com

Non-fiction for young adults: history, biography, science. Curriculum-based series include *Profiles, Great Decisions, Innovators, Shaping America, Business Builders, In the Cabinet* and *Looking at Europe*. Clara House (division): books for younger readers on how things work.
   Submission details Interested in receiving proposals that fit into an established series. Submit proposal, a resume of previously published works and any applicable education or experience together with a writing sample similar to the reading level, style and subject to the book that is being proposed. No unsolicited MSS.

Orchard Books – see Scholastic Inc.

The Overlook Press*
141 Wooster Street, New York, New York 10012
tel 212-673-2210 *fax* 212-673-2296
website www.overlookpress.com
President & Publisher Peter Mayer

Non-fiction, fiction, children's books (*Freddy the Pig* series). Imprints: Ardis Publishing, Duckworth, Rookery Press. Founded 1971.

Richard C. Owen Publishers, Inc.
PO Box 585, Katonah, NY 10536
tel 800-262-0787 *fax* 914-232-3977
website www.rcowen.com
Children's Books Editor Janice Boland

Books for grades K–8. Subjects include science, technology, history and geography.

All work must be submitted as hard copy. Books for Young Learners: Seeks high-interest stories with charm and appeal that 5–7 year-olds can read by themselves. Interested in original, realistic, contemporary stories, as well as folktales, legends, and myths of all cultures. Non-fiction content must be supported with accurate facts. Length: 45–1000 words.

Oxford University Press Inc.*
198 Madison Avenue, New York, NY 10016
tel 212-726-6000 *fax* 212-726-6455
website www.oup.com/us
President Tim Barton

Fiction and non-fiction for children of all ages, including young adult. Subjects include art, biography and memoirs, history, literature, music, myths and fairy tales, poetry, reference, science, reference. Adults: all subjects, from agriculture to sociology.

Pacific View Press
PO Box 2897, Berkeley, CA 94702
tel 415-285-8538 *fax* 510-843-5835
email pvp2@mindspring.com
website www.pacificviewpress.com

Multicultural children's books, Traditional Chinese Medicine, Asia and Asian–American affairs.

Dragon Books (imprint)
Multicultural non-fiction and literature for children focusing on the culture and history of China, Japan,

the Philippines, Mexico, and other countries on the Pacific Rim. Books are intended to encourage pride in and respect for the shared history that makes a people unique, as well as an awareness of universal human experiences. Recent successes include *Cloud Weavers: Ancient Chinese Legends* by Rena Krasno and Yeng-Fong Chiang and *Exploring Chinatown: A Children's Guide to Chinese Culture* by Carol Stepanchuk, illustrated by Leland Wong. Founded 1992.

Parenting Press, Inc.

PO Box 75267, Seattle, WA 98175–0267
tel 206-364-2900 *fax* 206-364-0702
email office@parentingpress.com
website www.parentingpress.com
Acquisitions Carolyn Threadgill

How-to information for child guidance, problem solving, emotional competence, and children's personal safety issues. Recent successful picture books include *The Way I Feel* by Janan Cain (ages 18 months–8), *When You're Mad* and *You Know It* in the *Feelings for Little Children* series by Elizabeth Crary and Shari Steelsmith, illustrated by Mits Katayama (ages 1–3) and *What About Me?: 12 Ways to Get Your Parents' Attention Without Hitting Your Sister* by Eileen Kennedy-Moore, illustrated by Mits Katayama (ages 4–8).

Parragon Publishing

440 Park Avenue South, 13th Floor, New York, NY 10006
tel 212-629-9773 *fax* 212-629-9756
email info_northamerica@parragon.com
website www.parragon.com

Children's non-fiction books of all kinds, from activity to reference. Adult titles include cookbooks, lifestyle, gardening, history.

Peachtree Publishers

1700 Chattahoochee Avenue, Atlanta, GA 30318–2112
tel 404-876-8761 *fax* 404-875-2578
email hello@peachtree-online.com
website www.peachtree-online.com
President & Publisher Margaret Quinlin, *Submissions Editor* Helen Harriss

Specialises in children's books, from picture books to young adult fiction and non-fiction. Publishes 30–35 titles each year. Recent successes include *Dad, Jackie and Me* by Myron Uhlberg and Colin Bootman. No adult fiction. Founded 1977.

Submission details For children's picture books, send complete MSS; for all others, send query letter with 3 sample chapters and table of contents to Helen Harriss with sase for response and/or return of material. For illustrations, query with samples, résumé, slides, colour photocopies to keep on file. Samples returned with sase.

Pearson Education*

One Lake Street, Upper Saddle River, NJ 07458
tel 201-236-7000 *fax* 201-236-6549
email communications@pearsoned.com
website www.phschool.com, www.pearsoned.com

Educational secondary publisher of scientifically researched and standards-based instruction materials for today's Grade 6–12 classrooms with a mission is to create exceptional educational tools that ensure student and teacher success in language arts, mathematics, modern and classical languages, science, social studies, career and technology, and advanced placement, electives, and honors. Part of the Curriculum Division of Pearson Education, Inc.

Pearson Scott Foresman

One Lake Street, Upper Saddle River, NJ 07458
tel 201-236-7000 *fax* 201-236-6549
website www.pearsonschool.com

Elementary educational publisher. Teacher and student materials: reading, science, mathematics, language arts, social studies, music, technology, religion. Its educational resources and services include textbook-based instructional programs, curriculum websites, digital media, assessment materials and professional development. Part of the Curriculum Division of Pearson Education Inc. Founded 1896.

Pelican Publishing Company*

1000 Burmaster Street, Gretna, LA 70053
tel 504-368-1175 *fax* 504-368-1195
email editorial@pelicanpub.com
website www.pelicanpub.com, www.epelican.com
Publisher/President Milburn Calhoun

Children's books. Also travel guides, art and architecture books, biographies, holiday books, local and international cookbooks, motivational and inspirational works, social commentary, history.

Submission details Send a query letter and sase. No queries or submissions by email. No unsolicited MSS. Most young children's books are 32 illustrated pages when published; their MSS cover about 4pp when typed continuously. Proposed books for middle readers (ages 8+) should be at least 90pp. Brief books for readers under 9 may be submitted in their entirety. Founded 1926.

Penguin Group (USA), Inc.*

375 Hudson Street, New York, NY 10014
tel 212-366-2000 *fax* 212-366-2666
email online@penguingroup.com
website www.us.penguingroup.com
President Susan Petersen Kennedy, *Ceo* David Shanks

Consumer books in both hardcover and paperback for adults and children; also maps, calendars, audiobooks and mass merchandise products.

Adult imprints: Ace Books, Alpha Books, Avery, Berkley Books, Daw, Dutton, Gotham Books,

HPBooks, Hudson Street Press, Jove, New America Library, Penguin, Penguin Classics, The Penguin Press, Perigee, Plume, Portfolio, G.P. Putnam's Sons, Riverhead, Sentinel, Signet Classics, Jeremy P. Tarcher, Viking.

Penguin Books for Young Readers (division)

Children's picture books, board and novelty books, young adult novels, mass merchandise products. Imprints: Dial Books for Young Readers, Dutton Children's Books, Firebird, Grosset & Dunlap, Philomel, Price Stern Sloan, Puffin Books, G.P. Putnam's Sons, Speak, Viking Children's Books, Frederick Warne. Founded 1997.

Dial Books for Young Readers (imprint)

Children's fiction and non-fiction, picture books, board books, interactive books, novels. Publishes 35 picture books, 3 young reader titles, 6 middle reader titles and 9 young adult titles each year. Recent successes include *A Year Down Yonder* by Richard Peck (fiction, age 10+), *The Sea Chest* by Toni Buzzeo, illustrated by Mary Grand (fiction picture book, all ages), *A Strong Right Arm* by Michelle Y. Green (non-fiction, age 10+) and *Dirt on Their Skirts* by Doreen Rappaport and Lyndall Callan (non-fiction picture book, ages 4–8).

Submission details For picture books, send MSS. For longer works, query with no more than 10pp of MSS. Responds in 4 months. Send sase. No email queries. For illustrations, send samples with sase to Design Dept.

Dutton Children's Books (imprint)

Picture books, young adult novels, non-fiction photographic books. Publishes 50% fiction, mostly young adult and middle-grade. Recent successes include *Leonard: Beautiful Dreamer* by Robert Byrd (non-fiction), *The Boy Who Spoke Dog* by Clay Morgan (middle-grade fiction), *Skippyjon Jones* by Judy Schachner (picture book) and *PREP* by Jake Coburn (young adult fiction). Founded 1852.

Submission details Approx. 10% of books are by first-time authors. No unsolicited MSS. Send query letter only; responds in 3 months. For illustrations, query with samples. Samples returned with sase.

Firebird (imprint)

Teenage science fiction and fantasy.

Grosset & Dunlap (imprint)

Children's picture books, activity books, fiction and non-fiction. Publishes 175 books each year. Recent successes include *Zenda* (series) and *Strawberry Shortcake* (license). Imprints: Grosset & Dunlap, Platt & Munk, Somerville House USA, Planet Dexter. Founded 1898.

Submission details Only interested in material via literary agent.

Philomel Books (imprint)

Fiction and non-fiction for all ages. Publishes 18 picture books, 2 middle-grade books, 2 young readers and 4 young adult books each year. Founded 1980.

Submission details Approx. 5% of books are by first-time authors. No unsolicited MSS. Fiction length: picture books – 1000 words; young readers – 1500 words; middle readers – 14,000 words; young adult – 20,000 words. Non-fiction length: picture books – 2000 words; young readers – 3000 words; middle readers – 10,000 words. For illustrations, query with samples: send résumé and tearsheets. Responds in one month. Samples returned with sase.

Price Stern Sloan (imprint)

Children's novelty/lift-flap books, activity books, picture books, middle-grade fiction, middle-grade and young adult non-fiction, graphic novels, books plus. Recent successes include *Inside the Little Old Woman's Shoe* by Chuck Reasoner, *Fear Factor Mad Libs* and *Elf*. Founded 1963.

Submission details No unsolicited MSS. Send query; responds in 3 weeks.

Puffin Books (imprint)

Picture books, fiction for 5–8 and 9–12 year-olds, teenage fiction, series fiction and film/TV tie-ins. Publishes approx. 175–200 titles each year. Recent successes include *Rules of the Road* by Joan Bauer, *A Long Way from Chicago* by Richard Peck and *26 Fairmount Avenue* by Tomie dePaola. Imprints: Firebird, Sleuth, Speak. Founded 1941.

Submission details Approx. 1% of books are by first-time authors. Will consider unsolicited MSS for novels only. Send with sase to Submissions Editor. Seeking to publish mysteries.

G.P. Putnam's Sons (imprint)

Children's hardcover and paperback books. Recent successes include *Fat Kid Rules the World* by K.L. Going (ages 12+), *Locomotion* by Jacqueline Woodson and *Atlantic* by G. Brian Karas (ages 4–8, non-fiction). Founded 1838.

Submission details For fiction, query with outline/synopsis and 1–3 sample chapters. Fiction length: picture books – 200–1000 words; middle readers – 10,000–30,000 words; young adult – 40,000–50,000 words. For non-fiction, query with outline/synopsis, 1–2 sample chapters and table of contents. Non-fiction length: picture books – 200–1500 words. Responds to queries in 3 weeks and to MS in 2 months. Write for illustrator guidelines.

Viking Children's Books (imprint)

Fiction, non-fiction and picture books for preschool–young adult. Publishes 70 books each year. Recent successes include *Strange Mr Satie* by M.T. Anderson (ages 5–8, picture book), *Restless* by Richard Wallace (ages 12) fiction, and *Open Your Eyes: Extraordinary Experiences in Far Away Places* (ages 12+, non-fiction). Founded 1925.

Submission details Approx. 25% of books are by first-time authors; receives 7500 queries a year. No unsolicited MSS. Responds to artists' queries/submissions only if interested. Samples returned with sase.

Frederick Warne (imprint)
Original publisher of Beatrix Potter's *Tales of Peter Rabbit*. Founded 1865.

Philomel Books – see Penguin Group (USA), Inc.

Mathew Price Ltd
5013 Golden Circle, Denton, TX 76208
tel 940-565-9594 *fax* 940-565-9310
email mathewp@mathewprice.com
website www.mathewprice.com
Chairman Mathew Price

Illustrated fiction and non-fiction children's books for all ages for the UK and international market. Specialist in flap, pop-up, paper-engineered titles as well as conventional books. Unsolicited MSS accepted only by email. Founded 1983.

Price Stern Sloan – see Penguin Group (USA), Inc.

Puffin Books – see Penguin Group (USA), Inc.

Simon Pulse Paperback Books – see Simon & Schuster Children's Publishing Division

G.P. Putnam's Sons – see Penguin Group (USA), Inc.

Random House Inc.*
1745 Broadway, 10th Floor, New York, NY 10019
tel 212-782-9000 *fax* 212-302-7985
website www.randomhouse.com
Chairman/Ceo Peter Olson

General fiction and non-fiction, children's books. Subsidiary of Bertelsmann AG.

Random House Children's Books (division)
website www.randomhouse.com/kids, www.randomhouse.com/teens

Comprises 2 editorial divisions: Knopf Delacorte Dell Young Readers Group, and Random House/Golden Books Young Readers Group.

Knopf Delacorte Dell Young Readers Group
Editorial division of Random House Children's Books, incorporating Bantam Books, Beginner Books, Robin Corey, Crown Books, Delacorte Press Books for Young Readers, Doubleday Books for Young Readers, Dragonfly Books, David Fickling Books, First Time Books, Golden Books, Alfred A. Knopf Books for Young Readers, Landmark Books, Wendy Lamb Books, Laurel-Leaf Books, Picturebacks, Schwartz & Wade Books, Stepping Stone Books, Yearling Books.

Bantam Books (imprint)
website www.randomhouse.com/kids
Commercial paperbacks. Focus on TV and film.

Submission details Not seeking new MSS at the moment.

Crown Books (imprint)
Juvenile fiction and non-fiction for ages 0–18.
Submission details Send query letter with sase to Acquisitions Editor.

Delacorte Press Books for Young Readers (imprint)
Literary and commercial novels for middle-grade and young adult readers, and educational/general interest non-fiction. Authors include David Almond, Ann Brashares, Libba Bray, Caroline Cooney, Robert Cormier, Lurlene McDaniel, Phyllis Reynolds Naylor, Joan Lowery Nixon, Louis Sachar, Zilpha Keatley Snyder and R.L. Stine.
Submission details Approx. 90% of books are published via literary agents.

Doubleday Books for Young Readers (imprint)
Picture books for young readers and gift books for all ages.
Submission details Approx. 90% of books are published via literary agents.

Dragonfly Books (imprint)
Paperback picture books, ranging from concept picture books to read-together stories to books for newly independent readers.

David Fickling Books (imprint)
The first bicontinental children's book publisher. Publishes 12 books a year, all of which are chosen and edited in the UK.

Alfred A. Knopf Books for Young Readers (imprint)
Fiction and non-fiction for ages 0–18, from board books to novels to non-fiction. Authors and illustrators include Marc Brown, Robert Cormier, Leo and Diane Dillon, Carl Hiaasen, Leo Lionni, Christopher Paolini, Philip Pullman, Eric Rohmann, Judy Sierra and Jerry Spinelli.
Submission details Send query letter with sase to Acquisitions Editor.

Knopf Trade (imprint)
Paperback editions of middle-grade and young adult novels originally published in hardback by Alfred A. Knopf Books for Young Readers.

Wendy Lamb Books (imprint)
Acquisitions Wendy Lamb
Middle-grade and young adult fiction. Publishes 12 middle readers and young adult books each year. Authors include Christopher Paul Curtis, Peter Dickinson, Patricia Reilly Giff, Gary Paulsen, Meg Rosoff and Graham Salisbury. Founded 2002.
Submission details Approx. 15% of books are by first-time authors. Receives 300–400 submissions a year. Send query letter with sase and no more than 5pp (picture books) or 10pp (novels). Will review MS/illustrations packages from artists: query with sase for reply.

Laurel-Leaf Books (imprint)
Literature for teenagers, including reprints of contemporary and classic fiction, mystery, fantasy, romance, suspense, and non-fiction for ages 12+. Authors include Judy Blume, Caroline B. Cooney, Robert Cormier, Lois Duncan, S.E. Hinton, Lois Lowry, Scott O'Dell, Gary Paulsen, Philip Pullman and Jerry Spinelli. Laurel-Leaf also features the Readers Circle publishing programme.

Schwartz & Wade Books (imprint)
Directors Anne Schwartz, Lee Wade
Picture books. Authors include Tad Hills, Ronnie Shotter and Valorie Fisher. Founded 2005.

Yearling Books (imprint)
Affordable paperback books for 8–12 year-olds: contemporary and historical fiction, fantasy, mystery and adventure. Authors include Judy Blume, Christopher Paul Curtis, Patricia Reilly Giff, Norton Juster, Madeleine L'Engle, Lois Lowry, Gary Paulsen, Philip Pullman and Louis Sachar.

Random House/Golden Books Young Readers Group*
Association of American Publishers Inc.1745 Broadway, New York, NY 10019
tel 212-782-9000
website www.randomhouse.com/kids, www.randomhouse.com/golden
Editor-in-Chief of Random House Books for Young Readers Mallory Loehr
Editorial division of Random House Children's Books. Classic titles such as *Tootle* and *Scruffy the Tugboat*. Established 1942.

Random House Books for Young Readers (imprint)
Variety and 'value' books for ages 6 months to young adult. Books range from *The Story of Babar* (1933) and *Dr Seuss*, to *Magic Tree House* and the *Junie B. Jones* books, and the *Step Into Reading* series.
Submission details Approx. 2% of books are by first-time authors. No unsolicited MSS: reserves the right to not return unsolicited material. All acquisitions are made via literary agents.

Golden Books for Young Readers (imprint)
Children's classic titles, including *Tootle*, *The Saggy Baggy Elephant*, *Scuffy the Tugboat*, and *The Poky Little Puppy*.
Submission details Approx. 2% of books are by first-time authors. No unsolicited MSS: reserves the right to not return unsolicited material. All acquisitions are made via literary agents.

Disney Books for Young Readers (imprint)
Colouring and activity books, storybooks, novelty books and early readers based on Disney properties. Films include *Toy Story 2*, *The Little Mermaid*, *The Lion King*, *Atlantis*, *Monsters, Inc.*, and *Finding Nemo*. Founded 2001.

Random House Value Publishing (division)
Children's classics, Crescent, Derrydale, Gramercy, Testament, Wings.

Rayo – see HarperCollins Publishers

Rising Moon – Luna Rising
PO Box 1389, Flagstaff, AZ 86002–1389
tel 928-774-5251 *fax* 928-774-0592
email editorial@northlandbooks.com
website www.northlandbooks.com, www.nbnbooks.com

Illustrated, entertaining, and thought-provoking picture books for children, including Spanish–English bilingual titles.
Submission details Seeking fresh picture book MSS about contemporary everyday life of children: edgy, innovative, spirited (e.g. *Do Princesses Wear Hiking Boots?* and *It's a Bad Day*). Also seeking exceptional Latino-themed picture books about multicultural living, contemporary issues, Latino role models (e.g. *My Name is Celia* and *Lupe Vargas and Her Super Best Friend*). Additionally seeking picture books that relate to western and southwestern USA, original stories with a Southwest flavour, fractured fairytales (e.g. *The Treasure of Ghostwood Gully* and *The Three Little Javelinas*). Imprint of Cooper Square Publishing. Founded 1998.

Roaring Brook Press
175 Fifth Avenue, New York, NY10010
tel 212-375-7149
website www.roaringbookspress.com
Publisher Simon Broughton, *Publishers* Neil Porter, Lauren Wohl

Picture books, fiction (including graphic novels) and non-fiction for young readers, from toddler to teen. Publishes about 40 titles a year. Authors include Jacqueline Wilson. Recent successes include *My Friend Rabbit* by Eric Rohmann (2003 Caldecott Medal winner), and *The Man Who Walked Between the Towers* by Mordicai Gerstein (2004 Caldecott Medal winner). Imprint: First Second Books. Division of Holtzbrink Publishers.
Submission details Does not accept unsolicited MSS or submissions.

Running Press Book Publishers
2300 Chestnut Street, Suite 200, Philadelphia, PA 19103
tel 215-567-5080 *fax* 215-568 2919
email perseus.promos@perseusbooks.com
website www.perseusbooksgroup.com/runningpress
Publisher Jon Anderson, *Directors* Bill Jones (design), Greg Jones (editorial), Joanne Cassetti (production), Craig Herman (marketing)

General non-fiction, science, history, children's fiction and non-fiction, food and wine, pop culture, lifestyle, photo-essay, illustrated gift books. Imprints: Running Press, Running Press Miniature Editions, Running Press Kids, Courage Books. Member of the Perseus Books Group. Founded 1972.

Running Press Kids (imprint)
Picture books, activity books, young adult fiction. Recent successes: *Cathy's Key* by Sean Stewart and Jordan Weisman.

Scholastic Education*

557 Broadway, New York, NY 10012
tel 212-343-6100 fax 212-343-6189
website www.scholastic.com

Educational publisher of research-based core and supplementary instructional materials. A leading provider in reading improvement and professional development products, as well as learning services that address the needs of the developing reader – from grades pre-K to high school.

Publishes 32 curriculum-based classroom magazines used by teachers in grades pre-K–12 as supplementary educational materials to raise awareness about current events in an age-appropriate manner and to help children develop reading skills. Magazines include Scholastic News®, Junior Scholastic®, The New York Times Upfront®, Science World®, Scope® and others, covering subjects such as English, maths, science, social studies, current events, and foreign languages. The magazine's online companion, Scholastic News Online is the leading news source for students and teachers on the internet.

Scholastic Education has also developed technology-based reading assessment and management products to help administrators and educators quickly and accurately assess student reading levels, match students to the appropriate books, predict how well they will do on district and state standardised tests, and inform instruction to improve reading skills.

Its wholly owned operations in Australia, Canada, New Zealand and the UK have original trade and educational publishing programmes. Division of Scholastic Inc.

Scholastic Library Publishing (division)

90 Sherman Turnpike, Danbury, CT 06816
tel 203-797-3500
website www.scholastic.com
Editor-in-Chief Kate Nunn

Online and print publisher of reference products. Major reference sets include Encyclopedia Americana®, The New Book of Knowledge®, Nueva Enciclopedia Cumbre®, Lands and Peoples and The New Book of Popular Science.

Scholastic Inc.*

557 Broadway, New York, NY 10012
tel 212-343-6100 fax 212-343-6930
website www.scholastic.com
Editorial Director Elizabeth Szabla

Innovative textbooks, magazines, technology and teacher materials for use in both school and the home. Scholastic is a global children's publishing and media company with a corporate mission to instill the love of reading and learning for lifelong pleasure in all children. Founded 1920.

Scholastic Trade Books, Children's Book Publishing

557 Broadway, New York, NY 10012
tel 212 343 6100

website www.scholastic.com
Award-winning publisher of original children's books. Publishes over 500 new titles per year including the branding publishing properties Harry Potter® and Captain Underpants®, the series Clifford The Big Red Dog®, I Spy™, and Scholastic's The Magic School Bus®, as well as licensed properties such as Star Wars® and Scooby Doo™. Imprints: Blue Sky Press®, Michael di Capua Books, Cartwheel Books®, The Chicken House™, Graffix, Arthur A. Levine Books, Little Shepherd, Orchard Books®, Point, PUSH, Scholastic Paperbacks, Scholastic Press and Scholastic Reference™.

Blue Sky Press (imprint)

Hardcover fiction and non-fiction, including novels and picture books. Publishes 15–20 titles a year. Recent successes include To Every Thing There is a Season illustrated by Leo and Diane Dillon (all ages, picture book) and How Do Dinosaurs Say Good Night? by Jane Yolen, illustrated by Mark Teague.

Submission details Approx. 1% of which are by first-time authors. Not currently accepting unsolicited submissions due to a large backlog of books. For illustrations, query with samples or tearsheets. Responds only if interested; samples only returned with sase.

Cartwheel Books (imprint)

Fiction and non-fiction for very young readers. Non-fiction is mostly written on assignment or is within a series. Publishes 25–30 picture books, 30–35 easy readers and 15–20 novelty books each year.

Submission details Submissions via literary agents only: send complete MSS. Will respond in 6 months. All unsolicited material will be returned unread. Length: 100–3000 words (picture books, easy readers). For illustrations, send samples and tearsheets to the Art Director with sase.

Klutz

How-to books packaged with the tools of their trade (from juggling cubes to face paints to yo-yos). Includes an educational product line for pre K–Grade 4 children in maths, reading and general knowledge. Products are designed for doing, not just reading: 'We think people learn best through their hands, nose, feet, mouth and ears. Then their eyes. So we design multi-sensory books'.

Arthur A. Levine Books (imprint)

Fiction and non-fiction, including picture books and young adult titles. Recent successes include How Are You Peeling? Foods with Moods by Saxton Freymann and Joost Elffers. US publisher of Harry Potter titles.

Submission details Send query letter only in first instance. Founded 1996.

Orchard Books (imprint)

Picture books, fiction and poetry for children and fiction for young adults. Publishes approx. 50 books each year. Recent successes include *Stuart's Cape* by Sara Pennypacker, illustrated by Martin Matje and *Where Are You Going? To See My Friend!* by Eric Carle and Kazuo Iwamura (picture book). Founded 1987.

Submission details Approx. 10% of books are by first-time authors. Send query letter only (responds in 3 months): no unsolicited MSS. For illustrations, send tearsheets or photocopies (not disks or slides). Responds in one month. Samples returned with sase.

Scholastic Press (imprint)

Picture books, fiction for 5–8 and 9–12 year-olds, teenage fiction, poetry, religion and non-fiction for 3 year-olds–teenage. Publishes approx. 35–50 titles each year. Recent successes include *A Corner of the Universe* by Ann M. Martin, *Gregor the Overlander* by Suzanne Collins, *Zen Shorts* by Jon J. Muth, and *Old Turtle and the Broken Truth* by Douglas Wood and Jon J. Muth.

Submission details Will not consider unsolicited MSS. Send query letter or submit via an agent.

Schwartz & Wade Books – see Random House Inc.

Silver Moon Press

381 Park Avenue South, New York, New York 10016
tel 212-802-2890 *fax* 212-802-2893
email customerservice@silvermoonpress.com
website www.silvermoonpress.com

Children's book publisher: test preparation, science, multiculture, biographies, historical fiction. Recent successes include *Stories of the States, Mysteries in Time* and *Adventures in America* series.

Simon & Schuster Children's Publishing Division*

1230 Avenue of the Americas, New York, NY 10020
tel 212-698-7200 *fax* 212-698-2793
website www.simonsayskids.com
President Rick Richter, *Senior Vice-President & Publisher* Rubin Pfeffer, *Vice-President & Publisher* Valerie Garfield

Preschool to young adult, fiction and non-fiction, trade, library and mass market. Imprints: Aladdin Paperbacks, Atheneum Books for Young Readers, Libros para niños, Little Simon, Little Simon Inspirations, Margaret K. McElderry Books, Simon & Schuster Books for Young Readers, Simon Scribbles, Simon Pulse, Simon Spotlight. Division of Simon & Schuster, Inc. Founded 1924.

Aladdin Paperbacks (imprint)

Vice-President & Associate Publisher Ellen Krieger
Reprints successful hardcovers from other Simon & Schuster imprints (primarily). Recent successes include the *Pendragon* series and *Edgar & Ellen* series.

Submission details Accepts query letters with proposals for middle-grade series and single-title

fiction, beginning readers, middle-grade and commercial non-fiction. Send MSS for the attention of the Submissions Editor. Send artwork submissions to Debra Sfetsios.

Atheneum Books for Young Readers (imprint)

Vice-President & Associate Publisher Emma Dryden, *Editorial Directors* Ginnee Seo, Caitlyn Dlouhy
Picture books, chapter books, mysteries, biography, science fiction, fantasy, graphic novels, middle-grade and young adult fiction and non-fiction. Covers preschool–young adult. Publishes 20–30 picture books, 4–5 young readers, 20–25 middle readers and 10–15 young adult books each year. Successes include *Inexcusable* by Chris Lynch, *Once Upon a Time, the End (Asleep in 60 Seconds)* by Geoffrey Kloske and Barry Blittt, *Click Clack Quackity-Quack* by Doreen Cronin and Betsy Lewin, and *Kira-Kira* by Cynthia Kadohata. Includes Ginnee Seo Books and Richard Jackson Books.

Submission details Approx. 10% of books are by first-time authors. No unsolicited MSS. Send query letter only. Responds in one month. For illustrations, send résumé, samples and tearsheets to Ann Bobco, Design Dept.

Margaret K. McElderry Books (imprint)

Vice-President & Associate Publisher Emma Dryden, *Executive Editor* Karen Wojtyla
Picture books, easy-to-read books, fiction (8–12 year-olds, young adult), poetry, fantasy. Covers preschool–young adult. Publishes 10–12 pciture books, 2–4 young reader titles, 8–10 middle reader titles, 5–7 young adult books each year. Recent successes include *Bear Stays Up for Christmas* by Karma Wilson and Jane Chapman, *The Water Mirror* by Kai Meyer, *Freaks* by Annette Curtis Klause, and *Where Did They Hide My Presents: Silly Dilly Christmas Songs* by Alan Katz and David Catrow.

Submission details Approx. 10% of books are by first-time authors. No unsolicited MSS. Fiction length: picture books – 500 words; young readers – 2000; middle readers – 10,000–20,000; young adult – 45,000–50,000. Non-fiction length: picture books – 500–1000 words; young readers – 1500–3000 words; middle readers – 10,000–20,000 words; young adult – 30,000–45,000 words. For illustrations, query with samples to Ann Bobco, Executive Art Director. Responds in 3 months. Samples returned with sase.

Simon Pulse Books (imprint)

Associate Publisher Bethany Buck, *Executive Editor* Jen Klonsky
Young adult series and fiction (primarily) and some reprints of successful hardcovers from other Simon & Schuster imprints. Recent successes include the *Uglies* trilogy by Scott Westerfield and the *Au Pair* books by Melissa de la Cruz.

Submission details Accepts query letters. Send MSS for the attention of the Submission Editor. Send artwork submissions to Russel Gordon.

58 Books

Simon & Schuster Books for Young Readers (imprint)
Associate Publisher Justin Chandu, *Editorial Director* David Gale, *Executive Editor* Kevin Lewis

Fiction and non-fiction, all ages. Recent successes include the *Pendragon* series including *The Rivers of Zadaa* by D.J. MacHale, *Arthur Spiderwick's Field Guide to the Fantastical World Around You* by Tony DiTerlizzi and Holly Black, and *And Tango Makes Three* by Pete Parnell, Justin Richardson and Henry Cole.

Submission details No unsolicited MSS. Send query letter only. Responds to queries in 2 months. Seeking young adult novels that are challenging and psychologically complex; also imaginative and humorous middle-grade fiction.

Paula Wiseman (imprint)
email paulawiseman@simonandschuster.com
Vice-President & Editorial Director Paula Wiseman

Picture books, fiction and non-fiction. Publishes 10 picture books, 2 middle readers and 2 young adult titles each year. Recent successes include *Double Pink* by Kate Feiffer and the *Amelia Notebook* series by Marissa Moss.

Submission details Approx. 10% of books are by first-time authors. Submit complete MSS. Length: picture books – 500 words; others standard length. Considers all categories of fiction. Will review MS/illustration packages from artists. Send MS with dummy.

Sleeping Bear Press – see page 44

Sterling Publishing Co., Inc.
387 Park Avenue South, New York, NY 10016
tel 212-532-7160 *fax* 212-891-0508
email custservice@sterlingpublishing.com
website www.sterlingpublishing.com

Adult non-fiction and children's board books, picture books, juvenile fiction and non-fiction. Juvenile non-fiction includes: crafts, hobbies, games, activities, origami, optical illusions, mazes, dot-to-dots, science experiments, puzzles (maths/word/picture/logic), chess, card games and tricks, sports, magic. Fiction in the following categories only: riddles and jokes, ghost stories, mystery and detective short stories. Recent successes include *Sometimes I Like to Curl Up in a Ball* by by Vicki Churchill and Charles Fuge and *I Know a Rhino* by Charles Fuge.

Submission details Accepts children's fiction only in those categories listed above. For non-fiction write explaining the idea and enclose an outline and a sample chapter of the proposed book. Include information a bio with regard to the subject area and your publishing history, and a sase if you wish your material to be returned. No email submissions. Submissions should be sent FAO Children's Book Editor. Founded in 1949.

Gareth Stevens Publishing
1 Reader's Digest Road, Pleasantville, NY 10570
tel 914-242-4100 *fax* 914-242-4187

email info@gspub.com
website www.garethstevens.com
Publisher Robert Famighetti

Educational books and high-quality fiction for 4–16 year-olds. Subjects include atlases and reference, arts and crafts, emergent readers, nature, science, maths, social studies, history and Spanish/bilingual. Publishes approx. 300 new titles each year and has over 1000 in print. Part of Reader's Digest Association. Founded 1983.

Katherine Tegen Books – see HarperCollins Publishers

TOKYOPOP – see HarperCollins Publishers

Tor Books – see Tom Doherty Associates, LLC

Tricycle Press
PO Box 7123, Berkeley, CA 94707
tel 510-559-1600
website www.tricyclepress.com
President Philip Wood, *Publisher* Nicole Geiger

Children's picture books and board books, both fiction and non-fiction, and middle-grade novels. Subjects include life lessons and social skills, food and cooking, math, science, nature, language arts, history, multiculturalism. Recent successes include *Hugging the Rock* by Susan Taylor Brown, *Mama's Milk* by Michel Elsohn Ross and illustrated by Ashley Wolff, *Where in the Wild* by David Schwartz and Yael Schy with photography by Dwight Kuhn. Founded 1993.

Twenty-first Century Books – see Millbrook Press

Two-Can Publishing
11571 K-Tel Drive, Minnetonka, MN 55343
tel 952-933-7537 *fax* 952-933-3630
email mbohr@nbnbooks.com
website www.northlandbooks.com, www.nbnbooks.com

Non-fiction books and multimedia products to entertain and educate 2–12 year-olds. Imprint of Cooper Square Publishing.

Viking Children's Books – see Penguin Group (USA), Inc.

VSP Books
7402–G Lockport Place, Lorton, VA 22079
tel 703-684-8142 *fax* 703-684-7955
email mail@vspbooks.com
website www.vspbooks.com

Educational books for children about special and historic places. Recent successes include the *Mice Way to Learn* series and *Heartsongs* (poetry). Founded 1992.

Walker & Co.
175 Fifth Avenue, New York, NY 10010
tel 646-438-6078

website www.walkerbooks.com, www.walkeryoungreaders.com
Publisher Emily Easton (children's), George Gibson (adult)

Picture books, non-fiction and fiction (middle grade and young adult). Publishes 20 picture books, 5–8 middle readers and 5–8 young adult books each year. Recent successes include *Gone Wild* by David McLimans and *Skinny* by Ibi Kaslik. General publishers for adults: biography, popular science, health, business, mystery, history. Division of Bloomsbury Publishing. Founded 1960.

Submission details Approx. 5% of books are by first-time authors. Approx. 65% of books are acquired via literary agents. Particularly interested in picture books, illustrated non-fiction, middle grade and young adult fiction. No series ideas. Send 50–75pp and synopsis for longer works; send the entire MSS for picture books. Include sase for response only.

Frederick Warne – see Penguin Group (USA), Inc.

Weigl Publishers Inc.
350 5th Avenue, Suite 3304, PMB6G New York, NY 10118–0069
tel 866-649-3445 *fax* 866-449-3445
email linda@weigl.com
website www.weigl.com

Educational publisher: children's non-fiction titles. Recent successes include *The Backyard Animals* and *Learning to Write* series.

Albert Whitman & Company
6340 Oakton Street, Morton Grove, IL 60053–2723
tel 847-581-0033 *fax* 847-581-0039
email mail@awhitmanco.com
website www.albertwhitman.com

Books that respond to cultural diversity and the special needs and concerns of children and their families (e.g. divorce, bullying). Also novels for middle-grade readers, picture books and non-fiction for ages 2–12.

Submission details Currently not seeking MS for the *Boxcar Children® Mysteries* series. For picture books send complete MS; for longer works send a query letter with 3 sample chapters. Also interested in art samples showing pictures of children. Founded 1919.

John Wiley & Sons Inc.*
111 River Street, Hoboken, NJ 07030
tel 201-748-6000 *fax* 201-748-6088
email info@wiley.com

website www.wiley.com
President/Ceo William J. Pesce

Specialises in scientific and technical books and journals, textbooks and educational materials for colleges and universities, as well as professional and consumer books and subscription services. Subjects include business, computer science, electronics, engineering, environmental studies, reference books, science, social sciences, multimedia, and trade paperbacks. Founded 1807.

Wiley Children's Division
General K–12, K–12 teaching and learning, history, cooking, parenting. Recent successes include *Secrets of Ancient Cultures: The Inca: Activities and Crafts from a Mysterious Land* by Arlette N. Braman, *The Complete Handbook of Science Fair Projects* by Julianne Blair Bochinski and *The United States Cookbook: Fabulous Foods and Fascinating Facts From All 50 States* by Joan D'Amico and Karen Eich Drummond.

Paula Wiseman – see Simon & Schuster Children's Publishing Division

Wordsong – see Boyds Mills Press

Workman Publishing Company*
225 Varick Street, New York, NY 10014–4381
tel 212-254-5900 *fax* 212-254-8098
email info@workman.com
website www.workman.com
Ceo Peter Workman

Adult and juvenile books: art and architecture, biography and memoirs, BRAIN QUEST®, business, children's, cooking, food and wine, crafts, fiction, gardening, gift books, health, history, home reference/how-to, humour, film and TV, music, parenting and families, pets and animals, poetry, science, sport, travel. Founded 1968.

World Book, Inc.
233 North Michigan Avenue, Suite 2000, Chicago, IL 60601
tel 312-729-5800 *fax* 312-729-5600
website www.worldbook.com

Encyclopedias, reference sources, and multimedia products for the home and schools, including *World Book*. Recent publications include *World Book Student Discovery Encyclopedia*, a new *Childcraft – The How and Why Library* and *Animals of the World*. Founded 1917.

Yearling Books – see Random House Inc.

Children's audio publishers

Many of the audio publishers listed below are also publishers of books.

Abbey Home Media plc
435–437 Edgware Road, London W2 1TH
tel 020-7563 3910 fax 020-7563 3911
email emma.evans@abbeyhomemedia.com
Managing Director Anne Miles

Specialises in the acquisition, production and distribution of quality audio/visual entertainment for children. Bestselling children's spoken word and music titles are available on CD and cassette in the Tempo range including Postman Pat, Watership Down, Michael Rosen, Baby Bright, Wide Eye, SuperTed and Golden Nursery Rhymes.

Barefoot Books Ltd
124 Walcot Street, Bath BA1 5BG
tel (01225) 322400 fax (01225) 322499
email info@barefootbooks.co.uk
website www.barefootbooks.co.uk
Publisher Tessa Stickland, Group Project Manager Jo Collins

Narrative unabridged audiobooks, spoken and sung. Established 1993.

Barrington Stoke
18 Walker Street, Edinburgh EH3 7LP
tel 0131-225 4113 fax 0131-225 4140
email info@barringtonstoke.co.uk
website www.barringtonstoke.co.uk
Chairman David Croom, Managing Director Sonia Raphael, Editorial Manager Kate Paice

Short fiction and non-fiction, specially adapted and presented for reluctant, struggling and dyslexic readers, aged 8–13 and 13+, with reading ages of 6.5 to 8. Short fiction (15,000 words) for adults with a reading age of 8. No picture books, no unsolicited submissions. Founded 1998.

BBC Audiobooks – Children's
St James House, The Square, Lower Bristol Road, Bath BA2 3BH
tel (01225) 878000 fax (01225) 310771
email info@audiobookcollection.com
website www.bbcaudiobooks.com
Managing Director Paul Dempsey, Publishing Director Jan Paterson, Children's Commissioning Editor Kate Walsh

Spoken word entertainment for parents and children, from preschool nursery rhymes to modern classics such as The Chronicles of Narnia and His Dark Materials trilogy by Philip Pullman. Imprint of BBC Audiobooks Ltd. Other children's imprints include: Chivers Children's Audiobooks. Formed in 2003 from the amalgamation of Chivers Press, Cover To Cover and BBC Radio Collection.

BBC Cover to Cover
St James House, The Square, Lower Bristol Road, Bath BA2 3BH
tel (01225) 878000 fax (01225) 310771
website www.bbcaudiobooks.com, www.audiobookcollection.com

Unabridged children's bestselling titles. List includes readings of stories by today's major children's authors, such as Philip Pullman, Eoin Colfer and Jacqueline Wilson. Imprint of BBC Audiobooks Ltd.

Bloomsbury Publishing Plc
36 Soho Square, London W1D 3QY
tel 020-7494 2111 fax 020-7734 8656
website www.bloomsbury.com
Contact Sarah Odedina

A broad selection of fiction and non-fiction. Baby books, picture books and fiction for children of all ages.

Bolinda Publishing Ltd
2 Ivanhoe Road, London SE5 8DH
website www.bolinda.com

CDs and cassettes of children's, teenage and adult fiction titles. Based in Melbourne, Australia; established in the UK in 2003.

Chivers Children's Audiobooks
St James House, The Square, Lower Bristol Road, Bath BA2 3BH
tel (01225) 878000 fax (01225) 310771
website www.bbcaudiobooks.com

Both the adult and children's lists feature current bestselling fiction and popular classics by some of Britain and the USA's best authors, read by some of the world's most celebrated actors. In addition, there is an extensive monthly programme of titles available on CD. Chivers Press pioneered the recording of complete and unabridged books with the first titles being published in 1980 and it now has a backlist in excess of 3000 titles ranged from 2-cassette to 16-cassette formats. Imprint of BBC Audiobooks Ltd.

Cló Iar-Chonnachta Teo.
Indreabhán, Conamara, Co. Galway, Republic of Ireland
tel (091) 593307 fax (091) 593362
email cic@iol.ie
website www.cic.ie
Ceo Micheál Ó Conghaile, General Manager Deirdre O'Toole

Predominantly Irish-language children's books with accompanying CD/cassette of stories/folklore/poetry. Established 1985.

CSA Word
6A Archway Mews, London SW15 2PE
tel 020-8871 0220 fax 020-8877 0712
email info@csaword.co.uk
website www.csaword.co.uk
Managing Director Clive Stanhope, Audio Director
Victoria Williams

CDs of classic children's literature such as Just
William, Billy Bunter and Black Beauty; also adult,
classic and current literary authors. Founded 1991.

Dref Wen
28 Church Road, Whitchurch, Cardiff CF14 2EA
tel 029-2061 7860 fax 029-2061 0507
Directors Roger Boore, Anne Boore, Gwilym Boore,
Alun Boore, Rhys Boore

Welsh language audiobooks. Founded 1970.

The Educational Company of Ireland
Ballymount Road, Walkinstown, Dublin 12,
Republic of Ireland
tel (01) 4500611 fax (01) 4500993
email info@edco.ie
website www.edco.ie
Executive Directors Frank Maguire (Chief Executive),
Martina Harford (operations), Robert McLoughlin,
Publisher Frank Fahy

Irish language CDs and audiotapes. Trading unit of
Smurfit Kappa Group – Ireland. Founded 1910.

HarperCollins Audio Books
77–85 Fulham Palace Road, London W6 8JB
tel 020-8741 7070 fax 020-8307 4818
website www.harpercollins.co.uk
Director David Roth-Ey, Editorial Nicola Townsend

Publishers of a wide range of genres including fiction,
non-fiction, poetry, Classics, Shakespeare, comedy,
personal development and children's. All works are
read by famous actors. Established 1990.

Hodder & Stoughton Audiobooks
338 Euston Road, London NW1 3BH
tel 020-7873 6000 fax 020-7873 6024
website www.hodder.co.uk
Publisher Rupert Lancaster

Publishes outstanding authors from within the
Hodder group as well as commissioning independent
titles. The list includes fiction and non-fiction.
Children's titles include Winnie the Pooh, Wallace &
Gromit and the Magic Roundabout Adventures.
Founded 1994.

Ladybird Books
80 Strand, London WC2R 0RL
tel 020-7010 3000 fax 020-7010 6060
email ladybird@uk.penguingroup.com
website www.ladybird.co.uk
Marketing Director Rachel Partridge

Ladybird Books in book-and-CD format for children
aged 0–8 years, including nursery rhymes, fairytales
and classic stories as well as licensed character
publishing.

Macmillan Digital Audio
20 New Wharf Road, London N1 9RR
tel 020-7014 6040 fax 020-7014 6023
email a.muirden@macmillan.co.uk
website www.panmacmillan.com
Audio Publisher Alison Muirden

Children's titles include The Gruffalo by Julia
Donaldson and Axel Scheffler. Also adult fiction,
non-fiction and autobiography. Established 1995.

Naxos AudioBooks
40A High Street, Welwyn, Herts. AL6 9EQ
tel (01438) 717808 fax (01438) 717809
email naxos_audiobooks@compuserve.com
website www.naxosaudiobooks.com
Managing Director Nicolas Soames

Classic literature, modern fiction, non-fiction, drama
and poetry on CD. Also junior classics and classical
music. Founded 1994.

The Orion Publishing Group Ltd
5 Upper St Martin's Lane, London WC2H 9EA
tel 020-7520 4425 fax 020-7379 6158
email pandora.white@orionbooks.co.uk
Audio Manager Pandora White

Adult and children's fiction and non-fiction.
Established 1998.

Penguin Audiobooks
Penguin Books Ltd, 80 Strand, London WC2R 0RL
tel 020-7010 3000
email audio@penguin.co.uk
website www.penguin.co.uk/audio
Audio Publisher Jeremy Ettinghausen

The audiobooks list reflects the diversity of the
Penguin book range, including classic and
contemporary fiction and non-fiction,
autobiography, poetry, drama and, in Puffin
Audiobooks, the best of contemporary and classic
literature for younger listeners. Authors include
Cathy Cassidy, Charlie Higson, Lauren Child, Roald
Dahl and Eoin Colfer. Readings are by talented and
recognisable actors. Over 300 titles are now available.
Founded 1993.

Puffin Audiobooks – see Penguin Audiobooks

Random House Audio Books
The Random House Group Ltd,
20 Vauxhall Bridge Road, London SW1V 2SA
tel 020-7840 8400 fax 020-7931 7672
email zhowes@randomhouse.co.uk
website www.rbooks.co.uk
Commissioning Editor Zoe Howes

SmartPass Ltd
15 Park Road, Rottingdean, Brighton BN2 7HL
tel (01273) 300742
email info@smartpass.co.uk
website www.smartpass.co.uk,
www.spaudiobooks.com,
www.shakespeareappreciated.com
Managing Director Phil Viner, *Creative Director* Jools Viner

SmartPass audio education resources present unabridged plays, poetry and dramatisations of novels as guided full-cast dramas for individual study and classroom use. Student editions present the text with an explanatory commentary and Teacher editions offer audio commentary options and CD-Rom classroom materials. Titles include *Macbeth, Romeo and Juliet, Twelfth Night, Henry V, Othello, King Lear, Shakespeare the Works, A Kestrel for a Knave, Animal Farm, An Inspector Calls, Great Expectations, The Mayor of Casterbridge, Pride and Prejudice* and *War Poetry.*

Usborne Publishing Ltd
Usborne House, 83–85 Saffron Hill,
London EC1N 8RT
tel 020-7430 2800 *fax* 020-7636 3758
email mail@usborne.co.uk
website www.usborne.com
Publishing Director Jenny Tyler, *General Manager* Robert Jones
Founded 1973.

Walker Books Ltd
87 Vauxhall Walk, London SE11 5HJ
tel 020-7793 0909 *fax* 020-7587 1123
website www.walker.co.uk
Publisher Loraine Taylor

Audiobooks include bestselling fiction titles such as the *Alex Rider* series, *Judy Moody* and *Confessions of a Teenage Drama Queen*. For younger children, the *Listen and Join In* audio range comprises entertaining story-based activities based on favourite picture books, including *We're Going on a Bear Hunt, Guess How Much I Love You* and *Can't You Sleep Little Bear?*

Children's book packagers

Many modern illustrated books are created by book packagers, whose particular skills are in the areas of book design and graphic content. In-house editors match up the expertise of specialist writers, artists and photographers who usually work on a freelance basis.

Aladdin Books Ltd
2–3 Fitzroy Mews, London W1T 6DF
tel 020-7383 2084 *fax* 020-7388 6391
email alexandra.mew@aladdinbooks.co.uk
website www.aladdinbooks.co.uk
Directors Charles Nicholas, Bibby Whittaker

Full design and book packaging facility specialising in children's non-fiction and reference. Founded 1980.

The Albion Press Ltd
Spring Hill, Idbury, Oxon OX7 6RU
tel (01993) 831094 *fax* (01993) 831982
Directors Emma Bradford (managing), Neil Philip (editorial)

Produces quality integrated illustrated titles from the initial idea to printed copies. Specialises in children's books: poetry, fairy tales, myths, Native Americans. Produces 4 titles each year. Founded 1984.

Submission details Will not consider unsolicited MSS. Interested in seeing fine samples of illustrations but no cartoons or technical drawings. Include sae.

Nicola Baxter Ltd
PO Box 215, Framingham Earl, Yelverton, Norwich NR14 7UR
tel (01508) 491111
email nb@nicolabaxter.co.uk
website www.nicolabaxter.co.uk
Director Nicola Baxter, *Design Manager* Amy Barton, *Submissions* Sally Delaney

Full packaging service for children's books, from concept to disk or any part of the process in between. Produces both fiction and non-fiction titles in a wide range of formats, from board books to encyclopedias. Experienced in novelty books and licensed publishing. Opportunities for freelances. Founded 1990.

Bender Richardson White
PO Box 266, Uxbridge, Middlesex UB9 5NX
tel (01895) 832444 *fax* (01895) 835213
email brw@brw.co.uk
website www.brw.co.uk
Directors Lionel Bender (editorial), Kim Richardson (sales & production), Ben White (design)

Design, editorial and production of activity books, non-fiction and reference books. Specialises in non-fiction: natural history, science, history and educational. Packages approx. 60–70 titles each year. Founded 1990.

Submission details Writers should send a letter and synopsis of their proposal. Opportunities for freelances.

The Book Guild Ltd
Pavilion View, 19 New Road, Brighton BN1 1UF
tel (01273) 720900 *fax* (01273) 723122
email info@bookguild.co.uk
website www.bookguild.co.uk
Directors Carol Biss (managing), Paul White (financial), Janet Wrench (production)

Fiction for 5–8 and 9–12 year-olds. Produces approx. 10 children's titles each year. Offers a range of publishing options: a comprehensive package for authors incorporating editorial, design, production, marketing, publicity, distribution and sales; editorial and production only for authors requiring private editions; or a complete service for companies and organisations requiring books for internal or promotional purposes – from brief to finished book. Write for submission guidelines. Founded 1982.

Book Street Ltd
Foresters Hall, 25–27 Westow Street, London SE19 3RY
tel 020-8771 5115 *fax* 020-8771 9994
email graham@bwj-ltd.com

Designers and packagers of large format children's books for the international market.

Bookmart Ltd
Blaby Road, Wigston, Leicester LE18 4SE
tel 0116-275 9060 *fax* 0116-275 9090
email books@bookmart.co.uk
website www.bookmart.co.uk
Publishing Director Linda Williams

Colour illustrated titles: children's fiction and non-fiction, poetry, novelty books, pop-up books, activity books. Age groups: preschool, 5–10, 10–15.

Bookwork Ltd
Unit 17, Piccadilly Mill, Lower Street, Stroud, Glos. GL5 2HT
tel (01453) 752521 *fax* (01453) 751544
email bookwork@compuserve.com
Directors Louise Pritchard (editorial), Alan Plank (production), Jill Plank (design)

Creates innovative books for children of all ages: activity books, board books, picture books, how-to books, reference books. Also supplies a full editorial and design service to other publishers. Imprint: Pangolin.

Brainwaves Ltd

31 Chart Lane, Reigate, Surrey RH2 7DY
tel (01737) 224444 *fax* (01737) 225777
email keith@brainwavesbooks.co.uk
Editorial Director Keith Faulkner

Packager of activity books, board books, novelty
books, picture books, pop-up books and gift books.

Breslich & Foss Ltd

2A Union Court, 20–22 Union Road,
London SW4 6JP
tel 020-7819 3990 *fax* 020-7819 3998
Directors Paula G. Breslich, K.B. Dunning

Books produced from MS to bound copy stage from
in-house ideas. Specialising in children's non-fiction
and children's classics. Founded 1978.

John Brown Group – Children's Division

136–142 Bramley Road, London W10 6SR
tel 020-7565 3000 *fax* 020-7565 3060
email andrew.hirsch@johnbrowngroup.co.uk
website www.johnbrowngroup.co.uk
Ceo Andrew Hirsch (operations), Sara Lynn
(creative)

Creative development and packaging of children's
products including books, magazines, teachers'
resource packs, partworks, CD-ROMs and websites.

The Brown Reference Group Plc

1st Floor, 9–17 St Albans Place, London N1 0NX
tel 020-7424 5640 *fax* 020-7424 5641
email info@brownreference.com
website www.brownreference.com
Managing Director Sharon Hutton, *Children's
Publisher* Anne O'Daly

Specialises in high-quality illustrated reference books
and multi-volume sets for trade and educational
markets. Opportunities for freelances. Founded 1989.

Brown Wells & Jacobs Ltd

Foresters Hall, 25–27 Westow Street,
London SE19 3RY
tel 020-8771 5115 *fax* 020-8771 9994
email graham@bwj-ltd.com
website www.bwj.org
Director Graham Brown

Design, editorial, illustration and production of high-
quality non-fiction illustrated children's books.
Specialities include pop-up and novelty books.
Packages approx. 30–40 titles each year.
Opportunities for freelances. Founded 1979.

Cambridge Publishing Management Ltd

Burr Elm Court, Main Street, Caldecote,
Cambs. CB23 7NU
tel (01954) 214000 *fax* (01954) 214002
email initial.surname@cambridgepm.co.uk
website www.cambridgepm.co.uk

Managing Director Jackie Dobbyne, *Managing Editors*
Karen Beaulah, Catherine Burch, Diane Feillol

Creative and highly skilled editorial and book
production company specialising in complete project
management of education, ELT including special
needs and illustrated non-fiction titles, from
commissioning authors to delivery of final files to
printer. Freelancers should send their CVs to Karen
Beaulah. Founded 1999.

Cowley Robinson Publishing Ltd

(incorporating David Hawcock Books)
8 Belmont, Bath BA1 5DZ
tel (01225) 339999 *fax* (01225) 339995
email sales: anna.sainaghi@cowleyrobinson.com
Directors Stewart Cowley (publishing), David
Hawcock, Phil Fleming (finance)

Specialises in children's novelty and paper-engineered
formats for international co-editions. Licence and
character publishing developments. Information and
early learning. Founded 1998.

Creations for Children International

Steenweg op Deinze 150, 9810 Nazareth, Belgium
tel (9) 2446090 *fax* (9) 2446099
email info@c4ci.com, jan.meeuws@c4ci.com,
marc.jongbloet@c4ci.com
website www.c4ci.com, www.inkypress.com
Directors Marc Barbier (business & sales), Marc
Jongbloet (book publishing & sales), *Production
Manager* Joost Demuynck, *Chief Editor* Mr Jan
Meeuws

Packagers of high-quality mass market children's
illustrated books, including fairy tale and classic
adventure story books. Activity books, board books,
colouring books, pop-up books, novelty books,
picture books and non-fiction books.

Creative Plus Publishing Ltd

2nd Floor, 151 High Street, Billericay,
Essex CM12 9AB
tel (01277) 633005 *fax* (01277) 633003
email enquiries@creative-plus.co.uk
website www.creative-plus.co.uk
Managing Director Beth Johnson

Provides all editorial and design from concept to
finished pages for books, partworks and magazines.
Specialises in female interest, children's, illustrated
non-fiction. Opportunities for freelances. Founded
1989.

Design Eye Ltd

226 City Road, London EC1V 2TT
tel 020-7812 8601 *fax* 020-7253 4370
email info@designeye.co.uk
website www.quarto.com/co_ed_designeye_uk.htm
Publisher Sue Grabham

Co-edition publisher of innovative Books-Plus for
children and adults. Children's: highly illustrated

paper-engineered, novelty and component-based titles for all ages, but primarily children's preschool (3+), 5–8 and 8+ years. Mainly non-fiction, early concepts and curriculum-based topics for the trade in all international markets. Adults: highly illustrated component-based kits and books for arts, crafts, lifestyle and hobbies. Opportunities for freelance paper engineers, artists, authors, editors and designers. Founded 1988.

Elm Grove Books Ltd
Elm Grove, Henstridge, Somerset BA8 0TQ
tel (01963) 362498
email hugh@elmgrovebooks.com,
susie@elmgrovebooks.com
Directors Hugh Elwes, Susie Elwes

Packager of children's books. Founded 1993.

Graham-Cameron Publishing & Illustration
The Studio, 23 Holt Road, Sheringham, Norfolk NR26 8NB
tel (01263) 821333 *fax* (01263) 821334
email enquiry@graham-cameron-illustration.com
and Duncan Graham-Cameron, 59 Hertford Road, Brighton BN1 7GG
tel (01273) 385890
website www.graham-cameron-illustration.com
Partners Mike Graham-Cameron, Helen Graham-Cameron, Duncan Graham-Cameron

Offers illustration and editorial services for picture books, information books and educational materials. Handles activity books, picture books, non-fiction and reference. Illustration agency with 37 artists. No unsolicited MSS. Founded 1985.

Hart McLeod Ltd
14 Greenside, Waterbeach, Cambridge CB25 9HP
tel (01223) 861495 *fax* (01223) 862902
email inhouse@hartmcleod.co.uk
website www.hartmcleod.co.uk
Directors Graham Hart, Chris McLeod, Joanne Barker

Primarily educational and general non-fiction with particular expertise in reading books, school texts, ELT and electronic and audio content. Opportunities for freelances and work experience. Founded 1985.

Hawcock Books
Grafton House, High Street, Norton St Philip, Nr Bath BA2 7LG
tel (01373) 834055 *fax* (01373) 834622
website http://hawcockbooks.co.uk

Designs and produces highly creative and original pop-up art and 3D paper-engineered concepts. Most of its experience is in developing, providing editorial for, printing and manufacturing pop-up books and novelty items for the publishing industry. Also undertakes demanding commissions from the advertising world for model-making, point-of-sale and all printed 3D aspects of major campaigns.

HL Studios Ltd
17 Fenlock Court, Blenheim Office Park, Long Hanborough, Oxford OX29 8LN
tel (01993) 881010 *fax* (01993) 882713
email info@hlstudios.eu.com
website www.hlstudios.eu.com

Primary, secondary academic education (geography, science, modern languages) and co-editions (travel guides, gardening, cookery). Multimedia (CD-Rom programming and animations). Opportunities for freelances. Founded 1985.

Miles Kelly Packaging
The Bardfield Centre, Great Bardfield, Essex CM7 4SL
tel (01371) 811309 *fax* (01371) 811393
email info@mileskelly.net
website www.mileskelly.net
Directors Gerard Kelly, Jim Miles, Richard Curry

Publishers of high-quality illustrated non-fiction titles for children and family. See also page 14. Founded 1996.

Little People Books
The Home of BookBod, Knighton, Radnorshire LD7 1UP
tel (01547) 520925
email littlepeoplebooks@thehobb.tv
website www.thehobb.tv/postings/000182.php
Directors Grant Jessé (production & managing), Helen Wallis (rights & finance)

Packager of audio, children's educational and textbooks, digital publications. Parent company: Grant Jessé UK.

Marshall Editions Ltd
The Old Brewery, 6 Blundell Street, London N7 9BH
tel 020-7700 6764 *fax* 020-7700 4191
email dominicc@marshalleditions.com
website www.marshalleditions.com
Publisher Dominic Carman

Highly illustrated non-fiction for adults and children, including history, health, gardening, home design, pets, natural history, popular science.

Monkey Puzzle Media Ltd
Gissing's Farm, Fressingfield, Eye, Suffolk IP21 5SH
tel (01379) 588044 *fax* (01379) 588055
email info@monkeypuzzlemedia.com
Director Roger Goddard-Coote

Offers a full packaging service from concept or commission through to delivery of repro-ready disks or film. Specialises in children's non-fiction and reference. Produces approx. 60 titles each year. Will consider unsolicited MSS and copies of illustrations with an sae. Founded 1998.

Orpheus Books Ltd
6 Church Green, Witney, Oxon OX28 4AW
tel (01993) 774949 *fax* (01993) 700330

email info@orpheusbooks.com
website www.orpheusbooks.com
Executive Directors Nicholas Harris (editorial, design & marketing), Sarah Hartley (production & design)

Produces children's books for the international co-editions market: activity books, novelty books, non-fiction and reference. Produces 8–20 titles each year. Welcomes samples from illustrators and CVs from writers. Founded 1993.

Picthall & Gunzi Ltd

21A Widmore Road, Bromley BR1 1RW
tel 020-8460 4032 *fax* 020-8460 4021
email chez@picthallandgunzi.demon.co.uk, chris@picthallandgunzi.demon.co.uk
website www.picthallandgunzi.com
Managing Director Chez Picthall, *Editorial Director & Publisher* Christiane Gunzi

Offers a complete package, from initial concept to publication, producing high-quality, illustrated non-fiction for children of all ages: early learning, novelty, activity, board books, non-fiction.

Pinwheel

Alligator Books Ltd, Gadd House, Arcadia Avenue, London N3 2JU
tel 020-8371 6622 *fax* 020-8371 6664
email reception@alligatorbooks.co.uk
website www.pinwheel.co.uk
Directors Andrew Flatt (managing), Linda Cole (publishing), Paula Burgess (creative)

Packages unique and innovative children's books for the international market, across 3 imprints (see Alligator Books Ltd, page 5).

Playne Books Ltd

Park Court Barn, Trefin, Haverfordwest, Pembrokeshire SA62 5AU
tel (01348) 837073 *fax* (01348) 837063
email playne.books@virgin.net
Design & Production Director David Playne, *Editor* Gill Davies

Specialises in highly illustrated adult non-fiction and books for very young children. All stages of production undertaken from initial concept (editorial, design and manufacture) to delivery of completed books. Contact by email or include sae for return of work. Founded 1987.

Tony Potter Publishing Ltd

1 Stairbridge Court, Bolney Grange Business Park, Stairbridge Lane, Bolney, West Sussex RH17 5PA
tel (01444) 232889 *fax* (01444) 232142
email info@tonypotter.com
website www.tonypotter.com
Directors Tony Potter (managing), Christine Potter

Creates high-quality children's titles as a packager and occasionally publishes under its own imprint: Over the Moon. Opportunities for freelance editors, designers and illustrators. Also creates custom-designed books and innovative paper-based products for children and adults, particularly for own-brand. Founded 1997.

The Puzzle House

Ivy Cottage, Battlesea Green, Stradbroke, Suffolk IP21 5NE
tel (01379) 384656 *fax* (01379) 384656
email puzzlehouse@btinternet.com
Partners Roy Preston and Sue Preston

Editorial service creating crossword, quiz, puzzle and activity material for all ages. Founded 1988.

Quarto Children's Books Ltd

226 City Road, London EC1V 2TT
tel 020-7812 8626 *fax* 020-7253 4370
email quartokids@quarto.com
website www.quarto.com
Publisher Sue Grabham, *Art Director* Jonathan Gilbert

Co-edition publisher of innovative Books-Plus for children. Highly illustrated paper-engineered, novelty and component-based titles for all ages, but primarily preschool (3+), 5–8 and 8+ years. Mainly non-fiction, early concepts and curriculum-based topics for the trade in all international markets. Opportunities for freelance paper engineers, artists, authors, editors and designers.

Small World Design

72A Pope Lane, Penwortham, Preston, Lancs. PR1 9DA
tel (01772) 750885 *fax* (01772) 750885
email sue.chadwick@smallworlddesign.co.uk
website www.smallworlddesign.co.uk
Partners Sue Chadwick, David Peet

Offers a writing, illustration, design and packaging service for preschool material, books, novelty books, games, jigsaw puzzles, activity packs, licensed products, creative and educational products. Founded 1995.

Tangerine Designs Ltd

2 High Street, Freshford, Bath BA2 7WE
tel (01225) 720001
Managing Director Christine Swift

Packagers and co-edition publishers of children's books including novelty books and licensed titles. Concepts and cooperation proposals considered. Submissions only accepted if sae is enclosed. Member of the Publishers Association. Founded 2000.

Tango Books Ltd

PO Box 32595, London W4 5YD
tel 020-8996 9970 *fax* 020-8996 9977
email sheri@tangobooks.co.uk, edith@tangobooks.co.uk
website www.tangobooks.co.uk
Directors Sheri Safran, David Fielder, *Submissions* Edith Fricker (*tel* 020-8996 9973)

Creates and produces international co-productions of children's novelty books only (touch-and-feel, flaps, pop-ups, foils, etc). No flat picture books. Produces mainly for the 0–6 age group but some for up to age 12. Books are highly visual with lots of illustrations and minimal text, except for non-fiction where there is scope for longer texts. Big multicultural novelty book list. Founded 1983.

Submission details The max. word count for ages 0–6 is 750 words. Text should be for novelty format (repetition works well). No particularly British themes or characters. No poetry. Artwork: modern style, fresh and fun. Likes collage, bright and bold styles, pen and ink coloured in. Less keen on watercolour unless very special. Send submissions with ssae for their return. Allow one month for reply.

The Templar Company plc

The Granary, North Street, Dorking,
Surrey RH4 1DN
tel (01306) 876361 *fax* (01306) 889097
email rebecca.beves@templarco.co.uk
website www.templarco.co.uk
Managing Director Amanda Wood, *Sales & Marketing Director* Ruth Huddleston, *Publishing Manager* Rebecca Elliott

Publisher and packager of high-quality illustrated children's books, including novelty books, picture books, pop-up books, board books, non-fiction and gift titles. Lightning Source Children's Publisher of the Year 2008; The Van Tulleken Independent Publisher of the Year 2008.

Tiptoe Books

Bradley's Close, 74–77 White Lion Street,
London N1 9PF
tel 020-7520 7600 *fax* 020-7520 7606/7607
email enquiries@amberbooks.co.uk
website www.amberbooks.co.uk
Managing Director Stasz Gnych, *Deputy Managing Director* Sara Ballard, *Publishing Manager* Charles Catton, *Head of Production* Peter Thompson, *Design Manager* Mark Batley, *Picture Manager* Terry Forshaw

Illustrated non-fiction, multi-volume sets, calendars and sticker books for children of all ages. Subjects include history, ancient civilisations, the natural world, fantasy. Opportunities for freelances. Imprint of Amber Books Ltd.

Toucan Books Ltd

3rd Floor, 89 Charterhouse Street,
London EC1M 6HR
tel 020-7250 3388 *fax* 020-7250 3123
website www.toucanbooks.co.uk
Directors Robert Sackville West, Ellen Dupont

International co-editions; editorial, design and production services. Founded 1985.

Emma Treehouse Ltd

Little Orchard House, Mill Lane, Beckington,
Somerset BA11 6SN

tel (01373) 831215 *fax* (01373) 831216
email sales@emmatreehouse.com
website www.emmatreehouse.com
Directors David Bailey, Richard Powell (creative & editorial)

Specialist creator of novelty books for children aged 0–7: bath books, books with a sound concept, cloth books, novelty books, flap books, touch-and-feel books. Packager and co-edition publisher with international recognition for its innovative and often unique concepts. The company has produced over 30 million books, translated into 33 different languages. Opportunities for freelance artists. Founded 1992

Tucker Slingsby Ltd

5th Floor, Regal House, 70 London Road,
Twickenham TW1 3QS
tel 020-8744 1007 *fax* 020-8744 0041
email firstname@tuckerslingsby.co.uk
Directors Janet Slingsby, Del Tucker

Highly illustrated adult and children's books and magazines from concept to delivery of film, disk or finished copies. Produces for preschool to teenage: annuals, activity books, novelty books, picture books, film/TV tie-ins, non-fiction, religion and reference. Produces approx. 100 titles each year. Founded 1992.

Submission details Opportunities for freelances and picture book artists. Submit by post or email.

David West Children's Books

7 Princeton Court, 55 Felsham Road,
London SW15 1AZ
tel 020-8780 3836 *fax* 020-8780 9313
email dww@btinternet.com
website www.davidwestchildrensbooks.com
Proprietor David West, *Partner* Lynn Lockett

Packagers of children's illustrated reference books. Specialises in science, art, geography, history, sport and flight. Produces 40 titles each year. Opportunities for freelances. Founded 1986.

Working Partners Ltd

Stanley House, 6 St Chad's Place,
London WC1X 9HH
tel 020-7841 3939 *fax* 020-7841 3940
email enquiries@workingpartnersltd.co.uk
website www.workingpartnersltd.co.uk
Chairman Ben Baglio, *Managing Director* Chris Snowdon, *Creative Director* Rod Ritchie

Children's and young adult fiction series: animal fiction, fantasy, horror, historical fiction, detective, magical, adventure. Recent successes include *Animal Ark*, *Rainbow Magic* and *My Secret Unicorn*.

Submission details Unable to accept any MS or illustration submissions. Pays advance and royalty; retains copyright on all work created. Selects writers from unpaid writing samples based on specific brief provided. Always looking to add writers to database: contact writers@workingpartnersltd.co.uk to register details. Founded 1995.

Children's book clubs

Not all the companies listed here are 'clubs' in the true sense: some are mail order operations and others sell their books via book fairs.

Baker Books

Manfield Park, Cranleigh, Surrey GU6 8NU
tel (01483) 267888 *fax* (01483) 267409
email bakerbooks@dial.pipex.com
website www.bakerbooks.co.uk

School book club for children aged 3–13. Operates in the UK and in English medium schools overseas.

BFC Books for Children

BCA Groundwell, Hargreaves Road, Swindon, Wilts. SR25 5BG
tel (01793) 723 547
website www.booksforchildren.co.uk

Offers a wide range of books, tapes, toys and CD-Roms for babies through to teenagers. Books include fiction, non-fiction and national curriculum-related material. Membership gives access to Books for Children website, and 12+ colour magazines per year offering books for sale. Conditions of membership: at least 4 books in first year must be ordered through the website or magazine. Part of the BCA Group.

Bibliophile

5 Datapoint, South Crescent, London E16 4TL
tel 020-7515 9222 *fax* 020-7538 4115
email orders@bibliophilebooks.com
website www.bibliophilebooks.com
Secretary Annie Quigley

To promote value-for-money reading. Upmarket literature and classical music on CD available from mail order catalogue (10 p.a.). Over 3000 titles covering art and fiction to travel, history and children's books. Founded 1978.

The Book People Ltd

Catteshall Manor, Catteshall Lane, Godalming, Surrey GU7 1UU
tel (01483) 861144 *fax* (01483) 861256
email sales@thebookpeople.co.uk
website www.thebookpeople.co.uk

Popular general fiction and non-fiction, including children's and travel. Monthly.

Children's Poetry Bookshelf

website www.childrenspoetrybookshelf.co.uk

This poetry book club offers poetry for 7–11-year-olds and its membership schemes are for parents and grandparents (with a gift membership), teachers and libraries. Its open access website has a lively and child-friendly area. Runs the Children's Poetry Bookshelf Competition over National Poetry Day each year. See also page 173.

Disney Book Club

Customer services Grolier Ltd, PO Box 49, Norwich NR5 9PP
tel (0870) 240 4385
email customerservice@grolier.co.uk
website www.disneybookclub.co.uk

Offers books based on Disney characters, Disney storybooks, year books, calendars and supplements. Six free books on joining. New books sent every 4 weeks. Membership may be cancelled after acceptance of 3 shipments.

Letterbox Library

71–73 Allen Road, London N16 8RY
tel 020-7503 4801 *fax* 020-7503 4800
email info@letterboxlibrary.com
website www.letterboxlibrary.com

Specialises in children's books that celebrate equality and diversity. Also provides pre-selected packs for Sure Starts and nurseries. Quarterly annotated catalogues. Operates as a non-profit-driven workers' co-operative. Orders taken online, by fax or by post.

Puffin Book Club

Catteshall Manor, Catteshall Lane, Godalming, Surrey GU7 1UU
Freephone tel (0500) 454 444 (UK), (1) 800 340 131 (ROI)
email customerservice@puffinbookclub.co.uk
Customer services Edinburgh Gate, Harlow, Essex CM20 2JE
website www.puffinbookclub.co.uk, www.puffinbookclub.ie

A schools-based book club that gives parents and children access to a fantastic range of discounted books from all the top publishers. It also helps schools to fill their classrooms and libraries with the best books as Puffin Book Club matches their school order value with the same value of free books.

Red House

PO Box 142, Bangor LL57 4ZP
tel 0845 606 4280
email enquiries@redhouse.co.uk
website www.redhouse.co.uk

Helps parents to select the right books for their children at affordable prices. A free monthly magazine features the best of the latest titles on offer, young reader reviews and fascinating insight into the minds of popular children's writers. Sponsors the Red House Children's Book Award (page 370). Founded 1979.

Red House International Schools Book Club (ISBC)

Scholastic Ltd, Windrush Park, Witney,
Oxon OX29 0YD
tel (01993) 893474 *fax* (01993) 708159
email intschool@scholastic.co.uk
website www2.scholastic.co.uk/isbc

International book club service for schools worldwide.

Scholastic Book Clubs and Fairs

Euston House, 24 Eversholt Street,
London NW1 1DB
tel 020-7756 7756 *fax* 020-7756 7799
website www.scholastic.co.uk

Leading schools book clubs and fairs. Offers primary and secondary clubs and fairs.

Scholastic Book Fairs

Dolomite Avenue, Coventry Business Park,
Coventry CV5 6UE
tel 0800 212281 (freephone)

website www.scholastic.co.uk/bookfairs
Managing Director Miles Stevens-Hoare

Sells directly to children, parents and teachers in schools through 25,000 week-long events held in schools throughout the UK.

Travelling Book Company

(also known as Troubadour)
Express House, Crow Arch Lane, Ringwood,
Hants BH24 1PD
tel (0800) 7315758 *fax* (01425) 471797
email enquiries@travellingbooks.co.uk
website www.travellingbooks.co.uk

Book fair operation selling books to children in schools in the UK (Celtic Travelling Book Company in Ireland) through easy-to-manage, well-stocked bookcases containing a wide range of books for all age groups. An editorial team works closely with teachers and parents to ensure a balanced collection and is headed up by Fiona Waters, the well-known writer, reviewer, publisher and bookseller.

Children's bookshops

The bookshops in the first part of this list specialise in selling new children's books and are good places for writers and illustrators to check out the marketplace. Most of them are members of the Booksellers Association and are well known to publishers. A list of second-hand and antiquarian children's bookshops follows.

Askews
218–222 North Road, Preston, Lancs. PR1 1SV
tel (01772) 555947 fax (01772) 254860
email enquiries@askews.co.uk
website www.askews.co.uk
Libraries and schools supplier.

Badger Books
email info@badgerbooks.co.uk
website www.badgerbooks.co.uk
Proprietors Nic and Janet Tall

Internet business specialising in selling modern reprints of sought after children's books.

Bags of Books
1 South Street, Lewes, East Sussex BN7 2BT
tel (01273) 479320 fax (01273) 478404
email bagsofbooks@bags-of-books.co.uk
website www.bags-of-books.co.uk

Specialist children's bookshop including a mail-order service and school supply. Also distributes big books and some hard-to-get US children's books.

Blast-Off Books
103 High Street, Linlithgow, Scotland EH49 7EQ
tel (01506) 844645 fax (01506) 844346
email info@blastoffbooks.co.uk
website www.blastoffbooks.co.uk

A dedicated children's bookshop for babies through to young adults, also stocking support materials for the Standard Grades and Highers. An important aspect of the shop is the range of materials for parents of, and teachers working with, children with specific learning needs such as dyslexia, autism, ADHD and Down's Syndrome.

The Book House
93 High Street, Thame, Oxon OX9 3HJ
tel (01844) 213032 fax (01844) 213311
email anybook@the-book-house.demon.co.uk

Bookspread Ltd
6 Croxted Road, London SE21 8SW
tel (0845) 200 4954, 020-8658 9613
fax (0845) 200 4964, 020-8402 7886
email info@bookspread.co.uk
website www.bookspread.co.uk

A bookshop run by ex-teachers who offer advice and consultation as well as a mobile book service for schools. Also organises workshops and author visits to schools. Works in conjunction with the educational charity, the Children's Discovery Centre.

Bookworm Ltd
1177 Finchley Road, London NW11 0AA
tel 020-8201 9811 fax 020-8201 9311
email ruth.swindon@lineone.net
website www.thebookworm.uk.com

Bookworms of Reigate
45A Bell Street, Reigate, Surrey RH2 7AQ
tel (01737) 222358 fax (01737) 242189
website www.bookwormsofreigate.co.uk
Specialist children's bookshop.

Brook Green Bookshop
72 Blythe Road, Brook Green, London W14 0HB
tel 020-7603 5999
email brookgreenbooks@btconnect.com

Children's bookshop started by former Macmillan sales director Michael Halden and his wife Loma Slater in spring 2003, situated in West London.

Browns Books For Students
22–28 George Street, Hull HU1 3AP
tel (01482) 384660 fax (01482) 384677
email schools.services@brownsbfs.co.uk
website www.brownsbfs.co.uk

Supplies children's books and any book in print to schools, colleges and international schools. Full school servicing of books on request.

Chameleon Books
5 Milnyard Square, Peterborough PE2 6GX
tel (0870) 7704606 fax (01733) 370607
email info@chameleongroup.co.uk
website www.chameleongroup.co.uk
Specialises in the supply of books and learning materials for schools and nurseries.

Chapter One Bookshop
136 Crockhamwell Road, Woodley, Reading RG5 3JH
tel/fax 0118-944 8883
email chapteronebookshop@yahoo.co.uk
website www.chapteronebookboxes.co.uk

General bookshop with specialisation in children's titles and teaching resource books. Also provide book boxes for reluctant readers to schools in the UK.

Childrens@Blackwells
Blackwells Bookshop, 48–51 Broad Street,
Oxford OX1 3BQ
tel (01865) 333000
email mail.ox@blackwell.co.uk
website www.blackwell.co.uk

Children's Book Centre
14A Earls Court Road, Kensington High Street,
London W8 6EA
tel 020-7938 2552
email gee4@dircon.co.uk

Children's books, videos, tapes, audiobooks, toys and
multimedia products.

The Children's Bookshop
1 Red Lion Parade, Bridge Street, Pinner,
Middlesex HA5 3JD
tel 020-8866 9116 *fax* 020-8866 9116
email thechildrens.bookshop@virgin.net

Children's Bookshop (Huddersfield)
37–39 Lidget Street, Lindley, Huddersfield,
West Yorkshire HD3 3JF
tel (01484) 658013 *fax* (01484) 460020
email barry@hudbooks.demon.co.uk

Children's Bookshop (Muswell Hill)
29 Fortis Green Road, London N10 3HP
tel 020-8444 5500 *fax* 020-8883 8632
email admin@childrensbookshoplondon.co.uk

Chimp and Zee Bookshop, Bookshop by the Sea
51 Broad Street, Lyme Regis, Dorset DT7 3QF
tel (01297) 442233
website www.anholt.co.uk

Owned by bestselling author/illustrator team
Catherine and Laurence Anholt. Workshops and
events.

Enchanted Wood
3–5 Kings Road, Shalford, Guildford GU4 8JU
tel (01483) 570088 *fax* (0870) 7052342
email sales@enchanted-wood.co.uk
website www.enchanted-wood.co.uk

Glowworm Books & Gifts Ltd
Unit 4, Bishopsgate Business Park,
189A West Main Street, Broxburn,
West Lothian EH52 5LH
tel (01506) 857570 *fax* (01506) 858100
website www.glowwormbooks.co.uk

Specialises in supplying books for children, especially
those who find reading difficult due to physical or
special educational needs.

Golden Treasury (Southfields)
29 Replingham Road, London SW18 5LT
tel 020-8333 0167

email southfields@thegoldentreasury.co.uk
website www.thegoldentreasury.co.uk

Jubilee Books
31a Vanburgh Park, Blackheath, London SE3 7AE
tel 020-8293 6060 *fax* 056 0150 8125
email enquiries@jubileebooks.co.uk
website www.jubileebooks.co.uk

Offers a wide range of books and resources to
schools. Organises book-related events including
visits by the bookbus, author/illustrator sessions and
creative workshops for schools, LEAs and other
education organisations. Established 1996.

Madeleine Lindley Ltd
Book Centre, Broadgate, Broadway Business Park,
Oldham OL9 9XA
tel 0161-683 4400 *fax* 0161-682 6801
email info@madeleinelindley.com
website www.madeleinelindley.com

Supplies books to schools, provides information
services and runs open days for teachers. Hosts
author/publisher events for teachers and children.

The Lion and Unicorn Bookshop
19 King Street, Richmond, Surrey TW9 1ND
tel 020-8940 0483 *fax* 020-8332 6133
email services@lionunicornbooks.co.uk
website www.lionunicornbooks.co.uk

A specialist independent children's bookshop. Holds
regular author events, offers services to schools,
loyalty scheme and newsletter *The Roar*. Voted
Independent Bookseller of the Year, The British Book
Awards 2000. Established in 1977.

Norfolk Children's Book Centre
Alby, Norwich NR11 7HB
tel (01263) 761402 *fax* (01263) 768167
email marilyn@ncbc.co.uk
website www.ncbc.co.uk

Specialist children's bookshop for readers of all ages.
Offers services to schools in East Anglia including
storytelling, talks to children and parents, approval
services and INSET for teachers.

Oundle School Bookshop
13 Market Place, Oundle, Peterborough PE8 4BA
tel (01832) 273523 *fax* (01832) 274611
email bookshop@oundle.co.uk
website www.oundleschool.org.uk

Peters Bookselling Services
120 Bromsgrove Street, Birmingham B5 6RJ
tel 0121-666 6646 *fax* 0121-666 7033
website www.peters-books.co.uk

Libraries and schools bookseller who provides book-
related promotional material for schools such as
posters, information booklets and *tBkmag*, a reader
development magazine for 8–12 year-olds.

Rhyme & Reason
681 Ecclesall Road, Sheffield S11 8TG
tel 0114-266 1950
email richard@rhyme-reason.co.uk

New books for children of all ages. Special interest in social and emotional aspects of learning.

Roving Books Ltd (The Roving Bookshop)
Administration 3 Kirkby Road, Desford,
Leicester LE9 9GL
tel (01455) 822192 *fax* (07005) 982306
email support@rovingbooks.com
Showroom inside the Leicester Wholefood Co-op,
Unit 3, Freehold Street, Leicester LE1 2LX
tel 0116-251 2525
website www.rovingbooks.com, www.xybacard.com

Children's specialist bookseller, taking a comprehensive children's bookshop into schools for purchases by children, parents, teachers and schools. Promoting reading with the Jolly Roger Book Club and Xybacard. Specialist advice and supply of children's books for individuals and institutions.

Seven Stories – see page 339

Tales On Moon Lane
25 Half Moon Lane, London SE24 9JU
tel 020-7274 5759
email info@talesonmoonlane.co.uk
9 Princess Road, London NW1 8JN
tel 020-7722 1800
website www.talesonmoonlane.co.uk
Proprietor Tamara Linke

Specialist children's bookshop which runs yearly children's literature festivals in May and October, as well as weekly storytelling sessions for preschool children.

Victoria Park Books
174 Victoria Park Road, London E9 7HD
tel 020-8986 1124
email info@victoriaparkbooks.co.uk
website www.victoriaparkbooks.co.uk
Proprietors Jo and Cris De Guia

Specialist children's bookshop including dual language books. Reading groups for toddlers. Any title can be ordered.

The Well Wisher Children's Bookshop
51 Long Street, Devizes, Wilts. SN10 1NP
tel (01380) 722640
email wellwisher@btconnect.com
website www.wellwisher.biz
Contact Karen Hellewell

Specialist children's bookshop.

Willesden Bookshop
Willesden Green Library Centre, 95 High Road,
London NW10 4QU
tel 020-8451 7000 *fax* 020-8830 1233
email books@willesdenbookshop.co.uk
website www.willesdenbookshop.co.uk

Specialist supplier of multicultural children's books (including many unusual and imported titles) to schools, nurseries, libraries and professional development agencies.

Young Browsers Bookshop
33 The Thoroughfare, Woodbridge,
Suffolk IP12 1AH
tel (01394) 382832 *fax* (01394) 330700
email youngbrowsers@browersbookshop.com

CHILDREN'S BOOKSELLERS FOR COLLECTORS

Blackwell Rare Books
48–51 Broad Street, Oxford OX1 3BQ
tel (01865) 333555 *fax* (01865) 794143
email rarebooks@blackwell.co.uk
website www.rarebooks.blackwell.co.uk

The Rare Books Department within Blackwell deals in early and modern first editions of children's books, among other subjects. Catalogues are issued periodically, which include modern and antiquarian children's books.

Bookmark Children's Books
Fortnight, Broad Hinton, Swindon, Wilts. SN4 9NR
tel (01793) 731693 *fax* (01793) 731782
email leonora-excell@btconnect.com
Contact Anne Excell, Leonora Excell

A mail-order bookseller, specialising in books for collectors, ranging from antiquarian to modern. A wide range of first editions, novelty and picture books, chap-books, ABCs, annuals, etc. Also a selection of vintage toys, games, dolls and nursery china. Catalogues of children's books and related juvenilia issued. Book search service available within this specialist area. Member of PBFA, exhibiting at PBFA book fairs in London, Oxford and Bath. Send sae. Established 1973.

Mary Butts Books
219 Church Road, Earley, Reading, Berks. RG6 1HW
tel 0118-926 1793
email mary.butts@tiscali.co.uk

Secondhand bookseller specialising in 19th- and 20th-century children's books for readers and students rather than collectors. Mainly postal business, but bookroom available on request. Free book search.

Paul Embleton
12 Greenfields, Stansted, Essex CM24 8AH
tel (01279) 812627
email paulembleton@btconnect.com
website www.abebooks.com

Sells by post via the internet (some stock is on Abe) and sends subject lists to regular customers. Receives visitors by appointment. Specialises in books and ephemera for the picture postcard collector and maintains a good stock of children's books and ephemera, mostly Victorian and Edwardian chromolithographic by such publishers as Nister and Raphael Tuck, and items of any age by collectable illustrators.

Ian Hodgkins & Co Ltd
Upper Vatch Mill, The Vatch, Slad, Stroud, Glos. GL6 7JY
tel (01453) 764270 *fax* (01453) 755233
email i.hodgkins@dial.pipex.com
website www.ianhodgkins.com
Contact Simon Weager

Dealer in rare and out-of-print books and related material. Specialist in Beatrix Potter and fairy tales and 19th-century British art and literature. Free catalogues in all specialist areas published regularly.

Robert J. Kirkpatrick
6 Osterley Park View Road,
London W7 2HH (private premises)
tel 020-8567 4521
email rkirkpatrick.molesworth@virgin.net

Secondhand bookseller specialising in stories about boys' schools from 1800 to the present day. Also public school studies, histories, etc.

Marchpane Children's Books
16 Cecil Court, Charing Cross Road,
London WC2N 4HE
tel 020-7836 8661 *fax* 020-7497 0567
email enquiries@marchpane.com
website www.marchpane.com

Specialises in collectable illustrated children's books. Open Mon–Sat 11am–6.30pm.

Plurabelle Books
The Grey Barn (Building 3), Michael Young Centre, Purbeck Road, Cambridge CB2 2HN
tel (01223) 415671 *fax* (01223) 413241
email books@plurabelle.co.uk
website www.plurabelle.co.uk
Contact Michael Cahn

Secondhand bookseller specialising in academic books on literature, reading, history of education and children's literature. Free book search for out-of-print books. Catalogue published 3 times a year. Visitors welcome by appointment.

Ripping Yarns Bookshop
355 Archway Road, London N6 4EJ
tel 020-8341 6111 *fax* 020-7482 5056
email yarns@rippingyarns.co.uk
website www.rippingyarns.co.uk

Bookshop specialising in children's books – particularly in 19th and 20th century children's fiction, annuals, Puffins and picture books.

Henry Sotheran Ltd
2–5 Sackville Street, Piccadilly, London W1X 2DP
tel 020-7439 6151 *fax* 020-7434 2019
Contact Rosie Hodge

A large showroom with hundreds of important children's books spanning 2 centuries, specialising in first editions and attractive illustrated works by pivotal artists. Issues 2 specialist children's book catalogues free, on request.

Stella and Rose's Books
Monmouth Road, Tintern,
Monmouthshire NP16 6SE
tel (01291) 689755 *fax* (01291) 689998
email enquiry@stellabooks.com
website www.rosesbooks.com
Contact Maria Goddard

Bookshop specialising solely in rare out-of-print children's books and located in the international book town of Hay-on-Wye. Stock available via website. Catalogues and specialist lists issued on a regular basis. Open daily 9.30am–5.00pm. Free want match service. Children's books purchased – single items or collections. Established 1986.

Talatin Books
21 Parkstone Avenue, Emerson Park, Hornchurch, Essex RM11 3LX
tel (01708) 447561 *fax* (01708) 442238
email talatin-books@talk21.com
Contact Maggie Stevenson

Dealer in antiquarian and modern children's books. A wide range available, including reference books. Visitors are welcome by appointment (private premises, parking at door). Catalogues sent worldwide. Exhibits at the occasional book fair.

Notes from Jacqueline Wilson

Jacqueline Wilson shares her first experience of becoming a writing success.

I knew I wanted to be a writer ever since I was six years old. I thought it would be the most magical job in the world. You could stay at home by yourself and write stories all day long.

I loved making up stories. I had a serial story permanently playing in my head. I used to mutter the words, acting each imaginary character in turn, but I soon learnt that this made people stare or giggle. I mastered the art of saying the words silently, experiencing all sorts of extraordinary adventures internally, while I sat staring seemingly blankly into space. No wonder I was nicknamed Jacky Daydream at school. My Mum thought I wasn't all there, and was forever giving me a shake and telling me not to look so gormless. She laughed at me when I confided that I wanted to be a writer. 'Don't be so daft Jac! Who on earth would want to read a book written by *you?*' she said.

She had a point. I was a totally unexceptional little girl, shy and anxious, barely able to say boo to a goose. My Mum wanted a daughter like Shirley Temple. She even permed my wispy hair to try to turn it into a cloud of golden ringlets. I ended up looking as if I'd been plugged into a light socket. I couldn't sing like Shirley, I couldn't tap dance like Shirley, and although I could recite long poems with dutiful expression I got so nervous performing I once wet myself on stage.

I didn't *want* to perform, well, certainly not in public. I would act out my stories enthusiastically whenever I was by myself, but I was a total shrinking violet in front of other people. I wasn't the life and soul of the party at school. I didn't clamour to have my friends round to play. I preferred playing elaborate imaginary games all by myself.

I saw a writing career as a wonderful grown-up version of these games. I suppose in a way it *is* – but I had no idea what it's *really* like to be a children's author. I don't think I've had a quiet day at home writing my book for weeks!

I suppose it used to be like that long ago. I've been writing children's books for the past 35 years. For the first 20 years very few people had ever heard of me. I wrote several books a year for a whole variety of publishers. They were published, and if I hunted high and low I occasionally saw one title in a bookshop down at the end of the Ws. I got a few pleasant reviews, and I was stocked in libraries, but that was about it. I've got copies of my first 40 books and they're all first editions – because they didn't go into any other editions. Publishing was so different in those days. You were kept on lists even if your books barely covered their advances – although eventually my first publisher told me they didn't see the point in buying any more of my books because they were never ever going to be popular.

I was upset, of course, but I felt their remarks were justified. I wrote about lonely imaginative children, all of them odd ones out. I thought that only odd children themselves would want to read them. I was worried that I'd never find another publisher but very luckily for me I was taken on by Transworld (now Random House Children's Books). I had the idea of writing a story about a fierce little kid in a children's home desperate to be fostered. I decided to tell it as if this child herself was writing her own life story. I wanted her to have a contemporary quirky kind of name. Something like... Tracy Beaker.

I knew I wanted the book to have lots of black and white illustrations as if Tracy herself had drawn them. I wanted several to a page, even in the margins. David Fickling was my editor then and he's always been very open to suggestions. 'Brilliant!' he said, rubbing his hands. 'I think I know just the chap too. He's done some wonderful illustrations for poetry books. His name's Nick Sharratt. Let's all meet.'

So Nick and I met in the publishing offices. We were both very shy at first. Nick seemed lovely and very talented but I wasn't quite sure he was wacky enough for Tracy-type illustrations. Then I needed to bend down to get a pen out of my handbag on the floor. I saw Nick's socks peeping out from his trouser hem – astonishingly bright canary yellow socks. I knew everything was going to be fine the moment I saw those amazing socks. In fact it became a running joke between us and I'd buy him ever more zany spotty stripy socks all colours of the rainbow.

We've worked on nearly 40 books together now and it's been just as magical as I'd hoped – but not at all as I'd imagined. I don't stay home all by myself and write my books. I have a beautiful book-lined study but I'm hardly ever in it. Most days I do my writing on trains or in the back of cars, scribbling frantically in my notebook on my way to endless meetings and events. I'm lucky enough to be able to write happily in these rather distracting conditions, though it's sometimes embarrassing if the train is crowded. I write in the first person, and my lovely Italian notebooks look like private journals. If a business man glances from his *Daily Telegraph* to my notebook, God knows what he thinks if he reads my fictional teenage girl musing; *I so fancy the boy I saw on the bus. How will I ever get to go out with him?*

People often ask me why I think my books have been so successful. I think there are several reasons, apart from sheer luck. They look great, with Nick's fantastic covers, and his lively black and white illustrations inside break up the text and make it less forbidding for inexperienced readers. I care passionately about language and play little word games with my readers, though I try to write in an immediate colloquial style through my child narrators. My publishers promote my books with energy and commitment. Nowadays they cosset me wonderfully when I embark on my three-week book tours, putting me up in luxurious hotels and giving me a delightfully cheery driver with a very comfortable car. But obviously you don't get this five-star treatment until your books sell in their millions. I believe the *real* secret of my success is the fact that I started doing many school and library visits early on, talking about my books. In fact I don't think there's a single county in the UK where I haven't given a talk.

I vividly remember my very first talk to a small docile group of Year 7s in a secondary school. I was so nervous I could barely eat breakfast beforehand. I hoped I acted like a reasonably competent sociable adult but inside I was still that shy little girl, terrified of performing. However, I could see the whole point of giving talks to children. It was a wonderful way of introducing them to the delights of reading in general, and to my own books in particular! That was why I was willing to put myself through this torture.

I didn't really know what to talk *about*. It seemed like terrible showing off simply talking about myself and my own work. I ended up reading an extract from Daisy Ashford's *The Young Visitors* to show that children could very occasionally have their work published, and then reading an extract from *Jane Eyre*, which had been my favourite book when I was 12. I realised soon enough that this was completely the wrong approach. The children thought the Daisy Ashford bizarre and *Jane Eyre* boring. They only livened up when I changed tack and talked about what I'd been like when I was young. I started to relate to them properly, and found I could tell them funny stories about myself as an earnest teenager, my experiences as a very junior journalist, and then chat to them about my latest book and how it came to be written.

I learnt how to give a talk – but it was a long time before I actually *enjoyed* doing it. I still got very fussed and anxious about it, and I hated it if I couldn't win every child over. After a while you learn that there will be an occasional kid who will give everyone a hard time. You just have to do your best and try to interest all the others. I slogged round several schools and libraries up and down the country every single week – and I learnt so much. This is where children's authors are so lucky. We can meet so many of our readers and find out what they like – and what they don't.

I only go to individual schools and libraries now as special favours to friends, but I still do many talks at festivals. Once you do something enough times you get so used to it you simply can't find it scary. I never get the slightest bit nervous now, even if I've got an audience of hundreds. I had to perform in the garden of Buckingham Palace in front of the Queen and 3000 children and even that wasn't too worrying. It's just part of my job and I find it great fun.

But I got it right when I was six years old. The *most* magical part of being a writer is staying at home by myself and writing stories all day long.

Jacqueline Wilson has sold millions of books which have been translated into over 30 languages and have won many major awards. She was the Children's Laureate 2005–7. *Jacky Daydream* (Random House 2007) is an account of her own childhood. Her website is www.jacquelinewilson.co.uk.

See also...

- *Getting started*, page 1
- *A word from J.K. Rowling*, page 77
- *How it all began*, page 78
- *Writing for girls*, page 111
- *Writing for different genres*, page 114
- *Writing for teenagers*, page 131
- *Teenage fiction*, page 135

A word from J.K. Rowling

J.K. Rowling shares her first experience of becoming a writing success.

I can remember writing *Harry Potter and the Philosopher's Stone* in a café in Oporto. I was employed as a teacher at the language institute three doors along the road at the time, and this café was a kind of unofficial staffroom. My friend and colleague joined me at my table. When I realised I was no longer alone I hastily shuffled worksheets over my notebook, but not before Paul had seen exactly what I was doing. 'Writing a novel, eh?' he asked wearily, as though he had seen this sort of behaviour in foolish young teachers only too often before. '*Writers' & Artists' Yearbook*, that's what you need,' he said. 'Lists all the publishers and… stuff' he advised before ordering a lager and starting to talk about the previous night's episode of *The Simpsons*.

I had almost no knowledge of the practical aspects of getting published; I knew nobody in the publishing world, I didn't even know anybody who knew anybody. It had never occurred to me that assistance might be available in book form.

Nearly three years later and a long way from Oporto, I had almost finished *Harry Potter and the Philosopher's Stone*. I felt oddly as though I was setting out on a blind date as I took a copy of the *Writers' & Artists' Yearbook* from the shelf in Edinburgh's Central Library. Paul had been right and the *Yearbook* answered my every question, and after I had read and re-read the invaluable advice on preparing a manuscript, and noted the time-lapse between sending said manuscript and trying to get information back from the publisher, I made two lists: one of publishers, the other of agents.

The first agent on my list sent my sample three chapters and synopsis back by return of post. The first two publishers took slightly longer to return them, but the 'no' was just as firm. Oddly, these rejections didn't upset me much. I was braced to be turned down by the entire list, and in any case, these were real rejection letters – even real writers had got them. And then the second agent, who was high on the list purely because I like his name, wrote back with the most magical words I have ever read: 'We would be pleased to read the balance of your manuscript on an exclusive basis…'

J.K. Rowling is the bestselling author of the *Harry Potter* series (Bloomsbury). The first in the series, *Harry Potter and the Philosopher's Stone*, was the winner of the 1997 Nestlé Smarties Gold Prize and *Harry Potter and the Goblet of Fire* (2000) broke all records for the number of books sold on the first day of publication. The final book in the series, *Harry Potter and the Deathly Hallows*, was published in July 2007.

See also...

- *Notes from Jacqueline Wilson*, page 74
- *How it all began*, page 78
- *Spotting talent*, page 83
- *Fiction for 6–9 year-olds*, page 119
- *Writing for teenagers*, page 131
- *Teenage fiction*, page 135
- *It could happen to you*, page 142
- *The amazing picture book story*, page 217

How it all began

Eoin Colfer shares his first experience of becoming a writing success.

I have in my time purchased several copies of the *Writers' & Artists' Yearbook*, yet there is only one copy on my bookshelf. This, I suspect, is a condition common to most authors. When other writers visit my bat-cave – sorry, office – they don't bother asking for a signed first edition of my book, instead they make off with my *Yearbook* secreted up their jumpers. This inevitably happens shortly after I have completed the laborious task of attaching colour-coded paperclips to pages of interest. I know what you're thinking. Colour-coded paperclips. That explains a lot.

My obsession with the *Yearbook* began in the dark era of glitter eye shadow and ozone-puncturing hairdos known as the Eighties. I had recently finished college, and like all males in their twenties, knew all there was to know about the world. The population in general, I decided with humble altruism, deserved the benefit of my wisdom. And the best way to reach my prospective public was through literature.

So I wrote a book. Not content with that, I designed the cover. Multi-tasking even before the phrase was coined. This book qualified as a book because it had many words and quite a few pages. Secure in my sublime self delusion, I got hold of an industrial stapler, bound the whole lot together and crammed a copy into the nearest postbox. One copy would be sufficient, to the country's foremost publishers. I settled back on the family chaise longue and waited for the publisher's helicopter to land in the garden.

Seasons passed and the helicopter never materialised. Not so much as a postcard from the honoured house. Sighing mightily I widened my net, sending copies of my book to several other publishers. I got some replies this time. Would that I had not. Most were civil enough. We regret to inform you, etc … the opening phrase that haunts every writer's dreams. Still, at least they were polite. But a few less generic replies dropped onto my doormat. There was one note in which the handwriting deteriorated in spots, as the editor suffered from sporadic fits of laughter. A pattern was beginning to emerge. Could it be possible that my manuscript was flawed? Was there a chance that my presentation was not all that it could be? Did genius have to be packaged?

Help arrived in the form of an editor's response. 'We regret to inform you …' it began. Nothing new there. I was becoming inured. But there was an addendum pencilled below the type. Get the *Writers' & Artists' Yearbook*. It's worth the investment.

Reluctant as any Irish man in his twenties is to take advice from anyone besides his mother, I decided to act on this particular recommendation. The *Yearbook* paid for itself almost immediately. The mere act of purchasing the fat volume made me feel like a legitimate writer. I left the shop, making certain that my grip did not obscure the book title.

At home, I was amazed to discover that the *Yearbook* was not just a list of publishers. Every possible scrap of information needed by the upcoming or established writer was included (for more details buy the book. And if there are paperclips on this book, it is mine: please return it!) but what I needed to know was detailed under the heading 'Submitting material'. Next time, I vowed. Next time.

Next time turned out to be nearly a decade later. My self esteem had recovered sufficiently to brave the sae trail once more. So I wrote an introductory letter and an interesting summary of the book, and included the first 50 pages – double-spaced.

It worked. Two weeks later I had a publisher. Now I can't put the entire thing down to the *Yearbook*, but it certainly played its part. In public of course, I take all the credit myself. I am a writer after all. But packaging and presentation in my opinion made the difference between desktop and trash, to use a computer analogy.

A few years later my brothers advised me that I needed an agent, as they were running short on beer money. Once again the *Yearbook* was consulted. Not only were the agents listed but they were categorised. These *Yearbook* people were cut from the same cloth as myself. I could almost imagine their desks stacked with coloured paperclips.

My research paid off, and within weeks I was sitting in a top-class hotel treating my new agent to a flute of champagne. Although she insists it was a glass of Guinness in a Dublin pub and she paid.

Since then, I haven't looked back. Things are going well enough for me to be invited to write this Foreword. If you are published and reading this book, hide it away and beware those with baggy jumpers. If you are as yet unpublished, then keep the faith and make sure that all around you can see the title.

Eoin Colfer has written several bestselling children's novels, including the *Artemis Fowl* series. The books have been translated into 43 languages and have won awards including British Children's Book of the Year, WHSmith Children's Book of the Year, Bisto Merit Awards and the South African Book Club Book of the Year. The first *Artemis Fowl* film is currently in production.

See also...

- *Getting started*, page 1
- *Notes from Jacqueline Wilson*, page 74
- *A word from J.K. Rowling*, page 77
- *Spotting talent*, page 83
- *Fiction for 6–9 year-olds*, page 119
- *Writing for teenagers*, page 131
- *Teenage fiction*, page 135
- *The amazing picture book story*, page 217

Notes from a successful children's author and illustrator

Lauren Child describes how *Clarice Bean, That's Me* came to be published and shares her experiences of taking advice from publishers and editors.

My first attempt at writing a children's book was when I was 18 – my friend Bridget and I had an idea. Everything seemed simple – we were going to write a book, get it published and get on with something else. Almost immediately, and by sheer fluke, we had an interested publisher. We were invited along for a 'working lunch' to discuss the story development. The editor made some suggestions for improvement which we were quite happy about – we really had no objection to rewriting; we were happier still with the business lunch and were fuelled by the confidence of youth that life would always be this easy. We did nothing, of course, and the whole thing fell through which, with hindsight, was a relief – I think we would both be squirming now. It was a number of years later before I even thought to write anything else.

Please yourself
The next time I learnt the hard way, by trekking around uninterested publishers with my portfolio – something it would be almost impossible to do now, as no one wants to see unsolicited work. I used any contacts I had, however distant. I forced myself to phone complete strangers to try to get appointments and advice – something I hated doing. When I met with publishers they seemed to have very set views on what a children's book should be. I listened to their advice and always tried to write the book they wanted me to write. But, whenever I went back to them with my work, there was always something missing – I could never write the book they had in mind.

So, unable to interest publishers, no matter how hard I tried to give them what they said they wanted, I forgot about the whole project and got on with other things. One day, having reached a rather low point in my life, and having looked at every possible career path, a friend suggested that I leave my portfolio of designs, drawings and ideas with her so she could show it to her business manager who had created and managed various successful companies. On meeting this woman, I mentioned I had an interest in film and animation and also designing products for children and, although I had no relevant training, she suggested that I try to write a children's book because, hopefully, it would prove I could create characters and invent a world for them. I think that I was just at a point where I was ready to listen – perhaps because she was very successful, perhaps because it made sense, perhaps because she was a complete stranger.

I started to write the odd sentence, then draw a character, then write a bit more... there was no order to it, no plot structure. I wasn't even sure what I was writing, all I knew was that I was interested when I hadn't been before. I think it helped enormously that I wasn't fixated on creating the perfect children's book – it was merely a means to an end, a way to get into something else. I stopped being self-conscious about what I was doing and stopped trying to please everyone else. When I took this book – *Clarice Bean, That's Me* – to publishers, the difference was very obvious – they were all interested! However, no one was willing to take it on – they all thought it was unpublishable and they told me so. But I knew I had written something that had at least got their attention.

Listening to publishers

Nearly every publisher made suggestions of what I should change in order for this book to be published, some of them quite fundamental. I was told to drop the illustrations and simplify the text. I was told that varying fonts and integrating text and pictures was too complicated, that it would confuse young readers. I listened to them all; I considered what they had to say, but I knew they were all wrong – I knew they were wrong because I knew I wouldn't be happy with the end result. Because I had written something which felt right to me, it seemed better not to be published at all than to publish a book that wasn't really mine. After four or so long years, I eventually found a publisher who was willing to take the book on pretty much as it was.

And I think this is one of the most important things to know – how far will you go, how far *should* you go to be published? When it comes to this you have to follow your gut instinct. Despite my experience, I do think it is important to listen to what publishers have to say – it is always wise to listen, but it is not always right to take it on board. In the end, they can give you the benefit of their experience, but they cannot write the book for you, and you cannot write the book for them. As the writer, the book has to come from you. Of course, if more than one or two people pick up on the same thing then it may be worth following that advice, but for me it is never worth making a change when, after much consideration, it still feels wrong.

Know who you are writing for

When it comes to the question of writing for the 6–9 year-old market, I would say there is no formula. I don't write for 6–9 year-olds, I write for myself. My books are for anyone who wants to read them. For me, writing young fiction is less about writing for a particular audience or age group and more about telling a story that interests me. I have never thought 'is this a book for 6–9 year-olds' or 'is this a book for 8–12 year-olds'. I feel the same when it comes to writing picture books; they are there to be enjoyed by both adults *and* children because while the child looks at the pictures it is the adult who usually reads the story.

How does a writer come up with the interesting ideas in the first place? As an adult writing a children's book, is it helpful – even necessary – to have children of your own? My own view is that it is simply irrelevant. First, we have all been children and anyone who wants to write for children must have strong feelings from his or her own childhood to draw upon. But more importantly, good fiction writing is not about imitation – it is about imagination. Just as having children does not mean you have anything to say to them in book form, so not having children is no bar to writing in a manner to which they will respond. Writing for anyone is about having something to say – a point of view. Writing for children is no different. When it comes to writing fiction, I think that any good writer will see children as people first, and as children second. Of course the context of childhood experiences is different from those of adults, but there is no emotion experienced as a child which is not felt equally in adult life.

Where to start

At the more practical level, I do not believe that there are any fixed rules. I know that many writers plot a book out before they start, and I had always been told that I needed to plot my books and understand where they were going if I was to write successfully. But I never begin writing a book knowing how it is going to end. I never normally know how it is going to start either. I generally just begin with a sentence taken at random. For me, it is all about an idea taking hold, and the writing tends to be more about a feeling than anything. *Clarice Bean, Don't Look Now* began as a book about love and ended up being a book more about loss than anything else. I wrote a few sentences about Clarice's inability to sleep and from that the whole mood of the book was determined. I started to write about insomnia and then wondered why Clarice might experience this, which led to thinking about her worries, which in turn led to the idea that she might be feeling very insecure and start questioning things around her. So, in a way, a few sentences shaped the whole plot because they reflected something that I felt personally at the time. I didn't try to force a story that I wasn't interested in writing; instead it became a book about Clarice's anxieties, her inability to explain the world to herself, and some recognition on her part that not only is life something which cannot be controlled, but it's also something which can only be imperfectly understood.

I write a lot of material and read it over and over, until I see what themes are emerging and then I look for a way to hang it all together. Once it has a solid plot, I start to cut. Writing picture books is a very good discipline for writing novels because with just 800 or so words to play with, you have to decide what is important and what isn't: what exactly is this book *about*? Writing picture books makes you much less frightened of editing out the bits that you love. You really can't be indulgent, and have to pare your writing down to the essence of what that story is about. Although of course a novel gives you much more freedom – *Don't Look Now* was 42,000 words – I still consciously try to make sure that every chapter is pushing the story forward and has something to say.

A good editor

That brings me on to another important part – your editor. I really have to trust who I am working with. I rely so much on my editor because of the patchwork way I work. A good editor will let you debate back and forth until you've finally reached a point where you know that you can't make something any better. You do have to trust them because it is so easy to lose your perspective about your own work. You may think it's great and not listen to criticism, but more often than not you will get doubtful and think it's all rubbish, and that's where an editor can keep you believing in your work.

If there's a single piece of advice I could offer for writing fiction, it would be to write from the heart. When I wrote *Clarice Bean, That's Me*, I became passionate about what I was writing and found it exciting. If you're bored when you're writing, you will write a boring book. And no matter how hard you find the early stages, keep going. You just need to write and write until you've written the imitation stuff out of you. It is hard but it is very rewarding too. Writing is one of the best things in the world – a licence to discuss ideas – even if it's just with yourself.

Lauren Child has published 24 books. Her picture books have won many awards, including the Kate Greenaway Medal in 2001 for *I Will Not Ever Never Eat a Tomato* (published 2001); the Smarties Gold Award in 2002 for *That Pesky Rat* (2002); and the Smarties Bronze Award for *Clarice Bean, That's Me!* (1999); *Beware of the Storybook Wolves* (2000); and *What Planet Are You From, Clarice Bean?* (2001). She published her first novel, *Utterly Me, Clarice Bean* in 2002, which was followed by *Clarice Bean Spells Trouble* (2004) and *Clarice Bean, Don't Look Now* (2006). Lauren has illustrated a new edition of Astrid Lindgren's *Pippi Longstocking* and her retelling of *Goldilocks* is upcoming. Three animated TV series of *Charlie & Lola* have been shown on CBBC and on channels around the world. Her website is www.milkmonitor.co.uk.

Spotting talent

Publishers and literary agents are not looking for what *they* like but for what children will like. Barry Cunningham famously accepted the manuscript of the first Harry Potter book which – as everyone knows – turned out to be the first of an international bestselling series. He explains here what he is looking for when he reads a new manuscript.

I'm a fan: I love reading and I love great stories. My background is in sales and marketing, and for many years I travelled with Penguin the length and breadth of the country – on tours with authors like Roald Dahl, to schools with the Puffin Book Club or to lonely writers' festivals.

It was during that time that I learnt the most important part of my trade – how children react to the books they love, the authors that they adore, and how they put up with the material that they are coerced into reading. Reluctant readers indeed!

So what I'm looking for is what *they* want, not what I like or what you think is good. More of this later.

First steps

All publishers get streams of brown envelopes – especially, like divorces, after Christmas or the summer holidays – when writers finally feel something must be done with that story they've been working on.

We read some part of everything we get. But, be warned, not every publisher does. So, ring up and find out what the publisher wants: sample, complete manuscript, or perhaps they won't accept it at all!

For most editors, first on the reading list are the submissions from agents, manuscripts recommended by other authors or by someone whose judgement they trust. So, if you know someone who knows someone – use the contact.

Next, know a little about the list you are submitting to: look at their catalogue or read some of their books. Let publishers know how much you like their publications (we all like those sorts of comments!) and how you think your novel might sit with the rest of their titles.

Then, write a short snappy synopsis – a page will do (I've had some that are as long as half the novel itself!). It should tell the publisher what the book is about, its characters and why they should read it.

Also include a little bit about you, the author. Don't forget that. It can be almost as important as anything else in these days of marketing and personality promotion (no, you don't *have* to be a vicar or an ex-glamour model, but it does give an impetus to read on…).

I worked with a very famous editor in my first job who was talking one day about her regular advice to first-time writers. Her advice began with a simple question – 'Have you thought of starting at Chapter 2?'

Strangely, I find myself repeating this regularly. Often I find the first chapter is tortured and difficult, before the writer relaxes into the flow of the story in Chapter 2. And often things improve if we start straight into the action, and come back and explain later. But more importantly, first novels often fail because the editor doesn't get past a poor opening section. Beginnings are crucial, because I know children won't persevere if the story has a poor start, either.

So what am I looking for?

Back to the heart of things…

There are writers who know a lot about children – they might be teachers or parents – so does this mean they can write more relevantly for young people? There are authors who know nothing about modern children, don't even really like children – does this mean they will never understand what a child wants? There are 'crossover' books that don't appear to be for real children at all. There are books with children in them that aren't children's books. Confused?

To me it's simple. Books that really work for children are written from a child's perspective through an age-appropriate memory of how the author felt and dreamed and wondered. The best children's writers carry that childhood wonder, its worry and concern, or even its fear and disappointment, around with them. They have kept the child within alive – so writing is not a professional task of storytelling for tiny tots but a simple glorious act of recreating the excitement of childhood.

That's part one of what you need. Part two, in my view, is a concentration on your audience. I've worked with adult writers too and there is a difference here. Children's authors are creating for a distinctly different readership – they need to think in a more *humble* way than if their work was for their contemporaries. What I mean is that they have to be mindful of how their work will impact on children. Characters must have convincing voices, descriptions must be good enough for children to visualise, and authors must be aware of things like children's attention span when it comes to detailed explanations.

But perhaps even more important is an awareness of the emotional effect of a story on a child. We must always remember their hunger for hope and a bright tomorrow, the closeness and importance of relationships – how easily a world can be upset by parents, or loss of an animal or a friend – and the way in which action really does speak to children, for fantasy and adventure is part of the process of literally growing an imagination.

(If all this means nothing to you, and writing for children is just another category, then I don't think you should bother. That's not to say all this should operate consciously in the mind of the new writer – but that's what a publisher seeks, and that's what I'm looking for.)

Categories and concepts

Everyone has read about the older children's market, and its lucrative crossover into the kind of children's book that adults buy for themselves. I think this will continue to be a growing phenomenon – but the best books in the field will still be clear in their intent: not looking 'over their shoulder' at adults, but true to themselves and their subjects.

I'm sure fantasy will continue to hold a firm following – but with the best books based around character and not simply wild lands and strange people. And historical fiction is poised for a come back for older children – showing the rich material and heritage we have in our shared everyday culture, as well as the 'big battles' of yore!

At last all kinds of young adult fiction has found a firm market and any number of clear voices: hard edged, romantic, comic, or a wild mixture of all three! Both here and in the United States the 13–17 age group has really started buying for themselves, and this is sure to demand more than just conventional 'problem issues' fare.

But my favourite category is the most neglected – real stories and novels for the 7–9 year-olds. This really was once the classic area of children's books, with the biggest names and the greatest longevity of appeal. Sadly, it has become the haunt of derivative series and boring chapter books. I predict a considerable revival, and it will be a great area for new talent.

Picture books seem to have had a much quieter time lately and are, perhaps, awaiting a revival with some newer attitudes. The success of cartoon novels and graphic story treatments for older readers must also hint at a new market here.

Language and setting
It's often said that, like exams, children's books are getting easier, that the language is getting 'younger' while the plots are getting more sophisticated. I don't think this is true. Certainly, for all markets, dialogue is more important than ever – and less time is taken in description.

Children are used to characters who say what they mean, and whose motivations and subtleties emerge in speech. But largely I think this makes for more interpretation and imagination. Descriptions now concentrate on setting and atmosphere, rather than telling us authoritatively what the hero or heroine feels. All to the good in my view, and something new writers for children should absorb.

Also welcome in contemporary children's books is the freeing up of the adult! These characters are no longer confined to small walk-on parts and 'parental' or 'villainous' roles. Nowadays, adults in children's novels are as well drawn as the children, sometimes as touchingly vulnerable people themselves. But as in life, the most potent and frightening image in any children's book remains the bad or exploitative parent.

International scope
Children's literature is truly one of our most glorious 'hidden exports'. British writers continue to be very successful around the world, particularly in the USA and Europe. It is worth remembering this – while setting is not so important as inspiration, obviously UK-centred plots, regional dialogue and purely domestic issues, if not absolutely necessary, are best avoided. But there is no need either – like a creaky old British film – to introduce 'an American boy' or mid-Atlantic slang to your work to appeal to another audience. This seldom works and is often excruciating!

The marketplace
The market still remains delightfully unpredictable. It is hopeless to look at last year's trends and try to speculate. The sound and timelessly good advice is to find your own voice and, above all, to write from the heart. If you can touch what moved you as a child or still moves the child within you, then there's your 'market appeal'. Whether it's aboard the frigate of your imagination or in the quieter, but equally dangerous seas of the lonely soul, skill and inspiration will win you your readership.

Oh, and finally, don't give up. As I once said to a certain young woman about a boy called Harry...

Barry Cunningham was the editor who originally signed J.K. Rowling to Bloomsbury Children's Books. He now runs his own publishing company, The Chicken House (see page 9), specialising in introducing new children's writers to the UK and USA. Notable recent successes include Cornelia Funke, Rod Gordon, Brian Williams and Sharon Dogar.

See also...
• *A word from J.K. Rowling*, page 77

Writing and the children's book market

Around 10,000 new children's titles are published in the UK every year. Chris Kloet suggests how a potential author can best ensure that their work is published.

The profile of children's books has never been higher, yet it can be difficult for the first-time writer to get published. It is a diverse, overcrowded market, with many thousands of titles currently in print, available both in the UK and from elsewhere via the internet. Children's publishers tend to fill their lists with commissioned books by writers they publish regularly, so they may have little space for the untried writer, even though they seek exceptional new talent. This is a selective, highly competitive, market-led business. Your work will be vying for attention alongside that of tried and tested children's writers, as well as titles from celebrities such as movie stars and pop singers, and the offerings for children from established writers for adults, who seize the opportunity to widen their audience. Since every new book is expected to meet its projected sales target, your writing must demonstrate solid sales potential, as well as strength and originality, if it is to stand a chance of being published.

Is your work right for today's market? Literary tastes and fashions change. Publishers cater to children whose reading is now almost certainly different from that of your own childhood. In the present digital age, few want cosy tales about fairies and bunnies, jolly talking cars or magic teapots. Nor anything remotely imitative. Editors choose *original*, lively material – something witty, innovative and pacey. They look for polished writing with a fresh, contemporary voice that speaks directly and engages today's critical, media-savvy young readers. These 'I want it and I want it now' children are used to multi-tasking across the media. Time poor, they are often easily bored.

Develop a sense of the market so that you can judge the potential for your work. Read widely and critically across the children's book spectrum for an overview, especially noting recent titles. Talk to children's librarians, who are expert in current tastes, and visit children's bookshops, both in the high street and online, and dedicated children's books websites, such as Achuka. As you read, pay attention to the different categories, series, genres and publishers' imprints. This will help you to pinpoint likely publishers. Before submitting your typescript, ensure that your targeted publisher currently publishes in your particular form or genre. Request catalogues from their marketing department; check out their website. Consult the publisher's entry under *Children's book publishers UK and Ireland* (see page 5). Many publishing houses now stipulate 'No unsolicited MSS or synopses'. Don't spend your time and postage sending work to them; choose instead a publisher who accepts unsolicited work.

You might consider approaching a literary agent who knows market trends, publishers' lists and the faces behind them. Most editors regard agents as filters and may prefer submissions from them, knowing that a preliminary critical eye has been cast over them.

Picture books

Books for babies and toddlers are often board books and novelties. Unless you are also a professional illustrator (see *Illustrating for children's books*, page 221) they present few opportunities for a writer. Picture books are aimed at children aged between two and five or six, and are usually 32 pages long, giving 12–14 double-page spreads, and illustrated in colour.

Although a story written for this format should be simple, it must be structured, with a compelling beginning, middle and end. The theme should interest and be appropriate for the age and experience of its audience. As the text is likely to be reread, it should possess a satisfying rhythm (but beware of rhymes). Ideally, it should be fewer than 1000 words (and could be much shorter), must offer scope for illustration and, finally, it needs strong international appeal. Reproducing full-colour artwork is costly and the originating publisher must be confident of achieving co-productions with publishers overseas, to keep unit costs down. It has to be said: it is a tough field.

Submit a picture book text typed either on single-sided A4 sheets, showing page breaks, or as a series of numbered pages, each with its own text. Do not go into details about illustrations, but simply note anything that is not obvious from the text that needs to be included in the pictures.

Younger fiction

This area of publishing may present opportunities for the new writer. It covers stories written for the post-picture book stage, when children are reading their first whole novels. Texts vary in length and complexity, depending on the age and fluency of the reader, but tend to be between 1000 and 6000 words long.

Some publishers continue to bring out titles under the umbrella of various series, each targeted at a particular level of reading experience and competency, although these are now often replaced by individual author series. Categories are: beginning or first readers, developing or newly confident, confident, and fluent readers. Note that these are not the same as reading schemes published for the schools market and do not require such a restricted vocabulary. Stories for the bottom end of the age range are usually short, straight-through narratives illustrated throughout in colour, whereas those for older children are broken down into chapters and may be illustrated in black and white. The table on page 88 lists publishers' requirements for some currently published series. Check that your material is correct in terms of length and interest level when approaching a publisher with a submission for a series.

General fiction

Many novels for children aged 9–12+ are published, not in series, but as 'standalone' titles, each judged on its own merits. The scope for different types of stories is wide – adventure stories, fantasies, historical novels (increasingly popular), science fiction, ghost and horror stories, humour, and stories of everyday life. Generally, their length is 20,000–40,000 words. This is a rough guide and is by no means fixed. For example, J.K. Rowling's *Harry Potter* novels weigh in at between 600–750+ closely printed pages, and publishers now seem more willing to publish longer texts, particularly fantasies, although the market is presently overloaded with hefty trilogies.

Perhaps more than in other areas of juvenile fiction, the individual editor's tastes will play a significant part in the publishing decision, i.e they want authors' work which *they* like. They, and their sales and marketing departments, also need to feel confident of a new writer's ability to go on to write further books for their lists – nobody is keen to invest in an author who is just a one-book wonder.

Publisher	Series name	Length	Age group	Comments
A&C Black	Chameleons	1200 words; 48 pages	5–7	Colour illustrations throughout
	Black Cats	14,000–17,000 words; 96–128 pages	8–12	B&w illustrations throughout
Egmont Books	Green Bananas	500 words; 48 pages	4+	Colour illustrations
	Blue Bananas	1000 words; 48 pages	5+	Colour illustrations
	Red Bananas	2000 words; 48 pages	6+	Colour illustrations
Franklin Watts	Tadpoles	70 words; 24 pages	4–6	Colour illustrations throughout
	Leapfrog	180 words; 32 pages	5–7	Colour illustrations throughout
	Hopscotch	350–400 words; 32 pages	5–8	Colour illustrations throughout
Hodder Children's Books	Bite	35,000+ words	12+	Contemporary fiction
Kingfisher	I Am Reading	1200 words; 48 pages	5–7	Colour illustrations throughout
Orchard Books	Crunchies	1000–1500 words	5–7	B&w line illustrations
	Colour Crunchies	300–1000 words	5–7	Colour illustrations
	Super Crunchies	2500–5000 words	7–9	B&w line illustrations
	Red Apples	15,000–50,000 words	8–12	
	Black Apples	30,000+ words	12+	
Penguin Group	Colour Young Puffin	2500 words; 64 pages	5–7	Colour illustrations
Walker Books	Walker Stories	1800 words; 64 pages	5+	B&w illustrations throughout
	Racing Reads	8000 words; 80–96 pages	7–9	B&w illustrations throughout

When submitting your work it is probably best to send the entire typescript. Although some people advise sending in a synopsis with the first three chapters, a prospective publisher will need to see whether you can sustain a reader's interest to the end of the book.

Teenage fiction

Some of the published output for teenaged readers is published in series but increasingly, publishers are targeting this area of the market with edgy, hard-hitting novels about contemporary teenagers, which they publish as standalone titles. There is also a current vogue for 'young adult' novels that have a crossover appeal to an adult readership. Indeed, recent award-winning titles such as Philip Pullman's *His Dark Materials* sequence, Mark Haddon's *The Curious Incident of the Dog at Night-time* and Markus Zusak's *The Book Thief*, have all been published in both juvenile and adult editions.

Non-fiction

The last few years have seen fundamental and striking changes in the type of information books published for the young. Hitherto the province, by and large, of specialist publishers catering for the educational market, the field has now broadened to encompass an astonishing range of presentations and formats which are attractive to the young reader. Increasingly, children who use the internet to furnish their information needs are wooed into learning about many topics via entertaining and accessible paperback series such as the *Horrible Histories* published by Scholastic, and highly illustrated titles by publishers such as Dorling Kindersley. In writing for this market, it goes without saying that you must research your subject thoroughly and be able to put it across clearly, with an engaging style. Familiarise yourself with the relevant parts of the National Curriculum. Check out the various series and ask the publishers for any guidelines. You will be well advised to check that there is a market for your book before you actually write it, as researching a subject can be both time consuming and costly. Submit a proposal to your targeted publisher, outlining the subject matter and the level of treatment, and your ideas about the audience for your book.

Chris Kloet is Editor-at-Large at Walker Books. She has written and reviewed children's books and has lectured widely on the subject.

See also...
- *The next big thing,* page 90
- *Year in view of children's publishing,* page 94
- *Writing for different genres,* page 114
- *Writing horror for children,* page 124
- *Illustrating for children's books,* page 221
- *Children's literary agents UK and Ireland,* page 192

The next big thing

Children's books have a higher profile than ever before and some authors have reaped huge successes. But anticipating what will be the 'next big thing' is difficult. Becky Stradwick outlines some of the factors to be taken into consideration when attempting to make such a prediction.

There's nothing that quite beats the thrill of opening a book, and as you read the first few sentences, a slow kind of magic steals over you. You turn the pages, slowly at first and then with a growing sense of wonder as you realise you have become completely hooked. Whether it's a young girl hiding in a room she shouldn't be in, an owl fluttering through the window of a house on a suburban drive, or a dead dog lying on a garden lawn, the sensation of plunging headfirst into a new and absorbing universe is the excitement all readers seek. And if you work in the book industry, whether writing, publishing, or selling, there is an added thrill in watching a manuscript, proof or book you love find an audience that falls in love with it too.

But predicting exactly what will create this chemistry for an audience is an inexact science and a huge challenge. And these days the bar seems to have been raised even higher than ever before. I first started working in children's books in 1997, the same year a story about a certain boy wizard first appeared. Little did anyone guess this book would be the catalyst for a major shift that would eventually change the perception of children's books and accelerate the industry to the massive £278 million that it was worth in 2007. It's also had a dramatic effect on the way books are marketed, talked about and sought after. This means, whilst competition is fierce, publishers are constantly looking for the best new talent to emerge and become, literally, the next big story.

Publishing tends to move in cycles. Crazes can be all-consuming, sweep all before them and almost saturate the market. And then it's on to the next thing and certain genres seem to almost disappear off the radar. One good example would be the horror genre. In the early 1990s there was a craze for the *Goosebumps* books by R.L. Stine and the *Point Horror* series (various authors), books that sold hundreds of thousands of copies. But that craze declined in subsequent years and they were no longer a major sales force in UK bookshops. But with the incredible success of Darren Shan and, more recently, the likes of Joseph Delaney and Tom Becker, the genre is thriving, getting bigger and blood thirstier all the time. And now *Goosebumps* are set to make a return, reincarnated and even darker than before.

And then of course there's the re-emergence of the wildly popular action hero category. An incredible number of spy books have been published, but from the leading properties of the *Alex Rider* and *Young Bond* series through to the more 'blonde Bonds', i.e. female spies, even to animal sleuths, sales show no sign of slowing. It makes me wonder what the Secret Seven's grandchildren might be up to nowadays…

And then there are the fairies. There was a time when you couldn't move in bookshops for pink and glittery titles, largely driven by the huge popularity of the *Rainbow Magic* series by Daisy Meadows. There is now a raft of books featuring our fluttering friends and though sales may have passed the initial fervour, you'd have to be mad not to still believe in fairies.

Given the success of these and other high-profile genres, publishers and retailers – as in any business model – are driven to recreate that success. Many authors have now become top brands and each new publication is an event, carefully timed so they don't clash with each other. There are certain 'slots' in the year when you know sales will be dominated by new titles from the likes of Jacqueline Wilson, Anthony Horowitz or Francesca Simon. But equally, with the increased footfall in bookshops and heightened interest in reading generated by those authors, there are opportunities for newer talents to benefit from a growing market and an army of readers hungry for more. Certainly a greater focus than ever is now being given to debut authors, both on publishers' lists and in bookshops across the country, and this can only be good news for the lifeblood of the industry. For that focus to translate into successful sales there can be any number of key factors at work.

From a book buyer's point of view, the first hint that a buzz is building might be word from the publisher that advance manuscripts are being passed excitedly around, or there are tales of early proof copies disappearing like hot cakes from the editor's office. Before this stage there may be an auction for the manuscript, sometimes hotly contested between various publishing houses, a bit like being the hot new band that every A&R man wants to sign. But this does seem to be relatively rare and has only an occasional bearing on the decision of the retailers to stock the book in question.

Once the publishers are firmly behind a book, key reviewers and buyers are sent copies, and in many cases early reactions can be critical. Booksellers, from the smallest independent to the largest chain, need to be persuaded to put a book into shops and hopefully in sufficient quantities for the customer to notice it. And it's not all about the largest chains either – 2007 saw a significant increase in the market share of independent bookshops and they play a crucial role in opinion forming and the hand selling of many authors. With a bewildering array of titles to choose from, customers look for recommendation and guidance to help them navigate the children's department. A bookseller who is convinced enough of a book's merit to recommend it to customers can go from selling one or two copies a week to dozens in one store alone. Once the success of that recommendation is replicated across a number of stores, the difference in sales will soon be considerable.

Production and design values can be crucial too – the look and feel of a book must make it catch a buyer's eye, and given the foils and finishes currently in vogue, there is a definite magpie effect going on in bookshops. Indeed, certain books that have been relatively unsuccessful or deemed not to have fulfilled their true potential are occasionally given a second chance and repackaged to reflect more current trends. For example, an historical book might be given a photographic look rather than an illustrative one, or a quieter retro jacket could be brought bang up to date in a style which reflects the latest Higson or Horowitz. Many teen novels are now designed in such a way to echo their adult equivalents – easily identifiable versions of Jodi Picoult or Andy McNab jackets are a subtler form of persuasion and a way of encouraging aspirational reading.

And then there are the more direct forms of marketing. Large-scale national advertising is of course expensive and therefore unfortunately rarer than authors, publishers and booksellers would all like, and so it's usually reserved for the more established authors. Space in the national press is always at a premium and so review space and news coverage for children's books is limited; at the moment it feels more like a nice surprise or bonus when a book is given major attention. But there are a number of passionate advocates who feel this needs to be addressed and are working to make sure this happens.

A recent example of this would be Channel 4's *Richard & Judy* children's books special which was screened in September 2007 in support of a literacy season of programmes on the same channel. Four different age groups looked at 12 selected titles and they were discussed on prime-time television. All of the authors involved benefited from an impressive uplift in sales and profile and, more importantly, kids' books were placed higher on the media agenda.

Sometimes it's all about timing. *Tunnels* by Roderick Gordon and Brian J. Williams was one of the big success stories of 2007 and is an undeniably cracking read, well-imagined fantasy that instantly transports the reader. But as it was published just before the seventh and final *Harry Potter* novel, journalists were falling over themselves to come up with a replacement to talk about and this was presented as the perfect contender. Publicity was massive, sales soared, the sequel is eagerly awaited and the film rights have been sold.

Sometimes an angle on the author helps generate coverage, if a previous profession proves to be of interest or if there is a particularly intriguing story behind their discovery. *Eragon* by Christopher Paolini was a huge success but much of the initial publicity was fuelled by the story that this was a teenage author, home-schooled by his parents, who had written a huge and complex fantasy novel.

Also important are the local and national book awards, particularly those where the judging panel is made up of children. A prize judged by the target audience is always going to be more direct and honest and therefore be the best indicator of what an audience actually wants (see *Children's book and illustration prizes and awards* on page 364) .

Viral marketing is an increasingly effective selling tool and is becoming ever more sophisticated. For example, a text message campaign focused a large amount of attention on Robert Muchamore's *Cherub* sequence, one of the bestselling series in recent times. Interactive phone or web content is undoubtedly seen as complementary to a book. In some cases auxiliary content can be a crucial selling point and this only looks set to increase in the coming years. Online clubs and societies can form the backbone of a fan base and provide important support for authors. Given how tech savvy this audience is, it's possibly even the best way to approach them.

All of which makes it difficult to judge exactly where the 'next big thing' will come from. As soon as a gap in the market is perceived, it's invariably swiftly filled. In recent years, publishers have focused heavily on fiction aimed at 5–8 year-olds – the classic storytime age – and this end of the market is now incredibly competitive. Also the growing teen market has been given a huge push, particularly with the success of authors like Meg Rosoff, Marcus Zusak and Linzi Glass – all authors who were published with dual edition jackets and sold in adult fiction sections as well. The crossover novel seems to be the Holy Grail for publishers but books that are genuinely suitable for both markets are few and far between.

Recent emerging trends have seen an insatiable appetite for more gothic romance where instead of girl meets boy, girl meets vampire, werewolf or zombie. And there's a new wave of slick, glamorous and slightly edgier stories featuring girls behaving badly at elite boarding schools or echoing the rich and famous WAG lifestyles that dominate the gossip magazines. These have become increasingly successful, proving that high fashion and low scruples are an irresistible cocktail.

But of course it's not all about following trends, otherwise we would all be reading about horrid fairies who go back in time to a magic boarding school where they are taught to spy on orphaned dragons by alien pirates. And nor is it all about marketing and promotion. The most hyped and heralded books can fail inexplicably, no matter how much time and money are spent on them, and even the loudest of publicity campaigns can fail to deliver. At the end of the day, the intended targets are a discerning and critical bunch and, well, you can't kid a kid. It's an arbitrary process: an author can take ten books to become an 'overnight success', or a debut might capture the zeitgeist perfectly and become an instant sensation. But the central ingredients vary rarely; an original voice, engaging characters and a narrative that fires the imagination. These will ensnare readers and ensure that the word-of-mouth is passed on. Sometimes it's the quiet ones that you need to keep an eye on…

Becky Stradwick started working as a children's bookseller in 1997 and worked in a number of Books etc stores before moving to Borders Head Office, where she is currently Head of Books.

See also…
- *Year in view of children's publishing,* page 94
- *Writing for different genres,* page 114
- *Children's books and the US market,* page 158

Year in view of children's publishing

Caroline Horn reviews the changes in the children's publishing industry.

As publishers emerged into a post-*Harry Potter* world at the start of 2008, the scenery was very different from that of the previous decade. Since the first book in the series was published in 1997, there have been major changes in the children's book world with new opportunities for children's fiction, more challenging books being published and a notable increase in publishing for boys.

Children's publishing has also moved closer to the adult business model, with the drive towards bestsellers, classic names and celebrity publishing replacing the 'midlist' publishing of old. Marketing budgets are directed towards fewer, bigger names as authors like Jacqueline Wilson and Anthony Horowitz achieve superstar status in the book world. Then there are the celebrity names: Katie Price (Jordan) and Geri Halliwell are among the latest names to join the list of celebrity authors with a children's book behind them.

However, there are still many changes to come – particularly in the emerging digital environment – and 2008 may be remembered as a year of scene-setting for the next decade of challenges.

The most pressing issue for publishers is the need to find new ways to sell children's books. To date, the *Harry Potter* books have generated high street sales of some £217.6 million (according to Nielsen BookScan) but despite their success, the overall value of children's book sales (excluding *Harry Potter*) has actually declined, from £382 million in 2006 to £367 million in 2007 (figures from Books and the Consumer report by Book Marketing Ltd).

Publishers now rely heavily on a handful of big author names, popular brands and film and TV tie-ins to help them maintain their market share. Scholastic, which publishes Philip Pullman's *His Dark Materials* trilogy, saw its sales rise nearly 40% in 2007 to £15 million, largely on the back of the film *The Golden Compass* (based on Philip Pullman's *Northern Lights*) and sales of the film tie-in books. The Daisy Meadow (*Rainbow Magic*) books contributed £4.6 million to Hachette Livre's £30 million turnover in 2007, while authors Terry Pratchett and Jacqueline Wilson together contributed over £14 million to Random House Children's Books' £23 million turnover (figures provided by Nielsen BookScan).

Despite the difficult market conditions, 2008 still began on a high following the government's announcement that 2008 would be the second National Year of Reading (NYR – see page 380), following the success of the first NYR in 1997. The government invested heavily in advertising NYR and reading has been on the agenda like never before.

A particular focus for NYR is families sharing reading time and publishers must hope that the emphasis on sharing books with younger children will be good news for the picture book and young fiction sectors. While sales of children's fiction (age 8+) have increased beyond anyone's expectations over the last decade, that success has been largely at the expense of picture book, young fiction and non-fiction sales.

Picture books

There are signs of change. Picture books, in particular, have enjoyed significant growth in the last few years after several years of decline. According to BML's Books and the

Consumer survey, sales of picture books have grown from 5.1 million to 7.5 million since 2004. This is partly thanks to demographics and a steadily increasing birth rate, but parents are also being encouraged by schools and the government to make story time a part of every child's day.

In addition, the Bookstart programme, which aims to give free books to very young children, now receives substantial government funding and the programme has been extended from babies and toddlers up to those starting school, through the Booktime project (with additional support from Pearson) – see page 338.

Publishers, though, remain cautious – many have made dramatic cuts in their picture book publishing and while there has been some resurgence in the last year or two, particularly by Walker Books, it remains very difficult for new authors and illustrators to break into this area. There is still a reliance on classic names such as Shirley Hughes, Julia Donaldson and Nick Butterworth, although more recent arrivals including Oliver Jeffers, Emily Gravett and Neal Layton are making their mark.

Newcomers to the illustrated market must be very talented and have broad appeal to international markets, which is making new picture book publishing in the UK very safe compared with European publishing. The Big Picture campaign (www.bigpicture.org.uk), managed by the charity Booktrust, aims to draw attention to picture books and to encourage tomorrow's budding authors and illustrators to make a career in picture books.

Young fiction

The story for young fiction is much more positive. Sparked by the commercial success of the *Rainbow Magic* series (Orchard) and Francesca Simon's *Horrid Henry* books (Orion), publishers have dramatically increased the number of books available to early readers. Boys in particular have benefited from series like *Astrosaurs* (Steve Cole) and *Dinosaur Cove* (Rex Stone).

However, it is children's core fiction for readers aged 8–12 years that continues to thrive. Publishers are still prepared to pay big advances for talented new voices in this sector and retailers are just as keen to support strong newcomers. For the past two or three years, publishers have focused on adventure stories that will appeal to boys but could also be read by girls. The *Percy Jackson* books (Rick Riordan) and *Jimmy Coates* series (Joe Craig) are typical of this genre. Fantasy, too, has maintained its grip on the sector, despite forecasts of its imminent decline for several years now.

Film companies have continued to draw on fiction as inspiration for family blockbusters, from Philip Pullman's *The Golden Compass* to Holly Black and Tony diTerlizzi's *Spiderwick Chronicles* and Cornelia Funke's *Inkheart*. None, though, has quite matched the success of the *Harry Potter* books, although Warner Brothers, the company behind the *Harry Potter* films, believes it has found a replacement *Harry Potter* in Angie Sage's *Septimus Heap* series, to which it bought the film rights last year.

Age guidance on book covers

One other initiative could have a significant impact on children's book sales. After years of discussion and debate, publishers have accepted that consumers need more guidance in selecting and buying children's books. The move follows consumer research showing that many parents and other book buyers want an indication of the reading age on a book, in a similar way to the age guidance given on children's toys and clothes.

The research, carried out at the end of 2006, showed that although many parents are comfortable choosing books for their children, many gift buyers were put off buying books because of their uncertainty over the age-appropriateness of the books they chose. Fiction was the hardest category to buy and the groups that found most difficulty in buying children's books were the light children's book buyers (buying between one and five books a year), non-working adults and low socio-economic groups.

Some 86% of the adult consumers questioned, including parents, grandparents and other gift buyers, thought age ranging was a good idea, with just 8% opposed to it. Another 40% of adults questioned in the research said that they would buy more books if books were age ranged.

Publishers believe that the argument for including an age range on book jackets is conclusive and they began to include age guidance on fiction titles in the summer of 2008. The suggested age ranges of 5+, 7+, 9+, 11+ and 13+ are now printed on the back cover of fiction titles; picture books and non-fiction are expected to follow.

The move, however, remains controversial with many vociferously opposed to age-ranging books, especially librarians, teachers and children's specialist booksellers. They argue that children's reading levels are simply too varied for this kind of classification and also that it will narrow the potential audience for particular titles. The *Alex Rider* titles by Anthony Horowitz, for example, are enjoyed by teenagers as much as by younger readers, but a classification of, say, 9+ could have put off those older fans.

The retail sector that is most likely to benefit from age guidance on book covers is supermarkets, where there are no specialist staff to help consumers with book choices. Supermarkets have also made it clear that they want to sell more books and age guidance on covers could be just what they need to do so.

The major high street book chains have also broadly welcomed the move, seeing it as an opportunity to increase sales among gift buyers such as aunts, uncles and grandparents who are often not familiar with a child's reading abilities.

Ebooks and online communities

The high street chains are facing increasing pressure on their margins as competition from supermarkets and online sales really begins to bite. The landscape they have chosen to fight the battle has been that of discounting. While the value of children's book sales for 2007 declined quite steeply from £382 million to £367 million, the volume of books sold was in fact slightly up in 2007 at 77.7 million compared to 76.7 million in 2006 (figures from BML's Books and the Consumer) as retailers fought for market share by heavily discounting top sellers.

However, there is a greater challenge for all book retailers just around the corner – that of digital downloads. Faced with the disastrous impact that downloads had on the music industry, the book chains and online retailers are taking the digital competition head-on. Borders, Waterstone's and Amazon all started to sell ebook devices this year but only time will tell if each of these devices – the iLiad, the Sony Reader and Amazon's Kindle respectively – will be commercially successful. Or, indeed, if book retailers can successfully take on the digital world in a way that music retailers failed to do.

This is of particular interest to the children's market because young people are generally early adopters of new technologies. The teen market, especially, is likely to embrace digital book downloads.

This fact, alongside the relentless challenge and costs of marketing through the high street retailers, has encouraged publishers to do more to market their books online. They are now as likely to market certain books through games websites for young people as via booksellers, and they are all developing their content ready for digital downloads.

More resources are now being devoted to promoting titles online – although publishers still have some way to go to catch up with other industries. They are developing dedicated websites for popular series and authors across all age ranges, from the *Astrosaurs* series (www.astrosaurs.co.uk) and David Melling's *Goblins* books (www.hiddengoblins.co.uk) for younger readers to Chris Ryan's website (www.chrisryanadventures.co.uk) and the *Young Bond* series website (www.youngbond.com) for older readers.

Publishers are also working hard to meet the demand of the new generation of readers by creating their own online communities such as Penguin's teen website (www.spinebreakers.co.uk), and by supporting independent children's books websites like www.readingzone.com, which aims to build online communities of young readers.

No one is yet quite sure how the digital world is going to change the face of the traditional publishing landscape but 2008 has shown that retailers as well as publishers are aware of the threat and preparing for it. Only time will tell if they are doing enough.

Caroline Horn is children's books editor at the *Bookseller* and editor of children's books website Reading Zone (www.readingzone.com).

See also...

- *Spotting talent*, page 83
- *The next big thing*, page 90
- *Categorising children's books*, page 162

Books for babies

Books for babies can be wonderfully enjoyable for both infant and reader, and can give the child a head start in learning to learn. Wendy Cooling looks at what makes a successful book for a baby.

In recent years reading has become big news with the phenomenal success of the *Harry Potter* series, *His Dark Materials*, *Lord of the Rings* and such memorable events as World Book Day and the Big Read. Children's books are now being read by adults and people outside the book business have stopped asking in sympathetic voices: 'Do you ever do anything with adult books?'. Within this context the baby book market has been an area of real growth.

For babies

Publishers are not the kinds of people who miss opportunities and they have responded with great creativity to this growing market. For five years the Sainsbury's Baby Book Award (now the Booktrust Early Years Awards; see page 365) has celebrated the rich achievements of this publishing and looked at what it is that makes a good book for a baby. The first winner was Helen Oxenbury's *Tickle, Tickle* (Walker Books); it has been hugely successful and demonstrates many of the ingredients that add up to a really good book for a baby. The text is a joy to read aloud – very necessary as anyone with children will know that favourite books must be read again, and again, and again. Children don't understand all the words but they respond to the sound of the voice of someone who loves them and to the sound of the words. 'Splish, splash' and 'Tickle, tickle' resonate in the head because they sound good, they're great words to say and help the very youngest children to develop an ear for language that will later take them into reading. The invitation to adult and child to join in with the 'Tickle, tickle' is a winner too as the shared reading experience is always better if there's an element of fun and interaction. The illustrations are a delight as babies rule in this book; they fill every page as they squelch in the mud, splash in the bath and take readers through the pages to bedtime. Helen Oxenbury draws wonderful babies, both black and white, yet children just starting to talk will point to every one of them saying, 'Me, me, me, me.' So this is a book, a tough board book, for a baby to listen to, look at, play with and enjoy in the first two years of life. And, for those parents who worry excessively about learning, children who've enjoyed this book will find that they understand such things as alliteration and onomatopoeia when they come to them at school!

Even before *Tickle, Tickle* babies needed books made from cloth, books for the bath and books with no words at all. Helen Oxenbury's wordless books, first published in 1981, are still the best as her pictures are perfectly observed yet deceivingly simple. *Dressing* (Walker Books) is a good example as it really encourages the adult to talk as each page reveals a clear picture of a toddler progressing with the very complicated business of getting dressed. Many others have tried the wordless book but to do it well is no easy task. My favourite bath book is a small duck-shaped book *My First Duck* (published long ago by Blackie and now sadly out of print). It fits into a baby's hand and feels squidgy and wonderful when wet; it's a great first book as it tells a simple story in clear words and pictures. With a book like this babies learn to love books before they have any real idea about what books and stories – and ducks – are. They just know that the experience is fun and the voice of mum or dad is lovely and they want more of it!

Cloth books too are quite a creative challenge. A good one is *Farm* (Baby Campbell), a stuffed cloth book that crackles and crinkles as it's touched and uses black and white alongside just a little red – colours good for the very young child to pick out.

For innovation it's hard to beat another Baby Book Award winner, *Baby Faces* (Baby Campbell). This is a small board book with round pages joined by a string on which there is also a rattle. You can't move this book, or even turn a page without it making a noise – great, for shared reading with tiny children is often not quiet time! The title of this book describes it accurately as each round page reveals a baby's face and a minimal text as babies say 'hello', demonstrate moods and say 'goodbye'. This time the illustrations are black and white photographs, by Sandra Lousada, and they really do appeal to babies. The publisher has put lots of thought into this, picked up on the research that tells us that babies can focus on black and white long before they can pick out colours, and produced a superb first book for any baby. Baby Campbell also gave us another winning innovation – the buggy buddies – a series of tiny board books that can be attached to a buggy, cot or high chair and so always be accessible to the baby. These books look good and are very close to being toys but with them babies and toddlers learn how books work, learn to turn the pages and to look at the pictures even when no one has time to read to them.

Nursery rhymes

Nursery rhymes, traditional songs and action rhymes are great for all preschool children but there are never enough good, small collections for the very young. Some rhymes are quite violent but many are ideal to start with – hopefully they remind adults of the rhymes they listened to when they were young, because of course talking and singing to children is just as good as reading to them. Too often, nursery rhyme books are packed so full of words and pictures that they're too much for the early years, although children will of course love all the detail on the page as they get older. *Head, Shoulders, Knees and Toes*, illustrated by Annie Kubler (Child's Play), another prize-winner, is a good example for the youngest of children. It is quite a large board book and Annie Kubler's babies fill every page as they touch their head, shoulders, and laugh and giggle as they do it! This is a book that absolutely demands participation and is totally focused on the baby and on fun!

For a more sophisticated edition of a well-known rhyme there's *Twinkle, Twinkle!* (Templar). 'Twinkle, twinkle little star' is told on uncluttered backgrounds with star-shaped cut-outs that are perfect for little fingers to feel and explore. This is a tough and stylish board book that invites talk about shapes as it introduces a traditional poem – it's part of the excellent amazing baby series.

For a big nursery rhyme book it's hard to beat Sam Childs' *The Rainbow Book of Nursery Rhymes* (Hutchinson), for its generous page design, clear and warm pictures and wide range of rhymes – this is a book to last, a book for the bookshelf so it can be dipped into again and again well up to starting school. There is, however, no doubt that babies under one year old prefer the small book that they can hold themselves and keep in the toy box.

For toddlers

As babies grow into toddlers and develop better coordination there's nothing they like more than the lift-the-flap book – unless it's the touch-and-feel book! A newish one for really young children is Debi Gliori's *Where, oh where, is Baby Bear?* (Orchard Books), offering a good introduction to her positive dad character, Mr Bear. Mr Bear is searching for Baby Bear and there's a flap to be lifted on every page until Baby Bear is discovered on the last page – and in the most obvious place. This is great for under one year-olds, with its delicious pictures and good rhyming text that children will try and gurgle along with before they start to talk. There are several bigger board books featuring Mr Bear for babies to move on to.

It's probably not necessary to mention two long-time winning lift-the-flap titles but I must. Eric Hill's *Where's Spot?* (Puffin) shows exactly what it takes to make a lasting baby book and so does *Dear Zoo* by Rod Campbell (Macmillan and Puffin) These books are worth examining by all would-be authors and illustrators of books for babies. What is it that makes children want to look and listen again and again once they know exactly where Spot is, and what will make the perfect pet?

Young children love to find characters they can read more and more about. As well as Spot and Mr Bear, current stars are Lucy Cousins' Maisy (Walker), Mick Inkpen's Kipper (Hodder), David McKee's Elmer (Andersen) and Tony Ross' Little Princess (Andersen). These characters all appear in board books as well as picture books and will still be enjoyed as children start school. *Weather*, a Little Princess board book, is one of the most delightful non-fiction books ever produced for babies; children who know her will happily learn with her many of the important things of life. All the characters mentioned are drawn with charm and love; all are very original and have the capacity to become friends. Many characters lack these qualities and never get beyond the third book.

What makes a classic picture book?

Babies who experience these exciting early books – and there are many more I could have mentioned – will soon be taking off into wonderful classic picture books such as *Each Peach Pear Plum* by Janet and Allan Ahlberg, *Where the Wild Things Are* by Maurice Sendak, *We're Going on a Bear Hunt* by Michael Rosen and Helen Oxenbury, and Eric Carle's *The Very Hungry Caterpillar*. If you're contemplating a career as an author and/or illustrator of picture books, look at these and at other great picture books carefully for there's a lot to learn – not least that every single word counts in a book for the very young.

What doesn't make a good picture book? The perfect picture book that has been reduced to board book format (why do publishers do it?) simply doesn't work – picture books are more sophisticated than that. Texts that lack rhythm and so really can't be read aloud should not be used. Crowded pages packed with the sort of detail that will intrigue a six year-old are obviously inappropriate for babies. Illustration that lacks quality and offers no interest to the child – and certainly none to the adult – should be abandoned.

So what *does* make a good picture book? Let's have great language packed with fine-sounding words that children will enjoy listening to. Let's have rhythm and rhyme that makes the reader want to turn the page and look/read on. Let's remember that the books are for the babies – it helps if adults enjoy them too but the baby must be at the heart of it. Let's value books for babies and celebrate them – they take children into a love of books and the start of a life as readers, and what could be more important? The right books can be nothing but good for babies, parents, carers, authors, illustrators and publishers – they make commercial and social sense.

About Bookstart

We've always known that an enormous amount of learning takes place in the preschool years and that reading books to babies can do nothing but good. Yet it took the Bookstart research to really prove to us all that sharing books with children from a very early age can give them a positive advantage when they start school and can change family attitudes to books and book-buying. Bookstart was piloted by Booktrust in Birmingham in 1992 and aimed simply to give books to families when they attended the 7–9 month health check at their Health Centre, and to invite them to join the local public library.

Professor Barrie Wade and Doctor Maggie Moore of Birmingham University evaluated the project and continue to follow the progress of the first babies involved with Bookstart. When they started school this group of children were way ahead of the control group in all literacy-based tests and, rather unexpectedly, in all the numeracy tests. The children who had been read to at home were really ready for school and were able to start with confidence. They knew about stories, about rhyme and rhythm, and about shapes and numbers and most importantly, they knew that books could give great pleasure and that sharing could be fun – their learning from this early book experience was accidental, but very important learning.

Bookstart became established and with government support grew into a nationwide project now giving three packs of books and information about reading to preschool children. Not all Bookstart parents have enrolled their babies at the library but many more than ever before have, and many are buying books whether it be in bookshops, by mail order or at car boot sales, which has to be good for books and for babies.

Wendy Cooling is a highly respected children's book consultant and reviewer, and winner of the 2006 Eleanor Farjeon Award. She taught English in Inner London comprehensives for many years before becoming head of the Children's Book Foundation (now Booktrust) where she initiated the Bookstart project. She is a regular guest on book-related radio and television programmes, and is the compiler of several children's fiction and poetry anthologies.

See also...
- *Writing and illustrating picture books*, page 213
- *Booktrust*, page 338

Writing books to read aloud

Bestselling author Anne Fine looks at why and how books are read aloud to children.

The first thing to say about writing books to read aloud is that they should be as much of a pleasure to read alone silently as any other story. Indeed, at first it's difficult to see where any differences might lie. Certainly when it comes to stories for the very young we tend to have a picture in our heads of the exhausted parent inviting the child to 'clean your teeth, hop into bed, and I'll read you a story'. And since all days are long for a parent, nobody wants their offspring to be worked into a frenzy all over again. So, in the classic bedtime stories for the younger child, there's very often a softer humour and a gentler tone, and a satisfactory and fulfilling ending.

And for the older child, there often isn't.

So, same old story really. No rules (or having to face the fact that rules appear to be there only for some other writer to irritate you intensely by making a fortune breaking them). But there are always the basic guidelines.

Keep things as simple as they can be for your particular story. With picture books you can of course assume that the child is propped up beside the reader, sharing each illustration as it comes along. But by the time the child is six, maybe they would prefer to snuggle down and shut their eyes to listen. So do you really have to take half a dozen sentences to describe the rigging, and the number and nature of the sails, and exactly how the ship was armed? Couldn't you just refer to it as 'the most magnificent galleon that ever sailed the seas' and leave it at that? After all, if those cannon ever come to be fired, we'll hear about it later.

Listeners are easily distracted. One minute they're all ears; the next, they're actually more interested in tracking the progress of a fly across the ceiling. Of course they're not going to admit they've lost the thread of the story, in case the parent snatches the opportunity to suggest they're too tired to listen and makes for the door, or the teacher decides it's time to move on to the workbooks. But their attention does stray. So it is best to try (as ever) to order your tale so you can start at the beginning and move on in sequence, steering clear of flashbacks.

On this matter of keeping things simple, does it sound mad to say that plots can be overrated? And never more so than in books designed to be read aloud to the young. In my own very short chapter book, *It Moved!*, Lily takes a stone in for Show and Tell and claims it sometimes moves, and we just get to see who in the class believes her and who doesn't, and how they all react over a day of watching it. In the *Stories of Jamie and Angus*, Jamie is an amiable child of about four in a perfectly normal household. His favourite soft toy is a little Aberdeen Angus bull. In the first story, Angus ends up in the washing machine when he's supposed to be 'dry clean only'. In another, the pair sort out the books in their bedroom according to their own rather strange shelving preferences. In yet another, they do little more than draw 'angry eggs'. The stories almost couldn't be more plain and domestic, and yet we still run through joy and misery, jealousy, anxiety, distress, fear, empathy, generosity, self-sacrifice, fury, resentment – the entire mercurial gamut of pre-school emotions. So do be confident that, especially for the very young, a tremendous amount can be forged from what seems, at first sight, not very much at all. With writing – just as with practically everything else in life – it's not what you do but the way that you do it.

Children, like adults, have to *care* about what's being read. We adults tend to ask the 'Can I be *bothered* with these people?' question before returning a book, half-read, to the library. It's a test even harder to pass when you're writing for young ones. Remember Robert Browning:

If you want your songs to last
  Base them on the human heart

because children love to identify with someone or something in the story – it doesn't really matter what. It could be another child, or a puppy, or even a lost pebble. But they do have to care. So perhaps it's best to make sure that, all the way through, your listener knows what your character (or puppy, or pebble) is feeling. And make sure that these are thoughts and emotions they will recognise. A child of six isn't 'disappointed that the weather is unpleasant'. It's all far more immediate. He feels the tears pricking because his socks are wet and his woolly hat is itching and his coat's too tight under his armpits. Ever heard them moan?

Joan Aiken once remarked that anyone who writes for the young 'should, ideally, be a dedicated semi-lunatic'. But you can go too far. The problem is one of differing – and shifting – levels of sophistication. What makes one child hoot with laughter will cause another to sneer, and there is in any case an entirely undefinable line between cashing in on a child's acceptance of the unlikely or the magical, and offering them something they think of as simply being 'stupid'. You might, for example, get away with the idea that the horse the child rescued from its cruel owner is being secretly kept in the garage, only to find your young readers baulking at the suggestion that Mum could walk in to fetch a screwdriver and not even notice it.

Avoid being arch. Of course there are differing levels at which many shared books can be read. The older reader often gets a sly chuckle out of things that sail right over the head of somebody smaller. But the joke does usually have to be at least potentially inclusive, so that, the tenth time around, out comes the thumb, down comes the chubby hand to stop you turning the page, and out comes the question: 'Daddy was just teasing them, really, wasn't he?' 'Mum *really* wanted to get back to reading the paper, didn't she?' In the be-nighted language of the National Curriculum, the child's already 'drawing inferences from text' (or, as we used to call it back in the good old days, 'reading').

Does it help to read your work aloud to children to see how it goes down? Not really, no. For one thing most children are notoriously polite and gentle with people they love, or strangers who come into class. And the sheer joy of having their opinions canvassed can send them haywire. One says, 'I liked this bit!' You beam, and all the other hands shoot up. 'I liked that bit!' 'And I liked that bit!' Everyone wants to have a go at the pleasure of shouting out to the visitor.

So trust your own judgement. You are the writer, after all. Try reading it aloud to an imaginary son or daughter or class. You'll soon notice which bits you're rushing through because they're tiresome, and which of the sentences you're tripping over because they're too clumsy or long. You'll realise that, yes, you *can* put that rather ambitious word into a story for four year-olds because the very context and the way in which it will be read out will make its meaning transparent.

Are there subjects best avoided in books to be shared between adults and children? Again, it's hard to say. Some parents will read anything the child demands. Others, like teachers, will beach up on things like 'pottymouth' poetry ('Well, *you* just said bogey! And you just said poo *twice*!'). Or books that appear to encourage the child to relish – or, worse, be amused by – cruelty and the infliction of pain. I watched as at least 30 parents with small children trooped out of a book fair when one enthusiastic author read out a passage from one of his history books about red hot pokers being driven up people's bottoms. (I wondered, frankly, why the others stayed.) He may justifiably argue that he's sold hundreds of thousands of copies, but I would guess that few of them have been read out aloud by squeamish parents to imaginative children before the lights go out. So use your sense.

What about *how* a book is read aloud? Should that make a difference to how you write it? I don't see how it can. After all, some readers treat the words in the old- fashioned way, and simply speak them with intelligence and inflections sympathetic to the meaning. They read, in short, as if it were a *book*. Others go half-mad, acting out every sentence, doing all the voices in different accents, shouting the yells and whispering the quiet bits. They treat the pages in front of them pretty well as a script for a stage performance. Like every other author whose work has been professionally recorded, I've shuddered through one actor's butchering of my work with his frantic showing off, and also been startled to find tears pricking as another has used her skills to mine a poignancy I had forgotten about or never even realised was there. It's their own voice that most writers hear in their head as they put down the words, so go along with that.

And that's the root of all writing, when it comes down to it. Your own voice. Children are strange. Ralph Waldo Emerson defined them as 'curly dimpled lunatics'. They assume that they're immortal. (Why else do adults have to step in so smartly and often, simply to keep them alive?) And children are at one with eternity. (When did you last see a nine year-old glance at a clock and say, 'My God! It's three already! And I've got nothing done!') Their lives may change immeasurably. See how the language of their stories has moved so seamlessly over the centuries from tumbledown cottages in dark forests, through secret gardens and kind governesses, to the babysitter and the stepbrother. But in their essential nature – however individual and various those natures may be – children have barely changed at all.

So the successful children's authors will always be those who can best make their work chime in with the child's capacity to understand and enjoy it. And since, like Walt Whitman, all children 'contain multitudes', that gives the writer enormous scope to get it very, very wrong or very, very right.

Anne Fine is one of the best known and most popular writers for children of all ages and was Children's Laureate 2001–3. She has twice won both the Carnegie Medal and the Whitbread Children's Book of the Year Award and at the Galaxy British Book Awards has twice been voted Children's Author of the Year. She has also won the *Guardian* Children's Fiction Prize and dozens of other awards in the UK and abroad. Her work is translated into over 40 languages. Anne also writes for adults. Her website is www.annefine.co.uk.

Writing for boys

Everyone knows that boys and girls develop differently, and their reading preferences are similarly as diverse. Russell Ash writes about non-fiction and explains what boys like to read.

Reluctant readers?

A few years ago my annual *Top 10 of Everything* (Hamlyn) was chosen by the American Library Association (ALA) as a 'Book for Reluctant Young Adult Readers'. I admit I initially felt slightly miffed. Then I realised it was something of an accolade: getting someone who didn't generally read books to read one is something of an achievement. Another of my books, the US edition of *Whitaker's World of Facts* (A&C Black), was added to the list in 2007.

As well as my books, the ALA's recent non-fiction picks for reluctant readers have included subjects of which the following is a random selection: basketball, film plots, biographies of rap and pop stars, manga comics, volcanoes, natural disasters, *Star Wars*, vampires, tattoos, young people's rights, Spider-Man and other superheroes, aliens, monsters, robots, James Bond, the artist M.C. Escher, phobias, skeletons, the *Titanic*, motorcycles and racing cars. Among the 2008 nominations is a book aptly titled *For Boys Only*.

Note the common thread? Predominantly, though not exclusively, these represent 'boys' interests'. And since American culture is closer to our own than many would like to think, the interests of British boys would not diverge much. Nor are the reluctant readers' subjects likely to be that different from those of the enthusiastic readers: the latter just read more and their tastes may be somewhat broader.

Although my books are not deliberately targeted at boys (nor even only at children), they constitute the majority of readers because they fulfil several criteria of 'things boys like', including lists, amazing facts, records and trivia. As both a male author of non-fiction books and the father of two teenaged boys, I have a sense of what we/they appreciate – though I stress at the outset that these views are my own and are inevitably generalisations: there are plenty of 'boy' subjects that girls like too, and *vice versa*. Also, many comments that relate to books are also relevant to magazine articles.

A century of non-fiction for boys

We have just celebrated the centenary of the publication of one of the bestselling non-fiction boys' books of all time, Robert Baden Powell's *Scouting for Boys* (1908). It was written at a time when, firstly, its mildly double-entendre title was not even considered, and, secondly, there was a very clear distinction between boys' and girls' interests, and hence their books.

In my own pre-computer youth, boys' fiction was often set in public schools or featured militaristic heroes such as Biggles, pirates and cowboys, while boys' non-fiction similarly reflected the actual or imagined interests of boys – transport, warfare, science, exploration and endeavour and so on. Boys' pursuits were firmly acknowledged as totally different from those of their female peers: we shot airguns, built things guided by books with titles like *Hundreds of Things a Boy Can Make* or played with Meccano. Girls probably had other obsessions – dolls? ponies? ballet? – we never discovered, since we were too busy devoting incalculable boy-hours to constructing unfeasibly huge gantry cranes.

Ward Lock's endless series of Wonder Books often included '...for Girls and Boys' in their titles, but their subjects (*Railways, Aircraft* – even the *Wonder Book of Wonders*) belied the claim. By 1960, over five million copies of them had been sold. Yet despite such numbers, juvenile non-fiction remained the poor relative of 'proper' books – novels. A US survey of books that had sold more than a million copies up to 1975 could muster only a handful of children's non-fiction bestsellers, including an atlas, a dictionary, a cookbook and, perhaps surprisingly, a sex manual for teenagers published in 1950 – although all of them had, astonishingly, outsold *Mary Poppins* and *Winnie-the-Pooh*.

From the 1970s onwards, in both juvenile fiction and non-fiction, various initiatives were launched to overcome gender stereotyping, but it really didn't work, and since the 1990s, the focus in schools at least has shifted from this issue to the problem of underachieving boys, which is today a worldwide phenomenon, irrespective of national variations in school systems.

It's different for boys

'Boys often prefer non-fiction; illustrated books; and "fun facts" material.'
(*Boys into Books* 2007)

In 2007 the School Library Association and Department for Education and Skills published *Riveting Reads: Boys into Books*. This report (available for download from www.sla.org.uk/boys-into-books) identifies 167 books that appeal to boys aged 11–14, from which state school libraries could select any 20 free of charge. Only 17 of the total are non-fiction titles, with my *Top 10 of Everything* heading the list of books of fascinating facts (one of the advantages of having a surname that begins with 'A'!). The themes presented in the other books encompass unusual phenomena and oddities, science, animals, nutrition, machines, things to know and things to do and lists of unusual facts and trivia. If there is a common thread to this disparate group, it is the enthusiastic voice of the author – someone who can entertain and inform his or her readership and carry them along with them, but without appearing to lecture. Although targeted at teachers and school librarians, the report contains a wealth of information that any would-be children's author will find useful.

A survey of reading habits generally by the National Literacy Trust showed that among children in early years education, one girl in five said she would rather read than watch television or use computers, but fewer than one boy in ten expressed this preference. Some 63% of boys and 82% of girls liked reading at home, but the boys' stronger preference for non-fiction revealed itself. When provided with a list of genres from which to select, 28% of boys chose non-fiction as one of their top three genres, but only 13% of girls did so.

Children's non-fiction author John Malam put it succinctly: 'Non-fiction is definitely a "boy thing" more than a "girl thing". In the past I've been commissioned to write specifically for boys on subjects that should appeal to them (cars, planes, trucks, football, etc). In some cases the books were high-low readers, targeted at boys with high ages but low reading abilities, where the choice of pictures seems to be as critical as the choice of facts (pictures being the hook to lure them in to reading captions, then the main text).'

Research by the Exeter Extending Literacy Project (EXEL) showed that boys were more likely than girls to be reading non-fiction books (a ratio of 56.6% boys to 43.3% girls), but the gender difference was far greater among those choosing information books as their favourite category (61.9% to 38.0%).

All the evidence shows that girls develop differently from boys. In her *Differently Literate: Boys, Girls and the Schooling of Literacy* (RoutledgeFalmer 1997), Elaine Millard explains: 'The largest contrast is between boys' interest in action and adventure, and girls' preference for emotion and relationships.' Girls' reading skills are often superior to those of boys, they enjoy reading fiction more, socialise and discuss their feelings about the books more readily, whereas boys want to interact with the world and expend their surplus energy

Popular non-fiction themes for boys

Adventure – thrilling true-life stories of exploration and survival against the odds

Biographies – the lives of heroes and individuals whose achievements boys respect

Cars, trucks, and big machines

Computer games-based books

Cooking – chefs such as Jamie Oliver and Gordon Ramsay have made cooking 'cool' for boys

Crime and criminals – general villainy (pirates and other free spirits are as popular in books as on the screen, especially since the huge success of the *Pirates of the Caribbean* trilogy; Anna Nilsen's *Pirates* (Little Hare) was the second most-borrowed book in 2005/6 and still seventh in 2006/7) and the work of the police and detectives

Fact books – generally, and especially books of lists and statistics, are perennially popular; from such almost exclusively male activities as memorising cricket scores to train-spotting, boys in particular have long been fascinated by numbers and rankings, so information books like *Guinness World Records*, my own books and those that compare and contrast things are of special appeal, while such books have the advantage of selling into the 'crossover market' (children and adults), some even attracting a good proportion of girl readers. *Blue Peter* offers an annual award for the 'Best Book with Facts' – the latest shortlist included the Science Museum's graphically titled *Why is Snot Green?*, *The Worst Children's Jobs in History* and *A Little Guide to Wild Flowers*

Fitness – despite alarmist press reports about levels of childhood obesity, many boys are concerned with achieving the levels of fitness required to compete in their favourite sports

History – provided it is presented in an amusing and entertaining style, popular history is an exceptionally strong genre, with Ancient Egypt, Rome, the Middle Ages and World War II among the most notable periods. Almost deserving of a case study of its own, Public Lending Right (PLR) data indicate that history titles are the most-borrowed children's non-fiction in public libraries, but this should be qualified by noting that at the last count (2006/7) Terry Deary occupied the No 1 place with *The Woeful Second World War*, plus ten of the top 20 places! He describes his enormously popular style as, 'Look, kids, I am not an expert – but you'll never guess what I discovered about these people!' – a far cry from the 'I'm the expert, so listen to me...' approach of more traditional school history textbooks. Deary has his imitators, but he would be a hard act for any would-be writer to follow unless they come up with an approach as refreshingly original as the one he has created

Hobbies – as with their choice of magazines and comics, at age 11–16 some 34% of boys compared with 15.38% of girls choose books because they relate to their hobby

Humour – boys respond well to humour and (especially sick) joke books

Magic tricks – a long-standing and ever-popular genre among boys

Military – warfare, derring-do, chivalry, weapons, the work of the SAS, and so on. Three books specifically on the Second World War appear in the PLR top 20

Music – especially guitars, bands and music technology for the iPod generation

Mysteries – from unsolved crime to the occult fringe (aliens, ghosts, the Bermuda Triangle, etc)

Nature – boys are notably fond of killer creatures, sharks, dinosaurs and creepy-crawlies

Science – including inventions, technology, how things work technically and computers; the Royal Society Prizes for Science Books has a junior award (see page 370) – the 2008 winner was *The Big Book of Science Things to Make and Do* by Rebecca Gilpin and Leonie Pratt (Usborne)

Sport – football and 'cool' sports such as basketball, extreme sports (surfing, skateboarding, mountain biking, etc) and martial arts have a captive boy audience: a study showed that 46.55% of boys aged 11–16 like to read about sport, compared with only 6.15% of girls!

through sport and other activities. They are much less inclined to 'curl up with a book' – but they can surprise: one of my sons didn't read a book for months, then suddenly became absorbed in Antony Beevor's 500-page account of the Siege of Stalingrad.

Boys, in the words of non-fiction author Anna Claybourne, '...don't like to be fobbed off, they want the real thing... boys at schools I visit are the ones who say (for example, of a picture in a book), "Is that a *real* operation, is that a *real live* person cut open... cool". Boys don't just like non-fiction, they like genuine reality and of course that's where things like oversensitive US restrictions can be really depressing – when I'm told not to show an arrow sticking through a soldier's neck, or elephant seals tearing each other apart, or photos of shark-inflicted wounds, for fear of being frightening or distressing, I always think "boring for the boys"! I know some girls (and probably some boys) may find such pictures distressing, but I also think that's often a cultural affectation, whereby girls demonstrate their femininity by reacting with stage horror to things like that, when in fact they are interested too – so I think it's important to keep these things in non-fiction books.'

This concern for 'reality' extends into other attributes that are typically male and are often considered in non-fiction. As exemplified by 'gross-out' films and television shows, boys like yuckiness – a well-known series of books often featured a minuscule person sitting on a toilet, posing a *Where's Wally?*-type challenge to its (mainly male) readers. Such elements may actually be a plus or a minus: with children, the ultimate reader is often not the purchaser, since books are bought by parents and other relatives or by teachers and librarians who may find offensive the very thing boys consider 'cool'.

Boys love the 'wow!' factor – the discovery of some remarkable fact they can quote as a sort of one-upmanship. The quoting of such facts and statistics, telling jokes, reciting comic catch-phrases and exchanging stickers for sticker books reinforces the bonds among many boys: it is a shared activity that forms part of their social development, with non-fiction books a source and component of the whole equation.

Danger zone

When I was a boy, we made fireworks and explosives, went camping in woods armed with air rifles, trapped animals, took birds' eggs and chloroformed butterflies. Since most of these pursuits are now illegal, I have not encouraged my own sons to do them, but there is a clear desire among boys in particular for a less prescriptive world, in part the nostalgia of their parents, in part an envious 'why can't we do what you did?' from the young people themselves as an escape from an environment in which they are often overprotected – taken to school by car, playing computer-based games, watching endless television – while forbidden from activities that may be deemed dangerous. *The Dangerous Book for Boys* by Conn and Hal Iggulden (HarperCollins 2006, www.dangerousbookforboys.com) brilliantly identified a yearning for a perceived 'golden age' of edgy activities. Voted Book of the Year in 2007, its sales have topped half a million copies in the UK. Its success has inevitably started a bandwagon rolling, with several other 'us too' publishers clambering aboard. Whether this boy's adventure genre is a flash in the pan or a new and exciting area for children's non-fiction authors to enter remains to be seen.

Facts about non-fiction

Illustrated non-fiction has a see-at-a-glance advantage over fiction in that the child can tell instantly whether this is a book that appeals, whereas they might get pages into a novel before they find they don't like it. A clear subject focus also has an obvious advantage – if a boy is interested in trucks, he will respond well to a book that is targeted at this specific interest (and being aware of his enthusiasm will make it easier to buy a book for him).

Non-fiction has the advantage that it can be read non-lineally – readers can dip in and select what they read in portions to suit their reading ability. While fiction may be read aloud to younger children, many are left to their own devices with an integrated text and picture information book – although the opportunities for questions and discussion about the content are actually often greater with non-fiction subjects. We should emphasise to children of both sexes that non-fiction is an important means of obtaining information, that the internet is not the only source, and that looking up and checking facts in books are skills worth acquiring.

A third of boys in the UK say they never read for enjoyment. When they do read they tend to go for magazines and comics rather than books. However, neither should be discounted as 'unsuitable' since they may be the stepping stones to books. We must also face up to the fact that not all children are going to become avid readers: all we can do is provide the tools and encourage them. Some parents, teachers and librarians still retain the prejudice that non-fiction books are not 'proper' books, and it remains true that many lists of recommended books are restricted to fiction (despite its positive promotion of non-fiction, 90% of those included in the *Boys into Books* survey are in the fiction category). The force-feeding of fiction to the exclusion of non-fiction may hamper the progress of the reluctant reader: fiction reading and comprehension skills highlight gender differences and revealing boys' relatively poor skills in this area may embarrass them and cut them off still further.

Certain other prejudices and often unwitting censorship also persist: librarians often refuse to stock books about wars and weaponry (just as many parents discourage their children from playing with toy guns, whereupon the child fashions one out of Lego). And – though, again, this is a generalisation – many publishers' commissioning editors are women to whom 'boys' interests' are to some extent unknown territory.

The publisher's perspective

In the UK some 10,000 new children's books are published every year, while 225 million were sold in 2007. The statistics do not separate children's fiction and non-fiction as precisely as adults', but Public Lending Right figures suggest a ratio of almost four fiction borrowings to every one non-fiction. A visual check in the average children's bookshop indicates that the space devoted to non-fiction is smaller than that for fiction, but whatever the figures, children's non-fiction – with boys as its principal consumers – is big business.

As the publishers' listings in this *Yearbook* show (see page 5), most companies produce non-fiction for children. Whether they exert positive discrimination and commission writers with boys specifically in mind is less apparent. However, while publishers rarely indicate that a book is aimed squarely at boys, its presentation and content are often clearly designed with boys as the perceived principal readers. (There are, of course, certain differences between books created for schools, where teachers use them as both literacy and learning tools, and trade books where the emphasis is more on impulse purchase.)

In an ideal world, publishers would like to sell their fiction and non-fiction to both sexes, but as with books for adults, if the reality is that girls gravitate to fiction and boys to non-fiction, whether tacitly or avowedly, they target each group separately in terms both of topic and presentation (the latter is graphically shown by such signs as the sea of pink on the girls' shelves and the graffiti-style lettering on the boys' books).

The illustrative content and style of illustration in non-fiction is paramount – boys respond well to a magazine-style presentation: captioned pictures and short entries can overcome the often short concentration spans of boys (frankly, we literate adults have to grin and bear this – there is no way the average boy is going to read swathes of narrative text). The high illustrative content of boys' non-fiction is also a response to the psychological facts of the case: because they are better at it than girls, boys prefer to decode meaning from visual symbols rather than words, this advantage often compensating for or masking their inferior reading skills.

Perhaps unfortunately for the novice author, in terms of commissioning (and unlike fiction where publishers tend to wait for books to come along from existing authors, agents, and – vary rarely – from unpublished authors) with non-fiction they customarily identify the gaps in the market themselves, create the ideas and seek an (often well-established) author. Much less commonly a publisher responds positively to an approach from a writer with a convincing idea – unless it is overwhelmingly original and obviously commercial.

Writing for boys

Do you feel competent to write about the themes listed in the box on page 107, or allied areas? If so, consider whether – although you may be a specialist, perhaps with a teaching background – you are able to convey information entertainingly to boys. Even if you do not possess specialist skills, research ability counts for a lot: many non-fiction titles can be written by non-specialists provided they undertake their research conscientiously.

Can you accommodate girl readers without alienating the boys? Anna Claybourne again: 'As for traditionally "girly" stuff, I think boys can cope with it in a book on a general topic – for example, I won't eschew mentioning painting your nails in a book on the human body, a fashion picture when dealing with silk moths, or romantic love in a biography, where it adds interest. Firstly, boys can identify this as "for the girls" and choose to perceive it from the outside; secondly, as with the reverse situation, boys will sneer at things like this to assert masculinity, but they may well strike a chord with them internally. So the more inclusion of both "girl" and "boy" things in a non-fiction book the better; the more variety and extremes the better; the more restriction and uniformity and dumbing-down, the worse.'

With the filtering out of content from many National Curriculum subjects, creating entertaining and informative non-fiction books for boys could be your opportunity to give them the facts they crave. It is not an overcrowded market and the rewards from a successful book or series, where books can stay in print and sell steadily for many years, can be considerable. Good luck!

Russell Ash is the author of *Top 10 of Everything* (Hamlyn, annual, 1989–) and *Whitaker's World of Facts* (A&C Black, annual 2005), as well as over 100 other non-fiction titles for boys (and girls, and adults). For further information see www.russellash.com, www.top10ofeverything.com, www.whitakersworld.com, www.whitakersworld.co.uk.

Further reading

Young People and Reading, National Literacy Trust, 2005, www.literacytrust.org.uk/Research/Reading_Champions_survey.pdf

Children's and Young People's Reading Habits, National Literacy Trust, 2005, www.literacytrust.org.uk/Research/Reading_Connects_survey.pdf

Writing for girls

Louise Rennison shares her thoughts about writing books for girls.

It still amuses me *a lot* when so called grown-ups have to read the titles of my books out loud. At one of my book launches, a middle-aged respectable-looking bloke in a suit was forced to say: 'And we are really looking forward to seeing *It's OK I'm Wearing Really BIG Knickers* at the top of the bestselling list'. Tee hee hee. I had to be practically carried to the loos because I was laughing so much when the same bloke announced the publication of my newbook *Knocked Out By My Nunga-Nungas*. And this you see, in a nutshell, is the secret of my geniosity. I don't have to unleash my teenager within when I write Georgia's diaries because it is already unleashed and wandering around like a fool. (As I write this I am wearing my fluffy mules and a tiara, just in case I suddenly get asked to a party.) It is very restful being yourself(ish).

One of my first readings was in a bookshop in Brighton. It was a mixed adult and teenage audience and as usual I did *ad hoc* rambling. I told the audience that everything in the books was based on real life – my life – and that I had written *Angus, Thongs and Full Frontal Snogging* really quickly and used real people's names. I said I meant to change them before the book was published but forgot.

For instance, my loony school caretaker was nicknamed 'Elvis' because he once came to a school dance and did some exhibition twisting on stage until his back went and he had to be taken to casualty. Well, in the book he is called 'Elvis Attwood'. And guess what his name was in real life? Yes, Mr Attwood. Now you get the picture. Ditto 'Nauseating P. Green' and 'Wet Lindsay'.

Anyway, I was telling the audience that all the characters were real and the family in the book was my family in real life and so on and a woman said 'Well, how does your family feel about having all of their secrets revealed?' My mum was in the audience and I replied 'I don't know. Mum, how do you feel about having all of your secrets revealed?' Mum was slightly flustered by this because she wanted to be proud but also wanted to keep her distance, so she said 'Well, on the whole I think this is a very good book but of course the bits about me are grossly exaggerated.'

Another member of the audience said 'So did you really go to a fancy dress party dressed as a stuffed olive?' And, sadly, I had to admit it was true. I made the 'olive' bit out of green crêpe paper and chicken wire to make the round shape. Then I dyed my face, neck and head red for a pimento effect. It was quite funny at the time – well, it was when I was still in my room. The difficulty came when I tried to get out of my room. I had to go down the stairs sideways and I couldn't get in dad's Volvo. He told me I'd have to walk but offered to drive really slowly alongside me. I announced I would walk there by myself in that case and he got all dadish and said 'I don't want you wandering around the streets at night by yourself.' And I replied 'What would I be doing wandering the streets at night dressed as a stuffed olive? Gate crashing cocktail parties?'

But he didn't get it. Anyway, when I did get to the party (walking with dad driving his Volvo alongside me at five miles an hour) I had a horrible time. Initially, everyone laughed but later ignored me. I did have a dance by myself, but things kept crashing to the floor around me. In the end, the host asked me to sit down. I tried – but failed. Still, I did find out that I am not on my own *vis à vis* childishosity. At the end of the reading, a woman confided in me that she'd gone to a fancy dress party as a fried egg! We both shared a chuckle and I said 'Blimey what were we like?'And she replied 'No Louise, you don't understand, this was last week!'

What was I rambling on about? Oh yes – writing for girls. It's a hoot and I thoroughly recommend it. All you do is think about jokes, boys, snogging and lipstick. Perfect. I wish I had a useful tale to tell about how to write for girls, but the fact is that everything I have done has been sort of accidental. I wasn't intending to write books. In fact, years ago, I used to perform my own show entitled 'Stevie Wonder felt my face'. (He did actually feel my face... hang on a minute... 'Stevie Wonder' was also based on my real life. I am sensing a theme here...) Anyway, I was at the Edinburgh Festival doing my show and my first instinct was to reply 'Oooh no, I don't want to be stuck in a room writing by myself'.

I did eventually write my first book in 1999. I was a columnist on the London *Evening Standard* and I wrote a piece about having to have my shoes surgically removed. (Once again based on a real incident. I had forced my big fat feet into tiny strappy stilettoes out of sheer vanity, and then I fell out with my boyfriend and clip clopped off home in a high dudgeon (I lived on the other side of London). When I eventually got home, in the early hours, I fell asleep on the sofa fully clothed and still wearing my shoes. I woke up in the morning to find my feet had swollen up and my shoes were cutting into my feet. The shoes were embedded in my feet. I had shoefeet. My friends carried me to Charing Cross Hospital casualty to have them cut off.

The day after publication, Brenda Gardener from Piccadilly Press phoned me up and asked me to write a teenage girls diary and I asked why me? She said 'Because I have never read anything so childish and self obsessed as your article and I think you could do a really good job.' And the rest is historosity. But not very good advice for getting a book deal!

When I attempted to write the book, quite a few people pointed out that I am in fact not a teenager and haven't been one for quite some time. A very long time. A very very long time. Their advice was that I go and talk to some teenagers. I tried this straight away because I assumed it was possible to talk to teenagers – but it isn't – it is a hopeless task. You can't get any sense out of them at all and very often they do that helpless laughing thing. They know they should just stop it because if they don't someone will kill them, but they still can't stop. Anyway, I did attempt to speak to them for 'research' purposes. I asked one group of girls if they still did snogging. And they looked at me as if I had fallen out of someone's nose. They said 'SNOGGING? You say snogging. Snogging? How sad is that?' Then when I asked another group of girls, they looked at me in the same way and said 'Yeah, we say snogging, what else would you say you sad person?'

So, on the whole I more or less ignore what 'the youth' say. When I do readings and signings I am very often asked which are my favourite teenage books. My answer is – none. I don't read teenage books because I am not a teenager. In truth, I really am very ignorant about the whole 'teen' thing and that's how I want to stay. I deliberately don't read anyone else's books. I just plug into what I remember about my own teen times.

I recall parts of my teens very vividly. When I was 15 my family emigrated from Leeds to Whakatane, New Zealand. I'm sure I remember things around that time because of the high drama of what I went through. But I think that if I hadn't had any major drama to star in I would have made some up for myself. After all, every teenager is the star of their own melodrama. *Everything* matters and can potentially ruin your life – the way your fringe lies, a spot under your skin (*aka* a lurker) and I won't even go into the nose slimming measures.

Having an excellent memory definitely helps and I do credit myself with a head made for trivia. Did you know that your memory is like a muscle? The more I go back in time to remember, for example, my teenage friend's and my scoring system for snogging (graded one to ten – number five being a three-minute kiss with no breaks) the more I remember.

Of course, it helps if you are still on speaking terms with other people who were there at the same time. I am still in touch with my 'Ace Gang' from school and they can sometimes fill in the gaps in my memory. For instance, I was talking to my friend Rosie about one of our school teachers, Herr Kamyer. He had the double comedy value of being the only male teacher in an all-girls school and being German. I recalled a physics experiment he did using billiard balls on a tea towel to explain how molecules vibrate. At the time, I found this very funny and I put my hand up and said 'Herr Kamyer, what part does the tea towel play in the molecular structure?' And Herr Kamyer made his fateful mistake and replied 'Ach no, I merely use the tea towel to keep my balls still.' It was absolute pandemonium. I could not stop laughing even as I was taken to see the headmistress. Anyway, while Rosie and I were talking about this incident, she remembered something else about Herr Kamyer that I had completely forgotten. She recalled when he had taken our class by train to the Lake District. The train had slam doors on each side of the carriage and when the train pulled into the station Herr Kamyer leapt up said 'Ach here ve are' and stepped out of the door on the wrong side of the train and disappeared onto the track. Oh – happy days.

Writing for teenage girls is somehow timeless. The rites of passage that my mates and I went through in the Sixties are not so very different – emotionally – from girls now. Fashions have changed and the bands have different names but girls still strop around worrying about boys liking them and ignoring their long-suffering dads. Somewhere, even as I write this, a girl will be thinking 'For the teenage vampire party I could make one big eyebrow out of theatrical fur. That will be vair vair funny.'

Louise Rennison is the author of nine books for teenage girls. Her most recent book is *Stop in the Name of Pants!* (HarperCollins 2008). Her other books are *Angus, Thongs and Full-Frontal Snogging, It's OK I'm Wearing Really Big Knickers, Knocked Out by My Nunga-Nungas, Dancing in My Nuddy-Pants, And That's When it Fell Off in My Hand, Then He Ate My Boy Entrancers, Startled by His Furry Shorts!* and *Love is a Many Trousered Thing*. A film based on the first two books is due to be released in 2008, called *Angus Thongs and Perfect Snogging*.

See also...
- *Writing and the children's book market*, page 86
- *Writing for boys*, page 105
- *Writing for different genres*, page 114
- *Teenage fiction*, page 135
- *Writing for the school market*, page 138
- *Creating graphic novels*, page 207

Writing for different genres

Malorie Blackman looks at the different genres of children's books with a view to helping writers decide what kind of story they could write.

Take a trip to your local library or bookshop and peruse the children's section. (Also check out the books for young adults.) The books will probably be sorted into age ranges, for example books for babies and toddlers, books for the 5+ age range, books for 7+, 9+, 11+ and books for young adults or 14+. Take a closer look. There will probably be a separate poetry section (but not always) and a separate non-fiction or reference section. Take an even closer look. Are the books in the fiction section divided by genre? Probably not. There are so many different genres (and sub-genres) and so many books which span more than one genre that it would be a thankless task to sort books in this way. But we all have views on the types of stories we like to read – and write.

For the purposes of this article (and my sanity), I shall only be looking at the main fiction genres for children. My genre list is by no means definitive or exhaustive, but what I want to do is present some guidelines for some of the genres and some examples of books for further reading. Let me say straight away that a number of the books I've listed below quite happily overlap other genres as well. Take my own book for young adults, *Noughts and Crosses*, as an example. The story is about the friendship of two teenagers, Callum and Sephy, which eventually turns into a deep, undying love. Does that make it a romance/ love story? The story takes place in an alternative version of contemporary Britain. So it's a fantasy story – right? Callum is a 'Nought' (white) and Sephy is a 'Cross' (black) and their society has strict demarcation lines where the two groups are not encouraged to integrate. Noughts are the minority and historically the ex-slaves of the Crosses. As the book takes an angled look at modern-day racism, does that make it a real life/contemporary story? Genre can be a hard one to pin down.

One of the first pieces of advice I received when I started writing was 'write about what you know'. Even though this advice is a useful starting point, I don't necessarily agree with it. After all, that's why we have imaginations, to take us outside of our own limited realm of experience. My advice would be to write what you *care* about rather than what you know. If you care about it, but don't know too much about it, then you'll take the trouble to find out, to do proper research. And if you care about it, then you'll write with a passion and a heart that will shine through.

Beware of choosing to write in a genre simply because it appears to be 'currently fashionable'. You may feel that you'll have more chance of being published or making money that way, but it's unlikely to be true. If you don't truly believe and feel every word you write, it will show. And what is 'currently fashionable' may not be so in one or two years' time. For a while in the mid to late 1990s, horror stories were the thing. Over the last few years, fantasy has been even bigger. But that also means there is more competition as every writer hoping to make some fast money jumps on that bandwagon. What makes your story more original, inventive and readable than the next one? If you can't answer that question, think long and hard about the type of story you are writing – and why.

Thrillers

Under this heading, I include the sub-genres of crime, ghost and horror stories. The key to thrillers is the battle between the protagonist or central character in your story and the antagonist or opponent. Your protagonist must have someone or something to battle against. Weak antagonists make for a weak story. Look at the *Harry Potter* stories for example (though they are not strictly speaking thrillers). Harry has to battle against the formidable Voldemort. Now if Voldemort was a weak enemy and easily vanquished, it would've made Harry's fight against him far less interesting. An antagonist doesn't have to be a person. It can be an organisation, the *status quo*, an object, but whatever it is, the reader should empathise with the protagonist's struggle against it.

Good examples: *I Am the Cheese* by Robert Cormier, *Cirque du Freak* series by Darren Shan.

Action

Always a favourite, action books are packed with incident. The most successful books in this genre certainly possess that page-turning quality which makes them incredibly hard to put down. Crime-busting spy thrillers are particularly popular. The protagonists are usually teenagers who invariably have to use their intelligence to get themselves out of myriad tricky situations.

Good examples: *Alex Rider* series byAnthony Horowitz, *Cherub* series by Robert Muchamore.

Mystery and adventure

These kinds of books catapult their readers into rip-roaring adventures. Most children love a puzzle element in a story and love the challenge of solving it. The puzzle element also provides that essential page-turning quality required for a successful book. The reader should not just want but *need* to know what is going to happen next. These types of stories, as well as thrillers, need endings which provide some resolution and a sense of closure. The puzzle presented in the story needs to be solved to be truly satisfying.

When I'm writing a mystery or an adventure story, I always make sure that the protagonist's troubles get worse in the middle of the story. Much worse. For example, in chapter one of my novel *Hacker*, one of the protagonists, Vicky, is accused of cheating in a Maths test by hacking into her teacher's computer to get the answers. But there's worse to come. When she gets home, she and her brother Gib find out that their dad has been arrested for siphoning off millions from the bank where he works. Worse is to come! Vicky and her brother have a huge bust up when Gib tells Vicky that her real parents drowned to get away from her and that she's not his sister and she never will be (Vicky is adopted). So not only does poor Vicky have her own school problems to deal with, she has to find a way to prove her dad innocent and find her own place within her family.

Good examples: *Wolf* by Gillian Cross, *Creepers* by Keith Gray.

Survival

Survival stories include stories where the protagonist finds himself or herself alone, with limited resources and having to rely on his/her wits to survive. These types of stories tend to involve a lot of interior monologue so that the reader can really get inside the head of the main character(s). The danger with this type of story is that the protagonist's plight can become a bit monotonous, so new, *believable* challenges have to be employed throughout the story and there has to be a real sense of jeopardy should the protagonist fail. These are great stories for having the protagonist learn a lot about themselves in the process. Characters in these books have to make a real emotional journey for the reader to care about them.

Good examples: *Wolf Brother* by Michelle Paver, *Kensuke's Kingdom* by Michael Morpurgo.

Animals and nature

There are two basic types of animal story – where real animals act in a 'realistic' way and anthropomorphosised animals, i.e. animals who are in fact humans. The latter allows children to identify with the main character(s) and to share in their adventures. Animals can be used to portray complex emotions in a way that is instantly identifiable to children but also one step removed. In this way, animals can be used to write stories about a number of difficult topics for younger children, such as bereavement or loneliness.

Good examples: *Watership Down* by Richard Adams, *The Sheep Pig* by Dick King Smith, *Fire, Bed and Bone* by Henrietta Branford.

Real life/contemporary

This is a vast genre which covers any kind of contemporary circumstance. These books – which are more than thrillers or mysteries – live or die by the central character(s). The protagonists don't necessarily need to be sympathetic, but we must empathise with them at least, otherwise readers won't bother to finish the book. This genre includes school and family stories, stories that deal with disfigurement or disability – the list is endless. When I write one of these stories, I always write a short five-page biography of each of my major characters: their favourite foods, their favourite types of music, their likes and dislikes, loves and hates, what their friends love about them, what their friends find annoying, etc. I will never start writing any novel until I know my main characters inside out. That way I'll know how they'll react in any given situation. And my characters become real people to me, and sometimes when I'm writing they'll behave in ways that surprise me. I take that as a good sign. It means my characters have really taken on a life of their own.

Good examples: *Holes* by Louis Sacher, *The Illustrated Mum* by Jacqueline Wilson, *Stone Cold* by Robert Swindells, *(Un)arranged Marriage* by Bali Rai, *Junk* by Melvin Burgess, *Speak* by Laurie Halse Anderson.

War

Unfortunately a genre which is always relevant. This genre allows the writer to examine the best and the worst of human nature.

Good examples: *Private Peaceful* byMichael Morpurgo, *I Am David* by Anne Holm, *Goodnight Mister Tom* by Michelle Magorian.

Romance and love stories

This is a popular genre for exploring relationships, and stories tend to be aimed at young adults.

Good examples: *Saskia's Journey* by Theresa Breslin, *Forever* by Judy Blume, *No Shame, No Fear* by Ann Turnbull.

Sports

This genre uses sport to illustrate and illuminate the major character(s) or society as a whole.

Good example: *Keeper* by Mal Peet, *McB* by Neil Arksey.

Fantasy

Hugely popular, this genre seems to have taken over from traditional myths and legends. It appeals to the sense that there is something inside or outside of us which we may or may not be able to control, and stories often contain a magical element.

Good examples: *Harry Potter* series by J.K. Rowling, *Artemis Fowl* by Eoin Colfer, *His Dark Materials* series by Philip Pullman.

Historical

Research, research, research. Do your research. For me, the best historical stories shine a light on the way we live now. This genre of course includes war, which is listed separately.

Good examples: *Hero* by Catherine Johnson, *Coram Boy* by Jamila Gavin.

Humour

Humour is always popular. It's easy and engaging to read but hard to do well. Anthony Horowitz's *Diamond Brother* series are fantastically funny crime novels and a particularly successful example of a fusion of genres. I've put them in this category though because for me, the antagonist in each of the *Diamond Brother* stories is almost incidental. I don't mean the books have weak antagonists; they don't. But it is the humour rather than the crimes in these stories that I more easily remember!

Good examples: *Angus, Thongs and Full Frontal Snogging* by Louise Rennison, *The Hundred Mile-an-Hour Dog* by Jeremy Strong, *I Know What You Did Last Wednesday* by Anthony Horowitz.

Science fiction

Science fiction is a vast genre. It can take you to other worlds, other times, other spaces and places, other minds. The writer who first turned me on to science fiction as a child was John Wyndham. I found his book *Chocky* totally mind-blowing. And it woke me up to the possibilities of science fiction. Science fiction isn't only spaceships and aliens from other planets – though there's nothing wrong with that! This genre allows for new technology and methodologies to be explored as in *Unique* by Alison Allen Grey, which explores the idea of cloning, or my own book, *Pig Heart Boy*, which uses as its starting point the whole notion of xenotransplantation (the transplantation of organs from one species into another). The title of my book gives away the species of the donor and the recipient!

Good examples: *Mortal Engines* by Philip Reeve, *Unique* by Alison Allen Grey, *Hex* by Rhiannon Lassiter.

Poetry/narrative verse

Over the last few years, there has been a welcome increase in the number of stories told in narrative verse. This genre is particularly useful for those children for whom unrelenting pages of prose can be quite daunting, but who still want to be told a story as opposed to reading a series of different poems on unrelated subject matter. Narrative verse stories contain all the drama and heart of prose stories but are an interesting form to use when telling the story. As a writer, you need to be very clear as to why you want to tell your story in this way. And bear in mind that narrative verse is very hard to translate, thus limiting foreign edition options – but don't let that stop you. If your story needs to be told in narrative verse – then go for it. Stories told this way should vary in rhyme, rhythm and cadence or they quickly become boring.

Good examples: *Love That Dog* by Sharon Creech, *Cloud Busting* by Malorie Blackman, *Locomotion* by Jacqueline Woodson.

Short stories

The sad fact is, short stories are a very hard sell. Random short stories across many different genres are an even harder sell. Short stories which focus on a particular genre may be easier to get published but not compared to writing a novel.

Good example: *A Thief in the Village and other stories* by James Berry.

Graphic novels

A number of well-known children's books have also had graphic novel editions published. These include *Stormbreaker* by Anthony Horowitz and *Artemis Fowl* by Eoin Colfer. Graphic novels are expensive to produce so it is rare for an unknown author to be published in this form by a children's publisher. Manga novels are becoming increasingly popular so this may change in the near future.

Fairy stories, myths and legends

These types of stories appear to have fallen out of fashion somewhat, which is a great shame. As a child I loved fairy stories and books of myths and legends from around the world. There was something very comforting in knowing that a true heart and a courageous spirit would eventually triumph over adversity. However as Rick Riordan shows, there's plenty of material in fairy stories and legends which can still be used and given a completely modern twist.

Good example: *Percy Jackson* series by Rick Riordan.

Malorie Blackman has written over 55 books for children, including picture books and novels for all ages and reading abilities. Her most recent book is *Double Cross*, the fourth in the *Noughts and Crosses* series. Malorie has received a number of awards including the FCBG Children's Book Award 2002 for *Noughts and Crosses*, a BAFTA for best children's drama *Pig Heart Boy* in 2000 (also shortlisted for the Carnegie Medal), and the Smarties Silver Book Award 2004 for *Cloud Busting*. Her websites are www.malorieblackman.co.uk and www.myspace.com/malorieblackman.

See also...

- *The next big thing*, page 90
- *Books for babies*, page 98
- *Writing for boys*, page 105
- *Writing for girls*, page 111
- *Fiction for 6–9 year-olds*, page 119
- *Writing humour for young children*, page 121
- *Writing horror for children*, page 124
- *Writing historical novels for children*, page 127
- *Writing for teenagers*, page 131
- *Writing for the school market*, page 138

Fiction for 6–9 year-olds

Alison Stanley is an experienced commissioning editor of young fiction. She gives here what she regards as essential components of a good fiction book for younger readers.

When teaching six year-olds in the mid-1970s, 'reading' was something that involved a queue of children at my desk, waiting to be heard struggling through their less than stimulating reading-scheme books. There had to be a better way of developing reading skills, especially as the delight of sharing real books with the children during 'storytime' at the end of the day, was such a marked contrast. I had no idea in those days about the business of publishing, and I certainly never imagined that many years later I would be commissioning books for that very same age group to read and enjoy. But without that classroom experience, I doubt that I would have begun to appreciate the needs of the young beginner reader. Nor would I have experienced that magical moment when a child just breaks through the reading skills barrier and begins to read unaided for the very first time. The anticipation in excitedly turning over the page to find out what happens next; the thrill of a guessed word being right; and the beginning of reading for pleasure are all magical moments to witness.

Books for younger readers

Here are some of my favourite books for younger readers that have stood the test of time. Read them and you'll know what I mean!

Happy Families series by Janet and Allan Ahlberg (Puffin)

Horrid Henry series by Francesca Simon (Orion)

The Littlest Dragon by Margaret Ryan (Collins)

Mr Majeika series by Humphrey Carpenter (Puffin)

The Worst Witch by Jill Murphy (Puffin)

Spider McDrew by Alan Durant (Collins)

The Black Queen by Michael Morpurgo (Random House)

Morris the Mouse Hunter by Vivian French (Collins)

Clarice Bean by Lauren Child (Orchard Books)

Lizzie Zipmouth by Jacqueline Wilson (Random House)

There's a Viking in My Bed by Jeremy Strong (Puffin)

Beginner readers

What makes a good book for children just beginning to read on their own – one that will stimulate and motivate them, and let them know that reading is an enjoyable and rewarding activity?

Firstly and simply – beginner readers need good stories. Strong plots that are easy to follow, so that when faced with an unrecognisable word, the child can predict what is going to happen and be able to have a go at reading that 'difficult' word. Lively and appealing characters are essential too, especially if featured in more than one book.

Beginner readers like stories that reflect their experiences of the world but also ones that will stretch their imaginations. Stories with a fantasy element rooted in the real world where something ordinary becomes extraordinary in a familiar world, are always popular. The language of the stories should be rhythmic with plenty of repetition and alliteration. Sentences need to be short enough so they don't get split by a page turn, but long enough so that the story doesn't read in a stilted fashion.

Books for beginner readers require a generous typeface and good clear layout with plenty of illustrations giving clues to the text. This will help make the transition from shared picture books to reading alone a smooth one.

Last, but definitely not least, there is one vital thing to remember when writing stories for the beginner reader... beginner readers read *slowly*. Wacky, fast-paced humour within the text does not work when read word for word, very slowly. Humour in the text needs to be obvious, relate to the child's world and work when read at a snail's pace (see *Writing humour for young children* on page 121 for inspirational advice on writing funny fiction).

Top 10 questions

To summarise, the ten questions I ask when assessing manuscripts for younger readers are:

Plot
• Is it a good story?
• Will it make sense when read slowly?
• Will it keep the reader wanting to turn over the pages?
• Is the story strong enough to stand up to the competition?

Setting
• Is the story set in a world that children will be familiar with?
• Are there events in the story that children will relate to?

Characters
• Are the characters appealing and original?
• Are the characters rounded enough for the beginner reader to want further books about them?

Language
• Is the vocabulary suitable for the young beginner reader?
• Is there plenty of repetition, alliteration and rhythmic writing?

I would also want to know about the author. I'd want to know if the manuscript was written by a published author, and if so, do his or her books sell? (Never forget that publishing is a commercial venture!) If it is a new author, I'd like to know if he or she is seen to be a major new talent who will progress to write further books.

The editorial process can help with many of these points, but the originality and unique-ness of a story belong to the author. Because there are so many books written for this age group, it takes a special author to create something new and appealing, something that will stand the test of time.

Confident readers

Once children become fluent readers, there's usually no stopping them in their quest to read more, and soon move on to longer novels. It's at this stage that they are exploring the different genres – humour, horror, adventure, or themes such as school stories, animal stories and football stories, amongst others. They're also finding out which authors they like to read and will be actively seeking out new books by that author. Confident readers come in all shapes, sizes, ages and with different backgrounds and personalities and it is essential that this is reflected in a broad range of reading matter.

Alison Stanley was a commissioning editor at Puffin Books and at HarperCollins Children's Books, where she was responsible for developing the younger end of the fiction list.

See also...
• *Books to read aloud*, page 102
• *Categorising children's books*, page 162

Writing humour for young children

Like most adults, children love humour. But in both cases the joke will fall flat unless it is aimed at the right audience. Jeremy Strong has ten rules for writing humour for young children.

The snappy bit: some simple rules

1. Never allow your bum to become gratuitous.
2. Write wrong.
3. Self mutilation is highly recommended.
4. Words are essential.
5. Pulchritude? No way.
6. Inside every 20-plus there's an eight year-old trying to get out.
7. You calling me a wozzer? Mankynora!
8. Just who do you think you're talking to?
9. Surprise!
10. Ha! I laugh at death.

The expansive bit. We begin at the beginning, with Rule Nine. Surprise! Ha ha! That's pretty much self explanatory.

Rule Six: Inside every 20-plus there's an eight year-old trying to get out.

Years ago, when I first began writing for children, I was often asked (by adults) why it was that the stories I wrote seemed to appeal to children. You have to imagine an adult asking this question, in a tone of voice that mixes one part admiration to ten parts complete bewilderment. I used to answer, fairly truthfully, that only my exterior had aged along with my chronological age, and that I was still aged about eight inside. The adult would usually laugh and would go away as bewildered as they were before they'd asked the question. The point here is, I think, that it isn't possible to really understand except from a child's viewpoint. If you have forgotten what it was like to be a child then you're unlikely to understand.

Rule One: Never allow your bum to become gratuitous.

To make matters worse, adults often think the things that make children laugh are puerile. To some extent this is true and it is easy to make a child laugh by playing 'lowest common denominator' jokes – jokes that refer to farts, snot, bums, knickers, etc. But whilst employing these guaranteed tickle-sticks it is easy to forget that children also like quite sophisticated jokes.

As for the bums and farts, it's okay to pop them in here and there but, for the sake of at least some self respect, keep them to a minimum. Never let your bum be gratuitous.

Rule Four: Words are essential.

Children love word play, and they love 'knowing' jokes – for example, jokes that are aware of how bad they are, or referential jokes that make use of things familiar to them, the things that mark out their lives, such as school, parents, family.

Then there is the matter of what children can read and understand. Obviously, this is going to vary not only with age but with ability. Anyone who has taught junior age children knows that there are children of six who can read like 11 year-olds, and vice versa, with all shades in between and quite frequently further beyond. Nevertheless, as a writer, you need to aim towards the centre. In this article I am going to concentrate on 6–11 year-olds because those are the ages I taught for 17 years.

Let's look at language. Things need to be fairly simple. Shorter, rather than longer sentences work best. But like all rules this one can be deliberately misused. For example, at some appropriate point in a story you might wish to hurl yourself into some ever-increasing sentence that just seems to plunge on and on at a relentless pace and with reckless abandon like a runaway car because that happens to be one of the best ways your writing can capture the manic activity that is going on in your story at that particular point. Maybe it is a description of a runaway car. You get the point. Children respond to this positively because, anchored as it is in a normally short and simple style of writing, the over-long sentence becomes not only a writing device, but also a source of humour.

Rule Ten: Ha! I laugh at death.

As with comedy for other age groups, nothing is held sacred. You will, however, have to obey the obvious rules that generally apply to writing for children, and also steer clear of the PC police. You can be smutty, but not dirty. You can be unkind to animals, but they mustn't be in a circus, unless you're a signed up freedom fighter for 'Say no! to performing dumb creatures'.

You can laugh about death. (It's an emotional release. Honest.) You can even have stereotypes and clichés – but in this instance don't expect to get published.

Rule Two: Write wrong.

Children love to recognise things that are wrong, and this is where word play often has great effect. Characters that get their words or spellings wrong are a good source of humour, not only because it is funny in its own right, but because children love the empowerment of recognising what's wrong. (You will, incidentally, lose brownie points for using words like 'empowerment'.)

Rule Seven: You calling me a wozzer? Mankynora!

Invented words can also be a terrific source of enjoyment for both writer and reader, especially when they are used as expletives – sort of coded (and therefore safe) swear words. Mankynora! Wozzer yourself! Let's also take a look at sophistication. You have to ask yourself, am I writing a joke for an adult or a child? I know for a fact that I am guilty of putting jokes for adults in some stories – jokes I know only an adult will understand. (Or sometimes a joke that a child will get on one level, but where the adult will see a second 'hidden' joke or implication.) The reason I do this is because (a) I can't resist the temptation if it's a good one, (b) I like to remember that many of my books are read to children by adults, and so I am putting in something to make it more enjoyable for them, and (c) I don't do it often and I make sure that the vast majority of the humour is firmly in the child's grasp.

Rule Five: Pulchritude? No way.

Whilst on the subject of sophistication it is worth thinking about the words you use. With each word you need to ask yourself: can a child of 'x' years read and understand this word? Apply a bit of common sense. There are some words a child might not understand but it might be worthwhile introducing it to them, allowing the context to help reveal its meaning.

The word sophistication itself is a reasonable example. Many junior children would not understand it but, although it's long, it's not too difficult to work out what it says and you could argue that it's a good word for a child to know. On the other hand, the word 'pulchritudinous' is not only very hard for a child to work out but it is extremely unlikely you would need to use such a word when writing for junior children and if you do then you seriously need to reconsider what you are doing.

Rule Three: Self mutilation is highly recommended.

You have to be rigorously self disciplined about this. No matter how good a joke is you have to cut it out if it's not actually funny to your audience. The humour also needs to arrive and leave quickly. Anything that takes pages to set up is not worth it and the longer it takes the more likely it is that your writing will become increasingly false and unnatural as you struggle with all the scaffolding you require to hold up the joke.

Rule Eight: Just who do you think you're talking to?

It is a mistake to think that the things adults laugh at in children make good material for children's books. They don't, for the simple reason that it's funny to the adult watching the child, and not the other way round. All of this points to one of the cardinal rules for writing anything: be aware of your audience. Keep that firmly in mind and you can't go far wrong. I was going to finish by writing: May the fart be with you. Then I realised that it would be out of place and one fart too many. See what I mean?

Jeremy Strong writes humorous fiction for 8–11 year-olds. His books include *The Karate Princess* titles, and three Viking stories which were made into a popular television series. Jeremy won the Federation of Children's Book Groups Children's Book Award for *The Hundred-Mile-an-Hour Dog*. His first book for young teenagers, *Stuff*, won the 2006 Manchester Book Award. *Beware! Killer Tomatoes* was shortlisted for two book awards in 2008. New titles published by Puffin include *Weird* (for teenagers), *Lost! The 100 mph Dog* and *The Battle for Christmas*.

See also...

• *Writing for different genres*, page 114
• *Writing comedy for children's television*, page 277

Writing horror for children

'Nine stories you'll wish you'd never read' it warns on the cover of *Horowitz Horror*. Anthony Horowitz writes about writing horror for children and, aware of children's thirst for blood and intestines, airs the question of just how far an author can go.

As much as it's fun to be asked to write about writing, I hope anyone reading this will take it all with a medium-sized pinch of salt. The only incontrovertible law of writing I ever came upon was set down by my great hero, the American screenwriter William Goldman in *Adventures in the Screen Trade*. NOBODY KNOWS ANYTHING. It deserves the capital letters. If you're setting out to write a horror story for children, what follows may be useful. But your own instincts are probably better. Anyway, here is my experience for what it's worth.

I am currently about halfway through writing a series of supernatural thrillers with the overall title of *The Power of Five*. The hero is a 14-year-old boy called Matt Freeman and in the first book, *Raven's Gate*, he finds himself arrested for attempted murder and sent on a fostering programme which lands him in the middle of a Yorkshire village, inhabited – as it turns out – by a coven of witches. Matt is chased by ferocious devil dogs and by the animated skeletons of dinosaurs. He is sucked into a bog, kidnapped and set up to be sacrificed. Anyone who tries to help him dies horribly. A policeman is killed in a car accident. A farmer is frightened to death. His own parents, of course, died long ago.

The second volume, *Evil Star,* begins with a madwoman immolating herself in a petrol tanker, shortly after murdering her live-in lover. The villain is a South American businessman who has been purposefully mutilated at birth. This time, Matt is beaten up by Peruvian police, robbed, starved, attacked by savage condors and … well, you probably get the idea.

Children love horror. You need look no further than the worldwide success of writers like Darren Shan to see it. Years ago, the *Goosebumps* series had covers that promised far more than the contents ever delivered but for a time they were littered across every school yard and made their author – R.L. Stine – a millionaire. Even the *Harry Potter* films have become progressively darker until the most recent instalment, which had one character cutting off his own hand, the death of a teenager and the truly hideous appearance of 'he who should not be named'.

And yet, the first – indeed the most crucial – question you have to ask yourself is: how far can you go? This is something of which I'm always painfully aware. Go into a classroom and talk to the children and you will discover that far enough is never enough. They want the blood, the intestines, the knife cutting through the flesh … the full monty. The problem, of course, is that if you give it to them you risk alienating the school librarians, bookshop buyers and the parents, and your book may never actually reach its intended audience.

When I visit schools, I always advise children to keep their own writing blood-free. Teachers don't like it, I tell them. I remind them that the scariest moment in any horror film is when the hand reaches for the door handle in the dark. That's when the music jangles and your imagination runs riot. What happens after the door is open is almost incidental. It seems to me that what you imagine will always be scarier than what you see – and this is a rule I apply to my own writing. For my money, the most effective passage in *Raven's Gate* comes when Matt gets lost, cycling through a wood in the dark. Every road brings him back to the same point. Slowly he begins to realise that he is never going to escape. There's no blood. No monsters. But it seems to work.

But at the same time – if you don't actually deliver, you're going to disappoint and so lose your audience. In my view, this is what went wrong with *Goosebumps* and it's the reason why they're no longer so popular. There has to be blood. How much of it and how far you go is up to you. Like I say, there are no rules. Take a look at the opening of Darren Shan's *Lord Loss*. The death of the parents leaves nothing to the imagination but teachers still love him. I don't know how he gets away with it.

Perhaps it's a question of context. A random act of violence or mutilation might seem very horrible in a book by, say, Jacqueline Wilson. But that's because her characters are so real, her world so recognisable. But when you write a horror story, you have a different departure point. Even before your readers buy the book, they know what to expect and they open it in exactly the same way as they might get on a ghost train at a fairground. They expect a certain number of skeletons and monsters and read the book in the knowledge that (a) it's only a ride, and (b) it will eventually deliver them back into the daylight.

The daylight, though, I think is important. I was genuinely shocked by the death of the teenager – Cedric Diggory – in *Harry Potter and the Goblet of Fire*. Not that J.K. Rowling needs to worry about the rules. But I've always thought that although it's reasonable to slap around your heroes, to frighten them and to hurt them, it's somehow irresponsible and wrong to kill them. No children have ever died in any of my books. Actually, none of them have ever felt real pain – again, because of the context. A child being chased by devil dogs through the swamps of Yorkshire may seem to be having a tough time. But that's nothing compared to a child in a London supermarket being slapped and screamed at by his mother. That, to me, is real horror.

Enough of these generalities. If you're thinking of writing something dark and scary for a young audience, here are just a few thoughts that might help.

• **You need an original story**. It may seem obvious but the realm of horror is stuffed with haunted castles, wicked stepmothers, evil magicians and all the rest of it. I know because I've used plenty of them myself. But a strong, simple idea will set you apart from the pack. Look at Justin Somper's success with *Vampirates*, a clever collision of swashbuckling and the supernatural. Or Garth Nix (*Mister Monday*) who time and time again comes up with hugely imaginative universes, completely new ideas.

• **Think about your central characters.** If they're likeable enough and idiosyncratic enough, you can – and will – get away with murder. There are some quite horrible things in Philip Pullman's *Northern Lights* with children kidnapped, stripped of their souls and turned into zombies. But we never doubt that Will and Lyra will win through.

• **Don't lose your sense of humour**. Mixing a few laughs in with the general mayhem doesn't lessen the horror. It helps the reader to deal with it. Paul Jennings, the Australian author, has produced some wonderfully twisted stories that would be far nastier if he didn't write with a smile.

• **Forget that you're writing for children**. This advice may seem incompatible with what I've already written but for me it's always been vital. If you sit at your desk with children in mind, it's all too easy for your work to become patronising and flabby. Of course it's important to consider levels of violence, what sort of language is applicable, how far you can go – but these should all be at the back of your mind. When I write horror, I try to scare myself. Darkness, solitude, the sense of being lost, the figure glimpsed out of the corner of your eye. I'm pretty sure that what scares children scares adults too. There's no need to cherry-pick, or to filter, the frissons!

• **Think visually.** The awful truth is that children are seeing more and more horror films with a 15 certificate, and they're also playing computer games with an incredible amount of electronic gore. Both films and games have a language which, I think, translates well to books. My generation was literary. Today's generation is visual. That's my theory, anyway, and I hope my audience will 'see' as much as read my work.

My intention has always been to entertain children – by which I mean neither educating them, improving them nor terrorising them. As to the last of these, I only ever got it wrong once. I wrote a short horror story (it's in *Horowitz Horror 2*) where the first letter of each sentence spelled out a message to the reader. That message went something along the lines of: 'As soon as you have read this, I'm coming to your house to kill you.'

About a year later, I received a note from a very angry and distressed mother who told me that she now had a traumatised daughter. My story, she said, was wilfully irresponsible and she suggested that I write a letter to her daughter, apologising.

I totally agreed. The next day I wrote a nice letter to the girl, explaining that I had intended to be mischievous rather than malevolent, that it was only a story, that she shouldn't have taken it so seriously.

Unfortunately, the first letter of every sentence in my letter spelled out: 'I am going to kill you too.'

Anthony Horowitz knew he wanted to be a writer when he was eight years old and was published for the first time when he was 22. He is perhaps best known for his *Alex Rider* novels, the first of which, *Stormbreaker*, was released as a major film in 2006. He has also written extensively for television, creating *Midsomer Murders* and *Foyle's War*. Four of his books were published in 2007: *Nightrise*, the third volume in *The Power of Five* series, *Snakehead* and *Point Blanc: Graphic Novel* in the *Alex Rider* series, and *The Greek That Stole Christmas*. His website is www.anthonyhorowitz.com.

See also...

• *Writing for boys*, page 105
• *Writing for different genres*, page 114
• *Writing for teenagers*, page 131

Writing historical novels for children

Michelle Paver shares her thoughts on how to approach writing historical novels for children and the importance of focusing on the story.

Books about how to get published sometimes advise new writers to research the market thoroughly. Read the competition, see what sells – that sort of thing. If that appeals to you, fine but I've never liked the idea and have never done it. In my view it isn't necessary, or even a good thing. You might just find it confusing and intimidating, and it could put you off what you really want to write.

I think it's better to concentrate on the story *you* want to write. The characters. The premise. The historical setting. You may not even know *why* you want to write it. But you do, and that's the main thing.

The period

Before you make a start, though, it's worth asking yourself why you want to set the story in your chosen historical period. Are you especially attracted to it? Did you day-dream about it as a child; maybe you still do? Or does it simply have a vague appeal, perhaps based on having seen a few films or read some novels set in that time?

There's no harm in being drawn to a particular period for tenuous reasons. But if that is the case, I'd suggest that you become a little more familiar with it before deciding whether to use that time for your story. You'll need to know your chosen period pretty thoroughly; and if you decide halfway through writing your novel that it isn't quite as fascinating as you'd thought, then the chances are that the reader will think so too, and your story probably won't work. In short, you must be prepared to live and breathe it for months or even years.

The story is king

This would seem to be the logical point to talk about research, but I'm going to leave that for later because I don't think it's the most important thing. The most important thing is the story. Always. And particularly for children. In general, children don't read a book because it got a great review in *The Times*, or because they want to look impressive reading it on the train. They read it because they want to know what's going to happen next.

That might seem trite, but it's amazing how easy it is to forget, especially when you've done a ton of research on a particular period, and there are so many terrific things about it that you just can't wait to share with everybody else.

So it's worth reminding yourself that the basics of any good story need to be firmly in place: characters about whom you care passionately; a protagonist who wants or needs something desperately; perhaps a powerful villain or opposing force which poses a significant threat. Big emotions: anger, envy, pride, hate, loyalty, love, grief. And just because the book will be read by children, don't shy away from the bad stuff (although obviously, you'll need to handle it responsibly). Death, violence, neglect, loneliness. Children want to know. They're curious about everything.

The beginning

Everyone knows that the first page of a story is critical, but this is especially so for children. In fact, the first paragraph is even more critical. And the first sentence is the most critical of all.

This poses a special challenge if you're writing a historical novel. How do you root the story in the past without getting bogged down in clunky exposition?

There's no magic formula, but the idea of 'show, don't tell' is a good place to start. Perhaps you could begin with a situation that's specifically of that period, like a witch-burning. Or, as part of the story, weave in an object of the period, like a flint knife.

You might be tempted to write a 'prologue', like the ones they used to have at the beginning of old movies ('London, England. The Cavaliers and Roundheads are at War…'). By all means write one of these. I did, for the first draft of *Wolf Brother*. But you may well ditch it before you finish the final draft. You may find that by then it has done its work by helping to anchor you, the writer, in the period. If you leave it in, it might have a distancing effect for the reader, diminishing the immediacy of the story.

Telling the story

What I said about the beginning of the story goes for the rest of it, too. The challenge for the writer of historical novels is to make the reader 'live' the story along with the characters. Somehow you've got to make them see, feel, touch, taste that period – without resorting to wodges of boring description that might slow things down, or overdone 'period' dialogue which is tiring to read and may distance the reader.

Again, there's no formula, but a good guiding principle is to make the essential exposition an integral part of the story. Make this a story that couldn't really have happened at any other time in history – even though the emotions involved are universals with which the reader can readily identify.

If you do this, then it'll become fairly clear what needs to stay in and what should come out. And there will probably be a lot of cutting. Pare down the exposition to what's essential. For instance, you may not need to explain the background to the entire war; just the particular skirmish in which your heroine has been caught up.

And for the essential exposition, it can help to introduce it in a highly charged emotional way: perhaps an argument or a fight. 'Exposition as ammunition' was a favourite motto of the film-maker Ingmar Bergman and it's one that can serve you well. But don't get so hung up on explaining things that you lose sight of the emotional focus of the scene.

The same goes for 'period atmosphere'. I would think long and hard before including anything for this reason alone. Try to make your period details part of the story. Then cut them back, then cut them back some more. What you need is a swift, vivid, unforgettable image with *just* enough detail to bring it alive – but no more.

Research

Which brings me (finally) to research. Some novelists don't do any. If that works for them, that's great. But if you're setting your story in the past, I don't think you can get by without doing at least some. And probably rather a lot. You need to know, intimately, what it was like to live back then. It's the little everyday details which interest readers, particularly children. What did people eat, wear, live in? How did they fight, travel, work, entertain themselves? What did they *think*? How were they similar to us? How were they different? And the more you can actually experience some of this for yourself the better – for example, by location research, trying out the food of the period – because it will give you all sorts of intriguing ideas and insights that you couldn't have got in a library.

Bear in mind, too, that research isn't just a matter of getting the details right. It'll probably spark ideas for the story itself: incidents, twists, particular scenes. These are gold dust. Use them. (Provided, of course, that they work in the context of the story as a whole.)

Perhaps the hardest thing about research is that the vast bulk of what you've lovingly unearthed isn't going to make it into the final draft. Be ruthless about keeping *only* those details that you really need: either to move the story along, or to develop character, or to set the scene. And shun any whiff of teaching; this is a story, not a history lesson.

This means that you'll probably go through a rather painful process of cutting over the course of your first, second, and successive drafts. But don't grieve too deeply for your lost treasures. *You* know all that background, and your in-depth knowledge will give your writing an assurance that it wouldn't otherwise have.

Language and style

This can be especially tricky: a kind of balancing act between keeping the story and the characters accessible, while leaving the language with just enough special vocabulary or dialogue to remind us that we're in another time. All this without distancing us too much, or (just as bad) without obvious anachronisms.

I'm often asked if I write differently when I'm writing for children, as opposed to when I'm writing for adults. The answer is, no, not at all. For me, it's the nature of the story that dictates the language and the style. If you're writing a story set in a middle-class Victorian home, your vocabulary and style will be utterly different from that which you'd use if you were writing about a forest of the Stone Age.

Having said that, if children are going to be among your readers, one important thing to bear in mind is that lengthy flashbacks can weaken the force of a story by reducing its immediacy. Because children read to know what's going to happen next, it helps too, to have unexpected twists, surprises, action, high emotion, flashes of humour, and lots of dialogue, as well as the odd cliff-hanger chapter ending. You've got to give them a reason to turn the page; and to keep turning the pages, all the way to the end.

Who are you writing for?

'What age group are you "aiming" at?' is a frequently asked question. For myself, the answer is: none. Apart from a general idea that I'm not writing a picture book for six-year-olds, I prefer to leave age groups to editors and publishers, and concentrate on the story.

Besides, once you start thinking in terms of 'aiming' a story at a particular group of people, where does it end? For instance, say you're 'aiming' a story at 9–12 year-olds. Well, what kind of 9–12 year-olds? They're not a homogeneous mass. Boys or girls, or both? And what kind? Middle-class or underprivileged? Immigrant or home-grown? Gifted, average, or special needs? If you start thinking like that, you run the risk of killing your story.

The same thing goes for the publisher's Holy Grail of the 'crossover' novel that's read by both adults and children. If you have this at the forefront of your mind when you're writing, it's unlikely that you'll do justice to the story. It may well end up being a mess which *nobody* will want to read.

Although this may sound a bit uncompromising, I have the same view when it comes to trying out your story on your own children – if you have them – or on others. In my view, this is risky and I prefer not to do it. (Well, in my case, I couldn't, because I don't have children, and don't know any very well!) In fact, quite a few children's writers don't have children of their own, but what many do have is a strong memory of what it was like to be a child and an ability to write from a child's perspective. That's what you need. Not market research.

Being true to your story, knowing your chosen period inside out but only including the most telling of details.... Of course, none of this is going to guarantee success. But with luck, it'll improve your chances on the slush pile. *And* you'll have a lot more fun than if you'd been slavishly studying the market!

Michelle Paver is the author of the bestselling *Chronicles of Ancient Darkness* series, which has been published in 37 languages. The first book in the series, *Wolf Brother*, was published in 2004 and a film of it is in development with Ridley Scott for Twentieth Century Fox. The second book is *Spirit Walker* (2005), the third is *Soul Eater*, the fourth is *Outcast*, and the fifth book, *Oath Breaker*, is due to be published in September 2008 by Orion Children's Books. The books have also been recorded as audiobooks read by Ian McKellen.

See also...
- *Writing for different genres*, page 114

Writing for teenagers

Meg Rosoff describes how she came to write *How I Live Now* and offers some suggestions to bear in mind when writing for teenagers.

Despite the optimistic title of this piece, I know hardly anything about writing for teenagers.

Here's a metaphor. Let's say you have sex, get pregnant, and give birth to a baby who grows up to be a successful actor/scientist/politician. Everyone wants to know how you did it. You ponder the question. Was it the organic food? Piano lessons? Good genes? State school? Was it benign neglect? Fish oil? Dumb luck?

It may be possible to post-rationalise success, but it rarely rings true. How did I manage to write a book adolescents like? I read a lot. Procrastinated for years. Had five careers. Am a foreigner. Found a good agent. Was desperate.

The answer is probably all of the above, plus a few hundred things I haven't thought of yet. Writing does come easily to me, which (let's face it) helps a lot. I always *wanted* to be a writer. And much as I hate to give it any credit at all, my disastrous career in advertising turned out to be an excellent apprenticeship. I was also desperate to get out of advertising, which helped in a different way. But I never thought I could write a novel.

For one thing, I was never interested in plot and could never figure out where people got their ideas for stories. I am not the sort of mother with an endless supply of charming bedtime tales. I can't even tell a decent joke.

To make matters worse, I compared myself incessantly to the people I most admired – Jose Saramago, George Eliot, Shirley Hazzard – and knew I'd never be able to write a book *that good*. Which turned out to be true enough, but (in retrospect) blindingly irrelevant.

As for writing for teenagers, I am uniquely ill-equipped by virtue of my advanced age. I'm 50, which disqualifies me from talking like a teenager or knowing much about how teenagers act or dress or think, except insofar as I observe them walking past my North London home most mornings on the way to school, leaving a trail of incomprehensible slang and McDonald's wrappers behind them. My daughter (aged four when I wrote *How I Live Now*) is now ten, which thankfully hints at, but does not yet provide concrete evidence of, the workings of the teenage mind.

So. The answer doesn't lie in storytelling ability, youth, or confidence. Nor will you find it in my powers of observation (mediocre, at best). I don't have an exceptional ear for dialogue or significant recall for past events. I'm terrible at history and hate research.

However … I have always had a morbid imagination (I can imagine a disaster in the most cheerful of scenarios) and a tendency to think like an adolescent. For me, teenage angst and midlife crisis got all caught up together at about the age of 20, and have been going along hand-in-hand ever since.

And I'm not the only hybrid freak around, the phenomenon of the middle-aged teenager is everywhere. Much of my generation was brought up on the idea that we never had to grow up, that we could wait forever to have children (whom we would raise as friends) that we could marry late or not at all, have powerful, well-paid jobs to which we would wear jeans and T-shirts, give ourselves grown-up toys for Christmas and birthdays (wide screen televisions, iPods, snowboarding kit, lava lamps) and never develop the gravitas our parents seemed to acquire magically and effortlessly at age 20.

When I was 25 (at which age my mother had married, bought a house and was pregnant with her second child) my friends and I were mooching around New York City, living in cockroach-riddled apartments, having affairs with inappropriate men, applying to art school, swapping illegal substances and going to all-night clubs. I married so late, my parents were convinced I was a lesbian. (How old was I? 33.)

My professional life followed a similar path. After seven jobs, three careers and a series of disastrous attempts to conform, I ended up in advertising, home to the hipsters at the end of the universe. Here was immaturity taken to its extreme: departments full of so-called creatives with goatee beards and stupid spectacles who played Xbox all day and called it work. The boys were joined by a tiny minority of females who changed their names from Susan and Mary to Cherokee and Zeus. And everyone pretended day after day that selling stuff nobody wanted was incredibly cool.

I got fired a lot from advertising, which seems fine today but at the time was discouraging. In retrospect, my relationship with advertising reminds me of a bad love affair – the sort that happens repeatedly when you lack the insight to realise that your taste in men (or in my case, careers) stinks. Being stuck in perpetual adolescence is all about lacking insight: lacking perspective, lacking wisdom, lacking everything in fact, except an enthusiasm that transcends failure. After failure. After failure.

As I moved from a 30-something adolescent to a 40-something adolescent, I ran up against the sobering consideration of having children. If your kids have parents who wear jeans, listen to Kings of Leon, and still don't understand the stock market, how are they supposed to act? My daughter started asking how to buy a house and the difference between credit and debit cards when she was six. She advises her father and me on how to dress, what car to drive, how to behave in public. She says she'd like to live in the American suburbs when she grows up, with a huge 4 x 4 and a spray-on tan. All her father and I can do is laugh (through our tears) and hope it passes.

But recently, something strange happened. Around my 40th birthday, I began to notice I wasn't quite so lacking in perspective as before. I began to make certain observations, certain wise observations, like: *Life is short. I hate my job. Perhaps I should write a book.*

In July 2002, I gave myself a deadline: two years.

I took a two-month leave of absence from work, stole a plot from the horse books I loved as a kid and wrote a practice novel. It wasn't the finest work of literature, and I sincerely hope it will never see the light of day, but it worked. It had a story (an old story, but a story) and a bunch of characters. It moved smoothly from A to B, was moderately funny and faintly poignant. It looked like a book, it read like a book, and I thought, it may not be Henry James, but it ain't advertising either.

With that book I found myself an agent, who suggested I write another book (she didn't say, 'a better one' but I read between the lines). And when I asked for advice on how to write a 'proper book' for teenagers, she said 'Write the best book you can write'. If I had to condense this long rambling autobiography-disguised-as-advice into seven words, that would be it. Nothing wiser has come my way since.

Having stuck with me so far, you are no doubt panting for the good old-fashioned, opinionated, bullet-pointed advice on how to write for teenagers that this article promises and I'm more than happy to give it a shot. Remember, however, your grain of salt, and that for each suggestion that follows, I can already think of an exception.

• **There are no rules.** There are books for teenagers with sex and drugs and unhappy endings. There are 100-page books and 700-page books, moral and immoral world-views, books with no children in them, books that tackle the Spanish Inquisition, the holocaust, adultery, suicide, football. If you don't believe me about this lack of rules, take note of how many panel discussions at literary festivals are devoted to the subject 'What Makes a Young Adult Novel?' The reason they continue to ask the question is that nobody knows the answer.

• **Know how to write.** Really, it helps. If your true talent lies in baking bread, open a bakery.

• **If you're not lucky enough to be immature, regress.** Haul yourself back to the days when the world was opaque.

• **On the other hand, be wise**. The more you experience in life, the more wisdom you unconsciously stockpile. The broken relationships, the family rows, the children you raise, the friends you manage to hang on to (or not), the careers you try, the journeys you take – all these things separate you, the writer, from a genuine adolescent. I may not know much, but I do know that having to read a book written by an actual 15 year-old makes my blood run cold.

• **Cut to the chase.** Ten pages of exposition will lose all of your readers. Five pages will lose most of them. Even two paragraphs is dicey. So start fast. The average attention span of a 12 year-old these days is about half as long as whatever you're trying to tell them. (And having judged prizes for teenage books, I can tell you that judges with 50 books to read aren't much better.)

• **Don't try to write cool.** You will almost inevitably fail. Even if you have eight teenagers at home, your writing will somehow manage to expose you as the middle-aged person you are. At which point you will embarrass your friends and family and particularly your teenage children. They will gag and run out of the room and shout that you've ruined their lives, and they will be correct. I've often been asked how I managed to write like a teenager in *How I Live Now*. The answer is, I didn't. I wrote like an old jaded person thinking like a teenager.

• **Get a life.** OK, I'm prejudiced. But it helps to know something about a subject, any subject. And despite failed careers in journalism, PR, politics, publishing and advertising, I managed to pick up a great deal of useful training for writing novels, articles, screenplays, etc on the way.

• **Have a good story.** This is true of writing for anyone. It's amazing how many people forget. And as someone who's good at character but lousy at plot, I feel your pain. Steal a plot, if you have to. After all there are only two: (1) Stranger Comes to Town, and (2) The Journey.

• **Don't look for issues, they will find you.** I challenge anyone to write for teenagers without coming up against at least one of the following subjects: sex, drugs, the meaning of life, family conflict, friendship, the future of the world, self-image, self-loathing, difficult siblings, impossible parents, bullying, depression, overachievement, please someone stop me! *Animal Ark* is a wonderful series of books about fixing hurt animals and that's why five to nine year-olds love it; but there's a reason that adults look back on Vonnegut and Dostoevsky and Kundera novels and say their lives were never quite the same afterwards.

• **Lie about everything except emotions.** England can be at war. Boys can read minds. Pigs can fly. But if you can't remember what it felt like to be depressed/vulnerable/in love, get a job writing *Animal Ark*.

• **Be passionate (see above).** Readers are.

• **Listen to what other people have to say.** OK, OK. So 15 publishers turned down *Harry Potter*. But if 15 people say your story is dull, heavy handed and badly written, it's probably not the next *Harry Potter* in its current form.

• **Don't worry about your connections (or lack thereof).** Ask any agent, editor or bookseller and they'll all tell you the same thing: there is not an overabundance of terrific books around. So if you think you can write something amazing, don't worry about selling it. When you're ready to show it around, someone will sit up and take notice.

• **Write the best book you can write.**

It worked for me, anyway.

Meg Rosoff was born in Boston, USA, and lived in New York City for ten years before moving to London in 1989. She was fired from an impressive variety of jobs before writing *How I Live Now*, which won the Guardian Children's Fiction prize in 2004. *Just in Case* won the 2007 Carnegie Medal. Her third novel is *What I Was* (Puffin 2007). Her website is www.megrosoff.co.uk.

See also...
• *Teenage fiction*, page 135
• *Categorising children's books*, page 162

Teenage fiction

Gillie Russell writes about teenage fiction from a publisher's pespective.

People often ask what the difference is between writing for teenagers and writing for adults. For me, the one significant difference is that teenagers come to books without a life experience. They are on the brink of self discovery, never having been plunged into the everyday grind of earning a living. They are open, honest and questioning as an audience and this, I believe, is why so many terrific writers want to write for this age group. Teenagers are challenging to write for and satisfyingly able to digest complex ideas. This often means that there are far too many 'issue'-based books on the market – not that these are badly written, often completely the reverse. But every major book fair will offer teenage books on incest, bullying, sibling rivalry, parental separation and drugs. Of course these kinds of books are important, but teenagers, like adults, need a varied diet. Teenagers like well-crafted stories in many genres – they love humour and history and fantasy, just as much as they like books which reflect their own worlds. They like inspirational and aspirational books where they can identify with the protagonists in a real way.

Getting teenagers to read

To lump teenage readers into one, all-encompassing bracket is not only dangerous but will ultimately reduce the choice of books available to them. We all know that teenagers who read don't necessarily want to continue reading 'children's books', that some seem to move seamlessly on to authors as varied as Agatha Christie and Isobel Allende, Ian Rankin and Margaret Atwood. This is partly because, though there are many wonderful writers for teenagers, no self-respecting young adult wants to venture into the 'children's' section of a bookshop – they would much rather hang out in Body Shop or HMV, or find books in the adult book displays or, sadly, stop reading books, entirely.

To attract teenagers to read at all is difficult; they don't like to feel manipulated, and life in secondary school nowadays makes it difficult to find time to read anything other than the books they are studying, The lead-up to major exams and the required reading tends to dominate their lives. This is why it is so important for children to develop the reading habit and reading stamina earlier in their lives – something which, hopefully, will never leave them, and the desire to lose themselves in a book.

As teenagers move away from the influence of their parents, it is important that, as well as having teachers to motivate and inspire them to read, there are bookshops which do the same. In the USA, for example, there are large areas devoted to 'young adult' books, sections of the bookshops which feel right for them, and are 'cool' places to be. Here in the UK it is sadly not the case. In most of the high street chains the children's areas are dominated by books for the much younger child. Hidden in amongst the books for the 8–12 year-olds there may be a few 'teenage' gems – but few teenagers venture into these areas and discover them. How about bookshops ranging teenage books like CDs, for example – in a rack, facing outwards – and organised by theme, with some short reviews?

Variety is the key

It is true that when we talk about books for teenagers, we tend to think automatically of gritty, contemporary fiction – rather like Melvyn Burgess's *Junk*, for example. But there are lots of books that young people like that are not specially written for teenagers. We need to remember that books for teenagers are any books, any genres, for the 12-plus age group. This band of children – from 12 up to young adult – can have any variety of tastes; they may like historical fiction, such as Celia Rees's *Witch Child*, humour, like Louise Rennison's *Angus, Thongs and Full Frontal Snogging* (to name just one of her deliciously funny and timeless teenage books), Philip Pullman's *His Dark Materials*, and David Almond's *Skellig*. A variety of genres, easy visibility in bookshops, the right covers and 'packaging' – all these things are hugely important to attract teenage readers. They are an intelligent and discerning audience, and when they discover an author they like, extremely loyal. Surely this is reason enough to make retailers think about being more imaginative in attracting teenage buyers?

The 'crossover' book

We talk a great deal these days of the 'crossover' book where an adult market has been identified for a children's book, a phenomenon which started with Harry Potter. Perhaps this is because publishers are desperately trying to attract a bigger section of the market for their authors, to make a double killing with one book. How true this *actually* is, I'm not sure, though occasionally a book which is stunningly original and exceptional, like *The Curious Incident of the Dog in the Night-Time*, can appeal to both markets, and even be successful in two editions. Another example of a 'crossover' book is *Across the Nightingale Floor* by Lian Hearn, which to some may feel more 'adult' than 'child', but which is hugely appealing to teenagers and doesn't feel at all patronisingly like a 'children's' book marketed at teens. How we market, package and position these 'crossover' books, such as Isobel Allende's *City of Beasts*, for example, occupies publishers constantly. Should they do one edition, sold into both adult and children's sections, or should there be two separate editions, one following the other? Or will teenagers who read discover Isobel Allende anyway, and thus make the publishing of a 'children's' edition completely redundant? Publishers certainly don't want to cannibalise their own book sales.

Is reading cool?

What we can say, post Harry Potter, is that reading is still 'cool' – that it is OK to be seen with a book on a bus or train. This can only be a good thing. It can only be fantastically exciting that there are queues outside bookshops for authors like Jacqueline Wilson, Philip Pullman, Darren Shan and, of course, J.K. Rowling.

Where do we go from here?

So where does this leave teenage fiction? How do we enable wonderful writers to reach their target audience? We try to keep publishing the talented authors who are offered to us, people like Mark Haddon who make a difference, who may write about 'issues' but don't set out to do so, but simply set out to write an engaging and compelling book. We keep trying to persuade retailers to recognise the importance of good teenage books – and I sincerely believe this is ultimately empowering, liberating and vital to their adult lives – and we have to be as innovative and imaginative as possible in the ways we think about presenting these books to our readers. Fewer books, better publishing, strong authors writing in different genres – this can be the only way forward. We have to keep on trying to publish the culturally important with the commercially successful in order to be able to produce books for our teenagers. We need to remember that, even in this relatively small area of our market, children need variety, complexity and vitality; they need adventure and fantasy and history and thrillers, humour and grit – everything, of course, that adult readers need, too.

We are privileged in our country to have truly wonderful authors writing for the teenage market – Michael Morpurgo's *Private Peaceful*, for example, which shows how world events impact on ordinary lives; Adele Geras, whose novel *Troy* is better than any history lesson; Peter Dickinson, Anthony Horowitz, Sherry Ashworth, Melvyn Burgess, Kevin Brooks, Nicky Singer… one can go on and on. There is new talent emerging all the time. Children's authors are now dominating the market in a way that was unheard of a few years ago, and this can only be a thrilling time for teenage fiction.

Gillie Russell is Fiction Publishing Director at HarperCollins Children's Books.

See also...
- *Notes from Jacqueline Wilson*, page 74
- *A word from J.K. Rowling*, page 77
- *How it all began*, page 78
- *Writing for different genres*, page 114
- *Writing for teenagers*, page 131

Writing for the school market

Changes made to the National Curriculum provide educational writers with the opportunity to create up-to-date teaching aids. Jim Green outlines the relationship between the writer for schools and the publisher.

Picture the scene: a typical school classroom; a teacher, pupils, desks, chairs, a computer in the corner of the room, the atmosphere noisy and intense. The typical classroom is a boisterous environment with a learning focus. What makes this so clearly a place of learning? The presence of a teacher and pupils of course; but it's their interaction with the vast range of available learning resources that makes this such a special place. It's the textbooks, the revision aids, the educational software, the posters on the walls and the vast array of published materials to be found in every classroom that, when expertly used by teachers and eagerly consumed by pupils, make this a centre for learning. How did all these resources find their way into the classroom? Whose thought, creativity and effort went into their development? And how would someone approach the challenge of creating materials that will one day find their way into this exciting environment?

The short answer to all these questions is that most educational resources are the result of an involved collaboration between a writer and a publishing company. A motivated individual wanted to create new materials and a publishing company saw an opportunity to develop and produce them. Individual schools are free to select their own resources and to use a broad range of materials from a number of sources. However, schools in the state sector are obliged to follow the National Curriculum, and it is the context of a National Curriculum that is most significant in determining the nature of published materials for the educational sector.

The National Curriculum

The National Curriculum is an educational framework that covers the entire Primary and Secondary school age range, establishing specific subject-by-subject requirements, desired learning outcomes and thus a very clear route map through the educational system followed by teachers and learners. Published materials must be compliant with, and supportive of, the requirements of the National Curriculum in order for them to be viable for use in the classroom. The template provided by the National Curriculum can be seen as both a very useful guide to an individual school's resource requirements and, less positively, as a rather constricting straitjacket which allows little individuality either in the preparation of resources or the teaching of course subject matter. My favourite National Curriculum analogy is that it can be likened to a classical symphony or a haiku – both have a clear and somewhat rigid framework within which there is infinite space for the creation of uniquely individual content. Indeed, it is the creation of unique content within the framework of the National Curriculum that is the essential challenge facing all prospective educational writers and publishers.

Whilst teachers might find reassurance in the overall structure offered by the National Curriculum, its ongoing development gives teachers the problem of implementing curriculum changes into their classroom teaching on a regular basis. Many teachers complain that the evolving curriculum creates one of their largest challenges – no sooner have they updated teaching notes, assimilated new learning outcomes and developed their own strategies for teaching the curriculum requirements, than the process begins again. However, it is curriculum change that presents the greatest single opportunity for new writers to create new materials and to get them into use in the classroom. Indeed, it is in helping teachers deliver emerging areas of the curriculum that writers and publishers can be of most value to the teaching community. Curriculum change can generally be anticipated some time in advance of implementation, giving prospective writers time to prepare materials and publishers time to assess both the market and the proposed materials. Focusing time and effort on areas of the curriculum that are changing makes good sense for all interested parties – teachers, writers and publishers.

What do publishers look for when assessing educational materials?

The single, overarching requirement is an understanding of the requirements of teachers and learners, which can also be described as market knowledge. What do schools need? What will help teachers do an even better job of delivering the curriculum? What will enhance the educational experience of pupils? A writer with clear and compelling answers to these questions will be of great interest to publishing companies. Other criteria publishers apply when assessing educational materials include:

• **Writing ability**. Is the material coherent, clear and appropriate for the target age group?
• **Knowledge of subject**. Is the writer an expert in the subject matter?
• Does the writer have **experience teaching the material**?
• Is the writer **a known authority in the field**, whose published work will be recognised as coming from an authoritative source? (For example, materials created by a subject examiner are widely coveted by publishers.)
• **Is the material well organised?** Does it have a logical structure?
• How much thought has the writer given to the **visual presentation of the content**? Are there sample illustrations, diagrams or photographs?
• **Is theoretical content applied in a motivating way?** Are the examples relevant and interesting? Do examples clarify or confuse?
• **Will the end product have an advantage** over the products currently available to schools? Is this clear in the materials?
• **Will the writer be fun to work with?** The best resources grow from a genuine partnership between writer and publisher.
• **Does the material give the motivated learner opportunities to go further and learn more?** This could, for example, take the form of a suggested further reading list, a series of links to relevant websites or optional activities that extend the learners' understanding of subject matter.

What publishers do

Assuming the prospective writer has given thought to the above, that there is a curriculum need for the materials and that a publisher is keen to invest in development and production, what happens next? Or more succinctly, what is it that publishers actually do?! Publishers manage every stage of the development, production and promotion of a project. The publisher role is to shape an original idea into an end product that articulates the original idea, whilst also supporting the curriculum and providing teachers with a resource that enhances the way they teach. The writer generally provides the creative impetus, the hard work of writing core content and, frequently, support to the sales and marketing of the end product. A more detailed list of the activities undertaken by a publisher includes:

• 18–24 months before publication: development of proposal; from an author's original idea the proposal is finalised, a contract agreed and the development timeline created.

• 6–24 months before publication: this phase includes the bulk of the writing and is when the writer's involvement is greatest. The publisher will provide input, feedback and guidance to the writer.

• 12 months before publication: initiation of marketing and promotional activities.

• 6–8 months before publication: coordination of reviews of the first draft of the manuscript. An editor will read the typescript and may also take advice from independent reviewers.

• 6–8 months before publication: copy-editing and preparing the typescript, commissioning of artwork, appointment of a picture researcher and clearance of copyright permission for sourced material.

• 6–8 months before publication: internal design and page layout.

• 6 months before publication: publisher will provide the author with a set of proofs for checking, these will also be sent to a professional proof reader and necessary corrections made to typescript.

• 4 months before publication: printing and binding.

• 2 weeks before publication: warehousing and release to market.

This is an overview of the process of creating educational materials that will hopefully be of use to anyone commissioned to write for the education market. However, we still need to look at the challenge of getting commissioned in the first place. This process will vary by publisher, indeed this process will vary between editors working at the same publishing house. What follows is a list of suggestions that will be of help to writers hoping to be commissioned to write for the school sector.

• **Make personal contact with the relevant editor**. The name of the editor responsible for a specific subject area will be available from the company switchboard. Call the editor to introduce yourself and your proposal prior to sending in sample materials. Materials sent to a generic 'Dear Sir/Madam' are rarely published.

• **When the time comes to send in sample materials, follow the publisher's requirements as closely as possible**. Most publishers will request a written overview of the project plus some comments on the needs of the prospective audience, as well as a draft table of contents and sample chapter. It's important to note that sending in too much material to an editor can be as unhelpful as sending in too little.

• **Ensure the material is 'fit for purpose'**. Does it solve a teaching problem? Does it meet an emerging curriculum requirement? Is it obvious to the reader that the material solves a problem/meets a curriculum requirement?

• **Ensure the end product has an advantage over currently available resources**. The existence of the National Curriculum means that there are ever smaller differences between the competing resources. A new product needs an 'edge', a point of distinction, that makes it more attractive to a teacher than the resource they currently use.

Summary

My intention is to provide helpful information that will assist in overcoming the challenges ahead. Should you feel daunted by any of the above it's important to remember that thousands of new products are published for the school market each year and many thousands of once-aspiring writers are now successfully published authors. The average classroom is packed with resources and this breadth of materials gives a lot of scope for new writers. Remember the classroom from the start of this article? A typical classroom will contain the work of around 100 different writers. Of course there will be long, lonely hours involved in the writing itself but once a publisher has committed to your project you'll be working as part of a team. The joy of making a direct contribution to education will make the effort worthwhile and when things get tough just imagine the excitement and interest created by well-written, well-published and genuinely motivating educational resources.

Jim Green has worked extensively in educational publishing in both the UK and North America. He has been involved in creating a broad range of educational resources for schools, most recently as Managing Director of Collins Education.

It could happen to you

Hundreds of manuscripts are sent to literary agents each week and luck and perseverance both play a part in their fate. Matthew Skelton tells the story of how his book was published.

My story begins with three unlikely words: 'No unsolicited manuscripts.' The stark warning appears next to many of the publishers and agents listed in the *Writers' & Artists' Yearbook* and filled me with trepidation each time I daydreamed my way through the guide as an aspiring author. How was I supposed to interest anyone in my manuscript if I couldn't send even the smallest portion without permission? It seemed impossible.

I was fortunate. One of my friends had completed a creative writing course at a UK institution and provided me with the names of two agents I might like to approach. My manuscript was already longer than the suggested word count for its age group, but I followed the rules in the *Yearbook* as closely as possible: I drafted a short synopsis of the plot and requested permission to submit my manuscript at the earliest convenience. I chose the longer-established agency first – more from a sense of reverence than anything else. (I had studied the rise of literary agents in the 1890s as part of my doctoral dissertation and I'd read some of the founder's letters to famous authors at the turn of the century. It seemed as good a connection as any.)

There was only one thing left to do: wait.

And wait.

No answer came.

I waited for more than four months, but I received no invitation to submit my manuscript. Was my proposal *that* bad? At this point, I was unemployed and living in a borrowed room. My confidence was at an all-time low. I didn't have the nerve to pick up the phone to check that my letter had arrived. I didn't even have a phone.

I took this as a sign. My book wasn't going to be published. I had failed. I hid my manuscript from all but my family and closest friends and tried to find that equally elusive thing: an academic job.

Once again, I was lucky. Another friend read my manuscript and urged me to approach the second agent. The text was far from perfect, she agreed with me, but there was something promising inside it … something just waiting to get out. When I pointed out that this agency was located a few streets away from where we stood, she put her foot down and said, 'If you don't send it, I will.'

And that's what she did. With my permission, of course, she printed the first 40 pages and delivered them, together with a revised copy of my covering letter, to the local agency.

In my case, I was extremely lucky. The first person to look at my manuscript took an instant liking to one of my central characters, Duck – a precocious girl who is unwilling to take off her bright yellow raincoat in case it causes her parents to split up. Within days, I had received a reply: the agency asked to see the rest of the manuscript. The name of the reader didn't match the name of the agent I had approached in my letter, but this didn't matter. I was in with a chance...

Once again, my friend came to my aid. She printed the whole manuscript for me and delivered it in person. This time, the wait was longer.

Something promising

What are agents looking for? As my friend wisely suggested, they're looking for something promising … something just waiting to get out. 'Something promising' can take a variety of forms: a gripping storyline; an intriguing character; a new, unusual, or confident voice; or something else completely... I can't presume to know. I wrote my first novel because my characters' lives depended on it. I wrote it for them – and for myself. I wrote it because I've known since I was a small boy that I wanted to be a writer and I had to keep on trying.

Had I realised, then, the number of manuscripts that are submitted to an agency in any given week I might have lost heart. Fortunately, these manuscripts *do* receive attention. Some are sent to the wrong kind of agent and so determine their own fate; others are so full of mistakes they make the agent's decision quite simple; but the majority come from hopeful, hardworking, aspiring writers – like me – and need some refinement before publishers will consider them seriously.

An agent is not merely an arbiter of good writing or potential marketability; increasingly, an agent is also an author's first editor, an experienced reader who happens to have an abundance of networks and contacts within the publishing industry. Someone, in short, who helps prepare a manuscript for its entrance into the fiercely competitive book world.

The wait

I went through the familiar gamut of emotions while I waited: excitement, incredulity, self-doubt... Four weeks later, I received a short note from the agent herself. Her verdict: we should meet.

The meeting was friendly, but professional. I was able to learn more about the kinds of books she represented (and to hear in advance about one of the following year's publishing sensations) while she asked me about my background and my aspirations as a writer. It was not dissimilar to a job interview, except that this was for a job I really wanted. We talked about the manuscript and she voiced many of my own reservations about the plot. She advised me not to give up my day job (well, in my case, my daily hunt for a day job), but more promisingly she told me to keep in touch.

Sadly, there is no instant metamorphosis from an aspiring author into a soon-to-be-published one. Securing an agent is just the first promising step of a long, often arduous process involving a lot of editing and endless daydreaming, but for me it made all the difference. I was back on my own, living in another borrowed room, revising my manuscript for what felt like the ten-thousandth time. Only I now had a renewed sense of hope and ambition. Even though we hadn't yet signed a contract, I had enticed the interest of a reputable agent and I was beginning to believe in my manuscript as a 'book'.

Three months of revision quickly lapsed into eight but something magical was happening: the plot was undergoing a radical transformation – a whole new dimension to the story was added, an historical element that connected most of the loose strands that had bothered me so much before. Every now and then, I would receive an encouraging, enquiring email from *my* agent (as I liked to think of her) which gave me the confidence to persevere, even when I feared my characters had led me into another dead end. It was the spur I needed: an approving voice telling me I was on the right track. Little did I realise, of course, that she was already 'selling' the book in quarters I could never hope to reach on my own: editorial offices, book fairs, publishing houses – both in the UK and overseas. I still remember the occasion she told me that an editor in New York was keen to see the revised version of the text. I was so surprised I jumped up from my seat at the computer terminal in the local public library (where I'd set up my makeshift office) and walked straight into a wall of books.

Nothing, however, could have prepared me for what happened next – not even my agent's cautious optimism. Just a few weeks after I signed the agency's agreement and she submitted the manuscript to London publishers, I was meeting many of the people mentioned in the *Writers' & Artists' Yearbook* face-to-face, hearing flattering things said about my writing, and receiving offers from various countries for translation rights. I was also learning rapidly about other components of the publishing world: interviews, launch parties, power lunches… And now I'm being asked to write an article for the *Children's Writers' & Artists' Yearbook* on how it feels to be published. Life is sometimes as strange as fiction.

Thanks to the advice of friends, the timely intervention of my agent (who decided when I should stop revising my manuscript and allow other people to read it) and no end of good luck, my first novel appeared in March 2006. Of course, the really hard work is only now beginning. There are publicity tours, television and radio interviews and school visits to consider … as well as Book Number Two! Nevertheless, I have achieved what initially felt impossible: I've got my foot in that elusive, allusive door. And that's just the start.

(As for the first agent on my list: I received a response – asking to see the manuscript – less than two weeks after I met my current agent. My letter had been buried in a pile of manuscripts. Of course, I wouldn't change a thing. My story had its own very happy ending.)

Matthew Skelton's first novel, *Endymion Spring* (Puffin 2006), has been translated into more than 20 languages.

See also...
• *The amazing picture book story*, page 217

What does an editor do?

Yvonne Hooker describes the varied and exciting aspects to an editor's job.

What does an editor do? Good question. Answers have ranged from reading all day to drawing the illustrations. However, baldly put, an editor's job is to acquire new titles and to oversee a book's progress from acquisition to publication, bringing the book in on time and on budget. Where the book goes, the editor follows – from finance and contracts, through design and production, to sales and publicity – making sure that their book, their baby, is getting the best possible treatment and the maximum attention. An editor is the book's champion throughout its life.

Acquiring

The demise of the publisher's slush pile in recent years means that most new books now come via agents. No editor wants to miss out on seeing the latest find from an agent. It's always possible that she will turn down a manuscript that will later become a runaway bestseller – publishing remains a gambling business – but the worst scenario of all is just not to have been offered the book in the first place. So, it is absolutely vital for the editor to be on close terms with all the relevant agents. She must make sure that the agent knows her tastes and is generally confident of her editorial skills and judgements, so that when a real plum of a book arrives, the agent will immediately think, 'Ah, x is just the editor for this,' and send it off.

No one can be an editor and not thrill to the sight of a new manuscript, so finding something you want to publish is a pulse-racing moment. What the editor has to do immediately is to get everyone else's pulse racing as well. She has to start the internal buzz. No book is going to succeed unless all the publishing departments are firmly behind it and it is the editor's job to get the enthusiasm going by talking the book up to key figures, and by presenting the book at the publisher's acquisitions meetings.

The editor will probably have to prepare some kind of financial spreadsheet showing that the book can be expected to make a profit. Figures are needed from sales, marketing, rights and so on and, in order to get the best possible forecasts, the editor has to convince all these other departments that here is a terrific new book which is an absolute must for the list.

In the meantime, the editor will have rung the agent to express her enthusiasm. Usually agents will say whether they are sending books to other publishers as well, but it's always prudent to check and to find out if interest has been expressed from any other quarter. If it has, and an auction situation is developing, then the editor has to make sure that everyone is aware of this, and that the offer is going to be ready on time. In these circumstances, the editor may prepare a particular pitch for the book: a presentation which will convince the author that this is the true home for the book with people who really understand it.

Although many other departments will be involved in the mechanics of the offer, it is the editor who will present it to the agent and who will negotiate all the terms of advance, royalties and rights. It would be rare for an offer for a book by a new author to be accepted as it stands. A certain amount of haggling will be expected and this is one instance where a cool head will serve an editor rather better than unbridled enthusiasm.

Sometimes, before the deal is concluded, the agent will want to have a beauty parade and take the author round to meet competing publishers. This is the editor's chance to woo the author face-to-face and, very often, though not always, the choice of editor will be the deciding factor. The author should be well aware that this is the person with whom he or she will be working most closely and that this will be a vital and all-important relationship. It is, of course, a professional one, and it is perfectly possible for author and editor to work together harmoniously even if they would never choose each other's company outside of publishing, but it does help to have a sense of rapport. No one else has as much contact with the author, and no one else fights as fiercely for the author's voice to be heard. Once the book is hers, the editor will be the author's champion. But she also has to remember that the book is required to make money for the publisher as well as the author.

Editing

The first stage the manuscript of the book goes through is editing: the process to arrive at a final text which is agreed upon by both the editor and the author. This is, rightly, a stage largely hidden from the rest of the world though, for both author and editor, it is the most rewarding part of the whole process. The editor is the first professional reader of the manuscript and her aim is to make the book the best it can possibly be. She will read it with a fine critical eye, checking for problems and seeing what can be done to put them right. These can range from the simple glitch (a week that lasts ten days or a dog that changes breed in the course of the story), to the emotional core (does a relationship have enough depth, would this character actually do or say this, is the emotional focus clear enough?) and the overall narrative structure (is the beginning punchy enough, does it take too long to get going, does it feel rushed at the end?).

This is the stage which cements the relationship between editor and author. It is a curiously intimate process, relying as it does on a basis of trust and a sharing of the creative process. There has to be absolute trust between author and editor. The author has to feel that he or she can rely upon the editor's critical skill and judgement; the editor has to feel that the author will receive editorial suggestions with serenity. It is taken for granted that editors will not make changes for the sake of it. Nor will they try to rewrite the book as they would have written it. It is, and will remain, the author's book. The whole process should be one of discussion and cooperation, with author and editor working together to make the book the very best it can be.

Every author has a different way of working with his or her editor. Some like to submit a finished manuscript, while others like to send in first ideas and chapters for editorial input as they go along. Any way the author wants to play it is fine with the editor. Sometimes, even the most experienced authors get stuck for some reason – finding the right voice, for instance – and it helps to meet with and talk to the editor. This is a vital and important part of the editorial role as writing is an incredibly lonely occupation and to be able to talk problems through with an interested and experienced reader can be a lifeline. The author–editor relationship can develop to the point where the editor will be one of the first people to be told about quite personal things – impending marriages and babies – and her advice can be sought about things which have nothing to do with work: the best way to cook roast potatoes, for instance (this has actually happened!). Editorial trust can extend beyond the book!

Copy-editing and proofing

When a final manuscript has been agreed between the author and editor, the text is ready to be copy-edited. Not many editors do this themselves nowadays, though most will have copy-editorial experience. This is not just because they do not have the time but it's good to have a fresh eye on the manuscript at this stage. The copy-editor marks up the manuscript for the typesetter, checks the grammar and spelling and acts as a safety net for any glitches which may have slipped through. Any word changes are checked with the author and, in any case, most authors are given the opportunity of seeing the copy-edited manuscript. This is the last opportunity to get everything right before the manuscript is typeset (and changes start costing money) so it is vitally important that everyone should be happy with it at this stage.

The copy-edited manuscript will then go off to be typeset. The editor, with the designer or text designer, will have chosen an appropriate text setting and any flourishes to chapter heads. If the book is to be illustrated, the editor will have marked appropriate places in the text for the illustrations. Both editor and author will be involved in choosing an illustrator, but this aspect is the responsibility of the design department.

When the proofs arrive from the typesetter a set will be sent to the author and another set will be proofread by a professional proofreader. The editor will see the proofs but will very rarely proofread the text, though every editor has the skill. This is a last opportunity for another fresh eye on the text to check for any errors.

While all this is going on, the editor will be busy with other aspects of the book. Having a final manuscript or bound proofs, if there are any, is an opportunity to remind everyone how good the book is, making sure it's not forgotten as other, newer titles are coming through. The editor may send the book out to well-known people in the hope of getting a useful quote for publicity purposes.

The cover

Getting the right cover for a book is of paramount importance. Although this is the design department's province, the editor has a vital role to play. She will need to discuss the book with the designer, and with the sales and marketing teams. Together they will decide on the approach to take, though the choice of artist will generally be in the hands of the designer. The editor may also have to write the cover copy if the publishing house does not have a separate blurb-writing department.

Because getting the right cover is so important, other departments such as sales and marketing will be involved and will have to approve. Of course, publishers want authors to be happy with the covers but authors very rarely have final approval of covers; it is generally accepted that this is an area where the publisher's judgement is final. It is the editor's job to send roughs and visuals of the cover to the author and, in rare cases of disagreement, to persuade them that the cover is absolutely the right one, or to suggest acceptable compromises.

Proof covers have to be ready at least six months before publication to allow for sell-in time. If that date slips, then the publication date has to move, so getting the cover through on time is a major editorial preoccupation.

Publication

Once the cover is done and the final text is going through, the editor's major work on the book is done. But she must keep it in the forefront of everyone's minds and keep the internal buzz growing. She will present the book at internal launch meetings and possibly also at sales conferences and presentations of lead and highlight titles. She will also be liaising with publicity and marketing on their plans to launch the book and will make sure that the author knows the publisher's publicity contact.

About a month before publication, early finished copies of the book will arrive on the editor's desk, hopefully looking wonderful. The editor will check through to make sure that everything is all right, and send an early copy to the author.

All the editor has to do then is to send the author a card on publication day, raise a glass at the launch party if there is one, read the reviews circulated by the publicity department, and make sure that the book is entered for every relevant prize going.

An editor has to have sound judgement, a fine critical eye and enormous funds of patience and sensitivity. It also helps to be a fast reader! Above all, she must be a consummate juggler, handling books at all their different stages – yet be able to drop everything in a crisis to concentrate on the one thing that matters: getting an author's book absolutely right, the book that he or she always hoped it would be.

Yvonne Hooker was Senior Editor at Puffin Books 1996–2008. She has now retired.

See also...
- *Getting started*, page 1
- *A word from J.K. Rowling*, page 77
- *How it all began*, page 78
- *Marketing, publicising and selling children's books*, page 149

Marketing, publicising and selling children's books

The way in which books for children are marketed and publicised is different to the way the adult market is targeted. Rosamund de la Hey identifies the target audience for children's books and explains the various ways in which publishers can reach that audience.

What is marketing?

Marketing can be seen as an umbrella term that includes all the work a publisher does to promote or sell a book. Many people are not clear about the difference between marketing and publicity. Traditionally, marketing is categorised as anything paid for (posters, advertising, catalogues, etc) and publicity (such as review coverage and radio interviews) is free. There is a useful saying that every book must be sold three times – by the editor to the rest of the company, by the sales/marketing/publicity departments to the bookseller, and by the bookseller to the consumer.

How can authors help?

There are many ways authors can help to market their books from the start. Most publishers will send out an author questionnaire soon after acquiring the book. This will generally ask for information ranging from the name of his or her local bookshop, to background details which may offer a marketing or publicity hook. It can help to think of a biography as a series of tabloid headlines – for instance, a children's novelist whose previous career was that of a fighter pilot would be very interesting to teenage magazine editors with a young male readership. On the other hand, if there are areas an author would rather the press did not know about, he or she should tell the publicist, as otherwise innocent, but upsetting, mistakes may happen. Sometimes a mock interview with the publisher's publicist may help the author.

If a book covers a specialist area or issue – for example, Benjamin Zephaniah's *Face* deals with severe facial scarring – it's likely that the author will be able to give the publisher information about relevant organisations which would be interested in hearing about the book, and whose members may indeed buy it.

Events can form a crucial part of promoting a children's book. However, it's worth remembering that not all authors are comfortable in front of a room full of six year-olds.

Marketing children's books

One of the differences between marketing children's books and marketing adults' books is the timescale. Adult book launches are all tied round a very specific window of publication, whereas a children's publication, even if there is a splashy launch, tends to work more like a slow-burn candle.

Children's advertising is also dictated by both the target market – children and their parents – and by more limited budgets. While adult campaigns can assume that adults read a newspaper, take public transport and go shopping, children's sphere of influence tends to be more limited – school, the local sports centre, the library, the internet or television. Publishers must also decide whether they are targeting the child or the parent in advertising.

Publicity

In publicity terms, children's review space is more limited than for adult books, so the coverage happens when the space allows. Additionally, many of the important reviews for children's books happen in specialist magazines such as *Books for Keeps* and *Carousel* which are published only bimonthly or quarterly.

Libraries

Libraries often receive the books some time after publication as each book needs to be adapted for library use. In school libraries, budgets can also be very tight so it may be months or years after publication that a school can afford to stock new titles.

Events

Unlike adult authors who will normally only do a book tour around publication, many children's authors and illustrators spend a great deal of their time doing events and workshops in schools and bookshops, and at the numerous literary festivals around the country throughout the year (see *Children's literature festivals and trade fairs* on page 375). For those who do get involved, the word-of-mouth benefits are well worth the effort. One of the best examples of this is Jacqueline Wilson, who was visiting schools up to three times a week long before her books became bestsellers. She still visits schools regularly year round, as well as touring bookshops and festivals with her new publications.

Direct marketing to schools

The children's market lends itself to direct marketing more than many other areas of trade publishing. This is largely because there is a captive market sitting in school for much of the year. However, marketing directly to schools does have its drawbacks. Teachers are very busy people who have to wade through enough paperwork without being sent endless publishers' catalogues. So, it is important for publishers to be clear and realistic about why they are sending material to schools. A children's educational publisher which also publishes a trade fiction list, may be more likely to be picked up by the Head of English because he or she is expecting to order course books from that catalogue.

Mailing a full trade publisher catalogue to every primary school headteacher in the country is also a very expensive exercise, for potentially little return. Some publishers do have a schools sales force who sell their list directly into schools; others use freelance reps to sell a limited selection from their list into schools. The appropriateness of either of these approaches will depend entirely on the type of list a publisher has.

World Book Day, however, provides many trade publishers with a positive platform to market to schools. For the past few years, a schools' pack has been sent out giving information to teachers and their pupils about World Book Day. Publishers that support World Book Day have the opportunity to insert marketing material (flyers, posters, etc) into the schools pack and know that the investment is more likely to pay dividends because it's more targeted.

Advertising in schools

Media agencies now sell poster sites within schools themselves. Books are arguably the perfect 'product' to advertise in this way – the teachers are keen to encourage reading and hopefully the advertisement will spark the interest of the children. This is an example of where jacketdesign is crucial. If the jacket is not sufficiently strong, it's unlikely to make an eye-catching design that will stand up to the advertising-savvy children.

This type of advertising is not cheap and so is likely to be used rarely and be carefully timed. *Holes* by Louis Sachar, although winner of the prestigious Newbury Medal in the USA, was unknown in the UK until 1999. Bloomsbury marketed the hardback with a successful publicity-led campaign and when the paperback was published nine months later it targeted schools and ran a poster campaign within secondary schools. It is always hard to gauge the exact response to advertising of this type without commissioning expensive research (which is often more expensive than the original advertising costs). However, *Holes* has now sold half a million copies, helped in no small way by being extensively read for course work in schools.

Playground marketing

The phrase 'playground marketing' was widely used after the publication of *Harry Potter and the Philosopher's Stone* in 1997 and partly as a result of the book winning theGold Smarties Book Prize that year. It is very hard to pin down exactly how playground marketing works except to say that it is a combination of many factors: school events, word of mouth, in-school advertising and the prizes network all play their part. The latter is especially important when the children themselves are involved in selecting the winner of a book prize. This now happens for many prizes, from the big national ones such as the Nestle Children's Book Prize and the Children's Book Award, to strongly championed local prizes such as the Angus Book Award (see *Children's book and illustration prizes and awards* on page 364).

Playground marketing only works in tandem with mainstream publicity and child-focused campaigns. For example, when *Harry Potter and the Prisoner of Azkaban* was released in 1999, it was timed for 3.45pm, just after school finished for the day. This caused massive publicity as children streamed out of school and into bookshop queues to buy the book, giving the television cameras a visual hook.

Internet marketing

Many children's publishers are putting more emphasis on internet marketing. The reasons for this are fairly straightforward. In general, children are far more internet-aware than their parents, and tend to spend a lot more time on their computers than reading a book.

Most publishers have their own website and it's worth having a look at some examples to get an idea about what's out there. Some lead titles will be marketed on a specially created independent site as a key part of the overall marketing plan. For example, fantasy fiction often inspires addictive online games and quizzes, such as www.faeriewars.co.uk and www.artemisfowl.co.uk. However, these are expensive to set up and a great deal can be done to promote a book on the existing publisher website. Many publishers also use their sites to run readers' clubs and offer information to teachers.

Design

One of the key marketing tools for any book is the jacket image. If the book is fantastic but has a dull, or inappropriate jacket, not only will the bookseller be unwilling to stock it, but the reader will not be attracted to it, nor understand what kind of a reading experience it's 'selling'.

A good example of where a jacket can help to raise an already successful writer to the next level, is *Witch Child* by Celia Rees. Staring out of the jacket is the beautiful face of a young girl who commands the passer-by's attention with her piercing stare. The book jacket was cited by many booksellers as one of the key reasons why customers picked it up and it was subsequently shortlisted for the British Book Awards in their Book Cover image of the year.

Book jacket design is not only important in bookshops, it is also crucial in advertising. This is true for all advertising from standing out in a small trade advert in the *Bookseller* or *The School Librarian*, to staring down from the side of a London bus.

Trade sales and marketing

Sales and marketing have become more and more closely allied since the demise of the Net Book Agreement (NBA). This was abolished in 1995 and has meant the inexorable rise of the big discount as a way for booksellers to market to the consumer. The knock-on effect of this in the high street has been for publishers to compete with one another for their books to claim valued places in bookshop promotions, be they '3 for 2' offers or '£2 off' schemes. Although these do almost always generate higher sales for a title, they come at a price, and more and more publishers' marketing budgets are being devoted to funding bookshops to run these promotions.

As a result, the trend is for big books to get bigger and small titles to get lost and often disappear without trace. This in turn is polarising publishers' lists and making it a much harder business to break into.

Non-traditional book markets

Another knock-on effect of the NBA's demise is the rise of the supermarket as bookseller. Big supermarket chains such as Asda, Tesco and Sainsbury's are getting more and more involved in selling books, and it is now almost impossible to get onto the general bestseller lists without a supermarket presence for your title. They usually stock a very narrow range of titles but some, such as Asda, will occasionally try less well-known authors who publishers are pushing strongly. Bearing in mind that the likes of Tesco have in the region of 800 stores, this can transform the sales of a title on the basis of one retailer.

Book clubs/direct marketing sales

Book clubs have always marketed themselves using price and heavy advertising in the national press. Usually they offer deals whereby if you join you get several books very cheaply and you are then tied into a minimum level of book buying through the club for a specific period. Direct marketing companies such as The Book People have been incredibly successful in selling to customers in their workplace and through catalogues.

In the children's world, book clubs are especially important as there are more clubs devoted to children and their parents than there are for adults (see *Children's book clubs* on page 68). The children's market also has schools as a captive audience. Several clubs, including Scholastic and Troubadour, are set up to run 'book fairs' in schools in tandem with their mail order operations. They offer a hand-picked selection of what the club deems to be the most commercial and appropriate selection of titles. It is therefore crucial that any children's publisher has a very strong relationship with the clubs. They may stock a more narrow range than the high street, but they order in bulk and in many cases that one order can radically improve the viability of a book's print run.

The changing face of the children's marketplace

The past five or six years has seen a huge change in attitudes to children's publishing. One of the effects of this has been to generate far more high-profile – and expensive – marketing campaigns to launch new writers such as Eoin Colfer and Anthony Horowitz. In the past, these authors might have expected a publicity campaign and perhaps a poster for book-shops and libraries. However, for a small number of lead titles, now you will see major 'outdoor' advertising and read about them as front page news. Children's books are now winning the big prizes and taking up the kind of column inches that used to be reserved for the Salman Rushdies of this world.

However, this can distort the market and it should be emphasised that, generally speaking, children's books attract smaller marketing budgets than adults' books. This is down to simple economics: in general, children's books cost less than their adult equivalent. On the positive side, all this publicity has meant that the public awareness of good children's writing has been massively raised by the success of authors such as Rowling, Pullman and Wilson.

The 'crossover' book

The rise of the children's book prompted adults to find out what all the fuss is about and as a result the 'crossover' book was born. When Bloomsbury first published the Harry Potter books for the adult market with a specially designed discreet black and white jacket in 1998, it was for several reasons. Firstly, anecdotal evidence suggested that adults were reading the books already but that some felt embarrassed to be seen in public with a children's book. Secondly, even when *Harry Potter and the Chamber of Secrets* reached number one in the overall bestseller charts, booksellers refused to stock the books at the front of store. And finally, as a marketing concept, for fun, to see if it worked.

The results speak for themselves with the advent of adult editions of the Philip Pullman trilogy *His Dark Materials*, *Holes* by Louis Sachar and *Face* by Benjamin Zephaniah, the 'crossover' book has become a recognised marketing strategy that works when used for the right book.

This theory has been taken a step further by the simultaneous publication of Mark Haddon's *The Curious Incident of the Dog in the Night-Time* in 2003 when Jonathan Cape and David Fickling Books brought out editions for both markets. This has proved a huge critical and commercial success.

Champion the book

One thing that will never change in marketing children's books is the very first sale that is made – by the editor to the publishing company. He or she must be able to inspire people to read and love the book they champion. In children's books, as with adult books, a very great deal comes down to the individual championing of one book above all others. This passion can make all the difference in marketing and selling, and it costs nothing.

Rosamund de la Hey was formerly Children's Marketing Director of Bloomsbury Publishing Plc and has been responsible for marketing J.K. Rowling's *Harry Potter* books, as well as other notable successes such as *Holes* by Louis Sachar and *Witch Child* by Celia Rees. With her husband, Bill, Rosamund has just opened a bookshop, café and giftshop in the Scottish Borders called the Mainstreet Trading Company.

See also...

- *What does an editor do?* page 145
- *Children's books and the US market*, page 158
- *Categorising children's books*, page 162
- *Magazines about children's literature and education*, page 270

Notes from a successful self-publisher

Despite having proof that children liked what he had written, John Howard's novel was repeatedly rejected by literary agents. Undeterred, he self-published his book and drew upon his creative resources to gain national and international recognition.

When I dispatched three chapters of my children's novel *The Key to Chintak* to literary agents in late 2003, along with appreciative letters and emails from children who'd read and commented on it for me, I had very high hopes. The children's reaction to my book had been very enthusiastic, and to me that was the acid test. I hoped literary agents would take a similar view.

Then, after the usual long wait for a response, something amazing happened. Every single agent I'd contacted rejected it. It is hard to describe the feeling of continually being knocked back in this way, although I'm sure many aspiring authors know exactly what I'm talking about.

Time, I decided, to self-publish.

Writing the right book

Around 12 months earlier, I had decided the time was right to ditch my IT career and finally have a go at full-time writing. It's something I've always wanted to do, even though I'm dyslexic and because of that, failed my English 'O' level at school. So my plan was not necessarily a wise one, particularly from a financial point of view. But money wasn't the main motivation. If it was, I would have stuck with IT. But my wife and I had built up a healthy savings fund, and she fully supported my decision. For my part, I simply wanted to earn a fair living doing something that I loved – creating something new for children to explore and enjoy.

The basic plot of *The Key to Chintak* had been swirling around in my head for quite a while, and once I started writing my story – about a 12-year-old girl who can read the pages of a blank book no one else can see – it all came together fairly quickly. My idea was to write a story for children aged ten and over that mixed fact and fiction, and where the central character was a young girl, because in my view there aren't enough strong young heroines in modern children's literature.

Once it was written, I then took the radical decision to actually ask children if they liked it before, and after, submitting it to any literary agents. This was because in 1997, I'd had an earlier stab at writing, producing a few chapters of a novel about the life and adventures of a young James Bond. I had no experience of writing a book but my head has always been overflowing with ideas. Though immersed in full-time work at that time, I managed to snatch the odd hour here and there to pen my planned masterpiece. Alas, the many publishing agents I contacted did not agree with my future career plans. After months of waiting, all returned my work – 'Thanks but no thanks', basically.

To find out why, I phoned one up, only to be told that James Bond was 'old hat'. If I believed *that* was what children wanted to read, then I should stick to my day job. So I did.

Roll forward to 2004 to find that young James Bond clone Alex Rider, the teenage spy created by author Anthony Horowitz, is an international multi-million bestseller. And since then, Master Bond himself has topped the charts, compliments of Charlie Higson.

Looking back, I can now see that the writing wasn't up to scratch, but that wasn't the reason given to me for rejection. So, when it came to getting *The Key to Chintak* published, I decided to cut out the middle man and ask the children what they thought of my work. Apart from my experience with my young James Bond novel, I felt – and still do – that children need more involvement in the whole process of delivering a children's book. Most children's books are written by adults, reviewed by adults, and circulated by adults – with little input from the target audience.

For my own market testing exercise, I had 50 copies of *The Key to Chintak* printed, and after visiting two local schools near my home in East Sussex to distribute the copies and then talking directly to the children who'd read it, I came away certain I was on to a winner. They all absolutely loved the book. Hence my decision to go it alone having been knocked back by the agents.

On the self-publishing road

Self-publishing is, however, a minefield. To start with, a good cover and good editor – and both are essential – will set you back over £1000. But that's just one part of the jigsaw. If you want to succeed as a self-published author, you also need an iron will, outstanding marketing and presentation skills, and a good website. Most importantly, you must be able to deal with anyone or anything that blocks your way. And a lot will block your way.

From the off, I decided I wanted to sell an eye-catching number of books – at the time I thought around 1000 should be enough – to convince a publisher to take me on without an agent. To do this, I needed exposure and to get into the bookshops, fairly obviously. But don't think for a minute that as soon as you print your work, people will be queuing up to buy it. Once you have exhausted family and friends, who else knows your book exists?

I decided the best way to drum up sales was to continue touring schools around Sussex. To convince headteachers to take a chance on an unknown like me, I offered my services free – and soon built up a long list of schools willing to have me in. Visiting both primary and secondary schools, I'd talk for an hour or so to an interested and enthusiastic young audience about my struggle to get published, then read from the book and act out a scene or two.

I then used these visits, and the enthusiastic response I met with, to blag some local press coverage, and then used the local press to blag some local radio airtime. Oh, yes, I should mention, you need to be able to blag a lot. Yet initially, all of this effort did not sell me many books in the shops. Instead it filled up my email inbox with people telling me they couldn't get *The Key To Chintak* anywhere.

I'd signed up with a very helpful print-on-demand specialist and through this company managed to get my book listed at a distributor. But this system let me down, and cost me sales.

As I discovered, the system back then for supply of books is cumbersome and flawed when it comes to print-on-demand for a mass market title. The theory is fantastic but the reality is not. The theory goes like this: somehow convince people to go into a shop and ask for my book. Being print-on-demand it will not be on the shelf, but once ordered it will be printed overnight and shipped to the store the next day. Fantastic.

It turned out, though, that when people were going into bookshops and asking for *The Key to Chintak*, they were often told it was out of print. I remedied this by convincing the wholesaler to actually stock pre-printed copies of the book, and once this happened, sales started to move. So a golden rule for all aspiring self-publishers is to never let your stock drop to zero at the wholesaler otherwise you will lose sales.

Because a lot of people were requesting *The Key to Chintak,* some local stores then decided to stock it on their shelves. My delight at this was short-lived when I discovered that one shop, which had sold some 200 copies of my book, was not scanning it at the till but manually keying the price in. This makes a lot of difference, because if books are not scanned, they will not register on Nielsen BookScan (which records all book sales nation-wide). If your sales do not register with them, then it is very hard to prove that you've had any in the first place. And no sales equals no credibility. Apart from the bookshop scanning problem, I had also sold some 2500 books direct to schools. Nielsen would not accept these sales either. Only by hooking up with a local bookshop that supplied schools did I overcome this problem but it took months to remedy and lots of pushing.

However, according to Nielsen BookData, in the second quarter of 2006 *The Key to Chintak* was No 2 in the Children's Chart for Small Publishers. This is no mean feat as this chart includes the likes of Faber and Faber. Also, I finished 25th for the year – the only self-published book in the top 500. In addition to the sales recorded by Nielsen I have sold just as many books again into schools, libraries, independent bookshops, book clubs, etc. Thought you might like to know!

Gaining national recognition

By February 2006, I had visited 40 more schools around Sussex, and spoken to loads of local booksellers, journalists and television people. I had also received around a thousand glowing emails from readers through the book's website (www.zamorian.com). Sales were going well. There was one remaining problem: outside of Sussex, nobody knew me. I needed national exposure. Specifically I needed to convince a major book retailer to stock *The Key to Chintak* nationwide, expand my school tour to coincide with this, and a new cover.

Up until then, everything I earned went back into the deep hole in the ground that is self-publishing. Visiting schools free and printing bookmarks and posters takes its toll on the bank balance. With no marketing budget to speak of, I believed a fancy cover would help persuade people who knew nothing about me to pick up my book and give it a chance – providing I could get into the shops nationally, of course.

I sent a cold-call email to Scott Pack, the then head buyer at Waterstone's, who, according to at least one newspaper has a fearsome reputation. My email was written with a lot of tongue and a lot of cheek. I didn't have Scott's email address, as nobody at Water-stone's would give it to me, so I guessed a few and one got through.

Scott replied straight away, saying that if the book was any good, Waterstone's would stock it. After reading it, he ordered 3000 copies in March, and included it in the stores' 'three books for the price of two' promotion. Oh, how lovely it was to see that order! Airport branches of WHSmith followed suit, as did the Sussex schools library service. *The Key to Chintak* went on to outsell a lot of mainstream-published books in the same Wa-terstone's promotion as mine. To date, Waterstone's have sold all of their 3000 allocation and more besides. To coincide with this, I went on a tour visiting 30 schools scattered far and wide around the country.

Not all of my promotional approaches have worked but both Terry Wogan and Chris Evans were kind enough to spare me some time when, after standing in the rain for two hours, I pounced on them as they left the BBC Radio 2 studios. I have also exchanged emails with Amanda Ross at Cactus TV, the makers of *Richard & Judy*. I read somewhere that she was almost impossible to pin down and hard to deal with. I agree with the first point (I got escorted off the Cactus TV premises twice!), but not with the second. I found her to be charming and helpful, and I'm not just saying that to get on the show!

Even though I have now sold well over 10,000 copies of *The Key to Chintak*, I am well aware that it could still benefit greatly from the right editorial input. But being self-published, it is extremely hard to convince an editor of any note to take you on. It took me four years to hook up with the right person for me, and I intend to work with them through the *Zamorian Chronicles* series – including re-editing *The Key to Chintak*.

The good news is that I have sold the Italian rights to *The Key to Chintak* to Mondadori, the largest publisher in Italy, and have signed up with a US agent. Incidentally, I have also turned down a publisher, but am always open to offers! (Also, I have something very interesting on the boil, so please keep an eye on my website.)

After three years of trying, blagging, ducking, diving, rejection, rejection, rejection, and a lot of hard work, it is very tempting to say: 'Told you so' to the odd agent or publisher. But the truth is that I've still got a long way to go. I'll get there, though.

Mind you, I'll get there a lot quicker if everyone reading this article buys my book.

John Howard is author of *The Key to Chintak: The Zamorian Chronicles* and is available from all good bookshops. His website is www.zamorian.com.

Children's books and the US market

Richard Scrivener outlines the possibilities for breaking into the US children's book market.

As L.P. Hartley once said of the past, America is a foreign country, they do things differently there. It is the biggest territory in the world for books, with immense opportunities, but with just as many pitfalls. Of course, the Brits have those US senators to thank, who some 200 years ago decided to make English the national language of their young nation. This does give British writers an edge over their Italian and French counterparts, although the competition for places is intense. So this article will briefly consider and note the general state of the US market, and then offer some general thoughts on what awaits a British writer who finds themselves about to be published in the United States of America.

Getting through the door

It's an old joke: the British and the Americans find their respective sandwiches very amusing. We think theirs are ridiculously big, they think ours are ridiculously small. The good news for authors is that the 'big sandwich culture' has an enormous sales potential. The even better news is that, unlike their rock and pop counterparts, British authors have a brilliant track record in doing very well 'over there'. From A.A. Milne to J.K. Rowling, from Beatrix Potter to Philip Pullman, time and again the US market has shown itself more than receptive to the stories written on these wet islands. The knack is how to get in through the door.

I wouldn't recommend that a writer research the American market, then write a novel with that specifically in mind. One would most likely end up with a series of novels featuring a Christian wizard who loved *Star Trek* and looked after horses. No. As a writer, you simply have to write what you think is right. Practicalities say that you should begin with a UK publisher and editor in mind. However, you may choose to avoid subjects that might alienate the American market, though it's probably true to say the same issues apply in the UK.

The US market

Here are some basic facts and figures. (With apologies if this is a little like an economics lesson.) The US market is six times bigger than the UK's. The US publish just about the same number of titles as in the UK – somewhere a little north of 140,000, of which around a quarter are children's books in various formats. The independent bookshop is still viable in the US, and that's despite the massive growth of online sales via Amazon and the growing importance of retail chains such as Barnes and Noble and Borders. The library and institutional market whilst having suffered severe funding issues of late, still plays a stronger role in US publishing than its much ravaged British counterpart. The area of the greatest volume at retail, the mass market, is dominated by a couple of key players, with Walmart by far the largest company. The Asda-owning supermarket behemoth has a turnover larger than most countries. When it takes a book it will sell in great quantities.

Immediately one can see parallels with the UK, yet there is one noticeable difference and it's a crucial one for authors. In the delightful vicious pond that is the UK publishing market, publishers and retailers agree different discounts depending on the size of the account. In the US you can't do that. It's basically the same discount if you're Mr Barnes Books of Biloxi or if you're Mr Barnes and Noble, though of course there are various legitimate ways around this. Nonetheless it sets the tone for the business.

As in the UK, the US is dominated by the big 'conglomerate' publishers: Random House, Penguin, HarperCollins and Simon & Schuster. They all carry large lists, publishing sometimes as many as 800 books a year. Hardback publication is still the much preferred initial route for most novels and picture books with a paperback following sometime later. Review coverage in the US for children's books is noticeably better than in the UK. *Publishers Weekly* (the US equivalent of the *Bookseller*; see *Magazines about children's literature and education* on page 270) always carries a children's section and features many thoughtful – and detailed – reviews. It would certainly be worth getting hold of a few copies of this excellent magazine to get a sense of the US market.

Alongside the usual names are other publishers which are less well known in the UK, but highly respected in the US: Harcourt Brace, Farrar Straus-Giroux, Houghton Mifflin and Little, Brown. Some of these publishers have affiliates in the UK, others are part of major media companies. They have considerable clout in the marketplace and can certainly make things happen. For example: Farrar Strauss-Giroux is the US publisher of Louis Sachar's *Holes* and sold it to Bloomsbury in the UK which then published it to great acclaim. And then there was the film…

There are also a host of small hardback houses, independent general publishers who have children's lists, as well as mass market publishers who service the supermarkets. There is plethora of choice, each company with its own dynamic and ethos.

So how do I make it over there?

The principal question of interest to any author is how do I get published in the US? As Bill Clinton used to say: that depends. If your book has been sold in the UK and the publisher has world rights and if that publisher has a US affiliate then most likely the affiliate will be the first port of call. This has the advantage of them knowing who to send it to and the fact that it's being published in the UK by the sister company will help. There should be a financial benefit to the author too – in that the royalty is paid 'straight through'. From a marketing perspective it could also mean that the publisher feels a global ownership of the author, and that would certainly help justify the necessary marketing investment.

But publishing isn't always that simple. The US affiliate may not like your book but this needn't be an issue *per se*. Nor indeed should it be a problem if the UK publisher doesn't have a US office because a good rights department will look to sell the title elsewhere. The cost of doing this for the publisher and the author is reflected in the cut of the deal retained by publisher.

If you have an agent, he or she may suggest selling US rights separately, in which case your manuscript or book will be submitted direct to US publishers. If you're really lucky, the agent may even be able to conduct an auction, but you have to be confident the book concerned will generate sufficient interest. There's nothing more embarrassing than a one-publisher auction.

In the case of picture books – there is no question of the publisher *not* getting world rights. Co-editions will need to be set up, so as broad a territory as possible is required to offset the high origination costs of publishing in full colour.

Changes, changes

Once your book has been sold, be prepared for further editorial comments! American editors nearly always make changes to the text to Americanise it. For example, rubbish becomes garbage, nappy becomes diaper and sausage becomes hot dog. And it's not unusual for a US editor to give more line by line comments and even request a different ending. Take these in your stride, sometimes it will help sell the book. On other occasions you may think it's a bridge too far. You'll have to take each battle as it comes.

Covers, too, require a sharp intake of breath. Invariably the US cover will be different. For reasons no one can understand, British and American cover sensibilities vary considerably. It's best really to let them get on with it. You have to trust that the publisher will know what sells in Des Moines. It may not look pretty to you, but if it sells, does it matter?

As in the UK, marketing is a critical factor in determining a book's success. Dumpbins, publicity, review coverage all add to the mix. The key thing is to have an editor who's supportive and a publishing organisation which supports the editor. The best marketing plans in the world can fall flat, whilst the unexpected bestseller can come from nowhere.

Being published in the US means you'll get US fanmail! And, unless you happen to live there, you won't have that 'I'll just the check the stock in my local bookshop' opportunity, that is unless you have American friends prepared to do it for you. (Though if you ring your US publisher to tell them about this, expect the same frosty response as you'd get from your UK publisher.)

Schools

Another point of difference with the US is the schools market. School book clubs and book fairs are enormously important sales channels in the US. A typical order quantity would be 75,000 units. Through club mailings and touring fairs, the principal player in this market is Scholastic, reaching virtually every American child at some stage or other. These titles are often discounted and acquired under licence from US publishers who grant schools rights. Royalties are generated via the net receipts from the sale of those rights and the ongoing sale of the book.

How did they do it?

It all sounds very exciting doesn't it? So how do I get invited to the party? Luck as much as anything plays an important part. Certainly you can't sit down and think I'm going to write a children's bestseller. Did J.K. Rowling ever think: 'I bet kids in Montana are going to love a story about an orphan trainee wizard attending a summer public school?' Who would have thought that Philip Pullman's version of *Paradise Lost* in which religion is castigated and God dies, would have been so popular in a country with such a wide Bible Belt?

So write what you want to write. Certainly it might be an idea to have more than one book in mind. America is after all the ultimate consumer country, if they like one, they'll want another – quickly. Though not what it once was, series publishing is still popular in the US. *Goosebumps* holds the record for the largest number of books sold, at its peak subscribing over a million copies on publication. And most likely a popular series will be made into a television show or even film – and then there's merchandising. But that's a whole other story.

Genres

As anywhere in the publishing world, genres come and go out of fashion. Fiction has been a hot category for some time now, with a particular emphasis on fantasy. It may well be this bubble will burst as publishers' lists fill with titles featuring weird creatures in various forms. Picture books have had a tough few years, but that said there are writers and artists who continue to sell very well in the US. Again it will depend on the strength of the book – it will have to be outstanding. Probably the most difficult area is publishing for the 5–8 year-olds. These books tend to feature school scenarios or make assumptions about reading levels. It is very difficult to sell these books in the US, so I wouldn't have high hopes if that's your milieu. That's not saying, like a local wine, that there's anything wrong with it – it just doesn't travel long distances.

Teenage books have actually found a much greater audience in recent years. That's as much a British thing as an American factor. Though I personally would avoid writing what I call 'My Dad killed my Step Mum' fiction, there are plenty of American writers doing that. Non-fiction certainly can travel extremely well – although for some reason, humorous non-fiction is less successful.

In short, there are many reasons to be interested in the American market. And the obvious point is the sales potential. Imagine if all of Europe spoke English – okay they do, but at least no American cities have been trashed by English football fans. The infrastructure of US publishing is immensely impressive, it's full of talented and dedicated people who, like their British counterparts, love books. Find a home. Find an editor. Find a publisher. If you get all three in the US, you'd be lucky, you may earn a few pennies. But whatever, if you're successful you'll have the satisfaction of knowing you're better than Oasis and Robbie Williams. *You* made it in America.

Richard Scrivener is Commercial and Operations Director of the Templar Company Plc.

Categorising children's books

When you walk into any high street bookstore the range of children's books can seem overwhelming. Once you look beyond the promotions and offers on the centre tables, however, the selections and layout start to make sense. Caroline Horn explains.

Retailers generally organise their children's book displays according to age ranges, making it easier for buyers to go straight to the section they want, be it baby board books or teen fiction. This approach also reflects how publishers 'segment' their lists.

Categorising children's books according to age groups is helpful as these categories generally reflect children's interests and reading abilities at key stages in their development. A book's format and subject matter, the presence of illustrations and the size of text and pagination, signal the intended age of its reader. So, for example, toddlers and preschool titles comprise short, illustrated picture books while young fiction books are mainly black and white text with short chapters, large text and some illustrations.

Large publishing houses will tend to cover the whole gamut of age ranges for children, from naught to young adult. They want their titles to win the loyalty of new parents from day one and to keep that loyalty all the way through to that child's teen years. Smaller, specialist publishers will often focus their lists on specific areas of children's publishing that reflect their in-house skills. Piccadilly Press, for example, is strong in teen fiction while Templar Publishing has developed a strong range of baby books.

Broadly speaking, children's books fit one of the following age groups: baby books (one to two years), picture books (two to five years), beginner readers (five to seven years), young fiction (six to eight years) and core fiction (8–12 years).

Teen titles and 'crossover books' (those that appeal to children or teenagers, as well as to adults) are in the top age range, i.e. 12 years plus. Non-fiction is also categorised according to age range and, often, National Curriculum subject areas.

There are, though, always exceptions and children's varied abilities and interests will mean that young readers will often cross these age bands. This is why including age guidance on books themselves – as they do with children's toys and clothing – has been such a contentious issue, one that publishers have actively avoided until now because of the wide variation in children's abilities and also their interests.

A nine year-old boy with reading difficulties could, for example, find himself reading a title that he sees is recommended for a child aged six years, and there's nothing more guaranteed to put off a child from picking up another book – ever! New lists have been developed by publishers like A&C Black (*White Wolves* series) and Barrington Stoke to fill the gap for titles that can be enjoyed by older readers who are still struggling to read fluently, and reluctant readers.

In other cases, where perhaps an eight year-old child has the reading ability of an 11 or 12 year-old, that child would probably struggle with the subject matter intended for older readers.

Age ranging

However, while there are very good reasons for not giving specific age recommendations on book covers, this has not helped parents and other book buyers who are struggling to find the right title for children. Research by Book Marketing Ltd ('Expanding the Market') in 2004 indicated a high level of confusion by consumers when buying books for children. Until now, publishers have been heavily reliant on booksellers' ability to recommend the best book for individual children. This year, however, publishers bit the bullet and decided that they would introduce age guidance on fiction, and later picture books and non-fiction, with the aim of supporting consumers. From autumn 2008, new fiction titles have included an age guidance on the back cover, either 5+, 7+, 9+, 11+ or 13+.

Age ranging is the broadest tool publishers can use in categorising their lists but they will also build their lists' depth and range according to a variety of other factors, particularly genres that are popular such as fantasy, historical fiction, horror, thrillers, etc. Publishers will frequently revisit their lists to check where their 'gaps' are and how well each area is doing at any particular time. They pay special attention to how well their list serves the core market of 8–12 year-old readers.

Recent developments in fiction

In recent years, the British and American markets for children's fiction, particularly fantasy, have flourished thanks to authors such as J.K. Rowling (*Harry Potter*) and Philip Pullman (*His Dark Materials*) and the appetite among young readers for more 'big' fiction books seems insatiable. This has helped drive up author advances to unprecedented heights in the children's market, with the popularity of fantasy titles both here and in the US continuing to hold. This was not always the case. One of the reasons why *Harry Potter* was originally turned down was its length – publishers were wary of any books that were more than 40,000 words long, believing that children would not pick up hefty or challenging reads. Children's fantasy was also distinctly out of fashion, both among UK booksellers and foreign publishers, whereas today publishers are keen to find imaginative and challenging reads for children.

The market for 'crossover' fiction is another recent development – it was hard to envisage any demand by adults for children's books prior to *His Dark Materials* trilogy and *Harry Potter*. Today, though, publishers will look closely at a title's potential for crossover appeal. After all, selling to adults as well as to children instantly doubles a book's market. David Fickling Books and Random House exploited this by creating separate covers, for children and for adults, for *The Curious Incident of the Dog in the Night-time* by Mark Haddon – the text was identical for both versions. Although very few novels can do so successfully, titles like Jonathan Stroud's *Bartimaeus Trilogy* (Random House Children's Books) and Jennifer Donnelly's *A Gathering Light* (Bloomsbury) can appeal to both adults and children or teen readers, and publishers are keen to find more books like these.

A more recent development in how books are categorised is by author 'brand'. Authors such as Jacqueline Wilson, Michael Morpurgo, Dick King-Smith and Eoin Colfer are all regarded as brands in their own right and, although these authors write for many different age ranges, their titles will often be displayed together on an author's 'shelf' in bookshops. Waterstone's, for example, has introduced new display cases in its children's sections to do just that, highlighting bestselling authors' work in individual sections. These key author 'brands' have a guaranteed – and large – audience. Jacqueline Wilson, who has sold more than 20 million copies across her titles, will regularly outsell adult bestseller titles with sales of her children's titles averaging about 50,000 copies a month. Readers are also loyal to series and Lemony Snicket's *A Series of Unfortunate Events* (Egmont) as well as Darren Shan's *The Saga of Darren Shan* series (one million UK sales) have shown how successful these can be.

At the younger end of the market, sales of the *Horrid Henry* series by Francesca Simon (Orion) have encouraged publishers to develop more mass market series such as those based on the Felicity Wishes character (Hodder Children's Books) and *Rainbow Magic* (Orchard Books), as well as Random House Children's Books *Astrosaurs* series. Mass market series like these help to get children aged six to eight years into the reading habit because they can recognise the books they have enjoyed and go back for more. Since young fiction books also tend to be relatively thin, a set of five or six books will help them to stand out on booksellers' shelves. More 'literary' series have also been developed for younger readers, with the production quality of the *Judy Moody* titles by Megan McDonald (Walker Books) and *The Spiderwick Chronicles* by Tony DiTerlizzi and Holly Black (Simon & Schuster) ensuring that they stand out from the crowd.

The next 'big thing'

But publishers know that they would be unwise to focus exclusively on areas that are ahead in today's climate – children's books is a cyclical business and what works today could be out of favour a few months down the line. Dorling Kindersley's approach to production was key to driving non-fiction sales in the Eighties while *Guess How Much I Love You* by Sam McBratney and illustrated by Anita Jeram (Walker Books) achieved a similar status for the picture book in the Nineties. In today's climate, however, non-fiction and picture books are struggling but it will only take a new taste, design or development to turn that around. People could easily be saying the same thing about fantasy fiction just a few years from now.

Publishers will regularly revisit and reshape their lists as a result of market changes like these. Walker Books, a notable picture book publisher, has in recent years strengthened its fiction list with lead authors including Anthony Horowitz and Kate DiCamillo, while Bloomsbury, which has traditionally focused on fiction, is now strengthening its picture book list. Traditional non-fiction publishers Kingfisher and Usborne have both recently moved into the fiction market, reflecting the greater focus on fiction.

Demographics are also responsible for changing tastes and shifting emphasis in publishers' lists. The number of children aged under 12 years is falling while the teen market is growing and this accounts for the increasing interest in young adult and crossover books. The demographic picture is similar in the US, a key market for British publishers, so interest in teen fiction is likely to be maintained for some time. Teenage titles are, themselves, also categorised according to genres such as 'issue' books, crime, thrillers, etc. What is proving most successful among teen readers today, largely thanks to Louise Rennison's *Angus* series (Piccadilly Press, HarperCollins) and Meg Cabot's *Princess Diaries* (Macmillan Children's Books) are contemporary, humorous and very commercial books for teenage girls.

It goes without saying that writers need to know what areas a publisher specialises in before approaching them with manuscripts. A brilliant teenage title is likely to be rejected if the publisher's list does not include teenage books. Still worse, an inexperienced publisher could take on a teen novel but let it fall into oblivion by failing to market it to the correct audience.

That said, it is hard to second-guess what type of book publishers are looking for at any one time. A picture book publisher may still turn down a title, no matter how much they like it, if they have over-commissioned in that area or it is too similar to a title they are already publishing. Equally, even though booksellers' shelves are groaning under the weight of fantasy titles, a book that stands out from the crowd will always find a home – publishers are continuously hunting for talented 'new voices'. In fact, 'debut author' has almost become a category in its own right as publishers strive to get unknown but promising authors into retail outlets.

It is also worth remembering that across the board, large publishing houses are reducing their children's output and that their lists are more structured and more focused than ever before. If a company has filled the gap for a dragon fantasy for a ten year-old reader, then they won't be looking for any more. Another publisher, however, might be looking for exactly that.

Caroline Horn is children's books editor at the *Bookseller* and editor of children's books website Reading Zone (www.readingzone.com).

Poetry
Riding on the poetry roundabout

Poet and anthologist John Foster writes about the difficulties involved in getting children's poetry published and offers some practical advice.

Today's children's poetry roundabout started spinning in the 1960s, when it was given a push-start by Spike Milligan, gathered momentum in the 1970s and 1980s with helping hands from the likes of Roger McGough, Allan Ahlberg and Michael Rosen, and has been gathering speed ever since. You would think, therefore, that it might be easier for a new-comer to break in and to get their poems published these days than it was when I started anthologising and writing poetry some 25 years ago. Yet, in spite of the upsurge in children's poetry publishing in recent decades, for the aspiring children's poet it can seem as hard as ever to get your poems published.

One reason, of course, is that there are now many more people specialising in writing children's poetry than there used to be and the competition is more fierce. Another is that there's an increasing number of established children's poets and that those people inevitably stand much more chance of getting a collection of their poems into print than someone who is unknown.

That said, anthologists like myself are always on the lookout for new voices, and if a good poem is submitted for an anthology, it doesn't matter who has written it – it will go in. When you're starting out, you have far more chance of getting one or two of your poems into some of the anthologies that are published annually than you have of getting a complete collection of your poems published. So if you are keen to find a ride on the poetry roundabout, it is better to discover what anthologies are in the pipeline and what specific poems are required than to try to place a single author collection. I had been anthologising and contributing poems to other anthologies for over ten years before my first book of original poems, *Four O'Clock Friday*, was accepted. And there are some very good children's poets – Julie Holder and John Kitching, for example – who have contributed to anthologies for many years, yet have never had collections of their own published.

Ask a publisher why there are many more anthologies than single poet collections and they will give you a simple answer: anthologies sell more copies. It is much easier to sell an anthology of school poems, such as 'Why do we have to go to school today?' than it is to sell 'The Very Best of A.N.Other Children's Poet'.

Get inspired by children

If you are undaunted by what I have said so far and still determined that you are going to write children's poetry and get it published, what tips can I offer?

Starting with the most obvious, get to know children's language. If you are writing poems about children's experiences from a child's point of view you must get the language right. It is, perhaps, not surprising that many of the most successful children's poets are from a teaching background – for example, Tony Mitton, Wes Magee, Judith Nicholls, Paul Cookson and Brian Moses. Teachers not only know what children's interests are, but they also know how children think and how they express themselves. So steep yourself in children's language, not just the language of your children or the children of friends, but of children from all sorts of backgrounds and cultures.

Try to arrange to visit schools in different areas. But always go through the correct channels with a letter to the literacy coordinator, copied to the head teacher, explaining the reasons you would like to visit. Schools these days are, quite rightly, very security-conscious. Visiting schools will give you the opportunity not only to talk with children, but to try out your poems too. There's nothing like a deafening wall of silence greeting that punchline you thought they would find so amusing to let you know that, in fact, the poem doesn't work!

Schools are also a good source of ideas. Many a poem comes from a child's tale or a teacher's comment. In one school I met a teacher called Mr Little, who was six foot six inches tall. He told me a story about a girl who had asked him: Were you big when you were little? This led to my poem 'Size-Wise' (below).

Our teacher Mr Little's really tall.
He's twice the size of our helper Mrs Small.
'Were you big when you were little?'
Sandra asked him.
'I was Little when I was little,
but I've always been big!'
he said with a grin.
'Have you always been small?'
Sandra asked Mrs Small.
'No,' said Mrs Small.
'I was Short before I got married,
then I became Small.
But,' she added, 'I've always been little.'
'That's the long and the short of it,'
* said Mr Little.*
'I've always been big and Little,
but she used to be little and Short,
and now she's little and Small.'

Visiting schools is worthwhile, too, because you can bring yourself up to date with how poetry is being used in the classroom. The Primary Framework for Literacy requires that children be introduced in the primary years to a wide range of poetic forms. There is an educational as well as a trade market for children's poems and it is worth knowing what the educational publishers might be looking out for.

Anthologies

Successful children's poets will tell you that many of their poems have been triggered by an anthologist's request for a poem on a particular theme. What then is the secret of getting a poem into an anthology?

It may seem to be stating the obvious but the first thing to do is to read the submissions letter closely. My filing cabinets are full of poems that have been given only a cursory glance, because it has become apparent from the first line that they are neither relevant to the theme of the anthology in question nor appropriate for the age group at which the anthology is aimed.

Having read the letter, one's first impulse is to consider whether any of the poems you have already written are suitable. There may well be one or two, particularly among those that are already published, but simply trawling through your file of unpublished poems to see if some of them can be made to fit in with the anthologist's demands is less likely to be successful than actually writing something new.

The key very often is to come up with something slightly different. Let's say you have been asked to contribute to a book of poems about pirates. You probably stand more chance of getting your poem selected if you write a poem about pirates who have become film stars, specialising in gangster parts, than if you write a poem about traditional pirates burying their treasure or making a captive walk the plank. Similarly, if you are writing about dragons, you are more likely to succeed in placing a poem about young dragons having a flying lesson (as I have done myself), or about a young dragon doing his party trick of lighting the candles on his birthday cake (as Ian McMillan has done) than a poem about a dragon fighting a knight. The wackier and more bizarre your idea is, the more chance you will have of your poem being chosen.

Another way of making your poem stand out from the crowd is to write it in a more unusual form. For example, instead of writing your poem about St George and the dragon in couplets, you could write it in the form of an encyclopedia entry, as a series of extracts from St George's diary or even as a text message. The more contemporary the form, the more likely it is to appeal, both to the anthologist and the reader.

Getting the idea is, of course, the hardest part. If you are stuck for a humorous idea, one way of trying to find one is to look in a book of jokes. I was racking my brains to come up with a new poem for a book of magic poems, when I came across this joke: Why are the ghosts of magicians no good at conjuring? Because you can see right through their tricks! This led to:

The ghost of the magician said:
'I'm really in a fix.
The trouble is the audience
Sees right through all my tricks!'

A word of caution: whereas it can pay to be risqué, both in terms of getting your poem selected and entertaining your readers, don't be rude just for the sake of it and, especially, don't be crude. Besides, you could easily get yourself labelled! During a performance in Glasgow, I included one or two poems which made references to 'bottoms' and 'knickers', getting the usual delighted response from the audience. However, I was taken aback when I asked them to suggest why the publishers won't allow me to illustrate my poetry books. Instead of giving me the expected – and correct – answer that my drawings are no good, the first boy I asked said: 'Because your poems are dirty!'

Before sending off your poems, make sure your name and contact details are given clearly beneath every poem. It is usually better, too, to put each poem on a separate page. Check with the anthologist before you submit your poems by email. Many anthologists prefer to receive hard copies, since they assemble the anthology by hand, rather than on the computer, and it saves them the chore of having to print out the poems themselves.

Also, don't send too many poems. As a rule of thumb it's usually best to send about five, and not more than ten. Of course, you will include what you think is your best and most suitable poem. But don't be surprised if it's not chosen and another one is. I'm constantly being asked why that happens. Usually it's because someone else has written a poem that's similar in content or form to your best one and it would not be appropriate to include two such similar poems. Whereas, with regard to your other poem, it either looks at the topic from a different angle or fills a gap that needs to be filled.

You won't make a fortune from getting your poem into an anthology, but once it is in print there's also the chance that it will be picked up and used by another anthologist. So my advice is: be prepared to accept any minor changes that the editor proposes, even if you prefer your original version of the poem. My own experience is that nine times out of ten any changes that have been suggested to my poems have actually improved them. One established poet actually calls me 'the poetry surgeon' because on several occasions I have suggested cutting whole verses from some of his poems. Professional that he is, he has agreed to accept the cuts, even if privately he knows, and I know, that he does not totally agree with them. And, of course, he has pocketed the fee!

Finally, the big question: how do you get yourself onto the anthologists' mailing lists? A simple request to have your name added won't necessarily do the trick. The anthologist needs to know that it is worth taking the time to send you a letter. So it's worth sending a sample of your poems (about five is enough) with a covering letter. But don't expect to be flooded with requests. There are only a limited number of anthologies published annually. However, if the anthologist thinks your poems have potential, your name will be added to the list – the first step towards getting a ride on the children's poetry roundabout.

John Foster's latest collection of his own poems, *The Poetry Chest*, is published by Oxford University Press. 'Size-Wise' is from *Making Waves* (Oxford University Press) ©John Foster; 'The Ghost of the Magician' ©John Foster.

An interview with my shadow

Brian Patten talks about writing poetry.

Who are you?
I'm your shadow.

What's that you're eating?
It's the shadow of an apple.

Surely shadows can't detach themselves from walls and eat shadow-apples?
They can if they are writers' and poets' shadows.

Why do you write for children as well as for adults?
I don't know, it just happened that way. But I really do believe that writing for one is no easier than writing for the other. If somebody tries to write for adults and finds they aren't any good at it, then they will very likely be even worse at writing for children.

Can you really appreciate poetry at seven or even 11 years old?
Of course you can! Adults have no monopoly on feelings. I suspect that many adults never feel as intensely about things as they did when they were younger.

What are the best kinds of things to write about?
You can write about anything you want. Sometimes the weirder the better. At ten you will probably write very different poems than when you're 14 and when you are 40 you'll write different poems again.

How about telling stories through poems?
Very short stories, yes. But not long stories. For long stories children prefer prose, and quite rightly I think. Part of poetry is to do with condensing, not expanding. It is different if you are writing a series of poems about the same character or about a particular situation or unusual creatures, or seeing certain themes from different angles. Then snapshots can build up into a story. But there have been very few successful long story-poems written for children.

I thought poets were supposed to be daydreamers. Some people think poetry is a bit soft.
Modern poetry for children is usually anarchic – anything but soft. Having said this, there is an awful lot of bad so-called 'children's poetry' about. Almost as much as bad 'adult poetry'.

How so?
Well, there is more rhyme and word play in contemporary children's poetry than in contemporary adult poetry. People can make things rhyme, but they either don't or can't work on the scansion, and then the whole metrical structure falls apart. No matter how good an idea, it is the execution of the work that brings it to life.

Did you intend that last sentence to be ironic?
Yes. And it is true. Would-be writers forget it at their peril! Children won't be fobbed off with lazy work.

Why did you begin writing poetry? Did anyone teach you?

No, one day I just started writing things down. You see, as a child I lived in this tiny house with three adults. They were all unhappy people. My mother was young and couldn't afford a place of her own, so we lived with my grandmother. My grandmother wore callipers and she dragged herself round the house by her hands. I remember thinking they were like talons.

What has this got to do with poetry and beginning to write it?

Everybody in that little house was miserable and they didn't talk to each other, and although they knew they were miserable and why they were miserable, they couldn't explain why.

You mean they could not express themselves?

Yes, and because they could not express themselves they kept everything walled up inside them, where it hurt and festered for want of light.

Were you like this as well?

To begin with. I don't know how it happened, or why, but I realised the only way I could express my feelings was by writing them down. I think that is how I started to become a poet. I began writing down what I felt. So really, I began writing poetry before I even began reading it. I needed to express my feelings and writing poetry was like writing a very intense diary.

Would you say you were a 'real' poet at that age? I mean, when you began writing did you think that you would ever become a professional poet?

No. That happened when I began changing words and moving lines around. When you begin to *make* something out of the words is when the professional element comes into play. A good poem is something that carries your feelings and ideas inside it. People remember a good poem because of the way it is written, just as much as because of what it says.

Would you like a bit of my apple?

I'm not sure. What does a shadow-apple taste like?

Brian Patten was born and bred in Liverpool. He writes poetry for adults and children and his most recently published books are *Collected Love Poems* (Harper Perennial 2007) and *Selected Poems* (Penguin 2007).

Poetry organisations

Poetry is one of the easiest writing art forms to begin with, though the hardest to excel at or earn any money from. Paul McGrane, Membership Manager at the Poetry Society, lists below the organisations which can help poets take their poetry further.

WHERE TO GET INVOLVED

Academi
3rd Floor, Mount Stuart House,
Mount Stuart Square, Cardiff Bay, Cardiff CF10 5FQ
tel 029-204 72266
email post@academi.org
website www.academi.org
Coordinator Peter Finch

The Welsh National Literature Promotion Agency which has a huge resource available for poets and poetry. It organises events and tours, promotes poets and poetry, offers poetry advice, locates poetry publishers, offers financial help to poets and to organisers wishing to book poets, and much more. To take advantage of their services you have to live or be in Wales, which has the largest number of poets per 1000 population anywhere in the Western World.

The British Haiku Society
38 Wayside Avenue, Hornchurch, Essex RM12 4LL
website www.britishhaikusociety.org

The Society runs the prestigious annual James W. Hackett International Haiku Award, the Nobuyuki Yuasa Annual International Award for Haibun and the bienniel Sasakawa Prize worth £2500 for original contributions in the field of haikai. It is active in promoting the teaching of haiku in schools and colleges, and is able to provide readers, course/workshop leaders and speakers for poetry groups, etc. Write for membership details. Founded 1990.

Commonword
6 Mount Street, Manchester M2 5NS
tel 0161-832 3777
email cathy@commonword.org.uk
website www.commonword.org.uk
Contact Cathy Bolton

Commonword is a valuable resource for poets and writers in the North West. It provides support, training and publishing opportunities for new writers. It has helped to launch the careers of many of the region's leading poets and strives to seek out new talent in unexpected places.

Creative Arts East
Griffin Court, Market Street, Wymondham,
Norfolk NR18 0GU
tel (01953) 713390
email communications@creativeartseast.co.uk
website www.creativeartseast.co.uk

Creative Arts East is a fast-growing arts development agency which provides practical support to the arts community in Norfolk; directly promotes tours, exhibitions, and one-off performances and readings by professional artists and companies; and develops community-based arts projects which address social issues around isolation and disadvantage.

The agency was formally launched in 2002, and was set up to combine the collective expertise and energy of 4 smaller arts organisations: Rural Arts East, Norfolk Arts Marketing, Norfolk Literature Development and Create! Members receive the Norfolk Literature Network newsletter containing information, news, events listings and competitions.

The Poetry Book Society
4th Floor, 2 Tavistock Place, London WC1H 9RA
tel 020-7833 9247 *fax* 020-7833 5990
email info@poetrybooks.co.uk
website www.poetrybooks.co.uk,
www.poetrybookshoponline.com,
www.childrenspoetrybookshelf.co.uk
Director Chris Holifield

This unique book club for readers of poetry was founded in 1953 by T.S. Eliot, and is funded by the Arts Council England. Every quarter, selectors choose one outstanding publication (the PBS Choice), and recommend 4 other titles, which are sent to members, who are also offered substantial discounts on other poetry books. The Poetry Book Society also administers the T.S. Eliot Prize, produces the quarterly membership magazine, the *Bulletin*, and has an education service providing teaching materials for primary and secondary schools. In addition, the PBS runs the Children's Poetry Bookshelf, offering children's poetry for 7–11 year-olds, with parent, school and library memberships and a new child-friendly website.

The Poetry Business
Bank Street Arts, 32–40 Bank Street, Sheffield S1 2DS
email edit@poetrybusiness.co.uk
website www.poetrybusiness.co.uk
Contact Peter Sansom

Dedicated to helping writers reach their full potential by running supportive workshops.

The Poetry Can
12 Great George Street, Bristol BS1 5RH
tel 0117-943 6976
email admin@poetrycan.co.uk
website www.poetrycan.co.uk
Coordinator Colin Brown

The Poetry Can is one of the few literature organisations in the UK specialising in poetry. It organises events such as the Bristol Poetry Festival; runs a lifelong learning programme; offers information and advice in all aspects of poetry.

Poetry Ireland
2 Prouds Lane, Off St Stephen's Green, Dublin 2, Republic of Ireland
tel (01) 478 9974 *fax* (0) 478 0205
email info@iol.ie
website www.poetryireland.ie

Poetry Ireland is the national organisation dedicated to developing, supporting and promoting poetry throughout Ireland. It is a resource and information point for any member of the public with an interest in poetry and works towards creating opportunities for poets working or living in Ireland. It is grant-aided by both the Northern and Southern Arts Councils of Ireland and is a resource centre with the Austin Clarke Library of over 10,000 titles. It publishes the quarterly magazine *Poetry Ireland Review* and the bi-monthly newsletter *Poetry Ireland News*. Poetry Ireland organises readings in Dublin and nationally, and runs a Writers-in-Schools Scheme.

Poetry on Loan
Unit 116, The Custard Factory, Gibb Street, Birmingham B9 4AA
tel 0121-246 2770
email jonathan@bookcommunications.co.uk
website www.poetryonloan.org.uk
Coordinator Jonathan Davidson

Poetry on Loan is a scheme to promote contemporary poetry through libraries in the West Midlands. There are 30 participating libraries and the scheme supports events, displays, stock collections and commissions. It also runs poetry projects for young people.

The Poetry Society
22 Betterton Street, London WC2H 9BX
tel 020-7420 9880 *fax* 020-7240 4818
email info@poetrysociety.org.uk
website www.poetrysociety.org.uk

The Poetry Society was set up to help poetry and poets thrive in Britain and is a registered charity funded by the Arts Council England. The Society offers advice and information to all, with a more comprehensive level of information available to members. Members receive copies of the UK's most prominent poetry magazine, *Poetry Review*, and the Society's newsletter, *Poetry News*, each quarter. The Society's website provides information, news, poetry links and a useful FAQ page, as well as an interactive regional guide to poetry organisations, venues, publishers, magazines and bookshops around the UK through its Poetry Landmarks of Britain section.

The Society also publishes education resources (see later); promotes National Poetry Day; runs Poetry Prescription, a critical appraisal service available to members and non-members (20% discount to members); provides an education advisory and training service, school membership, youth membership and a website. A diverse range of events and readings frequently take place at the Poetry Café and the Poetry Studio at the Society's headquarters in London. The Society also programmes events and readings in other regions of the UK.

Competitions run by the Society include the annual National Poetry Competition, which is one of the largest open poetry competitions in the UK with a first prize of £5000, the biannual Corneliu M. Popescu Prize for European Poetry in Translation and the Foyle Young Poets of the Year Award. Founded 1909.

The Seamus Heaney Centre for Poetry
c/o School of English, Queen's University Belfast, Belfast BT7 1NN
tel 028-9097 1070
email shc@qub.ac.uk
website www.qub.ac.uk/heanycentre

The new Seamus Heaney Centre for Poetry (SHC) is designed to celebrate and promote poetry and artistic endeavour by poets from Northern Ireland. The Centre houses an extensive library of contemporary poetry volumes. It hosts regular creative writing workshops, a poetry reading group, and an ongoing series of readings and lectures by visiting poets and critics from all over the world. The SHC is chaired by the eminent poet, Ciaran Carson, and other resident poets include Medbh McGuckian.

Survivors Poetry
Studio 11, Bickerton House, 25–27 Bickerton Road, London N19 5JT
tel 020-7281 4654 *fax* 020-7281 7894
website www.survivorspoetry.org.uk

A national charity which promotes the writing of survivors of mental distress. A Survivor may be a person with a current or past experience of psychiatric hospitals, ECT, tranquillisers or other medication, or a user of counselling services, a survivor of sexual abuse and any other person who has empathy with the experiences of survivors.

WHERE TO GET INFORMATION

The first place to start is your local library. They usually have information about the local poetry scene. Many libraries are actively involved in promoting poetry as well as having modern poetry available for loan. Local librarians promote writing activities with, for example, projects like Poetry on Loan and Poetry Places information points in West Midlands Libraries.

Arts Council England

website www.artscouncil.org.uk

Arts Council England has 9 regional offices and local literature officers can provide information on local poetry groups, workshops and societies (see page 344). Some give grant aid to local publishers and magazines and help fund festivals, literature projects and readings, and some run critical services.

The Northern Poetry Library

tel (01670) 534514 (poetry enquiries), 534524 (poetry dept)
email npl@northumberland.gov.uk
website www.northumberlandlibraries.com
Membership Free to anyone living in Northumberland, Tyne and Wear, Durham, Cleveland and Cumbria.

The Northern Poetry Library has over 15,000 titles and magazines covering poetry published since 1945. For information about epic through to classic poetry, a full text database is available of all poetry from 600–1900. The library has free public internet access. Founded 1968.

The Poetry Library

Level 5, Royal Festival Hall, London SE1 8XX
tel 020-7921 0943/0664 *fax* 020-7921 0939
email poetrylibrary@rfh.org.uk
website www.poetrylibrary.org.uk
Membership Free with proof of identity and current address

The principal roles of the Poetry Library are to collect and preserve all poetry published in the UK since about 1912 and to act as a public lending library. It also keeps a wide range of international poetry. It has 2 copies of each title available and a collection of about 40,000 titles in English and English translation. The Library also provides an education service (see under 'Help for young poets and teachers', below).

The Library runs an active information service, which includes a unique noticeboard for lost quotations, and tracing authors and publishers from extracts of poems. Current awareness lists are available for magazines, publishers, competitions, bookshops, groups and workshops, evening classes and festivals on receipt of a large sae. The Library also stocks a full range of British poetry magazines as well as a selection from abroad. When visiting the Library, look out for the Voice Box, a performance space for literature; a programme is available from 020-7921 0906. Open 11am–8pm Tuesday to Sunday. Founded in 1953 by the Arts Council.

The Scottish Poetry Library

5 Crichton's Close, Canongate, Edinburgh EH8 8DT
tel 0131-557 2876
email reception@spl.org.uk
website www.spl.org.uk

The Scottish Poetry Library is the place for poetry in Scotland for the regular reader, the serious student or the casual browser. It has a remarkable collection of written works, as well as tapes and videos. The emphasis is on contemporary poetry written in Scotland, in Scots, Gaelic and English, but historic Scottish poetry – and contemporary works from almost every part of the world – feature too. They also have collections for the visually impaired. All resources, advice and information are readily accessible, free of charge. It holds regular poetry events, details of which are available on the library website. Founded 1984.

ONLINE RESOURCES

You can obtain a wealth of information at the click of a mouse these days. In addition to those listed above, good starting points are:

The Poetry Archive

website www.poetryarchive.org

The Poetry Kit

website www.poetrykit.org

The Poetry Society of America

website www.poetrysociety.org

WHERE TO GET POETRY BOOKS

See the Poetry Book Society, above. The Poetry Library provides a list of bookshops which stock poetry. For second-hand mail order poetry books try:

Baggins Books

19 High Street, Rochester, Kent ME1 1PY
tel (01634) 811651 *fax* (01634) 840591
email godfreygeorge@btconnect.com
website www.bagginsbooks.co.uk

Secondhand bookshop with over half a million books in stock.

The Poetry Bookshop

The Ice House, Brook Street, Hay-on-Wye HR3 5BQ
tel (01497) 821812

Peter Riley

27 Sturton Street, Cambridge CB1 2QG
tel (01223) 576422
email priley@dircon.co.uk

Sweetens of Bolton

86 Deansgate, Bolton, Lancs.
tel (01204) 528457

WHERE TO CELEBRATE POETRY

Festival information should be available from Arts Council England offices (see page 344). See also *Children's literature festivals and trade fairs* on page 375.

The British Council

Literature Department, The British Council,
10 Spring Gardens, London SW1A 2BN
tel 020-7389 3166 fax 020-7389 3175
website www.britishcouncil.org/arts-literature.htm

Send a large sae or visit the website for a list of
forthcoming festivals.

WHERE TO PERFORM

In London, Express Excess, Short Fuse and
Aromapoetry are 3 of the liveliest venues for poetry
performances and they regularly feature the best
performers. Poetry Unplugged at the Poetry Café is
famous for its open mic nights (Tuesdays 7.30pm).
Poetry evenings are held all over the UK and those
listed below are worth checking out. Others can be
found by visiting your local library or your Arts
Council office, or by visiting the Landmarks of
Britain section of the Poetry Society website
(www.poetrysociety.org.uk/content/landmarks).

Apples & Snakes Performance Poetry

Battersea Arts Centre, Lavender Hill, London SW11
tel 020-7801 9026
email info@applesandsnakes.org
website www.applesandsnakes.org

Carlton Poets

The Carlton Centre, Carlton Road,
Weston-Super-Mare
email marilynedbrooke@hotmail.com

CB1 Poetry

32 Mill Road, Cambridge CB1 2AD
tel (01223) 363271 ext. 2725
email cb1poetry@fastmail.fm
website www.cb1poetry.org.uk

Clitheroe Books Open Floor Readings

New Inn, Clitheroe, Parson Lane, Clitheroe,
Lancs. BB7 1JN
tel (01200) 444242

Coffee House Poetry

Troubadour Coffee House, 265 Old Brompton Road,
London SW5
tel 020-8354 0660
email coffpoetry@aol.com

Dead Good Poets Society

96 Bould Street, Liverpool L1 4HY
tel 0151-709 5221
email sarah@deadgoodpoetssociety.org.uk

Express Excess

The Enterprise, 2 Haverstock Hill, London NW3
tel 020-7485 2659
website www.expressexcess.co.uk

Hammer and Tongue

Hammer and Tongue HQ, 16B Cherwell Street,
Oxford OX4 1BG
tel (01865) 200550
email poetry@hammerandtongue.org
website www.hammerandtongue.co.uk

Poetry Café

22 Betterton Street, London WC2 9BX
tel 020-7420 9887

Shortfuse

The Camden Head, Camden Walk, Islington,
London N1
website www.20six.co.uk/shortfuse

Tongues and Grooves

The Florence Arms, Florence Road, Southsea
tel (02392) 734180
email enquiries@tongues-and-grooves.org.uk
website www.tongues-and-grooves.org.uk

Voice Box

Level 5, Royal Festival Hall, London SE1
tel 020-7960 4242

COMPETITIONS

There are now hundreds of competitions to enter and
as the prizes increase, the highest being £5000 (first
prize in the National Poetry Competition and the
Arvon Foundation International Poetry
Competition), so does the prestige associated with
winning such competitions.

To decide which competitions are worth entering,
make sure you know who the judges are and think
twice before paying large sums for an anthology of
'winning' poems which will only be read by entrants
wanting to see their own work in print. The Poetry
Library publishes a list of competitions each month
(available free on receipt of a large sae).

Literary prizes are given annually to published
poets and as such are non-competitive. An A–Z guide
to literary prizes can be found on the Booktrust
website (www.booktrust.org.uk). A current list of
competitions can be found at
www.poetrylibrary.org.uk/competitions

WHERE TO WRITE POETRY

Apples & Snakes

Battersea Arts Centre, Lavender Hill,
London SW11 5TF
tel 020-7223 2223

A vital performance poetry agency dedicated to giving
'voice to challenging, diverse and dynamic poets...'
Presents fortnightly shows at the Battersea Arts
Centre and holds occasional workshops. Founded
1982.

The Arvon Foundation
Lumb Bank – The Ted Hughes Arvon Centre,
Hebden Bridge, West Yorkshire HX7 6DF
tel (01422) 843714 *fax* (01422) 843714
The Arvon Foundation at Totleigh Barton,
Sheepwash, Beaworthy, Devon EX21 5NS
tel (01409) 231338 *fax* (01409) 231144
The Arvon Foundation at Moniack Mhor, Teavarren,
Kiltarlity, Beauly, Inverness-shire IV4 7HT
tel (01463) 741675 *fax* (01463) 741733
The Hurst – The John Osborne Arvon Centre,
Clunton, Craven Arms, Shrops. SY7 0JA
tel (01588) 640658 *fax* (01588) 640509
email hurst@arvonfoundation.org
website www.arvonfoundation.org

The Arvon Foundation's 4 centres run 5-day
residential courses throughout the year to anyone
over the age of 16, providing the opportunity to live
and work with professional writers. Writing genres
explored include poetry, narrative, drama, writing for
children, song writing and the performing arts.
Bursaries are available to those receiving benefits.
Founded in 1968.

Camden Poetry Group
Contact Hannah Kelly, 64 Lilyville Road,
London SW6

Meets in Hampstead one Saturday per month from
6.30pm. Examples of work should be sent with a
covering letter before coming to the first meeting.

Centerprise Literature Development Project
136 Kingsland High Street, London E8 2NS
tel 020-7254 9632 ext. 211, 214 *fax* 020-7923 1951
website www.centerpriseliterature.com
Contact Eva Lewin, Catherine Johnson

Offers a range of creative writing courses, events,
surgeries, advice and information resources plus links
with other writers' organisations. Groups include the
Women's Poetry Group and the Black Writers'
Group. The project is committed to developing new
writing from all community and ethnic groups.

City University Creative Writing and Poetry Courses
Northampton Square, London EC1V OHB
website www.city.ac.uk

Epsom Writers' Workshop
Epsom Centre, 1 Church Street, Epsom
Contact Stella Stocker *tel* 020-8668 3816

Kent & Sussex Poetry Society
Camden Centre, Market Square, Royal Victoria,
Tunbridge Wells
email info@kentandsussexpoetrysociety.org
website www.kentandsussexpoetrysociety.org

Lancaster University
Department of Continuing Education,
Lancaster University, Ash House, Lancaster LA1 4YT
tel (01524) 592623/4
website www.lancs.ac.uk/depts/conted

A range of part-time creative writing courses in
various genres and at levels to suit both beginners
and those with some experience.

Phoenix Poets
Abbey Community Centre, 34 Great Smith Street,
London SW1
Contact Colleen McMath *tel* 020-85043 2506

Meets on first Wednesday of each month, excluding
January and August, 1–2.30pm, £2 per session.

Poetry Round
The Barkston Gardens Hotel,
34–44 Barkston Gardens, London SW5 0EW
tel 020-7373 7851

Meets on Mondays, 7.30–9.30pm, £2/£1 per session.

The Poetry School
81–83 Lambeth Walk, London SE11 6DX
tel (0845) 223 5274
website www.poetryschool.com

Offers courses and workshops in London,
Manchester, York and the North East, Exeter and the
South West, exploring key elements of poetic
practice, complemented by lectures, discussions and
seminars with some of the most renowned poets
working today. Also international and online courses,
and a postal tutorial service with Judy Gahagan and
Myra Schneider.
  The website has extensive links to poetry
information and resources on the internet. The
Poetry School was founded in 1997 by 3 poets –
Mimi Khalvati, Jane Duran and Pascale Petit.

Poets Anonymous
Dog and Bull, Surrey Street, Croydon
Meets on first Friday of each month at 8pm, £2/£1.
Also at the Primary Room, United Reformed Church,
Addiscombe
Meets second Saturday of the month, 2.30–4pm,
£1.50.
email poets@poetsanon.org.uk
website www.poetsanon.org.uk

The Poet's House/Teach na hÉigse
Clonbarra, Falcarragh, County Donegal,
Republic of Ireland
tel (074) 65470 *fax* (074) 65471
email phouse@iol.ie

The Poet's House runs 3 10-day poetry courses in
July and August. An MA degree in creative writing is
validated by Lancaster University, and the Irish
Language Faculty includes Cathal O'Searcaigh. The

poetry faculty comprises 30 writers, including Paul Durcan and John Montagu.

Shortlands Poetry Circle
Ripley Arts Centre, 24 Sundridge Avenue, Bromley
email shortlands@poetrypf.co.uk
website www.poetrypf.co.uk/shortlands.html

South Norwood Writers' Workshop
South Norwood Centre, Sandown Road,
London SE24 4XC
Contact Stella Stocker tel 020-8668 3816

Meets on Wednesdays, 7.30–9.30pm.

Spread the Word
77 Lambeth Walk, London SE11 6DX
tel 020-7735 3111 fax 020-7735 2666
email info@spreadtheword.org.uk
website www.spreadtheword.org.uk

Surrey Poetry Circle
Guildford Institute of the University of Surrey,
Ward Street, Guildford GU1 4LH
Contact Pat Earnshaw tel (01483) 274389

Meets on first and third Thursday of the month,
7.30–10pm.

Ty Newydd
Taliesin Trust, Ty Newydd, Llanystumdwy,
Criccieth, Gwynedd LL52 0LW
tel (01766) 522811 fax (01766) 523095
email post@tynewydd.org
website www.tynewydd.org

Ty Newydd runs week-long writing courses encompassing a wide variety of genres, including poetry, and caters for all levels, from beginners to published poets. All the courses are tutored by published writers. Writing retreats are also available.

Wimbledon and Merton Poetry Group
Contact Russell Thompson tel (07969) 597967
email zzush@yahoo.co.uk

Meets on first Tuesday evening of each month.

GROUPS ON THE INTERNET

It is worth searching for discussion groups and chat rooms on the internet.

British–Irish Poets
website www.jiscmail.ac.uk/archives/british-irish-poets.html
Discussion list (innovative poetry).

The Poem
website http://thepoem.co.uk/discussion.htm
Discussion forum.

Poetry Free-for-all
website www.everypoet.org/pffa
Post your poems and comment on others.

The Poetry Kit
website www.poetrykit.org/wkshops2.htm
List of online workshop/discussion sites.

Local groups
Local groups vary enormously so it is worth shopping around to find one that suits your poetry. Up-to-date information can be obtained from Arts Council England regional offices (see page 344).

The Poetry Library publishes a list of groups for the Greater London area which will be sent out on receipt of a large sae.

The Poetry Society organises local groups for its members – visit www.poetrysociety.org.uk/content/membership/stanzas/ for details.

HELP FOR YOUNG POETS AND TEACHERS

National Association of Writers in Education (NAWE)
PO Box 1, Sheriff Hutton, York YO60 7YU
tel/fax (01653) 618429
email paul@nawe.co.uk
website www.nawe.co.uk

NAWE is a national organisation, which aims to widen the scope of writing in education, and coordinate activities between writers, teachers and funding bodies. It publishes the magazine *Writing in Education* and is author of a writers' database which can identify writers who fit the given criteria (e.g. speaks several languages, works well with special needs, etc) for schools, colleges and the community. Publishes *Reading the Applause: Reflections on Performance Poetry by Various Artists*. Write for membership details.

The Poetry Library
Children's Section, Royal Festival Hall,
London SE1 8XX
tel 020-7921 0664
website www.poetrylibrary.org.uk

For young poets, the Poetry Library has about 4000 books incorporating the SIGNAL Collection of Children's Poetry. It also has a multimedia children's section, from which cassettes and videos are available to engage children's interest in poetry.

The Poetry Library has an education service for teachers and writing groups. Its information file covers all aspects of poetry in education. There is a separate collection of books and materials for teachers and poets who work with children in schools, and teachers may join a special membership scheme to borrow books for the classroom.

Poetry Society Education

The Poetry Society, 22 Betterton Street,
London WC2H 9BX
tel 020-7420 9894 *fax* 020-7240 4818
email education@poetrysociety.org.uk
website www.poetrysociety.org.uk

The Poetry Society has an outstanding reputation for its exciting and innovative education work. For over 30 years it has been introducing poets into classrooms, providing comprehensive teachers' resources and producing colourful, accessible publications for pupils. It develops projects and schemes to keep poetry flourishing in schools, libraries and workplaces. Schemes like Poets in Schools, Poet in the City and Poetry Places (a 2-year programme of residencies and placements, funded by the Arts Council's 'Arts for Everyone' lottery budget) have enabled the Poetry Society to give work to hundreds of poets and allowed thousands of children and adults to experience poetry for themselves.

Through projects such as the Respect Slam and The Foyle Young Poets of the Year Award the Poetry Society gives valuable encouragement and exposure to young writers and performers.

Schools membership offers publications, training opportunities for teachers and poets, a free subscription to *Poems on the Underground* and a consultancy service giving advice on working with poets in the classroom. *Poetryclass*, an INSET training project, employs poets to train teachers at primary and secondary level. Youth membership is available to 11–18 year-olds and provides advice on developing writing skills, access to publication on the Poetry Society website, quarterly issues of *Poetry News*, and poetry books and posters.

YOUNG POETRY COMPETITIONS

Children's competitions are included in the competition list provided by the Poetry Library (free on receipt of a large sae).

Foyle Young Poets of the Year Award

The Poetry Society, 22 Betterton Street,
London WC2H 9BX
tel 020-7420 9894 *fax* 020-7240 4818
email education@poetrysociety.org.uk
website www.poetrysociety.org.uk

Free entry for 11–17 year-olds with unique prizes.

Christopher Tower Poetry Prize

Tower Poetry, Christ Church, Oxford OX1 1DP
tel/fax (01865) 286591
email info@towerpoetry.org.uk
website www.towerpoetry.org.uk/prize/index.html

An annual poetry competition from Christ Church, Oxford, open to 16–18 year-olds in UK schools and colleges. The poems should be no longer than 48 lines, on a different chosen theme each year. Prizes: £1500 (1st), £750 (2nd), £500 (3rd). Every winner also receives a prize for their school. Highly commended entries each receive £200.

FURTHER READING

Baldwin, Michael, *The Way to Write Poetry*, Hamish Hamilton, 1982, o.p.

Chisholm, Alison, *The Craft of Writing Poetry*, Allison & Busby, 1997, repr. 2001

Chisholm, Alison, *A Practical Poetry Course*, Allison & Busby, 1997

Corti, Doris, *Writing Poetry*, Writers News Library of Writing/Thomas & Lochar, 1994

Fairfax, John, and John Moat, *The Way to Write*, Elm Tree Books, 2nd edn revised, 1998

Finch, Peter, *How to Publish Your Poetry*, Allison & Busby, 3rd edn, 2000

Forbes, Peter, *Scanning the Century*, Penguin Books, 2000

Hamilton, Ian, *The Oxford Companion to Twentieth Century Poetry in English*, OUP, 1996

Hyland, Paul, *Getting into Poetry*, Bloodaxe, 2nd edn, 1997

Livingstone, Dinah, *Poetry Handbook for Readers and Writers*, Macmillan, 1992

O'Brien, Sean, *The Firebox*, Picador, 1998, o.p.

Reading the Applause: Reflections on Performance Poetry by Various Artists, NAWE, 1999

Riggs, Thomas (ed.), *Contemporary Poets*, St James Press, 7th edn, 2001

Roberts, Philip Davies, *How Poetry Works*, Penguin Books, 2nd edn, 2000

Sansom, Peter, *Writing Poems*, Bloodaxe, 1994, reprinted 1997

Sweeney, Matthew and John Williams, *Teach Yourself Writing Poetry*, Hodder and Stoughton, 3rd edn, 2008

Whitworth, John, *Writing Poetry*, A&C Black, 2001

USA

Breen, Nancy, *Poet's Market 2009*, Writer's Digest Books, USA, 2008

Fulton, Len, *Directory of Poetry Publishers 2007–2008*, Dustbooks, USA, 2008

Fulton, Len, *The International Directory of Little Magazines and Small Presses 2007–2008*, Dustbooks, USA, 2008

Preminger, Alex, *New Princeton Encyclopedia of Poetry and Poetics*, Princeton University Press, 3rd edn, 1993

Literary agents
How to get an agent

Because children's publishing is highly competitive and the market is crowded, in this article
Philippa Milnes-Smith explains that finding an agent isn't child's play.

If you are currently just experiencing a vague interest in being a writer or illustrator, stop now. You are unlikely to survive the rigorous commercial assessment to which your work will be subjected. If you are a children's writer or illustrator, do not think that the process of getting published will be any easier than for the adult market. It's just as tough, if not tougher, partly because a lot of writers and would-be writers see writing for children as an easy option. It can't be that difficult to write a kid's book, can it? After all, it is just for kids…

Nowadays, too, there is extra competition in the children's field: the high profile of successes such as J.K. Rowling's *Harry Potter* series and Philip Pullman's *His Dark Materials* have drawn the attention of many professional writers who have previously only written for the adult market and who see it as a new and lucrative area for their talents. So, before embarking on a children's book/script/proposal for an exciting new children's character, remember that it is a highly competitive and crowded market you are entering.

So, what is a literary agent and why would I want one?

You will probably already have noticed that contacts for many publishers are provided in the *Children's Writers' & Artists' Yearbook*. This means that there is nothing to prevent you from pursuing publishers directly yourself. Indeed, if you can answer a confident 'yes' to all the questions below, and have the time and resources to devote to this objective, you probably don't need an agent.
• Do you have a thorough understanding of the publishing market and its dynamics?
• Do you know who are the best publishers for your book and why? Can you evaluate the pros and cons of each?
• Are you financially numerate and confident of being able to negotiate the best commercial deal available in current market conditions?
• Are you confident of being able to understand fully and negotiate a publishing or other media contract?
• Do you enjoy the process of selling yourself and your work?
• Do you want to spend your creative time on these activities?
An agent's job is to deal with all of the above on your behalf. A good agent will do all of these well.

Is that all an agent does?

Agents aren't all the same. Some will provide more editorial and creative support; some will help on longer-term career planning; some will be subject specialists; some will involve themselves more on marketing and promotion. Such extras may well be taken into consideration in the commission rates charged.

If I am writing and/or illustrating for children's books, do I need a specialist children's agent?

Most specialist children's agents would probably say you definitely need a specialist; many general agents will say you don't really need a specialist. In the end you will have to make up your own mind about whether an individual agent is right for your work and right for you as an individual. Knowledge, experience and excellent industry contacts (in the right companies and the right categories) are essential qualities in an agent who is going to represent you. If you are writing younger fiction, an agent whose expertise is in adult books with a few forays into young adult fiction probably won't have a full grasp of its potential. If your project is really something specifically for the schools and educational market it may well require different representation than a project for the consumer market: the audience (children) may be the same but projects for educational publishers tend to have to be tailored to the educational syllabus in a very particular way. You will need an agent who understands this (and there are very few).

If you are only interested in illustrating work by other people rather than developing your own projects and would like to try illustration work across a broad range of genres and formats, you may be best served by an artists' agent rather than a literary agent (see *Illustrators' agents* on page 228).

I am writing a text for an illustrated book – do I need to send illustrations with it for an agent to consider it?

No, not unless you are an accomplished illustrator or intend to do the illustrations yourself. The wrong illustrations will put off an agent as they will a publisher. A good text should be able to speak for itself. And never, in any case, send in original artwork, only send copies.

What if I have a brilliant novelty proposal, like a pop-up book? Do I need to show how it is going to look it its finished state?

If you can do it competently and it helps demonstrate how different and exciting your project is, you can certainly do this. But be prepared for the fact that you may need to make more than one, as the original runs the risk of getting damaged through handling or, when the worst comes to the worst, getting lost.

I have decided I definitely do want an agent. Where do I begin?

When I left publishing and talked generally to the authors and illustrators I knew, a number of them said it was now more difficult to find an agent than a publisher. Why is this? The answer is a commercial one. Running an agency is a costly thing and an agent will only take someone on if they can see how and why they are going to make money for the client and themselves (and, of course, a client who is making no money tends quickly to become an unhappy client). To survive just the basic costs, an agent needs to make commission and if an agent needs to fund sales trips on clients' behalf, often internationally, they need more commission. An agent also knows that if he or she cannot and does not sell a client's work, the relationship isn't going to last long.

So the agent just thinks about money?

Well, some agents may just think about money. And it is certainly what some authors and artists think about a lot. *But* good agents do also care about the quality of work and the clients they take on. They are professional people who commit themselves to doing the best job they can. They also know that good personal relationships count – and that they help everyone enjoy business more. This means that, if and when you get as far as talking to a prospective agent, you should ask yourself the questions: 'Do I have a good rapport with this person? Do I think we will get along? Do I understand and trust what they are saying?' Follow your instinct – more often than not it will be right.

So how do I convince them that I'm worth taking on?

Start with the basics. Make your approach professional. Make sure you only approach an appropriate agent who deals with the category of book you are writing/illustrating. Phone to check to whom you should send your work and whether there are any particular ways your submission should be made (if it's not clear from the listings in this *Yearbook* – see page 192). Only submit neat typed work on single-sided A4 paper. Send a short covering letter with your manuscript explaining what it is, why you wrote it, what the intended audience is and providing any other *relevant* context. Always say if and why you are uniquely placed and qualified to write a particular book. Also, provide a CV (again, neat, typed, relevant). Think of the whole thing in the same way as you would a job application, for which you would expect to prepare thoroughly in advance. You might only get one go at making your big sales pitch to an agent. Don't mess it up by being anything less than thorough.

And if I get to meet them?

Treat it like a job interview (although hopefully it will be more relaxed than this). Be prepared to talk about your work and yourself. An agent knows that a prepossessing personality in an author is a great asset for a publisher in terms of publicity and marketing – they will be looking to see how good your interpersonal skills are. Do also take the chance to find out, if you are discussing children's projects in particular, how and where they submit their clients' work and how well they understand the children's market themselves. Also check that they have good relationships with the sort of publishers/media companies with whom you think your work belongs. Don't be afraid to question them on their credentials and track record. And if you have personal recommendations and referrals from other writers, publishers and other industry contacts, do follow these up. Ask, too, about representation overseas and at the key trade children's book fair(s) such as the one held annually in Bologna. If appropriate, ask about representation in other media. Is this agent going to get their clients' work noticed by the right people in the right places and sold for the best market rates?

Will they expect me to be an expert on children and the children's market?

Not as such, but they might reasonably expect you to have an interest in what children like and enjoy and show an understanding of a child's eye view of the world. Basically, an agent will be looking for a writer/illustrator who is in sympathy with the target audience. It also won't do any harm if you spend time at your local bookshop and/or library and befriend your local librarian or specialist children's bookseller to find out what books and authors are working well and if anyone is doing exactly what you plan to do. It's good, basic market research, as is browsing what else is available through internet retailers. For example, if you are planning a series of picture books about a ballet-dancing mouse you need to be aware that *Angelina Ballerina* is already out there.

And if they turn my work down? Should I ask them to look again? People say you should not accept rejection.

No means no. Don't pester. It won't make an agent change his or her mind. Instead, move on to the next agency who might feel more positive towards your work. The agents who reject you may be wrong. But the loss is theirs.

Even if they turn my work down, isn't it worth asking for help with my creative direction?

No. Agents will often provide editorial advice for clients but won't do so for non-clients. Submissions are usually sorted into two piles of 'yes, worth seeing more' and 'rejections'.

There is not another pile of 'promising writer but requires further tutoring'. To get teaching and advice, creative writing courses (see page 328) and writers' and artists' groups are better options to pursue. It is, however, important to practise and develop your creative skills. You wouldn't expect to be able to play football without working at your ball skills or practise as a lawyer without studying to acquire the relevant knowledge. If you are looking to get your work published, you are going to have to compete with professional writers and artists – and those who have spent years working at their craft.

There are particular considerations that need to be given in the craft of writing children's books. In a picture book, the text needs to work specifically with the illustrations: the fewer words there are, the more they matter. In writing fiction for a young age group, where language and sentence construction have to be simple enough for a seven year-old child, the writer often has to work much harder to generate emotion and excitement and give the story personality. When illustrating children's poetry, the artist has to be able to develop and enhance the meaning of the words to just the right level. Children's books are a demanding business.

Good luck!

Philippa Milnes-Smith is a literary agent and children's specialist at the agency LAW (Lucas Alexander Whitley). She was previously Managing Director of Puffin Books.

See also...

- *Do you have to have an agent to succeed?*, page 185
- *The role of a children's literary agent*, page 189
- *Children's literary agents UK and Ireland*, page 192
- *Children's literary agents overseas*, page 199

Do you *have* to have an agent to succeed?

Bestselling children's author Philip Ardagh has over 70 titles to his credit but chooses not have a literary agent to represent him. In this article he tells us why.

There are a lot of people out there who think that they're children's writers ('I was a child myself once, you know') and who send unsolicited manuscripts directly to publishers in their hundreds – possibly thousands – every year. These manuscripts usually end up on what is called the 'slush pile'. Some publishers won't even read them. Some do but, usually, only after a very long time. Many manuscripts are very badly written or very badly presented. Some are perfectly good but a little too much like something already out there in the bookshops, or they lack that indefinable something that makes them stand out from the crowd. Others are perfectly good but are sent to completely the wrong publisher. The best children's fantasy novel ever isn't going to appeal to a publisher specialising in adult DIY manuals, is it? Getting an agent cuts through this process.

Having an agent

Firstly, if an agent submits a manuscript it's going to be to the publisher they think that it's best suited to, and probably to the most suitable editor within that company – more often than not someone they know or have had dealings with in the past. So your manuscript is being seen by the right people at the right place. It's also neatly bypassed the slush pile. It will actually get read. Hurrah! The agent has acted as a filter. The publisher knows that, if you've been taken on by a reputable agent, your words are probably *worth* reading. You're ahead of the game.

And if a publisher wants to publish your work, an agent knows the ins and outs of advances, royalties, escalators, foreign rights, and a million and one other things that makes the humble writer's head spin. Agents know the 'going rates' and will get you the very best deal they can. And, should there be problems further down the line, your agent can play the bad guy on your behalf – renegotiating contracts and doing the number crunching – whilst you only deal with the nice fluffy creative side with your editor.

That's the theory, of course, and much of it is true. They take their 10–15% but they're not a charity and, if they're on a percentage of your earnings, it's generally in their interest to make you as much money as possible, isn't it?

The question is: is it possible to be a successful children's author without an agent? Of course it is. Anything's possible. I'm an agentless author and I'm doing fine, but not without help, advice, common sense, good luck and, as time has passed, experience.

So what are the disadvantages of having an agent? If you've got the right agent, the answer is probably very few, if any. Sure, you're not earning the full advance or royalty because you're giving them a percentage but your manuscript may never have become a book (or the advance and royalty may have been much lower) if they didn't represent you in the first place. If you don't have an agent you don't get directly involved in every aspect of negotiation and discussion with your publisher because you've handed that role over. And if you like the on-hands approach (for that read 'are a control freak'), you may miss out on that but, over all, the pros seem to outweigh the cons.

If you're *not* happy with your agent, though, it can be a very different story. You're not your agent's only client and you may feel – rightly or wrongly – that they're not giving you enough attention. Many is the writer and illustrator I know who has said, 'I find more work for myself than my agent does', or who isn't happy with the advance they've received and said, 'I'm not sure why my agent was so keen for me to agree to this deal.' Another familiar lament is, 'She seemed so enthusiastic when I first signed up, but now she's gone really quiet.' Your filter has become a barrier.

There may also be jobs which your agent is reluctant for you to take. In children's non-fiction, many authors are still paid flat fees, and small ones at that. Many agents will tell you not to touch them with a barge pole but – if you are at the beginning of your career – who knows what that little job might lead to? I once wrote the text to a book that owed its subsequent international success not to the beauty of my prose but to the illustrations and brilliant paper engineering. My fee was peanuts and, in immediate financial terms, it made no difference if the book sold three copies or 300,000. But it did my writing career the power of good. My name was associated with a successful title, I got known by various people within that particular publishing house, I went on to write many more books for them *with* royalties, and added to my reputation, generating interest from other publishers.

Going it alone

I enjoy that getting-to-know aspect of developing a relationship with publishers and, when it comes to contracts, I have a very useful not-so-secret secret weapon. I may not have an agent but I can call on the contracts experts at the Society of Authors (see page 335). As a member of the Society, they'll go through a contract line by line for me, free and for nothing, offering comments, suggestions and advice. They also publish excellent easy-to-understand pamphlets on various aspects of publishing. If you're not already a member, rush out and join immediately! If you don't understand something, don't be afraid to ask.

Remember, whatever impression a publisher might give, there is very rarely such thing as a standard contract, written in stone, that can't be altered; sometimes significantly. Be prepared to concede some minor points, maybe, in return for sticking to your guns over a point which may really matter to you. (Different things matter to different writers.)

My big break came by luck, but luck borne out of developing contacts and making real friendships in the course of my agentless foray into the children's publishing world. The bulk of my 70-or-more titles are non-fiction, but the bulk of my income and 95% of my recognition comes from my fiction, but one grew from the other. Because I was involved and enthusiastic, I was invited to promote one of my non-fiction titles at a sales conference. As a result of how I ad libbed at the conference, following a mighty cock-up, I was asked if I wrote fiction. *Awful End* (my first Eddie Dickens book) was pulled out of the drawer and a deal was done. One thing had, indeed, led to another. Eddie's adventures are in over 30 languages and read around the world, picking up a few literary awards along the way. Now plans are afoot for a series of Eddie Dickens films.

Your rights

Publishers love to have world rights to your books. Agents love to sell the rights separately. You can see why. An agent will argue that they can get more for you (and therefore more for them) by selling foreign rights separately to foreign publishers – perhaps creating a US auction for your fabulous book, for example – rather than your signing everything over to your UK publisher in one fell swoop. If, however, you sell the world rights to your publisher, and you have a good relationship with them, they're in effect acting as your agent on foreign deals and can still negotiate some excellent ones *in consultation with you*. And, having your world rights, they can share in your international success when it comes, so may be more keen to nurture you (and your money-generating, recognition-building world rights) in the future than, possibly, another writer whom they only publish in the UK.

And remember, an advance is an advance of royalties. If the advance is small and the book is a success, it simply means that the advance is earned out sooner and the cheques start rolling in. My advance for *Awful End* was just a four figure sum, but the money I've earned from additional royalties has been very-nice-thank-you-very-much. And my advances for the later Eddie Dickens books and other fiction were significantly larger.

Making the right decision

I know from friends and colleagues that, when you're starting out, you can find it as hard to get an agent as a publisher, which is why some people choose to go straight for the publishing houses. My advice – and this may surprise some of you – is to stick at trying to get an agent. If I was starting out now, I'd do that. Having an agent from the beginning makes sense.

If you're dead against the idea, feeling convinced that you can do a great job (see Philippa Milnes-Smith's check-list on page 181) or are exhausted trying, there are a few obvious things you can do. Even now, I sometimes ask myself 'Am I getting the very best deal?' and 'Could an agent do better for me?' Financially, the answers to these are probably 'Maybe not' and 'Yes', but are these the right questions? Surely what I need to ask is: 'Am I happy with this deal?' 'Is it a reasonable sum reflecting what I think I'm worth and showing the commitment and understanding of the publisher?' And the answer to that is, more often than not, 'yes'. And remember, money ain't the be all and end all. A good working relationship with an editor and publisher who understand you, consult with you, nurture you and your writing, promote and market you in a way you're happy with is beyond price.

Approaching a publisher

But let's not get ahead of ourselves. One of the most important, important *important* – it's important, get it? – things you need to be sure of before sending a manuscript to an agent *or* a publisher is that it's ready to be seen. Some unpublished writers are so keen to show their work to others in the hope of getting it published as soon as possible that it's still in a very raw state. They're not doing themselves any favours. In fact, they could be ruining their chances. Sure, there is such a thing as overworking a piece, but you really need to be confident that it's about as good as it's going to get, especially if you're bypassing the agent route and going direct to the publisher. With no agent 'filter', you've got to be sure that you're representing yourself, through your work, in the very best possible light.

Look in bookshops to find out who publishes what. Once you've chosen a publisher, look them up in this *Yearbook*, find out their submissions procedure and ring them up. Ask the receptionist the name of the person you should send your manuscript or sample chapters to. This way you can address and write a letter to a particular person, rather than taking the 'Dear Sir/Madam' approach.

The covering letter you should write to the publisher is almost identical to the one for writing to a prospective agent in *How to get an agent* (page 181) except, of course, that you should also include the reason why you think they'd be right people to publish your work.

Finally, do treat the business side of selling yourself as a business. It's not simply that 'the writing's the important bit' and that it'll 'sell itself'. Network, send in invoices on time, get in touch when you say you'll get in touch and be contactable (there's no excuse for dropping off the radar in this age of emails and mobile phones). If you're shy or don't like parties, still go to the ones you're invited to by your publisher. You never know what that chance meeting with that rather scruffy bloke by the chilli dips might lead to. He could end up turning your book into a 24-part television series.

Oh, and one last thing: never admit that, secretly, you enjoy writing so much that you'd happily be published for nothing. Ooops. Me and my big mouth!

Agented or agentless, good luck.

Philip Ardagh is probably best known for his Eddie Dickens novels, which are published in over 30 languages. He also writes children's non-fiction on subjects ranging from hieroglyphs to relativity, and wrote and edited BBC radio's first ever truly interactive drama series *Arthur Storey and the Department of Historical Correction*. He's an 'irregular regular reviewer' of children's fiction in the *Guardian* and he collaborated with Sir Paul McCartney on the ex-Beatles' first children's book.

See also...

- *How to get an agent*, page 181
- *The role of a children's literary agent*, page 189
- *Notes from a successful self-publisher*, page 154
- *Publishing agreements*, page 231
- *The amazing picture book story*, page 217

The role of a children's literary agent

Literary agents receive numerous submissions from aspiring authors every day so the agent's attention must be grabbed from the outset. Rosemary Canter, a literary agent, explains what she is looking for.

As a children's literary agent I'm involved in all the different aspects of a writer's or illustrator's professional life. This means looking after, firstly, a person and their artistic concerns (as cued by them): giving editorial advice or art direction; finding the best and most suitable publishers; advising on career strategies; explaining the publishing process; dealing with problems over jackets, marketing and the like. At the same time, I do all I can to maximise a client's revenue from their work, which involves exploiting the sale of rights in every possible way. Of central concern is the contract, to understand and negotiate the best possible deal in every fine detail. That said, the sale to a UK publisher is often only the first sale; an agent may, and often does, sell the UK publisher the right to publish in the UK and EC countries and certain traditional other territories. This leaves a whole range of other options to explore, for instance the sale of translation rights, of US rights, perhaps rights for film, TV, audio.

When I first became an agent, the head of the agency I worked for expressed the business aspect very neatly: a publisher's business is books, an agent's business is contracts. So what is it that I am going to contract? How do I choose my clients? Or, to put it the other way round – how are you going to come to my notice?

The importance of the accompanying letter

The words 'slush pile', as the unsolicited manuscripts are invariably called, has a disparaging ring to it, sounding like a soggy and undifferentiated mass, but I hope – no, expect – to find two or three seriously good and promising writers from it every year. The life blood of my job, one of the truly thrilling aspects, is the search for new writers.

Look at it from my point of view. The children's department in our agency receives about 2000 unsolicited manuscripts a year. We look at everything but unless I feel intrigued and engaged from the first few lines, I probably won't stay the course (there is always the tug of the rest of the pile and the pressure of time). Writing a good letter is the first and best way to grab my attention. Yes, I want to hear some specifics about your life and your writing, but what my antennae are waving for is a strong sense of who you are. A good writer writes a good letter and makes me feel in the presence of a personality who interests me. I am not just taking on a book, as a publisher may do, I'm taking on a person, a new client who I hope to work with (and for) for many years. I want immediately to sense the possibility of connection, both as a reader and on a personal level.

Also from your letter I want to know that this is not a one-off. I have not yet met a children's publisher who will want to go to the effort of acquiring a lone title and, likewise, I am not interested in a single effort. I will always try to negotiate a two-book deal for a new writer and I am looking for someone who wants to write, at least partly, as a career. I also want a sense that you have done some market research, that you know where your story might fit in the marketplace and, even better, that you have worked on your material, editing and rewriting.

So what am I looking for? When I'm reading I'm always listening out, listening for someone spinning a tale in a new and arresting way. I'm always after that spellbinding experience of childhood, of being lost in a story, in another world. I'm not looking for a perfect manuscript (we can work on it together later on) but I am looking for that experience – familiar and new and thrilling every time – of a truly original voice. I want to feel that you have something to say, but not in a didactic way – I'm sure children, like me, are allergic to that – and that themes will emerge from character and situation. I don't want to be stalked in bold letters from the off!

And what kind of writer are you? Some people undoubtedly want to write only what the muse dictates. But in children's books there are still great opportunities for writers who itch to exercise their craft as much as possible; there are commissions for series fiction, for packagers, for anthologists.

It used to be the view that children's writers, in that sour joke, took 20 years to be an overnight success. Is it still true? There are indeed plenty of writers who by consistency, energy and hard work end up successful in this way. But increasingly, we live in an era when, as in the adult market, new writers are singularly prized and hungrily sought out. The market is an impatient one, energetic as never before, and in many ways it closely resembles the world of adult books in its preparedness to pay (occasionally) large advances and back up the investment with expenditure on marketing and promotion.

The changing marketplace

The pace of change in children's books is extremely fast. As I write this I see that certain kinds of horror stories are coming back … fast-paced adventure stories for boys remain strong … the market is probably saturated with fairy books … fantasy continues to be popular, as long as it is distinctive. These generalisations may or may not remain true in six months or a year's time, but they're a background, and an essential one at that. It is a fundamental part of an agent's job to know what is going on in the market (a phrase we use glibly all the time). It is crucial knowledge which is a constant accompaniment to my reading.

So, all this sits within the 'marketplace'. What does it mean? For an aspiring writer, an agent or a publisher *is* the market. It is frightening to think that there are probably no more than 30 editors of trade fiction for children in the UK; these are the people who count, who form the market to which I sell. The editors are selling to their colleagues in marketing, sales, publicity and rights, a community of people with a view on whether a book will sell and how it will fit in the marketplace. They in turn are selling to retailers – who are selling to the consumer, the child who will actually read the book.

However, it's slightly more complicated than that because today there is the strangest blurring of boundaries – books initially intended for children are now, quite commonly, read by adults. It could even be said that 'children's books' is just another genre description within the adult market. We children's agents and publishers consider ourselves specialists, with a proper understanding of what children want to read, but we can never quite know. The Harry Potter phenomenon has made it abundantly clear that all kinds of readers, of all ages, can and do enjoy children's fiction. Teenage fiction in particular is loved by adults: in books for older children we have the genesis of the 'crossover' title – the book that can appeal universally. I also see increasing echoes of adult successes in children's fiction, science fiction titles and memoirs. But in my view, and experience, I don't think that anyone can set out to write a book that will be successful across a range of markets. If you want to write for children, write for children. Successful books have a clear, targeted age range: the rest is due to word of mouth and an elusive appeal that multiplies buyers of many disparate kinds.

Encouragingly, the younger children's and teenage marketplace is constantly hungry for new, often surprising subject matter. The old, restrictive rules about length and the nature of suitable stories no longer apply, though, in my view, strong moral imperatives remain, as does the need to give young readers hope. And happily, I also see a market for children's books that is very properly dealing with subjects that only children want to read about – silly and rumbustious stories, adventures, stories about families and pets, princesses and fairies.

And then there are picture books. Of all the material that publishers seek, this is the one where they most frequently use the word 'desperate'. There are many gifted and interesting illustrators around, but writers of picture book texts? Yoohoo! Where are you? I think this is the most demanding literary form there is: how do you write an original story that is no longer than, maybe, 300 words, with a beginning, middle and, often, a surprising and unexpected ending, with strong characterisation, in glowing language, that will bear repeated readings — and invite reflection on its deeper meanings? Oh, and allow scope for illustration to bring another wealth of meaning? Not at all easy, this miniaturisation. But for a writer happy to learn the craft, there will never be a shortage of offers.

The electronic future

The underpinning to everything I have written so far is the notion of a settled world of book publishing. But, increasingly, my preoccupations as an agent – and it's true of a vast swathe of the publishing community – are with the upheavals to this order provoked by the electronic future. I can't be very specific because by the time you read this things will, undoubtedly, have changed. But what will the word 'publishing' come to mean, when there are – as is happening already – a myriad ways for writing to be read online? What will the relationship be between these forms and the book? What form will content take? How will stories be read? As ebooks? On mobile phones?

The whole structure and apparatus of publishing is changing from a physical and solid world – the world of offices, warehouses, shops, the book itself – into something digital and ungraspable and constantly evolving. How will the words 'intellectual property rights' (which have themselves a solid, country house kind of feeling) in the virtual world be expressed or controlled or rewarded? It is more and more my role as a children's agent to try to understand these powerful changes and it feels curiously apposite, because for children, the electronic world simply is their world – it's a matter of indifference whether they read a story on a hand-held device or from a book.

However, as publishing develops and evolves, my role will continue to be to support, help and argue for the writers and artists who provide the essential emotional and intellectual nourishment for children and young adults.

Rosemary Canter is the children's specialist agent at literary agency United Agents.

Children's literary agents UK and Ireland

Cautionary note: The *Children's Writers' & Artists' Yearbook*, along with the Association of Authors Agents and the Society of Authors, takes a dim view of any literary agent who asks potential clients for a fee prior to a manuscript being placed with a publisher. We advise you to treat any such request with caution and to let us know if that agent appears in the listings below. However, agents may charge additional costs later in the process but these should only arise once a book has been accepted by a publisher and the author is earning an income. We urge authors to make the distinction between upfront and additional charges.

*Full member of the Association of Authors' Agents

The Agency (London) Ltd*
24 Pottery Lane, London W11 4LZ
tel 020-7727 1346 *fax* 020-7727 9037
email info@theagency.co.uk
Children's Books Executive Hilary Delamere, *Film/TV/Theatre Executives* Stephen Durbridge, Leah Schmidt, Bethan Evans, Julia Kreitman, Norman North, Katie Haines, Faye Webber, Nick Quinn, Ian Benson

Novelty books, picture books, fiction for all ages including teenage fiction and series fiction (home 15%, overseas 20%). All adult writers for theatre, film, TV and radio only. No unsolicited MSS. No reading fee. Will suggest revision. Works in conjunction with agents in USA and overseas. Founded 1995.

Aitken Alexander Associates Ltd*
18–21 Cavaye Place, London SW10 9PT
tel 020-7373 8672 *fax* 020-7373 6002
email reception@aitkenalexander.co.uk
website www.aitkenalexander.co.uk
Agent Kate Shaw

Children's fiction (home 15%, overseas 20%). Handles fiction for 9–12 year-olds and teenage fiction. Also handles adult fiction and non-fiction; 10% of list is for the children's market. Send preliminary letter with a short synopsis and 3–5 sample chapters with a sae. No reading fee. Will suggest revision. No picture books and no submissions by email.
Children's authors include: Helen Fox, Manjula Padma and Louise Rennison. Founded 1977.

Darley Anderson Literary, TV and Film Agency*
Estelle House, 11 Eustace Road, London SW6 1JB
tel 020-7385 6652 *fax* 020-7386 5571
email enquiries@darleyanderson.com
website www.darleyanderson.com,
www.darleyandersonchildrens.com
Contacts Darley Anderson (US and Irish fiction thrillers), Zoe King (non-fiction), Camilla Bolton

(crime), Ella Andrews (women's and general fiction), Julia Churchill (children's books), Emma White (Head of Rights), Madeleine Buston (Rights Manager), Rosi Bridge (Finance)

Commercial fiction and non-fiction; children's fiction and non-fiction (home 15%, USA/translation 20%, film/TV/radio 20%). No poetry or academic books. Send preliminary letter, synopsis and first 3 chapters. Return postage/sae essential for reply.
Overseas associates APA Talent & Literary Agency (LA/Hollywood), Liza Dawson Literary Agency (New York) and 21 leading foreign agents worldwide.
Clients include Cathy Cassidy, Lisa Clark, Adrienne Kress, Carmen Reid, Rob Stevens, Kate Wild, Ahmet Zappa.

Author Literary Agents
53 Talbot Road, London N6 4QX
tel 020-8341 0442 *mobile* (07767) 022659
Contact John Havergal

Novels, thrillers, faction, non-fiction, graphic novels, and children's books, and graphic and illustrated media edutainment concepts (home 15%, overseas/translations 20%, advertising/sales promotion one-third). Pitches to publishers and producers. Send first chapter, scene or section, and graphics samples (if any), plus a half to one page plot or topic outline together with sae. No reading fee. Founded 1997.

The Bell Lomax Moreton Agency
James House, 1 Babmaes Street, London SW1Y 6HF
tel 020-7930 4447 *fax* 020-7925 0118
email agency@bell-lomax.co.uk
Executives Eddie Bell, Pat Lomax, Paul Moreton, June Bell

Quality fiction and non-fiction, biography, children's, business and sport. No unsolicited MSS without preliminary letter. No scripts. No reading fee. Founded 2000.

Jenny Brown Associates*
33 Argyle Place, Edinburgh EH9 1JT
tel 0131-229 5334

email lucy@jennybrownassociates.com
website www.jennybrownassociates.com
Contact Lucy Juckes

Represents children's writers and illustrators. Also adult fiction and general non-fiction. No reading fee. See website for submission guidelines.

Felicity Bryan*

2A North Parade, Banbury Road, Oxford OX2 6LX
tel (01865) 513816 *fax* (01865) 310055
email agency@felicitybryan.com
website www.felicitybryan.com

Fiction for children aged 8–14, and adult fiction and general non-fiction (home 15%, overseas 20%). Translation rights handled by Andrew Nurnberg Associates; works in conjunction with US agents.

Children's authors include Jenny Downham, Sally Gardner, Julie Hearn, Liz Kessler, Katherine Langrish, Graham Marks, Meg Rosoff, Lauren St John, Matthew Skelton, Eleanor Updale, Jeanne Willis.

Celia Catchpole

56 Gilpin Avenue, London SW14 8QY
tel 020-8255 4835
email celiacatchpole@yahoo.co.uk
website www.celiacatchpole.co.uk

Specialises exclusively as agent for children's writers and illustrators (home 10%, overseas 20%). Handles picture books and fiction to age 12. Send complete picture book MS or first 2 chapters of longer novels with sae for return. No poetry or plays. No reading fee. Founded 1996.

Conville & Walsh Ltd*

2 Ganton Street, London W1F 7QL
tel 020-7287 3030 *fax* 020-7287 4545
email (firstname)@convilleandwalsh.com
Directors Clare Conville, Patrick Walsh

Picture books, fiction for 5–8 and 9–12 year-olds, teenage fiction, series fiction and film/TV tie-ins (home 15%, overseas 20%). Also handles adult literary and commercial fiction and non-fiction. Submit first 3 chapters, cover letter, synopsis and sae. No reading fee.

Children's authors include John Burningham, Kate Cann, Timothy Knapman, P.J. Lynch, Joshua Mowll, Jacqui Murhall, Peadar O'Guilin, Nicky Singer, Steve Voake. Founded 2000.

Creative Authors Ltd

11A Woodlawn Street, Whitstable, Kent CT5 1HQ
tel (01227) 770947
email write@creativeauthors.co.uk
website www.creativeauthors.co.uk
Director Isabel Atherton

Fiction, women's fiction, literary fiction, non-fiction, humour, history, autobiography, memoir, Mind, Body & Spirit, health, cookery, arts and crafts, crime, children's fiction (home 15%, overseas 20%). Also represents a small number of scriptwriters.

Authors include Tania Ahsan, Sharon Byrne, Melissa Garner, Peter Harrodine, Nicola Hill, Steve Hill, Ray Murray, Adele Nozedar, Feargus O'Sullivan, Mark Torrender, Dee Weaver. Established 2008.

Curtis Brown Group Ltd*

Haymarket House, 28–29 Haymarket,
London SW1Y 4SP
tel 020-7393 4400 *fax* 020-7393 4401
email cb@curtisbrown.co.uk
website www.curtisbrown.co.uk
Ceo Jonathan Lloyd, *Director of Operations* Ben Hall, *Directors* Jacquie Drewe, Jonny Geller, Nick Marston, Sarah Spear
Books Jonny Geller (Managing Director, Book Division), Camilla Hornby, Jonathan Lloyd, Jonathan Pegg, Vivienne Schuster, Elizabeth Sheinkman, Janice Swanson, Gordon Wise, *Foreign Rights (books)* Carol Jackson (Head of Rights), Kate Cooper, Betsy Robbins, Katie McGowan

Novels, general non-fiction, children's books and associated rights (including multimedia), as well as film, theatre, TV and radio scripts (home 15%, overseas 20%). Send outline for non-fiction and short synopsis for fiction with 2–3 sample chapters and autobiographical note. No reading fee. Return postage essential. No submissions by email. See website for further submission guidelines. Also represents playwrights, film and TV writers and directors, theatre directors and designers, TV and radio presenters and actors. Overseas associates in Australia and the USA. Founded 1899.

Eddison Pearson Ltd*

10 Corinne Road, London N19 5EY
tel 020-7700 7763 *fax* 020-7700 7866
email info@eddisonpearson.com
Contact Clare Pearson

Children's books, fiction and non-fiction, poetry (home 10%, overseas 15–20%). Small personally run agency. Email enquiries only; email for up-to-date submission guidelines by return. No reading fee. May suggest revision where appropriate.

Authors include Valerie Bloom, Sue Heap, Robert Muchamore.

Fraser Ross Associates

6 Wellington Place, Edinburgh EH6 7EQ
tel 0131-553 2759, 0131-657 4412
email lindsey.fraser@tiscali.co.uk, kjross@tiscali.co.uk
website www.fraserross.co.uk
Partners Lindsey Fraser, Kathryn Ross

Writing and illustration for children's books; also adult fiction and non-fiction (home 12.5%, overseas 20%). No reading fee. Founded 2002. Client list and submission guidelines on website.

Annette Green Authors' Agency*

1 East Cliff Road, Tunbridge Wells, Kent TN4 9AD
tel (01892) 514275 *fax* (01892) 558262

email enquiries@annettegreenagency.co.uk
website www.annettegreenagency.co.uk
Partners Annette Green, David Smith

Full-length MSS (home 15%, overseas 20%). Literary and general fiction and non-fiction, popular culture, history, science, teenage fiction. No dramatic scripts, poetry, science fiction or fantasy. No reading fee. Preliminary letter, synopsis, sample chapter and sae essential.

Children's authors include Meg Cabot, Mary Hogan. Founded 1998.

Greene & Heaton Ltd*

37 Goldhawk Road, London W12 8QQ
tel 020-8749 0315 *fax* 020-8749 0318
email info@greeneheaton.co.uk
website www.greeneheaton.co.uk
Contact Linda Davis

Children's fiction and non-fiction (home 15%, overseas 20%). Handles picture books, fiction for 5–8 and 9–12 year-olds, teenage fiction, series fiction, poetry and non-fiction. Also handles adult fiction and non-fiction. Send a covering letter, synopsis and the first 50pp (or less) with an sae and return postage. Email enquiries will be answered but submission attached to emails will not be considered.

Children's authors include Helen Craig, Joshua Doder, Amber Deckers. Founded 1963.

Marianne Gunn O'Connor Literary Agency

Morrison Chambers, Suite 17, 32 Nassau Street, Dublin 2, Republic of Ireland
email mgoclitagency@eircom.net
Contact Marianne Gunn O' Connor

Commercial and literary fiction, non-fiction, biography, children's fiction (home 15%, overseas 20%, film/TV 20%). No unsolicited MSS. Translation rights handled by Vicki Satlow Literary Agency, Milan.

A.M. Heath & Co. Ltd*

6 Warwick Court, London WC1R 5DJ
tel 020-7242 2811 *fax* 020-7242 2711
website www.amheath.com
Contact Sarah Molloy

Fiction and non-fiction from age 5 to young adult (home 15%, USA/translation 20%). Handles picture books, fiction for 5–8 and 9–12 year-olds, teenage fiction, series fiction, film/TV tie-ins and non-fiction. Also handles adult literary and commercial fiction and non-fiction; 20% of list is for children's market. Submit synopsis and sample chapters. No reading fee. Will suggest revision. Overseas associates in USA, Europe, South America, Japan and the Far East.

Children's authors include Nicholas Allan, John Dougherty, Nick Gifford, Joanna Nadin, Susan Price, John Singleton, Rose Wilkins, Leslie Wilson, the Estates of Noel Streatfeild, Helen Cresswell and Joan Aiken. Founded 1919.

David Higham Associates Ltd*

(incorporating Murray Pollinger)
5–8 Lower John Street, Golden Square, London W1F 9HA
tel 020-7434 5900 *fax* 020-7437 1072
email dha@davidhigham.co.uk
website www.davidhigham.co.uk
Managing Director Anthony Goff, *Books* Veronique Baxter, Anthony Goff, Andrew Gordon, Bruce Hunter, Lizzy Kremer, Caroline Walsh, *Foreign Rights* Ania Corless, *Film/TV/Theatre* Gemma Hirst, Nicky Lund, Georgina Ruffhead, Jessica Cooper

Children's fiction, picture books and non-fiction (home 15%, USA/translation 20%, scripts 10%). Handles novelty books, picture books, fiction for 5–8 and 9–12 year-olds, teenage fiction, series fiction, poetry, plays, film/TV tie-ins, non-fiction, audio and CD-Roms. Also handles adult fiction, general non-fiction, plays, film and TV scripts; 35% of list is for the children's market. Submit synopsis and 2–3 sample chapters with a covering letter. For picture books, send complete MS, CV and sae. Address all submissions to Children's Submissions. No email submissions. See website for submissions policy. No reading fee. Represented in all foreign markets.

Also represents 21 illustrators for children's book publishing (home 15%). Submit colour copies of artwork by post or via email. Include samples that show children 'in action' and animals.

Clients (children's market) include Jenny Alexander, Caroline Anstey, Antonia Barber, Julia Bell, Joe Berger, Julie Bertagna, Tim Bowler, Alan Brown, Mike Brownlow, Charles Causley, Kathryn Cave, Lauren Child, Peter Collington, Trish Cooke, Anne Cottringer, Cressida Cowell, Roald Dahl, Susie Day, Kady Macdonald Denton, Berlie Doherty, Jonathan Emmett, Anne Fine, Susan Gates, Jamila Gavin, Julia Golding, Kes Gray, Ann Halam, Carol Hedges, Leigh Hodgkinson, Meredith Hooper, Julia Jarman, Sherryl Jordan, Anna Kemp, Clive King, Bert Kitchen, Rebecca Lisle, Tim Lott, Geraldine McCaughrean, Richard MacSween, Hazel Marshall, Simon Mason, Gwen Millward, Pratima Mitchell, Tony Mitton, Michael Morpurgo, Coleen Murtagh Paratore, Jenny Nimmo, Martine Oborne, Liz Pichon, Tamora Pierce, Chris Powling, Lucy Daniel Raby, Gwyneth Rees, Adrian Reynolds, Catherine Robinson, Nick Sharratt, Emily Smith, Alexander McCall Smith, Jeremy Strong, Alan Temperley, Frances Thomas, Theresa Tomlinson, Ann Turnbull, Caroline Uff, Jenny Valentine, A.M. Vrettos, Martin Waddell, Alex Williams, Gina Wilson, Jacqueline Wilson and David Wojtowycz. Founded 1935.

Johnson & Alcock Ltd*

Clerkenwell House, 45–47 Clerkenwell Green, London EC1R 0HT
tel 020-7251 0125 *fax* 020-7251 2172
email info@johnsonandalcock.co.uk
website www.johnsonandalcock.co.uk
Contact Anna Power

Children's fiction and non-fiction; ages 9–12, teenage fiction, young adult, series fiction (home 15%, USA/translation 20%). Also accept adult fiction and non-fiction. No short stories, poetry or picturebooks. No unsolicited MSS. No response to email submissions. No reading fee but return postage essential. Founded 1956.

LAW (Lucas Alexander Whitley Ltd)*
14 Vernon Street, London W14 0RJ
tel 020-7471 7900 *fax* 020-7471 7910
website www.lawagency.co.uk
Contacts Philippa Milnes-Smith, Ayesha Mobin

Children's books (home 15%, overseas 20%). Handles novelty books, picture books, fiction for 5–8 and 9–12 year-olds, teenage fiction, film/TV tie-ins, non-fiction, reference and audio. Send brief covering letter, short synopsis and 2–3 sample chapters. For picture books, send complete text and/or copies of sample artwork. Do *not* send original artwork. Sae essential. No email or disk submissions. Overseas associates worldwide. Founded 1996.

The Leo Media & Entertainment Group
150 Minories, London EC3N 1LS
tel 020-8905 5191 *fax* (0870) 1330258
email info@leomediagroup.com
website www.leomediagroup.com
Managing Director Alex Sullivan

General fiction and non-fiction: historical, science fiction, children's, plus filmscripts, TV series and documentary ideas (home 15%, overseas 20%). No reading fee. Will suggest revision. Legal services can be provided in conjunction with Fuglers Solicitors LLP.
   Authors include Bev Kelly, John Hardman, Anthony Mirarchi, Mia Sperber, Anthony Williams, Julian Williams. Founded 2003.

Christopher Little Literary Agency*
Eel Brook Studios, 125 Moore Park Road, London SW6 4PS
tel 020-7736 4455 *fax* 020-7736 4490
email info@christopherlittle.net
website www.christopherlittle.net
Contact Christopher Little

Fiction for 9–12 year-olds and teenage fiction (home 15%, overseas 20%); no illustrated children's or short stories. Also handles adult fiction and non-fiction. Send synopsis and first 3 chapters with an sae. No reading fee.
   Children's authors include J.K. Rowling and Darren Shan. Founded 1979.

London Independent Books
26 Chalcot Crescent, London NW1 8YD
tel 020-7706 0486 *fax* 020-7724 3122
Proprietor Carolyn Whitaker

Specialises in teenage fiction (home 10–15%, overseas 20%). Handles fiction for 9–12 year-olds, teenage

fiction and non-fiction. Also handles adult fiction, show business and travel; approx. one-third of list is for the children's market. Submit 2 chapters and a synopsis with return postage. No reading fee. Will suggest revision of promising MSS.
   Authors include Simon Chapman, Joe Delaney, Keith Gray, Elizabeth Kay, Elizabeth Richardson, Craig Simpson, Chris Wooding. Founded 1971.

Jennifer Luithlen Agency
88 Holmfield Road, Leicester LE2 1SB
tel 0116-273 8863 *fax* 0116-273 5697
Agents Jennifer Luithlen, Penny Luithlen

Not looking for new clients. Children's fiction (home 15%, overseas 20%), performance rights (15%). Founded 1986.

Eunice McMullen Ltd
Low Ibbotsholme Cottage, Off Bridge Lane, Troutbeck Bridge, Windermere, Cumbria LA23 1HU
tel (01539) 448551
email eunicemcmullen@totalise.co.uk
website www.eunicemcmullen.co.uk
Director Eunice McMullen

Specialises exclusively in children's books, especially picture books and older fiction (home 10%, overseas 15%). Handles novelty books, picture books, fiction for all ages including teenage, series fiction and audio. No unsolicited scripts. Telephone enquiries only. No reading fee.
   Authors include Wayne Anderson, Sam Childs, Caroline Jayne Church, Jason Cockcroft, Ross Collins, Charles Fuge, Maggie Kneen, David Melling, Angela McAllister, Angie Sage, Gillian Shields. Founded 1992.

Andrew Mann Ltd*
1 Old Compton Street, London W1D 5JA
tel 020-7734 4751 *fax* 020-7287 9264
email info@andrewmann.co.uk
website www.andrewmann.co.uk
Contacts Anne Dewe, Tina Betts, Louise Burns

Children's fiction and non-fiction (home 15%, overseas 20%). Handles picture books, fiction for 5–8 and 9–12 year-olds, teenage fiction, series fiction, film/TV tie-ins and non-fiction. Also handles adult fiction and scripts for TV, cinema, radio and theatre; 20% of list is for children's market. Submit synopsis and first 30pp plus a sae. Email synopses submissions only; no attachments. No reading fee. Will suggest revision. Founded 1968.
   Children's authors include Gina Douthwaite, Joe Hackett, Judith Heneghan, Shirley Isherwood, Kate Lennard, Jude Wisdom, Sarah Mussi, Savita Kalhan.

Sarah Manson Literary Agent
6 Totnes Walk, London N2 0AD
tel 020-8442 0396
email info@sarahmanson.com
website www.sarahmanson.com
Proprietor Sarah Manson

Specialises exclusively in fiction for children and young adults (home 10%, overseas 20%). Send letter, brief author biography, one-page synopsis, first 3 chapters with sae. See website for full submission guidelines. Founded 2002.

Marjacq Scripts
34 Devonshire Place, London W1G 6JW
tel 020-7935 9499 *fax* 020-7935 9115
email enquiries@marjacq.com
website www.marjacq.com
Contact Philip Patterson (books), Luke Speed (film/TV)

All full-length MSS (home 10%, overseas 20%), including commercial and literary fiction and non-fiction, crime, thrillers, commercial, women's fiction, children's, science fiction, history, biography, sport, travel, health. No poetry. Send first 3 chapters with synopsis. May suggest revision. Film and TV rights, screenplays, radio plays, documentaries, screenplays/radio plays: send full script with 1–2pp synopsis/outline. Interested in documentary concepts and will accept proposals from writer/directors: send show reel with script. Sae essential for return of submissions.

Miles Stott Literary Agency
East Hook Farm, Lower Quay Road, Hook, Haverfordwest, Pembrokeshire SA62 4LR
tel/fax (01437) 890570
email miles.stott@virgin.net
Director Nancy Miles

Specialist in children's novelty books, picture books, fiction for 6–9 and 10–12 year-olds, teenage fiction and series fiction (from 10% home, 20% overseas). Send covering letter, brief synopsis and 3 sample chapters. For picture books send complete text and/or copies of sample artwork (do not send original artwork). No reading fee. No email submissions. Sae essential. Founded 2003.

William Morris Agency (UK) Ltd*
Centre Point, 103 New Oxford Street, London WC1A 1DD
tel 020-7534 6800 *fax* 020-7534 6900
website www.wma.com
Books Eugenie Furniss (head of book division), Rowan Lawton, Cathryn Summerhayes, Raffaella De Angelis (translation rights); *TV* Holly Pye (head of TV), Sophie Laurimore, Isabella Zoltowski; *Film* Lucinda Prain

Worldwide talent and literary agency with offices in New York, Beverly Hills, Nashville, Miami and Shanghai. Handles film and TV scripts, TV formats; fiction and general non-fiction (film/TV 10%, UK books 15%, USA books and translation 20%). Accepts email submissions only. Send a synopsis and three sample chapters (50 pages or fewer) to ldnsubmissions@wma.com. No reading fee. London office founded 1965.

PFD (The Peters Fraser & Dunlop Group Ltd)*
Drury House, 34–43 Russell Street, London WC2B 5HA
tel 020-7344 1000 *fax* 020-7836 9539 /7836 9541
email postmaster@pfd.co.uk
website www.pfd.co.uk
Chief Executive Officer Caroline Michel, *Managing Director* Lesley Davey, *Books* Caroline Michel, Michael Sissons, Annabel Merullo, Marcella Edwards, *Foreign Rights* Louisa Pritchard, *Film, TV, Theatre, Presenters and Public Speakers* Gemma Hirst, Jessica Cooper, Alexandra Henderson, Michelle Archer, *Children's Books* Suzy Jenvey, *Creative Director* Sue Douglas, *PFD New York* Erin Edmison

Represents authors of fiction and non-fiction, children's writers, screenwriters, playwrights, documentary makers, technicians, presenters and public speakers throughout the world. Has 85 years of international experience in all media. Outline sample chapters and author biographies should be addressed to the books department. Material should be submitted on an exclusive basis; or in any event disclose if material is being submitted to other agencies or publishers. Return postage essential. No reading fee. Response to email submissions cannot be guaranteed. See website for submission guidelines.

Pollinger Limited*
(formerly Laurence Pollinger Ltd, successor of Pearn, Pollinger and Higham)
9 Staple Inn, Holborn, London WC1V 7QH
tel 020-7404 0342 *fax* 020-7242 5737
email info@pollingerltd.com, permissions@pollingerltd.com
website www.pollingerltd.com
Managing Director Lesley Pollinger, *Agents* Joanna Devereux, Tim Bates, Ruth Needham, *Consultants* Leigh Pollinger, Joan Deitch

All types of general trade adult and children's fiction and non-fiction books; intellectual property developments, illustrators/photographers (home 15%, translation 20%). Overseas, media and theatrical associates. No unsolicited material.

Children's clients include Peter Clover, Bridget Crowley, Catherine Fisher, Phillip Gross, Frances Hendry, Kelly McKain. Founded 1935.

Redhammer Management Ltd*
186 Bickenhall Mansions, Bickenhall Street, London W1U 6BX
tel 020-7486 3465 *fax* 020-7000 1249
website www.redhammer.info
Vice President Peter Cox

Specialises in works with international potential (home 17.5%, overseas 20%). Unpublished authors must be professional in their approach and have major international potential, ideally book, film and/or TV. Submissions must follow the guidelines given on the website. Do not send unsolicited MSS by post. No radio or theatre scripts. No reading fee.

Children's clients include Donna Ballman, Peggy Brusseau, Gary Bushell, Brian Clegg, Maria (MG) Harris, Lucy Johnson, Amanda Lees, Michelle Paver, Kellie Santin, David Yelland. Founded 1993.

Rogers, Coleridge & White Ltd*
20 Powis Mews, London W11 1JN
tel 020-7221 3717 fax 020-7229 9084
website www.rcwlitagency.com
Chairman Deborah Rogers, Managing Director Peter Straus, Director Patricia White, Agent Catherine Pellegrino

Children's fiction and non-fiction (home 15%, USA 20%). Handles novelty books, picture books, fiction for 5–8 and 9–12 year-olds, teenage fiction, series fiction, non-fiction and reference. No unsolicited MSS. No submissions by fax or email. No reading fee. Will suggest revision.

Children's authors include Mary Hoffman, Rhiannon Lassiter, Michelle Magorian, Richard Platt, Karen Wallace. Founded 1967.

Elizabeth Roy Literary Agency
White Cottage, Greatford, Nr Stamford, Lincs. PE9 4PR
tel (01778) 560672 fax (01778) 560672
website www.elizabethroyliteraryagency.co.uk

Children's fiction and non-fiction – writers and illustrators (home 15%, overseas 20%). Send preliminary letter, synopsis and sample chapters with names of publishers and agents previously contacted. Return postage essential. No reading fee. Founded 1990.

Uli Rushby-Smith Literary Agency
72 Plimsoll Road, London N4 2EE
tel 020-7354 2718 fax 020-7354 2718
Director Uli Rushby-Smith

Fiction and non-fiction, literary and commercial (home 15%, USA/foreign 20%). No poetry, picture books, plays or film scripts. Send outline, sample chapters (no disks) and return postage. No reading fee. Founded 1993.

Rosemary Sandberg Ltd
6 Bayley Street, London WC1B 3HE
tel 020-7304 4110 fax 020-7304 4109
email rosemary@sandberg.demon.co.uk
Directors Rosemary Sandberg, Ed Victor

Children's writers and illustrators, general fiction and non-fiction. Absolutely no unsolicited MSS: client list is full. Founded 1991.

Caroline Sheldon Literary Agency Ltd*
London office 70–75 Cowcross Street,
London EC1M 6EJ
tel 020-7336 6550

Mailing address for MSS Thorley Manor Farm, Thorley, Yarmouth PO41 0SJ
tel (01983) 760205, 020 7336 6550
email carolinesheldon@carolinesheldon.co.uk, pennyholroyde@carolinesheldon.co.uk
website www.carolinesheldon.co.uk
Contacts Caroline Sheldon, Penny Holroyde

Adult fiction and non-fiction and children's books (home 15%, USA/translation 20%, film/TV 15%). All writing for children from picture books up through 7–9 year olds, 9–12 year olds to teenage fiction. All major genres including contemporary, comic, fantasy, historical and series fiction. Also non-fiction. Illustrators also represented.

Authors – send introductory information about yourself and your ambitions and the first 3 chapters. If submitting by email type Submission in subject line; if submitting by post enclose a large sae.

Illustrators – send introductory information about yourself with samples. If submitting by email type Artist's Submission in subject line and attach samples of your work and/or link to your website. If submitting by post include printed samples and/or a disk with images saved as jpeg or tiff files together with a large sae. If available, include texts or book dummies. Founded 1985.

Dorie Simmonds Agency*
Riverbank House, One Putney Bridge Approach, London SW6 3JD
tel 020-7736 0002
Contact Dorie Simmonds

Children's fiction (UK/USA 15%; translation 20%). No reading fee but sae required. Send a short synopsis, 2–3 sample chapters and a CV with writing/publishing background.

Clients include award-winning children's authors.

The Standen Literary Agency
53 Hardwicke Road, London N13 4SL
tel/fax 020-8889 1167
email info@standenliteraryagency.com
website www.standenliteraryagency.com
Director Yasmin Standen

Children's fiction for all ages and picture books (home 15%, overseas 20%). Seeking new writers of fiction for 5–8, 9–12 and teen/young adult age groups. Send first 3 chapters and synopsis (one side of A4) with a covering letter by post only in first instance (no submissions via email) and sae. No reading fee. Also handles literary and commercial fiction for adults. 70% of list is children's writing. See website for further information.

Authors include Zara Kane, Zoe Marriott, Andrew Murray. Founded 2004.

Abner Stein*
10 Roland Gardens, London SW7 3PH
tel 020-7373 0456 fax 020-7370 6316

Contact Caspian Dennis, Arabella Stein

Fiction, general non-fiction and children's (home 10%, overseas 20%). Not taking on any new clients at present.

United Agents*

12–26 Lexington Street, London W1F 0LE
tel 020-7166 5266
email info@unitedagents.co.uk
website www.unitedagents.co.uk
Agents Sarah Ballard, Rosemary Canter, Jessica Craig (adult foreign rights), Caroline Dawnay, James Gill, Pat Kavanagh, Robert Kirby, Rosemary Scoular, Simon Trewin, Charles Walker, Anna Webber, Jane Willis (children's foreign rights)

Fiction and non-fiction (home 15%, USA/translation 20%). No reading fee. Founded 2008.

Ed Victor Ltd*

6 Bayley Street, Bedford Square, London WC1B 3HE
tel 020-7304 4100 *fax* 020-7304 4111
Contact Sophie Hicks

Children's picture books, fiction for 5–8 and 9–12 year-olds, teenage fiction, series fiction, film/TV tie-ins, non-fiction and audio (home 10%, overseas 20%). No short stories or poetry. Also handles adult fiction and non-fiction. No reading fee. No unsolicited MSS. No response to submission by email.

Children's authors include Mary Arrigan, Herbie Brennan, Emma Clayton, Eoin Colfer, David Lee Stone, Oisín McGann and Kate Thompson. Founded 1976.

Wade and Doherty Literary Agency Ltd

33 Cormorant Lodge, Thomas More Street, London E1W 1AU
tel 020-7488 4171 *fax* 020-7488 4172
email rw@rwla.com, bd@rwla.com
website www.rwla.com
Directors Robin Wade, Broo Doherty

General fiction and non-fiction, children's books (home 10%, overseas 20%). No poetry, plays or short stories. See website for submission guidelines. Email submissions preferred. New authors welcome. No reading fee. Founded 2001.

Watson, Little Ltd*

48–56 Bayham Place, London NW1 0EU
tel 020-7388 7529 *fax* 020-7388 8501
email office@watsonlittle.com
website www.watsonlittle.com
Contact Mandy Little, James Wills

Fiction, commercial women's fiction, crime and literary fiction. Non-fiction special interests include history, science, popular psychology, self-help and general leisure books. Also children's fiction and non-fiction (home 15%, USA/translation 20%). No short stories, poetry, TV, play or film scripts. Not interested in purely academic writers. Send informative preliminary letter and synopsis with return postage. *Overseas associates* The Marsh Agency Ltd; *Film and TV associates* The Sharland Organisation Ltd and MBA Literary Agents Ltd; *USA associates* Howard Morhaim Literary Agency (adult) and the Chudney Agency (children's).

Children's authors or illustrators include Stephen Biesty, V.M. Jones, Margaret Mahy, Lynne Reid Banks, Stewart Ross.

AP Watt Ltd*

20 John Street, London WC1N 2DR
tel 020-7405 6774
fax 020-7831 2154 (books), 020-7430 1952 (drama)
email apw@apwatt.co.uk
website www.apwatt.co.uk
Directors Caradoc King, Linda Shaughnessy, Derek Johns, Georgia Garrett, Natasha Fairweather, Sheila Crowley, Rob Kraitt (associate)

Adults' and children's full-length MSS; dramatic works for all media (home 15%, overseas 20% including commission to foreign agent). No poetry. No reading fee. Does not accept unsolicited MSS or any other material. Send a query letter in first instance.

Authors include Quentin Blake, Melvin Burgess, Georgia Byng, Zizou Corder, Grace Dent, Helen Dunmore, Dick King-Smith, Philip Pullman, Philip Ridley. Founded 1875.

Eve White*

1A High Street, Kintbury, Berks. RG17 9TJ
tel (01488) 657656
email eve@evewhite.co.uk
website www.evewhite.co.uk
Contact Eve White

Picture books, fiction for 5–8 and 9–12 year-olds, teenage fiction and film/TV tie-ins (home 15%, overseas 20%). Also handles adult commercial and literary fiction and non-fiction; 50% of list is for the children's market. No submissions by email. No reading fee. Will suggest revision where appropriate. See website for up-to-date submission requirements.

Children's clients include Carolyn Ching, Susanna Corbett, David Corderoy, Jimmy Docherty, David Flavell, Margie Hann-Syme, Abie Longstaff, Gillian Rogerson, Andy Stanton. Founded 2003.

Children's literary agents overseas

Before submitting material, writers are advised to send a preliminary letter with a SAE or IRC (International Reply Coupon) and to ascertain terms.

AUSTRALIA

Altair-Australia Literary Agency
PO Box 475, Blackwood SA 5051
tel/fax (8) 8278 5585
email altair-australia@altair-australia.com
website www.altair-australia.com
Agent Robert N. Stephenson

Specialises in science fiction and fantasy; also children's literature, mainstream literature, crime and mystery and action/adventure fiction (15%–20%). Non-fiction material may be considered if queried first. Founded 1997.

Submission details Submit the first 3 chapters (up to 15,000 words) and a 2-page synopsis for fiction/ novel. Send whole MS plus reference details for non-fiction (do not include original graphics, films or photographs). Allow at least 12 weeks before querying.

Australian Literary Management
2–A Booth Street, Balmain, New South Wales 2041
tel (9) 818 8557 *fax* (9) 818 8569
email alpha@austlit.com
website www.austlit.com

Fiction, non-fiction, fantasy, young readers and cartoons (home 15%). Telephone first, then submit a short synopsis and 2 chapters. No reading fee. Do not email. Does not suggest revision.

Children's authors include Pamela Freeman, Christine Harris, Glyn Parry, Laurie Stiller. Established 1980.

Bryson Agency Australia Pty Ltd
PO Box 226, Finders Lane PO, Melbourne 8009
tel (613) 9620 9100 *fax* (613) 9621 2788
email agency@bryson.com.au
website www.bryson.com.au
Contact Fran Bryson

Represents writers operating in all media: print, film, TV, radio, the stage and electronic derivatives; specialises in representation of book writers. Query first before sending unsolicited MSS. Not accepting until further notice.

Jenny Darling & Associates
PO Box 413, Toorak, Victoria 3142
tel (03) 9827 3883 *fax* (03) 9827 1270
email jda@jd-associates.com.au
website www.jd-associates.com.au
Contact Jenny Darling

Represents only a few children's authors. Open to all genres and ages. For picture books and up to end primary school, send the complete MS. For young adult, send the first 10pp in the first instance. Submit material by post, including return postage. See website for submission guidelines.

Golvan Arts Management
PO Box 766, Kew, Victoria 3101, Australia
tel (03) 9853 5341 *fax* (03) 9853 8555
email golvan@ozemail.com.au
website www.golvanarts.com.au
Manager & Director Debbie Golvan, *Director* Colin Golvan

Children's fiction and non-fiction (10%+GST). Handles picture books, fiction for 5–8 and 9–12 year-olds, teenage fiction, series fiction, film/TV tie-ins, non-fiction and plays. Also handles adult fiction and non-fiction, plays, feature film and TV scripts, visual artists and composers; 60% of list is for children's market. Read 'general information' section on website before sending a brief letter. Material sent to agency from outside of Australia will not be returned. No reading fee. Will suggest revision. Works with French, Chinese and Korean agents.

Children's authors include Nan Bodsworth, Kim Caraher, Terry Denton, Janine Fraser, Paty Marshall-Stace, Sally Morgan, Wendy Orr, Greg Pyers, Alan Sunderland. Founded 1989.

CANADA

Melanie Colbert
17 West Street, Holland Landing, Ontario L9N 1L4
tel 905-853-2435
Contact Melanie Colbert

Children's authors and illustrators. Send initial query; no unsolicited MSS. Established 1985.

Anne McDermid & Associates Ltd
83 Willcocks Street, Toronto, Ontario M5S 1C9
tel 416-324 8845 *fax* 416-324 8870
email info@mcdermidagency.com
website www.mcdermidagency.com
Director Anne McDermid, *West Coast Associate* Lise Henderson

Literary fiction and non-fiction, and quality commercial fiction.

West Coast office Literary fiction, children's and young adult literature (home 15%, USA 15%, overseas 20%). No reading fee. Founded 1996.

Pamela Paul Agency

12 Westrose Avenue, Toronto, Ontario M8X 1Z9
tel 416-410-4395 fax 416-410-4949
email agency@interlog.com
Contact Pamela Paul

Children's fiction only. No unsolicited MSS.
Established 1989.

Carolyn Swayze Literary Agency Ltd

W.R.P.O. Box 39588, White Rock,
British Columbia V4B 5L6
tel 604-538-3478
email reception@swayzeagency.com
website www.swayzeagency.com
Proprietor Carolyn Swayze

Literary and commercial fiction, some juvenile and
teen books. No romance, science fiction, poetry,
screenplays, or picture books. Eager to discover lively,
thought-provoking narrative non-fiction, especially
in the fields of science, history, travel, politics, and
memoir.

Submission details No telephone calls: make
contact either by post or send short queries by email,
providing a brief résumé which describes who you
are. Include publication credits, writing awards,
education and experience relevant to your book
project. Include a one-page synopsis of the book and –
if querying via post – include sase for the return of
your materials. Do not include original photographs
or artwork. Include sase if acknowledgement of
receipt of materials is required. Will not open
unsolicited attachments. Allow 6 weeks or longer for
a reply. Founded 1994.

Transatlantic Literary Agency

72 Glengowan Road, Toronto, Ontario M4N 1G4
tel 416-488-9214 fax 416-488-4531
email marie@tla1.com, karen@tla1.com
website www.tla1.com
Contact Marie Campbell, Andrea Cascardi

Specialises in children's and young adult books:
fiction, non-fiction, illustrated books and picture
books. No unsolicited MSS. Founded 1993.

NEW ZEALAND

Glenys Bean Writer's Agent

PO Box 60509, Titirangi, Auckland
tel (09) 812 8486 fax (09) 812 8188
email g.bean@clear.net.nz
website www.glenysbean.com
Directors Fay Weldon, Glenys Bean

Adult and children's fiction, educational, non-fiction,
film, TV, radio (10–20%). Send preliminary letter,
synopsis and sae. No reading fee. Represented by
Sanford Greenburger Associates Ltd (USA).
Translation/foreign rights the Marsh Agency Ltd.
Founded 1989.

Michael Gifkins & Associates

PO Box 6496, Wellesley Street PO, Auckland 1141
tel (09) 523-5032 fax (09) 523-5033
email michael.gifkins@xtra.co.nz
Director Michael Gifkins

Literary and popular fiction, fine arts, children's and
young adult fiction, substantial non-fiction (non-
academic) co-publications (home 15%, overseas
20%). No reading fee. Will suggest revision. Founded
1985.

Richards Literary Agency

postal address PO Box 31–240, Milford,
North Shore City 0620
tel/fax (649) 410-0209
email rla.richards@clear.net.nz
Staff Ray Richards, Elaine Blake, Judy Bartlam,
Frances Plumpton

Children's fiction and non-fiction (home 15%,
overseas 20%). Handles picture books, junior and
teenage fiction, film/TV tie-ins, non-fiction and
reference; educational (primary). Also handles adult
fiction and non-fiction, and film, TV and radio;
approx. 50% of list is for the children's market.
Concentrates on New Zealand authors. Send book
proposal with an outline and biography. No reading
fee. Co-agents in London and New York.

Children's authors include Joy Cowley and Maurice
Gee – the agency has approx. 50 on books. Founded
1977.

Total Fiction Services

PO Box 46-031, Park Avenue, Lower Hutt
tel (04) 565 4429
email tfs@elseware.co.nz
website www.elseware.co.nz

General fiction, non-fiction, children's books. No
poetry, or individual short stories or articles.
Enquiries from New Zealand authors only. Email
queries but no attachments. Hard copy preferred. No
reading fee. Also offers assessment reports, mentoring
and courses.

SOUTH AFRICA

Cherokee Literary Agency

3 Blythwood Road, Rondebosch, Cape 7700
tel (021) 671 4508
email dklee@mweb.co.za
Director D.K. Lee

Children's picture books in translation (home 10%).
Founded 1988.

SPAIN

RDC Agencia Literaria SL

C Fernando VI, No 13–15, Madrid 28004
tel 91-308-55-85 fax 91-308-56-00

email rdc@idecnet.com
Director Raquel de la Concha
Representing foreign fiction, non-fiction, children's books and Spanish authors. No reading fee.

Lennart Sane Agency AB
Paseo de Mejico (65), Las Cumbres-Elviria, ES-29600 Marbella (Malaga)
tel 95-283-41-80 *fax* 95-283-31-96
email lennart.sane@lennartsaneagency.com
website www.lennartsaneagency.com
President Lennart Sane

Fiction, non-fiction, children's books, film and TV scripts. Founded 1965.

USA

*Member of the Association of Authors' Representatives

Adams Literary*
7845 Colony Road, C4 #215, Charlotte, NC 28226
tel 704-542-1440 *fax* 704-542-1450
email info@adamsliterary.com
website www.adamsliterary.com
Agent Tracy Adams

Exclusively children's: from picture books to teenage novels (home 15%, overseas 20%). Strictly no unsolicited submissions. See website for guidelines. Founded 2004.

BookStop Literary Agency
67 Meadow View Road, Orinda, CA 94563
tel 925-254-2664 *fax* 925-254-2668
email info@bookstopliterary.com
website www.bookstopliterary.com
Contact Kendra Marcus

Exclusively children's fiction and non-fiction (home 15%). Represents both authors and illustrators. No reading fee.
  Submission details Send complete MS, sase for return of material and cover letter (include contact information, a short paragraph about your background, publishing credits and brief synopsis of MS). For non-fiction proposals send outline with 2 sample chapters. Illustrators should send colour and b&w samples. Do not send originals. Founded 1984.

Andrea Brown Literary Agency
1076 Eagle Drive, Salinas, CA 93905
tel 831-422-5925
website www.andreabrownlit.com
President Andrea Brown, *Senior Agent* Laura Rennert, *Associate Agents* Caryn Wiseman, Jennifer Jaeger, Michelle Andelman

Exclusively all kinds of children's books. Represents both authors and illustrators.
  Submission details Email submissions only. See website for guidelines. Founded 1981.

Pema Browne Ltd
11 Tena Place, Valley Cottage, NY 10989
email ppbltd@optonline.net
website www.pemabrowneltd.com
President Pema Browne, *Vice President* Perry J. Browne

Fiction, non-fiction and juvenile books (home/ overseas 20%). Only published children's book authors will be accepted for review. Will only review MSS if never sent out to publishers; no simultaneous submissions to other agents. Send query with sase; no phone, fax or email queries with attachments. Founded 1966.

Browne & Miller Literary Associates*
(formerly Multimedia Product Development Inc.)
410 South Michigan Avenue, Suite 460, Chicago, IL 60605
tel 312-922-3063 *fax* 312-922-1905
email mail@browneandmiller.com
website www.browneandmiller.com
Contact Danielle Egan-Miller

General fiction and non-fiction (home 15%, overseas 20%). Select young adult projects. Works in conjunction with foreign agents. Will suggest revision; no reading fee. Founded 1971.

Maria Carvainis Agency Inc.*
1270 Avenue of the Americas, Suite 2320, New York, NY 10020
tel 212-245-6365 *fax* 212-245-7196
email mca@mariacarvainis.com
President & Literary Agent Maria Carvainis, *Literary Agent* Donna Bagdasarian

Adult fiction and non-fiction (home 15%, overseas 20%). Fiction: all categories except science fiction and fantasy, especially literary and mainstream; mystery, thrillers and suspense; historical, Regency, young adult. Non-fiction: biography and memoir, health and women's issues, business, finance, psychology, popular science, popular culture. No reading fee. Query first; no unsolicited MSS. No queries by fax or email. Works in conjunction with foreign, TV and movie agents.

The Chudney Agency
72 North State Road, Suite 501, Briarcliff Manor, NY 10510
tel/fax 914-488-5008
email mail@thechudneyagency.com
website www.thechudneyagency.com
Contact Steven Chudney

Children's books. Focuses particularly on picture books, middle-grade novels and teen fiction. No unsolicited submissions for non-fiction chapter books, middle-grade or teen novels. Not interested in board books or lift-the-flap books; fables, folklore, or traditional fairytales; poetry or 'mood pieces'; stories for 'all ages'; or heavy-handed message-driven stories.

Looking for author/illustrators (one individual), who can both write and illustrate picture books. They must really know and understand the prime needs and wants of the child reader.

Submission details Submit full text; include 3–5 art samples (not originals), a brief biography, and a sase for return of material. Founded 2002.

Curtis Brown Ltd*
10 Astor Place, New York, NY 10003
tel 212-473-5400
President Peter Ginsberg, *Ceo* Timothy Knowlton, *Contacts* Elizabeth Harding, Ginger Knowlton

Fiction and non-fiction, juvenile, film and TV rights. No unsolicited MSS; query first with sase. No reading fee; no handling fees.

Liza Dawson Associates*
350 Seventh Avenue, Suite 2003, New York, NY 10001
email aolswanger@lizadawsonassociates.com
website www.olswanger.com
Contact Anna Olswanger

Fiction and non-fiction for adults and children (home 15%, overseas 20%). Promotes books of Jewish interest. Send query with email address, sase and first 5pp of MS.

Sandra Dijkstra Literary Agency*
PMB 515, 1155 Camino Del Mar, Del Mar, CA 92104–2605
tel 858-755-3115 *fax* 858-794-2822
President Sandra Dijkstra, *Sub-agents* Elise Capron, Taryn Fagerness, Kevan Lyon, Jill Marsal, Kelly Sonnack

Young adult, middle grade, picture books and graphic novels. Fiction and non-fiction (home 15%, overseas 20%). Works in conjunction with foreign and film agents. All submissions must include synopsis and SASE or IRC. No reading fee. Founded 1981.

Dunham Literary, Inc.*
156 Fifth Avenue, Suite 625, New York, NY 10010–7002
website www.dunhamlit.com
Contact Jennie Dunham

Children's books (home 15%, overseas 20%). Handles picture books, fiction for 5–8 and 9–12 year-olds and teenage fiction. Also handles adult literary fiction and non-fiction; 50% of list is for the children's market. Send query letter in first instance by post, not by fax or email. Do not send full MS. No reading fee. Founded 2000.

Dwyer & O'Grady Inc.
PO Box 790, Cedar Key, FL 32625–0790
tel 352-543-9307 *fax* 603-375-5373
website www.dwyerogrady.com
Agents Elizabeth O'Grady, Jeff Dwyer

Exclusively children's books (home 15%, overseas 20%). Represents both authors and illustrators. Small agency; not looking for new clients.

Dystel & Goderich Literary Management*
1 Union Square West, New York, NY 10003
tel 212-627-9100 *fax* 212-627-9313
website www.dystel.com
Contact Michael Bourret

Children's fiction (home 15%, overseas 19%). Handles picture books, fiction for 5–8 and 9–12 year-olds, teenage fiction and series fiction. Looking for quality young adult fiction. Also handles adult fiction and non-fiction. Send a query letter with a synopsis and up to 50pp of sample MS. No reading fee. Will suggest revision.

Children's authors include Antonio Pagliarulo, Kelly Easton, Sara Zarr, Anne Rockwell, Bernadette Rossetti. Founded 1994.

Educational Design Services LLC
5750 Bou Avenue, Ste 1508, N. Bethesda, MD 20852
email blinder@educationaldesignservices.com
website www.educationaldesignservices.com
Contact B. Linder

Specialises in educational texts for K–12 market (home 15%, overseas 25%). No picture books or fiction. Send query with sase, or send outline and one sample chapter by email or with sase for return of material. Founded 1981.

The Ethan Ellenberg Literary Agency*
548 Broadway, Suite 5E, New York, NY 10012
tel 212-431-4554 *fax* 212-941-4652
email agent@ethanellenberg.com
website www.ethanellenberg.com
President & Agent Ethan Ellenberg

Fiction and non-fiction (home 15%, overseas 20%). Commercial fiction: thrillers, mysteries, children's, romance, women's, ethnic, science fiction, fantasy and general fiction; also literary fiction with a strong narrative. Non-fiction: current affairs, health, science, psychology, cookbooks, new age, spirituality, pop-culture, adventure, true crime, biography and memoir. No scholarly works, poetry, short stories or screenplays.

Will accept unsolicited MSS and seriously consider all submissions, including first-time writers. For fiction submit synopsis and first 3 chapters. For non-fiction send a proposal (outline, sample material, author CV, etc). For children's works send complete MS. Illustrators should send a representative selection of colour copies (no orginal artwork). Unable to return any material from overseas. For response include a sase with correct US postage. Submissions without a sase will receive only an email response if interested. Founded 1983.

Flannery Literary
1155 South Washing Street, Suite 202, Naperville, IL 60540–3300

Children's literary agents overseas 203

tel 630-428-2682 *fax* 630-428-2683
Contact Jennifer Flannery

Specialises in children's and young adult, juvenile fiction and non-fiction (home 15%, overseas 20%). Send query letter by post in first instance. Founded 1992.

Barry Goldblatt Literary LLC*

320 Seventh Avenue, PMB 266, Brooklyn, New York, NY 11215
tel 718-832-8787 *fax* 718-832-5558
email bgliterary@earthlink.net
website www.bgliterary.com
Contact Barry Goldblatt

Specialises in young adult and middle grade fiction, but also handles picture book writers and illustrators. No non-fiction. Has a preference for quirky, offbeat work. Query only.

Ashley Grayson Literary Agency*

1342 18th Street, San Pedro, CA 90732
tel 310-548-4672 *fax* 310-514-1148
email graysonagent@earthlink.net
Contact Ashley Grayson, Carolyn Grayson

Commercial fiction and literary fiction for adults and children. Handles foreign rights. No unsolicited MSS. Submit query letter and first 3 pages of MSS. No calls or queries. No reading fee.
   Clients include Bruce Coville, J.B. Cheany, David Lubar, Christopher Pike. Established 1976.

The Greenhouse Literary Agency

11308 Lapham Drive, Oakton, VA 22124
tel 703-865-4990
email submissions@greenhouseliterary.com
website www.greenhouseliterary.com
Director Sarah Davies

Children's fiction from age 5 through to teen/young adult (USA/UK 15%, elsewhere 25%). Represents both US and UK authors. No picture books or non-fiction. No reading fee. Will suggest revision. Contact by email or snail mail. Founded 2008.

John Hawkins & Associates Inc.*

(formerly Paul R. Reynolds Inc.)
71 West 23rd Street, Suite 1600, New York, NY 10010
tel 212-807-7040 *fax* 212-807-9555
website www.jhalit.com
President John Hawkins, *Vice-President* William Reiss, *Foreign Rights* Moses Cardona, *Other Agents* Warren Frazier, Anne Hawkins

Fiction, non-fiction, young adult. No reading fee. Founded 1893.

JCA Literary Agency Inc.*

174 Sullivan Street, New York, NY 10012
email tom@jcalit.com, tony@jcalit.com
website www.jcalit.com
Contacts Tom Cushman, Tony Outhwait

Adult fiction, non-fiction and young adult. No unsolicited MSS; query first.

The Kirchoff/Wohlberg Literary Agency*

866 United Nation Plaza, New York, New York 10017
tel 212-644-2020 *fax* 212-223-4387
website www.kirchoffwohlberg.com
Agent Liza Pulitzer-Voges

Children's fiction and non-fiction for all ages from baby to young adult. Represents authors and author/illustrators. Send query letter, outline and sample plus sase.

Barbara S. Kouts, Literary Agent*

PO Box 560, Bellport, NY 11713
tel 516-286-1278 *fax* 516-286-1538
email bkouts@aol.com
Owner Barbara S. Kouts

Fiction and non-fiction, children's (home 15%, overseas 20%). Works with overseas agents. No reading fee. No phone calls. Send query letter first. Founded 1980.

Gina Maccoby Literary Agency*

PO Box 60, Chappaqua, NY 10514
tel 914-238-5630
email gmacloby@aol.com
Contact Gina Maccoby

Specialises in children's books: fiction, non-fiction, picture books, MS/illustration packages for middle grade and young adult (home 10%, overseas 20%).
   Submission details Send query letter by post in first instance. Founded 1986.

McIntosh & Otis Inc.*

353 Lexington Avenue, New York, NY 10016
tel 212-687-7400 *fax* 212-687-6894
website www.mcintoshandotis.com
Head of Children's Dept Edward Necarsulmer IV

Fiction for 5–8 and 9–12 year-olds, teenage fiction, series fiction, poetry and non-fiction for children (home 15%, overseas 20%). Also handles adult fiction and non-fiction. No unsolicited MSS for novels; query first with outline, sample chapters and sase. No submissions by email. No reading fee. Will suggest revision. Founded 1928.

Barbara Markowitz Literary Agency

PO Box 41709, Los Angeles, CA 90041
Agents Barbara Markowitz, Judith Rosenthal

Children's fiction, middle grade, young adult (11–15 year-olds), historical fiction (home 15%, overseas 15%). Seeking contemporary and historical fiction 35,000–50,000 words for 8–11 and 11–15 year-olds. No fables, fantasy or fairytales; no illustrated books; no sci-fi.
   Submission details Send query letter with sase or outline with 3 sample chapters. Send sase for return of material. Founded 1980.

Mews Books

20 Bluewater Hill, Westport, CT 06880
tel 203-227-1836 *fax* 203-227-1144
email mewsbooks@aol.com
Agents Sidney B. Kramer, Fran Pollak

Children's fiction, non-fiction, picture books, middle grade and young adult books (home 15%, overseas 20%). Seeking well-written books of professional quality with continuity of character and story.
   Submission details Send query letter with sase or outline and 2 sample chapters by regular mail (no email). Send sase for return of material. Founded 1974.

William Morris Agency Inc.*

(incorporating the Writers Shop, formerly Virginia Barber Literary Agency)
1325 Avenue of the Americas, New York, NY 10019
tel 212-586-5100 *fax* 212-246-3583
website www.wma.com
Executive VP Owen Laster, *Senior VPs* Jennifer Rudolph Walsh, Suzanne Gluck, Joni Evans, Mel Berger, Jay Mandel, Tracy Fisher

General fiction and non-fiction (home 15%, overseas 20%, performance rights 15%). Will suggest revision. No reading fee.

Erin Murphy Literary Agency

2700 Woodlands Village, Suite 300–458, Flagstaff, AZ 86001–7127
tel 928-525-2056

Children's books: fiction, non-fiction, picture books, middle grade, young adult (home 15%, overseas 20%). No unsolicited queries or submissions; considers material only by referral or through personal contact such as at conferences. Founded 1999.

Muse Literary Management

189 Waverly Place, Suite 4, New York, NY 10014–3135
tel 212-925-3721
email MuseLiteraryMgmt@aol.com
website www.museliterary.com
Agent Deborah Carter

Children's and adult fiction and non-fiction (home 15%, overseas 20%). Looking for picture books, middle grade and young adult novels that bring something new to their bookselling category. Prefers writers who interact with the age group they are writing for. Originality and imagination are treasured. Actively persuing new writers with formal training and published authors who want to try something new. Prospective authors should be receptive to editorial feedback and willing to revise. Interested in intelligent books: no vulgar subject matter or books that copy others.

Alison Picard, Literary Agent

PO Box 2000, Cotuit, MA 02635
tel 508-477-7192

email ajpicard@aol.com
Adult fiction and non-fiction, children's and young adult (15%). No short stories, poetry, plays, screenplays or sci-fi/fantasy. No reading fee. Founded 1985.

Pippin Properties Inc.

155 East 38th Street, Suite 2H, New York, NY 10016
tel 212-338-9310 *fax* 212-338-9579
email info@pippinproperties.com
website www.pippinproperties.com
Contact Holly M. McGhee, Emily van Beek, Samantha Cosentino

Exclusively children's book authors and artists (home 15%, overseas 25%), from picture books to middle-grade and young adult novels. Query with sase or by email. Founded 1998.

Susan Schulman Literary & Dramatic Agents Inc.*

454 West 44th Street, New York, NY 10036
tel 212-713-1633 *fax* 212-581-8830
email schulman@aol.com

Agents for negotiation in all markets (with co-agents) of fiction, general non-fiction, children's books, academic and professional works, and associated subsidiary rights including plays and film (home 15%, UK 7.5%, overseas 20%). No reading fee. Return postage required.

Stimola Literary Studio, LLC*

306 Chase Court, Edgewater, NJ 07020
tel/fax 201-945-9353
email info@stimolaliterarystudio.com
website www.stimolaliterarystudio.com
Contact Rosemary B. Stimola

Children's fiction and non-fiction, from preschool to young adult (home 15%, overseas 20%).
   Submission details Most clients come via referral. Founded 1997.

Ann Tobias, Literary Agent

520 East 84th Street, Apt 4L, New York, NY 10028
Contact Ann Tobias

Exclusively children's fiction and non-fiction: picture books, middle grade, young adult, young readers (home 15%, overseas 20%). US authors only.
   Submission details For picture books send complete MS; for longer works send 30pp and synopsis. Include sase for return of material. No email, fax or phone queries. Founded 1988.

S©ott Treimel NY*

434 Lafayette Street, New York, NT 10003
tel 212-505-8353 *fax* 212-505-0664
email st.ny@verizon.net
Contact Scott Treimel

Exclusively children's books: middle grade, young adult novels and MS/illustration packages by artist/

illustrator only. No picture book MSS (home 15–20%, overseas 20–25%). Interested in seeing first chapter books, and middle-grade and teenage fiction. No religious books. Send query letter with sase; no fax or email queries. Founded 1995.

Ralph M. Vicinanza Ltd*

303 West 18th Street, New York, NY 10011-4440
tel 212-924-7090 *fax* 212-691-9644
Contacts Ralph Vicinanza, Christopher Lotts, Christopher Schelling

Fiction: literary, popular (especially science fiction, fantasy, thrillers), children's. Non-fiction: history, business, science, biography, popular culture. Foreign rights specialists. New clients by professional recommendation only. No unsolicited MSS.

Writers House LLC*

21 West 26th Street, New York, NY 10010
tel 212-685-2400 *fax* 212-685-1781
website www.writershouse.com
Chairman Albert Zuckerman, *President* Amy Berkower, *Juvenile & Young Adult Agent* Steven Malk

Fiction and non-fiction, including all rights; film and TV rights. No screenplays or software. Send a one-page letter in the first instance, saying what's wonderful about your book, what it is about and why you are the best person to write it. No reading fee. Founded 1974.

Wylie-Merrick Literary Agency*

1138 South Webster Street, Kokomo, IN 46902
tel 765-459-8258
email robertbrown@wylie-merrick.com, sharenembrown@wylie-merrick.com
website www.wylie-merrick.com
Partners Robert Brown, Sharene Martin and Ann Boyle

Adult and juvenile fiction and non-fiction (home 15%, overseas 20%). Interested in romance, sci-fi and fantasy, women's, gay/lesbian, suspense/thrillers. No picture books or graphic novels. Query by email only; no unsolicited MSS. See website for full submission guidelines. Founded 1999.

Illustrating for children
Creating graphic novels

Raymond Briggs has created many graphic novels and here he describes the process.

Book writers have such an easy time of it. They sit down, write their book and when they come to the end they send it off to the publisher. It might be long, it might be short, the publisher doesn't mind.

The writer needs no materials or equipment. He can do it all with a pencil and a Woolworth's pad. Even the typing may be done for him. Unlike the illustrator, he needs no paints, crayons, T-squares, set squares, brushes, dividers, spray cans, handmade paper and mounting boards, light boxes, cutting tables, guillotines, type scales, magnifier lamps, wall-to-wall display boards and masses of space. The writer can scribble it all in bed. (They often do.)

Drawing the book

For the picture book illustrator, when he has finished the writing, that is the easy bit done. His true task then begins.

First he has to design the book. Picture books have to be exactly 32 pages, not 33 or 31. This includes prelims. So the text has to be divided into fewer than 16 spreads. On rare occasions, the publisher may allow 40 pages, or on even rarer occasions 48, though this allowance may contain 'self-ends' which take up eight pages. (This is too technical to explain to book writers.)

Then, the illustrator becomes a typographer. He casts off the MSS, chooses a suitable font, decides on the type size, the measure and the leading, and has it set. Surprisingly, some writers I have met know nothing about typography. Some don't even know the name of the font their own book is set in! Some have never even set foot in a printer's.

If the book is strip cartoon with speech bubbles, the task is even greater as each speech bubble has to be individually designed. The size and shape of it is part of its expressive quality and once the bubble is finalised the illustrator becomes a hand-lettering expert and letters in, possibly many hundreds of words, trying to maintain a consistent style over many days' work. In America strip cartoon work is divided amongst several people: writer, pencilling-in artist, inker-in, and letterer. In England we are made of sterner stuff – 'blood, toil, tears and sweat' and we 'graphic novelists' do it all.

The illustrator then makes a dummy (a blank book) with the correct number of pages and of the exact size. If he is well established and commands respect from the publisher, the publisher may have a dummy made for him – but you need to be at least 60 years old to be granted this privilege. (You might have to show them your Bus Pass.) He then cuts up the type proofs (which used to be called 'galleys') and sticks them onto the dummy, imagining the pictures on the page as he does so. Again, for strip cartoons it is much more complicated – you have to consider not just what text goes on each spread but how many frames the text is to be divided amongst, and what size and shape the frames are to be.

This brings us to the next stage: designing the 'grid', i.e. how many rows of frames per page and the number of frames in each row there are to be. Places where small frames give way to a big picture, either vignetted or bled off, will be determined by the text itself, not only in terms of space but also by the feeling the text is trying to express.

Creating the action

When all this is done, it is time to stop book designing and start making the 'film'. You become the director. Who comes on from the left and who from the right? A slight nuisance is that the character on the left is the one who has to speak first. What are the characters doing and thinking and feeling? We have their words, but is there a subtext? Can this be expressed by body language? Is one of them angrily scrubbing the floor, whilst the other gazes moodily out of the window?

You then become the art director, designing the sets. Where does the scene take place? Indoors or outdoors? In the garden or in the street? What does a 1930s kitchen look like? How big is the room? What is the view from the window?

You also have to be the costume designer and the lighting designer. What would they be wearing at the time? Is it winter or summer? What were overcoats and hats like then? What did they wear on the beach? Should it be daylight or artificial light in this scene? What exactly was the look of gaslight? Does it need a dark ominous light or a happy morning light?

Then as the cameraman you have to decide where to shoot from. Close-up, long shot, or middle distance? Both characters in shot or one off-screen? Perhaps a speech bubble stays in the frame but the speaker is unseen, through a doorway or simply out of shot. Shall it be a high view looking down on the scene or a low angle looking up? It all depends on what the action is trying to convey.

Finally, you have to become the actor and feel yourself inside the character when you're drawing it. This is the essence of good narrative illustration. It is an odd bit of psychology. You have to be mentally in two places at once. One part of you is inside character, feeling what it is like to be huddled and running in the pouring rain, the other part of your brain is detachedly looking at this figure from a certain point of view, taking note of perspective. 'Ah yes, the lower leg will be foreshortened from this angle; we're looking down on the thigh and on the back; we can't see his face as his head is down and his arm is up. Will we see the sole of the shoe that is raised or is it edge on?'

The lucky writer need know nothing about human and animal anatomy, perspective, drawing, line tone or colour. All they have to do is write down some words! It's a doddle.

I wish I could do it.

Raymond Briggs is creator of *The Snowman*, *Fungus the Bogeyman*, *Father Christmas* and many other characters and stories for children, and *When the Wind Blows* for adults. Since leaving art school in 1957 he has been a writer and illustrator, mainly of children's books. He has written plays for the stage and radio and a few 'adult' books. In 2004 he designed the Christmas stamps for the Royal Mail, and was made a Fellow of the Royal Society of Literature, but his proudest achievement is going on the radio programme *Desert Island Discs*, twice. His fansite is www.toonhound.com/briggs.htm.

See also...
● *Notes from a successful children's author and illustrator*, page 80
● *Writing and illustrating picture books*, page 213

Eight great tips to get your picture book published

Tony Ross gives some sound advice for illustrators and writers of children's picture books.

I have always had the uncomfortable feeling that if I can get published, anyone can. A belief that being published is something that only happens to other people, holds some very good writers and illustrators back.

Assuming you have drawings – or a story – to offer, there are several ways to go about it. Probably the best way is to have a publishing house in the family! Failing that, all is not lost.

Work can be sent directly to a publisher's office. Most editors receive a good amount of unsolicited work, so be patient with them for a reply. A stamped addressed envelope for its return is always appreciated, bearing in mind that the majority of work submitted is refused. At the beginning of a career, refusal is quite normal and a great deal about yourself and your talent can be gleaned from this experience. Sometimes, advice gained at this stage can change your future.

Starting on a drawing career is an exciting time and I think it's a good idea to get yourself in perspective. Visit the library and some bookshops to look at all the styles that are around. Get a sense for what's out there: you don't want to regurgitate it, but to get a feel for the parameters. You can learn a lot, maybe more than you learned at art school, from looking at great artists such as Edward Ardizzone, E.H. Shepherd, Maurice Sendak and Chris Van Allsberg.

Great Tip No 1: Use black and white

There is great appeal in working in full colour but it's good to remember black and white. Sometimes a publisher may have a black and white project waiting for an illustrator, while all of the big interest is going into the coloured picture book list. Some of the greatest children's books are illustrated in black and white – A.A. Milne and E.H. Shepherd made one of the greatest partnerships with those tiny black ink drawings contributing so much to a great classic. Not a bad place to start, eh?

Ink drawing is simple, in the hands of a master, but not easy. That unforgiving fluid! Wonder at the uncomplicated, straightforwardness of the Pooh drawings. Consider Toad in *The Wind in the Willows*. When he applied to do the illustrations, Kenneth Graham said to Shepherd: 'I have seen many artists who can draw better than you, but you make the animals live.' Can you learn anything from that? Look at Ardizzone's ability to draw mood. He can show a summer afternoon, or a cold November morning, both using black ink. There is so much to look at, so much to learn from.

Try to include black and white work in your folder. Also include a series of perhaps 30 drawings, such as a fully illustrated story, where you show your ability to be consistent with the characters and the style, without repetition or irrelevance (like the radio programme *Just a Minute!*).

It is a duty of an illustrator to be able to read – that is to try and understand the writer's aims – and to help them rather than to inflict a totally different angle onto the book (think of the Milne and Shepherd partnership). Much of this comes down to being sensitive enough to recognise the tone of the writing, and skilful enough to draw in the same tone. So the importance of really taking an interest in the story cannot be overstressed. In the text, there will be either clues, or blatant instructions to help the drawings gel. Be very aware.

Great Tip No 2: Experiment

I have known illustrators who convinced themselves that they couldn't use black ink. Mostly this was because they were using the wrong ink, the wrong pen, and/or the wrong paper. Types of black ink vary: waterproof behaves differently from water soluble. Fine nibs and broad nibs each give a totally different result, as does an old fountain pen or a sharpened stick. Try ten different inks, 50 different nibs, odd sticks and all the papers you can find: tracing, layout, calendered, five different cartridges, smooth and rough water-colour, handmade, wrapping paper, anything at all. It's a case of finding the combination that suits your hand and your intention. Your own genius, unrecognised at art school, could surprise you.

Many of the points I've made about black and white work also apply to colour. The marriage of image to text will be in your hands, but it must work.

Great Tip No 3: Choose the right words

I am hesitant to give advice to writers. After all, there are few rules, and the next J.K. Rowling may read this. My own view is really quite simple, and rather obvious. I write mainly for under eight year-olds, so my stories are as short as I can make them. I feel that it is good to have a magnetic first sentence, and an ending that EXPLODES WITH SURPRISE. I think that the ending is the most important part of the story. The bit in the middle should waft the reader along, remembering that the *sound* of words and sentences can be a useful tool.

I like stories to be either funny or scary. *Very* funny, or *very* scary. To be dull is the worst thing in the world! That sounds so obvious, but it gets overlooked. If you are not excited with your work, maybe nobody else will be either.

A picture book has about 23 pages of text (but this can be flexible). I think those pages should have fewer than 2000 words; 1000–1500 is good. One word per page would be great, if the one word was brilliant. As brilliant as the story. Don't be frightened of editing out surplus words. One brilliant one will work better than a dozen mundane ones.

Don't fall into the mindset that writing for children is easy. It has all the disciplines of writing for adults, with the added problem of understanding a child's mind and world. The great writers have a passport to a child's world – think of Roald Dahl. I have seen many brilliant ideas, with less than brilliant pictures, make wonderful books. I have seen a bad idea saved by wonderful illustrations. So, writing style apart, be your own concept's greatest critic. It is quite natural to be protective of your baby, of your story. But try to remember that there are a lot of good editors out there and it will be in your own interest to consider their advice. So don't be a young fogey: be flexible, listen, understand experienced points of view. This can be a good time to change for the better, and to start a relationship with one publishing house that may serve you for a lifetime.

Great Tip No 4: Choose what you draw

Don't plan huge drawing problems into your submitted roughs. They may be accepted, and the editor will expect the final art to be better than the roughs.

I illustrate my own writing. This appeals to me for all sorts of reasons, few of them noble. Firstly, I get all of the available fee or/and royalty. I don't have to let half or more go to a writer. Secondly, if there is something I don't like to draw, I don't write about it! For instance, most of my stories take place in the summer, because I prefer to handle trees with their leaves on.

Illustrations being worked on to be published is not the place to practise your drawing. *Practise, change, experiment* all the time, but not in a publishing project. Your finished illustrations must be as good as you can make them. I know an illustrator who won't draw feet, always hiding the ends of legs in grass, water, behind rocks, etc. This is okay if the text will allow; a well-drawn puddle is better than a badly drawn foot any day. It is better to think around a drawing problem, than just to go along with it.

Great Tip No 5: Experiment with your main character
Before you start, try drawing your main character (the most important visual element of the story) in all sorts of ways. A day spent doing this can be so valuable. Getting the main character right can indicate ways to proceed with the whole book.

Great Tip No 6: Think global
Remember that editors react well to stories with wide appeal, rather than minority groups. Foreign sales are in everyone's interest, so try to allow your work to travel. Rhyme is sometimes difficult to translate, as are unusual plays on words.

Great Tip No 7: Plan the whole book
Do little mock-up books for yourself to plan what text goes on which page. This helps to get the story right throughout the book. A 32-page children's book (the most common extent for a picture book) includes covers, end papers, title and half-title pages. This leaves you 23–25 pages to play with. These little mock-ups are for your own use, not to be presented as roughs, so they can be quite work-a-day.

By working out what text goes on which page you will get some sort of an idea of which illustrations go where. Just as the drawings are creative, so is their use on the page. If you use a full double-page spread, another can be expected on the next page. But imagine the effect if the next page explodes with huge typography, and tiny pictures? I am not suggesting you do this, only reminding you that pages of a book are there to be turned, and the turning can be unpredictable and adventurous. Book design is important, along with everything else.

Great Tip No 8: Persevere
So much to do, so much to remember. The main thing is, every children's illustrator and writer I know who has kept trying has got there in the end and been published. But I've also seen great talents give up far too early. Remember that rejection is normal: it's only someone's point of view. Some great books have had long hunts for a publisher. Be open to change and always bear in mind that editors have the experience that you may lack and an editor's advice is meant to help you, not choke you off. However, not all of their advice may apply in your case, so try to recognise what applies to you. When I worked in advertising, I had an art director who said: 'Half of what I say is rubbish. Trouble is, I don't know which half.'

And a reminder
Don't waste time by sending work to publishers who don't publish material like yours. Libraries and bookshops are worth exploring to familiarise yourself with which publishing houses favour what types of work. Research of this kind is time well spent.

Try to show your work in person so that you get a chance to talk, and learn. Do not, however, just drop in. Make an appointment first and hope that these busy people have some time available.

There are also agents prepared to represent new talent (see *Illustrators' agents* on page 228). Of course, an agent will charge a percentage of work sold, but my dad used to say, 'Seventy-five per cent of something is better than 100% of nothing.'

I am troubled by giving advice. I can't help thinking of the young composer who approached the slightly older Mozart and asked, 'Maestro, how should I compose a concerto?' to which Mozart replied 'You are very young, perhaps you should start with a simple tune'. The young composer frowned, and argued. 'But, Maestro, *you* composed a concerto when you were still a child!' 'Ah yes,' said Mozart, 'but I didn't have to ask how?'

Tony Ross is a renowned illustrator of international repute and the creator of such classics as *The Little Princess* and *I Want My Potty*. His first book was published in 1976 and since then he has illustrated more than 700 books including the *Dr Xargle* series, created with the author Jeanne Willis and the *Horrid Henry* series written by Francesca Simon.

See also...
- *Notes from a successful children's author and illustrator,* page 80
- *Creating graphic novels,* page 207
- *Writing and illustrating picture books,* page 213
- *The amazing picture book story,* page 217
- *Illustrating for children's books,* page 221

Writing and illustrating picture books

Debi Gliori tells the story of how she started writing and illustrating children's books.

The prospect of spending your life making children's books has a great deal to recommend it, not least the fact that you will never have to buy those nasty big itchy rolls of rockwool to insulate the walls of your home ever again. Twelve thousand or so volumes will do the job far better. Following the children's books career path will ensure that books will pour into your home, year after year, yours and other people's; foreign editions and large-print versions; pop-ups and boards; collections and anthologies; so many that you might think about studying 'Elementary Bookshelf Building for Beginners and Fumblethumbs' before your piles of books reach to the ceiling. You will also be forced to develop a pronounced and sincerely apologetic grovel each time your postman staggers laden to your door – after all, his sciatica/lower back pain/slipped disc is *entirely your fault.*

Tottering heaps of hardbacks notwithstanding, I can say, with hand-on-heart, that being a children's author and illustrator is the best job in the world. I'm not alone in this opinion. Some years ago, a midwife visited me in the studio I work from in my garden and said, apropos of nothing: 'Eee lass, you've landed with your bum in the butter'.

Unsurprisingly, I looked suitably horrified. (What *was* this, pray? Surely not more indignities to be visited upon my person in the name of childbirth?) Seeing my expression, she hastily explained that what she had *meant* was that I was exceedingly fortunate to be paid to do what I love best. 'Bum in the butter' huh? Takes all sorts. But hey, Gentle Reader, it was not always thus. Back in the mists of that ghastly period of human history known as the Eighties when I set off on this Quest for Publication, I recall that I underwent a long period of major struggle during which many lentils were consumed. This was a lengthy phase which also involved dressing in the morning *in* bed, serious layering of woolly jumpers and, I kid you not, bathrooms so cold that one's toothbrush *froze.*

After graduation from Edinburgh College of Art, I trawled round London publishers with my too-big portfolio and quickly realised that good picture book texts were as rare as talking bears. While illustrators, such as I'd been studying to become, were everywhere in abundance. Encouraging, *not.*

Stubborn is my middle name. That's right, Debi Stubborn Gliori – I know it's weird, but parents... pffff, what can I say? Anyway, stubbornly I decided that there was no way that I was going to take on a badly paid job to 'support' my unpaid non-existent career in children's books. That would be *two* jobs. I mean, get real. Nor did I much fancy the kind of grinding-noble-poverty-consumption-in-a-garret artist's lifestyle afforded by a complete lack of cash. Mercenary little beast that I was, I picked up as many well-paid advertising jobs as possible (illustrating whisky labels and smoked salmon packaging, mainly) and in my spare time, hauled myself off to libraries and bookshops and did my research. Who was publishing what? Why were these books published rather than, say, *mine*? What was fashionable and why? Did retellings work? Were books for babies no-brainers? Trust me, it wasn't all that hard for me to see what was required from a good picture book. I won't insult your intelligence by telling you. You know this stuff. Or if you don't, you'll pick it up quickly.

So, armed with a rough idea of what first publishers, then parents and finally, children might want (the order is, sadly, significant), I holed myself up in a 1.2 square metre cupboard and wrote a book which, joy of joys, was picked off the Walker Books slush pile and published. Read my lips: at that point, I had no 'in' in publishing – no contacts, no money and no influence. I was a single parent living in a freezing cold, damp cottage waaaaay out in the sticks in Scotland. And yet, and yet, and yet, I managed to get my book published. The message here is Take Heart. It *can* be done.

Making a picture book the Gliori way

How I go about starting to make a book from scratch is another matter. All of us approach the process of creating picture books from a multitude of different directions. For what it's worth, here's how I go about it. Although I always start with the text, nine times out of ten the initial idea for a book arrives in my head as a couple of images that I know I'd love to paint. Unsurprisingly, I never experience a burning desire to make a book that involves cars or horses, mainly because I cannot draw either. On the other hand, I love landscapes. So, for example, there's a scene in one of my early books called *Mr Bear Babysits* in which Mr Bear is walking home by moonlight through trees, and all around him are baby animals, birds and insects being tucked in for the night. Immediately that image sparks off a series of questions. What season would this be set in? Answer – summer, because then I can draw golden moonlit fields and haystacks. What time is it? Probably after midnight. Why is Mr Bear out so late? Maybe he's having a *liaison dangereux* with Mrs Grizzle-Bear... or then again, perhaps not. Let's imagine he's been babysitting for the Grizzle-Bear cubs. How many? Three. Heavens, poor Grizzle-Bears, they must *really* need a night off. What are the cubs like? Rumbustious. Has Mr Bear got kids of his own? Is he going home? Is this the end or is it the beginning? You can see the process, can't you? By trying to supply answers to my own questions, I am effortlessly beginning to build a framework round which I could start to construct a narrative.

I wouldn't like you to think that it's easy though. Frequently, the entire framework begins to assume the tensile properties of overcooked tagliatelle, at which point I will decide that this is an idea that's not ready to be written yet. I have several of these raw and palely loitering things tucked away in various notebooks, and once in a while I'll drag them out into the unforgiving daylight; poke, prod and play with them until they turn to mush at which point, with deep regret, I'll put them back and try a different tack. Sometimes, to my delight, the poking and prodding succeeds and a picture book text emerges, oozing and flubby in parts, but with a decent story at its heart. Over the course of the next month, I'll return to that text and read it out loud until my ears bleed, because reading out loud is the single best way for me to expose flaws, glitches and bumpy bits before I self-edit what I blithely imagine to be a ruthlessly incisive fashion.

Afterwards, breathless and pink with the unaccustomed exertion, I type it out and email it to my editor. When I was a beginner, I would assemble a thick envelope in which I included the following items for editor-seduction purposes: one lovingly typed covering letter on headed stationery, one double-spaced (with Tippex blobs) manuscript, (both typed and corrected on an ancient manual typewriter bought in a junk shop), a set of thumbnail sketches showing how I anticipated pacing the text and pictures over 32 pages, two hideously expensive colour photocopies of two spreads of artwork and one sae for the return of said hideously expensive samples. And then I would wait... and wait... and wait.

These days, if my editor likes my initial idea, she usually lets me know the same day I emailed it. This has little to do with talent, and everything to do with expediency. These days my editor knows my work and she trusts me. From past experience, she is fairly certain that come hell or high water, or even both, simultaneously, along with some obstetric complications thrown in for good measure, three months after she has read and approved my text, I will deliver detailed black and white pencil roughs showing how I intend each spread to look. For her part, she will comment on the roughs, sending them back to me with a tactful and light powdering of post-it notes. Only *suggestions*, Debi. Put that axe down. Five months afterwards, I will deliver camera-ready artwork and ten minutes after that, my editor and I will be raising that first of many flutes of champagne to our lips in celebration. What, at ten o'clock in the morning? Damn straight.

Proofs and publication

Back when I was starting out, nothing much happened after I delivered a book. There was a lull and then the first proofs arrived – a stage I loved, and still love, because suddenly your whole book appears to fall into focus – it looks like a real book at last and it's one of many identical copies, thus saving me from my illustrator's artwork-related paranoia about someone accidentally dropping a slice of raw tomato onto it. Before you dismiss me as neurotic, Gentle Reader, let me say that this tomato-on-watercolour-artwork-falling-incident really happened. He'll never walk again without a limp, though. After the heady rush of seeing my work in proof form, came the not-so heady rush of publication day, which came... and went, unremarked. Sometimes there would be a wee card in the post, signed by everyone who'd had anything to do with the book; sometimes a bunch of flowers would arrive from my publisher, bestowing a kind of temporary London-glamour on my Scottish hovel. Sometimes I'd cook something special for my family, or bake a cake or just sit in my studio and gnaw my fingernails off one by one, wondering just how far we could make 10% of not a lot stretch.

These days, I'm so involved with my next project that I'll have achieved a measure of distance from the book just published; so much so that I have been known to stare at a beautiful bouquet of flowers and wonder if my publisher thinks I've had another baby. Surely not? Maybe I did – perhaps I'd better just go and check the pram, just in case...

The exact timing of Publication Day can become a bit blurred when your book is released early in order to maximise sales at, say, a book festival. Actually, given the levels of author hospitality on offer, *everything* can get a little blurred during book festivals. By the time you get to Publication Day it's quite hard not to feel a little anti-climatic. What happens to your book from now on is, by and large, out of your hands. It's the day that unpublished authors dream of: the day you see *your* book in print. Perhaps I'm just an old cynic, but seeing my book in mint condition in bookshops doesn't press any of my buttons whatsoever. No, what *I* want to see is *my* book being read till it *falls to bits*. I want to see the date-stamp page at the front of a library copy of one of my books full to the brim with the inky evidence of many withdrawals. *That's* the whole point. Being *read* – not being published.

But first you have to get published, and that's why we're here; you reading and me attempting to spout wisdom like an illustrator's version of the Delphic Oracle. Did anyone remember to bring me a goat, by the way? Problem is, I'm not an oracle, and nor am I a teacher. All that I know is based my own experience of the business. Your experience will be significantly different. Without sitting down beside you and looking over your text or your portfolio, the best advice I can give is *keep going*. Be stubborn – if you want to be published, you're going to have to be rhinoceros-like in your determination as well as acquiring a rhino-hide to shrug off those slings and arrows of unkind comment. Follow your own star, even if it's a redundant Russian satellite. Er, learn how to put up bookshelves and develop a series of nifty recipes for lentils. And good luck: like all the best things in life, the process of learning how to make picture books is well worth the effort.

Debi Gliori has written and illustrated many picture books and her best-loved titles include *No Matter What* and the *Mr Bear* series. She is also the author of the *Pure Dead...* series of novels for older children. She lives in Scotland and works from her International Shedquarters at the bottom of her garden.

See also...
- *Creating graphic novels,* page 207
- *The amazing picture book story,* page 217
- *Illustrating for children's books,* page 221
- *Notes from a successful children's author and illustrator,* page 80

The amazing picture book story

Oliver Jeffers tells the story of how his first picture book came to be published.

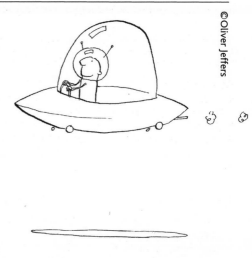

© Oliver Jeffers

In this, the 21st century, anything is possible. We drive flying cars, live in bubbles, go to the moon for our summer holidays and we can freeze and heat things instantly. People can do whatever they want, and in some cases get paid for it, even writing and illustrating children's books. And in this age of possibility, they can even be picked from the slush pile. That's what happened to me. Although I still believe I'm one of the luckiest people alive, and this article isn't much beyond bragging, hindsight and other people would suggest there is more to it than that. One thing that hasn't changed with all our technological advancements is the fundamental need for children's picture books on a number of levels. From educating enquiring young minds, and entertaining both children and adults alike at bedtime (and not just adults who have children, and not just at bedtime) to pushing the boundaries of style and content within the broader worlds of both art and literature. Children's books are art, and all true artists do what they love first and hope to make a living second. Creating a piece of work to the absolute best of an ability is an artist's priority. Getting paid is a bonus. The same goes for those who create children's books. (I bet if you were to ask someone like Tony Ross, if he wasn't getting paid to make children's books, would he do it anyway and just be poor? He'd probably say 'yes' but also have a second job working at the moon resort.)

Anyway, so back to me bragging about how I'm one of the luckiest people in the world and get to do what I love for a living. Well, sort of living as the money isn't great, and I sell proper paintings as well, and between the two I can pay my mortgage. But I do have a publisher that publishes my books and I'm going to tell you how that happened. The story itself is actually quite business-like and boring so I'll throw in a few creative exaggerations for effect.

The story begins

It all started when I had just defeated the Admiral of the Swiss Navy in a sword fight, and sat at the edge of the pier at the Sydney fish market for a think. I had known all along that I liked to draw pictures and I liked to write, and I had been putting the two together for a while in my paintings. I even bought and collected children's picture books both for my own enjoyment and as research for my paintings. But it wasn't until my good friend Ben suggested I attempt a children's book of my own that I seriously considered it as a direction to take my life. So, as I sat there dangling my legs off the pier, I had my first idea for a children's book, about a boy who tries to catch the reflection of a star in the water, much like the Brer Rabbit story of the *Moon and the Mill Pond*.

After a year out, I carried the idea into my final year studying Visual Communication (specialising in illustration) at the University of Ulster in Belfast in 2000, having to hold down a second job as a racecar driver to pay for my tuition. I developed self-portrait doodles to narrate my thesis that year, which eventually developed into the character used in the book. In the second half of my final year I used my picture book concept as a piece of coursework, deciding to see how far I could take it to a finished product. This involved getting the words right, and the pictures right, and more importantly, the balance between the two right.

Looking, thinking children's books

To get the words right, I read my manuscript to as many six year-olds as I could find (you'd be amazed how many there are: I reckon if they were all to jump at once something big would break, like London Bridge or at least a phone box or two), slowly tweaking the story based on the feedback I was getting. To get the pictures right I used the unending help of my older brother Rory who basically has a lot more sense than I do. And to get the balance right we both looked at hundreds of other picture books to see what everyone else had done. That was when the earthquake happened and Rory had to balance 58 books on his head to save them from falling down a crack to the molten core of the earth.

In the process of getting the balance right, I noticed a few things about how good picture books seem to work. The one that sticks out most is about how they seem to appeal across all ages without being forced. They aren't condescending, but at the same time they aren't inaccessible. There just seems to be a natural universal appeal to both children and adults – and let's face it, they need to appeal to adults, as however well a six year-old is doing, they're unlikely to stick their hand in their pocket and pull out a tenner in a bookshop!

OK, so in the second half of 2001, after I had finished developing my idea and finished my degree, and after the initial euphoria of never having to write another thesis in my life wore off, and during that slightly intimidating, 'I actually have to do something with my life now!' phase, I decided I would get my book published. I looked at what was

© Oliver Jeffers

around in the bookshops and thought that what I had created was as good as, if not better, than anything else that was out there, and confidence and self belief are important tools when you need to be self motivated. My first step was to buy the *Writers' & Artists' Yearbook* (and it's great to see this *Children's Writers' & Artists' Yearbook* out now) and I then began to look at which publisher would be lucky enough to receive my manuscript. Alright, I wasn't that confident, in fact, having worked in Waterstones for a few years and armed with a very minimal knowledge of the publishing world, I knew I was in for a long and trying road of numerous attempts contacting publishers, repeatedly saying 'have you read it yet?'

Apart from using the *Yearbook* to research which publishers I should send my idea to, I also referred to my own collection of children's picture books, the collection that would make any six year-old jealous. I looked to see who had published what, paying particular attention to my favourites, and which publishers popped up more often.

My next step was to figure out what exactly to send them. There are hundreds and thousands of unsolicited ideas that reach publishers every year and my objective was to stand out among those. To be noticed. By asking, I found that what publishers like to see in a proposal for a new book was the manuscript and a few samples of the illustrations to give a broad idea of the feel for the book. I invested a bit of money into producing 100 copies of a small spiral bound 'sample', with the manuscript at the start and ten full-colour illustrations after, which I put into an envelope with a letter outlining who I was and what I was trying to do, and a self-addressed envelope for them to contact me. I also included a small portfolio (and I mean small, eight prints that were 14cm square each) of other examples of my paintings and illustrations in the hope that if a particular publisher didn't pick up on my book idea, at least I might be able to get a few commissions while I was waiting.

A few phone calls later and I had found out who looked after the children's division in each appropriate publishing house, and addressed my envelope to them. The point being that it would arrive at a real person's desk instead of an anonymous room that was only used for hostage situations or when they ran out of chairs. I spent a while drawing up a big chart showing which publishers I had sent an envelope to, their contact name and number, date last contacted, and room for comments. I sent an envelope to the ten biggest publishers in the UK, and the ten biggest in USA, figuring I'd start at the top and work my way down.

© Oliver Jeffers

© Oliver Jeffers

The envelopes were opened

Expecting a healthy dose of being ignored and avoided, you can perhaps imagine my surprise when, the next afternoon, as I was entertaining the Sultan of Brunei and his wonderful wife Delilah, I received a phone call from a publisher in London during the course of which they expressed their desire to publish my book. It had arrived on the desk of a young editorial assistant: she had opened it, liked what she saw, and had immediately decided to do something about it. That offer was followed a week later by one from a US publisher in New York City, where something similar happened. I forgave the US publisher for their delay, as they are geographically further away.

And it was as simple as that. I met with both publishers, and between the three of us we were able to devise a cunning plan that would enable both of them to publish the book.

Told you I was lucky, I may as well have won the lottery. But as someone wiser than me once said, 'It's all about healthy measures of luck and hard work!' or was that 'work and hard luck?' I can't remember, but the point is that I set myself an objective and was quite methodical and logical in my efforts to get there. Like most businesses, I had an idea, I developed it, then invested time, thought, and money in selling it. But if I hadn't already sold it, I'd still be trying to, and I'd still be having the same ideas for my next books, only wearing cheaper shoes, eating Weetabix for dinner, and maybe sending off an application to the moon resort too.

The end. Or rather, the beginning...

Oliver Jeffers' first children's picture book, *How to Catch a Star*, was published in 2004. His second book, *Lost and Found*, was published in 2005 and won the Nestlé Children's Book Prize that year as well as being voted the Blue Peter Children's Book of the Year in 2006. Both books won the CBI Bisto Merit Award in 2005 and 2006 respectively. His most recent book is *The Incredible Book-eating Boy*, and all his books are published by HarperCollins.

See also...

- *Getting started*, page 1
- *Eight great tips to get your picture book published*, page 209
- *Writing and illustrating picture books*, page 213
- *Illustrating for children's books*, page 207
- *Notes from a successful children's author and illustrator*, page 80
- *It could happen to you*, page 142

Illustrating for children's books

The world of children's publishing is big business. The huge range of books published each year all carry artwork – lots of it. Maggie Mundy offers guidance for people who are at the start of their career in illustrating for children's books.

The portfolio

Your portfolio should reflect the best of you and your work, and should speak for itself. Keep its content simple – if too many styles are included, for instance, your work will not leave a lasting impression.

Include some artwork other than those carried out for college projects, for example an illustration from a timeless classic to show your abilities, and something modern which reflects your own taste and the area in which you wish to work.

If your strength is for black and white illustration, include pieces with and without tone and with or without a wash. Some publishers want line and tone and some want only line. As cross hatching and stippling can add a lot of extra time to an illustration deadline, it might be advisable to leave out these samples. If you can, include a selection of humour as it can be used effectively in educational books and elsewhere. It is best not to sign and date your work: some artworks can stand the test of time and still look good after a year or two, but if it looks dated ... so is the illustrator!

An A3 portfolio is probably the ideal size. Place your best piece of artwork on the opening page and your next best piece on the last page.

Looking at the market

Start by looking thoroughly at what is being published today for children. Take your studies to branches of big retail chains, some independent bookshops, as well as your local library (a helpful librarian should be able to tell you which are the most borrowed books). Absorb the picture books, explore the novelty books, look at the variety of colour covers, and note the range of black line illustrations inside books for children and teenagers. Make a list of the publishers you think may be able to use your particular style.

By making these investigations you will gain an insight into not only the current trends and styles but also the much favoured, oft-published classic children's literature. Most importantly, it will help you identify your market.

In books for a young age range every picture must tell the story – some books have no text and the illustrations say it all. Artwork should be uncluttered, shapes clear, and colour bright. If this does not appeal to you, go up a year or two and note the extra details that are added to the artwork (which still tells the story). Children now need to see more than just clear shapes: they need extra details added to the scene – for example a quirky spider hanging around, or a mouse under the bed.

Children are your most critical audience: never think that you can get away with 'any old thing'. Indeed, at the Bologna Book Fair it is a panel of children which judges what they consider to be the best picture book.

Current trends

Innovative publishers are always on the lookout for something new in illustration styles: something completely different from the tried and tested. More and more they are turning to European and overseas illustrators, often sourced from the Bologna Book Fair exhibitions and illustrators catalogue.

Always strive to improve on your work. Don't be afraid to try out something different and to work it up into acceptable examples. Above all, don't get left behind.

Making approaches for work

With your portfolio arranged and your target audience in mind, compile a list of publishing houses, packagers and magazines which you think may be suitable for your work.

An agent should know exactly where to place your work, and this may be the easier option (see below). However, you may wish to market yourself by making and going to appointments until you crack your first job.

Alternatively, you could make up a simple broadsheet comprising a black and white and two or three colour illustrations, together with your contact details, and have it colour photocopied or printed. Another inexpensive option is to have your own CDs made up and to send them instead. Send a copy to either the Art Director, the Creative Director or the Senior Commissioning Editor (for picture books) of each potential client on your list. Try to find out the name of the person you would like to see your work. Wait at least a week and then follow up your mailing with a phone call to ask if someone would like to see your portfolio.

Also consider investing in your own website which you can easily update yourself.

Know your capabilities

Know your strengths, but be even more aware of your weaknesses. You will gain far more respect if you admit to not being able to draw something particularly well than by going ahead and producing an embarrassing piece of artwork and having it rejected. You will be remembered for your professional honesty and that client may well try to give you a job where you can use your expertise.

Publishers need to know that you can turn out imaginative, creative artwork while closely following a text or brief, and be able to meet their deadline. It may take an illustrator three weeks to prepare roughs for 32 pages, three weeks to finish the artwork, plus a week to make any corrections. In addition, time has to be allowed for the roughs to be returned. On this basis, how many books can an illustrator realistically take on? Scheduling is of paramount importance (see below).

You will need to become familiar with 'publishing speak' – terms such as gutters, full bleed, holding line, overlays, vignettes, tps, etc. If you don't know the meaning of a term, ask – after all, if you have only recently left college you will not be expected to know all the jargon.

In the course of your work you will have to deal with such issues as contracts, copyright, royalties, Public Lending Right, rejection fees, etc. The Association of Illustrators, which exists to give help to illustrators in all areas, is well worth joining.

Organising your workload

When you have reached the stage when you have jobs coming through on a fairly regular basis, organise a comprehensive schedule for yourself so you do not overburden yourself with work. Include on it when roughs have to be submitted, how much work you can fit in while waiting for their approval, the deadline for the artwork, and so on. A wall chart can be helpful for this but another system may work better for you. It is totally unacceptable to deliver artwork late. If you think that you might run over time with your work, let your client know in advance as it may be possible to reach a new agreement for delivery.

Payment

There are two ways in which an illustrator may be paid for a commission for a book: a flat fee on receipt and acceptance of the artwork, or by an advance against a royalty of future sales. The advance offered could be less than a flat fee but it may result in higher earnings overall. If the book sells well, the illustrator will receive royalty payments twice a year for as long the book is in print.

You need to know from the outset how you are going to be paid. If it is by a flat fee, you may be given an artwork order with a number to be quoted when you invoice. Always read through orders to make sure you understand the terms and conditions. If you haven't been paid within 30 days, send a statement to remind the client, or make a quick phone call to ask when you can expect to receive payment.

With a royalty offer, a contract will be drawn up and this must be checked carefully. One of the clauses will state the breakdown of how and when you will be paid.

Once you have illustrated your first book you should register with the Public Lending Right Office (see page 238) so that you can receive a yearly payment on all UK library borrowings. You will need to cooperate with the author regarding percentages before submitting your own form. The PLR office will give you a reference number, and you then submit details to them of each book you illustrate. It mounts up and is a nice little earner!

Agents

The role of the agent is to represent the illustrator to the best of their ability and to the illustrator's best advantage. A good agent knows the marketplace and will promote illustrators' work where it will count. An agent may ask you to do one or two sample pieces to strengthen your portfolio, giving them a better chance of securing work for you.

Generally speaking, agents will look after you, your work schedules, payments, contracts, royalties, copyright issues, and try to ensure you have a regular flow of work which you not only enjoy but will stretch your talents to taking on bigger and better jobs. Without exposing your weaknesses, check that you have adequate time in which to do a job and that you are paid a fair rate for the work.

Some illustrators manage well without an agent, and having one is not necessarily a pathway to fame and fortune. Choose carefully: you need to both like and trust the agent and vice versa.

Agents' charges range from 25% to 30%. Find out from the outset how much a prospective agent will charge.

Finally

Do not be downhearted if progress is at first slow. Everyone starts by serving an apprenticeship, and it is a great opportunity to learn, absorb and soak up as much of the business as possible. Ask questions, get all the advice you can, and use what you learn to improve your craft and thereby your chances of landing a job. Publishers are always on the lookout for fresh talent and new ideas, and one day your talent will be the one they want.

Maggie Mundy has been representing illustrators for children's books since 1983. Her agency now represents ten European and British illustrators for children's books.

Children's character licensing

Joel Rickett gives an overview of children's character licensing across publishing, broadcasting and merchandising.

Characters that were once dreamt up by desperate parents in a bid to send their children to sleep are now big business. Names such as Peter Rabbit, Winnie the Pooh, Tintin, Babar and Mr Men are loved around the world. Their faces adorn T-shirts, soft toys, board games, pencil cases, milkshakes and even nappies. Barney and Kermit the Frog embark on world-wide stadium tours; in the summer of 2006 the Queen celebrated her 80th birthday by inviting Postman Pat, Mowgli and the BFG (Big Friendly Giant) to Buckingham Palace.

For this we can blame television series and films which carry these characters far and wide. They fuel a seemingly insatiable demand: in the UK alone, the children's licensing business is worth about £2.7 billion a year according to NPD Eurotoys (2004). About 22% of the money spent on children up to the age of 14 is absorbed by character-branded products; for four to five year-olds, that proportion rises to a third.

In this licensed world Disney reigns supreme. Yet many of Disney's characters began with books and inspire children to turn back to the printed page. The healthy two-way flow between books and broadcast has been bolstered by the *Harry Potter* phenomenon and Peter Jackson's *Lord of the Rings* films. The enduring appeal of stories such as *Thomas the Tank Engine* has led to a stream of revivals of old favourites – Noddy, Bagpuss, Basil Brush, Muffin the Mule. No character is safe from a nostalgic resurrection.

The companies that control rights to these characters are serious stock market players. The pioneer is Hit Entertainment, which created all-singing Bob the Builder, and took Angelina Ballerina from the cosy confines of Katherine Holabird's stories to television sets, dolls and duvet covers. Hit is followed by Chorion (owner of Noddy and Mr Men) and Entertainment Rights (Postman Pat, Basil Brush).

The first thing licensing companies seek, after television distribution deals, is publishing partners. Books are still seen as crucial for establishing the character, building its authority, and winning the goodwill of parents. Kathleen Caper, marketing executive at the Copy-rights Group, says: 'People hang on to their books and soft toys. Publishing is an essential part of childhood – DVDs become defunct and are not a family heirloom.'

Despite the dominance of television, characters can still exist outside it. Caper points out that only ten episodes of Peter Rabbit are screened each year, while Paddington Bear has no television series. 'But they still do well – they have longevity. I don't think Tele-tubbies will be a classic brand. Our aim is for our characters to still be here in 100 years.'

Publishing with character

Children's book and magazine publishers have reacted to and even led this boom in char-acter licensing. They work closely with authors, illustrators, animators and television pro-ducers to create a wide range of books and spin-off products around a central character. These span titles for the activity, leisure, educational and gift markets, across ages, and for different distribution channels (e.g. bookshops, supermarkets, school clubs, catalogues). Marketing and publicity strategies are tied closely to broadcast schedules.

Competition is fierce for the lead licences between a handful of UK publishing houses – Egmont, Scholastic, HarperCollins, Macmillan, Random House, Simon & Schuster and

Penguin, which runs Frederick Warne and the BBC's children's books operation. In 2005 the supermarket specialist Parragon poached the Disney books licence from Penguin – marking a significant mass market shift for the biggest brand generator.

But Parragon was too late to win one of the largest licensed franchises in recent years: Narnia. Back in 2000, HarperCollins paid tens of millions of pounds to the C.S. Lewis estate for the licence, gambling that the long-awaited Hollywood film would get the green light. So when Disney and Walden Media's production of *The Lion, the Witch and the Wardrobe* was finally scheduled for Christmas 2005 the publisher was determined to repeat its *Lord of the Rings* success. In the UK it ran pre-release advertisements with the strapline 'read it before you see it'. Then came 17 tie-in titles, from activity books and boxed sets to an official 'making of' guide, designed to appeal to new readers as well as fans of the classic books. For the main £400,000 campaign it created lampposts and life-sized lions for shops, as well as department store Christmas grottos.

Of course, if the film had been a flop then HarperCollins may have been left with piles of unsold stock. But despite a mixed critical reaction people flocked in their droves – it took $224 million in the US in its first three weeks, knocking *King Kong* from the number one spot. The debate around C.S. Lewis' Christian values – and Disney's $150 million marketing budget – also helped the publishing programme; in the UK HarperCollins sold more than 500,000 extra Narnia books and it posted a 24% increase in its fourth-quarter operating profits to $77 million.

Despite such juggernaughts there are still opportunities for smaller publishers in the licensing market. For example the late Max Velthuijs' *Frog* series from tiny Andersen Press is being brought to life as *Frog & Friends* by Telescreen. Tony Ross' *Little Princess*, also from Andersen, has been commissioned by Channel Five and is due to run at end of 2006.

Such screen transitions must be handled with care to avoid damaging perceptions of the original books. Deborah Forte, president of Scholastic's broadcast arm Scholastic Media, says the adaptors should first identify what is 'sacred' about the character or series. She cites Clifford, the preschool character that Scholastic took from bestselling picture books into a major US television show. 'We adapted the property but identified the fundamental values and what was sacred to the author. We did not throw away the look or the character, or change the core relationship between Clifford and [owner] Emily Elizabeth'. Clifford has been the number one preschool show in the US for five years running and sales of Clifford books in the US grew from £4 million a year to £45 million a year after the animation was first broadcast. Forte says a good adaptation can generate a new audience for books: 'If the essence of the storytelling is there, readers will be gained'.

Mobile markets

All the talk among children's character specialists is of new technologies, predominantly video-on-demand and mobile phone formats. While the CD-Rom goldrush led up a blind alley, and the internet has so far proved more a marketing tool than a profit source, there's a strong sense that these new areas will transform the way characters and series are sold and watched. In music, sales of mobile ringtones have already overtaken CD singles; in 2005 the irritating Crazy Frog became the first mobile character to have a number one hit.

Several start-up firms operating in mobile formats are approaching publishers with a view to licensing content; David McKee's Mr Benn books are already being developed for mobile phones and related merchandise. The challenge for publishers is to make the new technology draw people back to real books. To this end Walker Books has created a series of animated DVDs based on some of its best-loved picture books, including Lucy Cousins' *Hooray for Fish*, Sam McBratney's *Guess How Much I Love You* and Martin Waddell's *Owl Babies*. The animations have been created by King Rollo Films, the company behind the Maisie animations.

Selling the spin-offs

Multimedia brands are nothing new. Captain Pugwash started as a comic strip in the 1950s, then became a book, then a television series. It was revived in the late 1990s with a retro feel. The world's oldest literary licensing programme is of course from Beatrix Potter. Within two years of *The Tale of Peter Rabbit* being published in 1902, Mopsy, Cotton-tail and Peter had their own dolls. Now sales of Beatrix Potter products from ceramics to baby food are worth £333 million a year, which was quite likely enhanced by the biopic, *Miss Potter*, starring Renée Zellweger.

Kathleen Caper, whose Copyrights Group controls the Beatrix Potter spin-offs, believes its success underlines the need to keep brands consistent. 'In 1910 Peter Rabbit was about beauty and mischievous behaviour. We have been very careful to make sure those values have remained stable. We may brighten up the colours for a nursery age product, but we are still using the same artwork'. She contrasts this approach to *Winnie the Pooh*, where the values have become muddled under Disney's direction. 'He's still a successful character, but I'm not sure what he stands for now'.

So why do some book characters translate smoothly into spin-off products, yet others flop? Caper says there is no way to predict success: 'Sometimes the books do amazingly well, but licensing and merchandising don't'. The prime example is *Harry Potter*, where related products have failed to take off.

To minimise the risk, some licensers and publishers use focus groups to see how children react to new characters. They can then modify the character and advertising according to these 'play patterns' to ensure maximum pressure is put on parents. Some believe this approach has become overly aggressive but Dr Janine Spencer, director of the Centre for Research into Infant Behaviour (CRIB) says: 'Young children are attracted to novelty because that's how they learn. When you test children you find that they are drawn to any new object you introduce into a group of familiar objects. I think the industry should stop feeling guilty about selling to kids, because kids want things'.

One of the most successful UK spin-offs of recent years has been clothing and stationery based on the much-adored books from the former Children's Laureate Jacqueline Wilson and her long-time collaborator Nick Sharratt. Wilson told *Licensing* magazine: 'This not about cash. It's about doing delightful things that children will like. The products are extensions of the books'. Accordingly she took close interest in how they were developed: 'The products must be pretty and modern but also wholesome. I know that girls are conscious about the way they look and how they are seen but I am anxious not to encourage them to squeeze into little sexy tops and things like that. I don't think children need any encouragement to grow up faster than they need to'.

Tweens and tots

Wilson's comments highlight a relentless shift in the market over the last decade: the falling age of the 'consumer'. Whether due to media saturation or social and economic change, children are responsive to certain kinds of characters at ever-younger ages. For example the original Paddington Bear books were written for children aged eight and above, but Paddington has now become mainly a preschool character. 'Everything has shifted down,' Caper says. 'Kids are getting older younger.'

This has fuelled the 'tween' phenomenon, where girls aged 8–12 are fed a diet of music and fashion. But Wilson's series was successful because it provided an alternative to 'tween' marketing. Caper also notes a 'bounceback', where teenagers or adults again become absorbed by younger brands. Paddington T-shirts have recently become a hit with young teenage girls, and Bagpuss has just launched as a fashion brand to adults.

The preschool area has seen a character boom over the last five years, driven by frenetic competition between specialist broadcast slots such as CBeebies and Channel Five's Milkround. The names will be familiar to any parent: Boo-ba, Ballymory, Teletubbies, Pingu, Rubadubber, Fireman Sam. The market has been saturated, leaving little space for new brands.

This is mirrored in the picture book market, the source for much broadcast material. While star characters such as *The Gruffalo* (Julia Donaldson and Axel Scheffler) can shift more copies than ever, children's publishers have cut back heavily on their output. They are finding it tough to win shelf space in retailers who are slimming down their ranges to classic authors like Eric Carle (*The Hungry Caterpillar*) and Shirley Hughes. Picture books also suffer from a lack of media oxygen.

So with publishers and broadcasters both reluctant to take punts on untested properties, how can new creators break through? Caper says the answer is originality and persistence: 'Don't do a "me too" – it's about trying to create something that's original'. One route for young artists is stationery deals – for example winning a card license with a small greeting card house. There are myriad examples of characters that have gone from cards to books to television, such as *Scary Monsters*. Another idea is to self publish: you can then try to build your own audience, perhaps starting at local schools or bookshops.

Even if you make it into print and then sign a television deal, don't get overly excited: only an estimated 2% of optioned books ever reach development stage. As ever, books should be a labour of love and an end in themselves.

Joel Rickett is Deputy Editor of the *Bookseller*, and writes regular columns for the *Guardian* and *Screen International*. At the audiovisual content show Mipcom in 2005, he hosted a seminar on licensing links between children's books and broadcasting.

Illustrators' agents

Before submitting work, artists are advised to make preliminary enquiries and to ascertain terms of work. Commission varies but averages 25–30%. The Association of Illustrators (see page 346) provides a valuable service for illustrators, agents and clients.

*Member of the Society of Artists Agents
†Member of the Association of Illustrators

Advocate
39 Church Road, Wimbledon Village,
London SW19 5DQ
tel 020-8879 1166 *fax* 020-8879 3303
email mail@advocate-art.com
website www.advocate-art.com
Director Edward Burns

Has 5 agents representing 110 artists and illustrators. Supplies work to book and magazine publishers, design and advertising agencies, greeting card and fine art publishers, and gift and ceramic manufacturers. Also has an original art gallery, stock library and international licensing agency for the character 'Newton's Law'. Founded as a co-operative in 1996.

Allied Artists/Artistic License
mobile (07971) 111256
email info@allied-artists.net
website www.allied-artists.net,
www.umbrellapublishing.ca
Contacts Gary Mills, Mary Burtenshaw

Represents over 40 artists, all of whom illustrate children's books. Specialises in highly finished realistic figure illustrations and stylised juvenile illustrations for children's books. Extensive library of stock illustrations. Commission: 33%. Founded 1983.

Arena*†
Quantum Artists Ltd, 31 Eleanor Road,
London E15 4AB
tel (0845) 050 7600
email info@arenaworks.com
website www.arenaworks.com
Contact Tamlyn Francis

Represents 35 artists, half of whom produce children's material. Produces illustrations for picture books and children's fiction for all ages; also for book covers and design groups. Average commission 20%. Founded 1970.

The Art Agency (Wildlife Art Ltd)
The Lodge, Cargate Lane, Saxlingham Thorpe,
Norwich NR15 1TU
tel (01508) 471500 *fax* (01508) 470391
email info@the-art-agency.co.uk
website www.the-art-agency.co.uk

Represents more than 40 artists producing top-quality, highly accurate and imaginative illustrations across a wide variety of subjects and for all age groups, both digitally and traditionally. Clients are children's fiction and non-fiction publishers. Include sae with submissions. Do not email portfolios. Commission: 30%. Founded 1992.

The Artworks†*
40 Frith Street, London W1D 5LN
tel 020-7734 3333 *fax* 020-7734 3484
email info@theartworksinc.com
website www.theartworksinc.com
Contact Lucy Scherer, Stephanie Alexander

Represents 40 artists for illustrated gift books and children's books. Commission: 25% advances, 15% royalties.

Beehive Illustration
42A Cricklade Street, Cirencester, Glos. GL7 1JH
tel (01285) 885149 *fax* (01285) 641291
email info@beehiveillustration.co.uk
website www.beehiveillustration.co.uk
Contact Paul Beebee

Represents over 70 artists specialising in ELT (English Language Teaching) books, education and general publishing illustration. Commission: 25%. Founded 1989.

Celia Catchpole Ltd
56 Gilpin Avenue, London SW14 8QY
tel 020-8255 4835 *fax* 020-8255 4835
email celiacatchpole@yahoo.co.uk
website www.celiacatchpole.co.uk
Proprietor Celia Catchpole

Represents 9 artists specialising in artwork for picture books and storybooks for ages 0–12. Submit samples as A4 photocopies. Commission: 15%. Founded 1996. See also page 193.

The Copyrights Group Ltd
(now part of Chorion)
4th Floor, Aldwych House, 81 Aldwych,
London WC2B 4HN
tel 020-7061 3800 *fax* 020-7061 3805
email enquiries@copyrights.co.uk
website www.copyrights.co.uk
Chairman & Ceo Nicholas Durbridge, *Creative Director* Linda Pooley

Leading licensing organisation with an international team of staff working together to represent writers, artists and the owners of quality characters, fine art and brand names for licensing to manufacturers of consumer products and for consumer promotions. Properties include *Peter Rabbit, Paddington Bear, Spot, Flower Fairies, Maisy, Jacqueline Wilson, Horrible Histories, Ivory Cats, The Snowman, Father Christmas* and *The Wombles*.

Graham-Cameron Illustration

The Studio, 23 Holt Road, Sheringham, Norfolk NR26 8NB
tel (01263) 821333 *fax* (01263) 821334
email enquiry@graham-cameron-illustration.com
and Duncan Graham-Cameron, Graham-Cameron Illustration, 59 Hertford Road, Brighton BN1 7GG
tel (01273) 385890
website www.graham-cameron-illustration.com
Partners Mike Graham-Cameron, Helen Graham-Cameron, Duncan Graham-Cameron

Represents 37 artists. Undertakes all forms of illustration for publishing and communications. Specialises in educational, children's and information books. Telephone before sending A4 sample illustrations with sae. No MSS. Founded 1985.

David Higham Associates Ltd – see
page 194

John Hodgson Agency

38 Westminster Palace Gardens, Artillery Row, London SW1P 1RR
tel 020-7222 4468

Represents 6 artists producing children's material. Specialises in children's picture books for 0–8 year-olds. Phone before sending samples. Enclose an sae with samples. Commission: 25%. Founded 1965.

The Illustration Cupboard

22 Bury Street, London SW1Y 6AL
tel/fax 020-7976 1727
email john@illustrationcupboard.com
website www.illustrationcupboard.com
Chief Executive John Huddy

A London art gallery which specialises in the exhibition and sale of original book illustration artwork from around the world. It represents over 150 different leading illustrators and displays their work in group and single artist exhibitions with an annual catalogue produced every November. Founded 1996.

LAW (Lucas Alexander Whitley Ltd)

14 Vernon Street, London W14 0RJ
tel 020-7471 7900 *fax* 020-7471 7910
website www.lawagency.co.uk
Contacts Philippa Milnes-Smith, Ayesha Mobin

Illustrations for children's publishing for ages 0–16. Submit copies of samples (not originals) together

with an sae for their return plus a covering letter and CV. No submissions by email or disk accepted. Commission: 15% (20% overseas). Founded 1996.

David Lewis Illustration Agency

Worlds End Studios, 134 Lots Road, London SW10 0RJ
tel 020-7435 7762 *mobile* (07931) 824674
fax 020-7351 5044
email davidlewis34@hotmail.com
website www.davidlewisillustration.com
Director David Lewis, *Associate Director* Ramon Johns

All kinds of material for all areas of children's publishing, including educational, merchandising and toys. Represents approx. 25 artists, half of whom produce children's material. Send A4 colour or b&w copies of samples with return postage. Do not send CDs or emails. Commission: 30%. Founded 1974.

Frances McKay Illustration

18 Lammas Green, Sydenham Hill, London SE26 6LT
tel 020-8693 7006 *mobile* (07703) 344334
email frances@francesmckay.com
website www.francesmckay.com
Proprietor Frances McKay

Represents 20+ artists producing children's material, largely for book publishers and packagers. Also considers MSS for young children. Submit illustrations for age 4+ with an original slant, either as jpg files on CD, as low-res scans by email or send copies by post with sae. Commission: 25%–35%. Founded 1999.

NB Illustration

40 Bowling Green Lane, London EC1R 0NE
tel 020-7278 9131 *fax* 020-7278 9121
email info@nbillustration.co.uk
website www.nbillustration.co.uk
Directors Joe Najman, Charlotte Berens, Paul Najman

Represents 35+ artists, of whom 10% produce children's material for picture books and educational publishing. Submit samples either as web address by email or by post with an sae. Commission: 30%. Founded 2000.

The Organisation*†

The Basement, 69 Caledonian Road, London N1 9BT
tel 0845-054 8033 *fax* 020-7833 8269
email lorraine@organisart.co.uk
website www.organisart.co.uk
Contact Lorraine Owen

Represents 60 artists, 75% of whom produce children's material for all age ranges. Both traditional and digital illustration can be supplied to cover all markets, including the children's and educational book markets. Also produces illustrations for other print markets, advertising, packaging and editorial. Before submitting samples research the website. New artists must not have a similar style to one already represented. Send samples either by email or on a CD by post, or send printed images with sae. Average commission: 30%. Founded 1987.

Oxford Designers & Illustrators Ltd
Aristotle Lane, Oxford OX2 6TR
tel (01865) 512331 *fax* (01865) 512408
email richardcorfield@odi-illustration.co.uk
website www.o-d-i.com
Directors Peter Lawrence (managing), Richard Corfield, Andrew King

Studio of 20 staff working for educational publishers and businesses. Design for print and the web. All types of artwork including scientific, technical, medical, natural history, figures, 3-D, cartoons, animation, maps and diagrams – computer generated and hand drawn. Not an agency. Founded 1968.

PFD – see page 196

Plum Pudding Illustration
9 Lydden Road, London SW18 4LT
tel 020-3004 7135 *fax* 020-3004 7136
email info@plumpuddingillustration.com
website www.plumpuddingillustration.com
Contact Mark Mills

Children's publishing (all genres), advertising, editorial, greetings cards and packaging. See website for submission procedure. Represents 30+ artists. Commission: 30%. Founded 2006.

Linda Rogers Associates
163 Half Moon Lane, London SE24 9JG
tel 020-7501 9106
email lr@lindarogers.net
website www.lindarogers.net
Partners Linda Rogers, Peter Sims, Jess Sims

Represents approx. 65 illustrators producing children's material. Specialises in books and magazines, all types, all ages. Looking for contemporary, multi-racial, figurative work. Submit artwork samples by post with sae for their return, *not* by email. Will not view artists' websites. Commission: 25%. Founded 1973.

Elizabeth Roy Literary Agency
White Cottage, Greatford, Nr Stamford, Lincs. PE9 4PR
tel/fax (01778) 560672
website www.elizabethroyliteraryagency.co.uk

Handles illustrations for children's books. Only interested in exceptional material. Illustrators should research the children's book market before sending samples, which must include figure work. Send by post with return postage; no CD, disk or email submissions. See also page 197. Founded 1990.

SGA Children's Illustration Agency
9 Lydden Road, London SW18 4LT
020-3004 7137
email philip@sgadesignart.com
website www.sgadesignart.com
Director Mark Mills

Represents 40+ illustrators working in all genres of children's publishing, advertising, editorial, greeting cards and packaging. See website for submission details. Commission: 30%. Founded 1986.

Caroline Sheldon Literary Agency Ltd
London office 70–75 Cowcross Street,
London EC1M 6EJ
tel 020-7336 6550
Mailing address for MSS Thorley Manor Farm, Thorley, Yarmouth PO41 0SJ
tel (01983) 760205, 020-7336 6550
email carolinesheldon@carolinesheldon.co.uk, pennyholroyde@carolinesheldon.co.uk
website www.carolinesheldon.co.uk, www.carolinesheldonillustrators.co.uk
Contacts Caroline Sheldon, Penny Holroyde

Represents a select quality list of illustrators working mainly in children's books. Also author/illustrators. Send introductory information about yourself and samples by email (type Artist's Submission in subject line and attach samples and/or link to your website) or by post (include printed samples and/or a disk with images saved as jpg or tiff files and enclose a large sae). If available, send texts or book dummies. See also page 197. Founded 1985.

Specs Art
93 London Road, Cheltenham, Glos. GL52 6HL
tel (01242) 515951
email roland@specsart.com
website www.specsart.com
Partners Roland Berry, Stephanie Prosser

Represents 30 artists, all of whom produce children's material for all ages. High-quality illustration and animation work for advertisers, publishers and all other forms of visual communication. Specialises in licensed character illustration. Submit about 6 jpegs by email. Commission: 25%. Founded 1982.

Temple Rogers Artists' Agency
120 Crofton Road, Orpington, Kent BR6 8HZ
tel (01689) 826249 *fax* (01689) 896312
Contact Patrick Kelleher

Illustrations for children's educational books and magazine illustrations. Commission: by arrangement.

Vicki Thomas Associates
195 Tollgate Road, London E6 5JY
tel 020-7511 5767 *fax* 020-7473 5177
email vickithomasassociates@yahoo.co.uk
website www.vickithomasassociates.com
Consultant Vicki Thomas

Represents approx. 50 artists, three-quarters of whom produce children's material for all ages. Specialises in designing gift products and considers images for publishing, toys, stationery, clothing, decorative accessories, etc. Submit samples as photocopies with a covering letter. Commission: 25–30%. Founded 1985.

Publishing practice
Publishing agreements

Before signing a publisher's agreement, it should be thoroughly checked. Caroline Walsh introduces the key points of this very important contract.

So, you've done the difficult bit and persuaded a publisher to make an offer to publish your book. But how do you know if you're getting a fair deal? And what should you be looking out for on the contract? I would always advise an author or illustrator to engage an agent. An agent will ensure that the contract gives you the best possible chance of maximising your income from a book. Alternatively, the Society of Authors (see page 335) and the Writers' Guild of Great Britain (see page 363) will both check publishing agreements for their members. In addition, there are lawyers who specialise in publishing contracts and for those who prefer to go it alone, there are some useful books on the subject listed at the end of this article.

What follows is a whistle-stop tour around the key points of a publishing contract, especially for those writing for children. To begin, the offer from the publisher should come in writing clearly setting out exactly what rights the publisher wants to license and what they are willing to pay for those rights. A contract is a business agreement for the supply of goods or performance of work at a specified price. Normally, that payment comes as an advance against royalties. Occasionally, a flat fee payment is appropriate, but a royalty allows the author to share in the income from a book throughout its life and is therefore generally preferable. Perhaps the most important point of all is that you make sure you fully understand which rights are being licensed under the contract and aren't seduced merely into worrying about the advance and royalty (tempting though they may be!)

Publishers' agreements often have useful headings for each clause and I've used some of those headings here for ease of reference.

Licence

The very first thing to be clear about is what is being licensed to the publisher. For a new book one expects to grant to the publisher, for the legal term of copyright, the exclusive right to publish and sell the work in certain forms. The standard grant is of 'volume form', which means all book forms (hardback, paperback, other formats). However, the offer or contract may also state other forms, for example serial (newspaper and magazine rights) or audio rights. Some publishers' contracts include all-encompassing wording such as 'all media forms currently in existence and hereinafter invented'. This in effect hands control to the publisher of a wide range of rights, including electronic, dramatic (film, television, radio), merchandising and so on. In such a case, it's likely that the author's share of income from such rights will be less than it would be were the author to reserve those rights and have them handled separately.

Territory

Territory states *where* the publisher has the right to sell or sub-license the book. For picture books of all kinds, fiction and non-fiction, UK publishers generally require world rights as the UK market alone is not large enough to sustain the costs of four-colour printing. US publishers are lucky enough to have a sufficiently large home market to mean they are not reliant on foreign sales and therefore will not always require world rights.

For fiction (i.e. novels) a judgement needs to be made about which territories should be granted to the publisher. English language rights are made up of two large mutually exclusive territories: the UK and Traditional British Commonwealth (including or excluding Canada) on the one hand and the USA, its dependencies and the Philippines on the other. The rest of the world is considered an open market. One could grant Traditional British Commonwealth rights in the English Language to a publisher, thereby reserving American and translation rights to be sold separately. Or one could grant World English Language rights, so the publisher can sell on US rights while translation rights are held in reserve to be sold separately. Or again, one could grant world rights to the originating publisher.

When thinking of granting a wide range of territories to a publisher, it is worth checking out how proactive and successful their foreign rights department is. It may be possible to speak to the foreign rights manager and find out for yourself if they have a good track record. An agent will have an informed view on a publisher's expertise in this area and furthermore, they will probably either be experienced themselves in selling foreign and US rights, or will work with associate agencies in all the different language territories. Publishers will take 15–30% share on US and foreign sales and, if you have an agent too, their commission will also be deducted before you receive your percentage. Agents will generally charge 15–20% on US and foreign sales.

Advances

We've all read the newspaper headlines about huge advances, but the fact is most children's book advances currently fall within the range of £1000–£25,000. For books that will be published in the trade (i.e. by a mainstream publishing house and where the book will appear in bookshops) most offers are framed as an advance against royalties. Advances may be paid in one go, on signature, but don't be surprised if the publisher proposes paying half on signature and half on publication, or in thirds (signature, delivery and publication), or even in quarters (signature, delivery, hardback publication, paperback publication), though the latter is more common when the advance offered is substantial.

Royalties

As a very basic rule of thumb, hardbacks attract a 10% base royalty and paperbacks 7.5%. Bear in mind that on picture books these figures will be shared between author and illustrator. Sometimes, children's black and white illustrated fiction titles also bear a small royalty for the illustrator, which will come out of the total royalty. Most novelty books, including board books, work on a smaller royalty, for example 5% or even less because of the high production costs and relatively low retail price.

Ideally, the royalty will escalate to a higher level when a certain number of sales have been achieved and this can prove to be very important if a book becomes a long-running success.

For a trade book the royalties should ideally be based on the recommended retail price for home sales. Export sales and sales to book clubs or book fairs are usually calculated on the publisher's price received (or net receipts). The contract should set out each type of sale and list the appropriate royalty rate. Nowadays particular attention needs to be paid to 'high discount' clauses in contracts. However good the main home sales royalty is, a disadvantageous high discount clause can mean that disappointingly few of the sales attract the full royalty and consequently revenues will be much reduced. This is especially important now because retailers are pushing publishers hard on discounts. An agent will be used to negotiating carefully on precisely this kind of area to secure the best possible terms.

Co-edition royalties

As previously mentioned, picture books in the UK are very dependent upon publishers selling American and foreign language co-editions. Therefore, it is important to note on the contract what the author's share of any such co-edition deals will be. These generally fall under two categories in the contract:

• If the UK publisher prints for the foreign publisher, the books are usually sold for a fixed price per copy as 'royalty inclusive' and the author's and artist's share will be expressed as a percentage of the publisher's price received. These deals help to get the book published by bringing the unit cost down and they begin the process of earning out the advance.

• US and foreign language sales also fall under the heading of subsidiary rights. In this case, the UK publisher may or may not print the books, but the US or foreign publisher will have agreed to pay an advance and royalty for the right to sell the book in their territory (a 'royalty exclusive' deal). The author's and artist's share in this instance shouldn't be less than 50% and it could be much more. If a book is particularly sought after by foreign or US publishers, such a royalty exclusive deal could mean that the original UK advance is earned out immediately.

Subsidiary rights

Other subsidiary rights include reprint rights (large print, book club, paperback reprint, etc), serial rights (the right to publish in newspapers and magazines), anthology and quotation rights, educational rights, audio rights and so on. There will usually be a percentage listed against each right and that is the author's share of any deal. Generally the author receives at least 50% on these deals and more in the case of serial, US and translation rights. The rights listed in the sub-rights clause should be checked against the opening grant of rights clause to see that they conform.

Delivery and publication

There should be clauses in the contract that state the agreed delivery date of the book and give some indication of what is expected, for example 'a work for children to be written and illustrated by the said author to a length of not more than 25,000 words plus approximately 50 black and white line illustrations'. There should also be an undertaking by the publisher to publish the work within a stated time period, for example 'within 12 months from delivery of the complete typescript and artwork'. There might also be an indication of what the published price will be.

Copyright and moral rights

As you are licensing your work, you should retain copyright and there should be a clause that obliges the publisher to include a copyright line in every edition of the work published or sub-licensed by them. The author's moral rights are also often asserted within the contract.

Production

Though the publishers will generally insist on having the final decision regarding details of production, publication and advertising, they should agree to consult meaningfully with the author over the blurb, catalogue copy, jacket and cover design. There should also be an undertaking to supply the author with proofs for checking and enough time for the author to check those proofs.

Accounts

Publishers usually account to authors twice a year for royalties earned. Even if the advance has not earned out, the publishers should still send a royalty statement. Royalty statements are notoriously enigmatic and vary from publisher to publisher. Mistakes on royalty statements are more common than one might like to think and an agent will be used to checking royalty statements carefully and taking up any anomalies with the publisher.

In addition to the twice-yearly accounting, once the initial advance has been earned out, an agent will be able to ensure that any substantial income from sub-rights deals (e.g. in excess of £100) will be paid immediately.

Electronic or ebook rights

The electronic book market is in its infancy and norms have not yet been established. If a publisher insists on including these rights in the contract, one should aim to negotiate a royalty of 50% of the publisher's price received or, at the very least, only agree a lower rate for a fixed period of time, for example two years, after which it can be subject to review and renegotiation.

Reversion

It's important to ensure that the author can get back the rights to their book if the publisher either fails to stick to the terms of the contract or lets the book go out of print and leaves it out of print for six to nine months after receiving a written request to reprint it. It is well worth reclaiming rights to out of print books as it may be possible to re-license them later on.

Assignment

A small but important clause that may need to be added states that the publishers shall not assign the rights granted to them without the author's express written consent. This gives the author at least a degree of control over the book's destiny if the publishing company runs into trouble or is sold.

Educational publishers' contracts

Many children's authors begin as writers for educational publishers and quite a number continue to work in this field alongside producing books for the trade market. Educational publishers usually commission tightly briefed work. Advances are generally modest and the royalties are based on the publishers' price received. However, substantial sums can eventually be earned. Educational publishers usually expect to be granted a very wide range of rights and while it makes sense to grant audio or electronic rights where the publisher has the capacity to produce or license such formats for their market, it may be possible and desirable to reserve, for example, dramatic and merchandising rights. However, discretion is needed here. If, for example, the publisher is commissioning writers to create stories about a given set of characters created by the publisher, then the publisher will rightly expect to control such rights.

That really is a scratching of the surface of publishing agreements. Do take advice if you don't feel confident that the contract presented to you is fair. It seems a very obvious thing to say but always read a publishing agreement carefully before signing it and if anything in it isn't clear, ask for an explanation. Remember, too, that it's a negotiation and that despite publishers' talk of 'standard terms' and 'standard agreements', it is always possible to make amendments to contracts.

Caroline Walsh is a literary agent and a director of David Higham Associates Ltd (www.davidhigham.co.uk). She specialises in the children's book market.

Useful reading

Clark, Charles (ed.), *Publishing Agreements: A Book of Precedents*, Tottel Publishing, 7th edn, 2007

Flint, Michael F., *A User's Guide to Copyright*, Tottel Publishing, 6th edn, 2006

Legat, Michael, *An Author's Guide to Publishing*, Robert Hale, 3rd edn revised, 1998

Legat, Michael, *Understanding Publishers' Contracts*, Robert Hale, 2nd edn revised, 2002

FAQs about ISBNs

The ISBN Agency receives a large number of enquiries about the ISBN system. The most frequently asked questions are answered here.

What is an ISBN?

An ISBN (International Standard Book Number) is a product identifier used by publishers, booksellers and libraries for ordering, listing and stock control purposes. It enables them to identify a specific edition of a specific title in a specific format from a particular publisher. The digits are always divided into six parts, separated by spaces or hyphens. The six parts can be of varying length and are as follows:

Contact details

UK ISBN Agency
3rd Floor, Midas House, 62 Goldsworth Road, Woking GU21 6LQ
tel (0870) 777 8712 *fax* (0870) 777 8714
email isbn.agency@nielsen.com
website www.isbn.nielsenbookdata.co.uk

• EAN element – The first element of the ISBN is a three-digit number that is made available by EAN International. Prefixes that have already been made available by EAN International are 978 and 979, but there may be a further prefix allocation made in the future as required to ensure the continued capacity of the ISBN system.
• Prefix – Distinguishes the ISBN from other types of product identifier which are used for non-book trade products.
• Group Identifier – Identifies a national, geographic or language grouping of publishers. It tells you which of these groupings the publisher belongs to (not the language of the book).
• Publisher Identifier – Identifies a specific publisher or imprint.
• Title Number – Identifies a specific edition of a specific title in a specific format.
• Check Digit – This is always and only the final digit which mathematically validates the rest of the number.

Since January 2007 all ISBNs are 13 digits long. The older ten-digit format can be converted to the 13-digit format by adding the 978 EAN prefix and recalculating the check digit.

Do all books need to have an ISBN?

There is no legal requirement for an ISBN in the UK and it conveys no form of legal or copyright protection. It is a product identifier.

What can be gained from using an ISBN?

If you wish to sell your publication through major bookselling chains, or internet booksellers, they will require you to have an ISBN to assist their internal processing and ordering systems. The ISBN also provides access to bibliographic databases such as Nielsen Book's database and information services, which are organised using ISBNs as references. These databases are used by the book trade – publishers, booksellers and libraries – for internal purposes, to provide information for customers and to source and order titles. ISBNs are also used by Nielsen Book's sales analysis service to monitor book sales. The ISBN therefore provides access to additional marketing opportunities which assist the sales and measurement of books and other published media.

Where can we get an ISBN?

ISBN prefixes are assigned to publishers in the country in which the publisher is based by the national agency for that country. The UK and Republic of Ireland Agency is run by Neilsen Book. The Agency introduces new publishers to the system, assigns prefixes to new and existing publishers and deals with any queries or problems in using the system. The UK ISBN Agency was the first ISBN agency in the world and has been instrumental in the set up and maintenance of the ISBN. Publishers based elsewhere will not be able to get numbers from the UK Agency but may contact them for details of the relevant agency in their market.

Who is eligible for ISBNs?

Any organisation or individual who is publishing a qualifying product for general sale or distribution to the market is eligible (see 'Which products do not qualify for ISBNs?').

What is a publisher?

It is sometimes difficult to decide who the publisher is and who their agent may be, but the publisher is generally the person or body which takes the financial risk in making a product available. For example, if a product went on sale and sold no copies at all, the publisher is usually the person or body which loses money. If you get paid anyway, you are likely to be a designer, printer, author or consultant of some kind.

How long does it take to get an ISBN?

In the UK the 'Standard' service time is ten working days. There is also a 'Fast Track' service, which is a three-working day processing period.

How much does it cost to get an ISBN?

In the UK there is a registration fee which is payable by all new publishers. The fees during 2008 are £105.75 including VAT for the Standard service and £164.50 including VAT for the Fast Track service. A publisher prefix unique to you will be provided and allows for ten ISBNs. Larger allocations are available where appropriate.

ISBNs are only available in blocks. The smallest block is ten numbers. It is not possible to obtain a single ISBN.

Which products do not qualify for ISBNs?

Calendars and diaries (unless they contain additional text or images such that they are not purely for time-management purposes); greetings cards, videos for entertainment; documentaries on video/CD-Rom; computer games; computer application programs; items which are available to a restricted group of people, e.g. a history of a golf club which is only for sale to members, or an educational course book only available to those registered as students on the course.

Can I turn my ISBN into a barcode?

Prior to 2007, ISBNs were only ten digits long, whereas the appropriate barcode was 13 digits long and was derived from the ISBN by adding a prefix and recalculating the check digit. From 1 January 2007, the appropriate barcode number will be the same as the 13-digit ISBN. Further information about barcoding for books is available on the Book Industry Communication website (www.bic.org.uk).

What is an ISSN?

An International Standard Serial Number is the numbering system for journals, magazines, periodicals, newspapers and newsletters. It is administered by the British Library, *tel* (01937) 546959.

Public Lending Right

Under the PLR system, payment is made from public funds to authors (writers, translators, illustrators and some editors/compilers) whose books are lent out from public libraries. Payment is made once a year, and the amount authors receive is proportionate to the number of times that their books were borrowed during the previous year (July to June).

The legislation

Public Lending Right (PLR) was created, and its principles established, by the Public Lending Right Act 1979 (HMSO, 30p). The Act required the rules for the administration of PLR to be laid down by a scheme. That was done in the Public Lending Right Scheme 1982 (HMSO, £2.95), which includes details of transfer (assignment), transmission after death, renunciation, trusteeship, bankruptcy, etc. Amending orders made in 1983, 1984, 1988, 1989 and 1990 were consolidated in December 1990 (SI 2360, £3.90). Some further amendments affecting author eligibility came into effect in December 1991 (SI 2618, £1), July 1997 (SI 1576, £1.10), December 1999 (SI 420, £1), July 2000 (SI 933, £1.50), June 2004 (SI 1258 £3) and July 2005 (SI 1519, £3).

Further information

Public Lending Right
PLR Office, Richard House, Sorbonne Close, Stockton-on-Tees TS17 6DA
tel (01642) 604699 *fax* (01642) 615641
website www.plr.uk.com, www.plrinternational.com
Contact The Registrar
Application forms, information, publications and a copy of its *Annual Report* are all obtainable from the PLR Office. See website for further information on eligibility for PLR, loans statistics and forthcoming developments.

PLR Advisory Committee
Advises the Secretary of State for Culture, Media and Sport and the Registrar on the operation of the PLR scheme.

How the system works

From the applications he receives, the Registrar of PLR compiles a register of authors and books which is held on computer. A representative sample of book issues is recorded, consisting of all loans from selected public libraries. This is then multiplied in proportion to total library lending to produce, for each book, an estimate of its total annual loans throughout the country. Each year the computer compares the register with the estimated loans to discover how many loans are credited to each registered book for the calculation of PLR payments. The computer does this using code numbers – in most cases the ISBN printed in the book.

Parliament allocates a sum each year (£7,630,000 for 2007–8) for PLR. This Fund pays the administrative costs of PLR and reimburses local authorities for recording loans in the sample libraries. The remaining money is then divided by the total registered loan figure in order to work out how much can be paid for each estimated loan of a registered book.

Limits on payments

Bottom limit. If all the registered interests in an author's books score so few loans that they would earn less than £1 in a year, no payment is due.
Top limit. If the books of one registered author score so high that the author's PLR earnings for the year would exceed £6600, then only £6600 is paid. No author can earn more than £6600 in PLR in any one year.

Money that is not paid out because of these limits belongs to the Fund and increases the amounts paid that year to other authors.

The sample

The basic sample represents only public libraries (no academic, school, private or commercial libraries are included) and only loans made over the counter (not consultations of books on library premises). It follows that only those books which are loaned from public libraries can earn PLR and make an application worthwhile.

The sample consists of the entire loans records for a year from libraries in more than 30 public library authorities spread through England, Scotland, Wales and Northern Ireland. Sample loans represent around 20% of the national total. Several computerised sampling points in an authority contribute loans data ('multi-site' sampling). This change has been introduced gradually, and began in July 1991. The aim has been to increase the sample without any significant increase in costs. In order to counteract sampling error, libraries in the sample change every two to three years. Loans are totalled every 12 months for the period 1 July–30 June.

An author's entitlement to PLR depends, under the 1979 Act, on the loans accrued by his or her books in the sample. This figure is averaged up to produce first regional and then finally national estimated loans.

ISBNs

PLR depends on the use of code numbers to identify books lent and to correlate loans with entries on the register so that payment can be made. The system uses the International Standard Book Number (ISBN), which is required for all new registrations. Different editions (e.g. 1st, 2nd, hardcover, paperback, large print) of the same book have different ISBNs.

Summary of the 25th year's results

Registration: authors. When registration closed for the 25th year (30 June 2007) the number of shares in books registered was 422,330 for 35,052 authors and assignees.

Eligible loans. Of the 323 million estimated loans from UK libraries, 136 million belong to books on the PLR register. The loans credited to registered books – 42% of all library borrowings – qualify for payment. The remaining 58% of loans relate to books that are ineligible for various reasons, to books written by dead or foreign authors, and to books that have simply not been applied for.

Money and payments. PLR's administrative costs are deducted from the fund allocated to the Registrar annually by Parliament. Operating the Scheme this year cost £828,000, representing some 11% of the PLR fund. The Rate per Loan for 2007–8 was 5.98 pence and was calculated to distribute all the £6,660,000 available. The total of PLR distribution and costs is therefore the full £7.63 million which the Government provided in 2007–8.

The numbers of authors in various payment categories are as follows:

*359	payments at	£5000–6600
375	payments between	£2500–4999.99
797	payments between	£1000–2499.99
897	payments between	£500–999.99
3591	payments between	£100–499.99
17,923	payments between	£1–99.99
23,942	TOTAL	

* includes 242 authors where the maximum threshold applied.

Authorship

In the PLR system the author of a book is the writer, illustrator, translator, compiler, editor or reviser. Authors must be named on the book's title page, or be able to prove authorship by some other means (e.g. receipt of royalties). The ownership of copyright has no bearing on PLR eligibility.

Co-authorship/illustrators. In the PLR system the authors of a book are those writers, translators, editors, compilers andillustrators as defined above. Authors must apply for registration before their books can earn PLR. This can now be done online through the PLR website. There is no restriction on the number of authors who can register shares in any one book as long as they satisfy the eligibility criteria.

Writers and/or illustrators. At least one must be eligible and they must jointly agree what share of PLR each will take. This agreement is necessary even if one or two are ineligible or do not wish to register for PLR. Share sizes should be based on contribution. The eligible authors will receive the share(s) specified in the application. PLR can be any whole percentage. Detailed advice is available from the PLR office.

Translators. Translators may apply, without reference to other authors, for a 30% fixed share (to be divided equally between joint translators).

Editors and compilers. An editor or compiler may apply, either with others or without reference to them, to register a 20% share. Unless in receipt of royalties an editor must have written at least 10% of the book's content or more than ten pages of text in addition to normal editorial work. The share of joint editors/compilers is 20% in total to be divided equally. An application from an editor or compiler to register a greater percentage share must be accompanied by supporting documentary evidence of actual contribution.

Dead or missing co-authors. Where it is impossible to agree shares with a co-author because that person is dead or untraceable, then the surviving co-author or co-authors may submit an application without the dead or missing co-author but must name the co-author and provide supporting evidence as to why that co-author has not agreed shares.

The living co-author(s) will then be able to register a share in the book which will be 20% for the illustrator (or illustrators) and the residual percentage for the writer (or writers). If this percentage is to be divided between more than one writer or illustrator, then this will be in equal shares unless some other apportionment is requested and agreed by the Registrar.

The PLR Office keeps a file of missing authors (mostly illustrators) to help locate co-authors. Help is also available from publishers, the writers' organisations, and the Association of Illustrators.

Life and death. Authors can only be registered for PLR during their lifetime. However, for authors so registered, books can later be registered if first published within one year before their death or ten years afterwards. New versions of titles registered by the author can be registered posthumously.

Residential qualifications. With effect from 1 July 2000, PLR is open to authors living in the European Economic Area (i.e. EU member states plus Norway, Liechtenstein and Iceland). A resident in these countries (for PLR purposes) has his or her only or principal home there.

Eligible books

In the PLR system each separate edition of a book is registered and treated as a separate book. A book is eligible for PLR registration provided that:
• it has an eligible author (or co-author);
• it is printed and bound (paperbacks counting as bound);
• copies of it have been put on sale (i.e. it is not a free handout and it has already been published);
• it is not a newspaper, magazine, journal or periodical;
• the authorship is personal (i.e. not a company or association) and the book is not crown copyright;
• it is not wholly or mainly a musical score;
• it has an ISBN.

Notification and payment

Every registered author receives from the Registrar an annual statement of estimated loans for each book and the PLR due.

Sampling arrangements

To help minimise the unfairnesses that arise inevitably from a sampling system, the Scheme specifies the eight regions within which authorities and sampling points have to be designated and includes libraries of varying size. Part of the sample drops out by rotation each year to allow fresh libraries to be included. The following library authorities have been designated for the year beginning 1 July 2008 (all are multi-site authorities). This list is based on the nine government regions for England plus Northern Ireland, Scotland and Wales.
• East – Cambridgeshire;
• East Midlands – Leicestershire & Rutland;
• London – Lambeth, Redbridge/Havering/Tower Hamlets/Wandsworth;

- North East – Newcastle-upon-Tyne, Stockton-on-Tees;
- North West & Merseyside – Lancashire, St Helens;
- South East – Surrey, Brighton & Hove;
- South West – Wiltshire, Cornwall;
- West Midlands – Dudley, Staffordshire;
- Yorkshire & The Humber – Sheffield;

Most borrowed children's fiction titles

	Author	Title	Publisher	Year
1.	J.K. Rowling	Harry Potter and the Half Blood Prince	Bloomsbury	2005
2.	Jacqueline Wilson (illus. Nick Sharratt)	Candyfloss	Doubleday	2006
3.	Francesca Simon (illus. Tony Ross)	Horrid Henry and the Football Fiend	Orion Children's	2006
4.	Francesca Simon (illus. Tony Ross)	Horrid Henry's Underpants	Dolphin	2003
5.	Francesca Simon (illus. Tony Ross)	Horrid Henry and the MegaMean Time Machine	Dolphin	2005
6.	Francesca Simon (illus. Tony Ross)	Horrid Henry Meets the Queen	Orion Children's	2004
7.	Jacqueline Wilson (illus. N. Sharratt)	Sleepovers	Corgi Children's	2002
8.	Francesca Simon (illus. Tony Ross)	Horrid Henry and the Bogey Babysitter	Dolphin	2002
9.	Jacqueline Wilson (illus. Nick Sharratt)	Starring Tracy Beaker	Doubleday Children's	2006
10.	Julia Donaldson (illus. Axel Scheffler)	The Gruffalo's Child	Macmillan Children's	2004
11.	Jacqueline Wilson (illus. Nick Sharratt)	The Story of Tracy Beaker	Corgi Children's	1992
12.	Jacqueline Wilson (illus. Nick Sharratt)	Clean Break	Doubleday	2005
13.	Jacqueline Wilson (illus. Nick Sharratt)	The Mum-minder	Corgi Children's	1994
14.	Jacqueline Wilson (illus. Nick Sharratt)	Best Friends	Corgi Children's	2005
15.	Roald Dahl (illus. Quentin Blake)	The Twits	Puffin	2001
16.	Jacqueline Wilson (illus. Nick Sharratt)	The Worry Website	Corgi Children's	2003
17.	Francesca Simon (illus. Tony Ross)	Horrid Henry's Stinkbomb	Orion Children's	2003
18.	Julia Donaldson (illus. Axel Scheffler)	Gruffalo	Macmillan Children's	1999
19.	Francesca Simon (illus. Tony Ross)	Horrid Henry's Revenge	Dolphin	2001
20.	Jacqueline Wilson (illus. Nick Sharratt)	Lizzie Zipmouth	Corgi Children's	2000

• Northern Ireland – (all authorities) Belfast Education and Library Board, North Eastern Education and Library Board, South Eastern Education and Library Board, Southern Education and Library Board, Western Education and Library Board;
• Scotland – Edinburgh, East Lothian, Moray;
• Wales – Neath Port Talbot, Powys, Swansea.

Participating local authorities are reimbursed on an actual cost basis for additional expenditure incurred in providing loans data to the PLR Office. The extra PLR work mostly consists of modifications to computer programs to accumulate loans data in the local authority computer and to transmit the data to the PLR Office at Stockton-on-Tees.

Most borrowed classic children's titles

	Author	Title	Publisher	Year
1.	Roald Dahl (illus. Quentin Blake)	Charlie and the Great Glass Elevator	Puffin	2001
2.	Roald Dahl (illus. Quentin Blake)	The Witches	Puffin	2001
3.	Roald Dahl (illus. Quentin Blake)	James and the Giant Peach	Puffin	2001
4.	Roald Dahl (illus. Quentin Blake)	Danny the Champion of the World	Puffin	2001
5.	Roald Dahl (illus. Quentin Blake)	Matilda	Puffin	2001
6.	Roald Dahl (illus. Quentin Blake)	The BFG	Puffin	2001
7.	Roald Dahl (illus. Quentin Blake)	Charlie and the Chocolate Factory	Puffin	2001
8.	Roald Dahl	Charlie and the Chocolate Factory	Puffin	2005
9.	Korky Paul and Valerie Thomas	Winnie's Magic Wand	OUP	2002
10.	Roald Dahl (illus. Quentin Blake)	The Enormous Crocodile	Puffin	2001
11.	J.R.R. Tolkien (illus. David Wyatt)	The Hobbit	Collins	1998
12.	Roald Dahl (illus. Quentin Blake)	The Complete Adventures of Charlie and Mr Willy Wonka	Puffin	2001
13.	Enid Blyton	The Secret Seven	Hodder	2006
14.	Walt Disney Company	Peter Pan	Ladybird	2003
15.	Roald Dahl (illus. Quentin Blake)	The Vicar of Nibbleswicke	Penguin	1992
16.	C.S. Lewis (illus. Pauline Baynes)	The Lion, the Witch and the Wardrobe	Collins	1998
17.	Astrid Lindgren (illus. Tony Ross)	Pippi Longstocking	OUP	2002
18.	J.M. Barrie	Peter Pan	Puffin	1994
19.	Ian Beck	Chicken Licken	OUP	2003
20.	Roald Dahl (illus. Quentin Blake)	George's Marvellous Medicine	Cape	2003

Reciprocal arrangements

Reciprocal PLR arrangements now exist with the German, Dutch and Austrian PLR schemes. Authors can apply for German, Dutch and Austrian PLR through the Authors' Licensing and Collecting Society. Further information on PLR schemes internationally and recent developments within the EC towards wider recognition of PLR is available from the PLR Office or on the international PLR website.

Most borrowed children's non-fiction titles

	Author	Title	Publisher	Year
1.	Terry Deary (illus. Martin Brown)	The Woeful Second World War	Hippo	1999
2.	Mick Inkpen	Kipper's A to Z	Hodder Children's	2002
3.	Eric Hill	Spot Can Count	Puffin	2000
4.	Terry Deary (illus. Martin Brown)	The Ruthless Romans	Hippo	2003
5.	Felicity Brooks (illus. Jo Litchfield)	First Colours	Usborne	2006
6.	Fiona Watt (illus. Rachel Wells)	Dinosaurs	Usborne	2005
7.	Anna Nilsen	Pirates	Little Hare	2003
8.	Susannah Leigh (illus. Brenda Haw)	Puzzle Palace	Scholastic	2005
9.	Terry Deary, Neil Tonge (illus. Martin Brown)	The Terrible Tudors	Hippo	1993
10.	Fiona Land	Baby Touch Colours	Penguin	2006
11.	Annabel Karmel	Children's First Cookbook	Dorling Kindersley	2005
12.	–	Old Macdonald Had a Farm	Dorling Kindersley	2005
13.	Terry Deary (illus. Martin Brown)	The Groovy Greeks	Hippo	1996
14.	Illus. Kate Merritt	The Wheels on the Bus	Ladybird	2005
15.	Terry Deary (illus. Martin Brown)	The Rotten Romans	Hippo	1994
16.	Terry Deary (illus. Martin Brown)	The Vile Victorians	Scholastic	1994
17.	Terry Deary, Peter Hepplewhite (illus. Martin Brown)	The Awesome Egyptians	Scholastic	1993
18.	Terry Deary (illus. Kate Sheppard)	The Blitzed Brits	Hippo	1994
19.	Terry Deary (illus. Martin Brown)	The Villainous Victorians	Hippo	2004
20.	Terry Deary (illus. Martin Brown)	Even More Terrible Tudors	Hippo	1998

Copyright
Copyright questions

Copyright is a vital part of any writer's assets, and should never be assigned or sold without due consideration and the advice of a competent authority, such as the Society of Authors, the Writers' Guild of Great Britain, or the National Union of Journalists. Michael Legat answers some of the most commonly asked questions about copyright.

Is there a period of time after which the copyright expires?

Copyright in the European Union lasts for the lifetime of the author and for a further 70 years from the end of the year of death, or, if the work is first published posthumously, for 70 years from the end of the year of publication. In most other countries of the world copyright exists similarly for the lifetime and for either 50 years or 70 years after death or posthumous publication.

If I want to include an extract from a book, poem or article, do I have to seek copyright? How much may be used without permission? What happens if I apply for copyright permission but do not get a reply?

It is essential to seek permission to quote from another author's work, unless that author has been dead for 70 years or more, or 70 years or more has passed from the date of publication of a work published posthumously. Only if you are quoting for purposes of criticism or review are you allowed to do so without obtaining permission, and even then the Copyright, Designs and Patents Act of 1988 restricts you to 400 words of prose in a single extract from a copyright work, or a series of extracts of up to 300 words each, totalling no more than 800 words, or up to 40 lines of poetry, which must not be more than 25% of the poem. However, a quotation of no more than, say, half a dozen words may usually be used without permission since it will probably not extend beyond a brief and familiar reference, as, for example, Rider Haggard's well-known phrase, 'she who must be obeyed'. If in doubt, always check. If you do not get a reply when you ask for permission to quote, insert a notice in your work saying that you have tried without success to contact the copyright owner, and would be pleased to hear from him or her so that the matter could be cleared up – and keep a copy of all the relevant correspondence, in order to back up your claim of having tried to get in touch.

If a newspaper pays for an article and I then want to sell the story to a magazine, am I free under the copyright law to do so?

Yes, provided that you have not granted copyright or exclusive use to the newspaper. When selling your work to newspapers or magazines make it clear, in writing, that you are selling only First or Second Serial Rights, not your copyright.

If I agree to have an article published for no payment do I retain any rights over how it appears?

Whether or not you are paid for the work has no bearing on the legal situation. However, the Moral Rights which apply to books, plays, television and radio scripts, do not cover you against a failure to acknowledge you as the author of an article, nor against the mutilation of your text, when it is published in a newspaper or magazine.

I want to publish a photograph that was taken in 1950. I am not sure how to contact the photographer or even if he is still alive. Am I allowed to go ahead and publish it?

The Copyright, Designs and Patents Act of 1988 works retrospectively, so a photograph taken in 1950 is bound to be in copyright until at least 2020, and the copyright will be owned by the photographer, even though, when it was taken, the copyright would have belonged to the person who commissioned it, according to the laws then in place. You should therefore make every effort to contact the photographer, keeping copies of any relevant correspondence, and in case of failure take the same course of action as described above in relation to a textual extract the copyright owner of which you have been unable to trace.

I recently read an article on the same subject as one I have written. It contained many identical facts. Did this writer breach my copyright? What if I send ideas for an article to a magazine editor and those ideas are used despite the fact that I was not commissioned? May I sue the magazine?

Facts are normally in the public domain and may be used by anyone. However, if your article contains a fact which you have discovered and no one else has published, there could be an infringement of copyright if the author who uses it fails to attribute it to you. There is no copyright in ideas, so you cannot sue a writer or a journal for using ideas that you have put forward; in any case you would find it very difficult to prove that the idea belonged to you and to no one else. There is also no copyright in titles.

Does being paid a kill fee affect my copyright in a given piece?

No, provided that you have not sold the magazine or newspaper your copyright.

Do I need to copyright a piece of writing physically – whether an essay or a novel – or is it copyrighted automatically? Does it have to carry the © symbol?

Anything that you write is your copyright, assuming that it is not copied from the work of someone else, as soon as you have written it on paper or recorded it on the disk of a computer or on tape, or broadcast it, or posted it on the internet. It is not essential for the work to carry the © symbol, although its inclusion may act as a warning and help to stop another writer from plagiarising it.

Am I legally required to inform an interviewee that our conversation is being recorded?

The interviewee owns the copyright of any words that he or she speaks as soon as they are recorded on your tape. Unless you have received permission to use those words in direct quotation, you could be liable to an action for infringement of copyright. You should therefore certainly inform the interviewee that the conversation is being recorded and seek permission to quote what is said directly.

More and more newspapers and magazines have versions both in print and on the internet. How can I ensure that my work is not published on the internet without my permission?

Make sure that any clause granting electronic rights to anyone in any agreement that you sign in respect of your work specifies not only the proportion of any fees received which you will get, but that your agreement must be sought before the rights are sold. Copyright extends to electronic rights, and therefore to publication on the internet, in just the same way as to other uses of the material.

I commissioned a designer to design a business card for me, and I paid her well. Does the design belong to me or to her?

Copyright would belong to the designer, and not to the person who commissioned it (as is also true in the case of a photograph, copyright in which belongs to the photographer). However, copyright in the business card might be transferred to you if a court considered you to have gained beneficially from the card.

Michael Legat became a full-time writer after a long and successful publishing career. He is the author of a number of highly regarded books on publishing and writing.

See also...
* *The Society of Authors*, page 335
* *Authors' Licensing and Collecting Society*, page 250
* *Design and Artists Copyright Society*, page 252
* *The Copyright Licensing Agency Ltd*, page 248

The Copyright Licensing Agency Ltd

The Copyright Licensing Agency (CLA) licenses organisations to copy extracts from copyright publications on behalf of the authors, publishers and visual creators it represents. CLA's licences permit photocopying, scanning and emailing of articles and extracts from books, journals and magazines, as well as digital and online publications. The money collected is distributed to rights owners to ensure that they are properly rewarded for the use of their intellectual property.

Why was CLA established?

CLA was set up by its owners, the Authors' Licensing and Collecting Society (ALCS) and the Publishers Licensing Society (PLS) and has an agency agreement with the Design and Artists Copyright Society (DACS), which represents visual artists and illustrators.

Further information

The Copyright Licensing Agency Ltd
Saffron House, 6–10 Kirby Street,
London EC1N 8TS
tel 020-7400 3100 *fax* 020-7400 3101
email cla@cla.co.uk
website www.cla.co.uk

CLA exists to represent creators and publishers by licensing the copying of their work and promoting the value of copyright protection generally. This way CLA helps to protect the value of creativity.

How CLA helps artists and writers

CLA allows licensed users access to millions of titles worldwide. In return, CLA ensures artists and writers, along with publishers, are fairly recompensed by the licence fees which CLA collects and distributes to writers, artists and publishers.

The collective management of licensing schemes means that CLA can provide users with the simplest and most cost-effective means of obtaining authorisation for photocopying and scanning under strict copy limits.

CLA has licences which enable digitisation of existing print material. The licence enables users to scan and electronically send extracts from printed copyright works.

CLA has recently also launched a series of digital licences which enable users to re-use and copy from born digital electronic and online publications. Writers and publishers can benefit further from the increased income generated from these licences which operate under the same copy limits as the established photocopying licences.

Who is licensed?

CLA's licensees are aimed at three main sectors:
• education (schools, further and higher education);
• government (central, local, public bodies); and
• business (business, industry, professionals).

CLA develops licences to meet the specific needs of each sector and user groups within each sector. Depending on the requirement, there are both blanket and transactional licences available. Every licence allows the photocopying of most books, journals, magazines and periodicals published in the UK.

International activity

Many countries have established equivalents to CLA and the number of such agencies is set to grow. Nearly all these agencies, including CLA, are members of the International Federation of Reproduction Rights Organisations (IFRRO).

Through reciprocal arrangements with organisations from 25 countries CLA's licences also allow copying from an expanding list of publications in other countries. CLA receives monies from these territories for the copying of UK material abroad and forwards it to rights holders.

Distribution

The fees collected from licensees are forwarded to artists, authors and publishers via DACS, ALCS and PLS respectively, and are based on statistical surveys and records of copying activity. CLA is celebrating its 25th anniversary in 2008 and has distributed over £400 million to rights holders over this period. For the year 2006/7 over £47 million was paid to creators and publishers.

Respecting copyright

CLA believes it is important to raise awareness of copyright and the need to protect the creativity of artists, authors and publishers. To this end, CLA organises a range of activities such as copyright workshops in schools, seminars for businesses and institutions and an extensive programme of exhibitions and other events.

CLA believes in working positively together with all sectors, meaning legal action is rare. However, organisations – especially in the business sector – need to be aware that copyright is a legally enforceable right and not a voluntary option. CLA's compliance arm, Copywatch, is active in these sectors to educate users and seek out illegal copying.

Protecting the value of creativity

By supporting rights holders in the way described, CLA plays an important role in maintaining the value of their work, thereby sustaining creativity and its benefit to all. Through protection of this sort the creative industries in the UK have been able to grow to support millions of jobs and to produce over 8% of UK GDP.

Authors' Licensing and Collecting Society

The Authors' Licensing and Collecting Society is the rights management society for UK writers.

The Authors' Licensing and Collecting Society (ALCS) is the UK collective rights management society for writers. Established in 1977, the Society represents the interests of all UK writers and aims to ensure that they are fairly compensated for any works that are copied, broadcast or recorded.

A non-profit company, ALCS was set up in the wake of the campaign to establish a Public Lending Right to help writers protect and exploit their collective rights. Today, it is the largest writers' organisation in the UK with a membership of over 55,000 and an annual distribution of over £14 million in royalties to writers.

The Society is committed to ensuring that the rights of writers, both intellectual property and moral, are fully respected and fairly rewarded. It represents all types

Membership

Authors' Licensing and Collecting Society Ltd
The Writers' House, 13 Haydon Street,
London EC3N 1DB
tel 020-7264 5700 *fax* 020-7264 5755
email alcs@alcs.co.uk
website www.alcs.co.uk
Chief Executive Owen Atkinson

Membership is open to all writers and successors to their estates at a one-off fee of £25 for Ordinary membership. Members of the Society of Authors and the Writers' Guild of Great Britain have free Ordinary membership of ALCS. Operations are primarily funded through a commission levied on distributions and membership fees. The commission on funds generated for Ordinary members is currently 9.5%. Most writers will find that this, together with a number of other membership benefits, provides good value.

of writers and includes educational, research and academic authors drawn from the professions: scriptwriters, adaptors, playwrights, poets, editors and freelance journalists, across the print and broadcast media.

Internationally recognised as a leading authority on copyright matters and authors' interests, ALCS is committed to fostering an awareness of intellectual property issues among the writing community. It maintains a close watching brief on all matters affecting copyright both in the UK and internationally and makes regular representations to the UK government and the European Union.

The Society collects fees that are difficult, time-consuming or legally impossible for writers and their representatives to claim on an individual basis, money that is nonetheless due to them. To date, it has distributed over £157 million in secondary royalties to writers.

Over the years, ALCS has developed highly specialised knowledge and sophisticated systems that can track writers and their works against any secondary use for which they are due payment. A network of international contacts and reciprocal agreements with foreign collecting societies also ensures that British writers are compensated for any similar use overseas.

The primary sources of fees due to writers are secondary royalties from the following:

Photocopying
The single largest source of income, this is administered by the Copyright Licensing Agency (CLA – see page 248). Created in 1982 by ALCS and the Publishers Licensing Society (PLS),

the CLA grants licences to users for the copying of books and serials. This includes schools, colleges, universities, central and local government departments as well as the British Library, businesses and other institutions. Licence fees are based on the number of people who benefit and the number of copies made. The revenue from this is then split between the rightsholders: authors, publishers and artists. Money due to authors is transferred to ALCS for distribution. ALCS also receives photocopying payments from foreign sources.

Digitisation

In 1999, the CLA launched its licensing scheme for the digitisation of printed texts. It offers licences to organisations for storing and using digital versions of authors' printed works, which have been scanned into a computer. Again, the fees are split between authors and publishers.

Foreign Public Lending Right

The Public Lending Right (PLR) system pays authors whose books are borrowed from public libraries. Through reciprocal agreements with VG Wort (the German collecting society), Stichting Leenrecht (the Dutch collecting society) and Literar Mechana (the Austrian collecting society) ALCS members receive payment whenever their books are borrowed from German, Dutch, French and Austrian libraries. (Please note that ALCS does not administer the UK Public Lending Right, this is managed directly by the UK PLR Office; see page 238.)

ALCS also receives other payments from Germany. These cover the loan of academic, scientific and technical titles from academic libraries; extracts of authors' works in textbooks and the press, together with other one-off fees.

Simultaneous cable retransmission

This involves the simultaneous showing of one country's television signals in another country, via a cable network. Cable companies pay a central collecting organisation a percentage of their subscription fees, which must be collectively administered. This sum is then divided by the rightsholders. ALCS receives the writers' share for British programmes containing literary and dramatic material and distributes it to them.

Educational recording

ALCS, together with the main broadcasters and rightsholders, set up the Educational Recording Agency (ERA) in 1989 to offer licences to educational establishments. ERA collects fees from the licensees and pays ALCS the amount due to writers for their literary works.

Other sources of income include a blank tape levy and small, miscellaneous literary rights.

Tracing authors

ALCS is dedicated to protecting and promoting authors' rights and enabling writers to maximise their income. It is committed to ensuring that royalties due to writers are efficiently collected and speedily distributed to them. One of its greatest challenges is finding some of the writers for whom it holds funds and ensuring that they claim their money.

Any published author or broadcast writer could have some funds held by ALCS for them. It may be a nominal sum or it could run in to several thousand pounds. Either call or visit the ALCS website – see box for contact details.

Design and Artists Copyright Society

DACS promotes and protects the copyright and related rights of artists and visual creators.

About DACS

The Design and Artists Copyright Society (DACS) is the UK's not-for-profit copyright licensing and collecting society for artists and visual creators. It represents over 36,000 international fine artists, as well as 16,000 commercial photographers,

Contact details

Design and Artists Copyright Society (DACS)
33 Great Sutton Street, London EC1V 0DX
tel 020-7336 8811 *fax* 020-7336 8822
email info@dacs.org.uk
website www.dacs.org.uk

illustrators, craftspeople, cartoonists, architects, animators and designers.

DACS offers three services for artists and visual creators: Payback, Artist's Resale Right and Copyright Licensing. It makes an administrative charge on the revenue it receives on behalf of artists and visual creators in order to cover operating costs.

Payback

Payback is the annual service provided by DACS which pays artists, photographers, illustrators and many other visual creators (including their heirs and beneficiaries) a share of collective licensing revenue. Collective licensing is used in situations where it would be difficult or impossible for an individual to license their rights, such as photocopying of their work. DACS negotiates a share of this money on behalf of visual artists in the UK.

DACS' Payback service exists for all visual creators and not just those who are members of DACS. Any visual creator whose work has been reproduced in a UK book, magazine or included in a programme broadcast on terrestrial UK television can make a claim for their share of Payback royalties.

Artist's Resale Right

The Artist's Resale Right entitles an artist to a royalty each time their work is resold through an art market professional such as a gallery, dealer or auction house (subject to certain conditions). The right is applicable to all professional resales and can be transferred to heirs for up to 70 years after the artist's death. DACS collects and pays resale royalties 12 times a year at the end of each calendar month.

Copyright licensing

Creators of artistic works can exercise their exclusive rights by granting permission to another person to make copies of their work. Artists can appoint an agent or organisation such as DACS to manage their copyright licensing on their behalf, ensuring it is legally licensed, fairly paid for and its integrity respected. DACS takes away the administrative burden by negotiating fees, terms of reproduction and contractual arrangements.

Licensing clients come from a diverse range of sectors including advertising, publishing, broadcasting, multimedia, product design and merchandising. Members' works have been licensed for everything from greeting cards to film sets, from websites to silk scarves.

Copyright advice

DACS has a number of free copyright fact sheets available for download from its website. Artists and visual creators who join DACS for Artist's Resale Right and Copyright Licensing are also entitled to free telephone copyright advice.

Copyright facts

• Copyright is a right granted to creators under law.

• Copyright in all artistic works is established from the moment of creation – the only qualification is that the work must be original.

• There is no registration system in the UK; copyright comes into operation automatically and lasts the lifetime of the visual creator plus a period of 70 years after their death.

• After death, copyright is usually transferred to the visual creator's heirs or beneficiaries. When the 70-year period has expired, the work then enters the public domain and no longer benefits from copyright protection.

• The copyright owner has the exclusive right to authorise the reproduction (or copy) of a work in any medium by any other party.

• Any reproduction can only take place with the copyright owner's consent.

• Permission is usually granted in return for a fee, which enables the visual creator to derive some income from other people using his or her work.

• If a visual creator is commissioned to produce a work, he or she will usually retain the copyright unless an agreement is signed which specifically assigns the copyright. When visual creators are employees and create work during the course of their employment, the employer retains the copyright in those works.

See also...

• *Copyright questions*, page 245

Magazines and newspapers
Writing for teenage magazines

Teenage magazines can be a lifeline to adolescent girls but writing for this market is very specialised. Michelle Garnett explains what writers for teenage magazines need to know.

Life for teen girls is tough. Raging hormones, changing body bits, annoying boys and constant peer pressure, all gang up to present one huge challenge for them. And that's where teen magazines come to the rescue, providing escapism and reassurance for their confused readers.

But before even thinking about submitting your work to any teen mag, it's vital to get a firm grasp on what they're all about. Most mags tend to fall into two categories – 'Lifestyle' and 'Entertainment':

The Lifestyle titles (think *Bliss* and *Cosmogirl*) provide info on anything relevant to teen girls' lives, from reports on way-out new style trends and self-help features to dish out advice on coping with bullies to tips on bagging a buff boyfriend and gritty real life stories.

The Entertainment titles (think *It's Hot* and *Top of the Tops Magazine*) focus on celeb, music, TV and film gossip with lashings of star interviews, celeb quizzes, posters and song words.

Both categories tend to overlap slightly, with the Lifestyle titles including a juicy dollop of celebrity gossip and interviews and the Entertainment titles enjoying a sprinkling of fashion and self-help advice.

These days, with teens spending piles of their pocket money on mobile phone top-up cards and quick-fix junk food there's heaps of competition amongst the teen mags to be the one title that flies off the shop shelves like a rocket.

There's no excuse – covers *have* to be attention grabbing. Cover lines must offer exclusivity (e.g. a gripping heart-to-heart with the latest Big Brother star), fresh ideas (new revelations about the murky depths of teen boys' minds) and aspirational promises (easy steps to looking fab *whatever* your body shape). Cover images must be non-threatening (girls looking friendly, not bitchy), eye-popping (topless, and most importantly, hairless boy totty is usually a firm favourite) and colourful (you can't beat a flash of fluoro to help you stand out). Most mags also rely on 'free gifts' to help boost their 'come buy me!' appeal.

Teen mag readership

But who are these teen girls that we're trying to persuade to part with their precious pocket money? If you're intending to aim your features at this discerning group of individuals you'd better get to know all you can about them.

On the whole, teen readers are demanding, streetwise, fickle consumers who want to be treated with respect but view adulthood with apprehension, often clinging to the comforts of childhood to help them feel secure and safe when the pressure gets too much.

Here's the scientific bit… Did you know that typical teen readers tend to fall into four *very* revealing categories? First off, there's the 'Obsessive Fan'. This girl has to be the first to know any gossip. She'll usually be infatuated with one boy in particular – often this will be a celeb whose cute face will be plastered all over her bedroom wall, school locker, books, etc. She'll spend every last penny on anything (including mags) that contains a fleeting mention of him. Sometimes her affections will be focused on a 'real' boy – it's been known for Obsessive Fan types to keep a secret stash of her 'crush souvenirs', containing such gems as a dirty fork that he once used in the school canteen!

Next there's the 'Fashionista'. This girl is crazy about fashion. She'll spend hours flicking through the style pages desperate for inspiration for her weekly shopping trips to New Look and Top Shop. The more creative Fashionista will copy the step-by-step customising guides to give her outfits that individualistic edge. She'll be an expert with her make up brush and unsurprisingly, will be very image conscious. She might pretend that she doesn't need to read features on 'detox diets to make your skin glow' but she'll devour them in secret and then pass on her newly acquired tips to her gang.

Then there's the 'Reality Lover'. This girl is addicted to Jeremy Karl and TV soaps. She'll greedily devour tragic real life stories. It doesn't matter whether the tale relates to a famous celeb or an ordinary 15 year-old from Leeds – so long as it's majorly grim, with a positive ending, she'll be hooked. It's no surprise that she's a fan of reality TV shows and dramas and loves gossiping about the latest shocking antics on *I'm a Celebrity… Get Me Out of Here* or *Desperate Housewives*. In fact, it's reading about other people's lives that provides her with some comfort and reassurance about her own life.

Lastly, there's the 'Info Gatherer'. This girl is a true magazine junkie! She uses her mag fix to get high on knowledge that'll help her make sense of the world around her and will elevate her status in her gang. She's not fussy about what she reads, is less street-sussed than other girls in her class and becomes easily bored. She'll often have three different mags on the go at a time but will just as happily plough through her mum's mags too.

But in case you're thinking, 'Hey, I was a teen once – I *know* what they're like' just remember one thing... 21st century teen readers are very different from those even just ten years ago. These days' teens have much less to rebel about. The majority are actually best mates with their mothers and instead of shocking them with new pillar-box red highlights they'll be out shopping with their trendy mums and swapping clothes! They're also worldly wise and surprisingly ambitious about their future prospects.

Oh and don't think you can ever pull the wool over teen readers' eyes – they're sharp and quick to judge and if you get even the smallest fact wrong, they'll pick you up on it!

Considering writing for teen mags

So, now you've considered the kind of reader you'll be speaking to via your feature, it's time to get cracking, yes? No! It may sound mind-numbingly obvious but the first step when considering submitting material to a teen mag is to actually read a copy of that magazine! It's amazing how many times I've received suggestions for short fiction pieces when we don't actually feature those kind of stories in the magazine.

Familiarise yourself with the content, the look and the feel of the magazine. Many mags get revamped quite frequently to keep ahead of the competition, so it's wise to regularly browse through the latest issues to stay up to date.

A quick glance at the mag should tell you which kind of teen it's aimed at and therefore how you should tailor your copy or artwork to the targeted reader. As a writer it's vital to soak up the tone of the copy. Is it streetwise and fast-paced or cheesy and fun? Are there any phrases or words that pop up on a regular basis, giving an insight into the kind of language the average reader uses? Features for the older Lifestyle magazines tend to adopt a punchy, straight-talking approach with, where appropriate, more caring 'big sister' tone when tackling sensitive subjects. A magazine aimed at younger readers, such as *Top of the Pops Magazine*, veers towards a more excitable, upbeat tone, with the tendency to paint the pop world as bright, crazy and inoffensive.

Consider the tone of the actual subject matter too. Is it serious and gritty? Is it frivolous and tongue-in-cheek? Are there clear sections within the magazine which consist of a running theme? *Bliss* magazine features a strong 'real life stories' section which caters for their readers love for a dramatic, juicy read.

Another angle to reflect on is the topicality of the copy and pictures. When contributing ideas to a monthly mag think of a quirky spin you can give your idea to help give what could be a tried and tested subject a fresh makeover. If you're intending to submit ideas to a weekly mag then you need to prove that you've got your finger on the pulse. Think about how you can make your work up to date and relevant. Ask yourself, 'What's affecting teens' lives right *now*?' Are they crumbling under the pressure of exams? Is there a huge blockbuster film on the horizon that's set to capture their imaginations?

When the high school bitch-arama *Mean Girls* was released at the cinemas it was noticeable how several titles were quick to spot the potential popularity of the movie. Some magazines ran style spreads aping the main characters' preppy look plus features on how to get one better on the 'Mean Girls' at your own school. Similarly, by the time the final *Lord of the Rings* instalment hit the big screen, Hollywood star Orlando Bloom had firmly established himself as a teen heartthrob and his appearance in the movie as long-haired lovely Legolas encouraged a stream of Orli-inspired features to whet readers' appetites. Paparazzi and studio shots of the actor were in high demand and real life titbits and Orlando quizzes were a staple diet for several months.

And of course, think seasonal. A few months prior to the summer holidays, monthly teen titles will be dreaming up cover-worthy concepts for the ultimate boredom buster feature. Conjure up a trend-based, original idea and you could find yourself commissioned to produce a hefty eight-page special.

Getting noticed

Finally… how to get yourself noticed amongst a sea of competition from other freelancers. Sometimes it's all about timing. It may be worthwhile to find out if the mag you're hoping to submit work to has a set date each week or month when feature ideas are discussed so that you can ensure your suggestions land in the Features Editor's email box just when he or she is tuned into an ideas brainstorm. Don't go the bother of sending in a fully completed article. If your idea is strong, a catchy headline and brief synopsis will grab their attention and the sheer mention of a juicy real life case study will be enough to get them salivating! And if you have a specialist subject area (style, real life stories, celebrity interviews) it could be worth suggesting a meeting with the relevant team member – if you impress them with your expertise you could bag yourself a regular commission.

But most importantly of all – don't give up. If you don't hear back immediately it doesn't necessarily mean your idea's been discarded. Many teen mag offices are hectic environments in which pressured deadlines often take on a life of their own. Your contact is probably furiously chasing a lead on a reality TV star's love life trauma, while trying to persuade a gang of shy 14 year-old lads to confess their first date hells and batting around that ever niggling question: 'how am I going to make our lovely readers feel entertained, shocked, reassured and hooked by my magazine this issue?' And hopefully that's when *your* life-saving email will come to light!

Good luck!

Michelle Garnett was editor of *Sneak* magazine from April 2002 to May 2005. Previously, she worked for ten years in various roles in the entertainment industry including deputy editor of *Top of the Pops Magazine*, producer of *cd:uk news*, editor of *worldpop.com*, writer of pop band biographies and (her most bizarre job to date…) official news reporter for Reuters on the Backstreet Boys four-day round-the-world promotional trip (2000). She now freelances as a writer and editor for various publications.

See also…
• *Magazines and newspapers for children*, page 259

Magazines and newspapers for children

Listings of magazines about children's literature and education start on page 270.

Adventure Box

Bayard, 1st Floor, 2 King Street,
Peterborough PE1 1LT
tel (01733) 565 858 fax (01733) 427 500
email contact@bayard-magazines.co.uk
website www.bayard-magazines.co.uk
Editor-in-chief Simona Sideri, Art Director Pat Carter
10 p.a. £37 p.a.

Aimed at 7–9 year-old children starting to read on
their own. Each issue contains an illustrated chapter
story plus games, an animal feature, nature activity
and a cartoon. Length: 2500–3000 words (stories).
Specially commissions most material. Founded 1996.

Amy

BBC Worldwide Ltd, Room C100, Woodlands,
80 Wood Lane, London W12 0TT
tel 020-8433 1291
website www.bbcmagazines.com/amy
Editor Bea Appleby
Every 3 weeks £1.99

The little sister title to *Girl Talk*. Lifestyle magazine
for 5–8 year-old girls featuring CBBC characters such
as Tracey Beaker and programmes such as *Blue Peter*
and the *Really Wild Show*. Also includes film, arts and
crafts, stories, puzzles and quizzes. Founded 2006.

Animal Action

RSPCA, Wilberforce Way, Southwater, Horsham,
West Sussex RH13 9RS
tel (0300) 123 0100
website www.rspca.org.uk
Editor Ann Grain
Bi-monthly £1.99, £10 p.a.

RSPCA membership magazine for children under
13 years old with animal news, features, competitions
and puzzles.

Animals and You

D.C. Thomson & Co Ltd, Albert Square,
Dundee DD1 9QJ
tel (01382) 223131 fax (01382) 322214
email animalsandyou@dcthomson.co.uk
185 Fleet Street, London EC4A 2HS
tel 020-7400 1030 fax 020-7400 1089
Every 3 weeks £1.90

Features, stories and pin-ups for girls who love
animals. Founded 1998.

Aquila

New Leaf Publishing Ltd, PO Box 2518, Eastbourne,
East Sussex BN21 2BB

tel (01323) 431313 fax (01323) 731136
email info@aquila.co.uk
website www.aquila.co.uk
Editor Jackie Berry
Monthly £38 p.a.

Dedicated to encouraging children aged 8–13 to
reason and create, and to develop a caring nature.
Short stories and serials of up to 4 parts. Occasional
features commissioned from writers with specialist
knowledge. Approach in writing with ideas and
sample of writing style, with sae. Length: 700–800
words (features), 1000–1100 words (stories or per
episode of a serial). Payment: £75 (features); £90
(stories), £80 (per episode). Founded 1993.

Art Attack

Panini UK, Brockbourne House, Mount Ephraim,
Tunbridge Wells TN4 8BS
tel (01892) 500100 fax (01892) 545666
email paninicomics@panini.co.uk
website www.paninicomics.co.uk
Editor Simon Frith
Monthly £2.25

Magazine to complement the TV show *Art Attack*.
Step-by-step instructions on creative things to make
and do.

Astonishing Spider-Man

Panini UK, Brockbourne House, Mount Ephraim,
Tunbridge Wells TN4 8BS
tel (01892) 500100 fax (01892) 545666
email paninicomics@panini.co.uk
website www.paninicomics.co.uk
Editor Brady Webb
Every 4 weeks £2.50

The Avengers United

Panini UK, Brockbourne House, Mount Ephraim,
Tunbridge Wells TN4 8BS
tel (01892) 500100 fax (01892) 545666
email paninicomics@panini.co.uk
website www.paninicomics.co.uk
Editor Scott Gray
Every 4 weeks £2.50

Balamory Magazine

BBC Worldwide Ltd, BBC Woodlands,
80 Wood Lane, London W12 0TT
tel 020-8433 2000
website www.bbcmagazines.com/balamory
Editor Siobhan Keeler

Every 4 weeks £1.99

Based on the TV programme *Balamory*, each issue follows an exciting story through Balamory, with colouring, drawing, puzzles and games. *BBC Balamory Magazine* is featured in *Toybox Teach Me* magazine, along with lots of other CBeebies characters.

Barbie

Egmont Magazines, 239 Kensington High Street, London W3 6SA
tel 020-7761 3500 *fax* 020-7761 3510
website www.egmontmagazines.co.uk
Editor Rebecca Jamieson
Every 2 weeks £1.80

Magazine for 3–8 year-old girls. Provides the reader with news from the ever-changing world of Barbie from pretty princess to cool chic, with a constant focus on aspects of fashion, friends and fun.

Batman: Legends

Titan Publishing Group Ltd, Titan House, 144 Southwark Street, London SE1 0UP
tel 020-7620 0200 *fax* 020-7620 0032
website www.titanmagazines.co.uk
Editor Ned Hartley
Every 4 weeks £2.60

The Beano

D.C. Thomson & Co. Ltd, Albert Square, Dundee DD1 9QJ
tel (01382) 223131 *fax* (01382) 322214
185 Fleet Street, London EC4A 2HS
tel 020-7400 1030 *fax* 020-7400 1089
Editor Alan Digby
Weekly 99p

Comic strips for children aged 6–12. Series, 11–22 pictures. Artwork only. Payment: on acceptance.

Blast Off!

RNIB, PO Box 173, Peterborough PE2 6WS
tel (01733) 375000 *fax* (01733) 375001
email editorial@rnib.org.uk
website www.rnib.org.uk
Editor Racheal Jarvis
Monthly 22p (£1.43 overseas)

Braille general interest magazine for blind and partially sighted children aged 7–11. Also available on disk.

Bliss

Panini House, Coach and Horses Passage, The Pantiles, Tunbridge Wells, Kent TN2 5OT
tel (01892) 500106 *fax* (01892) 545666
email bliss@panini.co.uk
website www.blissmag.co.uk
Editor Leslie Sinoway
Monthly £2.30

Glamorous young women's glossy magazine. Bright, intimate, American A5 format, with real life reports, celebrities, beauty, fashion, shopping, advice, quizzes. Payment: by arrangement. Founded 1995.

Bob the Builder

BBC Worldwide Ltd, BBC Woodlands, 80 Wood Lane, London W12 0TT
tel 020-8433 2000 *fax* 020-8433 2941
website www.bbcmagazines.com/bobbuilder
Editor Siobhan Keeler
Every 3 weeks £1.85

Stories, puzzles, competitions and activities built around Bob and his team for children aged 4–6 and their parents.

Braille at Bedtime

RNIB, PO Box 173, Peterborough PE2 6WS
tel (01733) 375000 *fax* (01733) 375001
email editorial@rnib.org.uk
website www.rnib.org.uk
Editor Racheal Jarvis
Every 2 months 69p (£3.34 overseas)

Braille short fiction magazine for blind and partially sighted children aged 7–11.

Bratz

D.C. Thomson, Albert Square, Dundee DD1 9QJ
tel (01382) 223131 *fax* (01382) 322214
email bratzmag@dcthomson.co.uk
website www.dcthomson.co.uk
Editor Gillian Henny
Every 4 weeks £2.50

Bratz lifestyle magazine, covering hair, make-up, celebrity interviews, gossip and competition.

CBeebies Weekly Magazine

BBC Worldwide Ltd, Woodlands, 80 Wood Lane, London W12 0TT
tel 020-8433 2000
email cbeebiesweekly@bbc.co.uk
website www.cbeebiesmagazine.com
Editor Paddy Kempshall
Weekly £1.99

Magazine to 'enhance a child's experience of the CBeebies programming week'. Aims to encourage family interaction and promote the philosophy of learning through play. Includes a 'child-friendly' TV guide. Founded 2006.

Charlie and Lola

BBC Worldwide Ltd, Woodlands, 80 Wood Lane, London W12 0TT
tel 020-8433 2356
email charlieandlolamagazine@bbc.co.uk
website www.bbcmagazines.com
4-weekly £2.50

Interactive arts and crafts magazine for preschool children.

Commando

D.C. Thomson & Co. Ltd, Albert Square, Dundee DD1 9QJ

tel (01382) 223131 *fax* (01382) 322214
8 per month £1.25

Fictional war stories told in pictures. Scripts: about 135 pictures. Synopsis required as an opener. New writers encouraged; send for details. Payment: on acceptance.

Daisy

Egmont Magazines, 239 Kensington High Street, London W3 6SA
tel 020-7761 3500 *fax* 020-7761 3510
website www.egmontmagazines.co.uk
Every 4 weeks £1.85

Aimed at 4–7 year-old girls who like anything pretty or cute! A mix of favourite characters and animals, posters, and puzzles and activities. Founded 2005.

The Dandy

D.C. Thomson & Co. Ltd, Albert Square, Dundee DD1 9QJ
tel (01382) 223131 *fax* (01382) 322214
185 Fleet Street, London EC4A 2HS
tel 020-7400 1030 *fax* 020-7400 1089
Fortnightly £1.99

Comic strips and features for boys aged 7–10 years. Picture stories with 7–10 pictures per page, 1–4pp per story. Promising artists are encouraged. Payment: on acceptance.

Discovery Box

Bayard, 1st Floor, 2 King Street, Peterborough PE1 1LT
tel (01733) 565858 *fax* (01733) 427500
email contact@bayard-magazines.co.uk
website www.bayard-magazines.co.uk
Editor Simona Sideri
10 p.a. £37 p.a.

Photographs and short texts to introduce children aged 8–12 to animals and their habitats. Includes historical events retold as picture stories and a range of topics and experiments to develop children's scientific knowledge; also photographs showing the variety of lifestyles around the world. Plus games, fun facts, short story, recipe, quizz, cartoon. Specially commissions most material. Founded 1996.

Disney & Me

Egmont Magazines UK, 239 Kensington High Street, London W3 6SA
tel 020-7761 3500 *fax* 020-7761 3510
website www.egmontmagazines.co.uk
Fortnightly £1.99

Entertaining and fun reading source for 3–6 year-olds with authentic illustrations based on original Disney animation. Includes stories, games, puzzles, posters, colouring pages and reader's letters.

Disney Fairies

Egmont Magazines UK, 239 Kensington High Street, London W3 6SA

tel 020-7761 3500 *fax* 020-7761 3510
website www.egmontmagazines.co.uk
Monthly £1.99

Aimed at 5–7 year-old girls. Published under the Disney franchise spawned from the novels *Fairy Dust* and *The Quest for the Egg* by Gail Carson Levine. Founded 2006.

Disney's Princess

Egmont Magazines UK, 239 Kensington High Street, London W3 6SA
tel 020-7761 3500 *fax* 020-7761 3510
website www.egmontmagazines.co.uk
Every 2 weeks £1.80

Magazine for 4–7 year-old girls to enter the magical world of Disney heroines through stories, crafts and activities. Founded 1998.

DK FindOut!

Titan Magazines, Titan House, 144 Southwark Street, London SE1 0UP
tel 020-7620 0200 *fax* 020-7803 1803
website www.titanmagazines.co.uk
Editor Michelle Lee
Monthly £2.99

Information magazine covering geography and the natural world, art, history and science.

Doctor Who Adventures

BBC Worldwide Ltd, Woodlands, 80 Wood Lane, London W12 0TT
tel 020-8433 3386
email dwa@bbc.co.uk
Editor Moray Laing
Weekly £2.10

Magazine for 6–12 year-old fans of *Doctor Who*. Readers are immersed into the world of the Doctor, taking them on an adventure into time and space, with monsters and creatures, excitement, action, adventure and humour. Founded 2006.

Doctor Who Magazine

Panini UK, Brockbourne House, Mount Ephraim, Tunbridge Wells TN4 8BS
tel (01892) 500100 *fax* (01892) 545666
email paninicomics@panini.co.uk
website www.paninicomics.co.uk
Editor Tom Spilsbury
Every 4 weeks £3.99

Dora the Explorer

Egmont Magazines UK, 239 Kensington High Street, London W8 6SA
tel 020-7761 3500 *fax* 020-7761 3510
Editor Rebecca Jamieson
Monthly £1.75

Magazine for preschool children based on the Dora the Explorer character. Content includes puzzles, stories, posters and basic educational elements. Payment: by arrangement.

Essential X-Men

Panini UK, Brockbourne House, Mount Ephraim,
Tunbridge Wells TN4 8BS
tel (01892) 500100 *fax* (01892) 545666
email paninicomics@panini.co.uk
website www.paninicomics.co.uk
Editor Scott Gray
Every 4 weeks £2.50

Fifi and the Flower Tots

BBC Worldwide Ltd, Woodlands, 80 Wood Lane,
London W12 0TT
tel 020-8433 2000 *fax* 020-8749 0538
website www.bbcmagazines.com/fifiandtheflowertots
Editor Siobhan Keeler
Every 4 weeks £1.99

Magazine aimed at 3–5 year-old children and based
on the *Fifi and the Flowertots* TV programme. It
mirrors the values of fun, friendship and creativity
with activities and stories. Parent's notes are included
to encourage joint participation and added
enjoyment to the magazine. Founded 2006.

Fimbles

BBC Worldwide Ltd, Room A1130,
BBC Woodlands, 80 Wood Lane, London W12 0TT
tel 020-8433 2000 *fax* 020-8749 0538
website www.bbcmagazines.com/fimbles
Editor Stephanie Cooper
Monthly £1.99

Magazine aimed at 2–4 year-olds. The *Fimbles* are
always trying to find out new things and the magic of
discovery accompanies everything they do.

First News

First News House, 95 The Street, Horsley,
Surrey KT24 6DD
email newsdesk@firstnews.co.uk
website www.firstnews.co.uk
Editor Nicky Cox, *Editorial Director* Piers Morgan
Weekly Fri £1.10

An inspiring, educational and entertaining national
newspaper and website for 8–14 year-olds with news,
sport, showbiz, interviews and one in depth feature.
Among its aims, it aspires to raise the profile of
children's views and opinions in society. Launched
May 2006.

Fun to Learn Bag-o-Fun

Redan Publishing Ltd, Suite 2, Prospect House,
Belle Vue Road, Shrewsbury, Shropshire SY3 7NR
tel (01743) 364 433 *fax* (01743) 271 528
email info@redan.com
website www.redan.com
8 a year £3.85

Magazine for preschool children and their parents to
encourage early educational activities. Compiled of
popular characters including Mr Men, Brum, Spot,
Blues Clues and Oswald to help bring to life stories

and activities whilst developing basic educational
skills.

Fun to Learn Barney

Redan Publishing Ltd, Suite 2, Prospect House,
Belle Vue Road, Shrewsbury, Shropshire SY3 7NR
tel (01743) 364 433 *fax* (01743) 271 528
email info@redan.com
website www.redan.com
Every 4 weeks £1.99

An interactive magazine for girls and boys aged 3–7
with stories, activities and puzzles based on the
loveable purple dinosaur, Barney. It supports the
National Curriculum's Early Learning Goals and also
covers Barney's 5 pillars of sharing, caring, imagining,
dancing and learning.

Fun to Learn Discovery

Redan Publishing Ltd, Suite 2, Prospect House,
Belle Vue Road, Shrewsbury, Shropshire SY3 7NR
tel (01743) 364 433 *fax* (01743) 271 528
email info@redan.com
website www.redan.com
Twice yearly £1.99

A magazine covering the National Curriculum's Early
Learning Goals. It has a different theme every issue,
providing preschool children with stories and
activities on themes such as Lions & Tigers,
Dinosaurs, Cars & Lorries, Space, Witches & Wizards
and Father Christmas.

Fun to Learn Favourites

Redan Publishing Ltd, Suite 2, Prospect House,
Belle Vue Road, Shrewsbury, Shropshire SY3 7NR
tel (01743) 364 433 *fax* (01743) 271 528
email info@redan.com
website www.redan.com
Every 2 weeks £1.99

A magazine for preschool children compiled of
stories and activities using popular children's TV
characters including Dora the Explorer, Mr Men,
Sponge-Bob and Rupert. It includes a 24pp pull-out
workbook based on one of these characters for parent
and child inter-activity, with activities including
counting, matching, puzzles and colouring.

Fun to Learn Friends

Redan Publishing Ltd, Suite 2, Prospect House,
Belle Vue Road, Shrewsbury, Shropshire SY3 7NR
tel (01743) 364 433 *fax* (01743) 271 528
email info@redan.com
website www.redan.com
Every 2 weeks £1.99

Magazine for preschool children and their parents to
encourage early educational activities. Compiled of
stories and activities using popular children's TV
characters including Barney, Clifford's Puppy Days,
Dora the Explorer and Peppa Pig. Includes a 24-page
pull-out workbook based on one of these popular

characters for parent and child inter-activity, with activities including counting, matching, puzzles and colouring. The content supports the National Curriculum's Early Learning Goals.

Fun to Learn Letterland
Redan Publishing Ltd, Suite 2, Prospect House, Belle Vue Road, Shrewsbury, Shropshire SY3 7NR
tel (01743) 364 433 *fax* (01743) 271 528
email info@redan.com
website www.redan.com
Every 4 weeks £1.99

A magazine designed to complement the Letterland early reading skills scheme. It contains stories and activities to entertain and educate children using its story-based phonics system and characters designed to make learning fun.

Fun to Learn Peppa Pig
Redan Publishing Ltd, Suite 2, Prospect House, Belle Vue Road, Shrewsbury, Shropshire SY3 7NR
tel (01743) 364433 *fax* (01743) 271528
website www.redan.com
Editor Anita Cash
Every 3 weeks £1.99

Interactive magazine for girls and boys aged 3–7 with stories, activities and puzzles based on the TV show, *Peppa Pig*. Supports the National Curriculum's Early Learning Goals and includes a pull-out workbook, 4pp cut-out activities and stickers.

Futurama (UK)
Titan Publishing Group Ltd, Titan House, 144 Southwark Street, London SE1 0UP
tel 020-7620 0200 *fax* 020-7803 1803
website www.titanmagazines.com
Editor Andrew James
Monthly £2.50

Girl Talk
BBC Worldwide, Room A1130, Woodlands, 80 Wood Lane, London W12 0TT
tel 020-8433 1010 *fax* 020-8433 2941
email girltalk.magazine@bbc.co.uk
website www.bbcmagazines.com/girltalk
Editor Samantha Robinson
Fortnightly £1.75

Magazine for children aged 7–12 years old. Contains pop, TV and film celebrity features, personality features, quizzes, fashion, competitions, stories. Length: 500 words (fiction). Payment: £75. All material is specially commissioned. Founded 1997.

Go Girl Magazine
Egmont Magazines, 239 Kensington High Street, London W8 6SA
tel 020-7761 3500
website www.gogirlmag.co.uk
Editor Emma Prosser

Every 3 weeks £1.95

Magazine for 7–11-year-old girls including fashion, beauty, celebrity news and gossip. Payment: by arrangement. Founded 2003.

Goodie Bag Mag
D.C. Thomson & Co Ltd, Albert Square, Dundee DD1 9QJ
tel (01382) 223131 *fax* (01382) 225511
185 Fleet Street, London EC4A 2HS
tel 020-7400 1030 *fax* 020-7400 1089
Monthly (Thurs) £2.99

Features, fashion, puzzles pin-ups, stories, quizzes, competitions. Founded 2003.

Guiding magazine
17–19 Buckingham Palace Road, London SW1W 0PT
tel 020-7834 6242 *fax* 020-7828 5791
website www.girlguiding.org.uk
Editor Wendy Kewley
Monthly £2

Official magazine of Girlguiding UK. Articles of interest to women of all ages, with special emphasis on youth work and the Guide Movement. Articles on simple crafts, games and the outdoors especially welcome. Length: up to 600 words. Illustrations: line, half-tone, colour. Payment: £300 per 1000 words. Please contact editor with proposal first.

Headliners
Exmouth House, 3–11 Pine Street, London EC1R 0JH
tel 020-7833 2577 *fax* 020-7278 7722
email enquiries@headliners.org
website www.headliners.org
Director Fiona Wyton

An award-winning news agency charity (does not publish a magazine or newspaper) that offers young people aged 8–18 the opportunity to write on issues of importance to them, for newspapers, radio and TV. Founded 1995.

Horse & Pony Magazine
33 Broad Street, Stamford, Lincs. PE9 1RB
tel (01780) 754900
website www.horseandpony.com
Editor Sarah Whittington
Monthly £2.30

Equestrian magazine for girls aged 8–14 containing riding and horse-care know-how, games and competitions, top rider info and posters.

Junior Puzzles
Puzzler Media Ltd, Stonecroft, 69 Station Road, Redhill, Surrey RH1 1EY
tel (01737) 378700 *fax* (01737) 781800
email enquiries@puzzlermedia.com
website www.puzzler.co.uk
Editor Mike Murphy

6 p.a. £2.40

Entertainment for 7–12 year-old children with a variety of puzzles, e.g. spot the difference, wordsearch, kriss kross, dot to dot, crosswords, mazes.

Kids Alive! (The Young Soldier)

The Salvation Army, 101 Newington Causeway, London SE1 6BN
tel 020-7367 4911 *fax* 020-7367 4710
email kidsalive@salvationarmy.org.uk
website www.salvationarmy.org.uk/kidsalive
Editor Justin Reeves
Weekly 50p (£25 p.a. including free membership of the Kids Alive! Club)

Children's magazine: pictures, scripts and artwork for cartoon strips, puzzles, etc; Christian-based with emphasis on education re addictive substances. Payment: by arrangement. Illustrations: half-tone, line and 4-colour line, cartoons. Founded 1881.

KISS

Minjara, 2–4 Ely Place, Dublin 2, Republic of Ireland
tel (01) 480 4700 *fax* (01) 661 4629
website www.kiss.ie
Editor Susan Vasquez
Monthly €2.80

Articles on fashion and beauty, celebrities, entertainment, fashion and relationships for 13–18 year-old girls. Ireland's only teen magazine.

Learning is Fun!

BBC Worldwide Ltd, BBC Woodlands, 80 Wood Lane, London W12 0TT
tel 020-8433 2000 *fax* 020-8749 0538
website www.bbcworldwide.com
Deputy Editor Emma Goldhawk
Every 4 weeks £2.10

Educational magazine which aims to support children as they progress through KS1 of the National Curriculum, Literacy and Numeracy strategies. Each school subject is depicted in an exciting, fun and stimulating way with colourful illustrations, photographs of children and pictures. It includes a regular feature, written by the Education Editor, which tackles parent/school/child issues.

The Max

RNIB, PO Box 173, Peterborough PE2 6W7
tel (01733) 375000 *fax* (01733) 375001
email editorial@rnib.org.uk
website www.rnib.org.uk
Editor Racheal Jarvis
Monthly 40p (monthly £2.60 overseas)

Braille magazine for blind and partially sighted men aged 16–19. Also available in disk and email formats. Includes features on the music scene, sport, interviews with personalities and a problem page. Will consider unsolicited material but most material

has previously appeared in mainstream print magazines.

Mighty World of Marvel

Panini UK, Brockbourne House, Mount Ephraim, Tunbridge Wells TN4 8BS
tel (01892) 500100 *fax* (01892) 545666
email paninicomics@panini.co.uk
website www.paninicomics.co.uk
Editor Scott Gray
Every 4 weeks £2.50

Missy

RNIB, PO Box 173, Peterborough PE2 6WS
tel (01733) 375000 *fax* (01733) 375001
email editorial@rnib.org.uk
website www.rnib.org.uk
Editor Chris James
Monthly 40p (£2.78 export)

Braille general interest magazine for blind and partially sighted girls aged 12–15. Also available on disk.

Mizz

Panini UK, Brockbourne House, Mount Ephraim, Tunbridge Wells TN4 8BS
tel (01892) 500100 *fax* (01892) 545666
email mizz@panini.co.uk
website www.mizz.com
Editor Karen O'Brien
Fortnightly £1.95

Articles on any subject of interest to girls aged 10–14. Approach in writing. Payment: by arrangement. Illustrated. Founded 1985.

My Little Pony

Redan Publishing Ltd, Suite 2, Prospect House, Belle Vue Road, Shrewsbury, Shropshire SY3 7NR
tel (01743) 364433 *fax* (01743) 271528
website www.redan.com
Editor Jen Barker
Every 4 weeks £2.35

Magazine aimed at girls aged 4–9 containing stories, stickers, activities and puzzles, all based around the My Little Ponies and their friends.

The Newspaper

Young Media Holdings Ltd, PO Box 400, Bridgwater TA6 9DT
tel 0845-094 0646
email editor@thenewspaper.org.uk
website www.thenewspaper.org.uk
Editors Buffy Whiting, Tracey Comber
6 p.a. Subscription only

Newspaper aimed at 8–14-year-old schoolchildren for use as part of the National Curriculum. Contains similar columns as in any national daily newspaper. Not currently looking for new writers/articles. Founded 1999.

Noddy

Egmont Magazines, 239 Kensington High Street,
London W3 6SA
tel 020-7761 3500 *fax* 020-7761 3510
website www.egmontmagazines.co.uk
Editor Rebecca Jamieson
Monthly £1.85

Preschool magazine. Noddy and his friends introduce
children to the basic skills they need before they start
school via a variety of stories, activities, colouring,
rhymes and games. Founded 1992; relaunched 2006.

Play & Learn Thomas & Friends

Egmont Magazines, 239 Kensington High Street,
London W3 6SA
tel 020-7761 3500 *fax* 020-7761 3510
website www.egmontmagazines.co.uk
Fortnightly £1.99

Magazine for 3–6 year-old children with activities
and stories involving Thomas characters. A
companion to KS1 programmes of study.

Pokemon World

Highbury Entertainment Ltd, Paragon House,
St Peter's Road, Bournemouth BH1 2JS
tel (01202) 299900
email nickr@paragon.co.uk
website www.paragon.co.uk/mags/pokemon.html
Managing Editor Nick Roberts
Monthly £3.99

Magazine devoted to Pokémon. It covers every aspect
of the phenomenon, from games and movies through
to merchandise and trading cards.

Pony Magazine

Headley House, Headley Road, Grayshott,
Surrey GU26 6TU
tel (01428) 601020 *fax* (01428) 601030
Editor Janet Rising
13 issues p.a. £2.60

Lively articles and short stories with a horsy theme
aimed at readers aged 8–16. Technical accuracy and
young, fresh writing essential. Length: up to 800
words. Payment: by arrangement. Illustrations:
drawings (commissioned), photos, cartoons.
Founded 1949.

Postman Pat

Panini UK, Brockbourne House, Mount Ephraim,
Tunbridge Wells TN4 8BS
tel (01892) 500100 *fax* (01892) 545666
email paninicomics@panini.co.uk
website www.paninicomics.co.uk
Editor Toby Orton
Every 3 weeks £1.85

Power Rangers

Egmont Magazines, 239 Kensington High Street,
London W3 6SA

tel 020-7761 3500 *fax* 020-7761 3510
website www.egmontmagazines.co.uk
Monthly £1.95

Energetic magazine for *Power Rangers* fans, aimed at
3–7 year-old boys. Features puzzles, stories, games,
posters and colouring of the characters.

Pure

RNIB, PO Box 173, Peterborough PE2 6WS
tel (01733) 375336 *fax* (01733) 375001
email editorial@rnib.org.uk
website www.rnib.org.uk
Editor Chris James
Monthly 40p (£2.60 export)

Braille magazine for blind and partially sighted girls
aged 16–19. Also available in disk and email formats.
Includes real life stories, celebrity interviews and
beauty features. Will consider unsolicited material
but most material has previously appeared in
mainstream print magazines.

Puzzler Quiz Kids

Puzzler Media Ltd, Stonecroft, 69 Station Road,
Redhill, Surrey RH1 1EY
tel (01737) 378700 *fax* (01737) 781800
email reception@puzzlermedia.com
website www.puzzler.co.uk
Editor Jackie Guthrie
6 p.a. £2.40

Puzzles and quizzes for 7–11 year-old children to
help build reading, writing and mathematical skills.

Royal National Institute of the Blind

PO Box 173, Peterborough, Cambs. PE2 6WS
tel (0845) 7023153 *fax* (01733) 375001
textphone (0845) 7585691
helpline (0845) 7669999
email cservices@rnib.org.uk
website www.rnib.org.uk

Published by the Royal National Institute of the
Blind, the following titles are available via email and
in braille, unless otherwise stated. *3FM*, *Access IT*,
Aphra, *Big Print newspaper* (large print only), *Blast
Off!* (children's magazine), *Braille at Bedtime* (7–11
year-olds; braille), *Broadcast Times* (email and disk),
Channels of Blessing (disk and braille), *Chess
Magazine* (braille), *Compute IT*, *Contention*,
Conundrum (disk and braille), *Cricket Fixtures*, *Daily
Bread* (disk and braille), *Daisy TV Listings* (Daisy
format), *Football Fixtures* (email, Daisy and braille),
Good Vibrations, *Insight* (clear print, audio CD,
braille, email), *The Max* (boys aged 16–19), *Missy*
(girls aged 12–15), *Money Matters*, *Music Magazine*
(disk and braille), *NB* (print, email, Daisy, audio CD,
braille), *New Literature on Sight Problems* (print and
email), *New Product Guide* (braille, email, Daisy),
Journal of Physiotherapy, *Physiotherapy* (disk, cassette
tape, braille), *Physiotherapy Frontline* (cassette tape),
Piano Tuners' Quarterly (email, tape, braille),

Progress, Proms Guide, Pure (girls aged 16–19), *Radio Guide, Ready, Steady, Read* (for new readers of braille in braille only), *Rhetoric, Scientific Enquiry* (disk and braille), *Shaping Up, Shop Window, Shop Window Christmas Guide, Short Stories, SP, Television Guide, Theological Times* (disk, cassette tape, braille), *Upbeat, Vibe* (boys aged 12–15), *You & Your Child, Vision* (clear print, email, braille, Daisy format).

Scooby-Doo
Panini UK, Brockbourne House, Mount Ephraim, Tunbridge Wells TN4 8BS
tel (01892) 500100 *fax* (01892) 545666
email paninicomics@panini.co.uk
website www.paninicomics.co.uk
Editor Kate Rhead
Monthly £1.99

Shout
D.C. Thomson & Co. Ltd, Albert Square, Dundee DD1 9QJ
tel (01382) 223131 *fax* (01382) 200880
email shout@dcthomson.co.uk
185 Fleet Street, London EC4A 2HS
tel 020-7400 1030 *fax* 020-7400 1089
Editor Maria Welch
Fortnightly £2.20

Colour gravure magazine for 11–14 year-old girls. Pop, film and 'soap' features and pin-ups; general features of teen interest; emotional features, fashion and beauty advice. Payment: on acceptance. Founded 1993.

Simpsons Comics
Titan Publishing Group Ltd, Titan House, 144 Southwark Street, London SE1 0UP
tel 020-7620 0200 *fax* 020-7803 1803
website simpsonsmail@titanemail.com
website www.titanmagazines.com
Editor Rona Simpson
Monthly £2.99

Reprints the US *Simpsons Comics* material with localised letters page and some other features.

Simpsons Comics Presents
Titan Publishing Group Ltd, Titan House, 144 Southwark Street, London SE1 0UP
tel 020-7620 0200 *fax* 020-7803 1803
email simpsonsmail@titanemail.com
website www.titanmagazines.com
Editor Rona Simpson
Monthly £2.99

Sparkle World
Redan Publishing Ltd, Canon Court East, Abbey Lawn, Shrewsbury SY2 5DE
tel (01743) 364 433 *fax* (01743) 271 528
email info@redan.com
website www.redan.com
Every 3 weeks £2.45

Magazine aimed at 4–9 year-old girls with stories and activities based on a dazzling selection of the most popular licensed characters, including Rainbow Magic, Littlest Petshop, Polly Pocket, Strawberry Shortcake, My Little Pony and Angelina Ballerina. A fun and educational magazine for young girls who love everything that glitters.

Spectacular Spider-Man
Panini UK, Brockbourne House, Mount Ephraim, Tunbridge Wells TN4 8BS
tel (01892) 500100 *fax* (01892) 545666
email paninicomics@panini.co.uk
website www.paninicomics.co.uk
Editor Ed Hammonds
Monthly £1.99

SpongeBob SquarePants
Titan Magazines, Titan House, 144 Southwark Street, London SE1 0UP
tel 020-7620 0200 *fax* 020-7803 1803
email spongebob@titanemail.com
website www.titanmagazines.co.uk
Editor Rona Simpson
Monthly £2.60

Star Trek Magazine
Titan Magazines, Titan House, 144 Southwark Street, London SE1 0UP
tel 020-7620 0200 *fax* 020-7803 1803
Editor Paul Simpson
6 p.a. £4.99

Up-to-date news about every aspect of *Star Trek*, including all TV series and films, cast interviews, behind-the-scenes features and product reviews. Payment: by arrangement. Founded 1995.

Star Wars Comic
Titan Publishing Group Ltd, Titan House, 144 Southwark Street, London SE1 0UP
tel 020-7620 0200 *fax* 020-7803 1803
email swcomicmail@titanemail.com
website www.titanmagazines.com
Editor Andrew James
Monthly £2.60

Features reprints of the *Dark Horse Star Wars* comics.

Star Wars Insider Magazine
Titan Publishing Group Ltd, Titan House, 144 Southwark Street, London SE1 0UP
tel 020-7620 0200 *fax* 020-7803 1803
email starwarsmail@titanemail.com
website www.titanmagazines.com
Editor Brian J. Robb
Bi-monthly £4.99

Interviews, features, pin-ups and merchandise round-ups.

Storybox
Bayard, 1st Floor, 2 King Street, Peterborough PE1 1LT

tel (01733) 565858 *fax* (01733) 4275000
email contact@bayard-magazines.co.uk
website www.bayard-magazines.co.uk
Editor-in-chief Simona Sideri
10 p.a. £37 p.a.

Aimed at 3–6 year-old children. A range of stories with rhyme and evocative pictures to stimulate children's imagination and introduce them to the delights of reading. Each issue presents a new, full-colour, 24-page story created by teams of internationally acclaimed writers and illustrators for laptime reading. A non-fiction section linked to a theme in the story follows, together with pages of games and craft ideas. Includes games, an animal feature, science and a cartoon. Founded 1996.

Submission details Length: 500–1000 words (stories). Requirements: rhyme, repetition, interesting language. Specially commissions most material. Payment: by arrangement.

Sugar
Hachette Filipacchi, 64 North Row,
London W1K 7LL
tel 020-7150 7000 *fax* 020-7150 7001
Editor Annabel Brog
Monthly £2.30

Magazine for young women aged 13–19. Fashion, beauty, entertainment, features. Send synopsis first. Will consider unsolicited material. Interested in real-life stories (1200 words), quizzes. Payment: negotiable. Founded 1994.

tBkmag
4 Froxfield Close, Winchester SO22 6JW
tel (01962) 620320
email guy@newbooksmag.com
website www.newbooksmag.com
Editor Helen Boyle, *Send material to* Guy Pringle, Publisher
Quarterly £1.99

Extracts and activities from the best new books for 8–12 year-olds. Specially commissions all material. Email for a free introductory copy. Founded 2001.

Teletubbies
BBC Worldwide Ltd, BBC Woodlands,
80 Wood Lane, London W12 0TT
tel 020-8433 1291 *fax* 020-8749 0538
website www.bbcmagazines.co.uk/teletubbies
Editor Sarah O'Neill
Monthly £1.99

Magazine for very young children (18 months+) who love the *Teletubbies*. The activities included are designed to build children's confidence, creativity and imagination and are clear, colourful and entertaining. Founded 1997.

Thomas & Friends
Egmont Magazines, 239 Kensington High Street,
London W8 6SA

tel 020-7761 3500 *fax* 020-7761 3510
website www.egmontmagazines.co.uk
Fortnightly £1.85

Magazine for 3–6 year-old children designed to encourage early reading skills and all-round child development using stories and activities involving Thomas and all his friends. Each issue contains posters, colouring pages, competitions and readers' letters and drawings as regular features.

Thomas & Friends: Thomas Express Special
Egmont Magazines, 239 Kensington High Street,
London W8 6SA
tel 020-7761 3500 *fax* 020-7761 3510
website www.egmontmagazines.co.uk
Every 4 weeks £2.25

Magazine for children aged 3–6 years. Collection of classic stories and rhymes.

Tom and Jerry
Panini UK, Brockbourne House, Mount Ephraim,
Tunbridge Wells TN4 8BS
tel (01892) 500100 *fax* (01892) 545666
email paninicomics@panini.co.uk
website www.paninicomics.co.uk
Editor Jason Quinn
Every 4 weeks £1.99

Top of the Pops
BBC Worldwide Ltd, Room A1136,
BBC Woodlands, 80 Wood Lane, London W12 0TT
tel 020-8433 3910 *fax* 020-8749 2763
website www.bbcworldwide.com/magazines
Editor Peter Hart
Monthly £2.25

'The celebrity gossip bible for teenagers.' Primarily aimed at teenage girls (ages 10–13), the magazine strives to provide all the celebrity knowledge teenagers could want. It aims to make the reader feel part of an exclusive club, to transport them behind the scenes so they get a real sense of what really goes on in the world of the stars. Founded 1995.

Toxic Magazine
Egmont Magazines UK, 239 Kensington High Street,
London W8 6SA
tel 020-7761 3500
website www.toxicmag.co.uk
Editor Matt Yeo
Fortnightly £2.25

Topical lifestyle magazine for 8–12 year-old boys. Includes competitions, pull-out posters, reviews and jokes. Covers boys' entertainments, sports, video games, films, TV, music, fashion and toys. Slapstick humour. Showcases latest products, events and trends. Payment: by arrangement. Founded 2002.

Toybox
BBC Worldwide Ltd, Room A1130,
BBC Woodlands, 80 Wood Lane, London W12 0TT

tel 020-8433 2000 *fax* 020-8433 2941
website www.bbcworldwide.com
Associate Publisher Stephanie Cooper
Monthly £15.50 p.a.

Fun and interactive magazine for 3–5 year-olds with stories, activities, games and colouring-in. Features a variety of star characters from the BBC.

Tractor Tom
Panini UK, Brockbourne House, Mount Ephraim,
Tunbridge Wells TN4 8BS
tel (01892) 500100 *fax* (01892) 545666
email tractortom@panini.co.uk
website www.paninicomics.co.uk
Editor Patrick Bishop
Every 4 weeks £1.85

Tweenies
BBC Worldwide Ltd, BBC Woodlands,
80 Wood Lane, London W12 0TT
tel 020-8433 2356 *fax* 020-8433 2941
website www.bbcmagazines.com/tweenies
Editor Stephanie Cooper
Fortnightly £1.85

Magazine based around the *Tweenies* for children aged 2–5, with stories and activities including songs to sing, things to make and colouring-in.

2000 AD
The Studio, Brewer Street, Oxford OX1 1QN
email publicrelations@2000adonline.com
website www.2000adonline.com
Weekly, Wed £1.90

Cult sci-fi comic. A multi-award-winning cocktail of explosive sci-fi and fantasy, infused with a mean streak of irony and wry black humour, 2000 AD has been a proving ground for young writers and artists, and many of the biggest names in comics today honed their skills within its pages. It has won the Best British Comic award at the UK Comic Art Awards, National Comics Awards and Eagle Awards many times. Founded 1977.

Ultimate Spider-Man & X-Men
Panini UK, Brockbourne House, Mount Ephraim,
Tunbridge Wells TN4 8BS
tel (01892) 500100 *fax* (01892) 545666
email paninicomics@panini.co.uk
website www.paninicomics.co.uk
Editor Brady Webb
Every 4 weeks £1.99

Vibe
RNIB, PO Box 173, Peterborough PE2 6WS
tel (01733) 375000 *fax* (01733) 375001
email editorial@rnib.org.uk
website www.rnib.org.uk
Editor Racheal Jarvis
Monthly 38p (£2.65 export)

Braille general interest magazine for blind and partially sighted boys aged 12–15. Also available on disk.

The Voice
6th Floor, Northern & Shell Tower, 4 Selsdon Way,
London E14 9GL
tel 020-7510 0340 *fax* 020-7510 0341
email newsdesk@the-voice.co.uk
website www.voice-online.co.uk
Head of News Andrew Clunis, *Arts & Entertainment Editor* Russell Myrie, *Sports Editor* Rodney Hinds
Weekly 85p

Weekly newspaper for black Britons. Includes news, features, arts, sport and a comprehensive jobs and business section. Illustrations: colour and b&w photos. Open to ideas for news and features on sports, business, community events and the arts. Founded 1982.

Young Voices
website www.young-voices.co.uk
Editor Dionne Grant
Monthly, 2nd Tues of each month £2.40
News, features, reviews, showbiz highlights and current affairs for 11–19 year-olds. Founded 2003.

Winnie the Pooh
Egmont Magazines, 239 Kensington High Street,
London W3 6SA
tel 020-7761 3500 *fax* 020-7761 3510
website www.egmontmagazines.co.uk
Monthly £1.99

Interactive early learning magazine (2–5 year-olds) involving parent and child in a visually entertaining read.

W.I.T.C.H.
Panini UK, Brockbourne House, Mount Ephraim,
Tunbridge Wells TN4 8BS
email witch@panini.co.uk
website www.clubwitch.co.uk
Editor Alex Cooper
Monthly £2.10

Comic magazine featuring 5 young teenage girls who have special magical powers and want to save the world. They are also interested in all the things teenage girls are interested in – including fashion, boys and gossip. The magazine reflects the W.I.T.C.H. brand values of friendship, magic, action and drama, and features a mix of comic characters and real-life girls with whom the readers can identify.

Wolverine and Deadpool
Panini UK, Brockbourne House, Mount Ephraim,
Tunbridge Wells TN4 8BS
tel (01892) 500100 *fax* (01892) 545666
email paninicomics@panini.co.uk
website www.paninicomics.co.uk
Editor Scott Gray
Every 4 weeks £2.50

Young Scot

Rosebery House, 9 Haymarket Terrace,
Edinburgh EH12 5EZ
tel 0131-313 2488 *fax* 0131-313 6800
email info@youngscot.org
website www.youngscot.org
Editor Fiona McIntyre
Quarterly Free with *Scottish Daily Record* and at
selected venues

The latest news, features, discounts, and competitions
for Youngs Scots aged 12–26. Young Scot offers
incentives, information and opportunities to people
in this age group to help them make informed
choices, play a part in their community, and make
the most of their free time and learning.

Young Writer

5th Floor, 31–32 Park Row, Leeds LS1 5JD
tel (0113) 200 2929 *fax* (0113) 200 2928
email jtelfer@writersnews.co.uk
website www.youngwriter.org
Editor Jonathan Telfer
3 p.a. £3.75 (£10 p.a.)

Specialist magazine for young writers under 18 years
old: ideas for them and writing by them. Includes
interviews by children with famous writers, fiction
and non-fiction pieces, poetry; also explores words
and grammar, issues related to writing (e.g. dyslexia),
plus competitions with prizes. Length: 750 or 1500
words (features), up to 400 words (news), 750 words
(short stories – unless specified otherwise in a
competition), poetry of any length. Illustrations:
colour – drawings by children, snapshots to

accompany features. Payment: most children's
material is published without payment; £25-£100
(features); £15 (cover cartoon). Free inspection copy.
Founded 1995.

Your Dog Magazine

BPG (Stamford) Ltd, Roebuck House,
33 Broad Street, Stamford, Lincs. PE9 1RB
tel (01780) 766199 *fax* (01780) 766416
website www.yourdog.co.uk
Editor Sarah Wright
Monthly £3.25

Articles and information of interest to dog lovers;
features on all aspects of pet dogs. Length: approx.
1500 words. Illustrations: colour transparencies,
prints and line drawings. Payment: £80 per 1000
words. Founded 1994.

Your Horse

Bauer Consumer Media, Bushfield House,
Orton Centre, Peterborough PE2 5UW
tel (01733) 465644 *fax* (01733) 288163
email justine.thompson@bauerconsumer.com
Editor Justine Thompson
Every 4 weeks £3.50

Practical horse care and riding advice for the leisure
rider and horse owner. Send feature ideas with
examples of previous published writing. Specially
commissions most material. Welcomes ideas for
articles and features. Length: 1500 words. Payment:
£120 per 1000 words. Founded 1983.

Magazines about children's literature and education

Listings of magazines and newspapers for children start on page 259.

Armadillo
Mary Hoffman, c/o Patricia White Rogers, Coleridge & White, 20 Powis Mews, London W11 1JN
email armadillo@maryhoffman.co.uk
website www.armadillomagazine.com
Editor Mary Hoffman
4 p.a.

Magazine about children's books, including reviews, interviews, features and profiles. After 5 years of publication as a paper magazine it is now available only online. New issues will be posted at the end of March, June, September and December. New reviewers and writers are always welcome but the magazine does not pay a fee; reviewers keep the books. Publishers please note: books are *not* to be sent to the editor; she instructs reviewers to obtain specific titles direct from publishers. Founded 1999.

Books for Keeps
1 Effingham Road, London SE12 8NZ
tel 020-8852 4953 fax 020-8318 7580
email enquiries@booksforkeeps.co.uk
website www.booksforkeeps.co.uk
Editor Rosemary Stones, Send material to Richard Hill
Bi-monthly £25.50 p.a.

Features, reviews and news on children's books. Readership is both professionals and parents. Founded 1980.

The Bookseller
VNU Entertainment Media Ltd, 5th Floor, Endeavour House, 189 Shaftesbury Avenue, London WC2H 8TJ
tel 020-7420 6006 fax 020-7420 6103
email joel.rickett@bookseller.co.uk
website www.thebookseller.co.uk
Editor-in-Chief Neill Denny, Features Editor Liz Bury
Weekly £4.40, £170 p.a.

Journal of the UK publishing and bookselling trades. The *Children's Bookseller* supplement is published regularly and there is news on the children's book business in the main magazine. Produces the *Children's Buyer's Guide*, which previews children's books to be published in the following 6 months. The website holds news on children's books, comment on the children's sector, author interviews and children's bestseller charts. Founded 1858.

Carousel – The Guide to Children's Books
The Saturn Centre, 54–76 Bissell Street, Birmingham B5 7HX
tel 0121-622 7458
email carousel.guide@virgin.net
website www.carouselguide.co.uk
Editor Jenny Blanch
3 p.a. £11.25 p.a. (£16 p.a. Europe; £19 p.a. rest of world)

Reviews of fiction, non-fiction and poetry books for children, plus in-depth articles; profiles of authors and illustrators. Length: 1200 words (articles); 150 words (reviews). Illustrations: colour and b&w. Payment: by arrangement. Founded 1995.

Child Education PLUS
Scholastic Ltd, Villiers House, Clarendon Avenue, Leamington Spa, Warks. CV32 5PR
tel (01926) 887799 fax (01926) 883331
website www.scholastic.co.uk/childedplus
Editor Mike Ward
Monthly £4.25

For teachers concerned with the education of children aged 4–7. Articles by specialists on practical teaching ideas and methods. Length: 600–1200 words. Payment: by arrangement. Profusely illustrated with photos and artwork; also two A2 colour posters. Founded 1924.

Early Childhood Today
Scholastic Canada Ltd, 175 Hillmount Road, Markham, Ontario L6C 1Z7
email ect@scholastic.com
website www.scholastic.ca

Addresses and anticipates the needs of early childhood educators (pre-K–K). Each thematic issue focuses on a specific aspect of early childhood development, such as literacy or creativity, and provides a 'mini-workshop' on that topic: updates on current research, interviews with leading experts, and easy-to-implement activities broken down by age group.

Mary Glasgow Magazines
Scholastic UK Ltd, 24 Eversholt Street, London NW1 1DB
tel 020-7756 7756 (01926) 815563
email email@maryglasgowmags.co.uk
website www.maryglasgowmagazines.com

Publisher of 16 magazines for learners of English, French, German, and Spanish. Also publishes a series of resource books for teachers of English as a foreign language. Wholly-owned subsidiary of Scholastic Inc.

Inis – The Children's Books Ireland Magazine

Children's Books Ireland,
17 North Great George Street, Dublin 1
tel (1) 872 7475 *fax* (1) 872 7476
email info@childrensbooksireland.com
website www.childrensbooksireland.com
Editor Ms Paddy O'Doherty
Quarterly €4

Reviews and articles on Irish and international children's books. Readership of parents, teachers, librarians and children's books specialists. Founded 1989.

Instructor

Scholastic, c/o Scholastic Inc., P.O. Box 713, New York, NY 10013
fax (212) 343 4799
website www.teacher.scholastic.com

Professional magazine for elementary (Grades 1–8) classroom teachers that keeps educators abreast of the latest and best ideas about how children learn, and translates that thinking into effective classroom practice. Includes tips, activities, and strategies to better meet the needs of teachers.

Junior

Future Living, Berwick House, 8–10 Knoll Rise, Orpington BR6 0EL
tel (01689) 899023 *fax* (01689) 899266
email editorial@juniormagazine.co.uk
website www.juniormagazine.co.uk
Editor Catherine O'Dolan
Monthly £4.90

Glossy up-market parenting magazine aimed at mothers of children aged 0–8 and reflects the shift in today's society towards older mothers and fathers who have established their careers and homes. Intelligent and insightful features and the best in fashion. Specially commissions most material. Welcomes ideas for articles and features. Payment: £150 per 1000 words (articles/features/short fiction), £300 per feature (colour and b&w photos/artwork). Founded 1998.

Junior Education

Scholastic Ltd, Villiers House, Clarendon Avenue, Leamington Spa, Warks. CV32 5PR
tel (01926) 887799 *fax* (01926) 883331
email juniored@scholastic.co.uk
website www.scholastic.co.uk/magazines,
www.scholastic.co.uk/junioredplus
Editor Michelle Guy
Monthly £4.25

For teachers of 7–11 year-olds. Articles by specialists on practical teaching ideas, coverage of primary education news; posters; photocopiable material for the classroom. Length: 800–1000 words. Payment: by

arrangement. Illustrated with photos and drawings; includes 2 A2 colour posters. Founded 1977.

The Lion and the Unicorn

Project MUSE, 2715 North Charles Street, Baltimore, MD 21218-4319
tel 410-516-6989 *fax* 410-516-6968
email muse@muse.jhu.edu
website www.press.jhu.edu/journals/lion_and_the_unicorn/
3 p.a.

A theme- and genre-centred journal of international scope committed to a serious, ongoing discussion of literature for children. The journal's coverage includes the state of the publishing industry, regional authors, comparative studies of significant books and genres, new developments in theory, the art of illustration, the mass media, and popular culture. It has become noted for its interviews with authors, editors, and other important contributors to the field, such as Mildred Wirt Benson, Robert Cormier, Chris Crutcher, Lensey Namioka, Philip Pullman, and Aranka Siegal. Special issues have included 'Violence and Children's Literature' and 'Folklore In/And Children's Literature.' Includes a book review section and each year publishes a general issue and 2 theme issues. Project MUSE is part of the Johns Hopkins University Press.

Literacy

UK Literacy Association, 4th Floor, Attenborough Building, University of Leicester, Leicester LE1 7RH
tel 0116-229 7450 *fax* 0116-229 7451
email admin@ukla.org
website www.ukla.org, www.blackwellpublishing.com
Editor Kathy Hall, Department of Education, University College Cork, Lee Holme, Donovan's Road, Cork, Ireland (*email* k.hall@ucc.ie)
3 p.a. (subscription only)

The official journal of the United Kingdom Literacy Association (see page 361) and is for those interested in the study and development of literacy. Readership comprises practitioners, teachers, educators, researchers, undergraduate and graduate students. It offers educators a forum for debate through scrutinising research evidence, reflecting on analysed accounts of innovative practice and examining recent policy developments. Length: 2000–6000 words (articles). Illustrations: b&w prints and artwork. Formerly known as *Reading – Literacy and Language*. Published by Blackwell Publishing. Founded 1966.

Literacy Time

Scholastic Ltd, Villiers House, Clarendon Avenue, Leamington Spa, Warks. CV32 5PR
tel (01926) 887799 *fax* (01926) 883331
website www.scholastic.co.uk/magazines
Editor Helen Watts *tel* (01789) 292112
email helenwatts@redclose.demon.co.uk

Teachers' magazine with articles and lesson ideas. Online resources to download and use in the classroom offering a range of interactive texts. A2 posters for whole class work and multiple group reading leaflets, created to meet specific learning objectives for the National Literacy Framework. There are 3 levels: ages 5–7, ages 7–9 and ages 9–11. Texts include narrative, non-fiction, playscripts and poetry. Contact the Editor before submitting material.

NATE News (National Association for the Teaching of English)

NATE, 50 Broadfield Road, Sheffield S8 0XJ
tel 0114-255 5419 *fax* 0114-255 5296
email info@nate.org.uk
website www.nate.org.uk
Editor Ian McNeilly
3 p.a.

The official newsletter of the National Association for the Teaching of English (NATE), available as part of its membership. The newsletter is a topical mix of news of NATE activities and views on current issues. NATE also publishes a magazine, *English Drama Media* (3 p.a.) and an academic journal, *English in Education* (3 p.a.).

Nursery Education Plus

Scholastic Ltd, Villiers House, Clarendon Avenue, Leamington Spa, Warks. CV32 5PR
tel (01926) 887799 *fax* (01926) 883331
email earlyyears@scholastic.co.uk
website www.scholastic.co.uk/nurseryedplus
Editor Helen Dean
Monthly £39.99 p.a.

News, features, professional development and practical theme-based activities for professionals working with 0–5 year-olds. Activity ideas based on the Early Learning Goals. Material mostly commissioned. Length: 500–1000 words. Illustrations: colour and b&w; colour posters. Payment: by arrangement. Founded 1997.

Nursery World

22 Bute Gardens, London W6 7HN
tel 020-8267 8400
website www.nurseryworld.co.uk
Editor Liz Roberts
Weekly £65 p.a.

For all grades of primary school, nursery and child care staff, nannies, foster parents and all concerned with the care of expectant mothers, babies and young children. Authoritative and informative articles, 800 or 1300 words, and photos, on all aspects of child welfare and early education, from 0–8 years, in the UK. Practical ideas, policy news and career advice. No short stories. Payment: by arrangement. Illustrations: line, half-tone, colour.

Practical Parenting

Magicalia Publishing, Berwick House, 8–10 Knoll Rise, Orpington BR6 0EL
tel (01689) 899200 *fax* (01689) 899266
website www.practicalparenting.co.uk
Editor Susie Boone
Monthly £2.70

Articles on parenting, baby and childcare, health, psychology, education, children's activities, personal birth/parenting experiences. Send synopsis with sae. Illustrations: colour photos, line; commissioned only. Payment: by agreement. Founded 1987.

Publishers Weekly

360 Park Avenue South, New York, NY 10010
tel 646-746-6758 *fax* 646-746-6631 *fax* 646-746-6738
website www.publishersweekly.com
Editor-in-Chief Sara Nelson, *Contact* Isabell Taylor for general editorial enquiries *tel* 646-746-6758,
email i.taylor@reedbusiness.com *Children's Books Senior Editor* Diane Roback *tel* 646-746-6768

The international news magazine of the $23 billion book industry. Covers all segments involved in the creation, production, marketing and sale of the written word in book, audio, video and electronic formats. In addition to reaching publishers worldwide, it influences all media dealing with the acquisition, sale, distribution and rights of intellectual and cultural properties.

Children's Books Books for review, from preschool to young adult, should be sent to Diane Roback, Children's Books Editor – all reviews are prepublication. Also send her story suggestions on children's publishing, new trends, author or illustrator interviews, etc for the weekly *Children's Books*. Diane also edits the listings for new children's books twice a year for the Spring and Fall Children's Announcements issues. Fax (do not email) any story pitches or queries concerning review submissions of children's books, review enquiries and editorial guidelines for submission of children's books for review. Founded 1873.

Publishing News

7 John Street, London WC1N 2ES
tel (0870) 870 2345 *fax* (0870) 870 0385
website www.publishingnews.co.uk
Editor Liz Thomson, *Deputy Editor* Roger Tagholm, *Children's Editor* Graham Marks
Weekly by subscription only

Articles and news items on the book publishing and bookselling industry. Approx. 12 articles about children's publishing each year in the special features section. Articles by agreement only. Founded 1979.

Report

ATL, 7 Northumberland Street, London WC2N 5RD
tel 020-7930 6441 *fax* 020-7930 1359
email report@atl.org.uk
website www.atl.org.uk
Editor Alex Tomlin
9 p.a. £2.50 (£15 p.a. UK; £27 p.a. overseas) Free to members

The magazine from the Association of Teachers and Lecturers (ATL). Features, articles, comment, news about nursery, primary, secondary and further education. Payment: minimum £120 per 1000 words.

Right Start
Ten Alps Publishing, 9 Savoy Street, London WC2E 7HR
tel 020-7878 2338 fax 020-7379 6261
Editor Lynette Lowthian
Bi-monthly £10.90 p.a.

Features on all aspects of preschool and infant education, child health and behaviour. No unsolicited MSS. Length: 800–1500 words. Illustrations: colour photos, line. Payment: varies. Founded 1989.

The School Librarian
The School Library Association, Unit 2, Lotmead Business Village, Lotmead Farm, Wanborough, Swindon SN4 0UY
tel (01793) 791787 fax (01793) 791786
email info@sla.org.uk
website www.sla.org.uk
Editor Nancy Chambers
Quarterly £45 p.a.

Official journal of the School Library Association. Articles on school library management, use and skills, and on authors and illustrators, literacy, publishing. Reviews of books, CD-Roms, websites and other library resources from preschool to adult. Length: 1800–3000 words (articles). Payment: by arrangement. Founded 1937.

The TES
26 Red Lion Square, Holborn WC1R 4HQ
tel 020-3194 3000
fax 020-3194 3202 (news), 020-3194 3200 (features)
email newsdesk@tes.co.uk, features@tes.co.uk
website www.tes.co.uk
Editor Karen Dempsey
Weekly £1.40

Education newspaper. Articles on education written with special knowledge or experience; news items; books, arts and equipment reviews. Check with the news or picture editor before submitting material. Outlines of feature ideas should be emailed. Illustrations: suitable photos and drawings of educational interest, cartoons. Payment: standard rates, or by arrangement.

TES Magazine
Weekly Free with TES
Magazine for teachers focusing on their lives, inside and outside the classroom, investigating the key issues of the day and highlighting good practice. Length: 800 words max.

The TES Cymru
Sophia House, 28 Cathedral Road, Cardiff CF11 9LJ
tel 029-2066 0201 fax 029-2066 0207
email cymru@tes.co.uk
website www.tes.co.uk/cymru
Editor Nicola Porter
Weekly £1.40

Education newspaper. Articles on education, teachers, teaching and learning, and education policy in Wales. Length: up to 800 words (articles). Illustrations: line, half-tone. Payment: by arrangement. Founded 2004.

The TESS
Scott House, 10 South St Andrew Street, Edinburgh EH2 2AZ
tel 0131-557 1133 fax 0131-558 1155
website www.tes.co.uk/scotland
Editor Neil Munro
Weekly £1.30

Education newspaper. Articles on education, preferably 800–1000 words, written with special knowledge or experience. News items about Scottish educational affairs. Illustrations: line, half-tone. Payment: by arrangement. Founded 1965.

The Times Educational Supplement – see The TES

The Times Educational Supplement Scotland – see The TESS

Under 5
Pre-school Learning Alliance, The Fitzpatrick Building, 188 York Way, London N7 9AD
tel 020-7697 2500 fax 020-7697 8607
website www.pre-school.co.uk
Contact Anna Roberts
10 p.a. £30 p.a.

Articles on the role of adults – especially parents/ preschool workers – in young children's learning and development, including children from all cultures and those with special needs. Length: 600–1200 words. Founded 1962.

Young Writer – see page 269

Television, film and radio

Commissioning for children's television

Anna Home offers guidelines for writing for children's television programmes.

What are the classic children's television titles? *Blue Peter*, of course, *Magpie*, *Bagpuss*, *Grange Hill*, *My Family Are Aliens*, *Bob the Builder*, *Teletubbies*, etc. Children's television embraces a multitude of different kinds of programming, all of which requires writers. *Blue Peter* is not the kind of programme which gets commissioned cold – it evolved over the years through various production teams – but what is fundamental to its success is its makers' knowledge of its audience and how that audience has changed over the years. *Teletubbies*, and more recently *In the Night Garden*, are exactly the same: their creator Anne Wood spent months researching the target audience and testing ideas before committing to them. So....

• **Rule One.** Know your audience and the age range that you are aiming for.

• **Rule Two.** Know the schedules. Be aware of the available slots and the kind of programmes which go into them, and study the output and the varying requirements of the different channels. CITV has commissioned almost no new programmes since 2007 and seems unlikely to do much more in the immediate future. CBBC and CBeebies are the main commissioners catering for their specific age ranges; Five only caters for preschool. Nick, Cartoon Network and Disney do commission in the UK but only on a small scale. CBBC now has a 360 degree policy, i.e. all programmes need to be created with a variety of platforms and outlets in mind. They only have one commissioning round a year, although they are happy to discuss ideas at other times. Also go to 'Meet the Commissioner' meetings, network, and study the broadcasters' websites.

• **Rule Three.** Learn how to write proposals and how to pitch them (remember that commissioners receive hundreds and hundreds of proposals in a year). Presentation, clarity and passion are all important. This is a very competitive world and if you get an opportunity to pitch in person know how to do it as it may be your only chance to impress. Rehearse well, have your props prepared (if appropriate) and don't waffle. You have to convince the commissioner that your project has a real USP (unique selling point) and that you can deliver it.

• **Rule Four.** Have some idea of what your project is going to cost and be prepared to defend that costing. Few broadcasters fully fund commissions any more and you need to be aware of how to find matching deficit funding. Sometimes a writer may team up with an independent producer who will cover this part of it (see page 295 for listings). As a writer you will probably already have an agent, but that agent may not be an expert in terms of accessing television or film work. Check this out as many writers have two agents – one for their publishing activities and another for television and film.

Children's television drama

The BBC is now virtually the only commissioner of children's drama. The current policy is to concentrate on investing in big event dramas which will differentiate the channel –

for example *The Roman Mysteries*. There are a limited number of Sunday teatime slots, for example *Clay* by David Almond.

Smaller scale adaptations are still commissioned especially if they have a long running potential, for example *Tracy Beaker*. If you find a book which you think would work for television, you'll have to buy an option before you take it to the producer or commissioner. As a result of the huge success of *Harry Potter*, *Lemony Snickett*, etc, the cost of optioning children's books has risen steeply and the potential 'biggies' are snapped up before publication. However, there are a number of excellent children's books published every year which could make good television and you might pick up the next 'big thing', so keep an eye on what is happening in the children's publishing world, read the trade magazines and try to get to know children's publishers. When you are looking at books consider whether they have potential beyond one book or a limited series. Commissioners are always looking for something which has the possibility to go to more than one series and to become a franchise or brand. Once you have secured your option write a brief treatment of how you see the television version working and submit it together with the book either to an independent producer, or to a commissioner – remembering the rules outlined above.

Animation

Animation is the most prolific and potentially the most financially rewarding children's genre, but it is rather specialised. There are certain things that work in cell or model animation and there are things that don't, so it is well worth studying successful animated series. Remember that this really is a visual medium and often words are minimal – think *Pingu*! In fact, the *Yoko Toto Yakamoto* series (which has no words) has won two BAFTA Children's Writer Awards. The alternative is to start with a book or a series of characters and then approach an animation production house. You don't have to provide the visuals, but you do need to remember that animation needs to be a minimum of 26 episodes in the first series with the potential to go to 104 episodes or more. Animation also needs to have international appeal as most animated series are international co-productions. Lastly, if you can, its worthwhile trying to learn a little bit about how animation works technically – it will help you identify the right kind of books or ideas.

Comedy and comedy-drama

Comedy and comedy-drama has become an increasingly popular part of children's television output. It's mainly studio based, relatively cheap to make and it works well in the schedule. The same comments about potential longevity apply in terms of the series and you should always have this in mind. Having said all this however, the main thing is to write something that you really want to write and you think will work for the audience on television, something that you care about and are passionate about and are really able to visualise and able to sell to those cynical commissioners.

Good luck.

Anna Home is Chief Executive of the Children's Film and Television Foundation. Previously she worked in children's programmes at both the BBC and ITV. Latterly she was Head of CBBC for 11 years, responsible for commissioning all the children's output. Her career began on *Playschool*, she started *Grange Hill* and her last commission was *Teletubbies*.

Writing comedy for children's television

Adam Bromley looks at types of comedy, the parameters of writing comedy for children's television and describes the commissioning process.

Writing comedy for children's television presents numerous challenges: it is both liberating and restrictive. Today, this target audience is more discerning than ever and they have a wide choice of television channels and entertainment options. If a comedy show doesn't deliver in a few minutes viewers will look elsewhere and perhaps channel surf or switch on a games console. Budgets for making programmes are ratcheted downwards than upwards. Also, editorial restrictions for children's television are extensive and need to be considered at every stage in the writing process.

But don't be disheartened by these challenges because children are more imaginative than adults and as an audience they will be more receptive to more outlandish ideas than conservative adult audiences.

The first question

Before you start on the time-consuming, frustrating and drawn-out process of 'making it' as a comedy writer, there's one question you should ask yourself: 'Can I write funny material?' It's surprising how many aspiring comedy writers never take a moment to be objective about their own work. You have to be tough on yourself because the chances of getting a show commissioned are low. The majority of scripts never get past the initial filtering process by producers and script readers. At every stage the numbers are whittled down. So the odds of any given script actually becoming a television programme are stacked against a writer from day one. Hard work and dedication will take you a long way, but if you can't deliver the comedy then think again. Try out what you've written on children and observe their reaction. You can rely on children to display their honest opinions. Don't rely on adults to give you mere confidence-boosting words of encouragement about your work. You don't need to wow your audience with the first thing you write. But you do need to raise a laugh somewhere along the way. If, after looking at yourself objectively, you do reckon that you may have that potential, the next step is to find out more about your chosen medium.

Budgets and briefs

Children's television has two special features that a writer should be aware of at every stage of writing: low budgets and a restrictive editorial brief. Budgets for programmes are around a fifth of comparable adult television shows so it's worth considering programme budgets when devising an idea. Commissioners are more likely to be attracted to proposals that can be realised on these lower sums than shows with a cast of hundreds and requiring numerous special effects. But don't make the mistake of thinking that a lower budget means lower quality. For example, Monty Python's *Life of Brian* was shot on a very low budget. The use of coconuts clapped together in place of horses for the knights was an ingenious way of overcoming the lack of funds for the horses. Whilst it's not a writer's job to get mired in the detail of how a scene could be shot, you should try to get a sense of what to avoid. Complex ideas which require large casts, major set builds and extensive use of special effects or large amounts of expensive post production are the obvious pitfalls.

The other unique aspect to children's television is its editorial concerns, which are wide ranging and can be tricky to master. In terms of content, swearing, sexual references, blasphemy or realistic violence are absolutely taboo. Your point of reference should be the content of a U or PG-rated film at the cinema. Watch a good variety of children's television and films to get an innate sense of what the boundaries are. As with the budgets, it's more productive to see these editorial rules as something that will force you to be a better writer than just a burden. Often new comedy writers rely on dark, violent scenarios because mastering a scene that relies on word play and a clever premise is beyond them. This tighter control of content means that the writer cannot fall back on shock tactics or explicit language to achieve a reaction which is, in the long run, a better way to progress.

There is an additional concern known as 'imitative behaviour'. Children are more suggestible and have a lower sense of risk and personal safety. In anything you write avoid any action that, if copied by children, might harm them, for example swallowing lots of tablets, forcing things into their mouths, throwing household objects at people. This may pose problems if you've got slapstick gags, which are a reliable mainstay of children's comedy. Be wary of any highly realistic scenarios as opposed to cartoonish ones. If the above sounds limiting, the flipside is that children will readily make greater leaps of imagination than adults. Don't forget that you're writing for an audience that remains fresh and open-minded in a way few adults are. Working within these ground rules is a small price to pay for an appreciative audience.

Comedy writing itself naturally divides into three main areas: sketches, scripted comedy and gag writing.

Scripted comedy

Scripted comedy covers a number of forms, including comedy narrative that has an unfolding story which links week by week and sitcom in which each episode is largely self contained. The three keys to writing good scripted comedy are number one: character; number two: character; and number three: character.

Everything starts and ends with your principal characters. Witty one-liners and elaborate plot structures are worthless unless they flow from strong central characters. For creating comedy characters, it's useful to think of them as embodying certain key personality traits and to make that inform everything they do. As we're dealing with comedy, don't make your characters too pleasant. There's nothing very amusing, for example, about a family sitcom where everyone gets on wonderfully well, is understanding, supportive and helpful. That may be a good environment to raise children, but it makes for tedious television. Characters don't work in isolation so put together a mix of characters that will spark against one another. Comedy, like drama, needs tension. So if you have a dysfunctional family that lives in a house so huge they never need to interact with one another, there's no friction for comedy to happen. But if you put them in a pokey flat where they're always getting in one another's way, then you've got fertile comic territory.

If you want to devise characters that will appeal to a children's audience, a mix of adults and children will be the most likely to work, preferably of different generations. Children won't be interested in mid-life crises, office politics or single women in their twenties looking for love. Generational conflict with families is an ideal starting point. But as with everything, there are no rules.

So long as your audience can find some point of connection, there's no reason why your lead couldn't be an alien or from another century. It all depends on how that character is presented so consider how your characters will connect with the wider audience. A child's frame of reference is different to that of an adult and children want comedy that reflects that. Remembering that you're writing not just for yourself but for hundreds of thousands of strangers will help guide you towards broader, more accessible characters. Make sure that the comedy flows from the characters themselves and doesn't just happen around them. Your comic leads need to initiate much of the action. In comedy things should go wrong most of the time so the leads should be the authors of their own misfortunes rather than having random events simply happen.

Sketch writing

Sketch writing presents other challenges, not least that many ideas have been done before. Common mistakes new writers make with a sketch is to start with a confused or muddled premise. Alternatively, they have a good premise and do nothing with it. The premise of a sketch is the one-line summary of a funny idea. If you can't summarise the sketch into one line and if that summary doesn't make you laugh, then there's probably something at fault with the original idea. Once you've got a promising sketch idea, it should develop as the piece unfolds. Even though the sketch may be only two minutes of airtime, you'll have to give some kind of twist or progression to sustain the audience's interest over that period. Even ten seconds of dead air in a television programme can feel like an eternity. Write your sketches longer and then trim them back. Another good rule is to not let a sketch run for longer than two minutes.

Gag writing

Gag writing is a discipline all of its own. When writing standalone jokes, practise does make perfect and it's critical that you test your material on audiences. It can be intimidating but there's no better way to find out if what you've written makes audiences laugh. Your main avenue for gag writing is the scripted links in entertainment shows.

The commissioning process

Once you have material ready to submit, understanding the commissioning process can save a lot of wasted effort. The first hurdle for a writer is to get anyone, whether it's a producer or an agent, to take an interest in their work. Getting a programme commissioned is a long, frustrating process and it's integral to that process to have someone promoting your cause – typically a producer.

From a new writer's perspective, agents can help from an the early stage to get your script past the initial filtering stage. Producers and development executives are generally more receptive to scripts sent to them by agents, as they act as a form of quality control. Don't despair, if you send an unsolicited script or proposal to a producer or editor, it will be read… eventually.

One mistake writers often make is to send out copies of their script to every producer working in children's television with a general covering letter. This is never a good idea. It sends out a signal that the writer in question couldn't be bothered to do some research on who might be interested in their script. Finding out who makes which shows is relatively easy as all the major channels have information lines if you miss the end credits of shows. A bit of research goes a long way. You should follow up that script with a phone call or email. Although your script may represent months of hard toil to you, remember that producers work on other shows and that reading scripts is a low priority for them.

If you are able to get a producer to take an interest in your work, often the next natural step is not to immediately pitch your own programme ideas but to work on existing shows, perhaps writing episodes of a long-running sitcom, devising sketch ideas or writing additional material for entertainment shows. This is a good bridging stage as you'll get a better feel of the production and commissioning process. It's also a great opportunity to improve your writing craft without the exposure of a solo project. Nearly all comedy writers started out writing on other people's shows. The longer you spend writing in a professional environment, the better you'll get. Meeting deadlines and turning work around in a short time frame are not disciplines new writers acquire by writing on their own but they are an important part of being a successful television writer. Being funny on demand is a tough task and it's part of the craft.

In the long run most writers are more interested in getting their own solo ideas commissioned. Be prepared for a lot of frustration and disappointment if you follow this route. There are relatively few programme slots available in any given year. Commissioners tend to favour tried and tested writers over new names. There's no conspiracy to exclude new talent, however. When money is in short supply, opting for a safe pair of hands is a form of insurance policy. All of which means that, as a new writer, you'll have to be that much more impressive than an established one to get noticed. In spite of all this, if you deliver funny, original and accessible scripts, sooner or later you'll be noticed and they will make it on screen.

Adam Bromley is a freelance producer and director. He produced *Tiny and Mr Duk's Huge Show* and *Stupid* for CBBC, *Bash* for BBC3 as well as numerous hit comedies for BBC Radio 4, including *Think the Unthinkable*, *The Now Show*, *Hut 33* and *Double Science*.

See also...
- *Commissioning for children's television*, page 275
- *Writing humour for young children*, page 121

Children's literature on radio and audio

The spoken word and the written word in literature require different handling. Neville Teller looks at the radio and audiobook media and explores what a writer for the microphone needs to know and how to break into this market.

'Read me a story' – one of childhood's perennial calls. Parents found little relief from this cry (palming it off on grandma or auntie was perhaps the best bet) until radio appeared on the scene. But from its very beginning radio included in its schedules stories read aloud for children, and the loudspeaker, for part of the time at least, was able to provide a fair substitute for mummy or daddy by presenting professional actors reading literature specially prepared for performance at the microphone.

Very early on, actors learned that performing at the microphone was a new skill that had to be acquired – the techniques were quite different from those required on the stage. Writers, too, had to acquire a whole range of new skills in preparing material for radio. Two things quickly became apparent. First, literature simply read aloud from the printed page often failed to 'come across' to a listening audience, because material produced to be scanned by the eye is often basically unsuited to the requirements of the microphone. Secondly, the time taken to read a complete book on the air would be far too long to be acceptable, and in consequence most books would need to be abridged.

Today there are two main outlets in this country for aspiring radio/audio writers for children: BBC radio and audiobook publishers.

How has this market reached its present position?

Radio

Children's radio in the UK has certainly had its ups and downs. It came into existence in December 1922, just a few weeks after the BBC itself was born, and for some 40 years the daily Children's Hour became an established and much-cherished feature of life in this country. It is no exaggeration to say that during its heyday its presenters, and those who made its programmes, created an indelible impression on the childhood of millions of people.

However, in the 1960s the imminent death of radio was a generally accepted prognostication. So, starting in 1961, children's radio was slowly but surely strangled on the dubious, if not specious, grounds that children no longer had the time or inclination to listen to radio. Television, it was argued, was their medium of choice. So first the much-loved title 'Children's Hour' was dropped, then the time allotted to programmes 'For the Young' (as it was then called) was cut back. Finally, in March 1964, the programme was put out of its agony.

The demise of children's radio naturally evoked a massive groundswell of protest. In response – although the BBC of the day had clearly lost faith in it – they did grant some sort of reprieve. Stories had always featured strongly in its schedules, and *Story Time* – a programme of abridged radio readings – started life in the old Children's Hour slot with a strong bias towards children's literature. After a few years, however, its character changed.

More general literature began to be selected, and then the programme was moved to earlier in the afternoon. That decision, despite a brief experiment with a programme called *Fourth Dimension* and the continued existence of *Listen with Mother* till 1982, effectively left the Radio 4 schedules for nearly 20 years bereft of any specifically children's programmes.

The comeback started slowly, and then suddenly gathered momentum. Early in the new millennium the BBC – moved, doubtless, by mounting evidence of the undiminished popularity of radio – decided to reintroduce a regular programme for children. All they could offer at the time was a 30-minute programme each Sunday evening on Radio 4 called *Go4It*, a magazine-type show which would include a ten-minute reading. Children's literature had – to mix metaphors and create a glorious vision – re-established a toehold on the airwaves, and I found myself abridging books for the programme ranging from *The Lion, The Witch and the Wardrobe* by C.S. Lewis to *The Fall of Fergal* by Philip Ardagh and *The Wolves of Willoughby Chase* by Joan Aitken.

Much more was to follow, for in the autumn of 2002 the BBC launched its new digital radio channel, BBC7, and its schedules included, as a basic ingredient, daily programmes for children using live performers and incorporating readings from children's literature, both current and classic. These abridgements were specially prepared and read for the two daily shows: *The Big Toe Radio Show* for older children and – it goes without saying – *The Little Toe Radio Show* for the youngsters. I prepared a considerable number of books for young listeners for these programmes, including not only classical children's literature like *Robinson Crusoe, Huckleberry Finn, Black Beauty* and *The Prince and the Pauper*, but also more general classics specially prepared for younger listeners like *20,000 Leagues Under the Sea* and *Oliver Twist*. The Big Toe programme also featured up-to-the-moment favourites such as Anthony Horowitz's series about his boy secret agent, Alex Rider, the Artemis Fowl novels by Eoin Colfer, Terry Pratchett's *A Hatful of Sky*, Philip Ardagh's Awful End series and Jackie French's Callisto series. For younger listeners, I abridged books like the Whizziwig series by Malorie Blackman, the Lily Quench books by Natalie Jane Prior, and Kate Umansky's *The Silver Spoon of Solomon Snow*.

Children's radio had been re-established, and all seemed set fair. Then, towards the end of 2006, came news of major changes. The BBC's digital television channel for the youngest children, CBeebies, had been proving an enormous success. The BBC decided that the time was ripe to exploit this advantage. Lateral, not to say radical, thinking was applied. The outcome: a decision to convert *The Little Toe Radio Show* into a sort of radio extension of CBeebies – even to the extent of renaming the programme *CBeebies on BBC7*. The radio programme would be promoted on the television show, and children would be urged to tune in for more CBeebies on the air.

The new schedules began in March 2007. *CBeebies* now runs from 2–5pm every day, while *Big Toe* has been renamed *Big Toe Books* and is broadcast from 7–8am every morning.

Big Toe Books consists of readings drawn from the extensive archive of children's books built up over the past five years. These readings can be heard not only when transmitted, but for seven days afterwards through the 'Listen Again' facility on the BBC website. In addition to these books, the *Big Toe* website offers children a continually varying selection of about a dozen other books to listen to. A typical recent selection included *Johnny and the Dead* by Terry Pratchett, *The Butterfly Lion* and *Toro! Toro!* by Michael Morpurgo, *Thirteen Unpredictable Tales* by Paul Jennings, and *Blobheads Go Boing!* by Paul Stewart and Chris Riddell – three of which I recognise as past abridgements of mine.

As for *CBeebies on BBC7*, the golden rule is that readings will not last longer than ten minutes. For the new programme I have, accordingly, abridged quite a few shorter books written especially for younger children, like *The Lighthouse Keeper's Breakfast* by Ronda and David Armitage. Traditional fairy tales are also included in the schedule, and I have specially reconceived and rewritten ten of them to fit a five-minute reading time.

Other outlets

Oneword, the digital radio channel, stopped transmitting in 2007. Its programming consisted largely of audiobook readings and schedules included classical and new books for children.

A digital and online radio station directed specifically at younger children, Fun Radio, went on the air in 2005 with a varied programme of stories, songs and competitions. In January 2008, however, as part of cutbacks in DAB broadcasting made by its owners, Gcap Media, it was removed from most DAB multiplexes across the UK. It continues to broadcast online, and on DAB in Greater London only.

Audiobooks

Audiobooks are literary works of all types, some abridged, some unabridged, read by actors and now generally available in CD format (the audiocassette is becoming moribund). From what was virtually a standing start in the late 1980s, annual sales of audiobooks now top £70 million. In excess of five million audiobooks were purchased in the UK in 2007 and children's literature forms a significant proportion of that total.

Nowadays, it is common for major publishers to launch a fair number of their new books, including books for older children, in printed and audiobook form simultaneously. Publishers of books for younger children are also increasingly developing the 'twin pack' concept – packaging book and audiobook together – so that children can read and listen at the same time. This development has mushroomed since 2003 when Customs and Excise decided that such products could be zero-rated for VAT.

It was in May 2000 that a consortium thought of putting one modern development (audiobooks) together with another (digital radio), and came up with a revolutionary new radio concept. Oneword is a digital radio channel concerned above all with literature. The core of its programming is the transmission of audiobook readings, both abridged and unabridged, streamed into various segments throughout the day. Its schedules (which, like BBC7's, appear in *Radio Times* as well as in several newspapers) include classical and new books for children.

How children listen

The ways in which children can – and increasingly do – listen to the readings intended especially for them are multiplying. *Go4It* is transmitted on Radio 4 on Sunday evenings. Like all BBC programmes it can be accessed not only through normal AM or FM radio but also via digital radio through the so-called online 'simul-streaming' (that is, more or less at the same time as the direct radio transmission). In addition, the readings can be heard for a full week after transmission, by way of the 'Listen Again' facility.

BBC7, which carries *Big Toe* and *CBeebies*, is transmitted not only digitally, but also online (where it can be heard simul-streamed and through 'Listen Again'), and via television sets through Freeview, Sky and cable. In addition, electronic access to both digital radio and the internet is becoming increasingly available via new generation mobile phones, and evidence is mounting that children are taking advantage of this flexibility of access to read-aloud literature.

A comparatively new phenomenon which has made great strides over the past year is 'podcasting'. The BBC is enabling listeners (and viewers) to download an increasing range of programmes on MP3, iPod and similar systems, and this too is expanding children's access to read-aloud literature.

The downloading of audiobooks via the internet has also expanded greatly during the past year, and is set to grow even faster. Audible and iTunes have an enormous and expanding list of children's books available for downloading, and stories are proving a popular second-best to music for many children for their personal iPods. Subscribers either pay for downloads book by book, or pay a monthly fee for the right to download a specific number of titles. During 2008 in-car iPod playback, via the car radio, became widely available at very modest cost, and this method of listening is likely to rival the in-car audio or CD player for keeping children happy on long journeys.

The message of all this for writers is simply that the market seems poised for expansion, and if you are keen to break into it, it seems worthwhile to persevere.

Writing for the microphone

Putting unabridged audiobook readings to one side, what does the aspiring radio/audio children's writer need to know, and how can he or she break into the rather specialised world of abridging children's literature for the microphone?

As in all professional fields, the tyro is faced with the classic Catch-22 situation: radio producers and audio publishers are reluctant to offer commissions to people without a track record, while it is of course impossible to gain a track record without having won a commission or two. The only advice is to keep plugging away, hoping for that elusive lucky break – and the only consolation on offer is that even the most experienced of today's professionals was once a complete novice.

But what of the techniques that need to be applied in converting material produced for the printed page into a series of scripts that can be performed by an actor with ease at the microphone, and bring real listening pleasure to the child at the other end?

Getting to grips with abridging books for the microphone requires, in the first instance, the application of some simple arithmetic. Take a book of around 70,000 words. Children's radio usually devotes about ten minutes' airtime to its reading slot, and producers allow up to 14 episodes for each book. In ten minutes, an actor can read about 1450 words. It is clear, therefore, that normally the abridger will be required to reduce the wordage from 70,000 to no more than 20,300 words. In other words, one can be required to remove up to 70% of the original.

The audio field has different requirements. Books abridged for audio are produced increasingly in CD form, though they are also still sometimes presented as two double-sided cassettes. Each of the four cassette sides runs for about 45 minutes and uses 7000 words. Thus the normal audiobook contains some 28,000 words. CDs can accommodate well over 60 minutes of airtime, so the 180-minute abridgement is often also presented in the form of three CDs.

An abridgement – is that the same as a précis? I think not. A précis writer's objective is to reproduce the sense of an original in fewer words. The skill of the abridger lies in doing that while, in addition and quite as important, retaining the character of the original writing. That demands the capacity to respond sympathetically to the feel of an author's style and to be able to preserve it, even when large chunks of the original are being cut away. Abridging for radio goes beyond even this, for the writer must fulfil his or her commission through the medium of that highly technical artefact, the script.

Some abridgements intended for the printed page are able to boast 'only the words of the original are used'. Radio or audio abridgements that followed that principle could be disastrous. The requirements of eye and of ear do not always coincide; a message easily absorbed from the printed page can become surprisingly garbled if transmitted unamended at the microphone.

In crafting a radio/audio script the needs of the listener must be a prime consideration. The needs of the actor who will read it at the microphone are another. The writer must keep in the forefront of the mind the fact that the script has to be performed. The words must 'flow trippingly on the tongue'.

With audio the listener is in control, and can switch on or off whenever convenient. However, a radio script needs shape. On the air, ten minutes on an emotional plateau can be pretty boring. *Crescendi* and *diminuendi* are called for. A good plan is to provide a modest peak of interest about halfway through the script, and work up to a climax at the end, leaving the listener anxious for more of the story.

Principles, principles – what about practice? A modest illustration.

'How are you going?' Harriet said, stifling a yawn.

'The Oxford bus,' returned Pam.

Nothing wrong with that – on the printed page. If faced with it, though, the experienced radio or audio writer would feel it necessary to present it somewhat along the following lines:

Harriet stifled a yawn.

'How are you going?'

'The Oxford bus,' said Pam

Why? Let's take the points in order.

Harriet said.

If the speaker's name instantly follows a piece of reported speech, and especially a question, a moment of confusion can arise in the listener's mind. In this instance, it could be unclear for a second whether 'Harriet' is included in, or excluded from, the question. It might be: *'How are you going, Harriet... ?'*

The meaning is soon resolved, of course, but impediments to understanding are best eliminated.

'Stifling a yawn' is an indication of the way in which the words were said. If the actor is to provide that indication, he or she needs to know ahead of the speech how it is to be delivered. Moreover, taking the original version, if the actor stifles a yawn while saying Harriet's speech, and then reads 'said Harriet, stifling a yawn,' the passage becomes tautologous.

For this reason it is best to cut back to a bare minimum all indications in the text of how speeches are delivered. It is better to leave it to the actor and the producer to interpret most of them.

There are no apostrophes on the air. By and large, 'said' is the best radio indicator of speech. An alternative is to precede speech by some description of the speaker, and to insert the words spoken with no further indication of who is speaking. Thus:

Harriet stifled a yawn.
'*How are you going?*'
It is clearly Harriet speaking.
'*The Oxford bus,' returned Pamela.*
Two points here. Almost all the literary variants of 'said' ring false through the loud-speaker or headphones – cried, riposted, remarked, answered, etc. For reading purposes, most are best replaced with 'said' (or better, wherever possible, omitted altogether) and the speech in question left to the actor to interpret. In this instance, '*returned*' is particularly difficult for the listener – again, for no more than a moment – but is 'returned' part of the speech? '*The Oxford bus returned... ?*' It is surely best to eliminate obstacles to understanding.

This peek into the radio/audio abridger's toolbox might leave one thinking that the business is all gimmick and no heart – noses pressed up so hard against tree trunks that there is no time for the wood. It is certainly necessary that in this field, as in any other, basic techniques have to be acquired and then absorbed to the point where they become second nature. Only then can they be applied to ensure that the radio and audio media are used to interpret a writer's intentions as fully and as honestly as possible.

It is, though, equally essential that the abridger of children's books reproduces, as far as possible, the plot, atmosphere and character of the original. The aim must be to leave the listener with as complete a feeling of the original book as possible, given the technical limitations of time and wordage. It is, in short, an essential aspect of the radio/audio writer's craft to keep faith with the author.

Neville Teller MBE has been contributing to BBC radio for over 50 years. He has well over 250 abridgements for radio readings to his credit, some 50 radio dramatisations and over 150 audiobook abridgements. His most recent children's abridgements include *Bootleg* by Alex Shearer, *Kidnapped* by Robert Louis Stevenson, *Sunwing* by Kenneth Oppel, the Awful End series by Philip Adagh, *A Hatful of Sky* by Terry Pratchett, *Muddle Earth* by Paul Stewart and Chris Riddell, the Araminta Spook series by Angie Sage, the Callisto series by Jackie French, *The Lighthouse Keeper's Breakfast* by Ronda and David Armitage, *Fairytale News* by Colin and Jacqui Hawkins, *Captain Abdul's Little Treasure* by Colin McNaughton and *The Village of Round and Square Houses* by Anne Grifalconi. Neville Teller is a past chairman of the Society of Authors' Broadcasting Committee and of the Audiobook Publishing Association's Contributors' Committee. He was made an MBE in 2006 'for services to broadcasting and to drama'.

See also...
• *Children's audio publishers*, page 60
• *Writing to a brief*, page 287

Writing to a brief

Writing to a brief is an exacting process in which the writer has to produce work to satisfy others as opposed to exploring their own project ideas. The writer may work with others as part of a team when script writing or collaborate with an artistic director when adapting a play. Diane Redmond looks at three aspects of writing to a brief for children.

Writing to a brief is enormous fun! I never know what's going to land on my desk – it could be anything: a children's animation series, a set of books, a live action drama script or a stage play. For this kind of writing you must have the ability to absorb a lot of material quickly and you also have to be capable of putting your own ideas on the back burner. You can't twist the brief in order to accommodate what you want to write as opposed to what the commissioner is *paying* you to write.

Animation

Script writing for animation is energising writing – it makes you think in pictures and images which you have to transcribe into words. An animation series is usually commissioned in blocks of 26 or 52 ten-minute episodes. Once you've been invited to work on the series, background material is usually sent to you by the commissioning body. This outlining material is often referred to as the 'bible' and it contains everything the writer needs to know in order to write the manuscript: the number of characters, locations, props, sets and costumes. The 'bible' might contain a fully executed script, which is really useful as you can read for yourself a script that's been approved by the commissioner and thereafter use it as a guideline.

The writing team

The writing team meet with the commissioner (the person or company funding the show) to go through the 'bible' in some detail. The commissioner will be looking for scripts that contain humour, warmth, clarity and a real understanding of the age group the writers are pitching at. As a writer, you should never allow yourself to lose track of the main character and the central theme: if it's about garden gnomes then keep it in the garden; if it's about a builder then the building job will be essential to *every* story; if it's about a postman then he has to do his post round. I know it's obvious but you'd be astonished how often writers stray from the central plot in their obsession to create their *own* story! Most scripts, even if they're only ten minutes long, have a main plot and a sub-plot which have to reconciled. Make sure your sub-plot doesn't swamp your main plot and make doubly sure your main plot echoes the criteria of the series.

Storylines

Sometimes a few storylines are developed when the writing team is together – just enough to get the team kick-started. The writers may be invited to choose a storyline that excites them and develop it into a three- or four-page treatment, i.e. a scene-by-scene breakdown of the ten-minute episode. Alternatively, writers may be asked to think up and develop more storylines at home. When writing like this on a commission your contract should ensure that you're paid for each stage of the writing process.

The very first outline is often the hardest one of all. The writer may have seen the artwork, may even have seen a pilot script and heard a snatch of the opening music but she's coming to the first story *cold*. The characters aren't alive yet – it's the writer at this vital initial stage who breathes life into them. After a couple of scripts, and certainly after a series of 13 episodes, the characters will be alive and kicking! They will have taken up a space in your imagination and will inspire you with ideas for ten more series! You know what makes them tick because you've created them in the very act of writing. You'll find that within the writing team writers will favour particular characters and bring out the best in that character. It's a heart-lifting experience to work with a team of writers who are open and generous and willing to share their thoughts. By pooling your joint strengths and resources you generate ideas so don't hold back at the writers' meeting. If you've come up with one good idea, think of it as a springboard because you'll need at least another dozen hot on the heels of the first!

The script editor

The script editor is *vital*. He or she coordinates the scripts and makes sure the series has one voice. Four writers will have different styles, which is exactly why they've been chosen to do the job. However, the series itself has the voice – be it that of a ballerina, a robot, or a kind-hearted mule. The script editor has an overall view of the show and will make small changes to scripts so that idiosyncrasies are ironed out. She also has the sensitive task of liaising with the commissioner and the producer on the writers' behalf. Sometimes you *don't* want to see the notes the producer has made: they may be too abrupt or confusing. The script editor will expand and clarify these notes then pass them on to the writers who can then make the necessary alterations to their scripts based on the producer's wishes. The script editor should be valued because she does *a lot* for the writers in the team.

Stages of writing

After the initial idea, followed by a detailed outline (I usually précis mine scene by scene) you may be asked to reconstruct your outline based on changes the animators or the producer have requested. For instance, if you have written an elephant into your script and if that frame (containing your elephant puppet) will cost £8000 you can guarantee someone will want it to go! It's best to sort out all practical problems at this stage and a good producer will go through a script outline with a fine comb, looking for potential problem areas. The animators will tell you what they, in practical terms, can and cannot do so be prepared for notes from them and remember they're the ones who will be shooting the episode when you've been paid off. I usually find animators incredibly helpful, sometimes inspirational as they'll push their puppeteering to the limit and give me brilliant ideas in the process.

Writers expect to get detailed notes on their first draft scripts and shorter notes on their second draft scripts but if problems have been sorted out at the outline stage it's usually a wrap after two drafts. When you get the go-ahead to write the script the real *fun* begins! I have sat at my desk and laughed till I cried at some of the characters I've written for. Behind the lively dialogue there are other things happening simultaneously: movement within the set, expressions, little mutters and mumbles and music too. Sometimes your instructions to camera can be three times as long as a simple piece of dialogue like, 'Oh, all right then.' Occasionally you may wonder, 'How am I going to get all of that information to camera in such a small space?' It's an exacting rigour, which ultimately strengthens your overall writing skills. When your script is approved you get such a sweet feeling of relief. But then you'll start to miss your characters and so begin work on another script idea – and the business starts all over again.

Stage plays

As well as writing my own stage plays I've also adapted stage plays from the classics such as *Hard Times* by Charles Dickens and Homer's *Odyssey*. The Dickens play was commissioned by the Cambridge Youth Theatre for the Edinburgh Festival with a cast of 30, and *The Odyssey* was staged at the Polka Theatre for Children in London with a cast of six!

When briefed by an artistic director writers should listen hard to his or her requirements and it is imperative that they take on board the limitations of the budget. Theatres usually have to work on a shoestring budget. If too much is spent on props and costumes it may be at the cost of the funding for an actor, so be prepared to adapt and compromise.

Adapting from the classics

Adapting from a text such as a classic is an exacting exercise. The two books I adapted couldn't have been more different but the process was exactly the same. I read both books until I knew them backwards: with that knowledge under my belt I felt at liberty to explore the plotlines within the stories and look for modern day angles on how to dramatise them.

The brief for *The Odyssey* was to write a 90-minute play with a ten-minute interval for 8–12 year-olds. *The Odyssey* is full of sex! For instance, Odysseus loiters too long with Circe and nearly dies in his desire to reach the Sirens! In order not to shock my young audience I found a way around this sensitive area by bringing in the crew who made humorous references to Odysseus' behaviour. In one of my scenes Eurylochus says, 'It's time we set sail.' Castor nods towards Odysseus locked in the arms of Circe the Witch and says, 'I don't think the captain's ready for that yet, mate!' The language of Homer is hauntingly beautiful but certainly not pitched at children. The hardest part of writing the play was adapting the language and the plot so that the audience could understand what was going on without destroying the nobility of the original piece. Working closely with the artistic director, it took three drafts to get the tone of the play right but by that time I was so familiar with the gods and heroes of Ancient Greece that they felt like my extended family! It's a knowledge I've never lost and have since written four books based on classical Greek heroes. That's another great thing about writing: you can transpose a story from one art form to another!

Book series

A book series may be commissioned as a result of a writer pitching an idea to a publisher, or a publisher may have spotted a gap in the market which a writer has been invited to fill. The books vary in length depending on the age range – they could be anything from 2000 words to 40,000 words.

I've written three series of books based on football which I knew nothing about but finished up the world's expert on the offside trap! I went on to write several more series based on show jumping, a stage school, a veterinary practice, a drama queen, and an eight-book series based on bridesmaids! A lot of research goes into my books. With my show-jumping series I virtually lived at the livery yard, trailing the head groom and asking questions like, 'Where do show jumpers go when they're not show jumping? How do you treat a lame horse? What's the best fitness diet? Do show jumpers need special shoes and saddles?' I've always been very lucky in finding professionals who allowed me into their lives and let me watch them at work, though I have had a few nasty shocks in the process. Once I found myself masked and gloved in a vast operating theatre at a vet's surgery watching a Newmarket racehorse under the scalpel; but I fled the premises (and my note taking) when a couple brought in a large snake that needed treatment! You *really* do have to know your subject when you're writing this kind of specialist book. The readers certainly know their stuff and are very critical of any inaccuracies. I know this first hand because of all the letters I get from children who've read my series and appreciated the accuracy of them.

Diane Redmond is a prolific writer for children's television. She has worked for Aardman Animation, CBBC, CITV, HIT Entertainment, Cosgrove Hall, Milkshake, Nikelodeon, Nick Jn, CBC (Canada), Cyber Group (France) and Ki-Ka (Germany). Her credits include *Magic Roundabout, Bob the Builder, Postman Pat, Roary the Racing Car, Tweenies, Fifi Forget-me-Not* and *Angelina Ballerina*. She also writes for stage and radio and has published over a hundred books, and is a ghostwriter.

See also...
- *Children's literature on radio and audio,* page 281
- *What does an editor do?,* page 145

BBC children's television

During the day, BBC1 runs two children's channels – Cbeebies for a preschool audience and CBBC for older children. Both have designated early morning and afternoon time slots but programmes run continuously on individual channels on digital, cable and satellite networks. To find out about the commissioning process visit www.bbc.co.uk/commissioning

BBC writersroom

Grafton House, 379–381 Euston Road,
London NW1 3AU
tel 020-7765 2703
website www.bbc.co.uk/writersroom
Creative Director, New Writing Kate Rowland,
Development Manager Paul Ashton

BBC writersroom identifies and champions new writing talent and diversity across BBC drama, entertainment and children's programmes. It considers unsolicited scripts for TV drama, narrative comedy and children's drama/comedy, films, radio drama and comedy, and is also happy to read stage plays. Writers are strongly advised to read the submission guidelines and FAQs on the website before submitting scripts. BBC writersroom can only consider complete scripts of at least 10pp in hard copy (emailed scripts are not accepted). Post to the Development Manager, one at a time. In addition to submission guidelines, the comprehensive website provides advice on scriptwriting, contacts, interviews with prominent writers and BBC executives, formatting templates, free downloadable scripts from BBC productions, details of current opportunities and events, and useful links. Writers can sign up for the monthly newsletter on the homepage. From time to time national and regional open competitions for writers are held. All writers submitting scripts are considered for targeted professional writing schemes and workshops.

CBBC

Television Centre, Wood Lane, London W12 7RJ
tel 020-8743 8000
website www.bbc.co.uk/cbbc,
www.bbc.co.uk/commissioning/tv/network/channels/
cbbc.shtml

Controller Anne Gilchrist

CBBC is the brand for the primary school age group. It offers a distinctive schedule of original drama, animation, comedy, news, factual programming and events on a variety of platforms as well as interactive applications (online, WAP, SMS, enhanced TV) that allow children to get involved, to connect with CBBC and to explore topics further.

Visit the BBC's commissioning website for more details. Send presenter showreels to Sarah Hopper, Room E700 at Television Centre. Launched 2002.

CBeebies

Television Centre, Wood Lane, London W12 7RJ
tel 020-8743 8000
website www.bbc.co.uk/cbeebies,
www.bbc.co.uk/commissioning/tv/network/channels/
cbeebies.shtml
Controller Michael Carrington

CBeebies is the brand for 0–6 year-olds and aims to educate and entertain the BBC's youngest audience. CBeebies is the BBC's first truly tri-media brand, offering TV, radio and web services on all digital platforms. Offers a rich portfolio of content on its website, through its TV outlet and most recently via radio on BBC7.

The CBeebies digital TV channel (on satellite, cable and Freeview) is on-air daily 6am–7pm. CBeebies TV may also be found on BBC TWO.

Visit the BBC's commissionng website for more details. Send presenter showreels to Sarah Hopper, Room E700 at Television Centre. Launched 2002.

Independent children's television

A broad range of independently commissioned and scheduled programmes is available on terrestrial and digital, cable and satellite television networks. ITV, Channel 4 and Channel 5, have allocated children's morning, afternoon and weekend time slots, whereas the digital channels run back-to-back programmes between 12 and 24 hours a day. For channel information, contact Ofcom (www.ofcom.org.uk).

Boomerang

Turner House, 16 Great Marlborough Street,
London W1F 7HS
tel 020-7693 1000
website www.boomerangtv.co.uk

Cartoon entertainment broadcast 24 hours a day, including *Scooby-Doo, Tom and Jerry, The Flintstones* and *Looney Tunes*. Operated by Turner Broadcasting.

Cartoon Network

Turner Entertainments Network Ltd,
16 Great Marlborough Street, London W1F 7HS
tel 020-7693 1000
website www.cartoonnetwork.co.uk

Cartoon entertainment broadcast 24 hours a day, including *Ben 10, Foster's Home for Imaginary Friends, Codename: Kids Next Door* and *Ed, Edd n Eddy*. Operated by Turner Broadcasting. Established 1992.

Channel 4 Television Corporation

124 Horseferry Road, London SW1P 2TX
tel 020-7396 4444, 020-7306 8333 (viewer enquiries),
020-7396 4444 (E4 and FilmFour information)
fax 020-7306 8347
website www.channel4.com/entertainment/t4
Director of Television Kevin Lygo

Commissions and purchases programmes for broadcast during the whole week throughout the UK (except Wales). Also broadcasts subscription film channel FilmFour and digital entertainment channel E4.

Children's early morning viewing is approx. 6–7am and *The Hoobs* and *Spider-man* are programmes shown regularly. Programmes catering for teenagers, such as *Friends, Hollyoaks, Popworld, Shipwrecked, The OC* and *Big Brother*, are shown during weekday early evenings and on the weekend show *T4*.

CITV

200 Gray's Inn Road, London WC1X 8HF
tel 020-7843 8000 *fax* 020-7843 8158
website www.citv.co.uk

Encompasses ITV's dedicated children's programming, aimed at 2–12 year-olds, and CITV's new digital free-to-air commercial children's channel for 2–9 year-olds. Featuring CITV's existing slate of children's programming, the channel looks to expand commissioning opportunities and acquisitions. Programmes include drama, factual, preschool, entertainment, comedy and animation series which aim to both entertain and inform its audiences.

Discovery Kids

Discovery House, Chiswick Park, Building 2,
566 Chiswick High Road, London W4 5YB
tel 020-8811 3000
website www.discoverychannel.co.uk/kids

Satellite and cable network showing mainly science, documentary and nature programmes, such as *Mystery Hunters, History Busters* and *Sci-Busters*. Part of the Discovery Channel and owned by Discovery Communications.

Disney Channel UK

Chiswick Park, Building 12,
566 Chiswick High Road, London W4 5AN
tel (0870) 8807080
website www.disney.co.uk/disneychannel,
www.disney.co.uk/DisneyChannel/cinemagic,
www.disney.co.uk/DisneyChannel/playhouse

A cable and satellite network run by the Walt Disney Company. Disney Channel comprises 3 channels: Disney Channel, Disney Cinemagic (subscription) and Playhouse Disney. Features family-orientated programmes aimed at pre-teens and younger adolescents. Surprisingly, it does not feature many classic Disney cartoons but newer programmes such as *Lizzie McGuire, Hannah Montanna* and the *Higgletown Heroes*. Established 1973; UK version launched 1990s.

Five Broadcasting Ltd

22 Long Acre, London WC2E 9LY
tel 020-7550 5555, (08457) 050505 (comments)
fax 020-7550 5554
website www.five.tv
website www.five.tv/programmes/milkshake
website www.five.tv/programmes/shake
Director of Programmes Dan Chambers

The fifth and last national 'free-to-air' terrestrial 24-hour TV channel. Commissions a wide range of programmes to suit all tastes.

Milkshake! is Five's weekday children's programme slot, 6.30–9.25am. Programmes include *Noddy, Hi-5, Funky Valley* and *Peppa Pig*. Established 1997.

GMTV

London Television Centre, Upper Ground,
London SE1 9TT
tel 020-7827 7000 *fax* 020-7827 7001
email talk2us@gm.tv
website www.gm.tv
Director of Programmes Peter McHugh

GMTV is ITV's national breakfast TV service,
6–9.25am, 7 days a week. GMTV DIGITAL is
GMTV's digital, satellite and cable channel shown on
ITV4 daily, 6–9.25am. GMTV's children's
programming is called *Toonattik* and is broadcast on
Saturday 6–9.25am and Sunday 7.30–9.25am. GMTV
DIGITAL broadcasts children's programmes on
weekdays.

ITV Network Ltd/ITV Association

200 Gray's Inn Road, London WC1X 8HF
tel 020-7843 8000 *fax* 020-7843 8158
email info@itv.com
website www.itv.co.uk
Managing Director (Granada) Mick Desmond,
Managing Director (Carlton) Clive Jones, *Director of
Programmes* Nigel Pickard

Comprises 16 independent regional TV licensees,
broadcasting across 15 regions of the UK.
Commissions and schedules its own programmes and
from independent production companies, shown
across the ITV network. The ITV terrestrial channel is
ITV1. See also CiTV (listed) and the following
websites:

• **Anglia**
  website www.angliatv.co.uk
• **Border**
  website www.border-tv.co.uk
• **Carlton London, Central and West Country**
  website www.carlton.com
• **Channel Television**
  website www.channeltv.co.uk
• **Grampian**
  website www.grampiantv.co.uk
• **Granada**
  website www.granadatv.co.uk
• **HTV Wales**
  website www.htvwales.co.uk
• **HTV West**
  website www.htvwest.co.uk
• **London Weekend**
  website www.lwt.co.uk
• **Meridian**
  website www.meridian.co.uk
• **Scottish**
  website www.scottishtv.co.uk
• **Tyne Tees**
  website www.tyneteestv.co.uk
• **Ulster**
  website www.u.tv
• **Yorkshire**
  website www.yorkshire-television.co.uk

Jetix Europe

Chiswick Park, Building 12,
566 Chiswick High Road, London W4 5AN
tel (0870) 8807080
email info@jetix.co.uk
website www.jetix.co.uk

Owns and broadcasts programmes for children aged
2–14 in Europe and the Middle East. Programmes are
specifically aimed at the needs of different markets,
viewing habits, parental sensitivities and cultural
trends. Also offers localised websites. Launched 1996.

MTV Network UK & Ireland

17–29 Hawley Crescent, London NW1 8TT
tel 020-7284 7777
email pressinfo@mtvne.com
website www.mtv.co.uk

The world's largest 24-hour music TV network. It has
9 cable/satellite/digital channels in the UK: MTV,
MTV Dance, MTV Base, MTV Hits, MTV2, VH1,
VH2, VH1 Classic and TMF which show popular
rock and music videos. All channels except VH1
Classic are aimed at adolescents and young adults.
The company also produces other shows, including
animated cartoons such as *Beavis and Butthead* and
Daria, as well as reality shows and sitcoms such as
The Osbournes. Owned by Viacom.

Nick Jr

15–18 Rathbone Place, London W1T 1HU
tel 020-7462 1000
email letterbox@NickJr.co.uk
website www.nickjr.co.uk

Programmes for preschool children to promote social
and thinking skills through playful entertainment.
Nick Jr. policy is 'join in'. Programmes include
Maisy, Pepper Pig, Maggie and *Angelina Ballerina*, and
classics such as *Bagpuss, Mr Benn* and *The Wombles*.
Launched in 1999.

Nickelodeon UK

15–18 Rathbone Place, London W1H 1HU
tel 020-7462 1000
website www.nick.co.uk

Satellite network known for its innovative children's
programming. There are award-winning channels in
the UK: Nickelodeon, NickToons, Nick Jr, Nick Jr 2
and Nick Replay (programmes include *SpongeBob
SquarePants, Genie in the House, iCarly* and *Dora the
Explorer*). Established in the US in 1979; launched in
UK 1993. Owned by Viacom.

NickToons

15–18 Rathbone Place, London W1T 1HU
tel 020-7462 1000
website www.nick.co.uk

Channel solely devoted to Nick's own produced
children's cartoons (e.g. *SpongeBob SquarePants*).

Radio Telefís Éireann (RTÉ)

Donnybrook, Dublin 4, Republic of Ireland
tel (01) 208 3111 *fax* (01) 208 3080
email info@rte.ie
website www.rte.ie

The Irish national broadcasting service operating radio and TV.

Television Ongoing production of an urban drama serial, *Fair City*. Currently of interest: drama series for mainstream audiences, serials (preferably contemporary) and situation comedies (preferably set in Ireland or of strong Irish interest), with preferred length of commercial half hour or one hour. Proposals for serials and series suitable for a young adult RTÉ 2 audience, either cutting edge or humorous, which could exploit a low-cost DV production model are of particular interest. Full scripts will not be considered – treatments and series/ serial outlines only, except in cases where projects are already part funded. Before submitting material to the Drama or Entertainment departments, authors are advised to write to the department in question to establish initial interest, timing of commissioning rounds, etc.

Radio The RTÉ Radio 1 arts, features and drama department regularly produces documentaries, short stories and radio plays. Email ideas or proposals for future radio documentaries (documentaries@rte.ie). RTÉ Radio 1 holds annual competitions for short stories and radio plays; see the RTÉ Radio 1 website (www.rte.ie/radio1) for details. For further information on submissions email radio1@rte.ie

S4C

Parc Ty Glas, Llanishen, Cardiff CF14 5DU
tel 029-20747444 *fax* 029-20754444
email s4c@s4c.co.uk
website www.s4c.co.uk

Chief Executive Iona Jones, *Director of Commissioning* Rhian Gibson

Welsh language channel S4C is one of the UK's five public service broadcasters. A mixed-genre channel, programming includes drama, sport, children's factual, news, entertainment and culture. Programmes are commissioned from independent production companies with content also produced by BBC Wales and ITV Wales. The channel is available on all digital TV platforms, plus broadband, and has a video-on-demand service. There are subtitles for non-Welsh speakers and learners with signing for the deaf and the hard of hearing.

Smash Hits Channel

Mappin House, 4 Winsley Street, London W1W 8HF
tel 020-7436 1515
email letters@smashhits.net
website www.smashhits.net

24-hour, non-stop music channel where the viewer decides what is played.

Trouble

Flextech Television, 160 Great Portland Street, London W1W 5QA
tel (0870) 043 4027, 020-7299 5000
email enquiries@trouble.co.uk
website www.trouble.co.uk

Channel for teenagers. Shows US programmes such as *Girlfriends* and *Veronica Mars*. Also has interactive programmes such as *Talk to the Hand*. The website claims to have some of the busiest teen chatrooms. Owned by Flextech Television, the content division of Telewest Braodband.

Children's television and film producers

The recommended approach for submitting material is through a literary agency. However, if you choose to submit material direct, first check with the company that they may be interested in your work and whether they would like to receive it.

Aardman Animations
Gas Ferry Road, Bristol BS1 6UN
tel 0117-984 8485 fax 0117-984 8486
email mail@aardman.com
website www.aardman.com
Produces animated TV series, TV specials, short films, feature films, interstitials and commercials. Specialists in model animation. Considers screenplays for cinema and TV. No unsolicited submissions. Only considers proposals via an agent. Founded 1972.

Big Heart Media
Flat 4, 6 Pear Tree Court, London EC1R 0DW
tel 020-7608 0352 fax 020-7250 1138
website www.bigheartmedia.com
Contact Colin Izod
Creates TV drama and documentaries for young people. Founded in 1998.

Calon TV
3 Mount Stuart Square, Cardiff CF10 5EE
tel 029-2048 8400
email enquiries@calon.tv
website www.calon.tv
Managing Director Robin Lyons, Head of Creative Development Andrew Offiler
Animation and children's programmes for TV.

Children's Film and Television Foundation Ltd
Elstree Film and Television Studios, Shenley Road, Borehamwood, Herts. WD6 1JG
tel 020-8953 0844
email annahome@cftf.org.uk
Contact Simon George
Involved in the development and co-production of films for children and the family, both for the theatric market and for TV. Not currently taking on new projects. Founded 1951.

Chocmakers Productions
Unit 19, Silverburn House, Lothian Road, London SW9 6TY
tel 07990 573622
email info@chocmakers.com
website www.chocmakers.com
Directors Stefania Bochicchio, Valerio Baggio, Herbert Bussini

Preschool educational, animation and entertainment programmes for younger viewers.

Collingwood O'Hare Entertainment
10–14 Crown Street, London W3 8SB
tel 020-8993 3666 fax 020-8993 9595
email info@crownstreet.co.uk
website www.collingwoodohare.com
Contact Helen Stroud, Head of Development
Children's animation series for TV for ages 0–12, e.g. The Secret Show, Yoko! Jakamoko! Toto!, Gordon the Garden Gnome, Harry and His Bucket Full of Dinosaurs and Animal Stories. Will only consider material submitted via an agent. Founded 1988.

Cosgrove Hall Films Ltd
8 Albany Road, Chorlton-Cum-Hardy, Manchester M21 0AW
tel 0161-882 2500 fax 0161-882 2555
email animation@chf.co.uk
website www.chf.co.uk
Managing Director Anthony Utley
Screenplays for cinema and TV for animation (drawn, model or CGI) or a 'live action'/animation mix. Series material especially welcome, preschool to adult. Founded 1976.

The Walt Disney Company Ltd
3 Queen Caroline Street, London W6 9PE
tel 020-8222 1000 fax 020-8222 2795
website www.disney.com
Screenplays not accepted by London office. Must be submitted by an agent to The Walt Disney Studios in Burbank, California.

Endemol UK
Shepherd's Building Central, Charecroft Way, London W14 0EE
tel (0870) 333 1700 fax (0870) 333 1800
email info@endemoluk.com
website www.endemoluk.com
Incorporates Brighter Pictures, Cheetah Television, Initial, Zeppotron and Showrunner, which all specialise in a broad range of genres including factual entertainment, reality series, drama series, specialist factual, arts, live events, music entertainment, documentaries, youth shows and comedy.

The Farnham Film Company
34 Burnt Hill Road, Lower Bourne, Farnham GU10 3LZ

tel (01252) 710313 *fax* (01252) 725855
email info@farnfilm.com
website www.farnfilm.com

Television drama, documentaries and film. Particularly interested in children's programmes: drama, comedy and factual. See website for current requirements.

Ginger Productions

1st Floor, 3 Waterhouse Square, 138–142 Holborn, London EC1N 2NY
tel 020-7882 1020 *fax* 020-7882 1040
email ed.stobart@ginger.com
website www.ginger.com
Creative Director Ed Stobart

Entertainment, factual entertainment. Producers of *High School Project–USA* teen series. Part of SMG TV Productions.

HIT Entertainment plc

5th Floor, Maple House,
149 Tottenham Court Road, London W1T 7NF
tel 020-7554 2500 *fax* 020-7388 9321
website www.hitentertainment.com

One of the world's leading children's entertainment companies. Its activities span TV and video production (with studios in the US and the UK), publishing, consumer products, licensing (properties include *Bob the Builder*, *Thomas the Tank Engine*, *Barney*, *Angelina Ballerina*, *Pingu* and *Guinness World Records*) and live events. Founded 1989.

Libra Television Ltd

4th Floor, 22 Lever Street, The Northern Quarter, Manchester M1 1EA
tel 0161-236 5599 *fax* 0161-236 6877
email hq@libratelevision.com
website www.libratelevision.com
Contact Louise Lynch

Children's and education TV programmes.

Lion Television

Lion House, 26 Paddenswick Road, London W6 0UB
tel 020-8846 2000 *fax* 020-8846 2001
website www.liontv.co.uk

Light entertainment, documentaries, drama, children's, the arts, news/current affairs, religion.

Loonland UK Ltd

Royalty House, 72–74 Dean Street,
London W1D 3SG
tel 020-7434 2377 *fax* 020-7434 1578
email info@loonland.com
website www.loonland.com

See also Telemagination.

Lupus Films Ltd

Studio 212, Blackbull Yard, 24–28 Hatton Wall, London EC1N 8JH

tel 020-7419 0997 *fax* 020-7404 9474
email info@lupusfilms.net
website www.lupusfilms.net
Head of Development Ruth Fielding

High-quality children's programming across a variety of genre, from preschool animation to live-action family drama for up to 12 year-olds. Produces 1–2 programmes/films a year. Will consider screenplays for cinema and TV and for other TV programmes submitted *only* from reputable agents or publishers. 'Strong and original ideas will always push through. Watch children's TV and be aware of different channels' preferences and scheduling trends.' The company was set up by Camilla Deakin and Ruth Fielding, formerly the commissioning team for Arts and Animation at Channel 4 Television. Lupus prides itself on being the 'head not the hands' of the animation production process, acting not as a studio but as a production company, seeking out the best ideas and putting together talented teams by accessing their many useful contacts in the industry. Founded 2002.

Millimages

6 Broadstone Place, London W1U 7EN
tel 020-7486 9555 *fax* 020-7486 9666
email info@millimages-uk.com
website www.millimages.com
Managing Director John Reynolds

One of the main children's animation production companies in Europe.

Pesky Productions

11 Morecombe Street, London SE17 1DX
tel 020-7703 2080 *fax* 020-7703 8471
email claire@pesky.com
website www.pesky.com
Contact Claire Underwood

'One stop shop' for the development and production of original characters for licensing and print, interactive content for the internet and animation for games and TV. Productions include *The Amazing Adrenalini Brothers*, winner of BAFTA 2006 Best Animation. Founded 1997.

Praxis Films Ltd

Suite 3N, Leroy House, 436 Essex Road,
London N1 3QP
tel 020-7682 1865 *fax* 020-7682 1868
email info@praxisfilms.co.uk
website www.praxisfilms.co.uk
Contact Tony Cook

Documentaries, current affairs, educational, schools programming for TV. New Media, communications consultancy, media training. Founded 1985.

Ragdoll Productions Ltd

Timothy's Bridge Road,
Stratford-upon-Avon CV37 9NQ

tel (01789) 404100 *fax* (01789) 404136
email stratford@ragdoll.co.uk
website www.ragdoll.co.uk

Company set up by Anne Wood and best-known for *In the Night Garden, Teletubbies, Rosie and Jim, Badjelly the Witch, Boohbah, Brum, Tots TV* and *Pob.* Also works with marginalised children from around the world to create films through its charity, The Ragdoll Foundation.

Rubber Duck Entertainment
120 New Cavendish Street, London W1W 6XX
tel 020-7907 3773 *fax* 020-7907 3777
website www.rde.co.uk

A new division of the Contender Entertainment Group, its first animated series for children, *Tractor Tom*, has been broadcast.

SMG TV Productions
Pacific Quay, Glasgow G51 1PQ
tel 0141-300 3000
email website@smgproductions.tv
website www.smgproductions.tv

Drama, factual, factual/entertainment, entertainment and children's programming. The network TV production arm of SMG plc. Incorporates Ginger Productions.

Sunset & Vine
Elsinore House, 77 Fulham Palace Road, London W6 8JA
tel 020-7478 4700 *fax* 020-7478 7412
email enquiries@sunsetvine.co.uk
website www.sunsetvine.co.uk

Sports programmes. Music Box subsidiary produces entertainment and children's programming, including *Buzz* series, *Kerrang Awards, Popped In Crashed Out* and *Forever.* Sunset & Vine North subsidiary produces documentaries.

Talent Television
Lion House, 72–75 Red Lion Square, London WC1R 4NA
tel 020-7421 7800 *fax* 020-7421 7811
website www.talenttv.com
Managing Director Tony Humphries

Current affairs, entertainment, children's.

Telemagination
Royalty House, 3rd Floor, 72–74 Dean Street, London W1D 3SG
tel 020-7434 1551 *fax* 020-7434 3344
email mail@tmation.co.uk
website www.telemagination.co.uk, www.loonland.com
Managing Director Beth Parker

Producer of animated TV series for children such as *The Telebugs* and *The Animals of Farthing Wood.* One

of the UK's leading full-service animation studios, it has particular experience in large-scale international co-productions. Owned by TV-Loonland, a leading international producer and distributor of TV series and animation in the programming market for children, youth and families. Established 1984; bought by TV-Loonland in 2000.

Television Junction
Waterside House, 46 Gas Street, Birmingham B1 2JT
tel 0121-248 4466 *fax* 0121-248 4477
email info@televisionjunction.co.uk
website www.televisionjunction.co.uk

Education programmes for TV.

Tiger Aspect Productions
7 Soho Street, London W1D 3DQ
tel 020-7434 6700 *fax* 020-7434 1798
email general@tigeraspect.co.uk
website www.tigeraspect.co.uk
Chairman Peter Bennett-Jones, *Managing Director* Andrew Zein, *Head of Animation & Children's* Claudia Lloyd, *Head of Entertainment* Clive Tulloh, *Head of Drama & Co-Chairman, Tiger Aspect Pictures* Greg Brenman, *Head of Factual Group* Paul Sommers, *Finance Director* Dave Harries, *Commercial Director* Jamie Munro, *Head of Legal & Business Affairs* Emma Cockshutt, *Head of Comedy* Sophie Clarke-Jervoise, *Head of Talent* Sarah Shields, *Director of Factual Entertainment & Reality* Lisa Perrin, *HR Director* Helen Matthews

Programme genres include comedy, drama, entertainment, factual, animation, wildlife (Tigress) and feature films (Pictures). Children's programmes include *Star* and *Charlie and Lola.* All material should be submitted through an agent. Founded 1993.

Twofour Broadcast Ltd
Twofour Studios, Estover, Plymouth PL6 7RG
tel (01752) 727400 *fax* (01752) 727450
email enq@twofour.co.uk
website www.twofour.co.uk
Contact Melanie Leach (Managing Director)

Factual, factual entertainment, leisure and lifestyle, and children's TV programmes. Founded 1988.

WarkClements Children's and Youth
IWC Media, Children's, Family & Youth, 3–6 Kenrick Place, London W1U 6HD
tel 020-7317 2230 *fax* 020-7317 2245
website www.iwcmedia.co.uk
Director of Children's, Family & Youth Richard Langridge

Award-winning children's division of ICW Media. Programmes include *Captain Abercromby* and *Jeopardy*, both commissioned by the BBC and *Help! I'm a Teenage Outlaw* for CITV. Currently planning further ventures in children's programming in all areas, including comedy, factual and drama and family films. Founded 2001.

Children's radio

The BBC is the main outlet for radio writers with its strong relationship with children's literature. In addition to storytelling, the BBC commissions and produces dramatisations of children's classics and historically based fiction, as well as a wide range of significant works by contemporary children's authors.

BBC RADIO

BBC Children's Radio

Big Toe Books and Go4It Room 6015,
Broadcasting House, London W1 1AA
CBeebies Radio Room EG30, East Tower, Television
Centre, London W12 7RJ
website www.bbc.co.uk/bbc7/kids
Editor, Children's Radio, BBC Audio & Music Ruth
Gardiner

There are 2 children's radio programmes on BBC
Radio 7 and one on BBC Radio 4. *Big Toe Books* is on
every morning (7–8am) on BBC7 and offers 7–12
year-olds the charce to hear 5 episodes a day of
abridged stories from the very best classic and
modern authors.

CBeebies Radio is broadcast every day on BBC7,
2–5pm, and offers the youngest listeners stories,
songs, rhymes and quizzes.

Go4It on Radio 4 at 7.15pm every Sunday is hosted
by Barney Harwood who is joined by 3 children in
the studio who interview guests and take part in fun
and games.

BBC School Radio

Room 340, Henry Wood House,
3 & 6 Langham Place, London W1 1AA
email schoolradio@bbc.co.uk
website www.bbc.co.uk/schoolradio

Audio resources to support teaching across a wide
range of primary curriculum areas. The programmes
offer a varied and flexible, convenient resource with
learning outcomes which carefully target curriculum
objectives. Programmes are available in 3 ways: as
prerecorded CDs (due to rights restrictions these are
only available to schools in the UK); as 'audio on
demand' using the internet site; and transmission.

A range of programmes includes existing copyright
material while others require original scriptwriting.
Contact the Editor for further details.

INDEPENDENT RADIO PRODUCERS

Crosshands Ltd/ACP Television

Crosshands, Coreley, Ludlow, Shrops. SY8 3AR
tel (01584) 890893 *fax* (01584) 890893
email mail@acptv.com
Contact Richard Uridge
Radio and TV documentaries.

CSA Word

6ᴀ Archway Mews, London SW15 2PE
tel 020-8871 0220 *fax* 020-8877 0712
email info@csaword.co.uk
website www.csaword.co.uk
Audio Manager Victoria Williams

Produces readings, plays and features/documentaries.
Allow approx. 2 months for response to submissions.
Founded 1992.

Loftus Productions Ltd

2ᴀ Aldine Street, London W12 8AN
tel 020-8740 4666
email ask@loftusproductions.co.uk
website www.loftusproductions.co.uk
Contact Nigel Acheson

Produces features, documentaries and readings (no
drama) for BBC Radio. Programmes are mostly for
adults with approx. 5% of output for children aged
5–12, usually documentaries. Also produces audio
guides for museums and galleries, some specifically
for children. Founded 1996.

Lou Stein Associates Ltd

email info@lousteinassociates.com
Contact Lou Stein
Plays for BBC Radio. Founded 2000.

Theatre

Writing for children's theatre

Writing plays for children is not a soft option. David Wood considers children to be the most difficult audience to write for and shares his thoughts here about this challenge.

'Would you write the Christmas play?' These six words, uttered by John Hole, Director of the Swan Theatre, Worcester, unwittingly changed my life, setting me off on a trail I'm still treading 40 years later. It wasn't a totally mad question, even though I was then cutting my teeth as an 'adult' actor/director – and indeed I have managed to continue these so-called mainstream activities to a limited degree ever since. No, it had already struck me that children's audiences were important and, by doing magic at birthday parties since my teens, I had already developed an aptitude for and delight in entertaining children.

At Worcester I had organised Saturday morning children's theatre, inveigling my fellow repertory actors into helping me tell stories, lead participation songs and perform crazy sketches. And I was still

Further information

ASSITEJ UK
website www.assitejuk.org
The UK branch of the International Association of Theatre for Children and Young People. The website lists most of the companies currently in production. In association with Aurora Metro Press publishes *Theatre for Children and Young People* (see Further reading), a comprehensive collection of articles about the development of children's theatre and theatre-in-education in the UK over the last 50 years.

National Theatre Bookshop
National Theatre, South Bank, London SE1 9PX
tel 020-7452 3456 *fax* 020-7452 3457
email bookshop@nationaltheatre.org.uk
website www.nationaltheatre.org.uk

French's Theatre Bookshop
52 Fitzroy Street London W1T 5JR
tel 020-7255 4300 *fax* 020-7387 2161
website www.samuelfrench-london.co.uk

haunted by the memory of seeing, a couple of years earlier, a big commercial panto in which the star comedian cracked an off-colour joke to a matinee house virtually full of children, got an appreciative cackle from a small party of ladies in the stalls, then advanced to the footlights and said, 'Let's get the kids out of here, then we can get started!'. In the dark I blushed and my hackles rose. How dare this man show such disdain for the young audience whose parents' hard-earned cash had contributed towards his doubtless considerable salary? It set me thinking about how few proper plays were then written and performed for children. There were traditional favourites like *Peter Pan* in London, the occasional *Wizard of Oz, Toad of Toad Hall* and *Alice in Wonderland* in the regions but that was about it. Nothing new. Later I discovered my assessment had been too sweeping. There were several pioneers out there presenting proper plays for children, including Brian Way (Theatre Centre), Caryl Jenner (Unicorn), John Allen (Glyndebourne Children's Theatre) and John English (Midlands Arts Centre), but their work was not then widely recognised. Their contribution to the development of children's theatre in the UK cannot be overestimated. Also, in 1965, the Belgrade Theatre, Coventry had created the first theatre-in-education company, touring innovative work into schools; and early in 1967 I had acted in the first production of the TIE Company at the Palace Theatre, Watford.

So writing *The Tinder Box* for Christmas 1967 seemed a natural opportunity and, although I don't think it was very good, it paved the way for me to write around 70 (so far) plays that try to trigger the imagination, make children laugh, cry and think, and hopefully lead them towards a love of theatre. The journey hasn't always been easy. It is frustrating that children's theatre is still often perceived as third division theatre; funding for it is less than for its adult counterpart, even though it often costs as much, sometimes more, to put on, and always commands a lower seat price; critics generally ignore it; and most theatre folk seem to think it is only for beginners or failures, a ridiculous belief, since children are the most difficult and honest audience of all – and yet the most rewarding when we get it right.

Let's pause briefly to talk terminology. The phrase 'children's theatre' means different things to different people. Whereas 'youth theatre' clearly implies that young people are taking part in the play, 'children's theatre' can mean not only children performing but also (more correctly, in my view) theatre produced by adults for children to watch. And, although I have occasionally, and enjoyably, written plays for children to perform (*Lady Lollipop*, from Dick King-Smith's book) or for children to take part in alongside adults (*The Lighthouse Keeper's Lunch*, from Ronda and David Armitage's book and *Dinosaurs and All That Rubbish*, from Michael Foreman's book), the vast majority of my plays have been written for professional actors to perform for children. Don't get me wrong. Participation by children is hugely beneficial and worthwhile, but I like to feel my plays might provide the inspiration to encourage them to want to do it themselves. I believe that children respond to exciting examples that inspire them. I also believe that children are more likely to, say, want to learn to play a musical instrument if they see and hear the best professional musicians playing in a concert. They are more likely to want to excel at football if they see – live or on television – the best professional teams displaying dazzling skills.

So any advice I can offer about children's theatre is mainly aimed towards writers who would like to create plays for grown-ups to perform for children. Having said that, it has always surprised me that several of my professionally performed plays have been subsequently put on by schools and youth groups who cope, showing tremendous flair and imagination, with tricky technical demands. I sometimes wish I could write more plays specifically for schools and youth groups, but I think I might be tempted to oversimplify (which would be patronising) or to try to write enough roles for a very large cast, which might dilute the content and fail to provide a satisfying structure.

Encouragingly, the professional children's theatre scene today is much healthier than when I started. There are many more touring companies (see page 310) large and small, producing high-quality work for all ages. There has been an exciting explosion in the amount of work for under-fives. And at last we have two full-time children's theatre buildings – Unicorn and Polka – who put on their own plays as well as receive other companies' work. They are both in London, and the big hope is that there will in the future be many more such beacons in other cities and towns. Children are entitled to their own theatre, and creating theatre buildings especially for them, run by committed professionals, is the best way to improve the quantity, quality and status of the work. Alongside that, our major theatres, including the National and the Royal Shakespeare Company, should be setting an example by making children's theatre an integral part of their programming, rather than occasionally mounting a children's play as an optional extra. And this means more than coming up with an annual Christmas show.

Study the market

Go and see shows. Which companies are doing what? How many cast members can they afford? Are they looking for original plays as well as adaptations of successful books with big titles and box office appeal? Try to meet the artistic directors, to discuss what they might be looking for. What size spaces are the companies playing in? Studios? Large theatres? Do they have facilities for scene-changes? Is there flying? Incidentally, restrictions on cast size and staging possibilities are not necessarily a bad thing. Well-defined parameters within which to work can be a help not a hindrance. I was asked to write a play for the Towngate, Basildon, a theatre that had no flying, not much stage depth and virtually no wing space. And I was allowed a cast of only six. At first I despaired but then managed to think positively and wrote *The Gingerbread Man*, which ended up paying the rent for 30 years! The play is set on a giant Welsh dresser. No props or scenery come on or off stage during the show – the basic set is self-contained. And the six characters are joined by the off-stage voices (recorded) of the 'Big Ones', the human owners of the dresser.

It may be putting the cart before the horse to worry about where and how your play might be performed – before you've written it! But it really is foolish to start before finding out what might be practical and realistic. Quite frankly, a cast of 20, or even a dozen, is going to be out of the question for most professional companies, so if your idea demands such numbers, maybe you should approach a school, a youth drama group or an amateur dramatic society instead.

Rather than rely on others, might you be in a position to create your own openings? Many children's theatre practitioners, including myself, have had to start by 'doing it themselves'. I, like Richard Gill, Vicky Ireland and Annie Wood (former artistic directors of the Polka Theatre) not only write but also direct. And Richard Gill, Tim Webb (Oily Cart), Guy Holland (Quicksilver) and I (Whirligig), went as far as to create companies to produce our own work, because we knew we were unlikely to get other companies to put it on. The website of ASSITEJ UK (see box) lists most of the companies currently in production, and is a useful first port of call to see the scope of the work.

What 'works' for children?

A good, satisfying story makes a helpful start, told with theatrical flair. By that I mean that we should use theatrical techniques to spark the imagination of the audience – scenery, costume, sound, lighting, puppetry, magic, circus skills, masks, mime, dancing and music. The physical as well as the verbal can help to retain the attention and interest of children. Page after page of two characters sitting talking are likely to prove a turn-off. It's better to see them do something rather than just talk about it. I try to introduce lots of 'suddenlies' to help keep the audience riveted to their seats, wanting to know what happens next. I've often said that my life's work has been dedicated to stopping children going to the lavatory. Suddenlies – a new character appearing, a sound effect, a lighting change, a surprise twist, a musical sting – can be a huge help. Compare it to the page-turning appeal of a successful children's book.

Play ideas can be found in fairy tales, myths and legends, traditional rhymes and popular stories. Be careful, however, not to waste time adapting books in copyright, unless you have got the necessary permission – no public performances, paid or unpaid, can be given without this. Approach the publisher or the author's agent to discover if the stage ,rights are available and, if they are, how much it might cost to acquire them for a year or two.

Or you might use an incident from history, a pertinent modern social issue, such as conservation, or the real life of an inspirational or controversial person. Or you could explore a social problem especially relevant to children, like single-parent families or bullying.

In my book *Theatre for Children: A Guide to Writing, Adapting, Directing and Acting* I identify useful ingredients for children's plays. They are really fairly obvious – things that we know children respond to. They include animals, toys, fantasy, a quest, goodies and baddies, humour, scale (small characters in large environments and *vice versa*), a child at the centre of the story. And justice – think *Cinderella*. Children, like adults, have a strong sense of fairness and will root for the underdog. Roald Dahl's stories, six of which I have been lucky enough to adapt, all use this. Sophie (in *The BFG*), James (in *James and the Giant Peach*) and Boy (in *The Witches*) are all disadvantaged orphans whose strength of character leads them through immense difficulties to eventual triumph. They are empowered to succeed in an adult-dominated world, and children identify with them.

The use of audience participation is an option much argued about by children's theatre practitioners. Many hate it. For some plays, it would, indeed, be totally inappropriate. But for others it can be exciting and fun. I'm not talking about basic panto participation – 'he's behind you!' – though even this can be used on occasion with integrity. I'm talking about what I call 'positive participation', in which the audience contribute to the action by helping or hindering, by having ideas or by taking part in a 'set piece'. In *The Selfish Shellfish* they create a storm to fool an oil slick. In *Meg and Mog Show* (for very small children), they make springtime noises and movements to encourage Meg's garden to grow. In *The See-Saw Tree* they vote on whether to save an ancient oak or allow it to be cut down to make way for a children's playground. In *The Gingerbread Man* they help catch the scavenging Sleek the Mouse under an upturned mug. Their contribution is crucial to the development and resolution of the plot. In *The Twits* the audience fools Mr and Mrs Twit by making them think that they, the audience, are upside down. They all remove their shoes, put them on their hands and stretch their arms up while lowering their heads! The sight of a thousand children all doing this, with joy and not a shred of cynicism, is pure magic to me.

I don't believe that a children's play has to have a moral, a self-improving message for the audience. But I do believe a children's play should *be* moral, presenting a positive attitude and an uplifting, hopeful conclusion. And I resent the notion that children's plays should always be written to tie in with the national curriculum. Many do, but the educationalists shouldn't dictate our agenda – the tail shouldn't wag the dog.

Before you start

I strongly recommend that you create a synopsis, outlining the events in story order. This leads to clarity of storytelling, to the disciplined pursuit of a through-line, with not too many subplots that could end up as time-wasting, irrelevant cul-de-sacs. For myself it would be foolish to think I had the brilliance to start a play with only an initial idea and just let my imagination lead me through uncharted waters. I find it far better to let the juices flow during the synopsis stage and, when it comes to writing the play, to conscientiously follow through my original instincts with not too many diversions.

Good luck with getting your first play produced. Getting it published may need determination. It was a very special day for me when Samuel French accepted (after initial rejections) *The Owl and the Pussycat Went to See…*, my second play, co-written with Sheila Ruskin. After its first production at Worcester, I beavered away to get it on stage in London and, thanks to several friends helping financially, managed to produce it at the Jeannetta Cochrane Theatre. To save money I directed it myself. We were lucky enough to get two rave reviews. I approached Samuel French again. They came to see it and, hallelujah, offered to publish it. Since then their loyalty has been more than gratifying – they still publish most of my efforts. There are now several specialist ,children's play publishers, many of whom also act as licensees of amateur performances. The National Theatre Bookshop and French's Theatre Bookshop stock a fair number of plays and, when searching for a publisher, it is worth checking out their shelves. The internet can help too. Tap in the names of successful children's playwrights, like Mike Kenny, Charles Way or Adrian Mitchell and see what comes up.

I find that the challenge of writing a play for children never gets easier, however many times I go through the process. It certainly isn't a soft option, i.e. easier than writing a play for adults. And it carries, I believe, a big responsibility. I always worry that I haven't the right to fail! The last thing I want to do is write something that might put children off theatre for life. I'm aware that many in the audience will be first-time theatre-goers, some of whom never asked to come! It's so important to get it right, to enthuse them so much they can't wait to return. And this is where the passion comes in. Most children's theatre practitioners are passionate about what they do, with an almost missionary zeal to stimulate and delight their audience. Also, we all know that, unlike adult audiences who tend to sit quietly and clap at the end, even if they've hated the play, our children's audiences won't be – and shouldn't be – so polite. It is palpably obvious when we 'lose' them. We are dedicated to using our experience and instinct to 'hold' them, to help them enjoy the communal experience of a theatre visit and willingly enter the spirit of the performance. The buzz I get from being in an auditorium of children overtly having a great time – listening hard, watching intently, reacting, feeling, letting the play take them on a special, magical, unique journey – is a buzz I constantly strive for. I suppose that's really why I do it.

David Wood OBE has been dubbed 'the national children's dramatist' by *The Times*. His plays are performed regularly on tour, in the West End and all over the world. In 2006, for the Queen's 80th birthday party celebrations, he wrote *The Queen's Handbag*, which was broadcast live from Buckingham Palace Gardens and watched by 8 million viewers on BBC1. His website is www.davidwood.org.uk.

Further reading

Stuart Bennett (ed.), *Theatre for Children and Young People*, Aurora Metro Press, 2005
Wood, David, with Janet Grant, *Theatre for Children: A Guide to Writing, Adapting, Directing and Acting*, Faber and Faber, 1997

See also...
- *Adapting books for the stage*, page 304
- *Writing to a brief*, page 287

Adapting books for the stage

Stephen Briggs ponders the challenges and rewards of dramatising other people's novels.

Why me?

Stephen Briggs? Stephen Briggs? Who on earth is Stephen Briggs to write about adapting novels for the stage?

Well, many years ago I wrote a stage version of *A Christmas Carol* for my amdram group... no, stick with me on this.... *Then*, a few years later I adapted two Tom Sharpe novels (these were for one-off productions and the scripts are now long gone). *However*, my overwhelming – and more recent – experience has been with dramatising the novels of Terry Pratchett. I've now adapted 16 of Terry's books and 14 have so far been published – four for Transworld/Doubleday, two for Samuel French, two for Oxford University Press and six for Methuen Drama (now at A&C Black). These have been staged by amateur groups in over 20 countries from Zimbabwe to Antarctica (yes, really, Antarctica) and by professional groups in France and the Czech Republic. I also co-scripted *The Twelve Days of Hogswatch* for Sky One to promote their big budget television movie of Terry's *Hogfather*.

I have been involved in amateur theatre since I left school. Not just acting, but also directing, choreography, set design/construction, costume design/construction – even including brewing mulled wine for the audiences in our chilly medieval theatre. None of this makes me an expert, not by any interpretation of the word, but I was the one who had to make my scripts work on stage since I also directed them. I was also able to get useful and honest feedback from the original author. Hopefully I've learned a few lessons along the way, which I'm happy to pass on.

Dialogue

When you watch a film, a lot of screen time is taken up by fancy stuff – Imperial star cruisers roaring through space, ill-fated liners ploughing the waves, swooping pan shots over raddled pirate ships. In a play, you don't get any of that stuff. The dialogue has to drive the action.

The methods used to adapt a novel for the stage are as varied as the authors you try to adapt. Terry Pratchett, like Charles Dickens, writes very good dialogue and the scenes already leap from the page. Other authors make greater use of narrative which the adapter has to weave into the play as well, if they are to keep to the spirit of the original work. Terry is well known for his use of footnotes and, for some of the plays, I even included the Footnote as a 'character' – a Brechtian alienation device, for those who want a more literary justification.

Keep it simple

Terry Pratchett writes 'filmically' – his scenes cross-cut and swoop like a screenplay. On the silver screen, you can set a scene visually in a second. On the stage it can take longer, and you have to give the audience a chance to realise where they are if they are to have any chance of keeping up with the – often quite complex – plot.

It's important to remember that a theatre audience doesn't have the luxury of being able to re-read a page, or skip back to check a plot point – they (usually) get to see the play only once. It's vital, therefore, to ensure that important plot points are not lost along the way while one is tempted to keep in other favoured scenes from the much longer novel.

Keep it moving

Novelists are not constrained by budget – they can destroy cities, have characters who are 60-foot long dragons, write vital scenes involving time travel and other difficult concepts. These can initially appear to be a challenge for anyone without the budget of Industrial Light and Magic.

When I write, I have the good fortune to be writing for a theatre which has very limited space – on and off stage – and virtually no capacity for scenic effects. This makes staging the plays a nightma …, ahem … a challenge, but the benefit is that my adaptations can be staged virtually anywhere. I don't write them with essential big effects or big set changes. Of course, drama groups with huge budgets can go wild with all that – but the plays can work without it.

Plays which demand massive set changes or pose huge scenic problems are likely to put off many directors working to a tight budget. It's different if you're Alan Ayckbourn, of course… onstage swimming pool, floating river cruiser… no problem.

People say that radio has the best scenery. Allowing the audience to fill in the gaps can not only save on costly wood and canvas but, on occasions, can even be more effective than an expensive but stagey scenic effect. After all, Shakespeare's *Antony and Cleopatra* includes a sea battle between two great navies – all seen by two blokes standing on a hill.

The plays – like the books – have to keep moving. Scenes need to flow fairly seamlessly into one another. Set changes slow things down. I get to see large numbers of productions of my plays and the general rule is that the ones with frequent set-changes are the ones which plod.

Writing for schools

Two of my plays were written specifically for classroom use. I had to bear in mind that the plays were as likely to be used for reading in a classroom as well as for production on a stage. So I tried to keep the amount of stage directions to a minimum because I know all too well from reading plays with my own amateur drama group that the need to read through huge chunks of explanatory stuff in italics, interspersed with snippets of uninformative dialogue, is very tedious. Here is an example (not, I hasten to add, an extract from a real play):

> (*As Smithers looks out of the window, Bert rushes downstairs, carrying an aspidistra in a brass bowl. He passes, but fails to notice, the gorilla. He trips and falls, dropping the plant and pot on Smithers' head*)
>
> SMITHERS: Oof!
>
> (*Smithers picks up a broom from the floor and chases after Bert. They run into the kitchen and out again, up the stairs and across the landing. Bert takes a wad of banknotes out of his pocket and throws them at Smithers*)
>
> BERT: Take that!

It was also important to try to avoid characters with just 'one line and a cough'. Nothing is worse in a read-through than to be given the role of 'King of France' only to find that the character speaks one line on page one and then is silent for the rest of the play. Except, perhaps, being allocated a role meant for someone of the opposite sex and then finding it contains dialogue that will invite ridicule from the rest of the class…' I fink I've got a beard coming through' or 'Oh la, I feel so pretty; I do love wearing frilly pink underwear'.

I also try to ensure that whatever special effects are mentioned should be either easily achievable or not essential and again, that the plays can be performed with the minimum amount of scenery.

The two plays I wrote for OUP were the only ones I had written which I would not be staging myself. It was really fascinating (and quite gratifying) to see the plays staged by schools and to find that they *worked*.

How do I start?

• **I read the book.** Then I read the book again. I then put it down, leave it for a week and write down all the main plot points I can recall, and a rough list of scenes. That should give me a rough shape for the play. Anything I've forgotten to include can probably go high up on the list of potential material to cut.

• **I write it.** I sit down and write the script. At this stage I don't try to keep to a specific length; I just adapt the book, making mental notes of any scenes that show potential for trimming, cutting or pasting into another as I go along. My overall plan is to keep the play to around two hours. If, when I get to the end, the play is too long, I then go back and look again at each scene and character to ensure they can justify their place in the script.

• **I dump it.** Reducing a 95,000-word novel into a 20,000-word play means that there will have to be an element of trimming. The trick, I suppose, is to ensure that the cuts will not be too glaring to the paying audience ('I reckon if we cut out the Prince of Denmark, we can get *Hamlet* down to an hour and a half, no problem'). Hopefully, there will be subplots, not vital to the main story, which can be excised to keep it all flowing. But even so, occasionally tough decisions have to be made once all the fat's been removed and one is forced to cut into muscle and bone (as it were). It's important to let stuff go – even if it's a favourite scene in the book, or a favourite character.

• **I share it.** It's good then to let someone else read it. It's all too easy to get so far into the wood that you can no longer see the trees. Being challenged on the decisions you made in adapting the book is a very good thing. I'd certainly recommend anyone adapting a book to have the script read by someone who knows the book well, and who can point out any important plot omissions. It is also good to have your script read by someone who does *not* know the book and who can ask the 'what on earth does that mean?' questions.

It's useful for me that many of my drama club are not *Discworld* 'fans'. Their outsider's view of the script is extremely useful. I also then have the luxury of amending the script in rehearsal to tidy up scenes, add in bits and take bits out. This means that the script which is submitted to the publishers is then fully tried and tested.

Some golden rules

It's difficult to be hard and fast about 'rules' for adapting books, but here are a few useful guidelines that I do try to stick to:

• **Don't change the principle plot** – there's no point in calling a play *Bram Stoker's Dracula* if you're then going to have Dracula surviving at the end and starting up a flourishing law firm in Whitby.

• **Never sacrifice 'real' scenes in order to add in some of your own** – after all, you've chosen to adapt the author's work because, presumably, you admire their writing. If you think you can improve on their humour/drama/characterisation you should really be writing your own plots and not torturing theirs!

• **Use the author's dialogue whenever possible** – same as the above, really. Also try to attribute it to the right character whenever practicable.

• **Don't add characters** – stick to the ones the author has given you.

• **Don't be afraid to cut material** – after all, you're trying to squeeze a 300-page novel into a two-hour play; you just can't fit everything in, so don't try. Anything which does not advance the main plot should be on your list for potential dumping if your play overruns.

• **If it doesn't** *need* **changing – don't change it!**

As well as the 16 plays he mentions in his article, **Stephen Briggs** is the co-author, with Terry Pratchett, and illustrator, of *The Discworld Companion, The Streets of Ankh-Morpork, The Wit & Wisdom of Discworld* and a small raft of other publications emanating from Terry Pratchett's *Discworld* books. He reads the unabridged audio versions of Terry's books for Isis (in the UK) and for HarperCollins (in the US). In 2005 he was awarded an Audie (a US industry award) for his reading of Terry's *Monstrous Regiment*. His website is www.cmotdibbler.com.

See also...

• *Writing to a brief*, page 287

Theatre for children

London and provincial theatres are listed below; listings of touring companies start on page 310.

LONDON

Polka Theatre
240 The Broadway, London SW19 1SB
tel 020-8545 8320 *fax* 020-8545 8365
email info@polkatheatre.com
website www.polkatheatre.com
Artistic Director Jonathan Lloyd

Exclusively for children between 0 and 13 years of age, the Main Theatre seats 300 and the Adventure Theatre seats 80. It is programmed 18 months–2 years in advance. Theatre of new work, with targeted commissions. Founded 1967.

Royal Shakespeare Company
1 Earlham Street, London WC2H 9LL
tel 020-7845 0515 *fax* 020-7845 0505
website www.rsc.org.uk
Artistic Director Michael Boyd, *Company Dramaturg* Jeanie O'Hare

Based in Stratford-upon-Avon, produce a core repertoire of Shakespeare alongside modern classics and new plays, and the work of Shakespeare's contemporaries. Commission adaptations of favourite novels and stories for their Christmas show. Produce a season in London each year of plays first produced in Stratford. Works with contemporary writers, encouraging them to write epic plays. The Literary department seeks out the playwrights to commission. Read unsolicited work, but do monitor work of emerging playwrights in production nationally and internationally.

The Company is currently undergoing a four-year rebuilding programme transforming the Royal Shakespeare Theatre and the entire Waterside complex of studios, rehearsal rooms, actors' cottages and workshops. The theatre is being re-modelled to create a thrust stage within a 'one room' theatre. Waterside is being re-modelled to create state-of-the-art facilities for artists.

Soho Theatre
21 Dean Street, London W1D 3NE
tel 020-7478 0117 *fax* 020-7287 5061
email erin@sohotheatre.com
website www.sohotheatre.com

Aims to discover and develop new playwrights, produce a year-round programme of new plays and attract new audiences. Producing venue (144-seat theatre) of new plays and comedy. The Writers' Centre offers an extensive unsolicited script-reading service and provides a range of development, the

Westminster Prize, a thriving Young Writers' Programme, commissions and seed bursaries and more. There is also a large self-contained studio space with 85-seat capacity plus theatre bar, restaurant, offices, rehearsal, writing and meeting rooms. Primarily for adults but has staged *The Gruffalo* and *Private Peaceful*. Founded 1972.

Theatre-Rites
Unit 202, The Blackfriars Foundry,
156 Blackfriars Road, London SE1 8EN
tel 020-7953 7102 *fax* 020-7953 7041
email info@theatre-rites.co.uk
website www.theatre-rites.co.uk
Artistic Director Sue Buckmaster

Creates theatre for young people using a mix of performance, installation, puppetry, video and sound. It 'feeds the imagination and encourages adults and children to share magical experiences'. Founded 1995.

Unicorn Theatre
147 Tooley Street, London SE1 2HZ
tel 020-7645 0500 *fax* 020-7645 0550
email stage.door@unicorntheatre.com
website www.unicorntheatre.com
Executive Director Christopher Moxon, *Artistic Director* Tony Graham, *Associate Artistic Director* Rosamunde Hutt, *Associate Director & Literary Manager* Carl Miller, *Associate Artist (Literary)* Charles Way

At the end of 2005 Unicorn moved into its new theatre near Tower Bridge, where it produces a year-round programme of theatre for children and young people (0–19 years). In-house productions of full-length plays with professional casts are staged across 2 auditoriums, alongside visiting companies and education work. Unicorn rarely commissions plays from writers who are new to it, but it is keen to hear from writers who are interested to work with the Unicorn in the future. Its aim is for its work to be artistically led, truthful, and insistent on the primacy of imagination. It asks: does the play matter to children; does it have a sense of poetry; does it contain a child's perspective; is it drama; can it transcend and transform?

Do not send unsolicited MSS as Unicorn does not have the resources to read and respond to them in appropriate detail. Send a short statement describing why you would like to write for Unicorn and a CV or a summary of your relevant experience.

Whirligig Theatre
14 Belvedere Drive, London SW19 7BY
tel 020-8947 1732 *fax* 020-8879 7648

email david.woodplays@virgin.net
Artistic Director David Wood

Formerly a touring company, it is open to suggestions from theatres for one-off productions.

Young Vic Theatre Company
66 The Cut, London SE1 8LZ
tel 020-7922 2800
email info@youngvic.org
website www.youngvic.org
Artistic Director David Lan

Metropolitan producing theatre producing great plays of the world repertoire. Founded 1969.

PROVINCIAL

The Byre Theatre of St Andrews
Abbey Street, St Andrews KY16 9LA
tel (01334) 476288 *fax* (01334) 475370
email enquiries@byretheatre.com
website www.byretheatre.com

Offers an exciting year-round programme of contemporary and classic drama, dance, concerts, comedy and innovative education and community events. Operates a blend of in-house and touring productions. Education programme caters for all ages with Youth workshops and Haydays (for 50+). Offers support for new writing through the Byre Writers, a well-established and successful playwrights group.

Chichester Festival Theatre
Oaklands Park, Chichester, West Sussex PO19 6AP
tel (01243) 784437 *fax* (01243) 787288
email admin@cft.org.uk
website www.cft.org.uk
Artistic Director Jonathan Church

Summer Festival Season April–Sept in Festival and Minerva Theatres together with a year-round education programme, autumn touring programme and youth theatre Christmas show.

Clwyd Theatr Cymru Theatre for Young People
Mold, Flintshire CH7 1YA
tel (01352) 701565 *fax* (01352) 701558
email education@clwyd-theatr-cymru.co.uk
website www.ctctyp.co.uk,
www.clwyd-theatr-cymru.co.uk
Director Terry Hands, *Associate Director* Tim Baker,
Literary Manager William James

An organisation dedicated to both enlightening young people through theatre and creating an audience for the future through theatre production and related activities. Also the home of Clwyd Theatr Cymru.

Contact Theatre Company
Oxford Road, Manchester M15 6JA
tel 0161-274 3434 *fax* 0161-274 0640

email raw@contact-theatre.org
website www.contact-theatre.org
Artistic Director John E. McGrath

Interested in working with and for young people aged 13–30. Send sae for writers' guidelines or see website.

The Egg
Sawclose, Bath BA1 1ET
tel (01225) 823409 (Egg reception), (01225) 823433 (Egg administration)
email egg.reception@theatreroyal.org.uk
website www.theatreroyal.org.uk/egg

Part of the Theatre Royal Bath, the Egg is a purpose-built theatre for young people and their families. It hosts and produces shows for children and young people alongside a year-round participation and outreach programme for people aged 2–25. Opened in 2005.

Everyman Theatre
Regent Street, Cheltenham, Glos. GL50 1HQ
tel (01242) 512515 *fax* (01242) 224305
email admin@everymantheatre.org.uk
website www.everymantheatre.org.uk
Chief Executive Geoffrey Rowe, *Artistic Director* Kirsty Davies

Regional presenting and producing theatre promoting a wide range of plays. Small-scale experimental, youth and educational work encouraged in The Other Space studio theatre. Contact the Artistic Director before submitting material.

Leeds Children's Theatre
c/o The Carriageworks Theatre, The Electric Press, 3 Millennium Square, Leeds LS2 3AO
email info@leeds-childrens-theatre.co.uk
website www.leeds-childrens-theatre.co.uk

One of the many amateur dramatic societies based at The Carriageworks Theatre. A member of the Leeds Civic Arts Guild, Leeds Children's Theatre stages 2 shows each year. It is dedicated to the principle of quality, affordable children's entertainment in order to encourage the introduction of the theatrical experience to young children. It covers most aspects of theatrical production. Membership is open to all young people. Workshops for children of all ages. Adult membership is also available. Founded 1935.

Leighton Buzzard Children's Theatre
12 Linslade Road, Heath and Reach, Leighton Buzzard, Beds. LU7 0AU
tel (01525) 237469
email sally@lbct.org
website www.lbct.org

A community-based group which exists to introduce young people to the joy of theatre, to develop theatre craft and to enhance enjoyment of performance through community involvement. It offers a unique opportunity to young people aged 5–18 to act, sing, dance, improvise, communicate, have fun and learn.

Library Theatre Company

St Peter's Square, Manchester M2 5PD
tel 0161-234 1913 *fax* 0161-228 6481
email ltcadmin@manchester.gov.uk
website www.librarytheatre.com
Contact Artistic Director

Produces mostly contemporary drama with a major play for children and families at Christmas. A recent family production was Neil Bartlett's version of *Oliver Twist*. Will consider scripts from new writers. Allow 4 months for response.

Norwich Puppet Theatre

St James, Whitefriars, Norwich NR3 1TN
tel (01603) 629921 (box office), 615564 (admin.)
fax (01603) 617578
email info@puppettheatre.co.uk
website www.puppettheatre.co.uk
General Manager Ian Woods

Norwich Puppet Theatre is the base for a professional company which creates and presents its own productions at the theatre, as well as touring to schools and venues throughout the UK and to international venues and festivals abroad. Founded 1979.

Nottingham Playhouse

Nottingham Playhouse Trust Ltd, Wellington Circus, Nottingham NG1 5AF
tel 0115-947 4361 *fax* 0115-947 5759
website www.nottinghamplayhouse.co.uk/playhouse
Chief Executive Stephanie Sirr, *Artistic Director* Giles Croft

Works closely with communities of Nottingham and Nottinghamshire. Takes 6 months to read unsolicited MSS.

Roundabout is the Theatre in Education company of Nottingham Playhouse. Produces plays and workshops for children and young people, and training and support for teachers. Since 1975 Roundabout has created over 250 plays, and performed to over half a million children.

Queen's Theatre, Hornchurch

(Havering Theatre Trust Ltd)
Billet Lane, Hornchurch, Essex RM11 1QT
tel (01708) 462362 *fax* (01708) 462363
email info@queens-theatre.co.uk
website www.queens-theatre.co.uk
Artistic Director Bob Carlton

500-seat producing theatre serving outer East London with permanent company of actors/musicians presenting 8 mainhouse and 4 TIE productions each year. Treatments welcome; unsolicited scripts may be returned unread. Also offers writer's groups at various levels.

The Queen's Youth Theatre Programme provides the opportunity for young people aged 7–18 to become involved in drama. There is no selection process on the basis of experience or ability.

Sherman Cymru

Senghennydd Road, Cardiff CF24 4YE
tel 029-2064 6901 *fax* 029-2064 6902
email admin@shermancymru.co.uk
website www.shermancymru.co.uk
Director Chris Ricketts, *General Manager* Margaret Jones, *Literary Manager* Sian Summers

Regional repertory theatre producing a third of its plays for children. Produces work for the very young (under 5s) and Christmas productions for 6–12 year-olds and teenagers. Also participatory work with youth theatres for 15–25 age range. Recent children's productions include *Impossible Parents Go Green* (Arad Goch) and *Big Bad Wolf*, adapted by Victoria Goddard (Theatr Nan-og). No unsolicited submissions. Founded 1987.

TOURING COMPANIES

Arad Goch

Stryd Y Baddon, Aberystwyth, Ceredigion SY23 2NN
tel (01970) 617998 *fax* (01970) 611223
email jeremy@aradgoch.org
website www.aradgoch.org
Artistic Director Jeremy Turner

The company performs in Welsh and English and tours nationally throughout Wales, and occasionally abroad. It uses a visual and imagistic style often drawing both on contemporary physical theatre and on traditional performance techniques. The company is particularly interested in enabling children and young people to recognise and appreciate their own unique cultural identity though theatre. Some of the company's work is based on traditional material and children's literature but it also commissions new work from experienced dramatists and new writers. As well as creating productions which are performed in theatres, Arad Goch also creates many theatre-in-education projects for junior and secondary schools and offers seminars/workshops about this specialist work to teachers and to college and university students. Founded 1989.

Booster Cushion Theatre

75 How Wood, Park Street, St Albans, Herts. AL2 2RW
tel (01727) 873874 *fax* (01727) 872597
email boostercushion@hotmail.com
website www.booster-cushion.co.uk

Theatre company formed specifically to work with children to encourage them to take a greater interest in books. It has performed to over 300,000 people in schools and theatres in the UK using pop-up books up to 3m tall and concertina books over 5m wide.

All shows are solo performing shows using mime, voice and some sign language. They involve a high level of audience participation on the part of the children and are designed to foster a feeling of strong involvement in the event by drawing the audience in. Each show is completely portable and can be performed inside or outside as the technical requirements are minimal. Founded 1989.

Cahoots NI
109–113 Royal Avenue, Belfast,
Northern Ireland BT1 1FF
tel (28) 9043 4349 *fax* (28) 9043 4339
email info@cahootsni.com
website www.cahootsni.com
Artistic Director Paul Bosco McEneaney

A professional children's touring theatre company which concentrates on the visual potential of theatre and capitalises upon the age-old popularity of magic and illusion as an essential ingredient in the art of entertaining. It aims to provide inspiring theatrical experiences for children and to encourage appreciation of the arts in children from all sections of society. Each production is at the centre of a body of outreach work designed to maximise artistic potential, customise the individual theatre experience and extend the imaginative life of the piece beyond the actual event. Founded 2001.

Classworks Theatre
The Junction, Clifton Way, Cambridge CB1 7GX
tel (01223) 249100
email info@classworks.org.uk
website www.classworks.org.uk
Contact Gayle Macgregor, General Manager

Professional touring company which focuses on new work for and with young people. Also provides supporting workshops. Tours locally and nationally to small- and mid-scale arts venues. Founded 1983.

Cornelius & Jones
49 Carters Close, Sherington,
Newport Pagnell MK16 9NW
tel/fax (01908) 612593
email admin@ corneliusjones.com
website www.corneliusjones.com
Co-directors Neil Canham and Sue Leech

A small touring theatre company which performs for children and adults in schools and theatres. The company creates its own productions and commissions scripts and music. Founded 1986.

CTC Theatre
Arts Centre, Vane Terrace, Darlington DL3 7AX
tel (01325) 352004 *fax* (01325) 369404
email ctc@ctctheatre.org.uk
website www.ctctheatre.org.uk
Artistic Director Paul Harman

Creates theatre experiences for children and young people which aim to contribute to their emotional,

spiritual and social development. The company promotes greater awareness of the value of theatre to children and young people by working with teachers and others through courses, events and publications. It tours professional theatre productions to schools and venues within Tees Valley, the North East and nationally. Organiser of the annual Take Off Festival since 1994.

The Hiss & Boo Company Ltd
1 Nyes Hill, Wineham Lane, Bolney,
West Sussex RH17 5SD
tel (01444) 881707 *fax* (01444) 882057
email ian@hissboo.co.uk
website www.hissboo.co.uk
Managing Director Ian Liston

Not much scope for new plays, but will consider comedy thrillers/chillers and plays/musicals for children. Produces pantomimes. No unsolicited scripts – telephone first. Plays/synopses will be returned only if accompanied by an sae.

Imaginate
45A George Street, Edinburgh EH2 2HT
tel 0131-225 8050 *fax* 0131-225 6440
email info@imaginate.org.uk
Director Tony Reekie, *General Manager* Tessa Rennie

Imaginate is an arts agency committed to promoting and developing performing arts for children in Scotland. See page 352 for further information.

Kazzum Arts Project
Studio 8, 4th Floor, The Old Truman Brewery,
91 Brick Lane, London E1 6QL
tel 020-7539 3500
email info@kazzum.org
website www.kazzum.org
Artistic Director Daryl Beeton

Creates playful theatre and participative arts for young people, using art forms that reflect international influences. The work embraces the beliefs, emotions and creativity of its audience. It is a theatre and participative arts company which applies an innovative approach to producing theatre that allows young people to become part of a captivating experience in a safe environment. These aims are achieved through:

• small-scale touring productions for audiences aged up to 8
• large-scale interactive installations for audiences aged 10+
• 'Pathways', a programme of arts activities for young people across Greater London's refugee community
• education and outreach work in schools and community settings
• research and development with artists of vision.
Founded 1989.

Konflux Theatre in Education
St Thomas's Parish Rooms, Neville Terrace,
York YO31 8NF

tel/fax (01904) 611355
email info@konfluxtheatre.com
website www.konfluxtheatre.com
Artistic Director Anthony Koncsol

Tours throughout the UK with workshops and performances for children and young people. Its Creative Learning Workshops (for Early Years through to KS2) and Play in a Day project (KS1–3) involve working interactively with groups in schools, arts centres and small receiving houses, using drama to enhance personal and social development whilst at the same time enriching and extending the National Curriculum.

The Philosophy for Children project, Stone Soup, blends performance and discussion and encourages children (KS2) to question what kind of role they play within their community. Konflux has also produced work which tackles environmental issues and it works with more than 1000 schools every year. Founded 1997.

Legend Theatre

31 Darley Road, London SW11 6SW
tel 020-8767 8886 fax 020-8767 8886
email admin@legendtheatre.com
website www.legendtheatre.com
Contact Bob Clayton

Tours primary schools and theatres throughout the UK with entertaining and educational productions. The emphasis is always on movement, mime, clowning, masks, puppetry. Productions are based around the education of a popular historical period relevant to KS2 and the National Curriculum. Founded 1990.

The Little Angel Theatre

14 Dagmar Passage, London N1 2DN
tel 020-7226 1787
email info@littleangeltheatre.com
website www.littleangeltheatre.com
Artistic Director Peter Glanville

The theatre is committed to working with children and families, both through schools and the local community. It is developing innovative projects to improve access to their work, offer opportunities for participation, and stimulate learning and creativity for all using puppetry. Every term it runs activities for children, families and schools, including the Saturday Morning Puppet Club, family workshops and schools projects such as the highly successful Puppet Power. It also runs puppetry courses for teenagers and adults, as well as INSET training for teachers.

Shows last about an hour and many are toured to theatres, arts centres and festivals. The Little Angel Education Programme works with schools, youth groups and Education Authorities; it is a strategic plank in the theatre's ongoing work with children and young people.

M6 Theatre Company (Studio Theatre)

Hamer C.P. School, Albert Royds Street, Rochdale, Lancs. OL16 2SU

tel (01706) 355898 fax (01706) 712601
email info@m6theatre.co.uk
website www.m6theatre.co.uk
Contact Dorothy Wood

Theatre-in-education company providing high-quality theatre for children, young people and community audiences.

Magic Carpet Theatre

18 Church Street, Sutton on Hull, East Yorks. HU7 4TS
tel (01482) 709939 fax (01482) 787362
email jon@magiccarpettheatre.com
website www.magiccarpettheatre.com
Director Jon Marshall

A small touring company which incorporates the traditional skills of variety theatre, the circus and puppets including clown, slapstick and physical theatre to make highly entertaining productions for schools and theatres. Founded 1982.

Moby Duck

12 Reservoir Retreat, Birmingham B16 9EH
tel 0121-2420400
email guyhutchins@blueyonder.co.uk
website www.moby-duck.org
Contact Guy Hutchins

Produces stimulating, challenging and accessible work for young people and adults that celebrates the common ground between cultures. Tours throughout the UK, presenting new cross art form cross-cultural work to young children and adults in small- and middle-scale theatres, arts centres, village halls and schools. Also performs in less conventional venues, e.g. a farm equipment museum, a Crown Court and a 3-hole Georgian privy! Performances are storytelling-led and have included live Karnatic music, western jazz, Bharatanatyam dance, masks, mime, puppetry, visual arts, digital media and Eastern and Western cooking. Founded 1999.

Oily Cart

Smallwood School Annexe, Smallwood Road, London SW17 0TW
tel 020-8672 6329 fax 020-8672 0792
email oilies@oilycart.org.uk
website www.oilycart.org.uk
Artistic Director Tim Webb

Touring company staging 2 children's productions a year. Multi-sensory, highly interactive work is produced, often in specially constructed installations for 2 specific audiences: children aged 6 months–6 years and young people with profound and multiple learning disabilities. Considers scripts from new writers but at present all work is generated from within the company. Founded 1981.

Pop-Up Theatre

27A Brewery Road, London N7 9PU
tel 020-7609 3339 fax 020-7609 2284

email admin@pop-up.net
website www.pop-up.net

Touring company that performs specially commissioned productions for young people. The vitality and relevance of the company's work is informed and enriched by working directly with children, and sensitively addresses relevant issues for its audience. The performances inspire discussion and show children that they are not alone in the thoughts and emotions they experience. The company plays to an annual audience of over 25,000 in theatres, art centres, schools and nurseries both in the UK and overseas.

Initiatives such as Equal Voice and Dramatic Links give opportunities for young people to develop skills for drama and for life and for adults to understand what a modern childhood is like. They also enable writers, directors and designers to key into young people's concerns and emotions and to actively integrate their responses into the company's touring shows. Founded 1982.

Proteus Theatre Company
Queen Mary's College, Cliddesden Road, Basingstoke, Hants RG21 3HF
tel (01256) 354541 *fax* (01256) 356186
email info@proteustheatre.com
website www.proteustheatre.com
Artistic Director Mary Swan

Small-scale touring company particularly committed to new writing and new work, education and community collaborations. Produces 3 touring shows per year plus several community projects. Founded 1979.

Quicksilver Theatre
4 Enfield Road, London N1 5AZ
tel 020-7241 2942 *fax* 020-7254 3119
email talktous@quicksilvertheatre.org
website www.quicksilvertheatre.org
Joint Artistic Director/Ceo Guy Holland, *Joint Artistic Director* Carey English

A professional touring theatre company which brings live theatre to theatres and schools all over the country. Delivers good stories, original music, kaleidoscopic design and poignant, often humorous, new writing to entertain and make children and adults think. Two to three new plays a year for 3–5 year-olds, 4–7 year-olds and children 8+ and their families. Mission: to make life-changing theatre to inspire and entertain. Founded 1977.

Red Ladder Theatre Company
3 St Peters Buildings, York Street, Leeds LS9 8AJ
tel 0113-245 5311 *fax* 0113-245 5351
email rod@redladder.co.uk
website www.redladder.co.uk
Artistic Director Rod Dixon

Theatre performances for young people (13–25) in theatre venues and youth clubs. Commissions 1–2

new plays each year. Runs the Red Grit Project, a theatre training programme for young people (18–25) in Yorkshire.

Replay Productions
Old Museum Arts Centre, 7 College Square North, Belfast BT1 6AR
tel (028) 9032 2773 *fax* (028) 9032 2724
email info@replayproductions.org
website www.replayproductions.org
Artistic Director Richard Croxford

Provides professional theatre that entertains, educates and stimulates children and young people. It produces educational theatre performances, activities and accompanying resource materials to primary, secondary and special schools throughout Northern Ireland and the Republic of Ireland. Founded 1988.

Sixth Sense Theatre for Young People
c/o The Wyvern Theatre, Theatre Square, Swindon SN1 1QN
tel (01793) 614864 *fax* (01793) 616715
email sstc@dircon.co.uk
website www.sixthsensetyp.co.uk

A professional theatre company prioritising work with young people. It promotes theatre and helps young people explore issues that are important to them. Each year, the company produces both issue-based and creative theatre productions and performs in schools, theatres and arts centres in Swindon and the South West region. These productions are supported by additional young people-led work, workshops, training sessions and other additional production projects.

Theatr Gwent Theatre
The Drama Centre, Pen-y-Pound, Abergavenny, Monmouthshire NP7 5UD
tel (01873) 853167 *fax* (01873) 853910
email gwenttie@vwclub.net
website www.gwenttheatre.com

Commissions, devises and tours productions for young people to schools and communities. Offers individually designed workshops and INSET for schools, work experience for young people, an advisory service for schools, theatre tours and youth theatre.

Theatr Iolo
The Old School Building, Cefn Road, Mynachdy, Cardiff CF14 3HS
tel 029-2061 3782 *fax* 029-2052 2225
email info@theatriolo.com
website www.theatriolo.com
Artistic Director Kevin Lewis

Aims to produce and programme the best of live theatre, making it widely accessible to children and young people in Cardiff and the Vale of Glamorgan, to 'stir the imagination, inspire the heart and challenge the mind'. The company works alongside teachers and subject advisers to enhance teaching and learning across the curriculum.

Theatre Centre

Shoreditch Town Hall, 380 Old Street,
London EC1V 9LT
tel 020-7729 3066 *fax* 020-7739 9741
email admin@theatre-centre.co.uk
website www.theatre-centre.co.uk
Director Natalie Wilson

New writing company producing 3 plays a year and touring nationally and internationally. All productions are for children and/or young people, staged in schools, arts centres and other venues. Recently produced *Trashed* by Noël Greig, *Walking on Water* by Sarah Woods, *Journey to the River Sea* by Carl Miller adapted from the novel by Eva Ibbotson, *God is a DJ* by Oladipo Agboluaje and *Romeo in the City* by Amber Lone. It also manages the Brian Way Award. Keen to hear from writers from ethnic minority groups. Response time to submissions can be lengthy. Founded 1953.

The Theatre Co Blah Blah Blah

The West Park Centre, Spen Lane, Leeds LS16 5BE
tel 0113-274 0030
email admin@blahs.co.uk
website www.blahs.co.uk
Artistic Director Anthony Haddon

Takes theatre to young people at youth centres and schools across the country and internationally. Productions combine creative freedom with stark realism. Founded 1985.

Theatre Is...

The Innovation Centre, College Lane,
Hatfield AL10 9AB
tel (01707) 281100 *fax* (01707) 281038
email info@theatreis.org
website www.theatreis.org
Contact Michael Corley

Challenging and creating new models of live performance by, with and for young audiences across the East of England.

Theatre Workshop

34 Hamilton Place, Edinburgh EH3 5AX
tel 0131-225 7942 *fax* 0131-220 0112
email info@theatre-workshop.com
website www.theatre-workshop.com
Contact Robert Rae

Cutting edge, professional, inclusive theatre company. Plays include new writing/community/children's/disabled. Scripts from new writers considered.

Travelling Light Theatre Company

13 West Street, Old Market, Bristol BS2 0DF
tel 0117-377 3166 *fax* 0117-377 3167
email info@travellinglighttheatre.org.uk
website www.travlight.co.uk
Artistic Producer Jude Merrill

A professional touring company performing at schools, theatres, community venues and festivals in the UK, Europe and beyond. It presents new work, either devised or commissioned scripts, exploring themes and issues of special interest and relevance to young people. The performance style is highly physical, visual and musical.

Tutti Frutti Productions

Space@Hillcrest Community Primary School,
Cowper Street, Leeds LS7 4DR
tel 0113-262 2662
email emma@tutti-frutti.co.uk
website www.tutti-frutti.co.uk
Artistic Director Wendy Harris

Professional theatre aimed specifically at family audiences (age 3+ and adults). Productions are adaptations of children's books or specially commissioned pieces and include original music together with different artforms, i.e. puppetry, dance, movement. Tours nationally and performs in a host of different small-scale venues, including arts centres, village halls, rural touring schemes and schools, undertaking approx. 200 performances a year. Founded 1991.

Resources for children's writers
Setting up a website

Suna Cristall explains the procedure for setting up a website and presents the options for its design. She includes points to consider if the target audience includes children.

Having your own personal website is a fantastic promotional tool and will allow you to display your work and achievements to a global audience spanning all age ranges, genders and economic stratums. The internet is increasingly becoming the first place people look to find information and, with a staggering 14.3 million households with internet access in the UK alone (according to the National Statistics website, www.statistics.gov.uk), it is worthwhile making yourself accessible through this media.

Setting up a website can seem like a daunting task, especially if you're not very technically literate. However, there is absolutely no need to feel intimidated as there are options available to suit all budgets and levels of web-programming skills (even if you have none to speak of).

Getting started

First things first – you will need a web address, otherwise known as a domain name. It is basically the equivalent of a home or business address; people can only come and visit if they have an address to navigate to. Try to keep your domain name as simple as possible as this will make it easier for people to remember. It should also be something relevant to you, or to your work. This is particularly pertinent not only so that people can make a clear connection between you and your web address, but to avoid any potential legal issues. For example, HarryPotter.com is indubitably a memorable domain name, but it is rather likely that the author's, publisher's, and film company's legal teams will have a few things to say about you using it for yourself.

If you decide to hire a professional designer he or she can take care of the actual purchasing for you, but do note that they will charge you further for the privilege. There are a multitude of different companies you can buy a domain name from, all unfortunately with varying prices, so it is highly recommended that you shop around. It is also advisable to confirm that the company is ICANN certified. ICANN is the Internet Corporation for Assigned Names and Numbers and acts as the regulatory body for domain registrars. A list of ICANN certified domain registrars can be found on their website: www.icann.org/registrars/accredited-list.html

Planning your website

As with any form of design there are certain principles to follow which will ensure your end product is successful. Even if you choose to hire someone to create your website for you, it is worth noting the following basic guidelines for good web design as they will help you make an informed decision when it comes to finalising your layout.

• **Clear navigation.** Your visitor could be aged nine or 90, but if they cannot easily navigate their way around your website they will be equally frustrated by the experience. If someone gets lost whilst browsing your website, it is likely that you will lose them completely – people are more liable to log off than persevere as few like their patience challenged in that manner.

• **Be consistent.** This goes hand in hand with keeping your site navigation clear as it helps your visitors recognise where they are. Changing the look and structure of your website from page to page will only serve to confuse and disorientate people. It is the online equivalent of having different wallpaper and flooring in every room in your house. You want your website to flow and appear organised, with a clear design concept executed throughout.

• **Structure your text.** The average individual spends approximately 20 seconds per web page, and tends to simply 'scan' it as opposed to reading every line. With this in mind, it is highly recommended that you label your sections clearly to help your visitors find the information they require more easily. Also, make points of interest bold and eye-catching. This does *not* mean using lots of flashing images or text as those sorts of devices tend only to be effective at irritating people. It is also worth noting that most children are reluctant to scroll, so try to keep your content concise and constrained to the immediate visual area of the screen.

• **Readability.** Dark text on light backgrounds is best for the purposes of reading onscreen as it is the easiest on the eyes but, whatever your colour choice, make sure there is a high contrast between these two elements otherwise your copy simply blends into the background. Make sure to apply an appropriate font size, so that text is large enough to be legible, but not so large it looks like you are SHOUTING.

• **Fonts.** Sans-serif fonts, such as Geneva, Arial or Helvetica are the easiest to read on a computer screen. As an added bonus, these also happen to be 'web-safe' fonts. Web-safe fonts basically refer to the standard fonts that are on every computer system. They may be prettier but non-web-safe fonts are not universally installed, and using one would be a gamble as you run the risk of your visitors' computers not being able to recognise your specified font.

• **Current content.** Be wary of your site 'dating' itself. The content may be current at the time of construction, but how will it read six months later? To avoid your content being classified as *passé*, use the present or present-perfect tense as much as possible. Likewise, try to update your site regularly as this will help to generate repeat visitors.

• **Screen size.** Monitors come in all different sizes, with varying default resolutions. With this in mind it is good practice to design your site for the smaller screens – 800 (width) by 600 (height) pixels. People with larger screens will still be able to view all of the content on your site, whereas the reverse will cause unsightly bottom and side scrollbars (a rather unfortunate web design *faux-pas* that is easily avoided).

• **Page size.** Download time varies according to file size and the speed of internet connection. Faster connections are rapidly becoming the norm for business and home use, but it is still advisable to keep your web pages as small as possible so that people with slow dialup connections can still access your site at a reasonable speed. Graphics, animations and audio clips are generally the biggest culprits for bumping up file sizes, so keep your image resolutions low and your sound bytes short. If you want to include things such as high resolution images, provide a thumbnail of the image with an option of clicking to download the larger version.

• **Accessibility.** Making websites accessible to disabled users is not only good practice, but with new legislations being regularly introduced, this will eventually be *standard* practice. To ensure your website is up to scratch on this level, you will need to provide basic text equivalents for things such as images, audio/video clips, animations, etc, describing what they are so that a web reader can process the information. ALT tags are the most commonly used for this purpose (these are the buttercup-yellow text boxes that pop up when you hover the cursor over an image).

Know your audience

Knowing who your website is targeted at is a key step in the process, as your design and content will alter depending on whom you wish to reach. Even though your creative work may be aimed at children you will need to make certain you do not alienate parents, teachers, or people offering potential commissions. Fortunately, what makes a successful website does not differ between age groups as much as one might think, although there are certain deviations worth noting. In a study conducted by the Neilsen Norman Group, interesting revelations were made regarding how both children (aged 6–12) and teenagers (aged 13–17) use the web and it highlighted the unique distinctions between the two groups as well as the general similarities. They discovered that the younger age group participants were able to successfully use the sites that were aimed at adults, such as Google, successfully as they are minimally designed with clear navigation. They also responded well to animation and sound effects – the fun stuff. If you would like to include these elements in your website, it is advisable you do so as add-ons and not at the expense of your navigation, as the children were uniformly flummoxed when the navigation was convoluted. Notably, the children rarely scrolled down a screen, but instead randomly moved their cursor over the page looking for clickable areas.

The teens were online more often on a regular basis, as they purported to utilise the internet for school projects, hobbies, news and information, and e-commerce as well as entertainment (which was the main reason given for use by the younger age group). They responded particularly well to cool looking graphics and clean designs.

Most importantly, both groups demanded an element of interactivity to hold their interest – sites lacking this component were quickly classified as boring and the children did not hang around. Interactivity can be achieved in an assortment of ways and it is essential to have at least one of these attributes on your website for children and teenagers:
• quizzes
• forums or message boards
• voting
• games
• contact details, such as an e-mail address.

Designing your site

Now that you've got your domain name, understand the basic principles of good web design and have somewhat of a clue as to what children want (at least pertaining to websites), you are ready to start building your website.

As previously mentioned, there are a variety of options available to you with regard to designing and building your site. There is a solution out there to suit every level of available finances and technical savviness. They can be divided into three groups: DIY, ready-made, and professional.

• **The DIY option.** Although this option is cost effective, it requires a basic knowledge of HTML (HyperText MarkUp Language) and some time and patience on your part. HMTL is a language like any other and can be learned should you have the inclination. It is this vernacular that formats your web page and allows the browser to interpret text styles, links, images, etc. If you have never encountered it before, it can certainly look rather complicated (like sci-fi robot-speak) but rest assured it really is quite straightforward and follows a very simple logic. Should you decide to learn some HTML or already have a basic knowledge, this will most certainly be an asset when it comes to creating and maintaining your website. There are some extremely helpful software programmes on the market to assist you in building your website. Two of the most popular are Macromedia Dreamweaver and Microsoft FrontPage. These programmes are designed to be as user-friendly as possible and code parts of your site automatically for ease. They also come equipped with pre-designed web templates, so if you are feeling slightly less adventurous, you can simply add your content and images within their pre-established parameters. As an added bonus, there are plenty of books, online tutorials and forums that offer assistance should you find yourself in need.

• **The ready-made option.** Realising that there are a vast amount of individuals and businesses that desire websites, but lack the technical ability, time and patience to create their own or have insufficient resources to hire a professional designer, a few companies have recently emerged offering a ready-made option (the greatest invention of convenience since the TV dinner). These companies have already gone to all of the trouble for you and have created a complete professionally designed website. You simply choose your design and add your content through their interface, which is purposefully constructed for even the most technically challenged amongst us. They tend to charge on a monthly basis, but are truly affordable. The main drawback with this option is that you are constrained by their design templates and it is likely that other people will have chosen the same template as you, so your visitors may be struck by a case of *déjà vu*. However, the instant gratification of having a complete and professional looking website in a matter of hours more than makes up for the lack of creative freedom.

In a similar vein, you might want to consider using a blogging or social network site, such as Blogger.com or MySpace.com. These are free to use once you register with the main site and open your blog or personal profile up to a pre-existing online community. Although these will not entirely replace having a personal website, they are a great way to instantly get yourself online.

• **Employing a professional.** It pains me to say that we're a dime a dozen, but there is no denying that there are a ridiculous number of web designers out there. A recommendation from a trusted source, as with anything, is always helpful. However, if one is not forthcoming, make a note of the name of design companies that have created sites you like. When choosing a designer, it's worth assessing them on:

• *examples of their previous work* – they may be your sister's husband's first cousin on his mother's side, but if you don't like their style of design, don't employ them; no rabbits will be pulled out of any hats just because you're 'family';

• *company history* – this will give you a better idea of their level of experience and professionalism;

• *references* – they are working for you, so do not be afraid to ask for testimonials of satisfied clients;

• *charges* – you need to clarify how much they will charge you for the initial build as well as if there are any further charges for updates, etc.

Going online

Once you have successfully built your website (or had it built for you) it is time to put it 'live'. To get your website online you will need to purchase a hosting package. Your website, for all intents and purposes, is a file and needs to be stored somewhere which will allow public access. This is where the hosting company comes in – they provide the crucial disk space on their servers which will host your website.

Again, much like with domain registrars, there are many hosting companies in operation with varying annual charges, so by all means, do your research and compare price plans. Obviously, this step is only applicable if you have designed the site yourself. Otherwise, you have duly paid for the luxury not to have to worry about these things.

As soon as you have chosen and paid for your hosting package, you will receive a confirmation e-mail supplying you with the information you need to transfer your files over to them. The first step will be to log into the account you created when you purchased your domain name and change the name server to the one specified by your hosting company. This is a straightforward process, but do not hesitate to contact your domain registrar if you need assistance. This change tends to take approximately 48 hours to propagate. Whilst you are waiting for this to happen you can proceed with uploading your website to your hosting account. This is achieved by using a FTP (File Transfer Protocol) client or your web page editor and again, is a very simple process but do feel free to contact your hosting company if you are having trouble.

All that is left for you to do now is to promote your website – people won't know to visit if they don't know it exists. Add your web address to your business cards, as your e-mail footer and post your web address on other websites that have relevance to yours. Also post it within blog comments, forums, message boards, and/or by requesting a link (offering a reciprocal link is polite and always appreciated). As well as increasing targeted awareness of your website, the links also serve to improve your search engine rating (i.e. how high on the search results page your website appears). It really pays to be proactive on this front as the more traffic you encourage, the more people will know about your work, which of course is the whole point of all this rigmarole.

Suna Cristall lives in London and works as a freelance web designer.

Learning to write for children

Many people have what they consider to be brilliant ideas for children's books but have no experience of writing. But lack of experience need not get in the way of bringing an idea to fruition as there is guidance available in the form of courses. Alison Sage demystifies what happens on a writing course for children and outlines the benefits to be gained.

Can you teach people to write for children?

There are quite a few who think you can't. There is an implicit idea that writing is a talent you are born with and that one day, sitting at the word processor in your kitchen (why is it always the kitchen?) your innate ability will suddenly surface like a lottery ticket, and you will write a bestseller that will pay your mortgage and take you on exotic holidays for life.

After many years working in publishing and talking to would-be writers, I have come to the conclusion that this is only a tiny fraction of the truth. Writing is like any other talent and it improves with being used. Dancers dance, musicians play and writers have to write and write and write to get better.

There is no doubt that some people have more aptitude for writing than others. But besides natural talent, a writer must have something to say.

Next, a writer needs to have the persistence and self belief to continue to write through all kinds of distractions and discouragement. And finally, if a writer wants to be published successfully, he or she needs a certain amount of luck.

The role of writing classes

First and most importantly, writing classes can give the writer a chance to explore different kinds of writing in a non-judgemental atmosphere. It is the job of the teacher to help students to experiment until they find what suits them.

Students can also meet other people in the same situation. Writing can be a very lonely pursuit. A writer's friends are usually embarrassed to give their honest opinion about a story because it is a recipe for falling out. Every writer knows the despair of writing something which at first sounds wonderful and then on re-reading sounds rubbish. Where can writers find an independent judgement? Whoever they ask must be someone they can trust to be impartial, someone who can suggest where their good ideas become woolly and perhaps even how they might go about improving things. However, these must always be *suggestions*. It is the writer who must decide how, where, and in what way to alter the manuscript.

In an ideal world, the publisher's editor would help new writers endlessly until they achieved a bestselling novel. The reality is that publishers' editors are too busy to nurture every single would-be talent. Therefore, it is up to the writer either to go it alone – which many do – or to find someone else to act as a sounding board. This is where writing classes can help.

Who benefits most from writing classes?

It is impossible to guess at the beginning of a course how far students will develop their talent or even who will actually get published. Obviously, different teachers suit different people, but I have found an astonishing range amongst my students. That is what makes it so exciting and rewarding – and so unpredictable. The only student who is unlikely to be happy is the one who says: 'Teach me to write a bestseller.' This is frankly impossible and anyone who believes that writing is an exact science is bound to be disappointed.

Interestingly enough, the one thing that can indicate how far a student will get – apart from their persistence, of course – is how flexible they are. Often, people who are highly educated are actually at a disadvantage. They believe they have been taught how to write correctly – and that there is a 'right' and a 'wrong' way to do it. Nothing could be further from the truth, particularly when writing for children. Therefore, I have seen an Oxford graduate watch enviously as another student, still at school, sends the whole class into fits of laughter with a perfect story. I have had students who were models, refugees, counsellors, puppeteers, housewives, diplomats, postmen, soldiers, office managers, nurses, with children, without children or simply out of work. One of my best students left school aged 15. He is now editing a magazine and I still wonder if he will ever write his children's novel… Another is now a published author/illustrator, through his own talent and a great deal of effort. Yet another is looking after her children – and one day perhaps the quiet brilliance of her writing will find a publisher.

A typical course outline

Every course is different because every student is asked what they hope to achieve and this obviously affects what we do. However, certain things are always included in some form.

It may sound self evident, but central to a writing course is getting students to write. Students develop through putting new ideas into practice. Therefore, every class includes about 15 minutes' writing time and students read out and talk about what they have written. Most students are nervous at first, because they feel they are unprepared. But this rarely lasts because writing on the spot seems to bring the group closer together. It also relaxes everyone, as no one can be expected to write a bestseller in 15 minutes and at this point, students invariably have brilliant ideas and express them unbelievably well. If anyone gets stuck, they simply explain that the topic hasn't worked for them. Different students shine at different topics and this helps to steer them towards what they ultimately want to write.

Finding a story

The first place to look for a story is in your own experience. All students are asked to write something about their first memories of their baby brothers or sisters because when students genuinely remember their own childhood, their language becomes simpler, their writing more powerful and direct. They write in a way they never would if they were consciously trying to 'write for children'. This is a very important step in trying to discover what is your own voice. Writers need to know not only what they want to say, but also how they are going to put it over.

The class then usually discusses what kinds of story are appropriate for different ages. Perhaps one of the most common mistakes made by new children's writers is that they write about very young topics in a very sophisticated fashion. If you are aiming to write a picture book for a three year-old, you need to understand a little of what a three year-old can cope with. It is no use writing a story that is 10,000 words long.

However, a nine year-old is not going to be interested in stories designed for a three year-old – even if technically they are suitable. In fact, a good rule of thumb is that children are interested in most of the things that adults are – except they are not used to dealing with concepts. A child may love a book about a character who is alone, or brave, or funny. They will not be so interested in loneliness, heroism or humour in the *abstract*. Children are also not very comfortable with irony until they are about nine or ten years old, tending to take the printed word at its face value. However, when they *do* discover it, they love it.

The beginning

The next thing to stress is the importance of the beginning. Many students think that page one is where a writer finds his feet and that the story proper starts about page six. This is not true. The first paragraph of a book is crucial. Children invest a lot of energy in reading a book and they want to be convinced pretty quickly that this effort is going to be worthwhile. A dull first page means that the book will be put down, never to be opened again. Even more to the point, perhaps, a busy editor reading an unsolicited manuscript will also lose interest if the beginning of the story is dull or confusing and they will make this the excuse they need to return it immediately. The beginning must draw the reader in. If a story is the solving of a problem, then the beginning must make that problem sound exciting and tantalising.

At this point, it is usually a good idea for the class to discuss strategies for keeping going with a story. Finishing a story gives a student a great boost and in itself, is a huge learning curve. Different strategies are helpful for different people. Some students need a writing routine – a special chair or table or cup of coffee. For others this is either no use or impossible to maintain. Some find writing notes at the end of each writing session is helpful, so that they can more easily get into the flow of ideas where they broke off. And most people find a notebook helpful, where they can record interesting ideas and experiences to be used as the raw material for future stories. If you are able to go into a school and help with reading, this can be a great eye opener as you will see first hand which stories children struggle over and which really work.

A vital ingredient

Another vital topic usually covered at this stage of the course is tension. Tension is what makes you want to continue reading and without tension, a story is as dull as a meal without salt. Just as a joke falls flat if the timing is wrong, so a fascinating story can become boringly muddled if the author does not build to a climax. It is about choosing selective details and using the reader's own imagination to create suspense. A description of the monster's claw grasping from behind the door is far more terrifying than a complete rundown of the whole creature.

If you think of your own favourite childhood story, it is often not the end that sticks in your mind. It is the bit just before the climax. That is when the tension and suspense should be strongest. At the end of the story, you can ask a question or add a twist, to give the impression that your characters will continue even after the book has been shut.

Talk about getting published

Finally, most students are interested in the mechanics of getting published, and this is a minefield for would-be authors. It is difficult to get your work singled out from a pile of unsolicited manuscripts and while (eventually) good writers are usually discovered, it can be a long and tortuous process.

There are things you can do to improve your chances and while they are mostly common sense, this is probably an area where a good writing class can help. Look in your local bookshop for the publishers which produce the kind of books you admire. There is an outside chance that if you like them, they might like you. Far too many good manuscripts are sent to the wrong places and if a publisher produces medical books, he or she is not likely to be interested in a children's manuscript, even if it is *Harry Potter*.

Sharing an interest

Perhaps the most important thing is to enjoy writing and to meet other people who are also interested. That way, students can keep each other going through the rejections and at the very least, improve at something they want to do. There are a great many courses which cater for all different kinds of interests, attitudes and expectations. The best place to look is probably at the local adult education institute. If there is no course specifically listed for writing for children, it is worth ringing up and asking if they would like to start one. You could also put up a notice in your local library for anyone else who might be interested and as soon as you are a group, the authority will take notice of you. You could even start your own independent writing group!

There are also several residential courses (such as the Arvon Foundation courses), and they are a very enjoyable and relaxing way to take your ambitions further. Look on the internet, as these courses constantly change and new ones are added every year. Several universities and colleges also run long and short courses in children's writing and you can achieve a diploma in Writing for Children, although this would take you at least a year.

So can writing be taught?

The debate will certainly continue, as people point out that teachers on courses rarely become as famous as some of their students. However, there *are* things which are helpful to discover when you are starting out as a children's writer. And perhaps the encouragement of the group will make sure that you continue writing until instead of your returned manuscript, it is the publisher's contract that drops through your letterbox!

Alison Sage is an experienced commissioning editor of children's books and has worked for a variety of publishers including Oxford University Press, HarperCollins and Random House. Alison is also a writer and anthologist and her *Treasury of Children's Literature* won the Children's Book of the Year Award in 1995. She has run many courses on creative writing for children for Kensington & Chelsea and Hammersmith adult education institutes.

See also...
• *Children's writing courses and conferences,* page 328
• *Online resources about children's books,* page 330

Indexing children's books

Valerie A. Elliston is a Fellow of the Society of Indexers.

What is an index?

An index is 'a systematic arrangement of entries designed to enable users to locate information in a document' (British Standard BS ISO 999: 1996). Unlike the general contents page, it is a key to far more specific detail. There are two basic categories of reader: those who have not read the book and those who have. A good index will help the former to decide whether the book suits his or her needs. It will help the latter to revisit any part of it without having to riffle through all the pages. These statements apply equally to publications for children as well as for adults; the benefits can be enjoyed by both, especially if the skill of using an index is learned in the early years.

Further information

Society of Indexers
Woodbourn Business Centre, 10 Jessell Street, Sheffield S9 3HY
tel 0114-244 9561 *fax* 0114-244 9563
email admin@indexers.org.uk
website www.indexers.org.uk
Administrator Wendy Burrow
Membership £92.50 p.a. UK/Europe, £116 outside Europe; corporate: fewer than 50 employees £185, more than 50 employees £278

Visit the website or contact the Administrator for further information. Publishers and authors seeking to commission an indexer should consult *Indexers Available* on the website.

Useful websites
www.nc.uk.net/nc/contents
www.standards.dfes.gov.uk/primary/publications

Why index children's books?

The vital importance of indexing information books for children has been highlighted over many years, at least since the mid-1930s. This was confirmed in a survey sponsored by the British Library Research and Innovation Centre (Williams and Bakewell 1997). All 16 publishers participating in this investigation rated this importance very highly. Yet, fewer than one-third said that they always included an index in publications for children, with reasons for exclusion given chiefly as restrictions on budget, time and space. Sometimes the contents page is considered sufficient, even though this lacks essential details.

Advantages of indexes

Firstly, the National Curriculum (2000) requires that children should be taught sound information retrieval practice, using organisational features and systems to locate texts. Secondly, the Primary National Strategy includes in its non-fiction objectives: understanding the purpose of contents pages and indexes; finding information by page numbers and initial letters of words. Later, the aim includes finding parts of text that give particular information. Children should also use dictionaries to find words by using initial letters, and the teacher is advised to demonstrate scanning the index for information, asking the children to familiarise themselves with the contents pages, indexes and glossaries of the information books. Thirdly, using an index is one of the earliest tools of independent research as well as helping to promote analytical skills. Despite increasing use of the internet, books will be with us for a long time yet, and children are being encouraged more and more to read them, not only for enjoyment but in preparation for future studies. Finally, skill in using indexes can help when searching for information on the internet.

Disadvantages of a book that lacks an index

The Williams and Bakewell survey found a number of negative effects, chiefly that children lose patience and interest if they have to spend time looking through a whole book for specific information. Younger ones often find scanning difficult, and can therefore fail to develop independent searching methods, remaining reliant on the teacher or librarian. The survey also found that primary school children viewed the index as a highly important feature and assumed that every non-fiction book would have one. An 11 year-old asked how they were supposed to find anything in a book without an index. Workshops conducted by an indexer in a secondary school confirmed children's intelligent interest in the use of indexes. They were quick to grasp the importance of choosing relevant terms and of keeping the number of page references to a minimum. In fact, by the end of each session, the participants were able to criticise a selection of books from the school library, rejecting those without an index and rating the rest according to the quality of the index while taking into account the overall layout and appropriateness of the entries. Another indexer worked with groups of 10–11 year-olds who examined a selection of books and decided which were the key topics on each page before checking in the index. They gave points for inclusion and accuracy, becoming ever more discriminating as they progressed.

Quality of the indexes

Indexes for children's books should be just as high quality as for adults' books, perhaps even more so as children need to be taught with the best examples against which future use can be measured. A clear, accurate and well-presented index can encourage their use, just as a disappointing one can reduce their interest. It follows, therefore, that the index should be carefully planned, not tacked on as an afterthought or made by a computer without any consideration for the particular needs of the young user.

• **Terminology** should be appropriate for the age group, using words that children would be expected to know. Most will be taken from the text, but sometimes thought has to be given to the choice between additional entries or cross-referencing which can be a problem for younger users. For example, the text might mention 'currency' but it would be helpful to also include 'money' in the index or to cross-reference it with '*see also* money', according to the age group.

• **Subheadings** should be avoided if possible as they can confuse younger children. However, they might be necessary to avoid using too many locators (i.e. page or paragraph numbers).

• **Indexing names** needs careful consideration as there are many options. Should rulers be indexed individually or be listed as subheadings under the main entries 'kings' and 'queens'? Should titles or surnames be inverted as in indexes to adult books? The most suitable form of the name should be chosen for the particular index (e.g. 'Geldof, Bob' as opposed to 'Geldof, Sir Robert'). Correct spelling is essential, of course.

• **Consistency** is also important: should singular or plural terms be used for countable nouns? The British Standard already quoted recommends the use of the plural form for 'countables' and singular for 'non-countables'. For example, the countables 'chairs', 'cars' not 'chair' and 'car'. The plural is unlikely to arise for non-countable nouns, e.g. 'furniture', 'traffic', 'coffee'. The British Standard recommends lower case initial letters except for proper nouns.

• **Omission** of key topics is a major fault as, if children cannot find the item in the index, they will often assume it is not dealt with in the text and will give up. The index needs to be attractive and reliable, to appeal to the eye yet remain an invaluable tool.

Presentation of indexes

Presentation is particularly important to children.

• **Length** is determined by length of text and space available but, ideally, the index should adequately reflect the book.

• If the **font size** is small in proportion to the text, this can make the index seem relatively unimportant and sometimes more difficult to read, another reason for giving up.

• **Alphabetical order** can be used in two ways: word by word or letter by letter, but the chosen style must be used consistently. Many children's books print the entire alphabet on the first or each index page to help them locate the initial letters. Space between each section beginning with the same letter can be helpful, especially if the section is headed with the appropriate large upper case letter.

• **Illustrations** should be indexed but the difference between references to text and references to illustrations needs to be distinguished, perhaps by use of bold or italic type for the latter. If illustrations are also used purely for decoration, confusion should be avoided; the index pages should be as clear as possible. Another source of confusion could be a combined index and glossary; keeping them separate emphasises the different functions of each.

• **Locators (page or paragraph numbers)** can be shown with each page listed individually (4, 5, 6, 7, 8, 10, 11, 12, i.e. a separate reference to the topic on each page) or in ranges indicated by hyphens or en-rules (4–8, 10–12, i.e. a continuous reference over more than one page). This practice can be explained to children early on in their study of indexes so that they become familiar with it as soon as possible.

• **Passing mention** of a topic should be ignored as it is frustrating for children who find it is mentioned only in connection with something entirely different. Again, here is another reason for children giving up using an index. A further source of frustration is a long string of page numbers; children in the index workshop mentioned above were quick to notice them, announcing that they would certainly give up checking each one. Here then, is a sound reason for making more main entries or using subheadings.

• **Cross-references.** Using 'see' and 'see also' is often a problem, especially to younger children for whom additional entries might be more straightforward. The Williams and Bakewell survey found that the majority of respondents were in favour of keeping these traditional terms so that children could become accustomed to them in preparation for using adult books. Others suggested using double or additional entries or introducing different phrases such as 'try the word . . .' or 'also look up . . .' but the latter solution means the children will still have to learn the traditional phrases later on.

In view of all the foregoing, it might not be surprising that one of the 21 recommendations in the Williams and Bakewell report on indexes to children's information books is that such indexes should be compiled by a professional indexer who should have some knowledge of the subject matter. These recommendations appear in the Society of Indexers 'Occasional Paper No 5' which is derived largely from that investigation.

Valerie A. Elliston is a Fellow of the Society of Indexers, and a former adult education lecturer in English Language and Literature.

Further reading

Bakewell, K.G.B. and Williams, Paula L. with contributions from Elizabeth Wallis MBE and Valerie A. Elliston, *Indexing Children's Books*, 'Occasional Paper on Indexing No 5', Society of Indexers, 2000

British Standards Institution, *Information and Documentation: Guidelines for the content, organization and presentation of indexes*, BS ISO 999: 1996, 1997

Department for Educational Standards, *Key Stages 1 & 2 of the National Curriculum*, DfES, 2000

Williams P.L. and Bakewell K.G.B., *Indexes to Children's Information Books: A study of the provision and quality of book indexes for children at National Curriculum Key Stage 2. Final Report on Project RIC/G/330 (British Library Research and Innovation Report 129)*, 1997

Children's writing courses and conferences

Anyone wishing to participate in a writing course should first satisfy themselves as to its content and quality. For day and evening courses consult your local Adult Education Centre.

The Arvon Foundation
Lumb Bank, The Ted Hughes Arvon Centre,
Heptonstall, Hebden Bridge,
West Yorkshire HX7 6DF
tel (01422) 843714 *fax* (01422) 843714
email lumbbank@arvonfoundation.org
website www.arvonfoundation.org
Contact Ilona Jones
Moniack Mhor, Teavarran, Kiltarlity, Beauly,
Inverness-shire IV4 7HT
tel (01463) 741675 *fax* (01463) 741733
email moniackmhor@arvonfoundation.org
Contact Lyndy Batty
The Arvon Foundation, Totleigh Barton, Sheepwash,
Beaworthy, Devon EX21 5NS
tel (01409) 231338 *fax* (01409) 231144
email totleighbarton@arvonfoundation.org
Contact Julia Wheadon
The Hurst – The John Osborne Arvon Centre
Clunton, Craven Arms, Shropshire SY7 0JA
tel (01588) 640658 *fax* (01588) 640509
email thehurst@arvonfoundation.org
Contact Dan Pavitt

Children's Literature International Summer School (Creating Children's Literature)
Roehampton University, Digby Stuart College,
London SW15 5PB
tel 020-8392 3008 *fax* 020-8392 3819
email l.atkins@roehampton.ac.uk
website www.ncrcl.ac.uk
Takes place every other July

Run to promote writing for children by bringing together leading academics and those involved internationally in the related spheres of writing, translating and publishing for children, and to offer a series of seminars and keynote lectures. There are places for 80 participants and en-suite accommodation is available on campus.

The Federation of Children's Book Groups Conference
Details Martin and Sinead Kromer,
2 Bridge Wood View, Horsforth, Leeds LS18 5PE
email info@fcbg.org.uk
website www.fcbg.org.uk
Takes place 3 days in April

Held annually, guest speakers include well-known children's authors as well as experts and publishers in the field of children's books. Publishers also exhibit their newest books and resources.

IBBY Congress
Nonnenweg 12, Postfach, CH-4003-Basel,
Switzerland
tel (4161) 272 2917 *fax* (+4161) 272 2757
email liz.page@ibby.org, ibby@ibby.org
British Section PO Box 20875, GB–London
SE22 9WQ
tel 020-8299 1641
email ann@lazim.demon.co.uk
website www.ibby.org

A biennial international congress for IBBY (International Board on Books for Young People) members and other people involved in children's books and reading development. Every other year a different National Section of IBBY hosts the congress and several hundred people from all over the world attend the professional programme.

Forthcoming congresses: 7–10 September 2008 to be held in Copenhagen, Denmark on the theme 'The Story in the History'; 2010 Congress to be held in Santiago de Compostela, Spain on the theme 'The Strengths of Minorities'; 2012 Congress to be held in London, UK on the theme 'Translations and Migrations'. See also page 353.

NCRCL British IBBY Conference
Roehampton University, Digby Stuart College,
London SW15 5PB
tel 020-8392 3008 *fax* 020-8392 3819
email l.atkins@roehampton.ac.uk
website www.ncrcl.ac.uk

Conference held annually in November on a specific theme.

Oxford University Day and Weekend Schools
Department for Continuing Education,
Oxford University, Rewley House,
1 Wellington Square, Oxford OX1 2JA
tel (01865) 270368
email ppdayweek@conted.ox.ac.uk
website www.conted.ox.ac.uk
Contact Day School Administrator

Effective Writing: a series of 3-day accredited courses for creative writing. Topics vary from year to year. Courses always held on Fridays.

Pitstop Refuelling Writers' Weekend Workshops – see The Winchester Writers' Festival Conference and Bookfair

Tŷ Newydd
Tŷ Newydd, National Writers' Centre for Wales, Llanystumdwy, Cricieth, Gwynedd LL52 0LW
tel (01766) 522811 *fax* (01766) 523095
email post@tynewydd.org
website www.tynewydd.org
Week and weekend courses on all aspects of creative writing. Full programme available.

The Winchester Writers' Festival Conference and Bookfair
University of Winchester, Winchester, Hants SO22 4NR
tel (01962) 827238
email barbara.large@winchester.ac.uk
website www.writersconference.co.uk
Conference Director Barbara Large MBE, FRSA, HFUW,
Honorary Patrons Jacqueline Wilson OBE, Maureen Lipman, Dame Beryl Bainbridge
Takes place University of Winchester, 26–28 June 2009; Workshops 29 June–3 July 2009

This Festival of Writing, now in its 29th year, attracts 65 internationally renowned authors, poets, playwrights, agents and commissioning editors who give mini-courses, workshops, talks, seminars and one-to-one appointments to help writers harness their creativity and develop their writing, editing and marketing skills. Fifteen writing competitions, including Writing for Children, are adjudicated and 64 prizes are awarded at the Writers' Awards Reception. All first place winners are published annually in *The Best of* series.

The Bookfair offers delegates a wide choice of exhibits including authors' and internet services, publishers, booksellers, printers and trade associations.

Pitstop Refuelling Writers' Weekend Workshops are planned for 13–15 March and 24–26 October 2009, including Writing Marketable Children's Fiction and Non-fiction; Editing and Marketing your Novel; and How to Self-Publish Your Book day courses on 8 May and 18 September 2009 at a major book production company.

Writers Advice Centre for Children's Books – see page 363

YLG Conference
Bromley Central Library, High Street, Bromley BR1 1EX
tel 020-8461 7193 *fax* 020-8313 9975
email ian.dodds@bromley.gov.uk
website www.cilip.org.uk/specialistinterestgroups
Secretary Ian Dodds
Takes place September

This annual conference run by the Youth Libraries Group (YLG) of CILIP is a forum for discussion and debate on current issues for everyone working with and for children in libraries. It also provides an opportunity for experts, authors, illustrators, publishers and all those involved in the children's book trade to meet informally.

POSTGRADUATE COURSES

Bath Spa University
School of English and Creative Studies, Bath Spa University, Newton Park, Newton St Loe, Bath BA2 9BN
tel (01225) 875875 *fax* (01225) 875503
email enquiries@bathspa.ac.uk
website www.bathspa.ac.uk

MA in Writing for Young People, taught by a team of published children's writers. Prize for most promising work awarded by literary agent Rosemary Canter at United Agents. Informal enquires to Julia Green, course leader (j.a.green@bathspa.ac.uk). Also MA in Creative Writing and PhD in Creative Writing.

University of Winchester
Winchester SO22 4NR
tel (01962) 827234 *fax* (01962) 827406
website www.winchester.ac.uk
Contact Course Enquiries & Admissions

MA in Writing for Children and MA in Creative and Critical Writing.

Online resources about children's books

This is a representation of some of the many websites relating to children's books and reading. Individual author websites can be accessed via the ACHUKA or Booktrusted websites. See *Societies, associations and organisations* on page page 344 for other resources.

About Children's Books
www.childrensbooks.about.com

Part of About.com, this site holds international information on children's books plus a newsletter.

ACHUKA Children's Books UK
www.achuka.co.uk

The most up-to-date and comprehensive online guide to children's books and what's new in children's publishing. With author interviews, children's book news across the globe plus links to many other sites.

Armadillo
email armadillo@siliconhenge.com
website www.armadillomagazine.com
Editor Mary Hoffman, *Website Editor* Rhiannon Lassiter
£5 for 4 issues

Magazine about children's books, including reviews, interviews, features and profiles. After 5 years of publication as a paper magazine posted to subscribers, *Armadillo* is now available only online. New issues will be posted at the end of March, June, September and December. Some material will be accessible as a free sample but full access to the magazine is by subscription. New reviewers and writers are always welcome but the magazine does not pay a fee; reviewers keep the books. Publishers please note: books are *not* to be sent to the editor; she instructs reviewers to obtain specific titles direct from publishers. Founded in 1999 by author Mary Hoffman as a review publication for children's books.

Amazon
www.amazon.co.uk, www.amazon.com

UK and US online bookstore with more than 3 million books available on their websites at discounted prices, plus a personal notification service of new releases, reader reviews, bestsellers and book information.

BBC Education
www.bbc.co.uk/schools

Information about UK schools' curriculum. Essential for those wishing to write for educational publishers but also for keeping abreast of curricular topics.

BBC Switch
www.bbc.co.uk/switch

The Best Kids Book Site
www.thebestkidsbooksite.com

US site 'where children's books, crafts and collectibles intersect with your interests.' Useful links to Children's Book Awards, children's series fiction and author websites. Also gives access to the Book Wizard, an information tool to help track down children's books.

Quentin Blake
www.quentinblake.com

The official Quentin Blake website. Find out about the illustrator who brought many favourite children's characters to life, from Mister Magnolia and Mrs Armitage to the BFG and Matilda. There's also news and information on new books and exhibitions, downloads for children and suggestions for teachers on using books in the classroom. A great site for children, parents, teachers and aspiring children's books' illustrators.

Book Reviews by Kids
www.bookreviewsbykids.com

Website dedicated to children's book reviews written only by children. A great website for children to get their say on the books that they read.

BookHive
www.plcmc.org/bookhive

US guide to children's books for children, parents, teachers or anyone interested in reading about children's books. Includes book reviews.

Bookheads
www.bookheads.org.uk

The website of the Booktrust Teenage Prize aims to encourage teenagers to express their views on their favourite books. It features celebrity interviews and details of past, present and future Booktrust Teenage Prize shortlists and winners. A good way of finding out what teenagers really like to read!

Books4Publishing
www.books4publishing.com

Shropshire-based e-agent which showcases authors' synopsis and first chapter and then auto-targets publishers and agents for a £49.95 fee.

Booktrusted
www.booktrusted.co.uk

Dedicated children's division of Booktrust and an essential site for professionals working with young readers. Information on events, prizes, books, authors, etc.

Bunyips
www.nla.gov.au/exhibitions/bunyips

National Library of Australia's fun site about Bunyips!

Canadian Children's Book Centre
www.bookcentre.ca

The site of the Canadian Children's Book Centre includes profiles of authors, illustrators, information on recent books, a calendar of upcoming Canadian events, information on publications and tips from Canadian children's authors.

Children's BBC
www.bbc.co.uk/cbbc

'Kid culture' website. Has a section on books, including a behind-the-scenes visit to, and information on, the Blue Peter Book Awards.

The Children's Book Council
www.cbcbooks.org

The Children's Book Council in the USA is an organisation dedicated to encouraging literacy and the enjoyment of children's books. The website includes reviews of children's books published in the USA, forthcoming publications, author profiles and features 'sneek peeks at publishers' newest and hottest titles.' A good site for checking out the US marketplace.

Children's Books Online: the Rosetta Project
www.childrensbooksonline.org

Antique children's books which can read read online or downloaded.

Children's Literature
www.childrenslit.com

The aim of this US site is to help teachers, librarians, childcare providers and parents make appropriate literary choices for children. Each month there are featured interviews with children's authors and illustrators and several sets of themed reviews. (These are licensed to Barnes & Noble and Borders for use on their websites.)

The Children's Literature Web Guide
www.acs.ucalgary.ca/~dkbrown/

Internet resources related to books for children and young adults created by the University of Calgary, Canada.

Classic Children's Stories
www.childhoodreading.com

Many classic stories that have carried on through generations, including illustrations.

Contemporary Writers
www.contemporarywriters.com

Searchable database containing up-to-date profiles of some of the UK and Commonwealth's most important living writers – biographies, bibliographies, critical reviews, prizes and photographs.

Cool Reads
www.cool-reads.co.uk

Find out what children think are cool reads! A website set up by teenagers with reviews, genres, ideas and much more.

Roald Dahl Club
www.roalddahlclub.com

Everything you ever wanted to know about Dahl's books with a section for teachers, children's activities plus the online Roald Dahl Club magazine *The Gobblefunk Gazette*.

enCompass
www.enCompassCulture.com

The British Council's online worldwide reading group is divided into 3 sections: books for children (ages 3–12), books for ages 12–18 and books for adults. It aims to provide up-to-date information about the contemporary UK and Commonwealth literature that is being talked about. There is the opportunity to read or write book reviews, follow related web links, read about books and to chat with the online reader-in-residence. Books can be selected from the best of contemporary UK and Commonwealth literature.

The Guardian
http://education.guardian.co.uk

The Guardian's education pages online.

Guy's Read
www.guysread.org

US web-based literacy programme to help boys find material they like to read.

Kids' Bookline
http://wbd.wbc.org.uk/PAL/?lang=en

Part of the Welsh Books Council's Children's Books Department. Activities for children, in both Welsh and English.

Kids' Open Book
www.kidsopenbook.co.uk

Independent site of online reviews of children's books and multimedia, set up by an experienced UK bookseller. Selective titles and personal choices.

Kids' Reads and Teen reads
www.kidsreads.com, www.teenreads.com

Two excellent US websites with information, reviews, author links and features on children's and teenage books. Part of The Book Report Network.

KidSpace@The Internet Public Library
www.ipl.org/div/kidspace

Reading Zone of the Internet Public Library (IPL), a public service organisation and learning/teaching environment at the University of Michigan School of Information, USA.

The Looking Glass
www.the-looking-glass.net

An online children's literature journal.

Mrs Mad's Book-a-Rama
www.mrsmad.com

Children's book reviews from an independent reviewer – great fun and informative.

National Curriculum Online
www.nc.uk.net

This site links every National Curriculum programme of study requirement to resources on the Curriculum Online.

National Literacy Trust
www.literacytrust.org.uk

Details of all the NLT's initiatives plus lots of news and information about children's books.

On-Lion for Kids!
http://kids.nypl.org

New York Public Library children's book site which includes 100 Picture Books Everyone Should Know and 100 Favourite Children's Books.

Picturing Books
http://picturingbooks.imaginarylands.org

A website about picture books.

Reading is Fundamental, UK
www.rif.org.uk

An initiative of the National Literacy Trust that helps children and young people (aged 0–19) to realise their potential by motivating them to read.

ReadingZone.com
ReadingZone.com

Dedicated to helping young people, parents and adults and teachers to find out about children's books. Each area on the site provides information about new and classic titles with expert advice to help you find the best children's books available.

Ricochet-Litterature Jeunesse
www.ricochet-jeunes.org

This library offers the reader a series of identification sheets about books, authors, illustrators and film adaptations of children's and young people's literature.

Scottish Writers Website
www.slainte.org.uk

Linked to the Scottish Writers project that provides a forum for young readers and Scottish professionals to exchange literary ideas. Includes online writers-in-residence.

Stories from the Web
www.storiesfromtheweb.org

A development between Leeds, Bristol and Birmingham Library Services and the UK office for Library and Information Networking to provide information on library clubs, stories, and a chance to email authors.

Storybook Web
www.itscotland.org.uk/storybook

Access to Scottish Children's authors and book-related activities for children.

TeenSpace@The Internet Public Library
www.ipl.org/div/teen/teenread

Information on books for teenagers on the IPL website (see Kidspace).

UK Children's Books
www.ukchildrensbooks.co.uk

Directory of authors, illustrators and publishers involved in children's books and reading promotion.

The Word Pool
www.wordpool.co.uk

Independent website which profiles authors of children's books and gives information and advice for aspiring writers. Access to the free monthly newsletter.

World of Reading
www.worldreading.org

Website created by Ann Arbor District Library in USA devoted to book reviews written by and for children around the world.

Write4Kids
www.Write4Kids.com

US site with articles and information about the art of writing children's books. Also *Children's Book Insider* newsletter.

YouthBOOX/The Reading Agency
www.boox.org.uk

A joint venture between The Reading Agency and National Youth Agency to promote reading for pleasure for teenagers through building on their own interests.

Books about children's books

There are many books written about children's books. Some offer practical advice on selecting books. Others provide invaluable research material for those pursuing degrees and diplomas in children's literature. Here is a small selection.

Best Book Guide for Children and Young Adults
Published by Booktrust
Paperback pub. annually
website www.booktrustchildrensbooks.org.uk

Booktrust's independent annual 'pick of the best' in children's paperback fiction published in the previous calendar year. It is designed to help parents, teachers, librarians, booksellers and anyone interested in children's reading to select books for children, from babies to teenagers. Printed in full colour, each book featured has a short review, colour coding to indicate reading age and interest level, and bibliographic information.

The 2008 edition ties in with Booktrust's Big Picture campaign and features some of the books by the selected ten Best New Illustrators. Downloadable from the website.

The Book about Books
by Chris Powling
Published by A&C Black
ISBN 9780713654790
Paperback 2001

Using interviews with authors and illustrators, this book asks: what makes a classic? How do you get a book published? How do writers come up with their ideas? A light-hearted and informative book for children, perfect as a resource for Children's Book Week.

The Cambridge Guide to Children's Books in English
Edited by Victor Watson
Published by Cambridge University Press
ISBN 9780521550642
Hardback 2001

Reference work providing a critical and appreciative overview of children's books written in English across the world. It includes the history of children's books from pre-Norman times to the present, taking on board current developments in publishing practices and in children's own reading. Entries on TV, comics, annuals and the growing range of media texts are included.

The Oxford Companion to Children's Literature
Edited by Humphrey Carpenter and Mari Prichard
Published by Oxford University Press

ISBN 9780198602286
Paperback 1999

An indispensable reference book for anyone interested in children's books. Over 900 biographical entries deal with authors, illustrators, printers, publishers, educationalists and others who have influenced the development of children's literature. Genres covered include myths and legends, fairy tales, adventure stories, school stories, fantasy, science fiction, crime and romance. This book is of particular interest to librarians, teachers, students, parents and collectors.

The Reading Bug – and how you can help your child to catch it
by Paul Jennings
Published by Penguin Books
ISBN 9780141318400
Paperback 2004

Paul Jennings is a well-known children's author. This book explains, in his unique humorous style, how readers can open up the world through a love of books. He cuts through the jargon and the controversies to reveal the simple truths, which should enable adults to infect children with the reading bug.

The Rough Guide to Books for Teenagers
Edited by Nicholas Tucker and Julia Eccleshare
Published by Rough Guides
ISBN 9781843531388
Paperback 2003, repr. 2005

A resource for teenagers who love reading, this *Guide* is also ideal for adults looking to recommend and buy books for teenagers. More than 200 books are reviewed – mainly fiction – ranging from classics such as *Wuthering Heights* to more controversial and bestselling titles such as Melvin Burgess's *Junk* and Judy Blume's *Forever*. Graphic novels and some narrative non-fiction are also included.

The Rough Guide to Children's Books 0–5
Edited by Nicholas Tucker
Published by Rough Guides
ISBN 9781858287874
Paperback 2002

Comprises reviews of books for this youngest of age groups, including picture books for babies through alphabets and nursery rhymes to classic stories. Each book has a brief synopsis and an evaluation of its special qualities and educational advantages.

The Rough Guide to Children's Books 5–11

Edited by Nicholas Tucker
Published by Rough Guides
ISBN 9781858287881
Paperback 2002

With over 200 entries, this book contains reviews of recommended titles from poetry, non-fiction and classic tales, to fiction dealing with contemporary issues. Each book is roughly subdivided by the different ages within each age band, and by subject matter and genre.

Sticks and Stones: The Troublesome Success of Children's Literature from Slovenly Peter to Harry Potter

by Jack Zipes
Published by Routledge
ISBN 9780415938808
Paperback 2002

Jack Zipes – translator of the Grimm tales, teacher, storyteller, and scholar – questions whether children ever really had a literature of their own. He sees children's literature in many ways as being the 'grown-ups' version' – a story about childhood that adults tell kids. He discusses children's literature from the 19th century moralism of Slovenly Peter (whose fingers get cut off) to the wildly successful *Harry Potter* books. Children's literature is a booming market but its success, this author says, is disguising its limitations. *Sticks and Stones* is a forthright and engaging book by someone who clearly cares deeply about what and how children read.

The Ultimate Book Guide

by Anne Fine
Edited by Daniel Hahn, Leonie Flynn and Susan Reuben
Published by A&C Black
ISBN 9780713667189

Paperback 2004 (new edition due Feb 2009)

Over 600 entries covering the best books for children aged 8–12, from classics to contemporary titles published up to the end of 2003. Funny, friendly and frank recommendations written for children by their favourite and best-known authors including Anthony Horowitz, Jacqueline Wilson, Celia Rees, Darren Shan, David Almond and Dick King-Smith. Plus features on the most popular genres.

The Ultimate First Book Guide

by Leonie Flynn and Daniel Hahn
Published by A&C Black
Paperback 2008
ISBN 9780713673319

Comprehensive reference to help children aged 0–7 with their first steps into the world of books. Covers board books and novelty books, through to classic and contemporary picture books, chapter books and more challenging reads. It includes recommendations and features from top authors and experts in the field of children's books, including Children's Laureate Michael Rosen, Tony Bradman, Malachy Doyle and Wendy Cooling. There are also special features on a variety of topics and themed lists, and a selection of cross-references to other titles children may enjoy.

The Ultimate Teen Book Guide

Edited by Daniel Hahn and Leonie Flynn
Published by A&C Black
Paperback 2006
ISBN 9780713673302

Listings of over 700 books that might interest teenage readers which have been recommended and reviewed by authors such as Melvin Burgess, Anthony Horowitz, Meg Cabot, Eoin Colfer and others. Reviews cover the classics to cult fiction, and graphic novels to bestsellers, and each is cross-referenced to other titles as suggestions of what to read next. The book also contains essays on areas of teenage writing including *Race in Young Adult Fiction* by Bali Rai and *Off the Rails* by Kevin Brooks. There are also the results of a national teen readers' poll, the first time such a comprehensive survey has been carried out among teenagers in the UK, plus many reviews from teen readers.

Societies, prizes and festivals

The Society of Authors

The Society of Authors is an independent trade union, representing writers' interests in all aspects of the writing profession, particularly publishing, but also broadcasting, television and film, theatre and translation.

Founded over 100 years ago, the Society now has more than 8500 members. It has a professional staff, responsible to a Management Committee of 12 authors, and a Council (an advisory body meeting twice a year) consisting of 60 eminent writers.

Specialist groups

There are specialist groups within the Society to serve particular needs: the Academic Writers Group, the Broadcasting Group, the Children's Writers and Illustrators Group (see below), the Educational Writers Group, the Medical Writers Group and the Translators Association. There are also groups representing Scotland and the North of England.

The Children's Writers and Illustrators Group

The Children's Writers and Illustrators Group (CWIG) was formed in 1963. Besides furthering the interests of writers and artists and defending them whenever they are threatened, the Group seeks to bring members together professionally and socially, and in general to raise the status of children's books.

The Group has its own Executive Committee with representation on the Management Committee of the Society of Authors. Meetings and socials are held on a regular basis. Speakers have so far included publishers, librarians, booksellers and reviewers, and many distinguished writers and illustrators for children.

The annual subscription to the Society of Authors includes membership of all its groups. Membership of the CWIG is open to writers and illustrators who have had at least one

Membership

The Society of Authors
84 Drayton Gardens, London SW10 9SB
tel 020-7373 6642
email info@societyofauthors.org
website www.societyofauthors.org
General Secretary Mark Le Fanu

Membership is open to authors who have had a full-length work published, broadcast or performed commercially in the UK and to those who have had a full-length work accepted for publication, but not yet published; and those who have had occasional items broadcast or performed, or translations, articles, illustrations or short stories published. The owner or administrator of a deceased author's copyrights can become a member on behalf of the author's estate. Writers who have been offered a contract seeking a contribution towards publication costs may apply for associate membership and have the contract vetted.

The annual subscription (which is tax deductible) is £90 (£85 by direct debit after the first year). There is a special rate for partners living at the same address. Authors under 35 not yet earning a significant income from writing, may pay a lower subscription of £64. Authors over 65 may pay at the reduced rate after their first year of membership.

Contact the Society for a membership booklet and copy of *The Author*, or visit the website for an application form.

book published by a reputable British publisher, five short stories or more than 20 minutes of material broadcast on national radio or television. Election is at the discretion of the Committee.

For further details contact info@societyofauthors.org.

What the Society does for members

Through its permanent staff (including a solicitor), the Society is able to give its members a comprehensive personal and professional service covering the business aspects of authorship, including:

> 'It does no harm to repeat, as often as you can, "Without me the literary industry would not exist: the publishers, the agents, the sub-agents, the accountants, the libel lawyers, the departments of literature, the professors, the theses, the books of criticism, the reviewers, the book pages – all this vast and proliferating edifice is because of this small, patronised, put-down and underpaid person."' – *Doris Lessing*

• providing information about agents, publishers, and others concerned with the book trade, journalism, broadcasting and the performing arts;
• advising on negotiations, including the individual vetting of contracts, clause by clause, and assessing their terms both financial and otherwise;
• helping with members' queries, major or minor, over any aspect of the business of writing;
• taking up complaints on behalf of members on any issue concerned with the business of authorship;
• pursuing legal actions for breach of contract, copyright infringement, and the non-payment of royalties and fees, when the risk and cost preclude individual action by a member and issues of general concern to the profession are at stake;
• holding conferences, seminars, meetings and social occasions;
• producing a comprehensive range of publications, free of charge to members, including the Society's quarterly journal, *The Author*. *Quick Guides* cover many aspects of the profession such as: copyright, publishing contracts, libel, income tax, VAT, authors' agents, permissions, indexing and self-publishing. The Society also publishes occasional papers on subjects such as film agreements and packaged books.

The Society frequently secures improved conditions and better returns for members. It is common for members to report that, through the help and facilities offered, they have saved more, and sometimes substantially more, than their annual subscriptions (which are an allowable expense against income tax).

Further membership benefits
Members have access to:
• books, hotels and other products and services at special rates;
• free membership of the Authors' Licensing and Collecting Society (ALCS);
• a group Medical Insurance Scheme with BUPA;
• the Retirement Benefit Scheme;
• the Contingency Fund (which provides financial relief for authors or their dependents in sudden financial difficulties);
• the Pension Fund (which offers discretionary pensions to a number of members);
• membership of the Royal Over-Seas League at a discount.

What the Society does for authors
The Society lobbies Members of Parliament, Ministers and Government Departments on all issues of concern to writers. Recent issues have included the operation and funding of

Public Lending Right, the threat of VAT on books, copyright legislation and European Union initiatives. Concessions have also been obtained under various Finance Acts.

The Society litigates in matters of importance to authors. For example, the Society backed Andrew Boyle when he won his appeal against the Inland Revenue's attempt to tax the Whitbread Award.

The Society campaigns for better terms for writers. With the Writers' Guild, it has negotiated 'minimum terms agreements' with many leading publishers. The translators' section of the Society has also drawn up a minimum terms agreement for translators which has been adopted by Faber and Faber, and has been used on an individual basis by a number of other publishers.

The Society is recognised by the BBC for the purpose of negotiating rates for writers' contributions to radio drama, as well as for the broadcasting of published material. It was instrumental in setting up the ALCS (see page 250), which collects and distributes fees from reprography and other methods whereby copyright material is exploited without direct payment to the originators.

The Society keeps in close touch with the Arts Councils, the Association of Authors' Agents, the British Council, the Institute of Translation and Interpreting, the Department for Culture, Media and Sport, the National Union of Journalists, the Publishers Association and the Writers' Guild of Great Britain.

The Society is a member of the European Writers Congress, the British Copyright Council, the National Book Committee and the Creators' Rights Alliance.

Awards

The Society of Authors administers:
• Travelling Scholarships which give honorary awards;
• three prizes for novels: the Betty Trask Awards, the Encore Award and the McKitterick Prize;
• two prizes for a full-length published work: the Somerset Maugham Awards and the *Sunday Times* Young Writer of the Year Award;
• two poetry awards: the Eric Gregory Awards and the Cholmondeley Awards;
• the Tom-Gallon and Olive Cook Awards for short story writers;
• the Authors' Foundation and Kathleen Blundell Trust, which give grants to assist authors working on their next book;
• two radio drama prizes: the Richard Imison Award for a writer new to radio drama and the Peter Tinniswood Award;
• awards for translations from Arabic, Dutch/Flemish, French, German, Greek, Italian, Portuguese, Spanish and Swedish into English;
• the Francis Head Bequest for assisting authors who, through physical mishap, are temporarily unable to maintain themselves or their families;
• medical book awards.

Booktrust

Booktrust is the largest literature organisation in the United Kingdom. It is supported by Arts Council England and has a broad range of activities aimed at promoting books and reading.

Booktrust is an independent national charity that encourages readers of all ages and cultures to discover and enjoy reading. Booktrust administers a number of literary prizes, including the Orange Prize for Fiction for adults, and the Booktrust Teenage Prize and Booktrust Early Years Award for children (see *Children's book and illustration prizes and awards*, page 364), as well as promoting books and reading for all ages through numerous campaigns such as Get London Reading.

Further information

Booktrust
Book House, 45 East Hill, London SW18 2QZ
tel 020-8516 2977 *fax* 020-8516 2978
email query@booktrust.org.uk
website www.booktrust.org.uk,
www.bookheads.org.uk, www.bookstart.org.uk,
www.booktime.org.uk, www.bookedup.org.uk,
www.childrenslaureate.org.uk,
www.bigpicture.org.uk

Booktrust and children

The Booktrust children's books website has a searchable database of more than 2000 book reviews, resources for teachers, an illustrators' gallery featuring the best artists currently working in children's books, and interviews with authors and illustrators.

• The 'booktrusted' website gives invaluable information on children's books and resources, including annotated booklists; information about organisations concerned with children's books; publishers; children's book news; and events listings for readings, festivals and other children's book events throughout the UK.

• Booktrust coordinates four national programmes. Bookstart gives free advice and books to parents/carers attending their baby's health checks (see *Books for babies*, page 98). Booktime promotes reading for pleasure by giving a book pack to children across the UK shortly after they start school. Booked Up encourages children to read for pleasure by providing each Year 7 child with a free book of their choice. The Letterbox Club provides a parcel of books and other materials for children aged 7–11 in foster families, every month for six months.

• Booktrust publishes the annual *Best Book Guide for Children and Young Adults*, which details the best in children's paperback fiction published in the previous calendar year. The best books of the year are chosen for inclusion in Booktrust's annual *Best Book Guide*, which is available as a free download from the website.

• Booktrust runs the Booktrust Early Years Awards (formerly the Sainsbury's Baby Book Award) which aims to celebrate, publicise and reward the exciting range of books being published today for babies, toddlers and preschool children. With Bookstart, Booktrust hopes to promote and make these books accessible to as wide an audience as possible.

• Booktrust runs the Writing Together programme, which aims to ensure that, during their life at school, every child encounters opportunities to work with professional writers who inspire them creatively.

• Booktrust administers the Children's Laureate (Michael Rosen 2007–9).

• Booktrust administers National Children's Book Week (see page 376).

Seven Stories, the Centre for Children's Books

At Seven Stories the rich heritage of British children's books is collected, explored and celebrated.

sevenstories
the centre for children's books

Once upon a time an idea was born on the banks of the Tyne to create a national home for children's literature – a place where the original work of authors and illustrators could be collected, treasured and celebrated. After ten years of pioneering work by founding directors Elizabeth Hammill and Mary Briggs, that dream became a reality. In August 2005 Seven Stories, the Centre for Children's Books, opened in an award-winning converted seven storey Victorian granary in the Ouseburn Valley, a stone's throw from Newcastle's vibrant quayside.

The collection

At the heart of Seven Stories is a unique and growing collection of manuscripts, artwork and other pre-publication materials. These treasures record the creative process involved in making a children's book and provide illuminating insights into the working lives of modern authors and illustrators. The collection focuses on work created in modern Britain. It already contains thousands of items by authors such as Peter Dickinson, Berlie Doherty, Jan Mark, Philip Pullman, Michael Rosen, Robert Westall and Ursula Moray Williams; illustrators like Edward Ardizzone, Faith Jaques, Harold Jones, Anthony Maitland, Pat Hutchins, Helen Cooper, Jan Ormerod and Jane Ray; and editors and other practitioners such as Kaye Webb. Many more bodies of work are pledged. A catalogue of the collection is available via the Seven Stories website.

Exhibitions

A celebration of creativity underpins the Seven Stories project: its collection documents the creative act, and its exhibitions and programmes interpret this original material in unconventional but meaningful ways. The aim is to cultivate an appreciation of books and their making, and inspire creativity in its audience.

Seven Stories, known during its development as the Centre for the Children's Book, has been mounting exhibitions since 1998 – first in borrowed venues and now in its own home. Here it provides the only exhibition space in the UK wholly dedicated to showcasing the incomparable legacy of British writing and illustrating for children. Its current exhibitions are *Snozzcumbers and Frobscittle: The Wonderful World of Roald Dahl and Quentin Blake*, *Up to Mischief with Horrid Henry*, and *From Toad Hall to Pooh Corner*. Seven Stories has been fulfilling its national remit by touring exhibitions since 2003. These include *What's in the Book?*, the 17 million books of Jane and Allan Ahlberg, *Miffy*, and *Snozzcumbers and Frobscottle*.

Throughout its seven storeys – from the Engine Room to the bookshop and café to the Artist's Attic, visitors of all ages are invited to engage in a unique, interactive exploration of creativity, literature and art. In this ever changing literary playground and landscape for the imagination, they can become writers, artists, explorers, designers, storytellers, readers or collectors, in the company of storytellers, authors, illustrators and Seven Stories' own facilitators and education team.

Seven Stories aims to place children, young people and their books at the heart of the UK's national literary culture. An independent educational charity, it is committed to access for all and has initiated several innovative participation projects. The centre has developed close links with the Newcastle and regional community, and is currently working with the Children's Literature Unit in the Department of English Literature, Language and Linguistics at Newcastle University to develop the Seven Stories collection and maximise its potential for research and display.

In Seven Stories, Britain has now found a long needed home dedicated to the celebration of children's literature.

Further information

Seven Stories, the Centre for Children's Books
30 Lime Street, Ouseburn Valley,
Newcastle upon Tyne NE1 2PQ
tel (0845) 271 0777 *fax* 0191-276 4302
email info@sevenstories.org.uk
website www.sevenstories.org.uk
Registered Charity No 1056812

Public opening hours Mon–Sat 10am–5pm, Sun 11am–5pm

Admission charges Adult (17 and over) £5; child/concession £4; family £15. Annual passes available.

The Children's Book Circle

Katie Jennings of the Children's Book Circle introduces the organisation.

Are you passionate about children's books? The Children's Book Circle (CBC) provides an exciting forum in which you can develop your interest, build your contacts and enrich your engagement with the children's book world. The CBC's mem-

bership consists of publishers, librarians, authors, illustrators, agents, teachers, booksellers and anyone with an active interest in the field. If you're an aspiring author or illustrator, you'll already know how important it is to become as knowledgeable as possible about the current marketplace for children's books. The CBC is the ideal place to broaden your knowledge. It's not the place to try for a publishing contract, but it will give you the opportunity to take part in discussions with people from the industry in an informal and enjoyable context.

The CBC meets regularly at a variety of venues in London. At our speaker meetings, invited guest speakers debate key issues relating to the world of children's books. Recent events have included a discussion on the subject of picture books between bestselling illustrator Axel Scheffler, author/illustrator David Roberts and Claire Cartey, senior picture book designer at Hodder, and a talk on the state of the children's book business from Kate Wilson, Managing Director of Scholastic UK. In addition to these meetings, an event at a primary school gave members a chance to quiz to a panel of 10–11 year-olds about their reading habits.

Members also have the opportunity to attend the annual Eleanor Farjeon award ceremony and reception, and the Patrick Hardy Lecture. The Eleanor Farjeon Award is awarded for an outstanding contribution to the world of children's books, either by an individual or an organisation, and is voted for by CBC members. Recent winners include Mallorie Blackman, Jane Nissen and Wendy Cooling. The Patrick Hardy lecture is delivered each year by a distinguished speaker on a relevant topic of their choice. Past speakers have included Michael Rosen, David Almond, Meg Rosoff and Anthony Horowitz.

Another highlight of the CBC calendar is the summer quiz, which offers members an opportunity to show off their children's book knowledge.

Federation of Children's Book Groups

The aim of the Federation of Children's Book Groups is to bring children and books together and have fun. Sinead Kromer of the FCBG introduces the organisation.

The Federation of Children's Book Groups (now a registered charity) was formed in 1968 by Anne Wood to co-ordinate the work of the many different children's book groups that were coming together across the country. Over the next eight years the organisation expanded and a system of regionalisation was introduced to link groups together in each part of the country.

In 1976 National Tell-A-Story-Week was introduced and became an immediate success. This has now grown into National Share-A-Story-Month and takes place in May. It enables groups to focus on the power of story and to hold events which celebrate this. Each year the National Launch is held in a different part of the country and in 2007 a one-day event was held at Belvoir Castle on the theme 'Make History', and the event was led by children's authors Adele Geras, Linda Newbury and Ann Turnbull.

In 1977, the first Federation anthology was published, and since then there have been nine more titles. Plans are under way to consider a new anthology.

In 1981 the Federation inaugurated one of its most successful ventures – the Children's Book Award, a prize given for the best book of the year judged entirely by children. The first winner was *Mr Magnolia* by Quentin Blake and the present holder is author Andy Stanton for his book *You're a Bad Man Mr Gum!*. The Award for 2007 was presented at the Hay Festival in June. This was only the second time that the Award had been presented at a major literary festival. Children from all over the country came together to celebrate all that is best in children's books. For the past six years the Award has been supported by Red House Children's Books and their financial commitment has enabled the Award to go from strength to strength, providing opportunities for children all over the country, who are not members of the Federation, to become involved in the final round of judging.

Each year the Federation invites a Group to organise the Annual Conference. This ensures that the Conference moves around the country and that its organisation involves many different members. Venues have included Edinburgh, Bradford, Plymouth, Stratford-upon-Avon, Brighton and Cirencester. The 2008 conference was held at Exeter University and was organised by the Plymouth Children's Book Group. Over 300 delegates attended during the weekend and listened to speakers as diverse as Mick Inkpen, Mal Peet, Kaye Umansky, Mini Grey, Derek Landy and Justin Somper.

The Children's Book Groups

So where are the book groups and who are its members? Federation Groups exist in many parts of England, Scotland and Wales; from Plymouth to Dundee; from Grantham to St David's and from York to Lewes. Membership of a book group is made up of parents, carers, teachers, librarians and, in some cases, children's authors and illustrators. The passion of Federation members for bringing books and children together is the reason that the organisation has continued and developed over the past 40 years. A new venture in

2006 was to have a presence at the Hay Festival throughout the ten days, where once again the Federation's aim – to bring children and books together and have fun – was at the forefront of the day's activities. The success of this venture caused us to

Further information

Federation of Children's Book Groups
email info@fcbg.org.uk
website www.fcbg.org.uk
Registered Charity No 268289

return in 2007 and again in 2008 when, once again, many Federation members willingly gave up their time to help.

Each of the member groups is self supporting in terms of money and organisation, but has the advantage of a parent body to support and encourage its activities. These are as varied and diverse as the book groups themselves, serving their own community's needs. They might include author visits, children's events and celebrations. But above all the Federation is an organisation that is passionate about children's books, bringing together ordinary book-loving families, empowering parents, grandparents, carers and their children to become enthusiastic and excited about all kinds of good books. Local book groups encourage everyone to talk about books and reading, and thus enthusiasm for good children's literature is passed on at all levels.

Societies, associations and organisations

The societies and associations listed here include appreciation societies devoted to specific authors (see also online resources on page 330), professional bodies and national institutions. Some also offer prizes and awards (see page 364).

Academi (Welsh Academy)
Main Office 3rd Floor, Mount Stuart House, Mount Stuart Square, Cardiff CF10 5FQ
tel 029-2047 2266 *fax* 029-2049 2930
email post@academi.org
and Academi Glyn Jones Centre, Wales Millennium Centre, Cardiff Bay, Cardiff CF10 5AL
tel 029-2047 2266 *fax* 029-2047 0691
email post@academi.org
North West Wales Office Tŷ Newydd, Llanystumdwy, Cricieth, Gwynedd LL52 0LW
tel (01766) 522817 *fax* (01766) 523095
email post@tynewydd.org
South West Wales Office Dylan Thomas Centre, Somerset Place, Swansea SA1 1RR
tel (01792) 463980 *fax* (01792) 463993
website www.academi.org
Chief Executive Peter Finch
Membership Associate: £15 p.a. (waged), £7.50 (unwaged)

Academi is the trading name of Yr Academi Gymreig, the Welsh National Literature Promotion Agency and Society of Writers. With funds mostly provided from public sources, it has been constitutionally independent since 1978. It runs courses, competitions (including the Cardiff International Poetry and Book of the Year Competition), conferences, tours by authors, festivals and represents the interests of Welsh writers and Welsh writing both inside Wales and beyond. Its publications include *Taliesin* (3 p.a.), a literary journal in the Welsh language; *A470* (bi-monthly), a literature information magazine; *The Oxford Companion to the Literature of Wales*, *The Welsh Academy English-Welsh Dictionary*, *Welsh Academy Encyclopaedia of Wales* and a variety of translated works.

Academi administers a range of schemes including Writers on Tour, Writers Residencies and Writing Squads for young people. Academi also runs services for writers in Wales such as bursaries, critical advice and mentoring. Founded 1959.

AccessArt
6 West Street, Comberton, Cambridge, CB23 7DS
tel (01223) 262134
email info@accessart.org.uk
website www.accessart.org.uk

A fun, creative and dynamic learning tool for pupils across all the key stages, and for home-users of all ages. AccessArt gives users access to arts educational activities that would otherwise reach only a small audience. The website allows access to:

• a series of visually exciting and innovative 'online workshops' which condense and articulate artist-led teaching which has taken place in schools, museums and galleries; and
• teachers notes and learners' printouts. Each online workshop is accompanied by explanatory notes for the educators and printable resource material which can be used directly by the learner.
• AccessArt membership – keep up to date, Holiday Club, etc.

Louisa May Alcott Memorial Association
Orchard House, 399 Lexington Road, PO Box 343, Concord, MA 01742–0343, USA
tel 978-369-4118 *fax* 978-369-1367
email info@louisamayalcott.org
website www.louisamayalcott.org

A private, not-for-profit corporation. The Association provides the financial and human resources required to conduct public tours, special programmes, exhibits and the curatorial work which continue the tradition of the Alcotts, a unique 19th century family. Founded 1911.

American Society of Composers, Authors and Publishers
One Lincoln Plaza, New York, NY 10023, USA
tel 212-621-6000 *fax* 212-724-9064
website www.ascap.com
President & Chairman Marilyn Bergman

Amgueddfa Cymru – National Museum Wales
Cathays Park, Cardiff CF10 3NP
tel 029-2039 7951 *fax* 029-2057 3321
website www.museumwales.ac.uk

Arts Council England
14 Great Peter Street, London SW1P 3NQ
tel (0845) 300 6200 *textphone* 020-7973 6564
fax 020-7973 6590
email enquiries@artscouncil.org.uk
website www.artscouncil.org.uk
Chief Executive Alan Davey

The national development agency for the arts in England, distributing public money from Government and the National Lottery. Arts Council England's main funding programme is Grants for the Arts, which is open to individuals, arts organisations, national touring companies and other people who use the arts in their work.

Arts Council England has one national and 9 regional offices. It has a single contact telephone and email address for general enquiries (see above). Founded 1946.

East
Eden House, 48–49 Bateman Street, Cambridge CB2 1LR
tel (0845) 300 6200 *textphone* (01223) 306893
fax (0870) 242 1271

East Midlands
St Nicholas Court, 25–27 Castle Gate, Nottingham NG1 7AR
tel (0845) 300 6200 *fax* 0115-950 2467

London
2 Pear Tree Court, London EC1R 0DS
tel (0845) 300 6200 *textphone* 020-7973 6564
fax 020-7608 4100

North East
Central Square, Forth Street, Newcastle upon Tyne NE1 3PJ
tel (0845) 300 6200 *textphone* 0191-255 8585
fax 0191-230 1020

North West
Manchester House, 22 Bridge Street, Manchester M3 3AB
tel (0845) 300 6200 *textphone* 0161-834 9131
fax 0161-834 6969

South East
Sovereign House, Church Street, Brighton BN1 1RA
tel (0845) 300 6200 *textphone* (01273) 710659
fax (0870) 2421257

South West
Senate Court, Southernhay Gardens, Exeter EX1 1UG
tel (0845) 300 6200 *textphone* (01392) 433503
fax (01392) 229229

West Midlands
82 Granville Street, Birmingham B1 2LH
tel (0845) 300 6200 *textphone* 0121-643 2815
fax 0121-643 7239

Yorkshire
21 Bond Street, Dewsbury, West Yorkshire WF13 1AX
tel (0845) 300 6200 *textphone* (01924) 438585
fax (01924) 466522

Arts Council/An Chomhairle Ealaíon
Literature Adviser, 70 Merrion Square, Dublin 2, Republic of Ireland

tel (01) 6180200 *fax* (01) 6761302
website www.artscouncil.ie
Arts Programme Director John O'Kane

The national development agency for the arts in Ireland. Founded 1951.

Arts Council of Northern Ireland
MacNeice House, 77 Malone Road, Belfast BT9 5JW
tel 028-9038 5200 *fax* 028-90661715
website www.artscouncil-ni.org
Chief Executive Roisín McDonough, *Literature Officer* Damian Smyth, *Visual Arts Officers* Iain Davidson, Suzanne Lyle

Promotes and encourages the arts throughout Northern Ireland. Artists in drama, dance, music and jazz, literature, the visual arts, traditional arts and community arts can apply for support for specific schemes and projects. The value of the grant will be set according to the aims of the application. Applicants must have contributed regularly to the artistic activities of the community, and been resident for at least 1 year in Northern Ireland.

Arts Council of Wales
9 Museum Place, Cardiff CF10 3NX
tel 029-2037 6500 *minicom* 029-2039 0027
fax 029-2022 1447
email info@artswales.org.uk
website www.artswales.org.uk
Chairman Prof. Dai Smith, *Arts Director* David Alston, *Head of Communications* Sian Phipps, *Wales Arts International Director* Eluned Haf

National organisation with specific responsibility for the funding and development of the arts in Wales. ACW receives funding from the National Assembly for Wales and also distributes National Lottery funds for the arts in Wales. From these resources, ACW makes grants to support arts activities and facilities. Some of the funds are allocated in the form of annual revenue grants to full-time arts organisations such as the Academi. It also operates schemes which provide financial and other forms of support for individual artists or projects. ACW undertakes this work in both the English and Welsh languages. Wales Arts International is the unique partnership between The Arts Council of Wales and British Council Wales, which works to promote knowledge about contemporary arts and culture from Wales and encourages international exchange and collaboration.

North Wales Regional Office
36 Princes Drive, Colwyn Bay LL29 8LA
tel (01492) 533440 *minicom* (01492) 532288
fax (01492) 533677

Mid and West Wales Regional Office
6 Gardd Llydaw, Jackson Lane, Carmarthen SA31 1QD
tel (01267) 234248 *minicom* (01267) 223496
fax (01267) 233084

South Wales Office
9 Museum Place, Cardiff CF10 3NX
tel 029-2037 6525 minicom 029-2039 0027
fax 029-2022 1447

Association for Library Service to Children
American Library Association, 50 East Huron, Chicago, IL 60611–2795, USA
tel 800-545-2433 ext. 2163 fax 312-280-5271
email alsc@ala.org
website www.ala.org/alsc

The Association for Library Service to Children develops and supports the profession of children's librarianship by enabling and encouraging its practitioners to provide the best library service to our nation's children.

Association for Scottish Literary Studies (ASLS)
c/o Dept of Scottish Literature, 7 University Gardens, University of Glasgow G12 8QH
tel 0141-330 5309
email office@asls.org.uk
website www.asls.org.uk
Hon. President Alan Riach, Hon. Secretary Lorna Borrowman Smith, Publishing Manager Duncan Jones
Membership £38 p.a. individuals, £10 UK students, £67 corporate

Promotes the study, teaching and writing of Scottish literature and furthers the study of the languages of Scotland. Publishes annually an edited text of Scottish literature, an anthology of new Scottish writing, a series of academic journals and a Newsletter (2 p.a.). Also publishes Scotnotes (comprehensive study guides to major Scottish writers), literary texts and commentary CDs designed to assist the classroom teacher, and a series of occasional papers. Organises 3 conferences a year. Founded 1970.

Association of American Publishers Inc.
71 Fifth Avenue, New York, NY 10003, USA
tel 212-255-0200 fax 212-255-7007
website www.publishers.org
President & Ceo Patricia S. Schroeder
Founded 1970.

The Association of Authors' Agents
18–21 Cavaye Place, London SW10 9PT
tel 020-7373 8672
email aaa@carolinesheldon.co.uk
website www.agentsassoc.co.uk
President Clare Alexander, Vice President Philippa Milnes-Smith, Treasurers Andrew Nurnberg and Caroline Montgomery, Secretary Penny Holroyd

Maintains a code of professional practice to which all members commit themselves; holds regular meetings to discuss matters of common professional interest; provides a vehicle for representing the view of authors' agents in discussion of matters of common interest with other professional bodies. Founded 1974.

Association of Authors' Representatives Inc.
676A, Suite 312 9th Avenue, New York, NY 10036, USA
tel 212-840-5777
website www.aar-online.org
Founded 1991.

Association of Booksellers for Children
ABC National Office, 6538 Collin Avenue #168, Miami Beach, FL 33141
tel 617-390-7759 fax 617-344-0540
website www.abfc.com
Executive Director Kristen McLean

A national membership association that offers a support network for professional independent children's booksellers who share the goal of encouraging quality and service within the children's book industry.

Association of Canadian Publishers
174 Spadina Avenue, Suite 306, Toronto, Ontario M5T 2C2, Canada
tel 416-487-6116 fax 416-487-8815
email admin@canbook.org
website www.publishers.ca
Executive Director Carolyn Wood
Founded 1976; formerly Independent Publishers Association, 1971.

The Association of Illustrators
2nd Floor, Back Building, 150 Curtain Road, London EC2A 3AT
tel 020-7613 4328 fax 020-7613 4417
website www.theaoi.com
Contact Membership Coordinator

Exists to support illustrators, promote illustration and encourage professional standards in the industry. Publishes Varoom magazine (3 p.a.); presents an annual programme of events; annual competition, exhibition and tour of Images – the Best of British Contemporary Illustration (call for entries: July/August). Founded 1973.

Audiobook Publishing Association (APA)
(formerly the Spoken Word Publishing Association)
tel (07971) 280788
email info@theapa.net
website www.theapa.net
Membership £60–£750 p.a. plus VAT
Administrator Charlotte McCandlish

The UK trade association for the audiobook industry, APA brings together all those involved – publishers, performers, producers, distributors, retailers, manufacturers. It aims to increase the profile of the audiobook in the media, the retail trade and among the general public, and to provide a forum for discussion. Founded 1994.

Australia Council

PO Box 788, Strawberry Hills, NSW 2012, Australia *located at* 372 Elizabeth Street, Surry Hills, NSW 2010, Australia
tel (02) 9215 9000 *fax* (02) 9215 9111
email mail@australiacouncil.gov.au
website www.australiacouncil.gov.au
Ceo Kathy Keele

Provides a broad range of support for the arts in Australia, embracing music, theatre, literature, visual arts, crafts, Aboriginal arts, community and new media arts. It has 7 Boards: Literature, Visual Arts, Music, Theatre, Dance, Major Performing Arts, as well as the Aboriginal and Torres Strait Islander Arts Board.

The Literature Board's chief objective is to support the writing of all forms of creative literature – novels, short stories, poetry, plays and literary non-fiction. It also assists with the publication of literary magazines, has a book publishing subsidies programme, and initiates and supports projects of many kinds designed to promote Australian literature both within Australia and abroad.

Australian Copyright Council

PO Box 1986, Strawberry Hills, NSW 2012, Australia
tel (02) 8815 9777 *fax* (02) 8815 9799
email info@copyright.org.au
website www.copyright.org.au

An independent non-profit organisation which aims to assist creators and other copyright owners to exercise their rights effectively; raise awareness in the community generally about the importance of copyright; research and identify areas of copyright law which are inadequate or unfair; seek changes to law and practice to enhance the effectiveness and fairness of copyright; foster cooperation amongst bodies representing creators and owners of copyright. The Council comprises 23 organisations or associations of owners and creators of copyright material, including the Australian Society of Authors, the Australian Writers Guild and the Australian Book Publishers Association. Founded 1968.

Australian Publishers Association (APA)

60–89 Jones Street, Ultimo, NSW 2007, Australia
tel (02) 9281 9788 *fax* (02) 9281 1073
email apa@publishers.asn.au
website www.publishers.asn.au
Ceo Maree McCaskill

Australian Writers' Guild (AWG)

8/50 Reservoir Street, Surry Hills, NSW 2010
tel (02) 9281 1554 *fax* (02) 9281 4321
email admin@awg.com.au
website www.awg.com.au
Executive Director Jacqueline Woodman

The professional association for all performance writers, i.e. writers for film, TV, radio, theatre, video and new media. The AWG is recognised throughout the industry in Australia as being the voice of performance writers. Established 1962.

Authors' Licensing and Collecting Society Ltd – see page 250

Barnardo's Image Archive

Tanners Lane, Barkingside, Ilford, Essex IG6 1QG
tel 020-8550 8822 *fax* 020-8551 6870
email dorothy.howes@barnados.org.uk
website www.barnardos.org.uk

Extensive collection of b&w and colour images dating from 1874 to the present day covering social history with the emphasis on children and child care. Also 300 films dating from 1905. Founded 1872.

Hilaire Belloc Society

Contact Dr Grahame Clough, 1 Hillview Cottage, Elsted, Nr Midhurst, West Sussex GU29 0JX
tel (01730) 825575
email hilairebelloc1@aol.com

Commemorates the French-born English writer of light verse, history, travel books, biography and fiction.

Enid Blyton Society

93 Milford Hill, Salisbury, Wilts. SP1 2QL
tel (01722) 331937
email tony@enidblytonsociety.co.uk
website www.enidblytonsociety.co.uk
Contact Anita Bensoussane

To provide a focal point for collectors and enthusiasts of Enid Blyton through its magazine *The Enid Blyton Society Journal* (3 p.a.) and the annual Society Day which attracts in excess of a hundred members each year. Founded 1995.

Book Publishers Association of New Zealand Inc.

Private Bag 102902, North Shore City 0745, Auckland, New Zealand
tel (09) 442-7426 *fax* (09) 479-8536
email admin@bpanz.org.nz
website www.bpanz.org.nz
Association Director Anne de Lautour

The Booksellers Association of the United Kingdom & Ireland Ltd

272 Vauxhall Bridge Road, London SW1V 1BA
tel 020-7802 0802 *fax* 020-7802 0803

email mail@booksellers.org.uk
website www.booksellers.org.uk
Chief Executive T.E. Godfray
Founded 1895.

Booktrust – see page 338

The British Council
10 Spring Gardens, London SW1A 2BN
tel 020-7930 8466 *fax* 020-7839 6347
website www.britishcouncil.org,
www.britishcouncil.org/arts,
www.contemporarywriters.com,
www.encompassculture.com,
www.literarytranslation.com
Chair The Rt Hon. Lord Kinnock, *Chief Executive* Martin Davidson, *Director of Arts* Venu Dhupa

The British Council connects people worldwide with learning opportunities and creative ideas from the UK, and builds lasting relationships between the UK and other countries. It has 7900 staff in offices, teaching centres, libraries, and information and resource centres in the UK and 110 countries and territories worldwide.

Working in close collaboration with book trade associations, British Council offices participate in major international book fairs.

The British Council is an authority on teaching English as a second or foreign language. It also gives advice and information on curriculum, methodology, materials and testing.

The British Council promotes British literature overseas through writers' tours, academic visits, workshops, conferences, seminars and exhibitions. It publishes *New Writing*, an annual anthology of unpublished short stories, poems and extracts from works in progress and essays; and a series of literary bibliographies, including *Tbooks: UK Teenage Literature, Crime Literature* and *Reading in the City*. Through its Literature Department, the British Council provides an overview of UK literature and a range of online resources (see above). This includes a literary portal, information about UK and Commonwealth authors, translation workshops and a worldwide online book club and reading group for adults, teenagers and children with over 10,000 books plus reading group advice.

The Visual Arts Department, part of the British Council's Arts Group, develops and enlarges overseas knowledge and appreciation of British achievement in the fields of painting, sculpture, printmaking, design, photography, the crafts and architecture, working closely with the British Council's overseas offices and with professional colleagues in the UK and abroad.

Further information about the work of the British Council is available from Arts Press at the above address, or from British Council offices overseas by emailing arts@britishcouncil.org.

British Museum
Great Russell Street, London WC1B 3DG
tel 020-7323 8000/8299

email information@thebritishmuseum.ac.uk
website www.thebritishmuseum.ac.uk

Explore – families and children
website www.thebritishmuseum.ac.uk/explore/families_and_children.aspx
Explore enables children to explore the British Museum's collections online. It incorporates a special childrens' search, activities and quizzes for use in the classroom, noticeboards for children's work, 'Ask the Expert' and articles written specially for 7–11 year-olds. It is also available on terminals in the Reading Room in the Museum's Great Court. Access to Explore is free. Alongside these terminals are quiz sheets for children and family groups. Children are encouraged to find objects on Explore and then go and look at them in the galleries in order to complete the quiz. Explore is also available on specially designed touchscreens in the Reading Room which have much more than the web version, including higher quality images, animations, 3D reconstructions and gallery plans.

Randolph Caldecott Society
Secretary Kenn Oultram, Clatterwick House, Clatterwick Lane, Little Leigh, Northwich, Cheshire CW8 4RJ
tel (01606) 891303 (office), 781731 (evening)
website www.randolphcaldecott.org.uk
Membership £10 p.a. individual, £15 p.a. families/corporate

Aims to encourage an interest in the life and works of Randolph Caldecott (1846–86), the Victorian artist, illustrator and sculptor. Caldecott produced 16 picture books, each based on the words of a nursery rhyme or well-known nonsense verse. Meetings held in Chester and London. Liaises with the American Caldecott Society. Founded 1983.

Canadian Authors Association
320 South Shores Road, PO Box 419, Campbellford, Ontario K0L 1L0
tel 705-653-0323, 866-216-6222 (toll free)
fax 705-653-0593
email admin@canauthors.org
website www.canauthors.org
President Joan Eyolfson Cadham, *National Director* Alec McEachern

The Canadian Children's Book Centre (CCBC)
Suite 101, 40 Orchard View Blvd, Toronto, ON M4R 1B9, Canada
tel 416975-0010 *fax* 416-975-8970
email info@bookcentre.ca
website www.bookcentre.ca

A national, not-for-profit organisation dedicated to encouraging, promoting and supporting the reading, writing and illustrating of Canadian books for young readers. CCBC programmes and publications offer a wide range of resources to anyone who is interested in quality reading for children and teens. Founded 1976.

Canadian Magazine Publishers Association

425 Adelaide Street West, Suite 700, Toronto, Ontario M5V 3C1, Canada
tel 416-504-0274 *fax* 416-504-0437
email info@magazinescanada.ca
website www.cmpa.ca
Chief Executive Mark Jamison

Canadian Publishers' Council

250 Merton Street, Suite 203, Toronto, Ontario M4S 1B1, Canada
tel 416-322-7011 *fax* 416-322-6999
email pubadmin@pubcouncil.ca
website www.pubcouncil.ca
Executive Director Jacqueline Hushion

CANSCAIP (Canadian Society of Children's Authors, Illustrators & Performers)

40 Orchard View Boulevard, Suite 104, Toronto, Ontario M4R 1B9, Canada
tel 416-515-1559
email office@canscaip.org
website www.canscaip.org
Administrative Director Lena Coakley
Membership $75 p.a. Full member (published authors and illustrators), $45 Insitutional Friend, $35 Friend

A non-profit support network for children's artists. Promotes children's literature and performances through Canada and internationally. Founded 1977.

Careers Writers' Association

Membership Secretary Ann Goodman,
16 Caewal Road, Llandaff, Cardiff CF5 2BT
tel 029-2056 3444 *fax* 029-2065 8190
email helen.scott@btinternet.com
website www.careerswriting.co.uk
Membership £40 p.a.

Society for established writers on the inter-related topics of education, training and careers. Holds occasional meetings on subjects of interest to members, and circulates details of members to information providers. Founded 1979.

The Lewis Carroll Society

Secretary Alan White, 69 Cromwell Road, Hertford, Herts. SG13 7DP
email alanwhite@tesco.net
website www.lewiscarrollsociety.org.uk
Membership £15 p.a. UK, £18 Europe, £20 elsewhere; special rates for institutions

Aims to promote interest in the life and works of Lewis Carroll (Revd Charles Lutwidge Dodgson)

(1832–98) and to encourage research. Activities include regular meetings, exhibitions, and a publishing programme that includes the first annotated, unexpurgated edition of his diaries in 9 volumes, the Society's journal *The Carrollian* (2 p.a.), a newsletter, *Bandersnatch* (quarterly) and the *Lewis Carroll Review* (occasional). Founded 1969.

Lewis Carroll Society (Daresbury)

Secretary Kenn Oultram, Clatterwick House, Clatterwick Lane, Little Leigh, Northwich, Cheshire CW8 4RJ
tel (01606) 891303 (office), 781731 (evening)
Membership £7 p.a.

Aims to encourage an interest in the life and works of Lewis Carroll (1832–98), author of *Alice's Adventures*. Meetings take place at Carroll's birth village (Daresbury, Cheshire). Founded 1970.

Lewis Carroll Society of North America (LCSNA)

11935 Beltsville Drive, Beltsville, MD 20705, USA
email andrewsellon@optonline.net
website www.lewiscarroll.org
Membership $35 p.a. USA; $50 elsewhere
  President Andrew Sellon

An organisation of Carroll admirers of all ages and interests and a centre for Carroll studies. It is dedicated to furthering Carroll studies, increasing accessibility of research material, and maintaining public awareness of Carroll's contributions to society. The Society has a worldwide membership and meets twice a year. The Society maintains an active publication programme and members receive copies of the Society's magazine *Knight Letter*. An interest in Lewis Carroll, a simple love for Alice (or the Snark for that matter) qualifies for membership. Founded in 1974.

The Center for Children's Books (CCB)

Graduate School of Library and Information Science, University of Illinois at Urbana–Champaign, 501 East Daniel Street, Champaign, IL 61820, USA
tel 217-244-9331 *fax* 217-333-5603
email ccb@uiuc.edu
website http://ccb.lis.uiuc.edu

CCB houses a non-circulating collection of more than 16,000 recent and historically significant trade books for children, plus review copies of nearly all trade books published in the USA in the current year. There are over 1000 professional and reference books on the history and criticism of literature for youth, literature-based library and classroom programming, and storytelling. Although the collection is non-circulating, it is available for examination by scholars, teachers, librarians, students, and other educators.

Centre for Literacy in Primary Education (CLPE)

Webber Street, London SE1 8QW
tel 020-7401 3382/3 *fax* 020-7928 4624

email info@clpe.co.uk
website www.clpe.co.uk

A centre for children's language, literacy, literature and educational assessment which provides in-service training for teachers and courses for parents and contains a reference library of children's books plus teachers' resources. CLPE also publishes booklists and teaching resources relating to literacy in the primary classroom.

Department for Children, Schools and Families

Sanctuary Buildings, Great Smith Street, London SW1P 3BT
tel (0870) 000 2288 *fax* (01928) 794248
email info@dcsf.gsi.gov.uk
website www.dcsf.gov.uk

Aims to help build a competitive economy and inclusive society by creating opportunities for everyone to develop their learning potential and achieve excellence in standards of education and levels of skills. The department's main objectives are to give children an excellent start in education and enable young people and adults to develop and equip themselves with the skills, knowledge and personal qualities needed for life and work.

The Department also sponsors 11 non-departmental public bodies across a variety of professional disciplines and educational services.

The Children's Book Circle – see page 341

The Children's Book Council (CBC)

12 West 37th Street, 2nd Floor, New York, NY 10018–7480, USA
tel 212-966-1990 *fax* 212-966-2073
email info@cbcbooks.org
website www.cbcbooks.org

The non-profit trade association of publishers and packagers of trade books and related materials for children and young adults. The goals of the CBC are to make the reading and enjoyment of children's books an essential part of America's educational and social goals; to enhance public perception of the importance of reading by disseminating information about books and related materials for young people and information about children's book publishing; and to create materials to support literacy and reading encouragement programs and to encourage the annual observance of National Children's Book Week.

Children's Book Council of Australia

PO Box 3203, Norwood, SA 5067, Australia
tel (08) 8332 2845 *fax* (08) 8333 0394
website www.cbca.org.au

Aims to foster children's enjoyment of books through managing the Children's Book of the Year Awards; providing information on and encouragement to

authors and illustrators; organising exhibitions and activities during Children's Book Week; supporting children's library services; and promoting high standards in book reviewing.

The Children's Book Guild of Washington DC

website www.childrensbookguild.org
President Edith Ching

A regional association of writers, artists, librarians and other specialists dedicated to the field of children's literature. Its aims are to uphold and stimulate high standards of writing and illustrating for children; to increase knowledge and use of better books for children in the community; and to cooperate with other groups having similar purposes. Founded 1945.

Children's Books Ireland

17 North Great Georges Street, Dublin 1, Republic of Ireland
tel (01) 872 7475 *fax* (01) 872 7476
email info@childrensbooksireland.com
website www.childrensbooksireland.com
Director Mags Walsh, *Administrator* Jenny Murray
Membership €30/£20 p.a. individual, €50/£35 p.a. institutions, €45/£30/$55 p.a. overseas individual, €60/£40/$70 p.a. overseas institutions, €20/£15 p.a. student

Dedicated to ensuring that books are at the centre of young people's lives, through advocacy, resource and innovative programming and outreach. Formed in 1996.

Children's Literature Association (ChLA)

PO Box 138, Battle Creek, MI 49016–0138, USA
tel 269-965-8180 *fax* 269-965-3568
email info@childlitassn.org
website www.childlitassn.org
Membership Open to both individuals and institutions. Individual membership $75 (US), $105 (non-US/Canada). Discounts available for concessions. Institutional membership $145 (US), $175 (non-US/Canada)

An organisation encouraging high standards of criticism, scholarship, research and teaching in children's literature. Individual members are entitled to the *ChLA Quarterly* and the annual volume of *Children's Literature*.

Children's Literature Centre

Martynas Mazvydas National Library of Lithuania, Gedimino pr. 51, LT–01504, Vilnius, Lithuania
tel (370) 5 2398560 *fax* (370) 5 2496129
email vaikai@lnb.lt
website www.lnb.lt

Martynas Mazvydas National Library of Lithuania Children's Department came into existence in 1963 and in 1994 was reorganised into the Children's Literature Centre (CLC).

It accumulates, processes, and stores children's literature, both original and in translation, as well as works on history, theory and literary criticism, informative and reference publications from various countries related to children's literature. The aim of CLC is to acquire, as fully as possible, earlier Lithuanian and translated children's books and books published by Lithuanian exiles. The CLC collection numbers approximately 102,000 volumes.

The Centre organises children's reading research, analyses book popularity, design, illustrations, quality of translations. CLC arranges international children's book exhibitions, seminars and conferences on children's book and reading. Presentation of new books, meetings with authors, publishers and designers are regularly carried out. CLC is the coordination and monitoring centre of children's libraries in Lithuania.

Children's Writers and Illustrators Group – see The Society of Authors, page 335

CLÉ – Irish Book Publishers' Association
25 Denzille Lane, Dublin 2, Republic of Ireland
tel (01) 639 4868
email info@publishingireland.com
website www.publishingireland.com
President Séan Ó Cearnaigh

Comhairle nan Leabhraichean/The Gaelic Books Council
22 Mansfield Street, Glasgow G11 5QP
tel 0141-337 6211 *fax* 0141-353 0515
email brath@gaelicbooks.net
website www.gaelicbooks.net
Chair Prof. Roibeard Ó Maolalaigh

Stimulates Scottish Gaelic publishing by awarding publication grants for new books, commissioning authors and providing editorial services and general assistance to writers and readers. Has its own bookshop of all Gaelic and Gaelic-related books in print and runs a book club. All the stock is listed on the website and a paper catalogue is also available. Founded 1968.

Cwlwm Cyhoeddwyr Cymru
c/o Mairwen Prys Jones, Gwasg Gomer,
Parc Menter Llandysul, Ceredigion SA44 4JL
tel (01559) 363090 *fax* (01559) 363758
email mairwen@gomer.co.uk
website www.cwlwmcyhoeddwyr.com (Welsh language only)

Represents and promotes Welsh-language publishers. Founded 2002.

Cyngor Llyfrau Cymru – see Welsh Books Council/Cyngor Llyfrau Cymru

Roald Dahl Foundation
81A High Street, Great Missenden, Bucks. HP16 0AL
tel (01494) 892192

website www.roalddahl.com, www.roalddahlfoundation.org

A UK-based registered charity offering a programme of grant-giving to charities, hospitals and individuals in the UK. It supports many varied projects, in the same way Roald Dahl did when he was alive, offering practical assistance to children and families in 3 areas: neurology, haematology and literacy.

The websites are illustrated with the artworks of Quentin Blake, Roald Dahl's principal illustrator and include full information about the author, his life and his works. The Roald Dahl website includes a free online club for children and the online magazine *Dahl-y Telegraph*.

The Roald Dahl Museum and Story Centre
81–83 High Street, Great Missenden, Bucks. HP16 0AL
tel (01494) 892192
website www.roalddahlmuseum.org

Housing Roald Dahl's unique archive, the Roald Dahl Museum and Story Centre has two biographical galleries and a hands-on Story Centre that inspires visitors to write creatively.

Walter de la Mare Society
PO Box 25351, London NW5 1ZT
tel 020-8886 1771
website www.bluetree.co.uk/wdlmsociety
Membership £15 p.a.

To promote the study and deepen the appreciation of the works of Walter de la Mare (1873–1956) through a magazine, talks, discussions and other activities. Founded 1997.

Discover
1 Bridge Terrace, Stratford, London E15 4BG
tel 020-8536 5555
email team@discover.org.uk
website www.discover.org.uk
Director Sally Goldsworthy

Discover is designed for children aged 0–8 years and their families, carers and teachers. Discover is about story-building – making stories together. Story-building helps children to use their imaginations and express themselves, both to each other and to grown-ups, through play. Speaking, listening, writing and acting become easy activities. Story-building is fun and breaks down barriers.

Discover has been running its outreach programmes to schools, libraries and community centres since 2000. The Story Garden opened in 2002 and the Story Trail opened in June 2003 in a renovated Edwardian building in the centre of Stratford. Story Trail is full of unique hands-on exhibits. Children's input at every stage of Discover's work is fundamental.

The Arthur Conan Doyle Society
Organisers Christopher and Barbara Roden,
PO Box 1360, Ashcroft, B.C., Canada V0K 1A0

tel 250-453-2045 *fax* 250-453-2075
email sirhenry@telus.net
website www.ash-tree.bc.ca/acdsocy.html

Promotes the study of the life and works of Sir Arthur Conan Doyle (1859–1930). Publishes *ACD* journal (bi-annual) and occasional reprints of Conan Doyle material. Occasional conventions. Founded 1989.

Educational Publishers Council

The Publishers Association, 29B Montague Street, London WC1B 5BW
tel 020-7691 9191 *fax* 020-7691 9199
email mail@publishers.org.uk
website www.publishers.org.uk

Provides a forum for publishers of printed and electronic learning resources for the school and college markets. It runs a series of events and meetings for its members and provides an information service. It also promotes the industry through the media.

Educational Writers Group – see The Society of Authors, page 335

English Association

University of Leicester, University Road, Leicester LE1 7RH
tel 0116-252 3982 *fax* 0116-252 2301
email engassoc@le.ac.uk
website www.le.ac.uk/engassoc/
Chair Maureen Moran, *Chief Executive* Helen Lucas

Aims to further knowledge, understanding and enjoyment of English literature and the English language, by working towards a fuller recognition of English as an essential element in education and in the community at large; by encouraging the study of English literature and language by means of conferences, lectures and publications; and by fostering the discussion of methods of teaching English of all kinds.

Federation of Children's Book Groups – see page 342

Federation of European Publishers

Rue Montoyer 31 Bte 8, B–1000 Brussels, Belgium
tel (2) 770 11 10 *fax* (2) 771 20 71
email info@fep-fee.eu
website www.fep-fee.eu
President Jonas Modig, *Director* Anne Bergman-Tahon

Represents the interests of European publishers on EU affairs; informs members on the development of EU policies which could affect the publishing industry. Founded 1967.

The Federation of Indian Publishers

18/1C Institutional Area,
Aruna Asaf Ali Marg (near JNU), New Delhi 110067, India

tel 26852263, 26964847 *fax* 26864054
email fip1@satyam.net.in
website www.fipindia.org
President Shri R.C. Govil

Federation of Spanish Publishers' Association

(Federación de Gremios de Editores de España)
Cea Bermúdez, 44–2 Dcha. 28003 Madrid, Spain
tel (91) 534 51 95 *fax* (91) 535 26 25
email fgee@fge.es
website www.federacioneditores.org
President Sr Djordi Obedai Bauló

French Publishers' Association

(Syndicat National de l'Edition)
115 Blvd St Germain, 75006 Paris, France
tel (1) 44 41 40 50 *fax* (1) 44 41 40 77
website www.sne.fr

The Gaelic Books Council – see Comhairle nan Leabhraichean/The Gaelic Books Council

The Greeting Card Association

United House, North Road, London N7 9DP
tel 020-7619 0396
website www.greetingcardassociation.org.uk
General Manager Sharon Little

The trade association for greeting card publishers. See website for information. 3D cards for GCSE Graphic Products students and greeting card finishes. Official magazine: *Progressive Greetings Worldwide*.

Guernsey Arts Council

PO Box 87, St Peter Port, Guernsey GY1 4BS
Chairman Michael Rivett-Carnac

The Hayward

Southbank Centre, Belvedere Road, London SE1 8XX
tel 020-7921 0813 *fax* 0871-663 2596
email customer@southbankcentre.co.uk
website www.southbankcentre.co.uk/visualarts

Imaginate

45A George Street, Edinburgh EH2 2HT
tel 0131-225 8050 *fax* 0131-225 6440
email info@imaginate.org.uk
website www.imaginate.org.uk
Director Tony Reekie, *General Manager* Tessa Rennie

An arts organisation that promotes and develops the performing arts for children and young people in Scotland. Its aim is that children and young people aged up to 18 have regular access to a diverse range of high-quality performing arts activity, from home and abroad, that will entertain, enrich, teach and inspire them. Its mission is to act as an advocate for the provision of high-quality performing arts for children across Scotland. Imaginate produces an annual programme of events and initiatives.

Imaginate produces the Bank of Scotland Imaginate Festival (see page 375). It also produces WYSIWYG (What You See Is What You Get), Scotland's showcase and conference of performing arts for children and young people that takes place every 2 years. In the intervening years, a laboratory event is held with presentations from leading thinkers in the industry, workshops and work in progress.

Other areas of Imaginate's work include: development opportunities for artists and producers, professional development for teachers and other educators, and strategic development, i.e. research, advocacy and initiatives to increase access and participation and enhance the experience for children and young people.

Imperial War Museum
Lambeth Road, London SE1 6HZ
tel 020-7416 5320
website www.iwm.org.uk

Independent Publishers Guild
PO Box 93, Royston, Herts SG8 5GH
tel (01763) 247014 *fax* (01763) 246293
website www.ipg.uk.com
Membership £160 + VAT p.a. min. Open to new and established publishers and book packagers; supplier membership is available to specialists in fields allied to publishing (but not printers and binders)

Provides an information and contact network for independent publishers. The IPG also voices the concerns of member companies with the book trade. Founded 1962.

Independent Theatre Council (ITC)
12 The Leather Market, Weston Street, London SE1 3ER
tel 020-7403 1727 *fax* 020-7403 1745
email admin@itc-arts.org
website www.itc-arts.org
Young People's Theatre Co-ordinator Roger Lang
Membership Prices vary according to type of membership

ITC represents a wide range of performing arts organisations, venues and individuals in the fields of drama, dance, opera, music theatre, puppetry, mixed media, mime, physical theatre and circus. These organisations predominantly work on the middle and small scale around the UK. It has around 700 members across the performing arts who are united by their commitment to producing innovative, contemporary work (24% of the membership work specifically in the educational field reaching over 2 million children and young people). Founded 1974.

International Board on Books for Young People (IBBY)
Nonnenweg 12, Postfach, CH–4003–Basel, Switzerland

tel (4161) 272 2917 *fax* (+4161) 272 2757
email ibby@ibby.org, liz.page@ibby.org
British Section PO Box 20875, GB–London SE22 9WQ
tel 020-8299 1641
email ann@lazim.demon.co.uk
website www.ibby.org

IBBY is a non-profit organisation which represents an international network of people from all over the world who are committed to bringing books and children together. Its aims are:

• to promote international understanding through children's books;
• to give children everywhere the opportunity to have access to books with high literary and artistic standards;
• to encourage the publication and distribution of quality children's books, especially in developing countries;
• to provide support and training for those involved with children and children's literature;
• to stimulate research and scholarly works in the field of children's literature.

IBBY is composed of more than 68 National Sections all over the world and represents countries with well-developed book publishing and literacy programmes, and other countries with only a few dedicated professionals who are doing pioneer work in children's book publishing and promotion. Founded in Zurich, Switzerland in 1953.

International Publishers Association
3 avenue de Miremont, CH–1206 Geneva, Switzerland
tel (022) 346-30-18 *fax* (022) 347-57-17
email secretariat@internationalpublishers.org
website www.internationalpublishers.org
President Ana Maria Cabanellas, *Secretary-General* Mr Jens Bammel

Founded 1896.

The Irish Book Publishers' Association – see CLÉ – Irish Book Publishers' Association

Irish Educational Publishers Association
c/o Gill and Macmillan Ltd, Hume Avenue, Park West, Dublin 12, Republic of Ireland
tel 353 1 500 9509 *fax* 353 1 500 9598
email amurray@gillmacmillan.ie
Contact Anthony Murray

Represents 13 publishers of educational materials in Ireland.

Irish Writers' Centre
19 Parnell Square, Dublin 1, Republic of Ireland
tel (01) 8721302 *fax* (01) 8726282
email info@writerscentre.ie
website www.writerscentre.ie
Director Cathal McCabe

National organisation for the promotion of writers and writing in Ireland. Runs an extensive programme of events at its headquarters; operates the Writer in Community Scheme, which funds events throughout Ireland; runs an education programme offering courses and workshops in writing; and operates an International Writers' Exchange Programme. See website for further details. Founded 1991.

The Kipling Society

Hon. Secretary Jane Keskar, 6 Clifton Road, London W9 1SS
tel 020-7286 0194
email Jane@keskar.fsworld.co.uk
website www.kipling.org.uk
Membership £24 p.a. (£22 p.a. standing orders; £12 under age 23)

Aims to honour and extend the influence of Rudyard Kipling (1865–1936), to assist in the study of his writings, to hold discussion meetings, to publish a quarterly journal, and to maintain a Kipling Library in London and a Kipling Room in The Grange, Rottingdean, near Brighton.

C.S. Lewis Society (Oxford)

Pusey House, St Giles, Oxford OX1 3LZ
email oulewis@herald.ox.ac.uk

Meets 8.15pm, Tuesday term-time at Pusey House, to promote knowledge of C.S. Lewis (1898–1963) and the writers who influenced him, including J.R.R. Tolkien, Charles Williams, Dorothy L. Sayers, G.K. Chesterton and George MacDonald. Open to non-University members.

The C.S. Lewis Society (New York)

Secretary Clare Sarrocco, 84–23, 77th Avenue, Glendle, NY 11385–7706, USA
email subscribe@nycslsociety.com
website www.nycslsociety.com

The oldest society for the appreciation and discussion of C.S. Lewis (1898–1963). Founded 1969.

Little Theatre Guild of Great Britain

National Secretary, Barbara Watson,
181 Brampton Road, Carlisle CA3 9AX
tel (01228) 522649
email chrysbar@tiscali.co.uk
website www.littletheatreguild.org

Aims to promote closer cooperation amongst the little theatres constituting its membership; to act as coordinating and representative body on behalf of the little theatres; to maintain and advance the highest standards in the art of theatre; and to assist in encouraging the establishment of other little theatres. Its yearbook is available to non-members for £5.

The Livesey Museum for Children

682 Old Kent Road, London SE15 1JF
tel 020-7635 5829 *fax* 020-7277 5384
email info@liveseymuseum.org.uk
website www.liveseymuseum.org.uk

An all-new interactive exhibition is shown every year for children under 12 years old, their families, carers and teachers. Children can learn things by experimenting and investigating, by using their imaginations – and by having fun! Exhibitions are designed to support the National Curriculum at Foundation Stage, KS1 and KS2.

L.M. Montgomery Heritage Society

L.M. Montgomery Institute,
University of Prince Edward Island,
550 University Avenue, Charlottetown,
Prince Edward Island, Canada C1A 4P3
tel 902-628-4346 *fax* 902-628-4305
email lmmi@upei.ca
website www.lmmontgomery.ca

The Society is dedicated to protecting L.M. Montgomery's (1874–1942) Prince Edward Island literary and historic legacy for the benefit, education and enjoyment of the public. The Society is a non-profit organisation made up of representatives from Island heritage sites and groups with a mutual interest in preserving and promoting Montgomery's Island home. As part of its mandate, the Society holds events honouring the life and times of Montgomery, including an annual birthday celebration held each November and the L.M. Montgomery Festival held each August. L.M. Montgomery is the author of *Anne of Green Gables* and *Emily of New Moon*. Founded 1994.

Museum of London

London Wall, London EC2Y 5HN
tel (0870) 444 3851 *fax* (0870) 444 3853
email info@museumoflondon.org.uk
website www.museumoflondon.org.uk

The Mythopoeic Society

Corresponding Secretary Edith Crowe,
The Mythopoeic Society, PO Box 6707, Altadena, CA 91003-6707
email correspondence@mythsoc.org
website www.mythsoc.org
Membership with Mythprint $20 p.a. (USA), $36 p.a. (rest of world)

A non-profit international literary and educational organization for the study, discussion, and enjoyment of fantastic and mythic literature, especially the works of Tolkien, C.S. Lewis, and Charles Williams. The word 'mythopoeic' (myth-oh-PAY-ik or myth-oh-PEE-ic), meaning 'mythmaking' or 'productive of myth', aptly describes much of the fictional work of the 3 authors who were also prominent members of an informal Oxford literary circle (1930s–1950s) known as the Inklings. Membership is open to all scholars, writers, and readers of these literatures. The Society sponsors 3 periodicals: *Mythprint* (a monthly bulletin of book reviews, articles and events), *Mythlore* (scholarly articles on mythic and fantastic literature), and *Mythic Circle* (a literary annual of original poetry and short stories). Each summer the Society holds an annual conference. Founded 1967.

National Art Library
Victoria and Albert Museum, South Kensington, London SW7 2RL
tel 020-7942 2400
email nal.enquiries@vam.ac.uk
website www.vam.ac.uk/nal

A major reference library and the Victoria and Albert Museum's curatorial department for the art, craft and design of the book. All are welcome to use the facilities.

National Association for the Teaching of English (NATE)
50 Broadfield Road, Sheffield S8 0XJ
tel 0114-255 5419 *fax* 0114-255 5296
email info@nate.org.uk
website www.nate.org.uk

The professional association for all those working in English education in the UK. NATE provides information about current developments, publications and resource materials. It also funds research, in-service training and holds an annual and regional conferences. Annual membership gives members 5 copies of NATE's journal, newsletter and pupil age-related magazines and well as discounts on publications, courses and conferences. See website for details of how to join.

National Association of Writers' Groups
Headquarters The Arts Centre, Biddick Lane, Washington, Tyne and Wear NE38 2AB
tel (01262) 609228
email nawg@tesco.net
Secretary Diane Wilson, 40 Burstall Hill, Bridlington, East Yorkshire YO16 7GA
website www.nawg.co.uk
Membership £30 p.a. plus £5 registration per group; £14 Associate individuals

Aims 'to advance the education of the general public throughout the UK, including the Channel Islands, by promoting the study and art of writing in all its aspects'. Publishes *Link* bimonthly magazine. Annual Festival of Writing held in Durham in September. Annual Creative Writing Competition. Founded 1995.

National Association of Writers in Education (NAWE)
PO Box 1, Sheriff Hutton, York YO60 7YU
tel (01653) 618429
email paul@nawe.co.uk
website www.nawe.co.uk
Director Paul Munden

Represents and supports writers, teachers and all those involved in the development of creative writing in education. Useful resource of writers who work in schools and communities is held on the website.

National Centre for Language and Literacy (NCLL)
University of Reading, Bulmershe Court, Reading RG6 1HY
tel 0118-378 8820
email ncll@reading.ac.uk
website www.ncll.org.uk

An independent organisation concerned with all aspects of language and literacy learning. The Centre supports teachers, parents and governors through its unique collection of resources, its publications, an extensive programme of courses and conferences and ongoing research.

National Centre for Research in Children's Literature (NCRCL)
Bede House, School of Arts, Digby Stuart College, Roehampton University, Roehampton Lane, London SW15 5PH
tel 020-8392 3008 *fax* 020-8392 3819
email g.lathey@roehampton.ac.uk, l.sainsbury@roehampton.ac.uk
website www.ncrcl.ac.uk

Facilitates and supports research exchange in the field of children's literature. The NCRCL is based in Roehampton University, which houses several collections held in the Children's Literature Centre and in the Froebel Archive for Childhood Studies. The website provides information on resources, activities and children's literature-related individuals and links to websites.

National Galleries of Scotland
National Gallery Complex, The Mound, Edinburgh EH2 2EL
tel 0131-624 6200, 0131-624 6332 (press office)
fax 0131-343 3250 (press office)
email pressinfo@nationalgalleries.org
Scottish National Portrait Gallery, 1 Queen Street, Edinburgh EH2 1JD
Scottish National Gallery of Modern Art, Belford Road, Edinburgh EH4 3DR
The Dean Gallery, Belford Road, Edinburgh EH4 3DS
website www.nationalgalleries.org

National Gallery
Information Department, Trafalgar Square, London WC2N 5DN
tel 020-7747 2885 *fax* 020-7747 2423
email information@ng-london.org.uk
website www.nationalgallery.org.uk

National Literacy Association
87 Grange Road, Ramsgate, Kent CT11 9QB
tel/fax (01843) 239952

email wendy@nla.org.uk
website www.nla.org.uk

Campaigns to raise awareness of the needs of underachievers and aims to ensure that school leavers will have adequate literacy for their needs in daily life. Produces publications and other resources including *The Guide to Literacy Resources*, which is distributed free to schools, parent groups, libraries and others.

National Literacy Trust
68 South Lambeth Road, London SW8 1RL
tel 020-7587 1842
email contact@literacytrust.org.uk
website www.literacytrust.org.uk, www.rif.org.uk, www.readon.org.uk, www.readingthegame.org.uk, www.talktoyourbaby.org.uk
Director Jonathan Douglas

An independent charity that changes lives through literacy. 1 in 5 people in the UK struggles to read and write. The Trust links home, school and the wider community to inspire learners and create opportunities for everyone. It brings together key organisations to lead literacy promotion in the UK and support those working with learners through information, research, and innovative programmes – Reading Is Fundamental, UK; the National Reading Campaign; Reading The Game; and Talk To Your Baby.

National Museum Wales – see Amgueddfa Cymru – National Museum Wales

National Museums Liverpool
127 Dale Street, Liverpool L2 2JH
tel 0151-207 0001 *fax* 0151-478 4790

Venues: World Museum Liverpool, Walker Art Gallery, The National Conservation Centre, Merseyside Maritime Museum, International Slavery Museum, Lady Lever Art Gallery, Sudley House.

National Museums Scotland
Chambers Street, Edinburgh EH1 1JF
tel 0131-247 4422 *fax* 0131-220 4819
website www.nms.ac.uk

National Portrait Gallery
St Martin's Place, London WC2H 0HE
tel 020-7306 0055 *fax* 020-7306 0056
email personnel@npg.org.uk
website www.npg.org.uk

National Society for Education in Art and Design
The Gatehouse, Corsham Court, Corsham, Wilts. SN13 0BZ
tel (01249) 714825 *fax* (01249) 716138
website www.nsead.org
General Secretary Dr John Steers NDD, ATC, PhD

The leading national authority concerned with art, craft and design across all phases of education in the

UK. Offers the benefits of membership of a professional association, a learned society and a trade union. Has representatives on National and Regional Committees concerned with Art and Design Education. Publishes *International Journal of Art and Design Education* (3 p.a.; Blackwells) and *Start* magazine for primary schools. Founded 1888.

Natural History Museum
Cromwell Road, London SW7 5BD
tel 020-7942 5000
website www.nhm.ac.uk

The Edith Nesbit Society
21 Churchfields, West Malling, Kent ME19 6RJ
email mccarthy804@aol.com
website www.the-railway-children.co.uk
Membership £7 p.a., £14 organisations/overseas

Aims to promote an interest in the life and works of Edith Nesbit (1858–1924) by means of talks, a regular newsletter and and other publications, and visits to relevant places. Founded 1996.

New Producers Alliance
The NPA Film Centre, 7.03 Tea Building, 56 Shoreditch High Street, London E1 6JJ
tel 020-7613 0440 *fax* 020-7729 1852
email queries@npa.org.uk
website www.npa.org.uk
Membership £85 p.a., concessions £55 p.a., corporate £275 p.a., 'gold' £750 p.a.

A national membership organisation and registered charity dedicated to providing essential training and networking opportunities for film-makers. Led by industry professionals, the NPA assists independent film-makers in developing their skills, contacts and creativity in line with working industry practices. Founded 1993.

New Writing North
Culture Lab, Grand Assembly Rooms, Newcastle University, King's Walk, Newcastle NE1 7RU
tel 0191-222 1332 *fax* 0191-222 1372
email mail@newwritingnorth.com
website www.newwritingnorth.com
Director Claire Malcolm

The literature development agency for the North East. Offers advice and support to writers of poetry, prose and plays. See website. Founded 1996.

Newcastle University Library
Robinson Library, Newcastle University, Newcastle upon Tyne NE2 4HQ
tel 0191-222 7662
email lib-readersservices@ncl.ac.uk
website www.ncl.ac.uk/library

Historical children's books and other material relevant to the history of childhood and education.

Societies, associations and organisations 357

Over 100 collections of material ranging from rare books and archives to woodblocks and illustrations, from the mid 15th–21st century.

The Special Collections
tel 0191-222 5146
email lib-specenq@ncl.ac.uk
website www.ncl.ac.uk/library/specialcollections
Contains many historical children's books as well as a wealth of other material relevant to the history of childhood and education, especially 18th and 19th century chapbooks (cheap, popular pamphlets sold by itinerant traders, and often used by children). Most of these are to be found in the internationally important Robert White Collection. Special collections of children's books – the Chorley Collection of over 200 books published in the 19th and early 20th centuries; the Meade Collection of 184 books written by the children's author L.T. Meade (1854–1914); the Joan Butler Collection of about 5000 children's books published up to the mid-20th century (uncatalogued). Other collections include the Wallis Collection which contains material designed for the instruction of children; the Crawhall Collection which includes items such as the children's ABC books illustrated with woodcuts by Joseph Crawhall; the Bradshaw-Bewick Collection which contains several books designed for children and illustrated with woodcuts by Thomas Bewick. It also holds collections built up by schools from North-East England since the 16th century.

Special Collections at the Robinson Library is working in conjunction with Seven Stories to collect and preserve neglected collections of historical children's books.

The Booktrust Collection
Since the 1970s, most UK publishers have sent copies of every children's book they publish to Booktrust (see page 338), so that these books may be inspected and researched by the public. The Booktrust Collection, which is not fully catalogued, is now housed in the library. The collection currently contains approx. 60,000 items, including examples of toy and board books, picture books, young fiction and non-fiction. This number grows substantially each year. The collection provides an overview of British children's book publishing of the recent period and therefore of illustration, pedagogy, printing, images of childhood, design, typography, and so on, i.e. all the many areas included in the making of books for children. This is as complete a collection of recent and contemporary British children's books as exists anywhere.

The Seven Stories Archive
Since 1997, Seven Stories (see page 339) has been forming a collection of manuscripts and artwork by British writers and illustrators for children, from 1945 to the present day. Some of this archive is housed in the library.

Office for Standards in Education (OFSTED)
Royal Exchange Buildings, St Ann's Square, Manchester M2 7LA
tel (08456) 404045 *fax* (07002) 693274
email enquiries@ofsted.gov.uk
website www.ofsted.gov.uk

A non-ministerial government department established under the Education (Schools Act) 1992. Since April 2001 OFSTED has been responsible for inspecting all educational provision for 16–19 year-olds to establish and monitor an independent inspection system for maintained schools in England. Its inspection role also includes the inspection of local educational authorities, teacher training institutions and youth work. In September 2001, OFSTED took over the regulation of childcare providers, from 150 local authorities.

The Office of Communications (Ofcom)
Riverside House, 2A Southwark Bridge Road, London SE1 9HA
tel 020-7981 3000 *fax* 020-7981 3333
email contact@ofcom.org.uk
website www.ofcom.org.uk

The independent regulator and competition authority for the UK communications industries, with responsibilities across television, radio, telecommunications and wireless communications services. Established 2003.

The Poetry Book Society – see page 173

The Poetry Library – see page 175

The Poetry Society – see page 174

Poetry Society Education – see page 179

The Beatrix Potter Society
Membership Secretary c/o The Lodge, Salisbury Avenue, Harpenden, Herts. AL5 2PS
tel (01582) 769755
email beatrixpottersociety@tiscali.co.uk
website www.beatrixpottersociety.org.uk
Membership £20 p.a. UK (£25 overseas), £25/£30 commercial/institutional

Promotes the study and appreciation of the life and works of Beatrix Potter (1866–1943) as author, artist, diarist, farmer and conservationist. Regular lecture meetings, conferences and events in the UK and USA. Quarterly newsletter. Small publishing programme. Founded 1980.

The Publishers Association
29B Montague Street, London WC1B 5BW
tel 020-7691 9191 *fax* 020-7691 9199

email mail@publishers.org.uk
website www.publishers.org.uk
Chief Executive Simon Juden, *Director of International Division* Simon Bell, *Director of Educational, Academic & Professional Publishing* Graham Taylor

Founded 1896.

Publishing Scotland

(formerly Scottish Publishers Association)
Scottish Book Centre, 137 Dundee Street,
Edinburgh EH11 1BG
tel 0131-228 6866 *fax* 0131-228 3220
email enquiries@publishingscotland.org
website www.publishingscotland.org
Chairman Dr Keith Whittles, *Treasurer* Christian MacLean, *Chief Executive* Lorraine Fannin, *Member Services & Marketing Manager* Liz Small, *Information & Training Administrator* Joan Lyle

Founded 1973.

Qualifications and Curriculum Authority (QCA)

83 Piccadilly, London W1J 8QA
tel 020-7509 5555 *fax* 020-7509 6666
email info@qca.org.uk
website www.qca.org.uk
Chief Executive Dr Ken Boston

An independent government agency funded by the DfES. It is responsible for ensuring that the curriculum and qualifications available to young people and adults are of a high quality and are coherent and flexible. Its remit ranges from the under-fives to higher level vocational qualifications.

The Arthur Ransome Society Ltd (TARS)

Abbott Hall Museum, Kendal, Cumbria LA9 5AL
website www.arthur-ransome.org
President Norman Willis

To celebrate the life, promote the works, and diffuse the ideas of Arthur Ransome (1884–1967), author of the world-famous *Swallows and Amazons* series of books for children. The Society seeks in particular to encourage children and others to engage, with due regard to safety, in adventurous pursuits; educate the public generally about Ransome and his work; sponsor research in relevant areas; be a communications link for those interested in any aspect of Arthur Ransome's life and works. Founded 1990.

Readathon

The Parsonage, St Mary's, Chalford, Stroud GL6 8QB
tel (0870) 240 1124
email reading@readathon.org
website www.readathon.org

Readathon was set up to encourage children to read more books. Children undertake to read books, or do other literacy-based activities, in return for pledges of money, for charity, from family and friends. Thousands of schools have contributed to this success, and have made the Readathon campaign Britain's largest sponsored literary event. On joining, a free pack containing everything needed to run a successful Readathon is supplied.

Since it began Readathon has raised well over £20 million, which has been shared equally between two charities, the Roald Dahl Foundation and Sargent Cancer Care for Children. Fundraising costs are kept to a minimum because Readathon receives support from booksellers, children's publishers, and many organisations concerned with books and reading. Founded 1984.

Reading Is Fundamental, UK

National Literacy Trust, 68 South Lambeth Road,
London SW8 1RL
tel 020-7820 6271 *fax* 020-7587 1411
email rif@literacytrust.org.uk
website www.rif.org.uk

An initiative of the National Literacy Trust that helps children and young people (aged 0–19) to realise their potential by motivating them to read. Working with volunteers, it delivers targeted literacy projects that promote: the fun of reading; the importance of book choice; and the benefits to families of sharing books at home.

Children in each project choose up to 3 free books a year to keep at special events involving families and local volunteers; receive a book bag, bookmark, bookplates and stickers; and enjoy fun activities that highlight the pleasures of reading and often involve authors, poets, storytellers and illustrators.

Established in 1996 following the success of RIF Inc. (the largest children's and family literacy programme in the USA), RIF, UK has distributed 815,000 books to over 276,000 children and young people, and currently supports around 300 projects reaching 24,000 children. RIF, UK projects are set up in schools, libraries, football clubs, early years centres, bookshops, after-school and study support centres, women's refuges, prisons and parents' groups.

RNIB National Library Service

Far Cromwell Road, Bredbury, Stockport SK6 2SG
tel 0845-762 6843 *minicom* 0845-758 5691
fax 0161-355 2098
email cservices@rnib.org.uk
website www.rnib.org.uk/library

The largest specialist library for readers with sight loss in the UK. It offers a comprehensive range of books and accessible information for children and adults in a range of formats including braille, Moon, large print and unabridged audio. It also provides free access to online reference material, braille sheet music, themed book lists and a quarterly reader magazine (see Magazines and newspapers for children).

The Malcolm Saville Society
6 Redcliffe Street, London SW10 9DS
email mystery@witchend.com
website www.witchend.com
Membership £10 p.a. (£12.50 Europe, £16 elsewhere)

Aims to remember and promote interest in the work of Malcolm Saville (1901–82), children's author. Regular social activities, book search, library, contact directory and magazine (4 p.a.). Founded 1994.

Scattered Authors Society
Secretary Yvonne Coppard, 35 Thornton Way, Girton, Cambridge CB3 0NL
email yvonnecoppard@aol.com

Aims to provide a forum for informal discussion, contact and support for professional writers in children's fiction. Founded 1998.

School Library Association
Unit 2, Lotmead Business Village, Lotmead Farm, Wanborough, Swindon SN4 0UY
tel 0870-777 0979 *fax* 0870-777 0987
website www.sla.org.uk

Promotes the development of school libraries and information literacy as central to the curriculum. It publishes booklists and guidelines for library and resource centres, a quarterly journal and provides training and an information service.

Science Museum
Exhibition Road, London SW7 2DD
tel (0870) 870 4868
email sciencemuseum@sciencemuseum.org.uk
website www.sciencemuseum.org.uk

Scottish Arts Council
12 Manor Place, Edinburgh EH3 7DD
tel 0131-226 6051, (0845) 603 6000 (help desk; local rate) *fax* 0131-225 9833
email help.desk@scottisharts.org.uk
website www.scottisharts.org.uk
Chairman Dr Richard Holloway, *Head of Literature* Dr Gavin Wallace, *Head of Visual Arts* Amanda Catto

The lead body for the funding, development and advocacy of the arts in Scotland. Offers a unique national perspective on the provision and management of the arts which seeks to balance the needs of all arts sectors and all parts of Scotland. The expertise and experience of Scottish Arts Council in developing sound policy and good practice includes the ability to make links between the intrinsic value of the arts and their instrumental value in delivering social and economic benefits at a national level. Also offers a focus on research, information provision and international working.

The Council is an executive non-departmental public body (NDPB), which is one of the main channels for government funding for the arts in Scotland. Funding mostly comes from the Scottish Executive but it also distributes National Lottery funds.

Scottish Book Trust (SBT)
Sandeman House, 55 High Street, Edinburgh EH1 1SR
tel 0131-524 0160 *fax* 0131-524 0161
email info@scottishbooktrust.com
website www.scottishbooktrust.com

With a responsibility towards Scottish writing, SBT exists to inspire readers and writers, and through the promotion of reading, to reach and create a wider reading public. Programmes include: management of Live Literature funding, a national initiative enabling Scottish citizens to engage with authors, playwrights, poets, storytellers and illustrators; Writer Development, offering mentoring and professional development for writers; an ambitious children's programme including national tours, a children's festival and the Royal Mail Scottish Children's Book Awards; and an international programme showcasing Scottish writing abroad. An information service for readers, writers and occasional exhibitions and publications all contribute to SBT's mission to bring readers and writers together.

The Scottish Storytelling Forum
The Scottish Storytelling Centre, 43–45 High Street, Edinburgh EH1 1SR
tel 0131-556 9579 *fax* 0131-557 5224
website www.scottishstorytellingcentre.co.uk

Scotland's national charity for oral storytelling, established to encourage and support the telling and sharing of stories across all ages and all sectors of society, in particular those who, for reasons of poverty or disability, were excluded from artistic experiences. The Scottish Storytelling Centre is the Forum's resource and training centre. The Storytelling Network has over 100 professional storytellers across Scotland. Founded 1992.

Seven Stories – the Centre for the Children's Book – see page 339

Society for Editors and Proofreaders (SfEP)
Office Riverbank House, 1 Putney Bridge Approach, London SW6 3JD
tel 020-7736 3278
email admin@sfep.org.uk
website www.sfep.org.uk

Works to promote high editorial standards and achieve recognition of its members' professional status, through local and national meetings, an annual conference, email discussion groups, a regular magazine and a programme of reasonably priced workshops/training sessions. These sessions help newcomers to acquire basic skills, enable experienced editors to update their skills or broaden their competence, and also cover aspects of professional practice or business for the self-employed. An online Directory of editorial services is available. The Society supports moves towards recognised standards of training and accreditation for editors and proofreaders and has developed its own Accreditation in Proofreading qualification. It has close links with the Publishing Training Centre and the Society of Indexers, is represented on the BSI Technical Committee dealing with copy preparation and proof correction (BS 5261), and works to foster good relations with all relevant bodies and organisations in the UK and worldwide. Founded 1988.

Society for Storytelling (SfS)

PO Box 2344, Reading, Berks. RG6 7FG
tel 0118-935 1381
email sfs@fairbruk.demon.co.uk
website www.sfs.org.uk

Provides information on oral storytelling, events, storytellers and traditional stories. SfS volunteers have specialist knowledge of storytelling in education, health, therapy and business settings. To increase public awareness of the art it promotes National Storytelling Week, which takes place in the first week of February. The SfS provides a network for anyone interested in the art of oral storytelling whether they are full-time storytellers, use storytelling in their work, tell for the love or it or just want to listen. It holds an annual conference each Spring and produces a quarterly newsletter, a *Directory of Storytellers* and a variety of books and fact sheets. Founded 1993.

Society of Artists Agents

website www.thesaa.com

Formed to promote professionalism in the illustration industry and to forge closer links between clients and artists through an agreed set of guidelines. The Society believes in an ethical approach through proper terms and conditions, thereby protecting the interests of the artists and clients. Founded 1992.

The Society of Authors – see page 335

Society of Children's Book Writers and Illustrators (SCBWI)

36 Mackenzie Road, Beckenham, Kent BR3 4RU
tel 020-8249 9716
email ra@britishscbwi.org
website www.britishscbwi.org
Regional Adviser, SCBWI–British Isles Natascha Biebow
Membership £30 p.a. plus a one-off fee of £5

An international network for the exchange of knowledge between professional writers, illustrators, editors, publishers, agents, librarians, educators, booksellers and others involved with literature for young people. Sponsors conferences on writing and illustrating children's books and multimedia – in

New York (February, annual), Los Angeles (August, annual) and Bologna (spring, bi-annual) – as well as dozens of regional conferences and events throughout the world. Publishes a bi-monthly newsletter, *The Bulletin*, and information publications, and awards grants for works in progress. The SCBWI also presents the annual Golden Kite Award for the best fiction and non-fiction books, which is open both to published and unpublished writers and illustrators.

The SCBWI British Isles region meets regularly for speaker or workshop events. Also sponsors local critique groups and publishes *Words and Pictures* quarterly newsletter, which includes up-to-date events and marketing information, interviews and articles on the craft of children's writing and illustrating in the British Isles. The yearly Writers' Day and Illustrators' Day includes workshops and the opportunity to meet publishing professionals. Founded 1971.

Society of Editors

Director Bob Satchwell, University Centre, Granta Place, Mill Lane, Cambridge CB2 1RU
tel (01223) 304080 *fax* (01223) 304090
email info@societyofeditors.org
website www.societyofeditors.org
Membership £230 p.a.

Formed from the merger of the Guild of Editors and the Association of British Editors, the Society has more than 450 members in national, regional and local newspapers, magazines, broadcasting, new media, journalism education and media law, campaigning for media freedom. Founded 1999.

Society of Young Publishers

Contact The Secretary, c/o The Bookseller, Endeavour House, 189 Shaftesbury Avenue, London WC2H 8TJ
email info@thesyp.org.uk
website www.thesyp.org.uk
Membership Open to anyone employed in publishing or hoping to be soon; Associate membership available to those over the age of 35

Organises monthly speaker meetings at which senior figures talk on topics of key importance to the industry today, and social and other events. Runs a job database which matches candidates with potential employers. Meetings are held in Central London, usually on the last Wednesday of the month at 6.30pm. Also a branch in Oxford. Founded 1949.

Speaking of Books

105 John Humphries House, 4 Stockwell Street, London SE10 9JN
tel/fax 020-8858 6616
email jan@speakingofbooks.co.uk

Arranges school visits by writers, illustrators and storytellers. Also in-service training days relating to literacy.

The Robert Louis Stevenson Club
Secretary Dr Alan Marchbank, 12 Dean Park,
Longniddry, East Lothian EH32 0QR
tel (01875) 852976 *fax* (01875) 853328
email alan@amarchbank.freeserve.co.uk
website www.rlsclub.org.uk
Membership £20 p.a., £150 10 years

Aims to foster interest in Robert Louis Stevenson's
life (1850–94) and works through various events and
its newsletter. Founded 1920.

The Swedish Institute for Children's Books (Svenska barnboksinstitutet)
Odengatan 61, SE–113 22 Stockholm, Sweden
tel (0)8-54 54 20 50 *fax* (0)8-54 54 20 54
email info@sbi.kb.se
website www.sbi.kb.se

A special library open to the public and an
information centre for children's and young people's
literature. The aim is to promote this kind of
literature in Sweden as well as Swedish children's and
young people's literature abroad. Founded 1967.

Tate
Tate Britain, Millbank, London SW1P 4RG
tel 020-7887 8888
email visiting.britain@tate.org.uk
Tate Modern, Bankside, London SE1 9TG
tel 020-7887 8888
email visiting.modern@tate.org.uk
Tate Liverpool, Albert Dock, Liverpool L3 4BB
tel 0151-702 7400
email visiting.liverpool@tate.org.uk
Tate St Ives, Porthmeor Beach, St Ives, Cornwall
TR26 1TG
tel (01736) 796226
email visiting.stives@tate.org.uk
website www.tate.org.uk

Teenage Magazine Arbitration Panel (TMAP)
28 Kingsway, London WC2B 6JR
tel 020-7400 7520 *fax* 020-7404 4167
email kerry.neilson@ppa.co.uk
website www.ppa.co.uk/tmap

The magazine industry's self-regulatory body which
ensures that the sexual content of teenage magazines
is presented in a responsible and appropriate manner.

Theatre Museum
Victoria and Albert Museum, Cromwell Road,
London SW7 2RL
tel 020-7942 2000 *fax* 020-7942 2733
email tmgroups@vam.ac.uk
website www.vam.ac.uk/tco

New exhibitions and permanent galleries devoted to
theatre and performance are being developed at the
V&A. See website for education programme for all
ages. Material in the Museum's unrivalled collection

of programmes, playbills, prints, photos, videos, texts
and press cuttings relating to UK performance, is
available by appointment through the Reading
Room, Blythe House, Kensington W14, where
research facilities are provided. Open Tues–Fri
10.15am–4.30pm. Email tmenquiries@vam.ac.uk for
appointments.

The Tolkien Society
Membership Secretary Marion Kershaw,
655 Rochdale Road, Walsden, Todmorden,
Lancashire OL14 6SX
email membership@tolkiensociety.org
website www.tolkiensociety.org
Membership £21 p.a. (Full), £10.50 p.a. (Associate),
£2 p.a. (Entings)

United Kingdom Literacy Association (UKLA)
4th Floor, Attenborough Building,
University of Leicester, Leicester LE1 7RH
tel 0116 229 7450 *fax* 0116 229 7451
email admin@ukla.org
website www.ukla.org

UKLA is a registered charity, which has as its sole
object the advancement of education in literacy. It is
committed to promoting good practice nationally
and internationally in literacy and language teaching
and research. Its activities include:
• a conference programme of international, national
and local conferences reflecting language and literacy
interests.
• an active publications committee. Members are kept
up to date via UKLA journals and website. Members
receive a copy of the newsletter, *Literacy News*
(3 p.a.), and the journal *Literacy* (see *Magazines about
children's literature*). For an additional subscription,
members can receive the *Journal of Research in
Reading*. Both of the UKLA journals are refereed and
include research reports, both qualitative and
quantitative research, and critiques of current policy
and practice as well as discussions and debates about
current issues. UKLA also produces a range of books,
written mainly with teachers and students in mind.
In addition UKLA offers *English 4–11* published
jointly with the English Association.
• regular responses to national consultations,
including those organised through the DfES or QCA.
Consequently, the UKLA often seeks information and
responses from its members, as well as establishing a
UKLA response to particular issues.
• promoting and disseminating research. UKLA
provides support and small grants for literacy
research.
• networking – UKLA helps its members to network
both in the UK and through its worldwide contacts.
UKLA's affiliation to the International Reading
Association enables it to keep members in touch with
events and ideas in other parts of the world. UKLA is
also involved in specific international projects such as

Project Connect, for which it provides some support for literacy education in Uganda.

Founded in 1963 as the United Kingdom Reading Association; renamed the United Kingdom Literacy Association in 2003.

V&A Museum of Childhood

Cambridge Heath Road, London E2 9PA
tel 020-8983 5235
(24-hour Information Line) *fax* 020-8983 5225
website www.museumofchildhood.org.uk

Holds one of the largest and oldest collections of toys and childhood artefacts in the world. As well as its permanent displays, the museum has temporary exhibitions, workshops and activities for all. See website for details.

Victoria and Albert Museum

South Kensington, London SW7 2RL
tel 020-7942 2000
email vanda@vam.ac.uk
website www.vam.ac.uk

Voice of the Listener & Viewer Ltd (VLV)

101 King's Drive, Gravesend, Kent DA12 5BQ
tel (01474) 352835 *fax* (01474) 351112
email info@vlv.org.uk
website www.vlv.org.uk
Chairman Jocelyn Hay, *Administrative Secretary* Sue Washbrook

Represents the citizen and consumer interests in broadcasting: it is an independent, non-profit-making society working to ensure independence, quality and diversity in broadcasting. VLV is funded by its members and is free from sectarian, commercial and political affiliations. It holds public lectures, seminars and conferences, and has frequent contact with MPs and other relevant parties. It provides an independent forum where all with an interest in broadcasting can speak on equal terms. It produces a quarterly news bulletin and holds its own archive and those of the former Broadcasting Research Unit (1980–90) and BACTV (British Action for Children's Television). It maintains a panel of speakers, the VLV Forum for Children's Broadcasting, the VLV Forum for Educational Broadcasting, and acts as a secretariat for the European Alliance of Listeners' and Viewers' Associations (EURALVA). VLV does not handle complaints. Founded 1984.

Volunteer Reading Help (VRH)

VRH Central Office, Charity House,
14–15 Perseverance Works, 38 Kingsland Road,
London E2 8DD
tel 020-7729 4087 *fax* 020-7729 7643
email info@vrh.org.uk
website www.vrh.org.uk

A national charity that exists to inspire disadvantaged children with poor literacy and communication skills

to become confident and literate for life. VRH recruits and trains volunteers to work one-on-one with up to three children, aged 6–11, in two half hour sessions every week.

Welsh Animation Group (WAG)

Details Georgia Anderegg, WAG Treasurer,
13 Bangor Street, Cardiff CF24 3LQ
tel 029-2048 1420
email enquiries@siriol.co.uk
website http://wag.sequence.co.uk
Chair Robin Lyons
Membership Waged £25, unemployed £15, student £5, studio/corporate £200

Aims to bring together everybody working in animation in Wales, 'to build on the creative and economic successes of animation in Wales… to promote Welsh animation both nationally and throughout the world… to lobby for economic growth and the creation of jobs in the industry, and nurture the creative talent that has already brought Welsh animation international acclaim.' Holds regular meetings where animators can show their work, network, and voice their opinions. Helps to organise the Animation Day at the International Film Festival of Wales. Founded 1999.

Welsh Books Council/Cyngor Llyfrau Cymru

Castell Brychan, Aberystwyth, Ceredigion SY23 2JB
tel (01970) 624151 *fax* (01970) 625385
email castellbrychan@cllc.org.uk
website www.cllc.org.uk, www.gwales.com
Director Gwerfyl Pierce Jones

A national body funded directly by the Welsh Assembly Government which provides a focus for the publishing industry in Wales. Awards grants for publishing in Welsh and English. Provides services to the trade in the fields of editing, design, marketing and distribution. The Council is a key enabling institution in the world of books and provides services and information in this field to all who are associated with it. Founded 1961.

The Henry Williamson Society

General Secretary Sue Cumming, 7 Monmouth Road,
Dorchester, Dorset DT1 2DE
tel (01305) 264092
email zseagull@aol.com
Membership Secretary Margaret Murphy, 16 Doran
Drive, Redhill, Surrey RH1 6AX
tel (01737) 763228
email mm@misterman.freeserve.co.uk
website www.henrywilliamson.co.uk
Chairman Andrew Sanders
Membership £12 p.a.

Aims to encourage a wider readership and greater understanding of the literary heritage left by Henry Williamson (1895–1977). Two meetings annually; also weekend activities. Publishes an annual journal. Founded 1980.

Working Group Against Racism in Children's Resources

Unit 34, Eurolink Business Centre, 49 Effra Road,
London SW2 1BZ
tel/fax 020-7501 9992
website www.wgarcr.org.uk

A registered charity dedicated to training anyone working with children in the identification and elimination of racist images, language and sterotypes in children's books, resources and play materials.

Writernet

(formerly New Playwrights Trust)
Cabin V, Clarendon Buildings, 25 Horsell Road,
London N5 1XL
tel 020-7609 7474 *fax* 020-7609 7557
email info@writernet.org.uk
website www.writernet.org.uk
Director Jonathan Meth, *Chair* Bonnie Greer,
Administrator Elizabeth Robertson

Provides writers for all forms of live and recorded performance – working at any stage in their career, and in diverse contexts – with a range of services that enable them to pursue their careers better. These include: a network connecting dramatic writers to the industry and to each other; online resources to support dramatic writers and those who work with them; providing a wide range of producers with the opportunity to make more informed choices to meet their needs; as well as a script-reading service, publications and guides. It aims to help writers from all parts of the country and a wide diversity of backgrounds to fulfil their potential both inside and outside the new-writing mainstream. Founded 1985.

Writers Advice Centre for Children's Books

16 Smith's Yard, Summerley Street,
London SW18 4HR
tel (07979) 9905353
email info@writersadvice.co.uk
website www.writersadvice.co.uk
Editorial Director Louise Jordan

Dedicated to helping new and published children's writers by offering both editorial advice and tips on how to get published. The Centre also runs an online children's writing correspondence course plus a mentoring scheme for both ideas and manuscripts. Founded 1994.

The Writers' Guild of Great Britain

Writers' Guild Centre, 15–17 Britannia Street,
London WC1X 9JN
tel 020-7833 0777 *fax* 020-7833 4777
email admin@writersguild.org.uk
website www.writersguild.org.uk
General Secretary Bernie Corbett
Membership is open to all persons entitled to claim a single piece of written work of any length for which payment has been received under written contract, in terms not less favourable than those existing in current minimum-terms agreements negotiated by the Guild. Candidate membership (£90) is open to all those who are taking their first steps into writing but who have not yet received a contract. The minimum subscription is currently £150, or 1% of an author's income earned from professional writing sources in the previous calendar year, with a cap of £1500. All Full members are automatically members of the Authors Licensing and Collecting Society (ALCS). The Guild is a corporate member of the ALCS and is represented on its board.

A trade union for all professional writers working in TV, radio, film, theatre, books and multimedia, it is affiliated to the Trades Union Congress (TUC) and has more than 2000 members. The Guild represents writers in matters such as terms of pay and credits for their work. The Minimum Terms Agreements and advice services aim to safeguard writers against exploitation. Also offered are professional, cultural and social activities to help provide writers with a sense of community, making writing a less isolated occupation. Members receive *UK Writer*, a glossy quarterly magazine, plus a weekly email bulletin containing news and work opportunities. Further information and advice for writers working in theatre, film, radio or TV can be found in *Writers' & Artists' Yearbook* (A&C Black).

Members receive the *UK Writers*, which carries articles, letters and reports written by members, plus an email newsletter every Friday. Other benefits include free entry to the British Library reading rooms, and reduced entry to the National Film Theatre and regional film theatres. Founded in 1958.

Youth Libraries Group (YLG)

Bromley Central Library, High Street,
Bromley BR1 1EX
tel 020-8461 7193 *fax* 020-8313 9975
email ian.dodds@bromley.gov.uk
website www.cilip.org.uk/specialinterestgroups/bysubject/youth
Secretary Ian Dodds

The YLG is open to all members of the Chartered Institute for Library and Information Professionals (CILIP) who are interested in children's work. At a national level its aims are:

• to influence the provision of library services for children and the provision of quality literature;
• to inspire and support all librarians working with children and young people; and
• to liaise with other national professional. organisations in pursuit of such aims.

At a local level, the YLG organises regular training courses, supports professional development and provides opportunities to meet colleagues. It holds an annual conference and judges the CILIP Carnegie and Kate Greenaway Awards (see page 366). It also produces the journal *Youth Library Review*.

Children's book and illustration prizes and awards

This list provides details of prizes, competitions and awards for children's writers and artists. See page 373 for a *Calendar of awards.*

The Hans Christian Andersen Awards

Details International Board on Books for Young People, Nonnenweg 12, Postfach, CH–4003 Basel, Switzerland
tel (61) 272 29 17 *fax* (61) 272 27 57
email ibby@ibby.org, liz.page@ibby.org
website www.ibby.org

The Medals are awarded every 2 years to a living author and an illustrator who by the outstanding value of their work are judged to have made a lasting contribution to literature for children and young people. 2008 award winners: Jürg Schubiger (author) and Roberto Innocenti (illustrator).

Angus Book Award

Details Moyra Hood,
Educational Resources Librarian,
Educational Resources Service, Angus Council,
Leisure Services, Bruce House, Wellgate,
Arbroath DD11 3TL
tel (01241) 435008
email hoodm@angus.gov.uk
website www.angus.gov.uk/bookaward

An annual award originally set up as an Angus Council initiative to encourage pupils to read and enjoy quality teenage fiction. It is based on pupils not only voting for the winner but actively participating in all aspects of the award from selection of the shortlist to the award ceremony. The award involves 3rd-year pupils from all 8 secondary schools in Angus in reading 5 shortlisted titles. The shortlist is selected by teachers, librarians and pupils from books appropriate for the 14–15 year-old age group, written by authors living in the UK and published in paperback between July and June of the preceding year. Titles are chosen that reflect the range of themes which interest teenagers whilst challenging and interesting both committed and less enthusiastic readers. As part of the shortlisting process authors agree to visit schools and attend the Award ceremony, which takes place in May. The winner receives a miniature replica of the Aberlemno Serpent stone and £500. 2008 winner: *Leaving Poppy* by Kate Cann (Scholastic). Launched 1996.

Arts Council England

Details The Literature Dept, Arts Council England, 14 Great Peter Street, London SW1P 3NQ
tel 0845-300 6200 *textphone* 020-7973 6564
fax 020-7973 6590
email enquiries@artscouncil.org.uk
website www.artscouncil.org.uk

Arts Council England presents national prizes rewarding creative talent in the arts. These are awarded through the Council's flexible funds and are not necessarily open to application: the Children's Award, the David Cohen Prize for Literature, the Independent Foreign Fiction Prize, John Whiting Award, Meyer Whitworth Award and the Raymond Williams Community Publishing Prize.

Arts Council England, London

Details Gemma Seltzer, Literature Administrator, Arts Council England, London, 2 Pear Tree Court, London EC1R 0DS
tel 0845-300 6200 *fax* 020-7608 4100
website www.artscouncil.org.uk

Arts Council England, London, is the regional office for the Capital, covering 33 boroughs and the City of London. Grants are available through the 'Grants for the arts' scheme throughout the year to support a variety of literature projects, concentrating particularly on:

• original works of poetry and literary fiction and professional development for individual writers, including writers of children's books;
• touring and live literature;
• small independent literary publishers; and
• literary translation into English.

Contact the Literature Unit for more information, or see website for an application form.

Arts Council YouWriteOn.com Book Awards

tel (07930) 553269
email edward@youwriteon.com
website www.youwriteon.com

Arts Council-funded publishing awards for new fiction and poetry writers with consideration by leading literary agents and publishers. New writers upload opening chapters, short stories and poetry and each month the 5 highest rated writers receive a free professional critique from established authors and editors at literary agents and publishers, including Curtis Brown, Orion and Bloomsbury. The highest rated writers of the year are published, 3 in each of the adult and children's categories. The novel publishing awards total £1000 and winners can opt for a cash award instead of the publishing award. One of 2007's award finalists achieved a six-figure book deal with Transworld. An anthology of short stories and poetry will also be published. Writers can enter at any time throughout the year by joining the website. Closing date: 31 December each year. Founded 2005.

2008 children's book winners: *Tiger-Mouse* by Wai Ian Mo, *Get Santa* by David Wardale and *The Scream Park* by Edwain Gorty.

Association for Library Service to Children Awards

American Library Association, 50 East Huron Street, Chicago, IL 60611, USA
tel 800-545-2433 ext. 2163 *fax* 312-944-7671
email alsc@ala.org
website www.ala.org

The following awards are administered by ALSC:

• The Caldecott Medal was named in honor of the 19th century English illustrator Randolph Caldecott. It is awarded annually to the artist of the most distinguished American picture book for children.
• The Newbery Medal was named after the 18th century British bookseller John Newbery. It is awarded annually to the author of the most distinguished contribution to American literature for children.
• The Theodor Seuss Geisel Award is given annually to the author(s) and illustrator(s) of the most distinguished contribution to the body of American children's literature known as beginning reader books published in the United States during the preceding year. The award is to recognise the author(s) and illustrator(s) of a beginning reader book who demonstrate great creativity and imagination in his/her/their literary and artistic achievements to engage children in reading. The Award is named for the world-renowned children's author, Theodor Geisel. 'A person's a person no matter how small,' Theodor Geisel, a.k.a. Dr Seuss, would say. 'Children want the same things we want: to laugh, to be challenged, to be entertained and delighted.' Established 2004.
• The Robert F. Sibert Informational Book Award is given annually to the author of the most distinguished informational book published in English during the preceding year.
• The Wilder Medal, a bronze medal, honors an author or illustrator whose books, published in the USA, have made, over a period of years, a substantial and lasting contribution to literature for children.

Bardd Plant Cymru (Children's Poet Laureate)

Welsh Books Council, Castell Brychan, Aberystwyth, Ceredigion SY23 2JB
tel (01970) 624151 *fax* (01970) 625385
email castellbrychan@wbc.org.uk
website www.cllc.org.uk

The main aim is to raise the profile of poetry amongst children and to encourage them to compose and enjoy poetry. Ifor ap Glyn is Bardd Plant Cymru 2009–10. During his term of office he will visit schools as well as helping children to create poetry through electronic workshops. Established by S4C, the Welsh Books Council, Urdd Gobaith Cymru, and the Academi.

Basic Skills Book Awards

Welsh Books Council, Castell Brychan, Aberystwyth, Ceredigion SY23 2JB
tel (01970) 624151 *fax* (01970) 625385
website www.cllc.org.uk

As part of the Welsh Assembly Government's National Basic Skills Strategy, awards are made in categories including Primary Age-group, Secondary Age-group and Adult.

The Bisto Book of the Year Awards – see The CBI Bisto Book of the Year Awards

Blue Peter Children's Book Awards

Details Award Administrator, Fraser Ross Associates, 6 Wellington Place, Edinburgh EH6 7EQ
tel 0131-553 2759
website www.bbc.co.uk/cbbc/bluepeter

Awarded annually, judged by a panel of adults and children. Three categories: The Book I Couldn't Put Down, The Best Book with Facts, The Most Fun Story with Pictures. Eligible books are published in paperback between 1 May and 31 May of preceding year. Winning books are announced on Blue Peter in late autumn. 2007 winners: *The Outlaw Varjak Paw* by S.F. Said (Overall Winner), *The Worst Children's Jobs in History* by Tony Robinson, *You're a Bad Man, Mr Gum* by Andy Stanton and David Tazzyman.

BolognaRagazzi Award

Piazza Costituzione 6, 40128 Bologna, Italy
tel (051) 282242/282361 *fax* (051) 6374011
email bookfair@bolognafiere.it
website www.bolognachildrensbookfair.com
Takes place 23–26 March 2009

Winners of the BolognaRagazzi Award are displayed at the Bologna Children's Book Fair. Prizes are given to encourage excellence in children's publishing in the categories of fiction, non-fiction and 'new horizons' (books from emerging countries). The books are judged on the basis of their creativity, educational value and artistic design.

Booktrust Early Years Awards

Details Booktrust, Book House, 45 East Hill, London SW18 2QZ
tel 020-8516 2972/2960 *fax* 020-8516 2978
email tarryn@booktrust.org.uk,
helen@booktrust.org.uk
website www.booktrust.org.uk
Contacts Tarryn McKay, Helen Hayes

The winners of each of 3 categories, Baby Book Award, Pre-School Award and Best Emerging Illustrator, will each receive a cheque for £2000 and a crystal obelisk. The winner of the Best Emerging Illustrator also receives a specially commissioned piece of artwork from a well-known children's illustrator. The winning publishers receive a commemorative award. Closing date: early May. Established 1999 (formerly the Sainsbury's Baby Book Award).

2007 winners: Baby Book Award – *Tucking In!* by Jess Stockham (Child's Play); Pre-School Award – *Penguin* by Polly Dunbar (Walker Books); Best Emerging Illustrator – *Monkey and Me* by Emily Gravett (Macmillan Children's Books).

The Booktrust Teenage Prize

Details Booktrust, Book House, 45 East Hill, London SW18 2QZ
tel 020-8875 4821 *fax* 020-8516 2978
email megan@booktrust.org.uk
website www.bookheads.org.uk
Contact Megan Farr

The first annual national book prize to recognise and celebrate the best in young adult fiction. The author of the best book for teenagers receives £2500 and is chosen from a shortlist of 6–8. Eligible books must be fiction, aimed at teenagers between the ages of 13 and 16 and written in English by a citizen of the UK, or an author resident in the UK. The work must be published between 1 July and 30 June by a UK publisher. Established 2003.

2007 winner: *My Swordhand is Singing* by Marcus Sedgwick (Orion).

The Branford Boase Award

Details The Administrator, 8 Bolderwood Close, Bishopstoke, Eastleigh SO50 5PG
tel (01962) 826658 *fax* (01962) 856615
email anne.marley@tiscali.co.uk
website www.branfordboaseaward.org.uk

An annual award of £1000 is made to a first-time writer of a full-length children's novel (age 7+) published in the preceding year; the editor is also recognised. Its aim is to encourage new writers for children and to recognise the role of perceptive editors in developing new talent. The Award was set up in memory of the outstanding children's writer Henrietta Branford and the gifted editor and publisher Wendy Boase who both died in 1999. Closing date for nominations: end of December each year. 2008 winner: *Before I Die* by Jenny Downham, edited by David Fickling (David Fickling Books). Founded 2000.

British Book Awards – see Galaxy British Book Awards

Carnegie Medal – see The CILIP Carnegie and Kate Greenaway Awards

The CBI Bisto Book of the Year Awards

Details The Administrator, Children's Books Ireland, 17 North Great Georges Street, Dublin 1, Republic of Ireland

tel (01) 8727475 *fax* (01) 8727476
email info@childrensbooksireland.com
website www.childrensbooksireland.com

Annual awards open to authors and/or illustrators who are Irish citizens or who are full-time Irish residents. Closing date: December 2009 for work published between 1 January and 31 December 2008. Winners announced in May. Founded 1990.

The CBI Bisto Book of the Year Award

An award of €10,000 is presented to the overall winner (text and/or illustration). 2008 award winner: Siobhan Dowd for *The London Eye Mystery* (David Fickling Books).

The CBI Bisto Honour Awards

A prize fund of €6000 is divided between 3 authors and/or illustrators. 2008 award winners: F.E. Higgins for *The Black Book of Secrets*, Oliver Jeffers for *The Way Home*, and Roddy Doyle for *Wilderness*.

The CBI Bisto Eilís Dillon Award

An award of €3000 is presented to an author for a first children's book. 2008 award winner: Tom Kelly for *The Thing With Finn* (Macmillan Children's Books).

The Children's Laureate

Details Booktrust, Book House, 45 East Hill, London SW18 2QZ
tel 020-8875 4580 *fax* 020-8516 2978
email childrenslaureate@booktrust.org.uk
website www.childrenslaureate.org,
www.booktrust.org

A biennial award of £10,000 to honour a writer or illustrator of children's books for a lifetime's achievement. It highlights the importance of children's book creators in developing readers and illustrators of the future. Children's Laureates: Michael Rosen (2007–9), Jacqueline Wilson (2005–7), Michael Morpurgo (2003–5), Anne Fine (2001–3), Quentin Blake (1999–2001). Founded 1998.

The CILIP Carnegie and Kate Greenaway Awards

CILIP, 7 Ridgmount Street, London WC1E 7AE
tel 020-7255 0650 *fax* 020-7255 0651
email ckg@cilip.org.uk
website www.carnegiegreenaway.org.uk

Recommendations for the following 2 awards are invited from members of CILIP (the Chartered Institute of Library and Information Professionals), who are asked to submit a preliminary list of not more than 2 titles for each award, accompanied by a 50-word appraisal justifying the recommendation of each book. The awards are selected by the Youth Libraries Group of CILIP.

Carnegie Medal

Awarded annually for an outstanding book for children (fiction or non-fiction) written in English and first published in the UK during the preceding year or co-published elsewhere within a 3-month time lapse.

2008 winner: *Here Lies Arthur* by Philip Reeve (Scholastic).

Kate Greenaway Medal

Awarded annually for an outstanding illustrated book for children first published in the UK during the preceding year or co-published elsewhere within a 3-month time lapse. Books intended for older as well as younger children are included, and reproduction will be taken into account. The Colin Mears Award (£5000) is awarded annually to the winner of the Kate Greenaway Medal.

2008 winner: *Little Mouse's Big Book of Fears* by Emily Gravett (Macmillan).

The CLPE Poetry Award

Details CLPE, Webber Street, London SE1 8QW
tel 020-7401 3382/3 *fax* 020-7928 4624
email ann@clpe.co.uk
website www.clpe.co.uk

An award that aims to honour excellence in children's poetry. Organised by the Centre for Literacy in Primary Education, it is presented annually in June/July for a book of poetry published in the preceding year. The book can be a single-poet collection or an anthology. Submissions deadline: end of February. 2008 winner: *Red, Cherry Red* by Jackie Kaye, illustrated by Rob Ryan (Bloomsbury).

Costa Book Awards

(formerly the Whitbread Book Awards)
Details The Booksellers Association, Minster House, 272 Vauxhall Bridge Road, London SW1V 1BA
tel 020-7802 0801 *fax* 020-7802 0803
email naomi.gane@booksellers.org.uk
website www.costabookawards.co.uk
Contact Naomi Gane

The awards celebrate and promote the most enjoyable contemporary British writing. Judged in 2 stages and offering a total of £50,000 prize money, there are 5 categories: Novel, First Novel, Biography, Poetry and Children's. They are judged by a panel of 3 judges and the winner in each category receives £5000. 9 final judges then choose the Costa Book of the Year from the 5 category winners. The overall winner receives £25,000. Writers must be resident in Great Britain or Ireland for 3 or more years. Submissions must be received from publishers. Closing date: end of June.

2007 Costa Children's Book Award winner: *The Bower Bird* by Ann Kelley (Luath Press Ltd).

George Devine Award

Submissions Christine Smith, 9 Lower Mall, London W6 9DJ
tel 020-7267 9793 (evenings)

This annual award of £10,000 is open to any promising playwright for an original new stage play,

which need not have been produced. TV and radio plays will not be considered. Applicants should submit 2 copies of the play plus sae for return of scripts and an outline of their their work to date. Closing date: 1 March. Set up in 1966 as a memorial to the life and talent of George Devine, Artistic Director of the Royal court 1956–65.

The Eleanor Farjeon Award

website www.childrensbookcircle.co.uk

An annual award of (minimum) £2000 may be given to an individual or an organisation. Librarians, authors, publishers, teachers, reviewers and others who have given exceptional service to the children's book industry are eligible for nomination. It was instituted in 1965 by the Children's Book Circle (page 341) for distinguished services to children's books and named after the much-loved children's writer. 2007 winner: Jane Nissen Books.

Foyle Young Poets of the Year Award – see page 179

Galaxy British Book Awards

Details Merric Davidson, PO Box 60, Cranbrook, Kent TN17 2ZR
tel (01580) 212041 *fax* (01580) 212041
email nibbies@mdla.co.uk
website www.britishbookawards.com

Referred to as the 'Nibbies' and presented annually, major categories include: Author of the Year (biography, crime thriller, popular fiction, non-fiction, etc), Publisher of the Year, Bookseller of the Year and WHSmith Children's Book of the Year – 2008 winner: *Horrid Henry and the Abominable Snowman* by Francesca Simon (Orion Children's Books). Sponsored by Galaxy. Founded 1989.

Grampian Children's Book Award

tel (01651) 871213
email marion.wands@aberdeenshire.co.uk
website www.aberdeenshire.gov.uk/libraries/young_people

This award is for best fiction book, judged solely by pupils in participating secondary schools in Aberdeen City, Aberdeenshire and Moray and children in Aberdeen Central Children's Library. The 2008 award will be given to a children's book published in paperback between July 2006 and June 2007. 2008 winner: *Girl Missing* by Sophie McKenzie (Simon & Schuster Children's Books).

Kate Greenaway Medal – see The CILIP Carnegie and Kate Greenaway Awards

The Guardian Children's Fiction Prize

tel 020-7239 9694
email books@guardian.co.uk

The *Guardian's* annual prize of £1500 is for a work of

children's fiction for children over 8 (no picture books) published by a British or Commonwealth writer. The winning book is chosen by the Children's Book Editor together with a team of 3–4 authors of children's books. 2007 winner: *Finding Violet Park* by Jenny Valentine (HarperCollins).

Kelpies Prize

New Scottish Writing for Children, Floris Books, 15 Harrison Gardens, Edinburgh EH11 1SH
tel 0131-337 2372 *fax* 0131-347 9919
email floris@florisbooks.co.uk
website www.florisbooks.co.uk/kelpiesprize

A prize open to writers of fiction suitable for both boys and girls aged 9–12. Stories must be set wholly, or mainly, in present-day Scotland and must not have been previously commercially published. The winner receives £2000 and their book will be published in the Floris Books *Contemporary Kelpies* series of Scottish fiction. Closing date: end of February. Winner announced in August. 2007 winner: *Hox* by Annemarie Allan (Floris Books).

The Petra Kenney Poetry Competition

Details Morgan Kenney, The Belmoredean Barn, Maplehurst Road, West Grinstead RH13 6RN
email morgan@kenney.uk.net
website www.petrapoetrycompetition.co.uk

This annual competition is for unpublished poems by young people between 14 and 18 years of age. Theme and style are open. Entry fee: £3 per poem. Prizes: £250 and £125. Closing date: 1 December each year. Founded 1995.

Lancashire County Library Children's Book of the Year Award

Details LCC, Library & Information Service, East Cliff, PO Box 162, Preston PR1 3EA
tel (01772) 534008 *fax* (01772) 534880
email library@lcl.lancscc.gov.uk
website www.lancashire.gov.uk/libraries/services/children
Contact Jake Hope

A prize of £1000 and an engraved decanter is awarded to the best work of fiction for 12–14 year-olds, written by a UK author and first published between 1 September and 31 August of the previous year. The winner is announced in June. 2008 winner: *Fearless* by Tim Lott (Walker Books).

The Astrid Lindgren Memorial Award

Swedish Arts Council, PO Box 27215, SE–102 53 Stockholm, Sweden
tel (08) 519 264 00 *fax* (08) 519 264 99
email literatureaward@alma.se
website www.alma.se

An award to honour the memory of Astrid Lindgren, Sweden's favourite author, and to promote children's and youth literature around the world. The award is

5 million Swedish crowns, the world's largest for children's and youth literature, and the second-largest literature prize in the world, and will be awarded each year to one or more recipients, regardless of language or nationality.

Authors, illustrators, storytellers and promoters of reading are eligible. The award is for life-long work or artistry rather than for individual pieces. The prize can only be awarded to living people. The body of work must uphold the highest artistic quality and evoke the deeply humanistic spirit that Astrid Lindgren treasured.

The winner is selected by a jury based on nominations for outstanding achievement from selected nominating bodies around the world. The jury has the right to suggest nominees of their own. Neither individuals nor organisations may nominate themselves. 2008 winner: Sonya Hartnett. The Astrid Lindgren Memorial Award is administered by the Swedish National Council for Cultural Affairs. Founded 2002.

The Macmillan Prize for Children's Picture Book Illustration

Applications Lindsey Evans,
Macmillan Children's Books, 20 New Wharf Road, London N1 9RR
tel 020-7014 6124
email lindsey.evans@macmillan.co.uk

Three prizes are awarded annually for unpublished children's book illustrations by art students in higher education establishments in the UK. Prizes: £1000 (1st), £500 (2nd) and £250 (3rd).

The Macmillan Writer's Prize for Africa

website www.writeforafrica.com

A biennial competition devoted to previously unpublished works of fiction by African writers and aims to promote and celebrate story writing from all over the continent. The prize focuses on original writing for children and young people. There are 2 main awards – for children's literature and teenage fiction – plus an award for new, previously unpublished writers. There is also an award for children'sillustrators in Africa.

Entrants may select freely from themes that they consider to be of interest and value to their intended readership but all stories should have a strong African flavour. Entries will be assessed on the depth and originality of the work, the quality of the writing and the story's appeal to its audience. The competition is open to all nationals or naturalised citizens of countries throughout Africa and to those born in those countries. The next competition runs in 2009. Sponsored by Macmillan Education.

2007/8 winners: Junior Award – *Long Juju Man* by Nnedi Okorafor-Mbachu (Nigeria); Senior Award – *E Eights* by Jayne Bauling (South Africa); New Children's Writer Award – *Kwansa and the Bandit*

Crabs by Ekow Kwegyir Bentum (Ghana). Launched 2005.

Macmillan Children's Illustrator Award for Africa

A competition to recognise the importance of pictures in children's books. 2007/8 winner: Olusola Akinseye (Nigeria). Launched 2005.

Marsh Award for Children's Literature in Translation

Administered by The English-Speaking Union, Dartmouth House, 37 Charles Street, London W1J 5ED
tel 020-7529 1550
email elizabeth_stokes@esu.org
website www.esu.org
Contact Elizabeth Stokes

This biennial award of £1000 is given to the translator of a book for children (aged 4–16) from a foreign language into English and published in the UK by a British publisher. Electronic books, and encyclopedias and other reference books, are not eligible. Next award: January 2009. 2007 award winner: Anthea Bell for *The Flowing Queen* by Kai Meyer (Egmont). Founded 1996.

The Mythopoeic Fantasy Award for Children's Literature

David Oberhelman, Award Administrator, The Mythopoeic Society, 3700 West 19th Street, Suite K3, Stillwater, OK 74074–1678, USA
website www.mythsoc.org

This Award honours books for younger readers (from young adults to picture books for beginning readers), in the tradition of *The Hobbit* or *The Chronicles of Narnia*.

2008 award finalists: Holly Black – *Tithe: A Modern Faerie Tale* (Simon & Schuster), *Valiant: A Modern Tale of Faerie* (Simon & Schuster); *Ironside: A Modern Faery's Tale* (Margaret K. McElderry); Derek Landy – *Skulduggery Pleasant* (HarperCollins); J.K. Rowling – *Harry Potter* series (Bloomsbury); Nancy Springer – *Dusssie* (Walker Books for Young Readers); Kate Thompson – *The New Policeman* (HarperTeen).

NASEN & TES Special Educational Needs Book Awards

Nasen House, 4–5 Amber Business Village, Amber Close, Amington, Tamworth B77 4RP
tel (01827) 311500
email janec@nasen.org.uk
website www.nasen.org.uk
Contact Jane Cobby

The Awards have been created to recognise the authors and publishers of high-quality books that inspire both children with special educational needs and their teachers. The awards will be presented in 5 categories: the Special Educational Needs Children's Book Award; the Special Educational Needs Academic Book Award; the Books for Teaching and Learning Award; the Inclusive Resource for Primary Classrooms Award; and the Inclusive Resource for Secondary Classrooms Award. A prize of £500 will be awarded to the winning author of each category and to the publisher a quarter-page advertisement in the *TES* worth £1200 at a ceremony to be held at the British Library.

All books submitted for entry in any category must have been published in the UK. For specific entry details, including deadlines, telephone or see website. A maximum of 3 books can be submitted per publisher. Special Educational Needs Children's Book Award 2007 winner: *The London Eye Mystery* by Siobhan Dowd (David Fickling Books).

New Zealand Post Book Awards for Children and Young Adults

Details c/o Booksellers New Zealand, Surrey House, 21–29 Borderick Road, PO Box 13248, Johnsonville, Wellington, New Zealand
tel (04) 478-5511 *fax* (04) 478-5519
email info@booksellers.co.nz
website www.nzpostbookawards.co.nz

Annual awards to celebrate excellence in, and provide recognition for, the best books for children and young adults published annually in New Zealand. Awards are presented in 4 categories: non-fiction, picture book, junior fiction and young adult fiction. The winner of each category wins $7500. One category winner is chosen as the *New Zealand Post Book of the Year* and receives an additional $7500. Eligible authors' and illustrators' books must have been published in New Zealand in the calendar year preceding the awards year. Closing date: December. Founded 1990.

North East Book Award

Details Eileen Armstrong, Cramlington High School, Cramlington, Northumberland NE23 6BN
tel (01670) 712311 *fax* (01670) 730598
email earmstrong@cchsonline.co.uk
website http://northeastbookaward.worldpress.com

Awarded to a book first published in paperback between May and the end of June the following year. The shortlist is selected by librarians, teachers and the previous year's student judges, and the final winner by Year 8 and 9 students. Winner announced in April. 2008 winner: *Skulduggery Pleasant* by Derek Landy (HarperCollins Children's Books).

North East Teenage Book Award

Details Eileen Armstrong, Cramlington High School, Cramlington, Northumberland NE23 6BN
tel (01670) 712311 *fax* (01670) 730598
email earmstrong@cchsonline.co.uk
website http://northeastbookaward.worldpress.com

Awarded to a book first published in paperback between May and the end of June the following year.

The shortlist is selected by librarians, teachers and the previous year's student judges, and the final winner by Year 9+ students. Winner announced in January. 2008 winner: *Berserk* by Ally Kennen (Marion Lloyd Books).

Nottingham Children's Book Awards

Nottingham City Libraries and Information Service, Sneinton Library, Sneinton Boulevard, Nottingham NG2 4FD
tel 0115-915 1173
website www.nottinghamchildrensbookaward.co.uk
Contact Elaine Dykes, Deborah Sheppard

Nottingham children choose their favourite paperbacks of the year. The award is in 3 age groups: Nursery, Emerging Readers and Developing Readers. It attracts upwards of 10,000 votes through libraries, schools and nurseries each year. A shortlist of 15 titles is drawn up by groups of children in November, the shortlisted books are made available in January, promotion takes place through the Spring term and voting takes place in early March. The Award culminates in a grand presentation and celebration day in April. Launched 1999.

Peterloo Poets Open Poetry Competition

Details Peterloo Poets, The Old Chapel, Sand Lane, Calstock, Cornwall PL18 9QX
tel (01822) 833473
email publisher@peterloopoets.com
website www.peterloopoets.com

This annual competition offers a first prize of £1500 and 13 other prizes totalling £2100. There is also a 15–19 age group section with 5 prizes each of £100. Founded 1986.

Phoenix Award

Children's Literature Association, PO Box 138, Battle Creek, MI 49016–0138, USA
tel 269-965-8180 *fax* 269-965-3568
website www.childlitassn.org

This Award is presented by the Children's Literature Association (ChLA) for the most outstanding book for children originally published in the English language 20 years earlier which did not receive a major award at the time of publication. It is intended to recognise books of high literary merit. 2008 award winner: *Eva* by Peter Dickinson (Delacorte 1988). Founded 1985.

The Red House Children's Book Award

Details Andrea Goodall, 45 Wick Avenue, Wheathampstead, Herts AL4 8PZ
tel (01582) 831506
email andrea@wickave.waitrose.com
website www.redhousechildrensbookaward.co.uk

This award is given annually to authors of works of fiction for children published in the UK. Children

participate in the judging of the award. 'Pick of the Year' book list is published in conjunction with the award. 2007 winners – Younger Children category: *Who's in the Loo?* by Jeanne Willis and Adrian Reynolds (Andersen); Younger Children category and overall winner: *You're a Bad man, Mr Gum!* by Andy Stanton (Egmont); Older Readers category: *Girl Missing* by Sophie McKenzie (Simon & Schuster). Founded in 1980 by the Federation of Children's Book Groups.

Royal Mail Awards for Scottish Children's Books

Scottish Book Trust, Sandeman House, Trunk's Close, 55 High Street, Edinburgh EH1 1SR
tel 0131-524 0160 *fax* 0131-524 0161
email anna.gibbons@scottishbooktrust.com
website www.scottishbooktrust.com/royalmailawards
Contact Anna Gibbons, Children's Programme Manager

Awards totalling £14,000 are given to new and established authors of published books in recognition of high standards of writing for children in 3 age group categories: younger children (0–7 years), younger readers (8–11 years) and older readers (12–16 years). A shortlist is drawn up by a panel of children's book experts and then a winner in each category is decided by children and young people by voting for their favourites in book groups in schools and libraries across Scotland. An award of £3000 is made for the winner in each category and £500 for runners-up. Books published in the preceding calendar year are eligible. Authors should be Scottish or resident in Scotland but books of particular Scottish interest by other authors are eligible for consideration. Posthumous awards cannot be made. Guidelines available on request. Closing date: 31 January. Award presented: November. Administered by Scottish Book Trust, in partnership with the Scottish Arts Council.

The Royal Society Prizes for Science Books

Details The Royal Society,
6–9 Carlton House Terrace, London SW1Y 5AG
tel 020-7451 2500 *fax* 020-7930 2170
email events@royalsociety.org
website www.royalsoc.org/sciencebooks

These annual prizes reward books that make science more accessible to readers of all ages and backgrounds. Prizes of up to a total of £30,000 are awarded in 2 categories: General (£10,000) for a book with a general readership; and Junior (£10,000) for a book written for people aged under 14. Up to 5 shortlisted authors in each category receive £1000.

Eligible books should be written in English and their first publication in the UK must have been between 1 January and 31 December each year. Seven copies of each entry should be supplied with a fully completed entry form. Publishers may submit any number of books for each prize. Entries may cover any aspect of science and technology but educational textbooks published for professional or specialist audiences are not eligible. 2008 prize winners: General – *Six Degrees – Our Future on a Hotter Planet* by Mark Lynas (Fourth Estate); Junior – *The Big Book of Science Things to Make and Do* by Rebecca Gilpin and Leonie Pratt (Usborne). The prizes are managed by the Royal Society in cooperation with the sponsor, Aventis. Founded 1988.

RSPCA Young Photographer Awards (YPA)

Details Publications Department, RSPCA, Wilberforce Way, Southwater, Horsham, West Sussex RH13 9RS
tel (0300) 123 0455 *fax* (0303) 123 0455
email publications@rspca.org.uk
website www.rspca.org.uk/ypa

Annual awards are made for animal photographs taken by young people in categories: under 12; 12–18 year-olds; Portfolio (5 pictures); Pets Personalities. Prizes: overall winner (high-end digital camera), age group winners (camera). Four runners-up in each age group receive a camera. Closing date for entries: 1 September 2008; 31 August 2009. Sponsored by Warners and Olympus Cameras. Founded 1990.

Sainsbury's Baby Book Award – see Booktrust Early Years Awards

Scottish Arts Council

Scottish Arts Council, 12 Manor Place, Edinburgh EH3 7DD
tel 0131-226 6051
email gavin.wallace@scottisharts.org.uk
website www.scottisharts.org.uk
Contact Gavin Wallace, Head of Literature

A limited number of writers' bursaries – up to £15,000 each – are offered to enable professional writers based in Scotland, including writers for children, to devote more time to writing. Priority is given to writers of fiction and verse and playwrights, but writers of literary non-fiction are also considered. Applications may be discussed with Gavin Wallace. See also Royal Mail Awards for Scottish Children's Books (page 370).

Sheffield Children's Book Award

Details Book Award Co-ordinator, Schools Library Service, Sheffield
tel 0114-250 6844
email jennifer.wilson@sheffield.gov.uk
website www.sheffield.gov.uk

Presented annually in November to the book chosen as the most enjoyable by the children of Sheffield. There are 3 category winners and one overall winner. 2007 winners – Picture Book and Overall Winner:

Who's In the Loo? by Jeanne Willis and Adrian Reynolds; Longer Novel: *A Swift Pure Cry* by Siobhan Dowd; Shorter Novel: *Help I'm a Classroom Gambler* by Pete Johnson.

WHSmith Children's Book of the Year – see Galaxy British Book Awards

South Lanarkshire Book Award

Details Literacy Development Co-ordinator, Libraries and Community Learning
tel (01355) 248581 *fax* (01355) 229365
email margaret.cowan@southlanarkshire.gov.uk
website www.slc-learningcentres.org.uk/bookaward

An annual award to encourage teenagers to enjoy reading and to read more widely. Young people vote for the winner having read all the shortlisted books. The shortlist is chosen by public and school librarians from books appropriate for 14–15 year-olds, by writers living in the UK and published for the first time in paperback between August and July of the previous year. The shortlisting process is confirmed only when authors agree to visit schools and attend the Award ceremony in March. 2008 winner: *Frozen Fire* by Tim Bowler (OUP). Founded 1998.

Tir na n-Og Awards

Details Welsh Books Council, Castell Brychan, Aberystwyth, Ceredigion SY23 2JB
tel (01970) 624151 *fax* (01970) 625385
email menna.lloydwilliams@cllc.org.uk
website www.cllc.org.uk

Established with the intention of raising the standard of children's and young people's books published during the year, and to encourage the buying and reading of good books. Three awards are presented annually:

• The best English language book of the year with an authentic Welsh background. Fiction and factual books originally in English are eligible; translations from Welsh or any other language are not eligible. Prize: £1000.
• Welsh language books aimed at the primary sector. Prize: £1000.
• Welsh language books aimed at the secondary sector. Prize: £1000.
    Sponsored by the Chartered Institute of Library and Information Professional and the Welsh Books Council. Founded 1976.
    2008 winners – English language books: *Finding Minerva* by Frances Thomas (Gomer/Pont Books); Welsh language books – Primary Sector: *Y Llyfr Ryseitiau: Gwaed y Tylwyth* by Nicholas Daniels (Dref Wen); Welsh language books – Secondary Sector: *Eira Mân, Eira Mawr* by Gareth F. Williams (Gwasg Gomer).

Christopher Tower Poetry Prize – see page 179

UKLA Children's Book Awards

Details Lynda Graham
tel (0116) 229 7450

email lynda_j_graham@hotmail.com
Submissions Administrator, United Kingdom Literacy
Association, 4th Floor, Attenborough Building,
University of Leicester LE1 7RH
website www.ukla.org

The award is presented for excellence in the field of
literacy. Literacy is interpreted here as being about
'the expression of meaning and ideas through
challenging use of language, imaginative expression,
illustration and other graphics'. The awards are given
for content, expression and to honour writers whose
use of language has a powerful impact on the reader.
The shortlist is decided by teachers based on which
books engage young readers. The shortlist is
announced in the Spring and the prize awarded at the
UKLA International Conference in July.

The V&A Illustration Awards

Enquiries The Word & Image Dept,
Victoria & Albert Museum, London SW7 2RL
tel/fax 020-7942 2291
email villa@vam.ac.uk
website www.vam.ac.uk/illustrationawards
Contact Martin Flynn

These annual awards are given to practising book and
magazine illustrators, for work first published in the
UK during the 12 months preceding the closing date
of the awards. Cash prizes will be awarded for best
book cover, illustrated book and newspaper,
magazine and comic illustration. Also student
illustrator of the year category. Closing date:
December.

Waterstone's Children's Book Prize

Waterstone's, Capital Court,
Capital Interchange Way, Brentford,
Middlesex TW8 0EX
tel 020-8996 4323
fax 020-8742 0215 (FAO Gary Deane)
email gary.deane@waterstones.com
website www.waterstones.com
Contact Gary Deane

This award of £1000 was created to uncover hidden
talent in children's writing. It is open to authors who
have written 3 or less books. Publishers, booksellers
and the public join forces to recommend their book
to a panel of judges. There are 3 categories: 5–8, 9–12
and Teenage. 2008 winner: *Ways to Live Forever* by
Sally Nicholls (Marion Lloyd Books).

Whitbread Book Awards – see Costa Book
Awards

Winchester Writers' Conference
Competitions

Faculty of Arts, University of Winchester,
Winchester, Hants SO22 4NR

tel (01962) 827238
email barbara.large@winchester.ac.uk
website www.writersconference.co.uk
Contact Barbara Large, *Honorary Patrons* Dame Beryl
Bainbridge, Jacqueline Wilson OBE, Maureen Lipman

Fifteen writing competitions are attached to this
major international Festival of Writing, which takes
place at the end of June (see page 329). Each entry is
adjudicated and 64 sponsored prizes are presented at
the Writers' Awards Dinner. In addition to the
Writing for Children Competition sponsored by
Little Tiger Press, other categories include the First
Three Pages of the Novel, Short Stories, Shorter Short
Stories, Writing for Children, A Page of Prose,
Lifewriting, Slim Volume, Small Edition, Poetry,
Retirement, Writing Can be Murder, Local History,
and Young Writers' Poetry Competition. Deadline
for entries: 5 June 2009.

Write A Story for Children
Competition

Entry forms The Academy of Children's Writers,
PO Box 95, Huntingdon, Cambs. PE28 5RL
tel (01487) 832752
website www.childrens-writers.co.uk

Three prizes (1st £2000, 2nd £300, 3rd £200) are
awarded annually for a short story for children,
maximum 1500 words, by an unpublished writer of
children's fiction. Send sae for details or see website.
Founded 1984.

Young Writers' Programme

Details Young Writers' Programme,
Royal Court Young Writers' Programme,
Sloane Square, London SW1W 8AS
tel 020-7565 5050 *fax* 020-7565 5001
email ywp@royalcourttheatre.com
website www.royalcourttheatre.com

Anyone aged 13–25 can submit a play on any subject.
A selection of plays are professionally presented by
the Royal Court Theatre with the writers fully
involved in rehearsal and production. Pre-Festival
Development Workshops are run by professional
theatre practitioners and designed to help everyone
attending to write a play. Playwriting projects run all
year round.

YouWriteOn.com – see Arts Council
YouWriteOn.com Book Awards

Calendar of awards

Announcements of awards are subject to change.

January
The Marsh Award for Children's Literature in Translation (biennial)
Costa Book Awards
The Macmillan Writer's Prize for Africa
Macmillan Children's Illustrator Award for Africa
North East Teenage Book Award

March
Blue Peter Children's Book Awards
Hans Christian Andersen Awards
South Lanarkshire Book Award

April
BolognaRagazzi Award
North East Book Award
Nottingham Children's Book Awards
WHSmith Children's Book of the Year (Galaxy British Book Awards)

May
Angus Book Award
The CBI Bisto Book of the Year Awards
Grampian Children's Book Award
The Macmillan Prize for Children's Picture Book Illustration
The Royal Society Prizes for Science Books
The V&A Illustration Awards

June
Lancashire County Library Children's Book of the Year Award
Red House Children's Book Award

July
The Branford Boase Award
Carnegie Medal
The CLPE Poetry Award
Kate Greenaway Medal
UKLA Children's Book Awards

August
Kelpies Prize

September
Booktrust Early Years Awards
The Guardian Children's Fiction Prize

October
NASEN & TES Special Educational Needs Book Awards
Tir na n-Og Awards

November
The Booktrust Teenage Prize
The Eleanor Farjeon Award
Royal Mail Awards for Scottish Children's Books
Sheffield Children's Book Award

See also...
• *Children's book and illustration prizes and awards*, page 364

Children's literature festivals and trade fairs

Some of the literature festivals in this section are specifically related to children's books and others are general arts festivals which include literature events for children.

Aspects Festival

Town Hall, The Castle, Bangor, Co. Down BT20 4BT
tel (028) 91 278032, 91 271200 (box office)
fax (028) 91 271370
website www.northdown.gov.uk
Contact Gail Prentice, Arts Officer/Festival Co-ordinator
Takes place 24–28 Sept 2008

An annual celebration of contemporary Irish writing with novelists, poets and playwrights. Includes writers' visits to schools and Young Aspects Showcase, where young people are given opportunity to publicly read their own work.

Bank of Scotland Imaginate Festival

45A George Street, Edinburgh EH2 2HT
tel 0131-225 8050 *fax* 0131-225 6440
email info@imaginate.org.uk
Takes place May

As the largest performing arts festival for children and young people in the UK, this annual festival provides the opportunity for schoolchildren and their teachers, families and industry professionals to see the best children's theatre the world has to offer. Produced by Imaginate (page 352), the festival's aim is that children and young people aged up to 18 have regular access to a diverse range of high-quality performing arts activity, from home and abroad, that will entertain, enrich, teach and inspire them. Each year the festival presents around 16 national and international productions attracting an audience of over 15,000, and tours to both rural and urban areas throughout Scotland. Founded 1990.

Bath Festival of Children's Literature

PO Box 4123, Bath BA1 0FR
email info@bathkidslitfest.co.uk
website www.bathkidslitfest.co.uk
Festival Directors John McLay, Gill McLay
Takes place 19–28 September 2008

A 10-day celebration of children's books and reading. Authors and illustrators taking part include Michael Morpurgo, Francesca Simon, Charlie Higson, Rick Riordan, Cathy Cassidy, Axel Scheffler and Jeremy Strong. In addition to big name authors, there will be events for the youngest readers and readers-to-be. Sponsored by *The Daily Telegraph* and Waterstone's Booksellers.

Bath Literature Festival

Bath Festivals, Abbey Chambers, Kingston Buildings, Bath BA1 1NT

tel (01225) 462231 *fax* (01225) 445551
email info@bathfestivals.org.uk
website www.bathlitfest.org.uk
Director Sarah LeFanu
Takes place 28 Feb–2 March 2009

An annual 9-day festival with leading guest writers. Includes readings, debates, discussions and workshops, and events for children and young people. Programme available from box office in December.

Beyond the Border: The Wales International Storytelling Festival

St Donats Arts Centre, St Donats Castle, Nr Llantwit Major, Vale of Glamorgan CF61 1WF
tel (01446) 799095 (marketing), 799100 (box office)
fax (01446) 799101
email enquiries@stdonats.com, davidambrose@beyondtheborder.com
website www.beyondtheborder.com
Programme Director David Ambrose
Takes place First weekend in July

A biennial international festival celebrating oral tradition and bringing together storytellers, poets and musicians from around the world. This is the largest event of its type in the UK. On the last day there is a competition for young storytellers aged 10–20 to be BTB Young Storyteller of The Year.

Bologna Children's Book Fair

Piazza Costituzione 6, 40128 Bologna, Italy
tel (051) 282242/282361 *fax* (051) 6374011
email bookfair@bolognafiere.it
website www.bolognachildrensbookfair.com
Takes place 23–26 March 2009

Held annually, the Bologna Children's Book Fair is the leading children's publishing event. Publishers, authors and illustrators, literary agents, TV and film producers, licensors and licensees, and many other members of the children's publishing community meet in Bologna to buy and sell copyrights, establish new contacts and strengthen their professional relationships, discover new illustrators, develop new business opportunities, learn about the latest trends and developments and explore children's educational materials, including new media products. Approximately 4000 professionals active in children's publishing attend from 70 countries. Entry is restricted to those in the publishing trade.

Selected by a jury, the Bologna Illustrators Exhibition showcases fiction and non-fiction children's book illustrators, both new and established, from all over the world. Many illustrators also visit the Fair to show their latest portfolios to publishers.

Winners of the BolognaRagazzi Award are displayed. Prizes are given to encourage excellence in children's publishing in the categories of fiction, non-fiction and 'new horizons' (books from emerging countries), and books are judged on the basis of their creativity, educational value and artistic design. Hans Christian Andersen Award is announced at the Fair.

Book Now! Literature Festival, Arts Service

Orleans House Gallery, Riverside,
Twickenham TW1 3DJ
tel 020-8831 6000 *fax* 020-8744 0501
email artsinfo@richmond.gov.uk
website www.richmond.gov.uk
Takes place for 4 weeks in November

An annual literature festival covering a broad range of subjects. Leading contemporary authors hold discussions, talks, debates and readings. There are also exhibitions and storytelling sessions for children and adults.

The Times Cheltenham Literature Festival

109–111 Bath Road, Cheltenham, Glos. GL53 7LS
tel (01242) 227979 (box office), 237377 (brochure), 775861 (festival office)
email christine.stein@cheltenhamfestivals.com
website www.cheltenhamfestivals.com
Book It! Director Jane Churchill
Takes place October

Book It! is the children's festival running as part of the main festival programme. Events include workshops for children, talks and performances.

Chester Literature Festival

55–57 Watergate Row South, Chester CH1 2LE
tel (01244) 674020
email info@chesterlitfest.org.uk
website www.chesterlitfest.org.uk
Festival Administrator Katherine Seddon
Takes place October

An annual festival commencing the first weekend in October. Events featuring international, national and local writers and poets are part of the programme, as well as a literary lunch and festival dinner. There is a poetry competition for school children, events for children and workshops for adults. A Cheshire Prize for Literature is awarded each year; only residents of Cheshire are eligible.

Children's Book Festival

Festival Office, Childrens Books Ireland,
17 North Great Georges Street, Dublin 1,
Republic of Ireland

tel (1) 872 7475 *fax* (1) 872 7476
email info@childrensbooksireland.com
website www.childrensbooksireland.com
Contact Tom Donegan, Festival Coordinator
Takes place 1–31 Oct 2008

Annual nationwide celebration of reading and books in Ireland for young people.

Children's Book Week

Booktrust, Book House, 45 East Hill,
London SW18 2QZ
tel 020-8516 2967 *fax* 020-8516 2998
email education@booktrust.org.uk
website www.booktrust.org.uk
Takes place First full week of October

The annual Children's Book Week celebrates the wonderful world of children's books. It focuses on the enjoyment of reading, with the aim of encouraging as many children as possible to enjoy books. The Week is based on the belief that designating a special day or week at school, in libraries and at home, for enjoyable book activities can help children to see reading as a source of pleasure – as well as trying to encourage them to write themselves, to discuss and share books and to explore libraries and bookshops. All over the UK, schools, libraries and bookshops hold events and activities.

Edinburgh International Book Festival

5A Charlotte Square, Edinburgh EH2 4DR
tel 0131-718 5666 *fax* 0131-226 5335
email admin@edbookfest.co.uk
website www.edbookfest.co.uk
Director Catherine Lockerbie
Takes place 15–31 Aug 2009

Now established as Europe's largest book event for the public. In addition to a unique independent bookselling operation, more than 700 writers contribute to the programme of events. Programme details available in June.

Essex Poetry Festival

tel (01702) 230596
email derek@essex-poetry-festival.co.uk
website www.essex-poetry-festival.co.uk
Contact Derek Adams
Takes place Oct

A poetry festival across Essex. Also includes the Young Essex Poet of the Year Competition.

Folkestone Literary Festival

Church Street Studios, 11 Church Street, Folkestone, Kent CT20 1SE
tel (01303) 211300 *fax* (01303) 211883
email info@folkestonelitfest.com
website www.folkestonelitfest.co.uk
Takes place 1–9 Nov 2008

An annual festival with over 40 events, including a Children's Day.

The Guardian Hay Festival

Festival Office, The Drill Hall, 25 Lion Street,
Hay-on-Wye HR3 5AD
tel (0870) 7872848 (admin)
email ruth@hayfestival.com
website www.hayfestival.com
Takes place May/June

This annual festival aims to celebrate the best in writing and performance from around the world, to commission new work, and to promote and encourage young writers of excellence and potential. More than 400 events over 10 days, with leading guest writers. Programme published April.

Guildford Book Festival

c/o Tourist Information Office, 14 Tunsgate,
Guildford GU1 3QT
tel (01483) 444334
email deputy@guildfordbookfestival.co.uk
website www.guildfordbookfestival.co.uk
Festival Director Glenis Pycraft
Takes place Last 2 weeks in October

An annual festival. Diverse, provocative and entertaining, held throughout the historic town. Author events, poetry, workshops for all age groups from 6 months onwards. Its aim is to further an interest and love of literature by involvement and entertainment. Founded 1990.

Hay Festival – see The Guardian Hay Festival

Ilkley Literature Festival

The Manor House, 2 Castle Hill, Ilkley LS29 9DT
tel (01943) 601210 *fax* (01943) 817079
email admin@ilkleyliteraturefestival.org.uk
website www.ilkleyliteraturefestival.org.uk
Festival Director Rachel Feldberg
Takes place First two weeks in Oct

The north of England's most prestigious literature festival with over 140 events, from author's discussions to workshops, readings, literary walks, children's events and a festival fringe.

Imagine: Writers and Writing for Children

Purcell Room, South Bank Centre, London SE1 8XX
tel 020-7921 0906 (administration), 020-7921 0971
(programme), (0870) 160 2520 (box office)
fax 020-7928 2049
email literature&talks@southbankcentre.co.uk
website www.southbankcentre.co.uk/festivals-series/
imagine
Takes place February

An annual festival celebrating writing for children. Three days featuring a selection of poets, storytellers and illustrators.

Jewish Book Week

Jewish Book Council, ORT House, 126 Albert Street,
London NW1 1NE
email info@jewishbookweek.com
website www.jewishbookweek.com
Administrator Pam Lewis
Takes place Feb/March

A festival of Jewish writing, with contributors from around the world and sessions in London and nationwide. Includes events for children and teenagers.

Lincoln Book Festival

City of Lincoln Council,
Dept of Development and Environmental Services,
City Hall, Beaumont Fee, Lincoln LN1 1DF
tel (01522) 873844 *fax* (01522) 873553
email Sara.Bullimore@lincoln.gov.uk
website www.lincolnbookfestival.co.uk
Contact Sara Bullimore (Arts & Cultural Sector Officer)
Takes place 8–17 May 2009

A festival that celebrates books but also includes other art forms that books initiate and inspire – comedy, film, performance, conversation. It aims to celebrate local, national and international writers and artists, historical and contemporary works of art as well as offering the public a chance to see both emerging and well-known writers and artists. Includes a programme of children's events.

London Literature Festival

Southbank Centre, Belvedere Road, London SE1 8XX
tel (0871) 633 2501
website www.southbankcentre.co.uk
Takes place July

A 2-week festival featuring international and prize-winning authors, historians, poets, performers and artists, children's events, specially commissioned work, debate and discussion, interactive and improvised writing and performance. Established 2007.

Lowdham Book Festival

c/o The Bookcase, 50 Main Street,
Lowdham NG14 7BE
tel 0115-966 4143
email info@fiveleaves.co.uk
website www.lowdhambookfestival.co.uk
Contact Janet Streeter, Ross Bradshaw
Takes place June

An annual 10-day festival of literature events for adults and children, with a daily programme of high-profile national writers. The last day always features dozens of free events and a large book fair.

Northern Children's Book Festival

22 Highbury, Jesmond,
Newcastle upon Tyne NE2 3DY
tel 0191-2813289
website www.ncbf.org.uk
Chairperson Ann Key
Takes place 10–22 Nov 2008

An annual festival to bring authors, illustrators, poets and performers to children in schools, libraries and community centres across the North East of England. About 36 authors visit the North East over the 2-week period for 2–8 days, organised by the 12 local authorities. The climax of the festival is a huge public event in a different part of the North East each year when over 4000 children and their families visit to take part in author seminars, drama workshops, and to enjoy a variety of book-related activities. The Gala Day will be on 22 Nov 2008 at The Civic Centre, Newcastle upon Tyne.

Off the Shelf Literature Festival

Central Library, Surrey Street, Sheffield S1 1XZ
tel 0114-273 4400 *fax* 0114-273 4716
email offtheshelf@sheffield.gov.uk
website www.offtheshelf.org.uk
Contact Maria de Souza, Su Walker, Lesley Webster
Takes place 11 Oct–1 Nov 2008

The festival comprises a wide range of events for adults and children, including author visits, writing workshops, storytelling, competitions and exhibitions. Programme available in September.

Oundle Festival of Literature

2 New Road, Oundle, Peterborough,
Northants PE8 4LA
tel (01832) 273050
email liz@oundlelitfest.org.uk
website www.oundlelitfest.org.uk
Contact Liz Dillarstone (Publicity)
Takes place March

Featuring a full programme of author events, poetry, philosophy, politics, story-telling, biography, illustrators and novelists for young and old. Includes events for children.

Oxford Literary Festival – see The Sunday Times Oxford Literary Festival

Readathon

The Parsonage, St Mary's Chalford, Stroud GL6 8QB
tel (0870) 240 1124
website www.readathon.org

Run in schools throughout the year, especially for Children's Book Week and World Book Day. Children undertake to read books for pledges of money. All the money raised is donated to children's charities. See page 358.

Redbridge Book and Media Festival

London Borough of Redbridge, Arts & Events Team,
3rd Floor, Central Library, Clements Road,
Ilford IG1 1EA
tel 020-8708 2855
website www.redbridge.gov.uk
Contact Arts & Events Team
Takes place April and May

Features author talks, performances, panel debates, Urdu poetry events, an exhibition, workshops, children's activities and events, and a schools outreach programme.

Royal Court Young Writers' Festival

The Royal Court Young Writers' Programme,
Sloane Square, London SW1W 8AS
tel 020-7565 5050
website www.royalcourttheatre.com
Contact Nina Lyndon, Administrator
Takes place Biennially (2010)

A national festival which anyone aged 13–25 can enter. Promising plays which arise from the workshops are then developed and performed at the Royal Court's Theatre Upstairs.

Scottish International Storytelling Festival

43–45 High Street, Edinburgh EH1 1SR
tel 0131-556 9579 *fax* 0131-557 5224
email reception@scottishstorytellingcentre.com
website www.scottishstorytellingcentre.co.uk
Festival Director Donald Smith
Takes place 24 Oct–2 Nov 2008

A celebration of Scottish storytelling set in its international context, complemented by music, ballad and song. The main theme of the 2008 Festival will be 'Sagalands: traditions of storytelling from Northern Europe'. Takes place at the Scottish Storytelling Centre and partner venues across Edinburgh and the Lothians.

StAnza: Scotland's Poetry Festival

tel (05600) 433847 (administration), (01334) 475000 (box office), (01592) 414714 (programmes)
email admin@stanzapoetry.org
website www.stanzapoetry.org
Festival Director Brian Johnstone
Takes place March 2009

The festival engages with all forms of poetry: read and spoken verse, poetry in exhibition, performance poetry, cross-media collaboration, schools work, book launches and poetry workshops, with numerous UK and international guests and weekend children's events.

Stratford-upon-Avon Poetry Festival

Shakespeare Centre, Henley Street,
Stratford-upon-Avon CV37 6QW
tel (01789) 204016 *fax* (01789) 296083
email info@shakespeare.org.uk
website www.shakespeare.org.uk
Takes place July

Now in its 55th year, this festival celebrates poetry past and present with special reference to the works of Shakespeare. Events include: evenings of children's verse, a Poetry Mass and a local poets' evening. Full details available on the website from May. Sponsored by the Shakespeare Birthplace Trust.

The Sunday Times Oxford Literary Festival

Christ Church, Oxford OX1 1DP
tel (01865) 276152
email info@sundaytimes-oxfordliteraryfestival.co.uk
website www.sundaytimes-oxfordliteraryfestival.co.uk
Festival Directors Angela Prysor-Jones, Sally Dunsmore
Takes place March/April

An annual 6-day festival for both adults and children. Presents topical debates, fiction and non-fiction discussion panels, and adult and children's authors who have recently published books. Topics range from contemporary fiction to discussions on politics, history, science, gardening, food, poetry, philosophy, art and crime fiction. An additional 2 days of events for schools.

Winchester Writers' Conference, Bookfair and Weeklong Workshops – see page 328

Word – University of Aberdeen Writers Festival

University of Aberdeen, Office of External Affairs, University of Aberdeen, King's College, Aberdeen AB24 3FX
tel (01224) 273874 fax (01224) 272086
website www.abdn.ac.uk/word
Artistic Director Alan Spence
Takes place May

Over 70 of the world's finest writers and artists take part in a packed weekend of readings, music, art exhibitions and film screenings. The festival hosts some of the UK's best-loved children's writers and some of the richest talents in Gaelic literature.

The Word's Out!

Perth and Kinross Council, AK Bell Library, York Place, Perth PH2 8EP
tel (01738) 444949
email cfbeaton@pkc.gov.uk
Contact Caroline Beaton (Community Libraries Manager)
Takes place 22–28 Nov 2008

A festival to celebrate books, reading and libraries. It has a significant Scottish emphasis but has authors attending from across the UK. Events for children and families.

World Book Day

c/o The Booksellers Association,
272 Vauxhall Bridge Road, London SW1V 1BA
tel 020-8987 9370
email cathy.schofield@blueyonder.co.uk
website www.worldbookday.com
Contact Cathy Schofield
Takes place 5th March 2009

An annual celebration of books and reading aimed at promoting their value and creating the readers of the future. Every schoolchild in full-time education receives a £1 book token. Events take place all over the UK in schools, bookshops, libraries and arts centres. World Book Day was designated by UNESCO as a worldwide celebration of books and reading, and is marked in over 30 countries. It is a partnership of publishers, booksellers and interested parties who work together to promote books and reading for the personal enrichment and enjoyment of all.

See also Readathon (page 358).

Young Readers Birmingham

Children's Office, Central Library,
Chamberlain Square, Birmingham B3 3HQ
tel 0121-303 3368 fax 0121-464 1004
email patsy.heap@birmingham.gov.uk
website www.birmingham.gov.uk/youngreaders
Contact Patsy Heap
Takes place 16–30 May 2009

An annual festival targeted at children, young people and families. It aims to promote the enjoyment of reading; to provide imaginative access to books, writers, performers and storytellers; to encourage families to share reading for pleasure; to provide a focus for the celebration of books and reading for children and young people and help raise the media profile of children's books and writing. Approximately 150 events take place.

National Year of Reading

The National Year of Reading is a year-long celebration of reading, in all its forms. Its Project Director, Honor Wilson-Fletcher, explains why it has been established.

The National Year of Reading aims to help build a greater national passion for reading in England – for children, families and adult learners alike. The year aims to encourage people to read in businesses, homes and communities around the country, providing new opportunities to read and helping people to access help and

Further information

Literacy Trust (National Year of Reading)
68 South Lambeth Road, London SW8 1RL
tel 020-7820 6261
tel 020-7587 1411
email contact@yearofreading.org.uk
website www.yearofreading.org.uk

support through schools and libraries. It was launched publicly in April 2008 and each month until December 2008 is accompanied by a monthly theme, which is designed to help plan activities throughout the year. See website for details of events.

Artists and writers are central to the ambitions of the National Year of Reading. Whether as an author, journalist, poet, dramatist, lyricist, scriptwriter or diarist, those who put words together with care, and with the specific intention of recording their thoughts and ideas to share with other people, are the real power under the bonnet for the National Year of Reading campaign – to convey the joy and benefits of reading and to get – and keep – people reading.

The main aim is to encourage all forms of reading during the year – anything from newspapers to novels, and across all age ranges. Teenagers and younger readers in particular have very fixed views about what 'proper' readers read and sadly many think that the exploration of reading is not for the likes of them, that they are somehow not 'good enough' for reading. This is not helped by the alarming percentage of well-intentioned adults (45% according to a recent survey) who regularly chastise young teens for not reading something 'proper' – literature which will contribute towards their education. The National Year of Reading hopes to alter views of both children and adults by promoting and encouraging all kinds of reading as part of the fabric of daily life. Everyone has the right to an omnivorous reading diet – one that fits the individual by enriching life through variety as well as depth and understanding. By celebrating, and therefore hopefully 'permissioning', the rich creativity and personal pleasure (and relevance) of all mediums of the written word, whether in magazines, books, song lyrics or the internet, the National Year of Reading aims to promote the simple message that everyone has the right to read what they want and to love what they read. And that the real 'education' of reading is lifelong, rich, varied and, most of all, fun. After all, it's better to read what's enjoyed than to not read at all.

Another message of the National Year of Reading is that it's never too late to learn to read. A significant number of adults in the UK are unable to read confidently or learned to read later in life. Research indicates the discomfort which accompanies this issue, ranging from strategies to avoid discovery to the awful prospect of not being able to share reading with one's own children. This is often the point at which many brave adults take the plunge and learn to read and by doing so enjoy the skills and joys which reading fosters and makes possible.

Finance for writers and artists

FAQs for writers

Peter Vaines, a chartered accountant and barrister, addresses some frequently asked questions.

What can a working writer claim against tax?

A working writer is carrying on a business and can therefore claim all the expenses which are incurred wholly and exclusively for the purposes of that business. A list showing most of the usual expenses can be found in the article on *Income tax*, starting on page 383 of this *Yearbook*, but there will be other expenses that can be allowed in special circumstances.

Strictly, only expenses which are incurred for the sole purpose of the business can be claimed; there must be no 'duality of purpose' so an item of expenditure cannot be divided into private and business parts. However, HM Revenue & Customs (formerly the Inland Revenue) is usually quite flexible and is prepared to allow all reasonable expenses (including apportioned sums) where the amounts can be commercially justified.

Allowances can also be claimed for the cost of business assets such as a motor car, personal computers, fax, copying machines and all other equipment (including books) which may be used by the writer. An allowance of 25% of the cost can be claimed on the reducing balance each year and for most assets (except cars) an allowance of 50% can be claimed in the first year of purchase. Some expenditure on information technology now benefits from a special 100% allowance. See the article on *Income tax* (page 383)for further details of the deductions available in respect of capital expenditure.

Can I request interest on fees owed to me beyond 30 days of my invoice?

Yes. A writer is like any other person carrying on a business and is entitled to charge interest at a rate of 8% over bank base rate on any debt outstanding for more than 30 days – although the period of credit can be varied by agreement between the parties. It is not compulsory to claim the interest; it is up to you to decide whether to enforce the right.

What can I do about bad debts?

A writer is in exactly the same position as anybody else carrying on a business over the payment of his or her invoices. It is generally not commercially sensible to insist on payment in advance but where the work involved is substantial (e.g. a book), it is usual to receive one third of the fee on signature, one third of the fee on delivery of the manuscript and the remaining one third on publication. On other assignments, perhaps not as substantial as a book, it could be worthwhile seeking 50% of the fee on signature and the other 50% on delivery. This would provide a degree of protection in case of cancellation of the assignment because of changes of policy or personnel at the publisher.

What financial disputes can I take to the Small Claims Court?

If somebody owes you money you can take them to the Small Claims Section of your local County Court, which deals with financial disputes up to £5000. The procedure is much less formal than normal court proceedings and involves little expense. It is not necessary to have a solicitor. You fill in a number of forms, turn up on the day and explain the background to why you are owed the money (see www.courtservice.gov.uk).

If I receive an advance, can I divide it between two tax years?

Yes. There used to be a system known as 'spreading' but in 2001 a new system called 'averaging' was introduced. This enables writers (and others engaged in the creation of literary, dramatic works or designs) to average the profits of two or more consecutive years if the profits for one year are less than 75% of the profits for the highest year. This relief can apply even if the work takes less than 12 months to create and it allows the writer to avoid the higher rates of tax which might arise if the income in respect of a number of years' work were all to be concentrated in a single year.

How do I make sure I am taxed as a self-employed person so that tax and National Insurance contributions are not deducted at source?

To be taxed as a self-employed person under Schedule D you have to make sure that the contract for the writing cannot be regarded as a contract of employment. This is unlikely to be the case with a professional author. The subject is highly complex but one of the most important features is that the publisher must not be in a position to direct or control the author's work. Where any doubt exists, the author might find the publisher deducting tax and National Insurance contributions as a precaution and that would clearly be highly disadvantageous. The author would be well advised to discuss the position with the publisher before the contract is signed to agree that he or she should be treated as self-employed and that no tax or National Insurance contributions will be deducted from any payments. If such agreement cannot be reached, professional advice should immediately be sought so that the detailed technical position can be explained to the publisher.

Is it a good idea to operate through a limited company?

It can be a good idea for a self-employed writer to operate through a company but generally only where the income is quite large. The costs of operating a company can outweigh any benefit if the writer is paying tax only at the basic rate. Where the writer is paying tax at the higher rate of 40%, being able to retain some of the income in a company at a tax rate of only 21% is obviously attractive. However, this will be entirely ineffective if the writer's contract with the publisher would otherwise be an employment. The whole subject of operating through a company is complex and professional advice is essential.

When does it become necessary to register for VAT?

Where the writer's self-employed income (from all sources, not only writing) exceeds £67,000 in the previous 12 months or is expected to do so in the next 30 days, he or she must register for VAT and add VAT to all his/her fees. The publisher will pay the VAT to the writer, who must pay the VAT over to the Customs and Excise each quarter. Any VAT the writer has paid on business expenses and on the purchase of business assets can be deducted. It is possible for some authors to take advantage of the simplified system for VAT payments which applies to small businesses. This involves a flat rate payment of VAT without any need to keep records of VAT on expenses.

If I make a loss from my writing can I get any tax back?

Where a writer makes a loss, HM Revenue & Customs may suggest that the writing is only a hobby and not a professional activity thereby denying any relief or tax deduction for the loss. However, providing the writing is carried out on a sensible commercial basis with an expectation of profits, any resulting loss can be offset against any other income the writer may have for the same or the previous year.

Income tax

Despite attempts by successive Governments to simplify our taxation system, the subject has become increasingly complicated. Peter Vaines, a chartered accountant and barrister, gives a broad outline of taxation from the point of view of writers and other creative professionals. The proposals in the March 2008 Budget are broadly reflected in this article.

How income is taxed

Generally

Authors are usually treated for tax purposes as carrying on a profession and are taxed in a similar fashion to other self-employed professionals. This article is directed to self-employed persons only, because if a writer is employed he or she will be subject to the much less advantageous rules which apply to employment income.

Attempts are often made by employed persons to shake off the status of 'employee' and to attain 'freelance' status so as to qualify for the tax advantages, such attempts meeting with varying degrees of success. The problems involved in making this transition are considerable and space does not permit a detailed explanation to be made here – individual advice is necessary if difficulties are to be avoided.

Particular attention has been paid by HM Revenue & Customs to journalists and to those engaged in the entertainment industry with a view to reclassifying them as employees so that PAYE is deducted from their earnings. This blanket treatment has been extended to other areas and, although it is obviously open to challenge by individual taxpayers, it is always difficult to persuade HM Revenue & Customs to change its views.

There is no reason why employed people cannot carry on a freelance business in their spare time. Indeed, aspiring authors, painters, musicians, etc, often derive so little income from their craft that the financial security of an employment, perhaps in a different sphere of activity, is necessary. The existence of the employment is irrelevant to the taxation of the freelance earnings although it is most important not to confuse the income or expenditure of the employment with the income or expenditure of the self-employed activity. HM Revenue & Customs is aware of the advantages which can be derived by an individual having 'freelance' income from an organisation of which he or she is also an employee, and where such circumstances are contrived, it can be extremely difficult to convince an Inspector of Taxes that a genuine freelance activity is being carried on. Where the individual operates through a company or partnership providing services personally to a particular client, and would be regarded as an employee if the services were supplied directly by the individual, additional problems arise from the notorious IR35 legislation and professional advice is essential.

For those starting in business or commencing work on a freelance basis HM Revenue & Customs produces a very useful booklet, *Starting in Business (IR28)*, which is available from any tax office.

Income

For income to be taxable it need not be substantial, nor even the author's only source of income; earnings from casual writing are also taxable but this can be an advantage, because occasional writers do not often make a profit from their writing. The expenses incurred in connection with writing may well exceed any income receivable and the resultant loss may then be used to reclaim tax paid on other income. There may be deducted from the income certain allowable expenses and capital allowances which are set out in more detail below. The possibility of a loss being used as a basis for a tax repayment is fully appreciated by HM Revenue & Customs, which sometimes attempts to treat casual writing as a hobby so that any losses incurred cannot be used to reclaim tax; of course by the same token any income receivable would not be chargeable to tax. This treatment may sound attractive but it should be resisted vigorously because HM Revenue & Customs does not hesitate to change its mind when profits begin to arise. In the case of exceptional or non-recurring writing, such as the autobiography of a sports personality or the memoirs of a politician, it could be better to be treated as pursuing a hobby and not as a professional author. Sales of copyright cannot be charged to income tax unless the recipient is a professional author. However, the proceeds of sale of copyright may be charged to capital gains tax, even by an individual who is not a professional author.

Royalties

Where the recipient is a professional author, a series of cases has laid down a clear principle that sales of copyright are taxable as income and not as capital receipts. Similarly, lump sums on account of, or in advance of royalties are also taxable as income in the year of receipt, subject to a claim for averaging relief (see below).

Arts Council awards

Arts Council category A awards
• Direct or indirect musical, design or choreographic commissions and direct or indirect commission of sculpture and paintings for public sites.
• The Royalty Supplement Guarantee Scheme.
• The contract writers' scheme.
• Jazz bursaries.
• Translators' grants.
• Photographic awards and bursaries.
• Film and video awards and bursaries.
• Performance Art Awards.
• Art Publishing Grants.
• Grants to assist with a specific project or projects (such as the writing of a book) or to meet specific professional expenses such as a contribution towards copying expenses made to a composer or to an artist's studio expenses.

Arts Council category B awards
• Bursaries to trainee directors.
• Bursaries for associate directors.
• Bursaries to people attending full-time courses in arts administration (the practical training course).
• In-service bursaries to theatre designers and bursaries to trainees on the theatre designers' scheme.
• In-service bursaries for administrators.
• Bursaries for actors and actresses.
• Bursaries for technicians and stage managers.
• Bursaries made to students attending the City University Arts Administration courses.
• Awards, known as the Buying Time Awards, made not to assist with a specific project or professional expenses but to maintain the recipient to enable him or her to take time off to develop his personal talents. These at present include the awards and bursaries known as the Theatre Writing Bursaries, awards and bursaries to composers, awards and bursaries to painters, sculptures and print makers, literature awards and bursaries.

Copyright royalties are generally paid without deduction of income tax. However, if royalties are paid to a person who normally lives abroad, tax must be deducted by the payer or his agent at the time the payment is made unless arrangements are made with HM Revenue & Customs for payments to be made gross under the terms of a Double Taxation Agreement with the other country.

Arts Council grants

Persons in receipt of grants from the Arts Council or similar bodies will be concerned whether or not such grants are liable to income tax. HM Revenue & Customs has issued a Statement of Practice after detailed discussions with the Arts Council regarding the tax treatment of the awards. Grants and other receipts of a similar nature have now been divided into two categories (see box) – those which are to be treated by HM Revenue & Customs as chargeable to tax and those which are not. Category A awards are considered to be taxable; awards made under category B are not chargeable to tax.

This Statement of Practice has no legal force and is used merely to ease the administration of the tax system. It is open to anyone in receipt of a grant or award to disregard the agreed statement and challenge HM Revenue & Customs view on the merits of their particular case. However, it must be recognised that HM Revenue & Customs does not issue such statements lightly and any challenge to their view would almost certainly involve a lengthy and expensive action through the Courts.

The tax position of persons in receipt of literary prizes will generally follow a decision by the Special Commissioners in connection with the Costa Book Awards (previously called the Whitbread Book Awards). In that case it was decided that the prize was not part of the author's professional income and accordingly not chargeable to tax. The precise details are not available because decisions of the Special Commissioners were not, at that time, reported unless an appeal was made to the High Court; HM Revenue & Customs chose not to appeal against this decision. Details of the many literary awards that are given each year start on Children's book and illustration prizes and awards, and this decision is of considerable significance to the winners of each of these prizes. It would be unwise to assume that all such awards will be free of tax as the precise facts which were present in the case of the Whitbread awards may not be repeated in another case; however it is clear that an author winning a prize has some very powerful arguments in his or her favour, should HM Revenue & Customs seek to charge tax on the award.

Allowable expenses

To qualify as an allowable business expense, expenditure has to be laid out wholly and exclusively for business purposes. Strictly there must be no 'duality of purpose', which means that expenditure cannot be apportioned to reflect the private and business usage, e.g. food, clothing, telephone, travelling expenses, etc. However, HM Revenue & Customs does not usually interpret this principle strictly and is prepared to allow all reasonable expenses (including apportioned sums) where the amounts can be commercially justified.

It should be noted carefully that the expenditure does not have to be 'necessary', it merely has to be incurred 'wholly and exclusively' for business purposes. Naturally, however, expenditure of an outrageous and wholly unnecessary character might well give rise to a presumption that it was not really for business purposes. As with all things, some expenses are unquestionably allowable and some expenses are equally unquestionably not allowable – it is the grey area in between which gives rise to all the difficulties and the outcome invariably depends on negotiation with HM Revenue & Customs.

Great care should be taken when claiming a deduction for items where there may be a 'duality of purpose' and negotiations should be conducted with more than usual care and courtesy – if provoked the Inspector of Taxes may well choose to allow nothing. An appeal is always possible although unlikely to succeed as a string of cases in the Courts has clearly demonstrated. An example is the case of *Caillebotte* v. *Quinn* where the taxpayer (who normally had lunch at home) sought to claim the excess cost of meals incurred because he was working a long way from his home. The taxpayer's arguments failed because he did not eat only in order to work, one of the reasons for his eating was in order to sustain his life; a duality of purpose therefore existed and no tax relief was due.

Other cases have shown that expenditure on clothing can also be disallowed if it is the kind of clothing which is in everyday use, because clothing is worn not only to assist the pursuit of one's profession but also to accord with public decency. This duality of purpose may be sufficient to deny relief – even where the particular type of clothing is of a kind not otherwise worn by the taxpayer. In the case of *Mallalieu* v. *Drummond* a barrister failed to obtain a tax deduction for items of sombre clothing that she purchased specifically for wearing in Court. The House of Lords decided that a duality of purpose existed because clothing represented part of her needs as a human being.

Allowances

Despite the above, Inspectors of Taxes are not usually inflexible and the following list of expenses are among those generally allowed.

(a) Cost of all materials used up in the course of preparation of the work.

(b) Cost of typewriting and secretarial assistance, etc; if this or other help is obtained from one's spouse then it is entirely proper for a deduction to be claimed for the amounts paid for the work. The amounts claimed must actually be paid to the spouse and should be at the market rate although some uplift can be made for unsocial hours, etc. Payments to a wife (or husband) are of course taxable in her (or his) hands and should therefore be most carefully considered. The wife's earnings may also be liable for National Insurance contributions and it is important to take care because otherwise you may find that these contributions may outweigh the tax savings. The impact of the National Minimum Wage should also be considered.

(c) All expenditure on normal business items such as postage, stationery, telephone, email, fax and answering machines, agent's fees, accountancy charges, photography, subscriptions, periodicals, magazines, etc, may be claimed. The cost of daily papers should not be overlooked if these form part of research material. Visits to theatres, cinemas, etc, for research purposes may also be permissible (but not the cost relating to guests). Unfortunately, expenditure on all types of business entertaining is specifically denied tax relief.

(d) If work is conducted at home, a deduction for 'use of home' is usually allowed providing the amount claimed is reasonable. If the claim is based on an appropriate proportion of the total costs of rent, light and heat, cleaning and maintenance, insurance, etc (but not the Council Tax), care should be taken to ensure that no single room is used 'exclusively' for business purposes, because this may result in the Capital Gains Tax exemption on the house as the only or main residence being partially forfeited. However, it would be a strange household where one room was in fact used exclusively for business purposes and for no other purpose whatsoever (e.g. storing personal bank statements and other private papers); the usual formula is to claim a deduction on the basis that most or all of the rooms in the house are used at one time or another for business purposes, thereby avoiding any suggestion that any part was used exclusively for business purposes.

(e) The appropriate business proportion of motor running expenses may also be claimed although what is the appropriate proportion will naturally depend on the particular circumstances of each case; it should be appreciated that the well-known scale of benefits, whereby employees were taxed according to the size and cost of the car (and are now taxed on the basis of their CO^2 emissions), do not apply to self-employed persons.

(f) It has been long established that the cost of travelling from home to work (whether employed or self-employed) is not an allowable expense. However, if home is one's place of work then no expenditure under this heading is likely to be incurred and difficulties are unlikely to arise.

(g) Travelling and hotel expenses incurred for business purposes will normally be allowed but if any part could be construed as disguised holiday or pleasure expenditure, considerable thought would need to be given to the commercial reasons for the journey in order to justify the claim. The principle of 'duality of purpose' will always be a difficult hurdle in this connection – although not insurmountable.

(h) If a separate business bank account is maintained, any overdraft interest thereon will be an allowable expense. This is the only circumstance in which overdraft interest is allowed for tax purposes and care should be taken to avoid overdrafts in all other circumstances.

(i) Where capital allowances (see below) are claimed for a personal computer, fax, modem, television, video, CD or tape player, etc, used for business purposes the costs of maintenance and repair of the equipment may also be claimed.

Clearly many other allowable items may be claimed in addition to those listed. Wherever there is any reasonable business motive for some expenditure it should be claimed as a deduction although it is necessary to preserve all records relating to the expense. It is sensible to avoid an excess of imagination as this would naturally cause the Inspector of Taxes to doubt the genuineness of other expenses claimed.

The question is often raised whether the whole amount of an expense may be deducted or whether the VAT content must be excluded. Where VAT is reclaimed from the Customs and Excise by someone who is registered for VAT, the VAT element of the expense cannot be treated as an allowable deduction. Where the VAT is not reclaimed, the whole expense (inclusive of VAT) is allowable for income tax purposes.

Capital allowances

Allowances

Where expenditure of a capital nature is incurred, it cannot be deducted from income as an expense – a separate and sometimes more valuable capital allowance being available instead. Capital allowances are given for many different types of expenditure, but authors and similar professional people are likely to claim only for 'plant and machinery'; this is a very wide expression which may include motor cars, personal computers, fax and photocopying machines, modems, televisions, CD, video and cassette players used for business purposes. Plant and machinery generally qualifies for a writing down allowance of 25% (reduced to 20% for expenditure after 5 April 2008) on the reducing balance. Expenditure on information technology for the purposes of the business now benefits from a special

100% allowance in the year of purchase and there is a new annual investment allowance of 100% for the first £50,000 of expenditure on plant and machinery introduced this year. Where the useful life of an asset is expected to be short, it is possible to claim special treatment as a 'short life asset' enabling the allowances to be accelerated.

The reason these allowances can be more valuable than allowable expenses is that they may be wholly or partly disclaimed in any year that full benefit cannot be obtained – ordinary business expenses cannot be similarly disclaimed. Where, for example, the income of an author does not exceed his personal allowances, he would not be liable to tax and a claim for capital allowances would be wasted. If the capital allowances were to be disclaimed their benefit would be carried forward for use in subsequent years. Careful planning with claims for capital allowances is therefore essential if maximum benefit is to be obtained.

As an alternative to capital allowances, claims can be made on the 'renewals' basis whereby all renewals are treated as allowable deductions in the year; no allowance is obtained for the initial purchase, but the cost of replacement (excluding any improvement element) is allowed in full. This basis is no longer widely used, as it is considerably less advantageous than claiming capital allowances as described above.

Leasing is a popular method of acquiring fixed assets, and where cash is not available to enable an outright purchase to be made, assets may be leased over a period of time. Whilst leasing may have financial benefits in certain circumstances, in normal cases there is likely to be no tax advantage in leasing an asset where the alternative of outright purchase is available. Indeed, leasing can be a positive disadvantage in the case of motor cars with a new retail price of more than £12,000. If such a car is leased, only a proportion of the leasing charges will be tax deductible.

Books

The question of whether the cost of books is eligible for tax relief has long been a source of difficulty. The annual cost of replacing books used for the purposes of one's professional activities (e.g. the cost of a new *Children's Writers' & Artists' Yearbook* each year) has always been an allowable expense; the difficulty arose because the initial cost of reference books, etc (e.g. when commencing one's profession) was treated as capital expenditure but no allowances were due as the books were not considered to be 'plant'. However, the matter was clarified by the case of *Munby* v. *Furlong* in which the Court of Appeal decided that the initial cost of law books purchased by a barrister was expenditure on 'plant' and eligible for capital allowances. This is clearly a most important decision, particularly relevant to any person who uses expensive books in the course of exercising his or her profession.

Pension contributions

Where a self-employed person makes contributions to a pension scheme, those contributions are usually deductible.

These arrangements are generally advantageous in providing for a pension as contributions are usually paid when the income is high (and the tax relief is also high) and the pension (taxed as earned income when received) usually arises when the income is low and little tax is payable. There was also the opportunity to take part of the pension entitlement as a tax-free lump sum. It is necessary to take into account the possibility that the tax advantages could go into reverse. When the pension is paid it could, if rates rise again, be taxed at a higher rate than the rate of tax relief at the moment. From 6 April 2006 a whole new regime for pensions was introduced to create a much simpler system. Each individual has a lifetime allowance (set at £1.65 million for 2008/9 but rising annually). When benefits crystallise, which will generally be when a pension begins to be paid, this is measured against the individual's lifetime allowance; any excess will be taxed at 25%, or at 55% if the excess is taken as a lump sum.

Each individual also has an annual allowance for contributions to the pension fund which is set at £235,000 for 2008/9 but will increase in later years. If the annual increase in an individual's rights under all registered schemes of which he is a member exceeds the annual allowance, the excess is chargeable to tax at 40%.

For most writers and artists this means that they can effectively contribute the whole of their earnings to a pension scheme (if they can afford to do so) without any of the previous complications. It is still necessary to be careful where there is other income giving rise to a pension because the whole of the pension entitlement has to be taken into account.

Flexible retirement is possible allowing members of occupational pension schemes to continue working while also drawing retirement benefits. As part of this reform, however, the normal minimum pension age will be raised from 50 to 55 by 6 April 2010.

Class 4 National Insurance contributions

Allied to pensions is the payment of Class 4 National Insurance contributions, although no pension or other benefit is obtained by the contributions; the Class 4 contributions are designed solely to extract additional amounts from self-employed persons and are payable in addition to the normal Class 2 (self-employed) contributions. The rates are changed each year and for 2008/9 self-employed persons will be obliged to contribute 8% of their profits between the range £5435–£40,040 per annum plus 1% on earnings above £40,040. This amount is collected in conjunction with the Schedule D income tax liability.

Averaging relief
Relief for copyright payments

For many years special provisions enabled authors and similar persons engaged on a literary, dramatic, musical or artistic work for a period of more than 12 months, to spread certain amounts received over two or three years depending on the time spent in preparing the work.

On 6 April 2001 a simpler system of averaging was introduced. Under these rules, professional authors and artists engaged in the creation of literary, dramatic works or designs may claim to average the profits of two or more consecutive years if the profits for one year are less than 75% of the profits for the highest year. This new relief can apply even if the work took less than 12 months to create and is available to people who create works in partnership with others.

The purpose of the relief is to enable the creative artist to utilise his allowances fully and to avoid the higher rates of tax which might apply if all the income were to arise in a single year.

Collection of tax
Self-assessment

In 1997, the system of sending in a tax return showing all your income and HM Revenue & Customs raising an assessment to collect the tax was abolished. So was the idea that you pay tax on your profits for the preceding year. Now, when you send in your tax return you have to work out your own tax liability and send a cheque; this is called 'self-assessment'. If you get it wrong, or if you are late with your tax return or the payment of tax, interest and penalties will be charged.

Under this system, HM Revenue & Customs rarely issue assessments; they are no longer necessary because the idea is that you assess yourself. A colour-coded tax return was created, designed to help individuals meet their tax obligations. This is a daunting task but the term 'self-assessment' is not intended to imply that individuals have to do it themselves; they can (and often will) engage professional help. The term is only intended to convey that it is the taxpayer, and not HM Revenue & Customs, who is responsible for getting the tax liability right and for it to be paid on time.

The deadline for sending in the tax return is 31 January following the end of the tax year; so for the tax year 2007/8, the tax return has to be submitted to HM Revenue & Customs by 31 January 2009. If for some reason you are unwilling or unable to calculate the tax payable, you can ask HM Revenue & Customs to do it for you, in which case it is necessary to send in your tax return by 30 September 2008.

Income tax on self-employed earnings remains payable in two instalments on 31 January and 31 July each year. Because the accurate figures may not necessarily be known, these payments in January and July will therefore be only payments on account based on the previous year's liability. The final balancing figure will be paid the following 31 January together with the first instalment of the liability for the following year.

When HM Revenue & Customs receives the self-assessment tax return, it is checked to see if there is anything obviously wrong; if there is, a letter will be sent to you immediately. Otherwise, HM Revenue & Customs has 12 months from the filing date of 31 January in which to make further enquiries; if it doesn't, it will have no further opportunity to do so and your tax liabilities are final – unless there is something seriously wrong such as the omission of income or capital gains. In that event, HM Revenue & Customs will raise an assessment later to collect any extra tax together with appropriate penalties. It is essential for the operation of the new system that all records relevant to your tax returns are retained for at least 12 months in case they are needed by HM Revenue & Customs. For the self-employed, the record-keeping requirement is much more onerous because the records need to be kept for nearly six years. One important change in the rules is that if you claim a tax deduction for an expense, it will be necessary to have a receipt or other document proving that the expenditure has been made. Because the existence of the underlying records is so important to the operation of self-assessment, HM Revenue & Customs will treat them very seriously and there is a penalty of £3000 for any failure to keep adequate records.

Interest

Interest is chargeable on overdue tax at a variable rate, which at the time of writing is 7.5% per annum. It does not rank for any tax relief, which can make HM Revenue & Customs an expensive source of credit.

However, HM Revenue & Customs can also be obliged to pay interest (known as repayment supplement) tax-free where repayments are delayed. The rules relating to repayment supplement are less beneficial and even more complicated than the rules for interest payable but they do exist and can be very welcome if a large repayment has been delayed for a long time. Unfortunately, the rate of repayment supplement is only 3%, much lower than the rate of interest on unpaid tax.

Value added tax

The activities of writers, painters, composers, etc are all 'taxable supplies' within the scope of VAT and chargeable at the standard rate. (Zero rating which applies to publishers, booksellers, etc on the supply of books does not extend to the work performed by writers.) Accordingly, authors are obliged to register for VAT if their income for the past 12 months exceeds £67,000 or if their income for the coming month will exceed that figure.

Delay in registering can be a most serious matter because if registration is not effected at the proper time, the Customs and Excise can (and invariably do) claim VAT from all the income received since the date on which registration should have been made. As no VAT would have been included in the amounts received during this period the amount claimed by the Customs and Excise must inevitably come straight from the pocket of the author.

The author may be entitled to seek reimbursement of the VAT from those whom he or she ought to have charged VAT but this is obviously a matter of some difficulty and may indeed damage his commercial relationships. Apart from these disadvantages there is also a penalty for late registration. The rules are extremely harsh and are imposed automatically even in cases of innocent error. It is therefore extremely important to monitor the income very carefully because if in any period of 12 months the income exceeds the £67,000 limit, the Customs and Excise must be notified within 30 days of the end of the period. Failure to do so will give rise to an automatic penalty. It should be emphasised that this is a penalty for failing to submit a form and has nothing to do with any real or potential loss of tax. Furthermore, whether the failure was innocent or deliberate will not matter. Only the existence of a 'reasonable excuse' will be a defence to the penalty. However, a reasonable excuse does not include ignorance, error, a lack of funds or reliance on any third party.

However, it is possible to regard VAT registration as a privilege and not a penalty, because only VAT registered persons can reclaim VAT paid on their expenses such as stationery, telephone, professional fees, etc, and even computers and other plant and machinery (excluding cars). However, many find that the administrative inconvenience – the cost of maintaining the necessary records and completing the necessary forms – more than outweighs the benefits to be gained from registration and prefer to stay outside the scope of VAT for as long as possible.

Overseas matters

The general observation may be made that self-employed persons resident and domiciled in the UK are not well treated with regard to their overseas work, being taxable on their worldwide income. It is important to emphasise that if fees are earned abroad, no tax saving can be achieved merely by keeping the money outside the country. Although exchange control regulations no longer exist to require repatriation of foreign earnings, such income remains taxable in the UK and must be disclosed to HM Revenue & Customs; the same applies to interest or other income arising on any investment of these earnings overseas. Accordingly, whenever foreign earnings are likely to become substantial, prompt and effective action is required to limit the impact of UK and foreign taxation. In the case of non-resident authors it is important that arrangements concerning writing for publication in the UK, e.g. in newspapers, are undertaken with great care. A case concerning the wife of one of the great train robbers who provided detailed information for a series of articles in a Sunday newspaper is most instructive. Although she was acknowledged to be resident in Canada for all the relevant years, the income from the articles was treated as arising in this country and fully chargeable to UK tax.

The UK has double taxation agreements with many other countries and these agreements are designed to ensure that income arising in a foreign country is taxed either in that country or in the UK. Where a withholding tax is deducted from payments received from another country (or where tax is paid in full in the absence of a double taxation agreement), the amount of foreign tax paid can usually be set off against the related UK tax liability. Many successful authors can be found living in Eire because of the complete exemption from tax which attaches to works of cultural or artistic merit by persons who are resident there. However, such a step should only be contemplated having careful regard to all the other domestic and commercial considerations and specialist advice is essential if the exemption is to be obtained and kept; a careless breach of the conditions could cause the exemption to be withdrawn with catastrophic consequences.

Further information concerning the precise conditions to be satisfied for exemption from tax in Eire can be obtained from the Revenue Commissioners in Dublin or from their website (www.revenue.ie).

Companies

When an author becomes successful the prospect of paying tax at the higher rate may drive them to take hasty action such as the formation of companies, etc, which may not always be to their advantage. Indeed some authors seeing the exodus into tax exile of their more successful colleagues even form companies in low tax areas in the naive expectation of saving large amounts of tax. HM Revenue & Customs is fully aware of the opportunities and have extensive powers to charge tax and combat avoidance. Accordingly, such action is just as likely to increase tax liabilities and generate other costs and should never be contemplated without expert advice; some very expensive mistakes are often made in this area which are not always able to be remedied.

To conduct one's business through the medium of a company can be a most effective method of mitigating tax liabilities, and providing it is done at the right time and under the right circumstances very substantial advantages can be derived. However, if done without due care and attention the intended advantages will simply evaporate. At the very least it is essential to ensure that the company's business is genuine and conducted properly with regard to the realities of the situation. If the author continues his or her activities unchanged, simply paying all the receipts from his work into a company's bank account, he cannot expect to persuade HM Revenue & Customs that it is the company and not himself who is entitled to, and should be assessed to tax on, that income.

It must be strongly emphasised that many pitfalls exist which can easily eliminate all the tax benefits expected to arise by the formation of the company. For example, company directors are employees of the company and will be liable to pay much higher National Insurance contributions; the company must also pay the employer's proportion of the contribution and a total liability of over 23% of gross salary may arise. This compares most unfavourably with the position of a self-employed person. Moreover, on the commencement of the company's business the individual's profession will cease and the possibility of revisions being made by HM Revenue & Customs to earlier tax liabilities means that the timing of a change has to be considered very carefully.

The tax return

No mention has been made above of personal reliefs and allowances; this is because these allowances and the rates of tax are subject to constant change and are always set out in detail in the explanatory notes which accompany the Tax Return. The annual Tax Return is an important document and should be completed promptly with extreme care, particularly since the introduction of self-assessment. If filling in the Return is a source of difficulty or anxiety, comfort may be found in the Consumer Association's publication *Money Which? – Tax Saving Guide*, which is published in March of each year and includes much which is likely to be of interest and assistance.

Peter Vaines FCA, ATII, barrister, is a partner in the international law firm of Squire Sanders & Dempsey LLP and writes and speaks widely on tax matters. He is Managing Editor of *Personal Tax Planning Review*, on the Editorial Board of *Taxation*, tax columnist of the *New Law Journal* and author of a number of books on taxation.

Social security contributions

In general, every individual who works in Great Britain either as an employee or as a self-employed person is liable to pay social security contributions. The law governing this subject is complicated and Peter Arrowsmith FCA gives here a summary of the position. This article should be regarded as a general guide only.

All contributions are payable in respect of years ending on 5 April. See box (below) for the classes of contributions.

Employed or self-employed?

The question as to whether a person is employed under a contract *of* service and is thereby an employee liable to Class 1 contributions, or performs services (either solely or in partnership) under a contract *for* service and is thereby self-employed liable to Class 2 and Class 4 contributions, often has to be decided in practice. One of the best guides can be found in the case of *Market Investigations Ltd* v. *Minister of Social Security* (1969 2 WLR 1) when Cooke J. remarked:

'... the fundamental test to be applied is this: "Is the person who has engaged himself to perform these services performing them as a person in business on his own account?" If the answer to that question is 'yes', then the contract is a contract for services. If the answer is 'no', then the contract is a contract of service. No exhaustive list has been compiled and perhaps no exhaustive list can be compiled of the considerations which are relevant in determining that question, nor can strict rules be laid down as to the relative weight which the various considerations should carry in particular cases. The most that can be said is that control will no doubt always have to be considered, although it can no longer be regarded as the sole determining factor; and that factors which may be of importance are such matters as:
• whether the man performing the services provides his own equipment,
• whether he hires his own helpers,
• what degree of financial risk he takes,
• what degree of responsibility for investment and management he has, and
• whether and how far he has an opportunity of profiting from sound management in the performance of his task.'

The above case has often been considered subsequently – notably in November 1993 by the Court of Appeal in the case of *Hall* v. *Lorimer*. In this case a vision mixer with around 20 clients and undertaking around 120–150 separate engagements per annum was held to be self-employed. This follows the, perhaps surprising, contention of the former Inland Revenue that the taxpayer was an employee.

Classes of contributions

Class 1 These are payable by employees (primary contributions) and their employers (secondary contributions) and are based on earnings.

Class 1A Payable only by employers in respect of all taxable benefits in kind (cars and fuel only prior to 6 April 2000).

Class 1B Payable only by employers in respect of PAYE Settlement Agreements entered into by them.

Class 2 These are weekly flat rate contributions, payable by the self-employed.

Class 3 These are weekly flat rate contributions, payable on a voluntary basis in order to provide, or make up entitlement to, certain social security benefits.

Class 4 These are payable by the self-employed in respect of their trading or professional income and are based on earnings.

Exceptions

There are certain exceptions to the above rules, those most relevant to artists and writers being:

• The employment of a wife by her husband, or vice versa, is disregarded for social security purposes unless it is for the purposes of a trade or profession (e.g. the employment of his wife by an author would not be disregarded and would result in a liability for contributions if her salary reached the minimum levels). The same provisions also apply to civil partners from 5 December 2005.

• The employment of certain relatives in a private dwelling house in which both employee and employer reside is disregarded for social security purposes provided the employment is not for the purposes of a trade or business carried on at those premises by the employer. This would cover the employment of a relative (as defined) as a housekeeper in a private residence.

In general, lecturers, teachers and instructors engaged by an educational establishment to teach on at least four days in three consecutive months are regarded as employees for social security purposes, although this rule does not apply to fees received by persons giving public lectures.

Freelance film workers

There is a list of grades in the film industry in respect of which PAYE need not be deducted and who are regarded as self-employed for tax purposes.

Further information can be obtained from the guidance notes on the application of PAYE to casual and freelance staff in the film industry issued by the former Inland Revenue. In view of the Inland Revenue announcement that the same status will apply for PAYE and National Insurance contributions purposes, no liability for employee's and employer's contributions should arise in the case of any of the grades mentioned above.

However, in the film and television industry this general rule was not always followed in practice. In December 1992, after a long review, the DSS agreed that individuals working behind the camera and who have jobs on the Inland Revenue Schedule D list are self-employed for social security purposes.

There are special rules for, *inter alia*, personnel appearing before the camera, short engagements, payments to limited companies and payments to overseas personalities.

Artistes, performers/non-performers

The status of artistes and performers for tax purposes will depend on the individual circumstances but for social security new regulations which took effect on 17 July 1998 require most actors, musicians or similar performers to be treated as employees for social security purposes, whether or not this status applies under general and/or tax law. It also applies whether or not the individual is supplied through an agency.

Personal service companies

From 6 April 2000, those who have control of their own 'one-man service companies' are subject to special rules. If the work that the owner of the company does for the company's customers would – but for the one-man company – be considered as an employment of that individual (i.e. rather than self-employment), a deemed salary may arise. If it does, then some or all of the income of the company will be treated as salary liable to PAYE and National Insurance contributions. This will be the case whether or not such salary is actually paid by the company. The same situation may arise where the worker owns as little as 5% of a company's share capital.

The calculations required by HM Revenue & Customs are complicated and have to be done very quickly at the end of each tax year (even if the company's year-end is different). It is essential that affected businesses seek detailed professional advice about these rules which may also, in certain circumstances, apply to partnerships.

In order to escape the application of these rules, a number of workers have arranged their engagements through 'managed service companies', etc where the promoter is heavily involved in all the company management to the exclusion of the workers themselves. Such companies are now subjected to similar, but different, rules from 6 April 2007 for tax and 6 August 2007 for NIC.

Pension age

The current pensionable age is 60 for women and 65 for men. From 6 April 2010 to 5 April 2020 the pensionable age for women will rise to 65. From 6 April 2024 the pensionable age for both men and women will rise to 66 (gradually over a two-year period), and likewise to 67 from 2034–6 and then to 68 from 2044–6.

Class 1 contributions

As mentioned above, these are related to earnings, the amount payable depending upon whether the employer has applied for his employees to be 'contracted-out' of the State earnings-related pension scheme; such application can be made where the employer's own pension scheme provides a requisite level of benefits for his or her employees and their dependants or, in the case of a money purchase scheme (COMPS) certain minimum safeguards are covered. Employers with employees contributing to 'stakeholder pension plans' continue to pay the full not contracted-out rate. Such employees have their contracting out arrangements handled separately by government authorities.

Contributions are payable by employees and employers on earnings that exceed the earnings threshold. Contributions are normally collected via the PAYE tax deduction machinery, and there are penalties for late submission of returns and for errors therein. From 19 April 1993, interest is charged automatically on PAYE and social security contributions paid late.

Employees liable to pay

Contributions are payable by any employee who is aged 16 years and over (even though they may still be at school) and who is paid an amount equal to, or exceeding, the earnings threshold. Nationality is irrelevant for contribution purposes and, subject to special rules covering employees not normally resident in Great Britain, Northern Ireland or the Isle of Man, or resident in EEA countries or those with which there are reciprocal agreements, contributions must be paid whether the employee concerned is a British subject or not provided he is gainfully employed in Great Britain.

Employees exempt from liability to pay

Persons over pensionable age are exempt from liability to pay primary contributions, even if they have not retired. However, the fact that an employee may be exempt from liability does not relieve an employer from liability to pay secondary contributions in respect of that employee.

Employees' (primary) contributions

From 6 April 2003, the rate of employees' contributions on earnings from the earnings threshold to the upper earnings limit is 11% (9.4% for contracted-out employments). Certain married women who made appropriate elections before 12 May 1977 may be entitled to pay a reduced rate of 4.85%. However, they will have no entitlement to benefits in respect of these contributions.

From April 2003, earnings above the upper earnings limit attract an employee contribution liability of 1% – previously, there was no such liability.

Employers' (secondary) contributions

All employers are liable to pay contributions on the gross earnings of employees. As mentioned above, an employer's liability is not reduced as a result of employees being exempted from contributions, or being liable to pay only the reduced rate (4.85%) of contributions.

For earnings paid on or after 6 April 2003 employers are liable at a rate of 12.8% on earnings paid above the earnings threshold (without any upper earnings limit), 9.1% where the employment is contracted out (salary related) or 11.4% contracted out (money purchase). In addition, special rebates apply in respect of earnings falling between the lower earnings limit and the earnings threshold. This provides, effectively, a negative rate of contribution in that small band of earnings. It should be noted that the contracted-out rates of 9.1% and 11.4% apply only up to the upper earnings limit. Thereafter, the not contracted-out rate of 12.8% is applicable. From 6 April 2003 to 5 April 2007 the contracted-out rates were 9.3% and 11.8% respectively.

Whilst the Chancellor of the Exchequer announced on 13 May 2008 an additional increase to the personal tax allowance for 2008–9 it is understood at the time of going to press that there will be no commensurate increase to the earnings threshold of £105 per week shown in the table below.

The employer is responsible for the payment of both employees' and employer's contributions, but is entitled to deduct the employees' contributions from the earnings on which they are calculated. Effectively, therefore, the employee suffers a deduction in respect of his or her social security contributions in arriving at his weekly or monthly wage or salary. Special rules apply to company directors and persons employed through agencies.

Items included in, or excluded from, earnings

Contributions are calculated on the basis of a person's gross earnings from their employment. This will normally be the figure shown on the deduction working sheet, except

Rates of Class 1 contributions and earnings limits from 6 April 2008

Earnings per week	Rates payable on earnings in each band			
	Not contracted out		Contracted out	
	Employee	Employer	Employee	Employer
£	%	%	%	%
Below 90.00	–	–	–	–
90.00–104.99	–	–	–(*)	–(*)
105.00–770.00	11	12.8	9.4	9.1 or 11.4
Over 770.00	1	12.8	1	12.8

* Special rebates deductible in respect of this band of earnings.

where the employee pays superannuation contributions and, from 6 April 1987, charitable gifts under payroll giving – these must be added back for the purposes of calculating Class 1 liability.

Earnings include salary, wages, overtime pay, commissions, bonuses, holiday pay, payments made while the employee is sick or absent from work, payments to cover travel between home and office, and payments under the statutory sick pay, statutory maternity pay, statutory paternity pay and statutory adoption pay schemes.

However, certain payments, some of which may be regarded as taxable income for income tax purposes, are ignored for Class 1 purposes. These include:
• certain gratuities paid other than by the employer;
• redundancy payments and some payments in lieu of notice;
• certain payments in kind;
• reimbursement of specific expenses incurred in the carrying out of the employment;
• benefits given on an individual basis for personal reasons (e.g. wedding and birthday presents);
• compensation for loss of office.

Booklet CWG 2 (2008 edition) gives a list of items to include in or exclude from earnings for Class 1 contribution purposes. Some such items may, however, be liable to Class 1A (employer only) contributions.

Miscellaneous rules

There are detailed rules covering a person with two or more employments; where a person receives a bonus or commission in addition to a regular wage or salary; and where a person is in receipt of holiday pay. From 6 April 1991 employers' social security contributions arise under Class 1A in respect of the private use of a company car, and of fuel provided for private use therein. From 6 April 2000, this charge was extended to cover most taxable benefits in kind. The rate is now 12.8%. From 6 April 1999, Class 1B contributions are payable by employers using PAYE Settlement Agreements in respect of small and/or irregular expense payments and benefits, etc. This rate is also currently 12.8%.

Upper Accrual Point

From 6 April 2009 there will be introduced a new Upper Accrual Point (UAP) from which entitlement to benefit (principally earnings-related state pension) will cease, even though main rate Class 1 contributions will continue to be due. This will impact on contracted-out employees in particular. The UAP is fixed at a constant cash amount of £770 per week and will eliminate any earnings-related element of the state pension by around 2031.

As the UAP will come into effect before this edition of the *Yearbook* is superseded, illustrative Class 1 rates and limits are set out below. It should be noted that all rates and limits may change – only the UAP itself is known at the time of writing.

Class 2 contributions

Class 2 contributions are payable at the weekly rate of £2.30 as from 6 April 2008. Exemptions from Class 2 liability are:
• A person over pensionable age.
• A person who has not attained the age of 16.
• A married woman or, in certain cases, a widow either of whom elected prior to 12 May 1977 not to pay Class 2 contributions.

• Persons with small earnings (see below).
• Persons not ordinarily self-employed (see below).

Small earnings

Application for a certificate of exception from Class 2 contributions may be made by any person who can show that his or her net self-employed earnings per his profit and loss account (as opposed to taxable profits):
• for the year of application are expected to be less than a specified limit (£4825 in the 2008/9 tax year); or
• for the year preceding the application were less than the limit specified for that year (£4635 for 2007/8) and there has been no material change of circumstances.

  Certificates of exception must be renewed in accordance with the instructions stated thereon. At HM Revenue & Customs' discretion the certificate may commence up to 13 weeks before the date on which the application is made. Despite a certificate of exception being in force, a person who is self-employed is still entitled to pay Class 2 contributions if they wish, in order to maintain entitlement to social security benefits.

Persons not ordinarily self-employed

Part-time self-employed activities (including as a writer or artist) are disregarded for contribution purposes if the person concerned is not ordinarily employed in such activities and has a full-time job as an employee. There is no definition of 'ordinarily employed' for this purpose but a person who has a regular job and whose earnings from spare-time occupation are not expected to be more than £1300 per annum may fall within this category. Persons qualifying for this relief do not require certificates of exception but may be well advised to apply for one nonetheless.

Method of payment

From April 1993, Class 2 contributions may be paid by monthly direct debit in arrears or, alternatively, by cheque, bank giro, etc following receipt of a quarterly (in arrears) bill.

Overpaid contributions

If, following the payment of Class 2 contributions, it is found that the earnings are below the exception limit (e.g. the relevant accounts are prepared late), the Class 2 contributions that have been overpaid can be reclaimed, provided a claim is made between 6 April and 31 January immediately following the end of the tax year. Such a refund may, however, prejudice entitlement to contributory benefits.

Illustrative rates of Class 1 contributions and earnings limits from 6 April 2009

Earnings per week	Rates payable on earnings in each band			
	Not contracted out		Contracted out	
	Employee	Employer	Employee	Employer
£	%	%	%	%
Below 93.00	–	–	–	–
93.00–107.99	–	–	– (*)	– (*)
108.00–769.99	11	12.8	9.4	9.1 or 11.4
770.00–830.00	11	12.8	11	12.8
Over 830.00	1	12.8	1	12.8

* Special rebates deductible in respect of this band of earnings.

Class 3 contributions

Class 3 contributions are payable voluntarily, at the weekly rate of £8.10 per week from 6 April 2008, by persons aged 16 or over with a view to enabling them to qualify for a limited range of benefits if their contribution record is not otherwise sufficient. In general, Class 3 contributions can be paid by employees, the self-employed and the non employed.

Broadly speaking, no more than 52 Class 3 contributions are payable for any one tax year, and contributions cannot be paid in respect of tax years after the one in which the individual concerned reaches state pension age (i.e. currently 65 for men and 60 for women). Class 3 contributions may be paid in the same manner as Class 2 (see above) or by annual cheque in arrears.

Class 4 contributions

In addition to Class 2 contributions, self-employed persons are liable to pay Class 4 contributions. These are calculated at the rate of 8% on the amount of profits or gains chargeable to income tax which exceed £5435 per annum but which do not exceed £40,040 per annum for 2008/9. Profits above the upper limit of £40,040 attract a Class 4 charge at the rate of 1%. The income tax profit on which Class 4 contributions are calculated is after deducting capital allowances and losses, but before deducting personal tax allowances or retirement annuity or personal pension or stakeholder pension plan premiums.

Class 4 contributions produce no additional benefits, but were introduced to ensure that self-employed persons as a whole pay a fair share of the cost of pensions and other social security benefits, yet without those who make only small profits having to pay excessively high flat rate contributions.

Payment of contributions

In general, Class 4 contributions are now self-assessed and paid to HM Revenue & Customs together with the income tax as a result of the self-assessment income tax return, and accordingly the contributions are due and payable at the same time as the income tax liability on the relevant profits. Under self-assessment, interim payments of Class 4 contributions are payable at the same time as interim payments of tax.

Class 4 exemptions

The following persons are exempt from Class 4 contributions:
• Persons over state pension age (i.e. currently 65 for men and 60 for women) at the commencement of the year of assessment (i.e. on 6 April).
• An individual not resident in the United Kingdom for income tax purposes in the year of assessment.
• Persons whose earnings are not 'immediately derived' from carrying on a trade, profession or vocation (e.g. sleeping partners).
• A child under 16 on 6 April of the year of assessment.
• Persons not ordinarily self-employed.

Married persons and partnerships

Under independent taxation of husband and wife from 1990/1 onwards, each spouse is responsible for his or her own Class 4 liability.

In partnerships, each partner's liability is calculated separately. If a partner also carries on another trade or profession, the profits of all such businesses are aggregated for the purposes of calculating their Class 4 liability.

When an assessment has become final and conclusive for the purposes of income tax, it is also final and conclusive for the purposes of calculating Class 4 liability.

Maximum contributions

There is a form of limit to the total liability for social security contributions payable by a person who is employed in more than one employment, or is also self-employed or a partner.

Where only not contracted-out Class 1 contributions, or not contracted-out Class 1 and Class 2 contributions, are payable, the maximum contribution payable at the main rates (11%, 9.4% or 4.85% as the case may be) is limited to 53 primary Class 1 contributions at the maximum weekly not contracted-out standard rate. For 2008/9 this 'maximum' will thus be £3876.95 (amounts paid at only 1% are to be excluded in making this comparison).

However, where contracted-out Class 1 contributions are payable, the maximum primary Class 1 contributions payable for 2008/9 where all employments are contracted out are £3300.31 (again excluding amounts paid at only 1%).

Where Class 4 contributions are payable in addition to Class 1 and/or Class 2 contributions, the Class 4 contributions payable at the full 8% rate are restricted so that they shall not exceed the excess of £2890.30 (i.e. 53 Class 2 contributions plus maximum Class 4 contributions) over the aggregate of the Class 1 and Class 2 contributions paid at the full (i.e. other than 1%) rates.

Further information

Further information can be obtained from the many booklets published by HM Revenue & Customs, available from local Enquiry Centres and on their website (www.hmrc.gov.uk).

National Insurance Contributions Office, Charities, Assets & Residency
Newcastle upon Tyne NE98 1ZZ
tel (08459) 154811 (local call rates apply)
Address for enquiries for individuals resident abroad.

Transfer of government departmental functions

The administrative functions of the former Contributions Agency transferred to the Inland Revenue from 1 April 1999. Responsibility for National Insurance contribution policy matters was also transferred from DSS Ministers to the Inland Revenue and Treasury Ministers on the same date. The DSS is now known as the Department for Work and Pensions (DWP). From 18 April 2005, the functions of the former Inland Revenue and former HM Customs and Excise were merged to become HM Revenue & Customs.

Peter Arrowsmith FCA is a sole practitioner specialising in National Insurance matters. He is a member and former chairman of the Employment Taxes and National Insurance Committee of the Institute of Chartered Accountants in England and Wales, and Consulting Editor to *Tolley's National Insurance Contributions 2008/9*.

Social security benefits

In this article K.D. Bartlett FCA summarises some of the more usual benefits that are available.

The social security benefits regime has undertaken major changes in the last few years and more changes are promised. There are now four types of State Benefits:
• Pension age benefits (for those aged 60 and over) are administered by the Pensions Service.
• Tax credits for families with children and people in work are administered by HM Revenue & Customs (formerly the Inland Revenue).
• Disability and carer benefits are administered by the Disability and Carer Benefits Scheme.
• Working age benefits (for those under the age of 60) are administered by Jobcentre Plus.

Family benefits

Child Benefit is payable for all children who are either under 16 or under 19 and receiving full-time education at a recognised educational establishment. The rate is £18.80 for the first or eldest child and £12.55 a week for each subsequent child. It is payable to the person who is responsible for the child but excludes foster parents or people exempt from UK tax.

Those with little money may apply for a maternity loan or grant from the Social Fund. Those claiming Working Families Tax Credit or Disabled Person's Tax Credit can apply for a Sure Start Maternity Grant of £500 for each baby expected, born, adopted or subject to a parental order. Any savings over £500 are taken into account. This grant will only be paid on the provision of a relevant certificate from a doctor, midwife or health visitor.

A Guardian's Allowance is paid at the rate of £13.45 a week to people who have taken orphans into their own family. Usually both of the child's parents must be dead and at least one of them must have satisfied a residence condition. The allowance can only be paid to the person who is entitled to Child Benefit for the child (or to that person's spouse). It is not necessary to be the legal guardian. The claim should be made within three months of the date of entitlement.

Pensions

The state pension is divided into two parts – the basic pension, presently £90.70 per week for a single person or £145.05 per week for a married couple – and Pension Credit.

Women paying standard rate contributions into the scheme are eligible for the same amount of pension as men but five years earlier, from age 60. The Pensions Act 1995 incorporated the provision for an equal state pension age of 65 for men and women to be phased in over a ten-year period beginning 6 April 2010. If a woman stays at home to bring up her children or to look after a person receiving Attendance Allowance she can have her basic pension rights protected without paying contributions.

Pension Credit is a new entitlement for people aged 60 or over. It guarantees everyone aged 60 and over an income of at least £124.05 a week for a single person; or £189.35 a week for those with a partner. ('Partner' means a spouse or a person with whom one lives as if married to them.)

People aged 65 and over will be rewarded for some of their savings and income they have for their retirement. In the past, those who had saved a little money were no better off than those who had not saved at all. Pension Credit will change this by giving new money to those who have saved – up to £19.71 for a single person, or £26.13 for those with a partner. The person who applies for Pension Credit must be at least 60 but their partner can be under 60.

Child Tax Credits

Child Tax Credits were introduced on 6 April 2003. To obtain them, a claim form has to be submitted (Tax Credits Form TC600 is available by either telephoning 0845 366 7820 or applying via Tax Credits Online – www.taxcredits.inlandrevenue.gov.uk).

Child Tax Credit has replaced the Children's Tax Credit previously claimed through tax paid. It is paid directly to the person who is mainly responsible for caring for the child or children. Apply online to ascertain your entitlement to tax credits.

Child Tax Credits are especially complicated for those on variable income and the self-employed.

Working Tax Credit

Working Tax Credit is paid to support people in work and is administered by HM Revenue & Customs. It is not necessary to have paid National Insurance contributions (NICs) to qualify. People over 16 who are responsible for a child or young person and work at least 16 hours a week qualify. People without children can claim if:
• They are over 25 and work at least 30 hours a week;
• They are aged 16 or over and work at least 16 hours a week and have a disability that puts them at a disadvantage in obtaining a job;
• A person or their partner are aged 50 or more and work at least 16 hours a week and are returning to work after time spent on obtaining a qualification.

Working Tax Credit is paid as well as any Child Tax Credit entitlement. The calculations for how much a person receives are complicated and depend on how many hours he/she works and his/her income or the joint income.

Employed people receive the payment via their employer and those in self-employment will be paid direct. To check eligibility to receive Working Tax Credit, either telephone 0845 764 6646 or visit Tax Credits Online (see above).

Benefits for the ill

Incapacity Benefit replaced Sickness Benefit and Invalidity Benefit. The contribution conditions haven't changed but a new medical test has been brought in which includes a comprehensive questionnaire. The rates from April 2008 are:

	£
Long-term Incapacity Benefit	84.50
Short-term Incapacity Benefit	63.75
Increase of long-term Incapacity Benefit for age:	
Higher rate	17.75
Lower rate	8.90

Carer's Allowance, formerly Invalid Care Allowance, is a taxable benefit paid to people of working age who cannot take a job because they have to stay at home to look after a severely disabled person. The basic allowance is £50.55 per week. An extra £9.00 is paid for the first dependent child and £11.35 for each subsequent child.

Disability Living Allowance

Disability Living Allowance (DLA) has replaced Attendance Allowance for disabled people before they reach the age of 65, and has also replaced Mobility Allowance. Those who are disabled after reaching 65 may be able to claim Attendance Allowance. The Attendance Allowance Board decide whether, and for how long, a person is eligible.

DLA is paid at different rates depending on how the disability affects the claimant. DLA is in two parts – the care component and the mobility component. It is possible to receive just one component or both.

Individual circumstances will affect how much a person can receive.

Care component	Weekly rate (£)
Highest rate	67.00
Middle rate	44.85
Lowest rate	17.75
Mobility component	
Higher rate	46.75
Lower rate	17.75

Widowed Parent's Allowance

This is a system of bereavement benefits for men and women introduced in April 2001. Women who were receiving benefits under the provisions scheme are unaffected as long as they still qualify under the rules. A Widowed Parent's Allowance is a regular payment based on the late husband's or wife's contributions, and is for widows or widowers bringing up children. The main conditions for receiving this benefit are:
• You must be aged over 45 and have a dependent child or children.
• If you were over the state pension age when you were widowed you may receive Retirement Pension based on the husband's or wife's NICs.
• If the spouse died as a result of their job, it is possible to receive bereavement benefits even if they did not pay sufficient NICs.
• You cannot receive bereavement benefits if you remarry or if you live with a partner as if you are married to them.
• Bereavement benefits are not affected if you work.
• The allowance is £90.70 for those over 55 and varies for those aged 45–54.

There are increases for dependent children of £9.00 for the oldest child who qualifies for Child Benefit and £11.35 for each child who qualifies.

Bereavement Payment and benefits

From 9 April 2001 bereavement benefits are payable to both widows and widowers but the benefits are only paid to those without children. Benefits are based on the NICs of the deceased. No benefit is payable if the couple were divorced at the date of death or if either of the survivors remarries or cohabits.

Widows and widowers bereaved on or after 9 April 2001 are entitled to a tax-free Bereavement Payment of £2000.

The death grant to cover funeral expenses was abolished from 6 April 1987. It has been replaced by a funeral payment from the Social Fund where the claimant is in receipt of Income Support, income-based Jobseeker's Allowance, Disabled Person's Tax Credit, Working Families' Tax Credit or Housing Benefit. The full cost of a reasonable funeral is paid up to a maximum of £700.

Jobseeker's Allowance

People of working age but unemployed and actively seeking work may be able to obtain Jobseeker's Allowance (JSA). To be eligible a person must be out of work or working less than 16 hours a week on average. He/she must also be capable of working, available for work, actively seeking work and below retirement age.

Jobseeker's Allowance is not paid to people under the age of 18 or full-time students. There are exceptions – particularly if a person looks after children – so it's worth checking with the local Jobcentre Plus.

Contribution-based JSA may be received by those who have paid, or are treated as having paid, enough NICs. A flat weekly rate is paid according to the recipient's age: £47.95 for people aged 18–24 and £60.50 for those aged 25 or over. Payments may be reduced if the recipient is receiving a pension, or delayed if he/she is getting final payments from their last job.

Income-based JSA may be paid to those who haven't paid enough NICs (or have only paid contributions for self-employment) and are on a low income. The maximum weekly rates are:

Status	£
Single people aged 18–24	47.95
Single people aged 25 or over	60.50
Couples and civil partnerships (both aged 18 or over)	94.95
Lone parents	60.50

Those with savings of over £6000 will receive less; and applicants with savings of over £16,000 probably won't qualify. If the applicant's partner or civil partner works 24 hours or more a week on average, income-based JSA is usually not allowed (contribution-based JSA isn't affected). If they work less than 24 hours, it may affect the amount received.

Unemployed 16- or 17-year-olds may be able to receive income-based JSA for a short period if, for example, they are forced to live away from their parents; will suffer severe hardship if they don't get JSA; or are part of a couple responsible for a child.

Statutory Maternity Pay

To help women to take time off work when they have a baby, Statutory Maternity Pay (SMP), a weekly payment from employers, may be paid. To qualify for SMP the woman must have been:
• employed by the same employer without a break for at least 26 weeks into the 15th week before the week the baby is due;
• earning an average of at least £90 a week (before tax).

Women not eligible for SMP may be able to get Maternity Allowance instead (see below). Those who do not qualify for either SMP or Maternity Allowance may be able to get some Incapacity Benefit or a Sure Start Maternity Grant instead if the woman or her partner or civil partner are claiming benefits or tax credits.
• SMP is 90% of the woman's average weekly earnings with no upper limit for the first six weeks of her maternity leave, and for the remaining 33 weeks either £117.18 or 90% of her average earnings, if this 90% rate is less than £117.18.

Statutory Paternity Pay

When a wife, partner or civil partner gives birth or adopts a child, a man may be able to obtain Statutory Paternity Pay (SPP), which is paid by his employer to help him take time off work. To qualify for SPP, all of the following must apply:
• The man must be the biological father or adopter of the child or be the mother's husband, partner or civil partner or have or expect to have responsibility for the child's upbringing.

406 Finance for writers and artists

• He must have continued to work for the same employer without a break for at least 26 weeks by the 15th week before the baby is due, or employed up to and including the week his wife, partner or civil partner was matched with a child.
• He must continue to work for that employer without a break up to the date the child is born or placed for adoption.
• He must be earning an average of at least £90 a week (before tax).

If the man's average weekly earnings are £90 or more (before tax), SPP is for one or two consecutive weeks at £117.18 or 90% of his average weekly earnings if this is less.

Maternity Allowance

If a woman is pregnant or has a new baby but doesn't qualify for SMP, she may be able to claim Maternity Allowance (MA). There are changes to MA that apply to women with babies due on or after 1 April 2007. A woman may be eligible for Maternity Allowance if:
• she is employed, but not eligible for SMP and is registered self-employed and paying Class 2 NICs, or holds a Small Earnings Exception certificate;
• she has been at work for at least 26 weeks of the 'test period' (66 weeks up to and including the week before her baby is due) – part weeks count as full weeks;
• she earned an average of £30 in any 13 of the weeks in the test period.

A woman who is entitled to Statutory Maternity Pay will not be eligible for Maternity Allowance.

Maternity Allowance pays a standard weekly rate of £117.18 or 90% of the woman's average weekly earnings (before tax), whichever is the smaller. Extra money for her husband, civil partner or someone else who looks after her children may be obtained, if that person is on a very low income.

K.D. Bartlett FCA qualified as a Chartered Accountant in 1969 and became a partner in a predecessor firm of Horwath Clark Whitehill LLP in 1972.

Index

Aardman Animations 295
Abbey Home Media plc 5, 60
Abingdon Press 38
Harry N. Abrams Inc. 38
abridgements, for radio and audio 284
Absey and Co. Inc. 38
Academi (Welsh Academy) 173, 344
AccessArt 344
accessibility 317
accounts, publishers' 234
ACER Press 27
action hero books 90, 115
Action Publishing, LLC 38
Adams Literary 201
Adams, Richard 116
adaptations
  for stage 304
  of classics 289
  of works 289
advances (against royalties) 163, 187, 223, 231–232,
  382, 384
Adventure Box 259
adventure stories 190
advertising 91
advertising in schools 150
Advocate 228
age
  groups 129
  guidance on book covers 95
  age ranging 96, 114
Agency (London) Ltd, The 192
agents
  illustrators' 182, 212, 222-3
  literary 2, 77, 83, 86, 142, 154, 155, 159, 181, 185,
    189, 232, 275, 279
  television and film 275
Agreements
  contracts 186, 189, 231
  minimum term 337
  publishing 2, 186, 231
Aiken, Joan 103
Aitken Alexander Associates Ltd 192
Aladdin Books Ltd 63
Aladdin Paperbacks 38
Albion Press Ltd, The 63
Louisa May Alcott Memorial Association 344
All About Kids Publising 38
Philip Allan 5
Allen & Unwin Pty Ltd 27
Allen, John 299
Allied Artists/Artistic License 228
Alligator Books Ltd 5
Altair-Australia Literary Agency 199
Alyson Publications, Inc. 38

amateur dramatic society 301
Amazon 96
Tiptoe Books (an imprint of Amber Books Ltd) 67
American Girl Publishing, Inc. 39
American Library Association (ALA) 105
American Society of Composers, Authors and
  Publishers 344
Americanisation 159
Amgueddfa Cymru – National Museum Wales 344
Amistad Press 39
Amy 259
Grupo Anaya 37
Hans Christian Andersen Awards, The 364
Andersen Press Ltd 5
Darley Anderson Literary, TV and Film Agency 192
Michelle Anderson Publishing Pty Ltd 27
Andrew Brodie Publications 5
Julie Andrews Collection, The 39
Andromeda Children's Books 5
Anglia Young Books 5
Angus Book Award 151, 364
Animal Action 259
animal and nature stories 116
Animals and You 259
animation 80, 276, 287, 317
Anness Publishing 5
Annick Press Ltd 29
Anova Children's Books 5
anthologies, poetry 167–168
anthologists 190
Anvil Books/Children's Press, The 5
Apples & Snakes Performance Poetry 176
Aquila 259
Arad Goch 310
Arcturus Publishing Ltd 5
Ardagh, Philip 185
Arena 228
Edizoni Arka srl 34
Armadillo 270
Armitage, Ronda and David 300
Arrowsmith, Peter 394
Art Agency (Wildlife Art Ltd), The 228
Art Attack 259
artistic directors 301
Artist's Resale Right 252
Arts Council England 173, 175, 338, 344, 364
  grants 385
Arts Council/An Chomhairle Ealaíon 345
Arts Council of Northern Ireland 345
Arts Council of Wales 345
Arts Council YouWriteOn.com Book Awards 364
Artworks, The 228
Arvon Foundation, The 177, 323, 328
  International Poetry Competition 176

Ash, Russell 105
Askews 70
Aspects Festival 375
ASSITEJ UK 301
Association for Library Service to Children 346
Association for Library Service to Children Awards 365
Association for Scottish Literary Studies (ASLS) 346
Association of American Publishers Inc. 346
Association of Authors' Agents, The 346
Association of Authors' Representatives Inc. 346
Association of Booksellers for Children 346
Association of Canadian Publishers 346
Association of Illustrators 241, 346
Astonishing Spider-Man 259
Atheneum Books for Young Readers 39
Atlantic Europe Publishing Co. Ltd 6
Atom 6
Attendance Allowance 402–403
auctions 91
audience participation 302
Audiobook Publishing Association (APA) 346
audiobooks 281, 283
Austin Clarke Library 174
Australia Council 347
Australian Copyright Council 347
Australian Literary Management 199
Australian Publishers Association (APA) 347
Australian Writers' Guild (AWG) 347
Author, The 336
Author Literary Agents 192
authors
    and marketing 149
    and production 234
    as brands 163
    tracing 251
Authors' Licensing and Collecting Society (ALCS) 244, 248, 250, 336
Authors' Licensing and Collecting Society Ltd 347
authorship 240
Autumn Publishing 6
Avengers United, The 259
averaging relief 382, 389
Avisson Press, Inc. 39
Avon Books 39
Award Publications Ltd 6

b small publishing limited 6
babies, books for 86, 98, 162
Badger Books 70
BAFTA Children's Writer Awards 276
Baggins Books 175
Bags of Books 70
Baker Books 68
Balamory Magazine 259
Bank of Scotland Imaginate Festival 375
Bantam Books 39
Bantam Press (children's) 6
Barbie 260
barcoding 237
Bardd Plant Cymru (Children's Poet Laureate) 365

Barefoot Books 39
Barefoot Books Ltd 6, 60
Barnardo's Image Archive 347
Barrington Stoke 6, 60
Barron's Educational Series Inc. 39
Bartlett, K. D. 402
Basic Skills Book Awards 365
David Bateman Ltd 35
bath books 98
Bath Festival of Children's Literature 375
Bath Literature Festival 375
Bath Spa University 329
Batman: Legends 260
Nicola Baxter Ltd 63
BBC Audiobooks – Children's 60
BBC Audiobooks Ltd 6
BBC Children's Books 6
BBC Children's Radio 281, 298
BBC Cover to Cover 60
BBC School Radio 298
BBC writersroom 291
Glenys Bean Writer's Agent 200
Beano, The 260
Bebop Books 39
Becker, Tom 90
Beehive Illustration 228
beginner readers 119, 162
Belair 6
Belgrade Theatre, Coventry 299
Bell Lomax Moreton Agency, The 192
Hilaire Belloc Society 347
Bender Richardson White 63
Benefits
    bereavement 404
    Child 402
    disability and carer 402
    incapacity 404, 406
    invalidity 404
    pension age 403
    social security 403
    state 403
    working age 403
bereavement benefits 404
Beyond the Border:Wales International Storytelling Festival, The 375
BFC Books for Children 68
Bibliophile 68
Bick Publishing House 39
Big Heart Media 295
Big Picture campaign 95
Big Read 98
Bisto Book of the Year Awards, The 365
A&C Black Publishers Ltd 6
Black, Holly, and diTerlizzi, Tony 95
Blackman, Malorie 117
Blackwater Press 7
Blackwell Rare Books 72
Blanch, David 342
Blast Off! 260
Blast-Off Books 70
Bliss 260
Blogger.com 318
blogging 318
Bloomsbury Publishing Plc 7, 60

Bloomsbury USA 40
Blue Balloon 35
Blue Peter Children's Book Awards 365
Blue Sky Press 40
Blume, Judy 116
blurb 234
Enid Blyton Society 347
board books 86, 98
Boardwalk Books 29
Bob the Builder 260
Bodley Head Children's Books 7
Bolinda Publishing Ltd 60
Bologna Book Fair 221
Bologna Children's Book Fair 183, 375
BolognaRagazzi Award 365
book chains, high street 96
book clubs 152
Book Guild Ltd, The 63
Book House, The 70
Book Industry Communication website 237
Book Marketing Ltd 94, 162
Book Now! Literature Festival, Arts Service 376
Book People Ltd, The 68
Book Publishers Association of New Zealand
    Inc. 347
Book Street Ltd 63
Bookmark Children's Books 72
Bookmart Ltd 63
Books
  action 90, 115
  baby 86, 98, 162
  barcoding 237
  bath 98
  board 86, 98
  cartoon 85
  categorising 162
  cloth 162
  crime 117
  crossover 84, 92, 129, 136, 153, 162, 190
  historical 117, 127
  horror 114, 190
  jackets 150-151, 234
  lift-the-flap 99
  manga 118
  novelty 221
  nursery ryhme 99
  picture books 82, 86, 94, 100, 102, 162, 191, 209,
    213, 219, 231
  pop-up 182
  read aloud, to 102
  reference 114
  spy 90, 115
  tax relief on 388
  toddlers 86, 99
  teenage 112
  wordless 98
  younger readers, for 87, 182, 221
Books and the Consumer report 94
Books for Keeps 1, 150, 270
Bookseller, The 152, 159, 270
Booksellers Association of the United Kingdom &
    Ireland Ltd, The 347
booksellers, children's 91, 96
bookshops, independent 91

Bookspread Ltd 70
Bookstart 95, 338
BookStop Literary Agency 201
Booktime project 95
Booktrust 95, 338, 348
  Early Years Awards 98, 338, 365
  Teenage Prize, The 366
Bookwork Ltd 63
Bookworm Ltd 70
Bookworms of Reigate 70
Boomerang 292
Booster Cushion Theatre 310
Borders 96
Boxer Books Ltd 7
Boyds Mills Press 40
boys
  publishing for 94
  writing for 105
Braille at Bedtime 260
Brainwaves Ltd 64
Branford Boase Award, The 366
Branford, Henrietta 116
Bratz 260
Breslich & Foss Ltd 64
Breslin, Theresa 116
brief, writing to a 287
Briggs, Raymond 207
Briggs, Stephen 304
Brilliant Publications 7
British Book Awards 152, 366
British Council, The 176, 348
British Haiku Society, The 173
British Museum 348
British Museum Company Ltd 8
Andrew Brodie 8
Bromley, Adam 277
Brook Green Bookshop 70
Jenny Brown Associates 192
John Brown Group – Children's Division 64
Andrea Brown Literary Agency 201
Brown Reference Group Plc, The 64
Brown Wells & Jacobs Ltd 64
Pema Browne Ltd 201
Browne & Miller Literary Associates 201
Browns Books For Students 70
Felicity Bryan 193
Bryson Agency Australia Pty Ltd 199
budgets 305
buggy buddies 99
Burgess, Melvin 116
Buster Books 8
Butterworth, 95
Mary Butts Books 72
Byre Theatre of St Andrews, The 309

Cahoots NI 311
Randolph Caldecott Society 348
Calkins Creek Books 40
Calon TV 295
Cambridge Publishing Management Ltd 64
Cambridge University Press 8, 36
Camden Poetry Group 177

Campbell Books   8
Canadian Authors Association   348
Canadian Children's Book Centre (CCBC),
   The   348
Canadian Magazine Publishers Association   349
Canadian Publishers' Council   349
Candlewick Press   40
CANSCAIP (Canadian Society of Children's Authors,
   Illustrators & Performers)   349
Canter, Rosemary   189
Jonathan Cape Children's Books   8
capital allowances   387
Careers Writers' Association   349
Carer's Allowance   403
Carl Hanser Verlag   33
Carlsen Verlag   33
Carlton Poets   176
Carlton Publishing Group   8
Carnegie Medal   366
Carolrhoda Books   40
Carousel   1, 150, 270
Lewis Carroll Society (Daresbury)   349
Lewis Carroll Society, The   349
Lewis Carroll Society of North America
   (LCSNA)   349
Cartoon Network   292
cartoons, cartoonists   85, 207
Cartwheel Books   40
Maria Carvainis Agency Inc.   201
Celia Catchpole   193, 228
categorising children's books   162
Caterpillar Books   8
Catnip Publishing Ltd   8
CB1 Poetry   176
CBBC   291
CBeebies   291
CBeebies Weekly Magazine   260
CBI Bisto Book of the Year Awards, The   366
Cengage Learning Australia   27
censorship   109
Center for Children's Books (CCB), The   339, 349
Centerprise Literature Development Project   177
Centre for Literacy in Primary Education
   (CLPE)   349
CGP   8
Chameleon Books   70
Channel 4 Television Corporation   292
Paul Chapman Publishing   9
Chapter One Bookshop   70
Charlesbridge Publishing   40
Charlie and Lola   260
Chart Studio Publishing (Pty) Ltd   36
Times Cheltenham Literature Festival, The   376
Cherokee Literary Agency   200
Cherrytree Books   9
Chester Literature Festival   376
Chicago Review Press   41
Chichester Festival Theatre   309
Chicken House, The   9
Child Benefit   402
Child Education PLUS   270
Child, Lauren   80
Child Tax Credits   403
Department for Children, Schools and Families   350

Children's Book Centre   71
Children's Book Circle   341, 350
Children's Book Council (CBC), The   350
Children's Book Council of Australia   350
Children's Book Festival   376
Children's Book Guild of Washington DC, The   350
Children's Book Week   376
Children's Books Ireland   350
Children's Bookshop, The   71
Children's Bookshop (Huddersfield)   71
Children's Bookshop (Muswell Hill)   71
Children's Film and Television Foundation Ltd   295
Children's Laureate, The   366
Children's Literature Association (ChLA)   350
Children's Literature Centre   350
Children's Literature International Summer School
   (Creating Children's Literature)   328
Children's Poetry Bookshelf   68
Children's Writers and Illustrators Group   351
Childrens@Blackwells   71
Child's Play (International) Ltd   9
Chimp and Zee Bookshop, Bookshop by the Sea   71
Chivers Children's Audiobooks   60
Chocmakers Productions   295
Christian Education   9
Chronicle Books   41
Chrysalis Children's Books   9
Chudney Agency, The   201
CILIP Carnegie and Kate Greenaway Awards,
   The   366
CITV   292
City University Creative Writing and Poetry
   Courses   177
Claire Publications   9
Clarion Books   41
classics, adapting from   289
classrooms, plays in   305
Classworks Theatre   311
CLÉ – Irish Book Publishers' Association   351
Clear Light Books   41
Clever Books Pty Ltd   36
Clitheroe Books Open Floor Readings   176
Cló Iar-Chonnachta Teo.   60
cloth books   99
CLPE Poetry Award, The   367
Clwyd Theatr Cymru Theatre for Young
   People   309
CMX   41
co-authorship   240
co-editions   159, 233
co-productions   276
Coffee House Poetry   176
Melanie Colbert   199
Cole, Steve   95
Colfer, Eoin   78, 117–118
Collingwood O'Hare Entertainment   295
Collins Education   9, 41
Colourpoint Books   9
comedy writing
   for children's television   276–277
   scripted   278
Comhairle nan Leabhraichean/Gaelic Books Council,
   The   351
Commando   260

commissioning of scripts 279
Commonword 173
company, operating as 382, 392
compilers 240
Contact Theatre Company 309
Continuum International Publishing Group Ltd, The 9
Continuum International Publishing Group Inc., The 41
contracts 186, 189, 231 *see also* Agreements
Conville & Walsh Ltd 193
David C. Cook 41
Cooling, Wendy 98
copy-editing 147
copying 251
copyright 233, 240, 245
  and libel 248
  assignment of 245
  duration of 245
  infringement of 246
  interviews, in 246
  photographs, in 246
  royalties 385
  use of symbol 246
Copyright, Designs and Patents Act (1988) 245
Copyright Licensing Agency (CLA) 248, 250
Copyrights Group Ltd, The 228
core fiction 162
Corgi Children's Books 9
Cormier, Robert 115
Corneliu M. Popescu Prize for European Poetry in Translation 174
Cornelius & Jones 311
Cosgrove Hall Films Ltd 295
Costa Book Awards 367
Joanna Cotler Books 41
courses, writing 142, 184, 320
covers 147, 150–151, 160
Cowley Robinson Publishing Ltd 64
cp publishing 9
Craig, Joe 95
Creations for Children International 64
Creative Arts East 173
Creative Authors Ltd 193
Creative Plus Publishing Ltd 64
Creech, Sharon 117
Cricket Books 41
crime novels 117
Cristall, Suna 315
Cross, Gillian 115
Crosshands Ltd/ACP Television 298
crossover books 84, 92, 129, 136, 153, 162, 190
Crown Books 41
Crown House Publishing Ltd 10
Editorial Cruilla 37
CSA Word 61, 298
CTC Theatre 311
Cunningham, Barry 83
Curtis Brown Group Ltd 193
Curtis Brown Ltd 202
cutting 306
Cwlwm Cyhoeddwyr Cymru 351
Cygnet 27
Cyngor Llyfrau Cymru 351

Roald Dahl Foundation 351
Dahl, Roald 302
Daisy 261
Dandy, The 261
Darby Creek Publishing 41
Jenny Darling & Associates 199
Dawn Publications 42
Liza Dawson Associates 202
DC Comics 42
De Agostini Editore 34
Walter de la Mare Society 351
Dead Good Poets Society 176
Dean 10
death grant 404
debts, bad 381
Delacorte Press Books for Young Readers 42
Delaney, Joseph 90
delivery date 233
Department for Work and Pensions (DWP) 401
design 147, 150–151, 207
  right 247
  templates 318
Design and Artists Copyright Society (DACS) 248, 252
Design Eye Ltd 64
designers 315
Destino Infantil & Juvenil 37
Deutscher Taschenbuch Verlag (DTV) 33
George Devine Award 367
Dial Books for Young Readers 42
dialogue 304
digital downloads 96
digitisation 251
Sandra Dijkstra Literary Agency 202
direct marketing 152
Disability Allowance (DLA) 403
disability and carer benefits 402
Disability and Carer Benefits Scheme 402
Disabled Person's Tax Credit 402, 404
disabled website users 317
discounting 96
Discover 351
Discovery Box 261
Discovery Kids 292
Disney & Me 261
Disney Book Club 68
Disney Books for Young Readers 42
Disney Channel UK 292
Disney Fairies 261
Walt Disney Company Ltd, The 295
Disney's Princess 261
DK FindOut! 261
Doctor Who Adventures 261
Doctor Who Magazine 261
Dog-Eared Publications 42
Tom Doherty Associates, LLC 42
domain name 315
Donaldson, Julia 95
Dora the Explorer 261
Dorling Kindersley 10
double taxation agreements 385, 392
Doubleday Books for Young Readers 42
Doubleday Canada 29
Doubleday Children's Books 10

Dover Publications Inc.   42
Arthur Conan Doyle Society, The   351
Dragon Books   42
Dragonfly Books   42
drama, for under-fives   300
dramatisations   304
Dref Wen   10, 61
Dundurn Press   29
Dunham Literary, Inc.   202
Dunmore Press Ltd   35
Dutton Children's Books   42
Dwyer & O'Grady Inc.   202
Dystel & Goderich Literary Management   202

e-books   191
Early Childhood Today   270
ebook devices   96
L'Ecole des Loisirs   32
EDCON Publishing Group   42
Eddison Pearson Ltd   193
Edinburgh International Book Festival   376
editors   82, 155, 190, 240
   publisher's   145, 153
Edizioni El/Einaudi Ragazzi/Emme Edizioni   34
Educational Company of Ireland, The   10, 61
Educational Design Services LLC   202
Educational Explorers (Publishers)   10
Educational Publishers Council   352
educational publishing   138
Educational Recording Agency (ERA)   251
Educational Writers Group   352
Edupress   43
Eerdmans Publishing Company   43
Egg, The   309
Egmont Books   10
electronic publishing   191
Ethan Ellenberg Literary Agency, The   202
Elliston, Valerie A.   324
Elm Grove Books Ltd   65
Paul Embleton   72
Enchanted Wood   71
Encyclopaedia Britannica Inc.   43
Endemol UK   295
English Association   352
English, John   299
Enslow Publishers, Inc.   43
Eos   43
Epsom Writers' Workshop   177
Essential X-Men   262
Essex Poetry Festival   376
Evan-Moor Educational Publishers   43
Evans Publishing Group   10
Everyman Theatre   309
Exeter Extending Literacy Project (EXEL)   106
expenses, claimed against tax   381, 385
Express Excess   176

Faber and Faber Ltd   11
fairy books   90, 190
fairy stories   118

CJ Fallon   11
family stories   116
fantasy   114, 116, 151, 163, 190
Eleanor Farjeon Award, The   367
Farnham Film Company, The   295
Farrar, Straus and Giroux, LLC   43
Federation of Children's Book Groups Conference,
   The   328, 342, 352
Federation of European Publishers   352
Federation of Indian Publishers, The   352
Federation of Spanish Publishers' Association   352
festivals, children's literature   150
David Fickling Books   43   11
Fickling, David   74
fiction   81, 92
   age ranges   96
   boys   105
   children's   87, 94, 190
   core   162
   general   87
   genres   114
   young adult   81, 94-95, 114-116, 162
Fifi and the Flower Tots   262
films   80, 95
Fimbles   262
finance   381
Fine, Anne   102
Firebird   43
First and Best in Education   11
First News   262
Fitzhenry & Whiteside Ltd   29
Five Broadcasting Ltd   292
Flame Tree Publishing   11
Flammarion   33
Flannery Literary   202
Floris Books   11
Flux   44
Folens Publishers   11   11
Folkestone Literary Festival   376
fonts   316
Foreman, Michael   300
Foster, John   167
Walter Foster Publishing Inc.   44
Foyle Young Poets of the Year Award   174, 179, 367
Fraser Ross Associates   193
Free Spirit Publishing   44
freelance (self-employed) status   383
French Publishers' Association   352
French, Samuel   302
French's Theatre Bookshop   303
Front Street   44
FTP (File Transfer Protocol)   319
Fulcrum Resources   44
David Fulton   12
Fun to Learn Bag-o-Fun   262
Fun to Learn Barney   262
Fun to Learn Discovery   262
Fun to Learn Favourites   262
Fun to Learn Friends   262
Fun to Learn Letterland   263
Fun to Learn Peppa Pig   263
funeral payment   404
Funke, Cornelia   95
Futurama (UK)   263

Gaelic Books Council, The   352
gag writing   279
Galaxy British Book Awards   367
Galaxy Children's Large Print   12
Gale Cengage Learning   44
Gallimard Jeunesse   33
Galore Park Publishing Ltd   12
games websites   97
Gardner Education Ltd   12
Garnett, Michelle   255
Gavin, Jamila   117
Geddes & Grosset   12
general fiction   87
genres   114
Laura Geringer Books   44
ghost stories   114
Michael Gifkins & Associates   200
Gill, Richard   301
Ginger Productions   296
Ginn   12
Girl Talk   263
girls, writing books for   111
Giunti Editore SpA   34
GL Assessment   12
Mary Glasgow Magazines   270
Glass, Linzi   92
Gliori, Debi   213
Glowworm Books & Gifts Ltd   71
Glyndebourne Children's Theatre   299
GMTV   293
Go Girl Magazine   263
Gold Smarties Book Prize   151
Barry Goldblatt Literary LLC   203
Golden Books for Young Readers   44
Golden Treasury (Southfields)   71
Golvan Arts Management   199
Gomer Press   12
Goodie Bag Mag   263
Google   317
Gordon, Roderick   92
gothic romance   92
W.F. Graham   12
Graham-Cameron Illustration   229
Graham-Cameron Publishing & Illustration   65
Grampian Children's Book Award   367
Granada Learning   12
Graphia   44
graphic novels   118, 207
graphic story treatments   85
Gravett, Emily   95
Gray, Keith   115
Ashley Grayson Literary Agency   203
Annette Green Authors' Agency   193
Green, Jim   138
Kate Greenaway Medal   367
Greene & Heaton Ltd   194
Greenhaven Press   44
Greenhouse Literary Agency, The   203
Greenwillow Books   44
Greeting Card Association, The   352
greetings cards   1
Grey, Alison Allen   117
Grosset & Dunlap   44
Gryphon House, Inc.   44

Guardian Children's Fiction Prize, The   367
Guardian Hay Festival, The   377
Guardian's Allowance   402
Guernsey Arts Council   352
Guiding magazine   263
Guildford Book Festival   377
Marianne Gunn O'Connor Literary Agency   194

Hachai Publishing   45
Hachette Children's Books   12, 27
Hachette Livre   94
Hachette Livre Australia Pty Ltd   27
Hachette Livre UK Ltd   13
Hachette Livre/Gautier-Languereau   33
Haldane Mason Ltd   13
Halliwell, Geri   94
Halse Anderson, Laurie   116
Hammer and Tongue   176
Handprint Books   45
Harcourt Canada Ltd   30
Harcourt School Publishers   45
Harcourt Trade Publishers   45
HarperCollins Audio Books   61
HarperCollins Publishers (Australia) Pty Ltd Group   27
HarperCollins Publishers Ltd   13, 30, 45
HarperCollins Publishers (New Zealand) Ltd   35
Harry Potter   92, 94–95, 115, 190
Hart McLeod Ltd   65
Hawcock Books   65
John Hawkins & Associates Inc.   203
Hay Festival   377
Hayward, The   352
Headliners   263
Health Press NA Inc.   46
A.M. Heath & Co. Ltd   194
Heinemann   13
David Higham Associates Ltd   194, 229
Hippo   13
Hiss & Boo Company Ltd, The   311
historical novels, writing for children   117, 127
History Compass LLC   47
HIT Entertainment plc   296
HL Studios Ltd   65
HM Revenue & Customs   402
Hodder & Stoughton Audiobooks   61
Hodder Children's Books   13
Hodder Education Group   13
Hodder Gibson   14
Hodder Headline Ltd   14
Ian Hodgkins & Co Ltd   73
John Hodgson Agency   229
Hole, John   299
Holiday House   47
Holland, Guy   301
Henry Holt and Company LLC   47
Hooker, Yvonne   145
Hopscotch Educational Publishing Ltd   14
Horn, Caroline   90, 162
Horowitz, Anthony   91, 94, 96, 115, 117–118, 124
horror, writing for children   90, 114, 124, 190
Horse & Pony Magazine   263

hosting company 319
Houghton Mifflin Company 47
Housing Benefit 404
Howard, John 154
HTML (HyperText MarkUp Language) 318
Hughes, Shirley 95
Human & Rousseau 36
humour 117, 125
  writing for young children 121, 161
John Hunt/O-Books Publishing Ltd 14
Hunter House Publishers 47
Hutchinson Children's Books 14
Hyperion Books for Children 48

IBBY Congress 328
Ideals Publications LLC 48
iLiad 96
Ilkley Literature Festival 377
Illumination Arts Publishing 48
Illustration Cupboard, The 229
illustrations, illustrators 2, 80, 86, 100, 147, 191,
  207, 209, 213, 217, 221, 240
  non-fiction 108
Imaginate 311, 352
Imagine: Writers and Writing for Children 377
Impact Publishers Inc. 48
Imperial War Museum 353
Incapacity Benefit 403, 405
Incentive Publications Inc. 48
Income Support 404
income tax 381, 383
  interest on overdue 390
  self-assessment 389
  tax return 390
  taxable 383
Independent bookshops 91
Independent Publishers Guild 353
Independent Theatre Council (ITC) 353
indexing, children's books 324
Inis – Children's Books Ireland Magazine, The 271
innovativeKids 48
Instructor 271
intellectual property rights 191
interactivity 317
International Board on Books for Young People
  (IBBY) 353
International Federation of Reproduction Rights
  Organisations (IFRRO) 248
International Publishers Association 353
internet 303, 315
  and copyright 246
  marketing to 151
  poetry groups on 178
Internet Corporation for Assigned Names and
  Numbers (ICANN) 315
interviews, copyright in 246
Invalid Care Allowance 403
Invalidity Benefit 403
Ireland, Vicky 301
Irish Book Publishers' Association, The 353
Irish Educational Publishers Association 353
Irish Writers' Centre 353

ISBNs 239, 241
  FAQs about 236
ISSNs 237
ITV Network Ltd/ITV Association 293

jacket, book 150–151, 234
Jacklin Enterprises (Pty) Ltd 36
James W. Hackett International Haiku Award 173
JCA Literary Agency Inc. 203
Jeannetta Cochrane Theatre 303
Jeffers, Oliver 95, 217
Jenner, Caryl 299
Jetix Europe 293
Jewish Book Week 377
Jobcentre Plus 402
Jobseeker's Allowance 404
John Kinsella's 178
Johnson & Alcock Ltd 194
Johnson, Catherine 117
Jolly Learning Ltd 14
Jubilee Books 71
Junior 271
Junior Education 271
Junior Puzzles 263
Just Us Books, Inc. 48

Kaeden Books 48
Kaléidoscope 33
Kar-Ben Publishing 49
Kazzum Arts Project 311
Miles Kelly Packaging 65
Miles Kelly Publishing 14
Kelpies Prize 14, 368
Petra Kenney Poetry Competition, The 368
Kenny, Mike 303
Kent & Sussex Poetry Society 177
Key Porter Books Ltd 30
KidHave Press 49
Kids Alive! (Young Soldier), The 264
Kids Can Press Ltd 30
kill fees 246
Kindle 96
King Smith, Dick 116, 300
Kingfisher 14, 49
King's England Press, The 14
Kingscourt/McGraw-Hill 14
Jessica Kingsley Publishers 15
Kipling Society, The 354
Kirchoff/Wohlberg Literary Agency, The 203
Robert J. Kirkpatrick 73
KISS 264
Kloet, Chris 86
Klutz 49
Alfred A. Knopf Books for Young Readers 49
Konflux Theatre in Education 311
Barbara S. Kouts, Literary Agent 203
Kube Publishing Ltd 15

Ladybird Books 15, 61
Wendy Lamb Books 49

Lancashire County Library Children's Book of the Year Award 368
Lancaster University 177
language and style 129
Lassiter, Rhiannon 117
Laurel-Leaf Books 49
LAW (Lucas Alexander Whitley Ltd) 195, 229
Layton, Neal 95
Learning is Fun! 264
Leckie & Leckie 15
Lee & Low Books, Inc. 49
Leeds Children's Theatre 309
Legat, Michael 245
Legend Theatre 312
Leighton Buzzard Children's Theatre 309
Lemniscaat BV 34
Leo Media & Entertainment Group, The 195
Lerner Publishing Group 49
Letterbox Library 68
Letts Educational 15
Arthur A. Levine Books 49
C.S. Lewis Society (New York), The 354
David Lewis Illustration Agency 229
Libra Television Ltd 296
libraries 96, 150, 380
  talks at 75
Library Theatre Company 310
Libros del Zorro Rojo 37
Editorial Libsa 37
licence to copy 248
licensing 231
lift-the-flap books 99
Lincoln Book Festival 377
Frances Lincoln Ltd 15
Astrid Lindgren Memorial Award, The 368
Madeleine Lindley Ltd 71
Lion and the Unicorn, The 271
Lion and Unicorn Bookshop, The 71
Lion Hudson plc 15
Lion Television 296
Literacy 271
Literacy Time 271
literary agents 2, 77, 83, 86, 142, 154, 159, 181, 185, 189, 232, 275, 279
literature festivals 1, 150
Little Angel Theatre, The 312
Little, Brown & Company 49
Little, Brown Book Group 15
Little Hare Books 28
Christopher Little Literary Agency 195
Little People Books 65
Little Theatre Guild of Great Britain 354
Little Tiger Press 15
Livesey Museum for Children, The 354
Livewire 15
Llewellyn Worldwide 50
Loftus Productions Ltd 298
London Independent Books 195
London Literature Festival 377
Longman 15
Loonland UK Ltd 296
Lowdham Book Festival 377
Lucent Books 50
Jennifer Luithlen Agency 195
Lupus Films Ltd 296

M6 Theatre Company (Studio Theatre) 312
Gina Maccoby Literary Agency 203
Anne McDermid & Associates Ltd 199
Margaret K. McElderry Books 50
McGraw-Hill Education 50
McGraw-Hill Book Company New Zealand Ltd 35
McGraw-Hill Education Ltd 28
McGraw-Hill Ryerson Ltd 30
McIntosh & Otis Inc. 203
Frances McKay Illustration 229
Macmillan Digital Audio 61
Macmillan Education Australia Pty Ltd 28
Macmillan Prize for Children's Picture Book Illustration, The 368
Macmillan Publishers Ltd 15
Macmillan Writer's Prize for Africa, The 368
Eunice McMullen Ltd 195
Macromedia Dreamweaver 318
Madison Press Books 30
magazines
  about children's literature and education 1, 159
  teenage 255
Magi Publications 16
Magic Carpet Theatre 312
Magorian, Michelle 116
Mallinson Rendel Publishers Ltd 35
manga novels 118
Andrew Mann Ltd 195
Sarah Manson Literary Agent 195
Mantra Lingua 16
manuscripts 3, 80, 86, 185, 189, 209
  unsolicited 80, 86, 185, 189, 209
Marchpane Children's Books 73
Marjacq Scripts 196
marketing 86, 91–92, 147, 149
  to US 158
  viral 92
Barbara Markowitz Literary Agency 203
Marsh Award for Children's Literature in Translation 369
Marshall Cavendish Benchmark 50
Marshall Cavendish Children's Books 50
Marshall Cavendish 16
Marshall Editions Ltd 65
Maskew Miller Longman (Pty) Ltd 37
Maternity Allowance 405–406
maternity
  loans and grants 402
  pay, statutory 406
Max, The 264
Kevin Mayhew Ltd 16
McNab, Andy 91
Meadows, Daisy 90
Meadowside Children's Books 17
Melling, David 97
memoirs 190
Mercier Press, The 17
Mews Books 204
Microsoft FrontPage 318
Midlands Arts Centre 299
Mighty World of Marvel 264
Miles Stott Literary Agency 196
Milet Publishing, LLC 50
Milkweed Editions 50
Mill Publishing 17
Millbrook Press 50

Millimages 296
Milnes-Smith, Philippa 181
minimum terms agreements 337
MINX 50
Missy 264
Mitchell, Adrian 303
Mitchell Lane Publishers, Inc. 50
Mizz 264
MM House Publishing 35
mobile phones 191
Mobility Allowance 403
Moby Duck 312
Arnoldo Mondadori Editore S.p.A (Mondadori) 34
Mondo Publishing 51
Monkey Puzzle Media Ltd 65
L.M. Montgomery Heritage Society 354
Morgan Reynolds Publishing 51
Morpurgo, Michael 116
William Morris Agency Inc. 204
William Morris Agency (UK) Ltd 196
MSS *see* manuscripts
MTV Network UK & Ireland 293
Muchamore, Robert 92, 115
Mundy, Maggie 221
Erin Murphy Literary Agency 204
Muse Literary Management 204
Museum of London 354
My Little Pony 264
mystery and adventure stories 115
Mythopoeic Fantasy Award for Children's Literature, The 369
Mythopoeic Society, The 354

Napoleon & Company 30
narrative 304
  verse 117
NASEN & TES Special Educational Needs Book Awards 369
NATE News (National Association for the Teaching of English) 272
National Art Library 355
National Association for the Teaching of English (NATE) 17, 355
National Association of Writers' Groups 355
National Association of Writers in Education (NAWE) 178, 355
National Centre for Language and Literacy (NCLL) 355
National Centre for Research in Children's Literature (NCRCL) 355
National Curriculum 103, 110, 138, 324
National Galleries of Scotland 355
National Gallery 355
National Insurance Contributions 382, 386, 389, 392, 395
  exemptions 400
  maximum 401
National Literacy Association 355
National Literacy Strategy 168
National Literacy Trust 106, 356
National Museum Wales 356
National Museums Liverpool 356

National Museums Scotland 356
National Poetry Competition 174, 176
National Poetry Day 174
National Portrait Gallery 356
National Share-A-Story-Month 342
National Society for Education in Art and Design 356
National Theatre 300
National Theatre Bookshop 303
National Union of Journalists 245
National Year of Reading (NYR) 94, 380
Natural History Museum 356
navigation 315
Naxos AudioBooks 61
NB Illustration 229
NB Publishers (Pty) Ltd 37
NCRCL British IBBY Conference 328
Neate Publishing 17
Neilsen Norman Group 317
Thomas Nelson Publisher 51
Nelson Thornes Ltd 17
Edith Nesbit Society, The 356
Net Book Agreement (NBA) 152
New Africa Books (Pty) Ltd 37
New Frontier Publishing 28
New Producers Alliance 356
New Writing North 356
New Zealand Council for Educational Research 35
New Zealand Post Book Awards for Children and Young Adults 369
Newcastle University Library 356
Newspaper, The 264
Nick Jr 293
Nickelodeon UK 293
NickToons 293
Nielsen 94
Nielsen BookScan 156
Jane Nissen Books 17
Nobuyuki Yuasa Annual International Award for Haibun 173
Noddy 265
non-fiction 94, 114, 186
  age ranges 96
  boys' 105
  children's 89
Norfolk Children's Book Centre 71
North East Book Award 369
  Teenage Book Award 369
Northern and Southern Arts Councils of Ireland 174
Northern Children's Book Festival 377
Northern Poetry Library, The 175
NorthWord Books for Young Readers 51
Norwich Puppet Theatre 310
Nottingham Children's Book Awards 370
Nottingham Playhouse 310
novels, adapting for stage 304
novelty books 221
Nursery Education Plus 272
nursery rhyme books 99
Nursery World 272

Oberon Books 18
O'Brien Press Ltd, The 18

Off the Shelf Literature Festival   378
Office for Standards in Education (OFSTED)   357
Office of Communications (Ofcom), The   357
Oily Cart   301, 312
Oliver Press, Inc., The   51
Oneword   283
online
    clubs and societies   92
    going   319
    sales   96
Orca Book Publishers   30
Orchard   95
Orchard Books   18, 51
Organisation, The   229
originality of work   125
Orion   95
Orion Publishing Group Ltd, The   18, 61
Orpheus Books Ltd   65
Oundle Festival of Literature   378
Oundle School Bookshop   71
Overlook Press, The   51
overseas, earnings from   391
Richard C. Owen Publishers, Inc.   51
Oxford Designers & Illustrators Ltd   230
Oxford Literary Festival   378
Oxford University Day and Weekend Schools   328
Oxford University Press   18
Oxford University Press Inc.   51
Oxford University Press Southern Africa   37

Pacific View Press   51
packagers   190
page size   316
Palace Theatre, Watford   299
Pan Macmillan Australia Pty Ltd   28
pantomime   299, 302
Paolini, Christopher   92
Parenting Press, Inc.   52
Parragon Books Ltd   18
Parragon Publishing   52
Patten, Brian   171
Pamela Paul Agency   200
Paternity, Statutory pay   406
Paver, Michelle   116, 127
Pavilion Children's Books   19
Payne-Gallway   19
PCET Publishing   19
Peachtree Publishers   52
Pearson   95
Pearson Education   19, 52
Pearson Education Australia   28
Pearson Education Canada   31
Pearson Education New Zealand Ltd   35
Pearson Scott Foresman   52
Pelican Publishing Company   52
Penguin Audiobooks   61
Penguin Group (Australia)   28
Penguin Group (Canada)   31
Penguin Group (NZ)   36
Penguin Group (UK)   19, 97
Penguin Group (USA), Inc.   52
Penguin Longman   19

pensions   388, 402, 405
    age benefits   402
    retirement   405
    state   403
Pension Credit   402
Pensions Act 1995   402
Pensions Service   402
permission to quote   245
personal service companies   395
Pesky Productions   296
Peterloo Poets Open Poetry Competition   370
Peters Bookselling Services   71
PFD (Peters Fraser & Dunlop Group Ltd), The   196, 230
Phaidon Press Ltd   19
Philomel Books   54
Phoenix Award   370
Phoenix Poets   177
photographs, copyright in   246
Alison Picard, Literary Agent   204
Piccadilly Press   20
Picoult, Jodi   91
Picthall & Gunzi Ltd   20, 66
picture books   82, 86, 94, 100, 102, 162, 191, 209, 213, 217, 231
    age ranges   96
Pinwheel   66
Pinwheel Children's Books   20
Pipers' Ash Ltd   20
Pippin Properties Inc.   204
Pippin Publishing Corporation   31
Pitstop Refuelling Writers' Weekend Workshops   329
Play & Learn Thomas & Friends   265
playground marketing   151
Playne Books Ltd   66
plays
    classrooms, in   305
    stage   289, 301
    writing for children   299, 303
playwrights   303
plot structure   80
plots   102
Plum Pudding Illustration   230
Plurabelle Books   73
poetry   104, 114, 117
    children's   167, 171, 173
Poetry Book Society, The   173, 357
Poetry Bookshop, The   175
Poetry Business, The   173
Poetry Café   176
Poetry Can, The   173
poetry, children's   171
Poetry Ireland   174
Poetry Kit   175, 178
Poetry Landmarks of Britain   174
Poetry Library, The   175–176, 178, 357
Poetry on Loan   174
Poetry Prescription   174
Poetry Round   177
Poetry School, The   177
Poetry Society, The   174, 357
Poetry Society Education   179, 357
Poetry Society of America   175

Poets Anonymous   177
Poet's House/Teach na hÉigse, The   177
Point   20
Pokemon World   265
Polka Theatre   300, 308
Pollinger Limited   196
Pont Books   20
Pony Magazine   265
Poolbeg Press Ltd   20
pop-up books   182
Pop-Up Theatre   312
portfolio   2, 221
Postman Pat   265
Beatrix Potter Society, The   357
Tony Potter Publishing Ltd   66
Power Rangers   265
Practical Parenting   272
Pratchett, Terry   94, 304
Praxis Films Ltd   296
presentation   3
Price, Katie (Jordan)   94
Mathew Price Ltd   54
Price Stern Sloan   54
Priddy Books   20
Prim-Ed Publishing   20
Prim-Ed Publishing Pty Ltd   28
print-on-demand   155
prizes and awards, book and illustration, tax
     position   385
production, author and   234
proofreading   147, 234
Proteus Theatre Company   313
Public Lending Right Act 1979   238
Public Lending Right Office   223
Public Lending Right (PLR)   109, 238, 250
     books eligible for   241
     foreign   251
     reciprocal arrangements   244
     sampling arrangements   241
publicity   150
publicity campaigns   93
publishers   303
     and ISBNs   237
     approaching   86, 142, 187, 209, 218
     educational   138
     US   159
Publishers Association, The   357
Publishers Licensing Society (PLS)   248, 250
Publishers Weekly   159, 272
publishing agreements (contracts)   2, 186, 231
     educational   234
Publishing News   272
Publishing Scotland   358
Puffin   20, 29
Puffin Audiobooks   61
Puffin Book Club   68
Puffin Books   54
Pullman, Philip   94–95, 117
Simon Pulse Paperback Books   54
Pure   265
G.P. Putnam's Sons   54
Puzzle House, The   66
Puzzler Quiz Kids   265

QED Publishing   20
Qualifications and Curriculum Authority
     (QCA)   358

Quarto Children's Books Ltd   20, 66
Queen's Theatre, Hornchurch   310
University of Queensland Press   29
Quentaris Chronicles, The   29
Quicksilver   301
Quicksilver Theatre   313

racism   114
radio   305
     writing for   281
Radio Telefis Éireann (RTÉ)   294
Ragdoll Productions Ltd   296
Ragged Bears Publishing Ltd   21
Rai, Bali   116
Rainbow Magic   94–95
Raincoast Books   31
Raintree   21
Random House Audio Books   61
Random House Australia Pty Ltd   29
Random House Children's Books   74, 94
Random House Group Ltd, The   21
Random House Inc.   54
Random House Mondadori   38
Random House New Zealand Ltd   36
Random House of Canada Ltd   31
Ransom Publishing Ltd   21
Arthur Ransome Society Ltd (TARS), The   358
Ravensburger Buchverlage   33
Rayo   55
RDC Agencia Literaria SL   200
readability   316
Readathon   358, 378
Reader's Digest Children's Publishing Ltd   21
reading aloud, books for   102
Reading Is Fundamental, UK   358
real life/contemporary stories   116
reciprocal arrangements, PLR   244
Red Bird Publishing   22
Red Deer Press   31
Red Fox Children's Books   22
Red House   68
     Children's Book Award, The   370
     International Schools Book Club (ISBC)   69
Red Kite Books   22
Red Ladder Theatre Company   313
Redbridge Book and Media Festival   378
Redhammer Management Ltd   196
Redmond, Diane   287
Reeve, Philip   117
reference books   114
rejection   154
Religious and Moral Education Press (RMEP)   22
Rennison, Louise   111, 117
Replay Productions   313
Report   272
research   127, 128
Retirement Pension   404
Rhyme & Reason   72
Richard & Judy   91
Richards Literary Agency   200
Rigby   22
Right Start   273

rights   186, 189, 231, 301
  artists' and visual creators'   252
  assignment of   234
  authors'   251
  electronic   234, 246
  foreign   159, 186, 232
  moral   233, 245
  reversion of   234
  serial   245
  subsidiary   233
  translation   189
Peter Riley   175
Riordan, Rick   118
Ripping Yarns Bookshop   73
Rising Moon – Luna Rising   55
Rising Stars   22
Roaring Brook Press   55
Linda Rogers Associates   230
Rogers, Coleridge & White Ltd   197
romance and love stories   116
Rosoff, Meg   92, 131
Ross, Tony   209
Roving Books Ltd (Roving Bookshop), The   72
Rowling, J.K   77, 117
Elizabeth Roy Literary Agency   230   197
Royal Court Young Writers' Festival   378
Royal Mail Awards for Scottish Children's
  Books   370
Royal National Institute of the Blind   265, 358
Royal Shakespeare Company   300, 308
Royal Society Prizes for Science Books, The   370
royalties   160, 232
  statements   234
RSPCA Young Photographer Awards (YPA)   371
RSVP Publishing Company   36
Rubber Duck Entertainment   297
Rubinstein Publishing   34
Running Press Book Publishers   55
Uli Rushby-Smith Literary Agency   197
Ruskin, Sheila   302
Russell, Gillie   135
Ryan, Chris   97

S4C   294
Sacher, Louis   116
Sage, Alison   320
Sage, Angie   95
SAGE Publications Ltd   22
Sainsbury's Baby Book Award   98, 371
Adriano Salani Editore S.p.A.   34
Salariya Book Company Ltd   22
sales figures   96
sampling arrangements, PLR   241
Rosemary Sandberg Ltd   197
Sandcastle Books   32
Lennart Sane Agency AB   201
Editions Sarbacane   33
Sasakawa Prize   173
Malcolm Saville Society, The   359
Scattered Authors Society   2, 359
scenery   305
Schofield & Sims Ltd   22

Scholastic Australia Pty Ltd   29
Scholastic Book Clubs and Fairs   69
Scholastic Book Fairs   69
Scholastic Canada Ltd   32
Scholastic Education   56
Scholastic Inc.   56
Scholastic Ltd   22, 94
Scholastic New Zealand Ltd   36
School Librarian, The   152, 273
School Library Association   359
school stories   92, 116
schools   380
  drama in   300
  in US   160
  marketing to   87, 138, 156, 182
  talks to   75
Susan Schulman Literary & Dramatic Agents
  Inc.   204
Schwartz & Wade Books   57
science fiction   117, 190
Science Museum   359
Scooby-Doo   266
Scottish Arts Council   359, 371
Scottish Book Trust (SBT)   359
Scottish International Storytelling Festival   378
Scottish Poetry Library, The   175
Scottish Storytelling Forum, The   359
SCP Publishers Ltd   23
screen size   316
screenplays   304
scripts   306
Scripture Union   23
Scrivener, Richard   158
Seamus Heaney Centre for Poetry, The   174
search engine ratings   319
self-employed status   382, 394
self-publishing   154
SEMERC   23
SEN Press Ltd   23
series fiction   190
series publishing   160, 163, 289
Seven Stories – the Centre for the Children's
  Book   72, 339, 359
SGA Children's Illustration Agency   230
Shan, Darren   90, 115
Sharpe, Tom   304
Sharratt, Nick   75
Sheffield Children's Book Award   371
Caroline Sheldon Literary Agency Ltd   230   197
Sherman Cymru   310
Short Books Ltd   23
short stories   117
Shortfuse   176
Shortlands Poetry Circle   178
Shout   266
Shuter and Shooter Publishers (Pty) Ltd   37
Sickness Benefit   403
Silver Moon Press   57
Dorie Simmonds Agency   197
Simon & Schuster Children's Publishing
  Division   57
Simon & Schuster UK Ltd   23
Simon, Francesca   91, 95
Simpsons Comics   266

420 Index

Simpsons Comics Presents   266
six-to-nine-year-olds, books for   119
Sixth Sense Theatre for Young People   313
Sjaloom & Wildeboer, Uitgevers   34
Skelton, Matthew   142
sketch writing   279
Sky One   304
Sleeping Bear Press   58
slush pile   185, 189
Small Claims   381
Small Earnings Exception   406
Small World Design   66
Smart Learning   24
SmartPass Ltd   62
Smash Hits Channel   294
SMG TV Productions   297
WHSmith Children's Book of the Year   371
Social Fund   402
social problems   302
social security
   benefits   402
   contributions   394
   pension credit   406
social security contributions   394
Society for Editors and Proofreaders (SfEP)   359
Society for Storytelling (SfS)   360
Society of Artists Agents   360
Society of Authors   186, 231, 245, 335, 360
   Children's Writers and Illustrators Group
   (CWIG)   335
Society of Children's Book Writers and Illustrators
   (SCBWI)   360
Society of Editors   360
Society of Young Publishers   360
Soho Theatre   308
Sony Reader   96
Le Sorbier   33
Henry Sotheran Ltd   73
sound effects   317
South Lanarkshire Book Award   371
South Norwood Writers' Workshop   178
Sparkle World   266
Speaking of Books   360
special effects   306
Specs Art   230
Spectacular Spider-Man   266
SpongeBob SquarePants   266
sports stories   116
Spread the Word   178
spy books   90
spy thrillers   115
Stacey International   24
stage plays   289
Standen Literary Agency, The   197
Stanley, Alison   1, 119
StAnza: Scotland's Poetry Festival   378
Star Trek Magazine   266
Star Wars Comic   266
Star Wars Insider Magazine   266
Start-Ups   29
state benefits   402
state pension   402
Statutory Maternity Pay (SMP)   405
Statutory Paternity Pay (SPP)   405

Abner Stein   197
Lou Stein Associates Ltd   298
Stella and Rose's Books   73
Sterling Publishing Co., Inc.   58
Gareth Stevens Publishing   58
Robert Louis Stevenson Club, The   361
Stichting Leenrecht   251
Stimola Literary Studio, LLC   204
Stine, R.L.   90
Stone, Rex   95
stories
   ghost   114
   historical   117, 127
   horror   90, 114, 124, 190
   real life/contemporary   116
   romance/love   116
   school   92, 116
   short   117
   sports   116
   survival   115
   war   116
Storybox   266
Storysack Ltd   24
Stradwick, Becky   90
Stratford-upon-Avon Poetry Festival   378
Stripes   24
Strong, Jeremy   117, 121
submissions   2, 142, 189
subplots   302, 306
suddenlies   301
Sugar   267
Sunday Times Oxford Literary Festival, The   379
Sunset & Vine   297
supermarkets, as booksellers   96, 152
Sure Start Maternity Grant   402, 405
Surrey Poetry Circle   178
survival stories   115
Survivors Poetry   174
Swan Theatre, Worcester   299
Carolyn Swayze Literary Agency Ltd   200
Swedish Institute for Children's Books (Svenska
   barnboksinstitutet), The   361
Sweetens of Bolton   175
Swindells, Robert   116
synopsis   89, 302

Talatin Books   73
talent, spotting   83
Talent Television   297
Tales On Moon Lane   72
Tangerine Designs Ltd   66
Tango Books Ltd   24, 66
Tarquin Publications   24
Tate   361
Tax – see also Income Tax
   Agreements   385, 392
   books purchased   388
   credits, child   402, 403
   disabled persons   403, 405
   expenses, claimed against   381, 386
   prizes and awards   386
   return   393

Tax *cont.*
  value added   382, 392
Taylor and Francis Group   24
tBkmag   267
teachers   96
teen market   92
teenage fiction   89, 131, 135, 161–162, 190
Teenage Magazine Arbitration Panel (TMAP)   361
teenagers   92, 96
  books for   112
  magazines for   225
Katherine Tegen Books   58
Telemagination   297
Teletubbies   267
television   92, 275
Television Junction   297
Teller, Neville   281
Templar Company plc, The   24, 67
Temple Rogers Artists' Agency   230
territory (granted to publisher)   231
TES, The   273
TES Cymru, The   273
TESS, The   273
text message campaign   92
Theatr Gwent Theatre   313
Theatr Iolo   313
theatre, amateur   304
Theatre Centre   299, 314
Theatre Co Blah Blah Blah, The   314
Theatre Is...   314
Theatre Museum   361
Theatre Workshop   314
Theatre-Rites   308
theatrical techniques   301
Thomas & Friends   267
Thomas & Friends: Thomas Express Special   267
Vicki Thomas Associates   230
D.C. Thomson & Co. Ltd – Publications   24
Thomson Nelson   32
thrillers   114–115
Ticktock Media   24
TIE Company   299
Tiger Aspect Productions   297
Times Educational Supplement, The   273
Times Educational Supplement Scotland, The   273
Tir na n-Og Awards   371
Titan Books   24
Ann Tobias, Literary Agent   204
toddlers, books for   86, 99
TOKYOPOP   58
Tolkien Society, The   361
Tom and Jerry   267
Tongues and Grooves   176
Top of the Pops   267
Top That! Publishing plc   25
Tor Books   58
Total Fiction Services   200
Toucan Books Ltd   67
touring companies   300
Christopher Tower Poetry Prize   179   371
Towngate Theatre, Basildon   301
Toxic Magazine   267
Toybox   267
Tractor Tom   268

Transatlantic Literary Agency   200
translation rights   189
translators   240
Transworld   74
Travelling Book Company   69
Travelling Light Theatre Company   314
Treehouse Children's Books   25, 67
S©ott Treimel NY   204
Trentham Books Ltd   25
Tricycle Press   58
Trotman Publishing   25
Trouble   294
T.S. Eliot Prize   173
Tucker Slingsby Ltd   67
Tundra Books Inc.   32
Turnbull, Ann   116
Tutti Frutti Productions   314
Tweenies   268
Twenty-first Century Books   58
2000 AD   268
two-book deals   189
Two-Can Publishing   58
Twofour Broadcast Ltd   297
Ty Newydd   178, 329
typography   207

UKLA Children's Book Awards   371
Ultimate Spider-Man & X-Men   268
Under 5   273
Unicorn   299
Unicorn Theatre   308
unique selling point (USP)   3
United Agents   198
United Kingdom Literacy Association (UKLA)   361
University of Western Australia Press   29
unsolicited manuscripts   80, 86, 185, 189, 209
Usborne Publishing Ltd   25   62

Vaines, Peter   381, 383
Van Goor   34
V&A Illustration Awards, The   372
V&A Museum of Childhood   362
VAT (value added tax)   391, 392
VG Wort   251
Vibe   268
Vicens Vives SA   38
Ralph M. Vicinanza Ltd   205
Ed Victor Ltd   198
Victoria and Albert Museum   362
Victoria Park Books   72
Viking Children's Books   58
viral marketing   92
Voice, The   268
Voice Box   176
Voice of the Listener & Viewer Ltd (VLV)   362
Volunteer Reading Help (VRH)   362
VSP Books   58

Wade and Doherty Literary Agency Ltd   198
Wade, Rachel, and Baker, Miranda   341

Walker & Co.   58
Walker Books   95
Walker Books Ltd   25, 62
Walsh, Caroline   231
war stories   116
Ward Lock Educational Co. Ltd   25
WarkClements Children's and Youth   297
Warne   26, 59
Warner Brothers   95
Waterstone's   96
    Children's Book Prize   372
Watson, Little Ltd   198
AP Watt Ltd   198
Franklin Watts   26
Watts Publishing Group Ltd, The   26
Way, Brian   299
Way, Charles   303
Wayland   26
web
    design   317
    page editor   319
Webb, Tim   301
websites   97, 156
    personal   222
    setting up   315
Weigl Publishers Inc.   59
Weldon Owen Education   36
Well Wisher Children's Bookshop, The   72
Welsh Animation Group (WAG)   362
Welsh Books Council/Cyngor Llyfrau Cymru   362
David West Children's Books   67
Whirligig   301
Whirligig Theatre   308
Whitbread Book Awards   372
Whitbread Literary Award   385
Eve White   198
Whitecap Books Ltd   32
Albert Whitman & Company   59
Widowed Parent's Allowance   404
John Wiley & Sons Inc.   59
Willesden Bookshop   72
Williams, Brian J.   92
Henry Williamson Society, The   362
Wilson, Jacqueline   74, 91, 94, 116
Wilson-Fletcher, Honor   380
Wimbledon and Merton Poetry Group   178
University of Winchester   329
Winchester Writers' Conference Competitions   372,
    379
Winchester Writers' Festival Conference and
    Bookfair, The   329
WingedChariot Press   26
Winnie the Pooh   268
Paula Wiseman   59
W.I.T.C.H.   268
Wizard Books Ltd   26

Wolverine and Deadpool   268
Women's Press, The   26, 32
Wood, Annie   301
Wood, David   299
Word – University of Aberdeen Writers
    Festival   379
wordless books   98
Word's Out!, The   379
Wordsong   59
Wordsworth Editions Ltd   26
working age benefits   402
Working Families Tax Credit   402, 404
Working Group Against Racism in Children's
    Resources   363
Working Partners Ltd   67
Working Tax Credit   403
Workman Publishing Company   59
World Book Day   98, 150, 379
World Book, Inc.   59
Write A Story for Children Competition   372
Writernet   363
Writers Advice Centre for Children's Books   329,
    363
Writers' Guild of Great Britain   231, 245, 337, 363
Writers House LLC   205
writing classes/courses   142, 184, 320
Wylie-Merrick Literary Agency   205
Wyndham, John   117

Y Lolfa Cyf.   26
Yearling Books   59
YLG Conference   329
York Notes   26
young adult fiction   81, 91–95, 114, 116, 162
Young Browsers Bookshop   72
Young Picador   26
Young Readers Birmingham   379
Young Scot   269
Young Vic Theatre Company   309
Young Writer   269, 273
Young Writers' Programme   372
younger readers, books for   87, 182, 221
Your Dog Magazine   269
Your Horse   269
Youth Libraries Group (YLG)   363
youth theatre   300
YouWriteOn.com   372

Zero to Ten Ltd   26
Zirkoon Uitgevers   35
ZooBooKoo International Ltd   26
Zusak, Marcus   92